Contemporary Authors
Autobiography Series

ISSN 0748-0636

Contemporary Authors

Autobiography Series

Joyce Nakamura
Editor

volume **14**

 Gale Research Inc. • DETROIT • LONDON

EDITORIAL STAFF

Joyce Nakamura, *Editor*

Shelly Andrews, Laura Standley Berger, and
Motoko Fujishiro Huthwaite, *Associate Editors*
Deborah A. Stanley, *Assistant Editor*
Marilyn O'Connell, *Editorial Associate*
Mark Zadrozny, *Contributing Editor*

Victoria B. Cariappa, *Research Manager*
Mary Rose Bonk, *Research Supervisor, Biography Division*
Jane Cousins, Andrew Guy Malonis, and Norma Sawaya, *Editorial Associates*
Mike Avolio, Patricia Bowen, Reginald A. Carlton, Clare Collins,
Catherine A. Coulson, Theodore J. Dumbrigue, Shirley Gates,
and Sharon McGilvray, *Editorial Assistants*

Peter M. Gareffa, *Senior Editor*

Mary Beth Trimper, *Production Manager*
Shanna Philpott Heilveil, *Production Assistant*

Art Chartow, *Art Director*
C. J. Jonik, *Keyliner*

Donald G. Dillaman, *Index Program Designer*
David Jay Trotter, *Index Programmer*

The paper used in this publication meets the minimum requirements of American National Standard for Information Sciences--Permanence Paper for Printed Library Materials, ANSI Z39.48-1984. ∞™

Copyright © 1991
Gale Research Inc.
835 Penobscot Bldg.
Detroit, MI 48226-4094

Library of Congress Catalog Card Number 84-647879
ISBN 0-8103-4513-7
ISSN-0748-0636

Printed in the United States of America

Published simultaneously in the United Kingdom
by Gale Research International Limited
(An affiliated company of Gale Research Inc.)

Contents

Preface

Each volume in the *Contemporary Authors Autobiography Series (CAAS)* presents an original collection of autobiographical essays written especially for the series by noted writers. *CAAS* has grown out of Gale's long-standing interest in author biography, bibliography, and criticism, as well as its successful publications in those areas, like the *Dictionary of Literary Biography, Contemporary Literary Criticism, Something about the Author,* and particularly the bio-bibliographical series *Contemporary Authors (CA),* to which this Autobiography Series is a companion.

As a result of their ongoing communication with authors in compiling *CA* and other books, Gale editors recognized that these writers frequently had more to say than the format of existing Gale publications could accommodate. Inviting authors to write about themselves at essay-length was an inevitable next step. Added to that was the fact that the collected autobiographies of current writers were virtually nonexistent. *CAAS* serves to fill this significant information gap.

Purpose

CA Autobiography Series is designed to be a meeting place for writers and readers--a place where writers can present themselves, on their own terms, to their audience; and a place where general readers, students of contemporary literature, teachers and librarians, even aspiring writers can become better acquainted with familiar authors and make the first acquaintance of others. Here is an opportunity for writers who may never write a full-length autobiography to let their readers know how they see themselves and their work, what carefully laid plans or turns of luck brought them to this time and place. Even for those authors who have already published full-length autobiographies there is the opportunity in *CAAS* to bring their readers "up to date" or perhaps to take a different approach in the essay format. Singly, the essays in this series can illuminate the reader's understanding of a writer's work; collectively, they are lessons in the creative process and in the discovery of its roots.

CAAS makes no attempt to give a comprehensive overview of authors and their works. That outlook is already well represented in biographies, reviews, and critiques published in a wide variety of sources. Instead, *CAAS* complements that perspective and presents what no other ongoing reference source does: the view of contemporary writers that is shaped by their own choice of materials and their own manner of storytelling.

Scope

Like its parent series, *Contemporary Authors,* the *CA Autobiography Series* sets out to meet the needs and interests of a wide range of readers. Each volume provides about twenty essays by writers in all genres whose work is being read today. We consider it extraordinary that twenty busy authors from throughout the world are able to interrupt their existing writing, teaching, speaking, traveling, and other schedules to converge on a given deadline for any one volume. So it is not always possible that all genres can be equally and uniformly represented from volume to volume, although we strive to include writers working in a variety of categories, including fiction, nonfiction, and poetry. As only a few writers specialize in a single area, the breadth of writings by authors in this volume also encompasses drama, translation, and criticism as well as work for movies, television, radio, newspapers, and journals.

Format

Authors who contribute to *CAAS* are invited to write a "mini-autobiography" of approximately 10,000 words. In order to give the writer's imagination free rein, we suggest no guidelines or pattern for the essay. We only ask that each writer tell his or her story in the manner and to the extent that feels most natural and appropriate. In addition, writers are asked to supply a selection of personal photographs showing themselves at various ages, as well as important people and special moments in their lives. Barring unfortunate circumstances like the loss or destruction of early photographs, our contributors have responded generously, sharing with us some of their most treasured mementoes. The result is a special blend of text and photographs that will intrigue even browsers.

A bibliography appears at the end of each essay, listing the author's book-length works in chronological order of publication. Each entry in the bibliography includes the publication information for the book's first printing in the United States, and if an earlier printing has occurred elsewhere, that information is provided as well. The bibliographies in this volume were compiled by members of the *CAAS* editorial staff from their research and the lists of writings that were provided by many of the authors. Each of the bibliographies was submitted to the author for review.

A cumulative index appears in each volume and cites all the essayists in the series as well as the subjects presented in the essays: personal names, titles of works, geographical names, schools of writing, etc. The index format is designed to make these cumulating references as helpful and easy to use as possible. For every reference that appears *in more than one essay*, the name of the essayist is given before the volume and page number(s). For example, W. H. Auden is mentioned by a number of essayists in the series. The entry in the index allows the user to identify the essay writers by name:

Auden, W.H.
 Allen **6:**18, 24
 Ashby **6:**36, 39
 Bowles **1:**86
 Burroway **6:**90
 Fuller **10:**120, 123
 Hall **7:**58, 61
 Hazo **11:**148, 150
 Howes **3:**143
 Jennings **5:**110
 etc.

For references that appear *in only one essay*, the volume and page number(s) are given but the name of the essayist is omitted. For example:

Stieglitz, Alfred **1:**104, 109, 110

CAAS is something more than the sum of its individual essays. At many points the essays touch common ground, and from these intersections emerge new patterns of information and impressions. The index, despite its pedestrian appearance, is an important guide to these interconnections.

Looking Ahead

Each essay in the series has a special character and point of view that sets it apart from its companions. A small sampler of anecdotes and musings from the essays in this volume hint at the unique perspective of these life stories.

Malay Roy Choudhury, remembering his aunt Kamala: "Dad's only sister, Kamala, lived in a single-room tenement at Ahiritola in Calcutta, adjacent to the red-light tourist spot Sonagachi. The room had a two-tiered bed for her eight children, seven of whom quit school to be found always on either of the tiers doing nothing by her husband, who would come back from his office every evening high on Goddess Kali brand rice liquor whistling a nineteenth-century tune, alerting neighbours to his drunkenness. It being the only place to stay during a visit to Calcutta, the floor of the room meant for guests was also where we sat and ate steamed rice, pigeon pea pulse, and shrimp fried in mustard oil served on brass plates. The toilet was slippery, without doors, and I used to keep coughing to notify my presence to any intruder. Aunt Kamala became blind yet continued her cooking routine believing, as she told me, the blindness was for having seen six toes on a woman's feet during a full moon. Her husband was found in a pool of blood on a summer morning in 1967 when he had nightwalked off a terrace during one of his spells; the remains of his body were scraped from the asphalt into a loincloth bundle for the postmortem."

Louis Dudek, on the survival of poetry in a world of popular culture: "There is nothing that bothers me more than the rattling off of numbers of copies sold and the huge profits made by popular books. Majority taste is not the only taste. There must be room in any society, as in fact there is, for the more highly demanding preferences of various minorities: it is only by minorities that chamber music, or fine art, or philosophical thought can be encouraged and maintained. And the same can be said, by and large, of poetry. Poetry is not an art that masses of people will turn to easily, unless it's sentimental or sensational in some obvious way, and therefore poetry must be nurtured and supported by the small audience for it which still exists naturally. Eventually, as good poetry ripens, and as its fame spreads through time, it may also reach great audiences. But for the time being we must be content with the readers that exist, and we must provide for them."

Steve Katz, reflecting about an impressionable episode from one of his scriptwriting jobs: "My poem sequence *Cheyenne River Wild Track* comes out of that experience, particularly from my contact on the set with Henry Crow-Dog, seventy-four years old, a full-blooded Sioux, over six feet tall, classic Native American face, long hair, from the Rosebud reservation, a shaman of the Native American Church, who was hired to be on the set as a 'spiritual adviser,' and to be seen in a couple of shots. He and I shared a cabin. It was one of those 'shocks of recognition' the first time I went to meet him at Crow-Dog's Paradise, where he lived and did sweats and peyote rituals. I walked into his amazing shack by the Little Rosebud River, built of old pieces of corrugated tin, and car parts, and salvaged windows, and refrigerator doors, because he refused to live in the BIA (Bureau of Indian Affairs) prefabs, and a couple of Navajo braves visiting him said 'How.' That greeting dropped like a stone through my consciousness. It was the first time in my life I was forced to separate these people from the cliche imprinted on me by white American mythology. Living with Henry I realized you didn't need to go to the Himalayas or Sri Lanka to find spiritual teachers. Henry was as exotic and esoteric in his spiritual codes as any yogi, and he was right here in South Dakota.''

Doris Lessing, describing the effects of war's aftermath as seen through a child's eyes: "There was one thing these nice people had in common that I didn't see then. They were survivors of World War I. The men had artificial arms or legs or an eye-patch where an eye had gone. They would discuss the whereabouts of various bits of shrapnel forever travelling about their bodies out of sight, but sometimes appearing from healthy tissue to tinkle into a shaving mug or onto a plate. One woman had had four sons and a husband killed in the Trenches, and was farming with the remaining son. She was dignified, stoical, and the house was full of photographs of dead men in uniform. Another family had two boys whom we played with, but photographs of a third dominated the house and the talk of the parents: he had been drowned in a torpedoed ship. There was a man with a steel plate keeping his brains in, and another who was rumoured to have a steel plate holding in his bowels. They talked about the war, both men and women--the war, the war, the war; and we children escaped into the bush away from it, just as, at home, my brother and I tried to shut our ears against what my father came to call, sarcastically, the Great Unmentionable: 'I don't want to bore you with the Great Unmentionable, God forbid that you should waste your time on anything so unimportant.'''

David McKain, recalling his precocious beginnings as a writer: "I began keeping a journal when I was in first grade. I don't know why I started, but on my fifth birthday my father gave me a bank envelope with a picture of George Washington smiling through an oval window of red berries and holly. The next day, my dollar buttoned safely inside my shirt pocket, I ran downtown to Woolworth's and bought a wooden pen, a bottle of blue-black Parker's ink, and a journal marked 'Ledger.' The book had a black-and-white marbled cover and swirling purple endpapers. Each page was tinted celery green with a thin red line down the margin and a wide blue line down the center. I didn't know why I bought the ledger, but keeping a record meant a great deal to me, . . . 'Why did you buy a ledger?' my mother asked, perhaps sensing my confusion. 'Do you want to become a businessman?' She looked at me and asked me to look at her. I could feel tears in my eyes, but I did not answer. I knew only that I wanted to write down things I had seen during the day so I would always have them, the way I saved oak leaves and horse chestnuts, special stones and rusty railroad spikes. I wanted to keep track of the changes in my life, whatever came into it and whatever went out, but I did not know that was what I wanted to do. I did not want to show her anything I had drawn or written down, so I hid the ledger in my desk. Keeping a ledger was a little like talking to God. It was secret.''

These brief examples only suggest what lies ahead in this volume. The essays will speak differently to different readers; but they are certain to speak best, and most eloquently, for themselves.

Authors Forthcoming in *CAAS*

Bella Akhmadulina
Russian poet, translator, and short-story writer

Claribel Alegria
Latin American poet and fiction writer

Mulk Raj Anand
Indian novelist, nonfiction writer, and critic

Russell Banks
American novelist

Germaine Bree
French-born translator, editor, and critic

Elizabeth Brewster
Canadian novelist, poet, and short-story writer

Ed Bullins
American playwright

Abelardo Delgado
Chicano poet and fiction writer

Paul Engle
American poet and educator

Charles Gordone
American playwright, actor, and director

Daniel Halpern
American poet and editor

Michael S. Harper
American poet

Rolando Hinojosa
Chicano novelist

John Hollander
American poet

Joanne Kyger
American poet

Walter Laqueur
German-born historian, journalist, and novelist

Leonard Michaels
American short-story writer, editor, and novelist

Jim Wayne Miller
American poet, essayist, and fiction writer

Bharati Mukherjee
Canadian novelist and short-story writer

Harry Mark Petrakis
American novelist and screenwriter

James Reaney
Canadian poet and playwright

Alastair Reid
Scottish poet, essayist, and translator

Ernesto Sabato
Argentinean novelist and essayist

Antonis Samarakis
Greek novelist and short-story writer

Sonia Sanchez
American poet

Lloyd Van Brunt
American poet

Anne Waldman
American poet

Acknowledgments

We wish to acknowledge our special gratitude to each of the authors in this volume. They all have been most kind and cooperative in contributing not only their talents but their enthusiasm and encouragement to this project.

Grateful acknowledgment is also made to those publishers, photographers, and artists whose works appear with these authors' essays.

Photographs/Art

Richard Bausch: p. 15, Karen Bausch.

Marvin Bell: p. 35, Berkeley Studios.

Dennis Brutus: p. 63, courtesy of Africa Network.

Judson Crews: p. 101, Walter Chappell; p. 104, Will S. Thompson, from the collection of F. D. Lisle; pp. 110, 113, Mildred Tolbert; p. 116, Anna Bush Crews; p. 117, Diana Huntress.

Louis Dudek: p. 121, Famous Studios, Montreal; p. 124, Adam Carter; p. 133, Betty Gustafson.

Robert Easton: p. 143, Sidney Webb; p. 154, U.S. Army; p. 158, Ellen Easton Brumfiel.

Steve Katz: p. 174, Lee Friedlander.

Doris Lessing: All photos courtesy of the author.

David McKain: p. 209, The cover of *Spellbound: Growing Up in God's Country,* by David McKain. Touchstone Edition, 1990. Copyright © 1988 by the University of Georgia Press. Reproduced by permission of the University of Georgia Press./ p. 214, copyright © Kelly Wise.

William Meredith: p. 219, copyright © 1988 Mimi Levine; p. 228, Murcier Studio, New York.

Edouard Roditi: p. 237, copyright © Mellon; p. 240, portrait by William Ablett; p. 252, portrait by Yankel Adler, courtesy of the Grunwald Center for the Graphic Arts, University of Southern California, Los Angeles (gift of Edouard Roditi); p. 266, portrait by Josef Herman; p. 271, portrait by Yüksel Arslan, courtesy of Emmanuel Sabbath; p. 279, portrait copyright © 1984 by Judith Clancy Johns; p. 283, copyright © Ira Cohen.

Eve Shelnutt: p. 291, Rawlins-Allen Studio.

Contemporary Authors

Autobiography Series

Richard Bausch

1945-

Autobiography holds almost no interest for me. Beyond this short article, I will probably never attempt anything like it. Aside from incidental details of place and time, my fiction is almost totally devoid of autobiographical matters; in fact, when something I'm working on begins to come too close to the life I actually lead, I can feel the pen begin to freeze up. For me, finally, the personal side of my lived experience is uninteresting *as itself*, which is to say that while I myself am obviously pitted in it, and engaged with all passion and earnest in a struggle not only to survive but to prosper and be happy, almost nothing of my daily life seems appropriate to write about directly. Or I should say that almost none of it appears to me to be anybody's business but mine. It is worth *my* time; it is worth all the intelligence and energy *I* can muster. But finally it is only what happens in my days; it is not what I see when I begin the process of dreaming up another story, long or short, and in consequence it comprises very little of what I end up with.

Having said this, I should also point out that I am not an impresario, either, and contrary to the apparent assumptions of certain critics, my subjects are not intellectually chosen. To a large extent, I do not choose what I write about; it chooses me. A part of my makeup is struck by something, some chord—a tone of voice, or a situation, or a word—and something else in me begins to empathize; my interest is engaged, I can sense myself becoming the character I will write about; I feel it through, *as though* it is me, and the story begins to emerge. Usually, when *anything* about the people or situation I find myself imagining surprises me, I know I have a story and not a mere cleverness, a mere idea for prose. Always, it is what is *made up* that gives me the necessary belief in the worth of the thing.

Regarding autobiography as a literary form, I have in the past made efforts to read some of the more famous examples, and I must confess that I have never finished one. I do in fact read plenty of history and biography because they are what I entertain myself with. But there is something about the memoir as a form which begs credibility.

Richard Bausch—"One of the earliest photos of me, taken in Georgia," about 1947

For instance, I have always been dubious about the prospect that anyone, regardless of other qualities or skills, could feel certain about what his first memory is; yet many autobiographers begin with such memories—and in great detail. The whole thing, I suppose, makes me suspicious, as I am and always have been suspicious of memory.

When I was three or four, my twin and I took a walk together up the Safeway. The Safeway, we thought, was the cracked, uneven, partially overgrown sidewalk at the end of the street—Geranium Street—where we lived in northwest Washington, D.C. Our father would say, "I'm going up to the Safeway," which was the name of the grocery store in the neighborhood, and since we didn't know about the store, and were old enough to understand vaguely what "safe" and "way" meant, we jumped to the obvious conclusion and went exploring. No doubt we went right past the grocery store—nothing is less

1

interesting than a grocery store—and happened upon what for almost sixteen years I was to remember as a wide prospect under a bridge: a depot, with nine parallel railroad tracks; the smell of coal and creosote and iron, and the sound of engines, several trains rolling through. A tremendous hubbub and confusion, and people moving among the clouds of steam and exhaust. That was how I remembered it, and that was how I told it for years—and one day when I was twenty, and we had come into Washington to visit family that had remained there, my father heard me tell it.

"We're not far from there," he told me. "Would you like to see it again?"

"What station is it?" I said.

"It's not a station."

I do not remember if he accompanied me there; I have no clear idea if anyone went with me, though I would guess that if my twin was there that afternoon, he certainly would have come along. In any case, what I found was a single, one-lane concrete bridge, and one lone track winding out of sight between two weedy banks. No station; no switching house or platform. Just the one neglected track. My imagination had provided the rest.

Hence, this circumspect and doubtful beginning—one which, I trust, properly asks for skepticism.

Once, when I was about fifteen, I put one of my father's hats on and pretended to be a newspaper reporter. I even fought with the old stiff keys of an Underwood typewriter my father had brought into the house. I remember being mildly interested in the fact that Underwood was also my maternal grandmother's married name. And I remember that I was quite literal-minded about everything—I expected the Second Coming momentarily because it was clear that Saint Paul did in the Epistles the priest read each Sunday at Mass.

Ours was a devout household; yet it was only at church that we got the prodigious guilt and fear of deep religion. At home, we said the rosary every night, and if the children were a little restless and distracted, we all sensed something of what it meant, and I believe we learned from that experience that words counted for everything: one could address them to the dark, to the night stars in faith that they would be heard and that they mattered.

There was love in the rooms, and a tremendous seriousness and magic, too—we were nearly destitute, yet never felt that way. The parents were Bob and Helen. Bob of the Piqua, Ohio, branch of the Bausch clan, and Helen of the Washington Sim-

monses and Roddys. Her father had died in the black-flu epidemic of 1918, so she never knew him. Her stepfather's name was Dick Underwood. Because her mother had to work to support her, she was substantially raised by her maternal grandmother, Minnie Roddy. Her mother married Dick Underwood and had another little girl, Florence.

Bob Bausch was the oldest of six children, five boys and one girl, all but two of whom survive at the date I am writing. His mother, Marguerite Leahy, who was widowed in 1968 when her husband Carl died at seventy-three years of age, lived until March of last year, when she quietly passed on in her sleep. She was ninety-seven.

In *our* family there were also six children: Barbara, the oldest, the twins, Bob and me, then Betty, and then the two younger ones, Steve and Tim. Timmy arrived when we lived on Valleywood Drive in Wheaton, Maryland—a little three-bedroom rambler atop three grass terraces. The older children—and then Steve and Tim when they were old enough—argued all the time, and we were often in trouble; we shouted and got things out in the open and sometimes we drove each other crazy, but we laughed a lot, too. It was a boisterous, confused place, and yet I have so many remembered instances where I'm talking with one or the other of my parents, and it seems that no one else is in the house.

Bob and I were born in Georgia, where my father was stationed at the end of World War II. We moved north and lived in Washington, D.C., for a time—on Geranium Street, the same street where my friend Susan Richards Shreve lived, though I probably didn't know her then. At some point during our time there, I saw a girl run over by a car. I was three or four. They put a blanket over her, and there was blood on the surface of the road, and a lot of people standing around. I seem to recall the girl as being fairly tall, with a page-boy haircut. I believe the thing happened, and that I must have turned just afterward. I have no specific memory of anyone being with me, but Bob remembers it too, so he must have been there. Anyway, in every circumstance, all my life, my mind shows me the possible bad outcome: someone walks down steps, and before I can do anything to head the image off, I see a fall, a catastrophe. It is always there, like a form of spiritual arthritis, and I'm so used to it I hardly notice it. (I might add that my life, the living of it, has given me little reason for other expectations, since at this writing I have lost in sudden death five people very dear to me.)

In 1950 we moved out to the suburbs—first to a place called Kenross Avenue in Silver Spring, Maryland, and then, in 1954, to Valleywood Drive in

*"Shortly after the arrival of my youngest brother, Tim; I'm seated at the far left,
with Steve, Barbara (holding Tim), Betty, and Robert," 1955*

Wheaton. My father was working with the Department of Agriculture in town, and every day he walked the mile to Viers Mill Road, where he would catch the bus in to work. We had no car. In the mornings, my father would kiss us good-bye—smelling of Mennen, always—and then we would watch him go down the long sidewalk toward Viers Mill, holding his hat against the wind. I believe the government was paying him about a hundred dollars a week.

One night I lay down to go to sleep and quite suddenly became convinced that there were cancer cells on my pillow. I had seen an article about the disease in a *Life* magazine, and hadn't read it—only looked at the pictures of victims. I thought the disease could be caught, like any germ-spread illness; the experience made me sleepless and very frightened of the nights. I was nine and ten and eleven years old, and my mother sat up with me, understanding it and patiently trying to explain it away. I didn't know how to tell her what I was really afraid of. I don't remember what I did tell her. Later, I grew to love baseball, since the games could last well into the hours after dark—if the score was tied it could go past

midnight—and on summer nights I was allowed to stay up until things were decided, which removed the necessity of facing the prospect of the night's bad sleep. I have a self-portrait from that time—we could all draw and paint, as could our mother—and there are dark circles under my eyes; I look like a very neurotic eleven-year-old.

I think now that I had simply begun to make the acquaintance of my imagination, which I have since learned to trust, recognizing the corrosive, self-digestive thing it can be if one is not turning it on the world outside: that is, I believe that when I am not writing, making up stories, my imagination begins to digest me. And sometimes I believe it is digesting me anyway.

At some point during all this, my fifth-grade teacher, Mrs. Jefferson, looked at me and said, "Ah, you're something." I lived on that for a year at least. It was one good signal from an outside world that had been mostly threatening. In the Catholic school, the nuns showed us slide shows of the Last Judgement, and a voice would say, "Listen to the screams of the damned." And we would do that, hearing, I guess, actors screech and wail. Then the little bong would sound, and there would be another slide. More shots of hell. I think they actually used Michelangelo. I was very small, and these things went to my imagination and grew; terrible things awaited us all. I was always seeing consequences; and I could not suppress all the impulses and imperfections that made me, I knew, a fitting candidate for those dramatic horrors.

Mrs. Jefferson had blond hair and had been to Europe, and taught us songs. There was something bright about everything she said and did. She was a person who liked people, and had no quarrel with their nature. A year earlier I had felt something like reverence for old Mrs. Day—whose sternness with another child at first made me fear her, but who turned out to be wonderfully benign at heart. She read to us from James Whitcomb Riley and the Bible, and her voice enunciated the words, caressed the syllables with something like the appreciation of someone enjoying delectable food. I can still see her cheeks, where the steel frames of her glasses cut in, and hear the timbre of her voice saying "And the Goblins'll get ya, ef'n ya don't watch out." Somehow, this threat was marvelously fun to hear, perhaps because it was so clearly part of a *story.* I was transported when she read to us, and was always sorry when she closed the book.

For her, I felt reverence; for Mrs. Jefferson, I felt the love of a friend.

At Christmas, my mother would read to us from Dickens, *A Christmas Carol,* and sometimes she would read other things, too. I have an image of her, pregnant with Tim, and I can still see the dark dress she wears; it's near Christmas, and the smell of pine is in the air, the sense of anticipation and delight. She sits in the light from a stand-up lamp and reads about there being no doubt that Marley was dead.

We moved to Virginia just after I graduated from high school. I thought I was going to be a radio announcer or an artist—having decided, like most Catholic boys my age, that I would not, after all, enter the priesthood. When I thought I *was* going to be a priest, I read Saints François de Sales and Ignatius Loyola, Thomas à Kempis, even some Aquinas, along with Bishop Fulton J. Sheen (everything), and Thomas Merton. I later read Thomas Merton's poems, and his *Asian Journals.* It was Sheen who led me to Dostoevsky, in a long passage from, I believe, *Peace of Soul* about how Feodor anticipated communism. I read Shakespeare because everybody was quoting him. And, all the late attacks on it from the Marxists and all the other "ists" and "isms" notwithstanding, I say here quite flatly that it is still the best

poetry in any language, anywhere (even space, other universes); and I love the fact that Tolstoy didn't like him, Tolstoy being the greatest fiction writer in any language.

At any rate, I began with the religious writers, and was led by their eloquence and their knowledge to the others—the great poets first, because I was beginning to think I wanted to be a poet. I had begun to be interested in folk music, and thought I might write song-poems. I had liked John Kennedy, and when he was killed drew several pictures of him that some people still have on their walls. I delivered one to the door of Robert Kennedy's residence in McLean, Virginia, and he invited me in. We had a very friendly conversation in his kitchen, and then I went on my way, feeling that I had stepped back out of history and into my life again. It was a curiously relieved sensation, if I can trust what I remember. (I also left a drawing with a Secret Service man outside Jackie Kennedy's Georgetown house in the summer of 1964; and I'll admit I find it rather satisfying, just for the vaguely circular feel of it, that I am in receipt of a letter with Doubleday's colophon on the masthead, dated 1988 and signed by the lady, asking me to supply a blurb for a novel she was publishing in her role as an editor there).

Anyway, I'd read that Jack Kennedy liked poetry, and, wanting to mirror that well-rounded sort of figure—the man who knows the world's history and can recite lines of poetry—I had begun to read it in earnest. It all started as self-improvement of a kind, I suppose. It was at least partly that.

There was also simply an always-present love of words, of what seemed to me to be language arranged gorgeously (many times I read with little understanding of what I was reading, but was moved by the combinations of sounds all the same). By this time I had begun to entertain vague thoughts of entering politics. I would write my own speeches. In early 1964 I was writing imitations of Francis Thompson's "The Hound of Heaven," and, believe it or not, Walt Whitman's "Song of Myself." I wrote with a quill-shaped, white ballpoint pen, and I offer my age as an explanation of the conceit: I was nineteen. When I had something I liked written down, I typed the results, hunting and pecking, as they say (I still type with two fingers, though now I can go more than seventy-five words a minute, and if you were in the next room and heard me, you would swear I was going at it with all ten). I had it in the back of my mind that I could do about anything I wanted, and while I accept the possibility that the fact that I was born white and male in the then blatantly racist and segregated America of the 1940s and '50s, I might also point out that I knew plenty of kids—also white and male—who had no such feeling at all about themselves.

Even so, I believe the reasons for this are not as complicated as one might suspect.

Once, when I was eleven or so years of age, and was interested in the great Joe Louis, and had with my father's encouragement sent away for a series of pamphlets about him, I announced to my father that I wanted to be one of two things when I grew up: an artist, (I was drawing the pictures in the Joe Louis books), or heavyweight champion of the world. My father went into what I then—and for decades afterward—believed was a perfectly unreasonable tirade about the dirty business of boxing and the corruption that was rife in it, the dishonesty of promoters and the opportunism of managers, and how the boxer was the victim in all cases, poor Joe Louis being hounded by creditors and tax men, after his amazing accomplishments in the ring. It took me more than thirty years to realize what a gift that was—a grown person taking my idle speculations about what I might do in the world as dead seriously as if it really *were* only a matter of deciding.

And I had, of course, the evidence of my mother's drawings and watercolors—though I was almost ten years old before I knew they even existed. She spoke of them as something she did to entertain herself when she was younger: but this was more than childish entertainment; these drawings, these paintings were brilliantly rendered portraits, still lifes, dramatic scenes—all of them quite true to the shape

Newlyweds Richard and Karen, May 3, 1969,
Champaign, Illinois

and texture of things, and with a sophisticated understanding of light and shade and color (one representation of Christ stands out in my memory). She said she didn't really do that anymore because she had six children and because by her own testimony she didn't want to; but it was always there if she *did* want to. And of course she showed such interest in *our* drawings.

Then, of course, for a long time during our eighth-grade year, Bob was writing a Civil War novel called "Hidden Glory." Barbara, the oldest, was spending evenings typing it up. There were a lot of illustrations by the author. Everybody was excited about it. It got up to more than 400 pages before Bob quit on it and, as I recall, he still had it with him almost fifteen years later in the trunk of a white Ford he and I drove all over the Midwest, during my time as a singer/songwriter/entertainer.

In any case, by the time Bob and I joined the air force on the buddy system in August of 1965, we were pretty sure we were going to be good at something.

Bob was interested in politics then, reading all the history he could get; I was writing poetry (or what I thought was poetry), and reading everything I could get my hands on that traveled under the name of literature: I loved the dramatists, and read everything by the Greeks—especially the tragedies—Shakespeare, of course, and all the moderns, too: Ibsen and Chekhov and Shaw; old, mad Strindberg; Goethe, Brecht and O'Neill, and Tennessee Williams and Arthur Miller. I had read Dostoevsky, and now I read Tolstoy for the first time, then Pushkin and Turgenev. For a time I even read the contemporary Russians—Mayakovski and Pasternak; Yevtushenko and the wonderful Voznesensky (whom I had the pleasure of meeting recently in Florida). I read Thomas Mann and Virginia Woolf and William Faulkner (I remember sitting cross-legged on the top bunk in a barracks room in Mississippi—where I had traveled to sing and perform in a talent show for the air force—and looking up from a page of *As I Lay Dying*, exclaiming to friends, "Look at this, man. Just look. That's a chapter. That's a whole damn chapter: 'My mother is a fish.'"), and of course there was all the Hemingway, all of my beloved F. Scott Fitzgerald (I still read *The Great Gatsby* every year, and every year I find some new gem or richness that I hadn't seen before, and each time it charms me all over again with its magical spell, its sheer audacity—for Fitzgerald *was* out to capture something essential and defining which he perceived in the American soul, and his expression of it is in fact all-inclusive; here we

"The move to Iowa. That's Karen, and Tom Philion; the little one is Wesley. Partly obscured by me is Sally Gorman," 1974.

have been all these years looking for the great American novel [read *BIG*], and all along it has been with us, in that slim, beautifully precise, understated, and perfect work of fictive art).

In the air force, I met a young man playing a guitar in the dayroom of a barracks at Chanute Air Force Base in Illinois. I didn't like him much; he seemed a bit supercilious, slouching back in one of those awful red-cushioned, metal-armed chairs, fingerboard surfing on the guitar, not listening to anyone in particular. Then he played something and we all sang along. We all talked idly about putting a group together, and this kid with the guitar allowed as how he had been on "The Merv Griffin Show." I asked his name, and he told me. David Marmorstein. I had never heard of him of course, and nor had anyone else in our company. "We were the Brockton Family Singers," he said.

I thought of the Family von Trapp.

During the tech-training phase of my few months in the air force, I had done some singing with another fellow who owned a twelve string—just singing along with him really. And that seemed to be what was

happening here. Dave played another song we all knew, and we sang it with him. But then it turned out that when everyone else had gone or lost interest, I was still there, and now he was teaching me a song. The song was "They Call the Wind Mariah."

Before long, we were getting together every day after our respective shifts, and practicing. I began to learn how to play harmonica (it took two days, which is twice as long as it ever took anybody else), and in a month we were doing a full show's worth of songs, arrangements and all. We began to write songs. And we began to entertain around the county. We sang together throughout my time in the air force, and in the summer of 1967 we paired up with two other guys, Pat Coffey and Mike Richardson, to form a group. We called ourselves the City Sounds, after a song Dave and I had written. We played all over southern Illinois, and in that summer we played the Hoopston Corn Festival, on the same stage as the fifty runners-up for the Miss America Contest; we sang a song we'd worked on in the car on the way down there; it was the first lyric I was really proud of, I think:

Lara Ann

Lara Ann, with your shining curls
What's it like, in your tiny world.
Night time dreams in your sleepy head
And your tiny hand, and your tiny hand in mine.

Lara Ann, with your baby things,
What's it like, having angel's wings.
How you cried, when you scraped your knee
As I dried your eyes, as I dried your eyes and mine.

Lara Ann, with your young-child's sleep
And your toys and your hide and seek,
Sleep my child, sleep and dream your dreams.
Soon you'll have to grow, soon you'll have to grow
  like me.

It sounded better than it reads; but after more than twenty years I still like the little suggestion of drama in the second verse, and the note of rueful adult regret in the last. Remember, I was only twenty-two. One thing I'm quite proud of: Pat Coffey, with whom I am still in touch, and who is still a marvelous musician, named his daughter after the song.

By the time I was getting ready to leave the air force, I had been entertaining either in a duo with Dave or with the City Sounds for three years wherever anyone would let us entertain; and because Dave Marmorstein had been shipped to Viet Nam, I had begun to learn the guitar, and was playing it around, performing alone. I'd had a long friendship and then a brief stormy romance with a rock singer and guitarist of great talent named Charlotte Vinnedge; I sang with her band, and we traveled some—with me serving as road manager and clown, and occasionally doing Dylan with them—"Like a Rolling Stone." We had a wonderful bond, the Luv'd Ones—as the group was called—and me. And they had a wonderful band. We traveled through Iowa and down to Mississippi, then over to Alabama for a week, then on up to Zenia, Ohio. We made two separate trips to Alabama, actually (those thirty days of leave the air force gave were takeable in ten-day increments, and using weekends you could make it two weeks with ease), and many things happened—storms and late-night forays and sleeplessness and exhaustion and several kinds of hallucination, all of which would take too long to describe. All the Luv'd Ones—Char and Chris, who were sisters, Faith and Mary—were generous in expressing their great faith in my talent as a writer, and I liked the pose of the young depressed poet, reading William Carlos Williams's *Paterson* and Hemingway's *For Whom the Bell Tolls* at the same time. We made up songs and sang them and we were in opposition to the forces of destruction all over the world. It was the summer before the summer of love.

And then it was the summer of love. Martin Luther King and Robert Kennedy were shot and killed, the bloody Chicago Convention went to pieces, and we in the air force were told that if we were not going to reenlist, they could not afford to pay us through August of 1969. We could be discharged six months early, in January, if we wanted to go. It was called an "early out."

I don't know of anyone who refused the early out.

And in October of that year, by previous arrangement, at a small apartment in Champaign, Illinois, my friend Ginny Sollars introduced me to someone named Karen Miller. Karen was wearing a light blue dress; her dark brown hair was shoulder length; she had her arms folded casually, and she nodded, looking at me with simple courtesy, and with a kind of gentle reassurance I have been trying to capture in words ever since, to no avail. She was quite simply and easily the most beautiful woman I have ever seen, and I had an image of her in another room somewhere else twenty years hence, my wife. We hit it off immediately in a friendly way, and I asked for a date. We were never willfully or happily apart afterwards.

We were married on May 3, 1969. Dave Marmorstein was in Viet Nam. Brother Bob was selling cars in Champaign. I was working in Walgreen's as the liquor manager, and playing guitar at night. Karen and I lived happily, happily, in a little converted garage that is still there, just beyond the railroad tracks in the east end of Urbana, Illinois. (I remember the first snow that winter, the winter of 1969–70: Karen woke me up to look at it out the living-room window of that little place; it was the middle of the night and we were warm and awake and young and in love and, to paraphrase the old Count in his greatest book, we were at that pitch of happiness where it is impossible to imagine anyone could have an ungenerous thought.)

At night, sometimes all night, I scribbled in a notebook what I thought were poems. Occasionally Karen would ask if I meant to go to sleep at all. What I was writing was *very* bad, of course; and even so I suspicioned that it wouldn't stay that way if I kept at it: I had seen the faces of people responding to lyrics I had written, and I didn't know enough to know how bad it all really was. I was still writing songs. We were waiting for Dave to come home from Viet Nam, so we could put together our brilliant and glamorous future as rock stars.

Dave did come home. We, the three of us, headed out in February of 1970 to Brockton, and Dave's family. We were already tentatively booked to play the summer fairs up and down the East Coast, Dave said. We made the trip, and Karen and I moved into a small two-and-a-half room place in the corner of one of those big shingle/slate-sided apartment houses in Brockton. Every night the "group" practiced: Dave and me, and the family—Dave's brothers and sisters. We were terrible. The only one of us with substantial musical talent, I believe, was Dave. And I was the only one with the words. There were conflicts, all of which became absurdly—almost pathetically—moot when Dave, driving home in the middle of the night after having too much to drink (Nam, he said, had given him a habit; but we were all drinking pretty heavily back then), fell asleep and ran into a wall. Karen and I went through all the awful details of the funeral, of saying good-bye that way to someone who had been like a brother, and then after I had got myself preregistered at Northeastern University in Boston, we came upon the realization that we both wanted badly to get out of Brockton: the truth was, nothing remained for us in New England. It seemed odd to us both that we could have considered staying to go to school.

So we sold everything but the books and a few pictures, packed a small U-Haul trailer, hitched it up, and headed for Virginia. We have never been back to New England.

By this time, though I was still composing songs, I'd decided that what I wanted most to do was to write stories. I studied in two Virginia colleges: Northern Virginia Community College and George Mason University. At the community college I studied with Joseph Maiolo, who was a student of Peter Taylor's and had just won the Houghton Mifflin Short Story Contest of the famous Hollins Writing Conference of 1970. He was starting a new fiction workshop at the school, and I took that course with him, then took another, which he offered through community services out where he lived in Reston, Virginia. I took still another in the fall of 1971. He introduced me to George Garrett, who had just finished *Death of the Fox*, and Fred Chappell—two writers whose work every literate American *ought* to know. In my mind, Maiolo was like these men, the real thing, and he had said to me that *I* was a writer. For this I was and remain grateful; and for all his work and advice I was also grateful. We became friends. The four of us—Joe, his wife Julie, Karen, and I—had a lot of fun together. And though, where writing and publishing is concerned, he didn't have the good fortune I had over the years, at the point that *I* began to sell novels and stories, no one was happier than he was. The friendship lasted twenty

years, through various levels of poverty and plenty. We were around for new additions to our families and for support when there was trouble; our children were like cousins; we celebrated each other's successes and mourned each other's losses and we laughed a lot. We were that kind of friends. It ended in 1989, in a bizarre spasm of acrimony which I won't go into, and perhaps our relationship was only dying a natural death, as Karen has suggested.

There are and have been other, finally truer, friends—and other concerns.

At George Mason, I studied with the poet Margaret Gibson, and though we seldom see each other these days, she was wonderfully encouraging and she introduced me to Peter Taylor, among others. Among the students at Mason, we met the Gormans, Jim and Sally, and Tom Philion. Gorman was a veteran, like me, on the GI Bill. He was studying philosophy; Sally was putting him through school by working at Fairfax Hospital as a nurse. Philion was just out of high school—a dark, stocky kid with already a huge knowledge of the world's music. Of all the world's music. The walls of his apartment were lined with records the way the Gorman's and ours were lined with books. We all spent long hours talking, talking, trying our ideas, being funny, being smart. Tom educated me in classical music, and Gorman educated me in philosophy.

The Gormans now live in Milwaukee, where Jim is pastor of Faith Church of Christ, and Sally still does health care, acting as a nurse at a pediatric home-care agency. It was Sally who walked with me back to the intensive care unit to see Wesley minutes after he was born. She still calls him "tootie," though he is now a good foot taller than she is. And Philion, after successful stints with at least one ballet company and several orchestras—including the National Symphony and the Cleveland Orchestra—is managing the Vermont Symphony.

In 1974, with a fourteen-month-old child and almost no money, Karen and I put everything we owned into an eighteen-foot Ryder truck, and drove out to Iowa, where I had been accepted at the Iowa Writers' Workshop. At Iowa, I was a teaching/writing fellow, and studied with Vance Bourjaily, John Leggett, and John Irving, among others. My classmates were Barbara Grossman (now senior editor at Charles Scribner's—and the mother of twins), Jane Smiley, Allan Gurganus, Douglas Unger, Richard Wiley, Joanne Meschery, Meredith Steinbach, Michael McGuire, Mark Jarman, and Robert Chibka; a pretty strong class, I think—and most of us are still in

"In Iowa, April 1975: (standing) Karen, me, Henry Bromell, Barbara Grossman, Jane Smiley, Meredith Steinbach, Robert Chibka; (kneeling) Joanne Meschery, Hope Landres, Allan Gurganus"

some kind of touch, some through the books that keep appearing every year.

In September of 1974, not long after our arrival in Iowa, my sister Barbara and her husband, Gerry, were killed in an automobile accident. As it was with Dave Marmorstein's death, we got the news in the middle of the night. We flew home the following morning. Barbara and Gerry had four children, ranging in age from eleven to three years old, and our parents took over the job of raising them (the oldest, Laura, has her own little boy now, and he lives with my father; so three generations of children have called that man "Daddy").

After Iowa, we had no work, save part-time teaching, without benefits, at the two Virginia colleges I had attended. We were poor, and so was everyone else we knew. The Gormans were living in Chicago, and Philion had moved to Connecticut with his first wife. He was managing the Hartford Symphony, and we talked on the phone a lot. I had met Susan

Richards Shreve, who had been hired over me as the writer at George Mason University. *A Fortunate Madness* had just come out, and she was finishing up *A Woman Like That*. She sought me out when she arrived, and we had an immediate chemistry—it has been a blessed friendship.

Some of the other writers I came to know that year were Tim O'Brien and John Gardner (both introduced to me by Susan), James Dickey (through Garrett and Maiolo), Frederick Busch, whose wonderful stories moved me to write him, and Dave Smith (introduced to me by Margaret Gibson).

In the spring of 1976 Karen was pregnant with Emily; I was spending the nights trying to write and doing all sorts of part-time work, in every kind of circumstance, to make extra money. There were angry phone conversations with bill collectors and credit companies, and then Wesley, at not quite three years old, wound up in the hospital with pneumonia. Having no medical insurance, we incurred more debt. I was making a little less than $530 a month, and it wasn't stretching a bit beyond the first two weeks of each month. We were worried all the time about whether or not we were going to be able to put food on the table, and even so we were happy. We had a dog my sister Betty had given us, and we had puppies from that dog, and we had Wes, Emily, and then, in October of 1977, Paul.

It was over Christmas of 1977 that I began what was to turn into *Real Presence*.

Earlier that December, we had been to Damascus, Maryland, to visit my parents (the journey there always takes us past the curve in the road—and the tree with its paint marks—where Barbara and Gerry died), and had gone to Mass with them at a little church in the Maryland countryside. The priest there began his sermon with a small sigh of what looked like exhaustion, and then asked that people not call him between the hours of six and seven each night, so he could have one hour to eat a meal in peace. His expression and the half-melancholic, half-exhausted tone of his voice gave me the first intimation of my old priest, Father Vincent Shepherd. I first thought of it as a story, and then as a possible short novel. I was working on a novel at the time—I was calling it "The Far Country." (It remains in longhand script in my desk drawer. One sketch from it later became a short story, "The Brace," which no magazine wanted, but which is, I think, the best story in my most recent collection.)

In any case, I worked on the new idea all through Christmas week of 1977—we were visiting with Karen's parents, Jay and Betty Miller of Champaign, Illinois—and they had fixed me up a room to work in. Indeed, through a lot of very unpromising time, those two people never once let on what must have been grave doubt about my prospects. They kept a respectful quiet in their own house while I entertained pipe dreams in the other room. At that time, it could have seemed nothing else. In any case, I stopped working only for meals, and in the first week I had around one hundred typescript pages. I was beginning to see that it would be a novel, and when we got home that beginning of 1978 I worked on it almost day and night—but mostly at night, and as I have said many times, that novel still has a nocturnal feeling about it. I worked on into the warmer months, finishing a draft sometime in June, I think. Karen took it upstairs and read it one Saturday morning, and when she came down she looked as though she might cry. "Honey," she said. "It's not ready."

And of course it wasn't.

I was so discouraged that I put it aside, and went back to work on "The Far Country," even typing some of it up to look at it. I believe it was the late summer before I looked at the priest novel again, and discovered that it wasn't so bad as I had thought. I went back to work on it, and completed a much longer draft that fall. Again, it wasn't right, and I knew it. So I began again, writing from the first page on, sometimes referring to what I had and sometimes not. In February or early March, just as we were learning that we were not going to be able to renew our lease on the house we were renting, I came upon the true architecture and matter for *Real Presence*, and finished it. The end surprised me, I remember. And I ran upstairs from the workroom I'd rigged in the downstairs den of this house we were about to be evicted from and read the last pages, shivering, to Karen.

By this time, I had an agent: Harriet Wasserman, who was then with the honorable old Russell and Volkening Agency. Gordon Lish, when he was at *Esquire*, liked one of the stories I sent him well enough to suggest me to her—I remember what he said exactly: "She has a good eye, and she's cracker jack at placing first novels." I still owe Mr. Lish for that great favor. Ms. Wasserman took me on on the strength of a single story, and she has been a dear and true friend, and a great business partner, for fifteen years now.

I sent the novel to her on April 1, 1979, and on April 9 she sold it to The Dial Press. We were official, as they say. The afternoon we received the news, I stood in the open front door of the house and shouted to the neighborhood: "Everybody listen up! I'm a novelist!" We called everyone we knew, of course, and we had a party. Tom Philion flew down

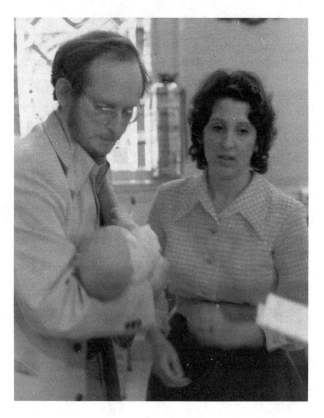

"Karen, Emily, and I at Emily's baptism: no money, no prospects, but we were happy anyway," 1976

from Connecticut, and later went to sleep in the bathtub. Karen and our friend Suzanne got him up and helped him into his room, tucked him in. Over the years, the joke is that he and I both have been gently aroused in this fashion by lovely women, at the predawn, tag-end of parties, and then escorted to bed and tucked in like babies.

People were kind and happy for us. There were cards and bottles of champagne and wine and late-night phone calls. Suzanne, who had been my student in the worst times, and wound up baby-sitting for the two older children when Paul arrived, had become like a member of the family—as I am proud to say students of mine do fairly regularly. Suzanne is still with us—she acted as the agent for us when we had this house in the country built—and her place is so familiar as to make it difficult to remember that she was ever sitting in my class.

We had several parties the week I sold *Real Presence*. At some point during all the festivities, my brother Bob leaned toward me and said, "Don't you wish Barbara were here to see this."

Yes. With all my heart.

I remember that at about four in the morning of the day after I had the news, I woke with a bad, deep feeling of dread. I have often jokingly said that if you were to have been standing in the doorway of the room and had seen me, you would have witnessed a physical incarnation of Edvard Munch's etching *The Scream*. I got up and paced and walked the house and worried. And then Emily had a nightmare and I went and got her out of her bed, the two of us shivering under a blanket on the sofa, cuddling, and I was talking to her softly, reassuring her, wanting to say that I was as frightened as she was, wishing I could go sit in my own father's lap.

Getting what you want after years of struggle toward it is frightening, and as I look over what I have written I see that I haven't come close to truly characterizing the nature of the lean years—when bill collectors were hounding us, and there was no money to be had and no hope for getting any money, and people who loved us were wondering how long we would persist in this foolishness—when I would give up and get a real job. I would have done so, too, if it hadn't been for Karen. During the worst of those times, when I had accepted a job with the government and was out of any other kind of work, she sat me down at the dining-room table of the shack we were living in at the time and began to list all the reasons why I should take the job—security, regular pay, medical benefits, etc.—and then listed the one reason she wanted me to turn the job down: I would hate it. And she said, "I'd rather have nothing and live with someone who's happy doing what he's doing."

But my favorite story about Karen involves the tax people, when we were called in to go over our return for 1981. I had sold *Real Presence* and *Take Me Back*—which arrived, like singing, over the summer of 1979—and we had used the money to pay back hospitals and credit people, and then Uncle Sam had come crashing down with his own estimate of what we owed him. We were living in another rented house and we didn't have five cents in the bank, and my salary at George Mason, where I had been invited to teach in the new writing program, was a good $22,000 *below* what the median salary range was in Fairfax, Virginia, at that time. Still, Uncle Sam felt he had to have a much larger cut than we had estimated we owed him, and so we had been sending $150 a month to the Internal Revenue Service, trying to make up the debt.

And they called us in. Karen has always handled the bills and the money, so we went in together, and we brought all three children. We sat in the waiting

area and let the children play, and finally the caseworker, a woman, asked us into her office. It was decided that Wesley, who was almost nine, would watch the other two children, and they would all stay in the reception area. Karen and I went into the caseworker's office and sat side by side in ladder-back chairs opposite the desk where a young woman looked over our file.

"How much money do you have in checking?" the woman asked.

"Eleven dollars," Karen said.

"And savings?"

"We have no savings."

"And do you have any money on you?"

Karen leaned forward, opening her purse, and with a brittle smile, and in a voice filled with pleasant hatred, said, "Well, I don't think so. Do you want me to go out and shake the children down?"

I still laugh when I think about it. I was so proud to be sitting next to her there, and I'm still proud.

As I said, *Take Me Back* arrived like singing. I can recall thinking that I would pay a price for the ease with which the thing was written. That summer, I'd get up lazily around ten in the morning, eat a bowl of cereal, then go to my desk and begin work. I had written the first few pages while at Chautauqua in New York State, and I had already begun typing the pages I'd done earlier. I'd sit at the desk and write longhand, then use the easy chair on the other side of the room. I worked well, all of the late morning and into the early evening, when I would break for dinner. There were nights when I played a little basketball outside—someone had put up a basket and backboard on the curb—and then I'd come back in and shower and play with the children a little, after which everyone went to bed and I'd work some more, usually until some past midnight. The next day, the whole cycle would begin again. I had written most of *Real Presence* at night—the last two drafts, anyway, in the hours after midnight, most nights—and this working all day was fun. I worked fifteen-hour days on the thing, and finished it in a little less than four months.

That was in September of 1979. I was to go from that time to October of 1983 before I was to sell another thing. False starts, failures, novels dying under my hand. Good things were happening: I had been invited to teach in the writing program at George Mason; *Real Presence* appeared in June of 1980 and was selected for the Book-of-the-Month Club and positively reviewed in *Time*. It went through two printings. *Take Me Back* appeared the following March and was nominated for a PEN/Faulkner

Award at about the time that Bob's first novel, *On the Way Home,* appeared. We were an item—the only identical twin novelists in the history of American letters. The *Washington Post* did a big article about us. I had written a first-person novel called *The Last Good Time,* and while there had been the small shock that Dial didn't want it, they offered me some good money for whatever was next. Harriet advised that we shop the novel around, but I decided to take the offer, since Karen and I were still in such straits financially, and I feared the prospect of a long wait while we looked for another publisher. I was confident; I had produced *Take Me Back* in four months, and the latest one, the one I was calling *The Last Good Time,* had taken about that long as well. I would take another four months and produce another novel. But then I ran into a strange period where the words seemed to dissolve as I wrote them—seemed to drain themselves of their old associations and meanings. It was as if I had turned myself to stone. I wrote every day, and I produced many pages of polished, adequate prose fiction; yet there was something dead at the heart of it, and through many revisions of various materials, I worked my way down to nothing.

I had another student, Cary Kimble, who had become a friend, and his humor and appetite for good talk, good food, good music had made some of the darker worries lighter; Karen and I had a lot of parties back then, and we wound up introducing him to another friend, also named Karen, who was working as a secretary in the English department at George Mason. They are my proudest social accomplishment, happily married since 1984, with two children, and I have laughed as hard with them as I have laughed with anyone on earth, with the possible exception of Philion.

In 1982 and part of 1983 I had produced a long piece of a novel I was calling "The Summer before the Wars," and had completed the manuscript of another novel, about 379 typed pages long, called *Spirits.* None of it was any good. I had also written 80 pages of a thing called "Winter House," which I still may go back to one day, and any number of fragments and pieces and attempts. Finally, in frustration, I sent off the one called *Spirits,* just to see what Harriet thought of it. I told Karen I would take a year without writing at all, just to educate myself again. I would just read. We were sitting in a restaurant, eating salad and soup.

"I give you one week," she said, smiling.

"I'm serious," I told her. "I mean it."

She didn't even look up from her soup. "Seven days. Tops."

Harriet said she liked *Spirits,* but I no longer liked it. It wasn't alive for me, somehow.

About this time, April of 1983, I was describing for Karen some of the difficulties I was encountering in trying to write at all, trying to get the themes straight, trying to make the novel *mean* something, and she said, "But don't you see, that's not you. That's not what you do as a writer, all that intellectual stuff. You're like Tennessee Williams—you write about people trying to get used to their pain."

I accepted the point, without subscribing to the similarity in any other way—being someone who would like to dream he might write something as filled with heart as Mr. Williams. In any case, about five days after our conversation in the restaurant I thought of Edward Cakes, with his little apartment and his picture of a flapper on the wall. I was interested in memory, I think. How the past looks from great distance. In any case, I made up my mind that I would simply tell a story: and I sat down at the kitchen table the next morning and wrote this sentence: "On the outskirts of a great northern city there lived an old man who kept a small apartment, alone, because that was the way his life had gone."

I had been thinking about the picture of the flapper on an apartment wall, without having any idea what it meant or exactly where it would take me. I began with the simplest wish merely to tell a story, and not to think about it being my third novel, or there being the necessity of some departure from myself, or from what I had already done. I remember feeling that it was a kind of capitulation, and just maybe it was—but I'm glad of it. It opened the gates, in a way. I was calling this novel "Edward Cakes and the Flapper," but I hadn't got far along with it before I discovered that one of the characters in it was the major character of the old first-person narration I had called *The Last Good Time.* So I incorporated most of the first thirty pages of that manuscript into the new one and changed the title. *The Last Good Time,* in its final form, was written from April to August of 1983. I shopped it around, looking for a buyout of the old Dial contract, but then in the fall of 1983 decided to give Dial the book. Allen Peacock accepted it, and then left to go to Simon and Schuster, with the new Linden Press imprint.

My new editor, Fran McCullough, suggested some revisions—actually, she thought it needed a couple more scenes toward the middle—and I supplied them. The novel was published in October of 1984, only months before Doubleday, in a corporate spasm, collapsed Dial Press, and fired all the editors and assistants.

That year, on the strength of *Real Presence* and *Take Me Back*, and the sale of a story (it was actually a late chapter of the novel *Spirits*) to the *Atlantic Monthly*, I was given a Guggenheim Fellowship. I took a year off teaching and swore that I'd get to the bottom of *Spirits*. I failed that fall to make any real progress. And I had begun to work stories a little—after years away. I wrote a piece called "What Feels Like the World," and in April of 1985 sold it to the *Atlantic*. I decided, at about this time, that I would make a collection of stories and call it *Spirits*, after the abortive novel.

And even so, the stories arrived at first without much of a sense that I was making a book. There were other things going on: my mother had been ill, and on August 4, 1985, she died suddenly. Karen and I were en route to Illinois, driving and stopping along the way, to visit her parents, and we didn't get the news—no one knew where to reach us on the road—until it was too late to go home again.

"She's not here, Son," my father said. "I don't want to worry about you trying to drive here. And you have your own family to worry about."

That end of summer is hard to remember clearly. We traveled on to Minnesota to see the Maiolos, and then to Wisconsin to spend a few days with the Gormans. I wasn't thinking of writing. And I don't remember when I did go back to work. Work is, after all, what one is given to do in the world.

I wrote "Police Dreams" next, I think. Perhaps it was the fall of 1985. Then "Wisemen at Their End"—that one I wrote mostly while lying in bed with a cold. I remember that I began a story about a hitchhiker one morning, got about two pages in—where the young woman, the hitchhiker, shoots a man—and then put it aside, feeling that it wasn't my kind of story at all. I worked on others, several of them at the same time—the title story, I recall, was done over different drafts of others as well—moving from story to story as I felt like it. When one took hold, I would stay with it until it was finished. One night while talking to a student about his story, I said, "You have to go with your subconscious, you have to trust it, let it take you wherever it seems to be taking you and don't question it until whatever it's going to be is written. *Then* is the time to be conscious and smart." And I thought of the story I had put aside. I went home and wrote the rest of "The Man Who Knew Belle Starr," following the subconscious where it wanted to go, and in the space of the rest of that night I substantially finished it.

The last story I worked on was one called "Letter to the Lady of the House." It was the transcription of a song I'd written back in my singer/entertainer days. I didn't like it much, and left it off the end of the book, which was completed in the summer of 1986. I had sold "Police Dreams" to the *Atlantic*, along with "The Man Who Knew Belle Starr." The earlier story, "What Feels Like the World," had been chosen for the O. Henry awards.

Since Dial had folded, and we were not thrilled with what Doubleday had done to *The Last Good Time*—Doubleday was a travesty of a publisher back then, the books so cheaply made that no one who knew books could fail to be appalled—we went up on auction with *Spirits, and Other Stories*, and a bare outline for a novel which was to become *Mr. Field's Daughter*. Allen Peacock, at Linden Press, made a preemptive bid in August of 1986, and we agreed to terms. It was the beginning of a very good period of productivity for me—which is still going on as I write this.

In the summer of 1986, after I had delivered *Spirits*, I wrote another story, "The Fireman's Wife." Gradually, while working on the new novel, which I was then calling "This Just Man" (I may still write that one, too), I kept writing stories, or simply working through sketches for stories. I had already decided that after I was through with the novel, I would do another collection.

During the summer of 1986, there was a little space where Karen thought she might be pregnant, and when it turned out that she wasn't, we were both so sad that we began to think about having another child. She traveled with me on the train to New York that September, when I went to sign contracts with Simon and Schuster; we stayed at the St. Moritz, in a lovely room overlooking Central Park. We like to think that Maggie was conceived there. In any case, she arrived the summer of 1987, and for the first time we had the experience of bringing a baby into a house we owned. We call her our yuppie baby; and this one has real literary pedigree, being the goddaughter of two of America's best writers: Mary Lee Settle and George Garrett. Her christening was held at a little chapel on the campus of Georgetown University. The celebrant was a young Jesuit, Father Edward Ingebretsin. It was a beautiful hour: Garrett and my pal Roland Flint read poems, and Mary Lee read from the Gospel of John; I played a choral rendition of Schubert's *Ave Maria* on a small tape player; we had communion, and then we all sang "Amazing Grace," led by Susan Richards Shreve's daughter Kate. My sister Betty and her family were there, and of course our older children. Afterward, we all went to Susan Shreve's for a

With George Garrett at the 1990 PEN/Malamud award ceremony—"Garrett was the honoree"

reception. And then George Garrett took us out to dinner.

We were all so imbued with the glow of what was happening that not one photograph was taken.

In the spring of 1988 I was nominated for the PEN/Faulkner Award again, this time for *Spirits*. I was hard at work revising *Mr. Field's Daughter*, and the revision was going slowly, seemed to be creating new problems with very sentence, and so everything was colored by that difficulty. We had received news that "Police Dreams," which had appeared in the *Atlantic*, had been chosen for inclusion in *Best American Short Stories*, and that another *Atlantic* story, "The Man Who Knew Belle Starr," was chosen for *New Stories from the South: The Year's Best, 1988*. That story also helped win the National Magazine Award for the *Atlantic*.

None of these things quite got through to me because of the trouble I was having with *Mr. Field's Daughter*. And then in the late summer of 1988, I had a breakthrough of sorts. Revision went very quickly after this, and I delivered the final manuscript in the early fall.

In the spring of 1989, thanks to Mary Lee Settle, I was sent to the Far East and on to Australia and New Zealand as part of the Voice of America program; I gave readings and lectures and was interviewed by the local papers. But the trip abroad taught me that the terrain I love best is the terrain of Karen and the children's faces. We were having a new house built out in the country; Karen was pregnant with our little accident, Amanda. Things were all up in the air about movers and whether or not the new house would be finished; we were waiting for the publication of *Mr. Field's Daughter*, and I had stopped work on what I began as one of the stories of the new collection, but which quickly showed itself to be another novel. I met wonderful people in Taipei, and in Australia and New Zealand, but I wanted to go home beyond the telling. One night in a hotel in Christ Church, I opened a closet and found perhaps thirty airport-sized bottles of liquor, and for perhaps the second or third time in my life made a conscious decision to get drunk. I opened the first one— bourbon—and savored it. The others, brandy and scotch and more bourbon, I didn't stop to taste.

Before the night was over I was lying on my back in the middle of the bed, completely blotto, laughing at absolutely nothing and thinking about the fact that I was in a country where I knew nobody at all, thousands of miles away from everyone I loved. It seemed ridiculously funny, but it was depressing, too. In one week, I would meet Karen in Hawaii. That week went by like evolution.

Mr. Field's Daughter was published to the best reviews I've ever had, and I'm told it did reasonably well in the stores. The experience of writing the novel was a little like arranging thrown cards in a deck—I worked on the end in the beginning, the middle at the end, the beginning in the middle. I never knew what was supposed to go where—it took good readings of it by Karen, and by Allen Peacock and Harriet, and a lot of encouragement and advice from all of them to get the thing where it needed to be. And it is the one novel of mine that I never was excited about: it felt like the most intractable work, and I was fighting all the time a battle not to be simply skillful with it, but to get down to where it engaged my heart. I did that, but at tremendous cost in energy and those resources you call on in the workroom. By the time it was published, I was exhausted, and did not want to look at it or have much at all to do with it.

This could be also that the collection I was working on had given me, in the middle of work on it, another novel, "Violence," at which I was hard at work throughout the summer of 1989. That was a busy summer: we moved out to the country, and Amanda was born (a speeding trip the thirty miles into Fairfax, with me holding Karen's hand and helping her breathe, and Karen saying "Hurry, hurry."), and I finished a version of "Violence." But it was going to need another time through. I had begun to write more stories and was having more luck selling them to the magazines, and I decided to complete the new collection and publish it first. Thus, in 1990, *The Fireman's Wife, and Other Stories*. Two of them had been in the *New Yorker*, two in the *Atlantic*, one in *Esquire*, and one in *Wigwag*. Still another, "Old West," was donated to Share Our Strength, and was printed in that anthology, all the proceeds of which go to helping the homeless. Two were included in the 1990 *Best American Short Stories*, and one was includ-

Richard Bausch—"Karen took the picture of all of the rest of us: Wesley holding Amanda, Emily, Maggie, Paul, and me," 1990

ed in the 1990 *New Stories from the South*. The last story, "Letter to the Lady of the House," the one I'd left off the end of *Spirits, and Other Stories*, was first of the two that were in the *New Yorker*; it won a National Magazine Award, and was the occasion of more letters than anything else I've ever written—it touched people in a way I could not have begun to anticipate, though of course I would like to pretend I had at least an inkling of it. I am the fellow who threw it away, though.

In an article for *Contemporary Authors*[1] I said, being cute, that I hated literary gatherings. Well, maybe there are certain kinds of literary gatherings I hate; but I do love the company of other writers, younger and older. I used to lean back and clasp my hands over my head and say, "Oh, God, but I do love being young and gifted." I have removed the word *young* from the phrase, but the sentiment still holds: Susan Richards Shreve, when we first met, told me she didn't know any writers and wanted to know who I might know. At the time I knew almost no one except my classmates at Iowa, only two of whom were publishing yet. Since then, Susan has gone on to serve as president of the PEN/Faulkner Foundation; I don't know any writers whose respect and admiration she does not have; working with her, I have come to know some wonderful poets and fiction writers: John Gardner, the wonderful Roland Flint, Henry Taylor, C. K. Williams, Robert Stone, Eudora Welty, Doris Grumbach, Richard Ford, Tim O'Brien, Raymond Andrews, Wesley Brown, and Peter Taylor, to name a few. It was Susan who introduced me to Stephen Goodwin, for the best part of ten years our colleague at George Mason. The three of us have presided over a writing program which brings us into contact with other writers, younger and older. We get paid to do this. Those two have been my allies through all the sometimes-treacherous turns of academic life, and I don't know what I would have done without them, though as Susan said once, we three would have been friends had we been dentists, too. Recently, we added

---

[1]*Contemporary Authors*, Vol. 101, Frances C. Locher, ed. (Detroit: Gale, 1981), 42.

Alan Cheuse to the gang. Another pal. And it was John Berryman, wasn't it, who said that what really nourished the soul of a writer was work and pals. "Bless everyone in the world," he said in a lovely prayer/poem, "Especially some, thou knowest whom."

Looking over all this, I see that it has come down to a sort of chronology of publications and arrivals of children, jobs, and friends. I don't know what else I ought to say. But it must be quite clear now that the charms of autobiography elude me. I offer everything, then, in the spirit of cooperation—suppressing an urge to wonder what anyone could find of interest in it, and hoping it provides at least diversion. As far as I can make out, these are some of the facts as I know them. When I set out, I wanted to write twenty books; that seemed a good round number. I have written six that I have published. The seventh is almost finished. The eighth and ninth, if my sketches and plans are any indication, should follow fairly quickly. I'm almost halfway there.

February 1, 1991

BIBLIOGRAPHY

Fiction:

Real Presence, Dial, 1980.

Take Me Back, Dial, 1981.

The Last Good Time, Dial, 1984.

Spirits, and Other Stories, Simon & Schuster/Linden, 1987.

Mr. Field's Daughter, Simon & Schuster/Linden, 1989.

The Fireman's Wife, and Other Stories, Simon & Schuster/Linden, 1990.

Short stories are represented in anthologies, including *Best American Short Stories* and *New Stories from the South*. Contributor of short stories to numerous magazines, including *Atlantic*, *Esquire*, *New Yorker*, and *Wigwag*. Author of songs.

Robert Bausch

1945-

LIFE THUS FAR

Robert Bausch—"In my office," 1982

My parents grew up during the depression and spent their early youth watching the world blow up and fall apart. My father was wounded twice overseas. He got hit in Africa, was nursed back to health in a hospital in Tunisia, then got wounded again in Sicily, and was returned to the front lines in time for action in Anzio. My sister Barbara was two years old before he ever saw her. My brother Richard and I were born in 1945, at Fort Benning, Georgia, where my father was stationed after they were done with him in Italy.

My father made up his mind that if he survived the war he would have a good life. The war taught him things. He knew what mattered. In spite of the fact that his generation painted pinup girls on bombers and believed that a woman's place was in the home, he was and still is a kind and loving man. Privately he was very religious, although he wasn't ever very evangelical about it. We were Catholic, and every Wednesday night we would all sit together and my father would lead us in the rosary. I can still hear his deep, reverent voice reciting the Hail Mary.

The heroes of my father's time were silent, stoic fellows who never said how they felt. People like Gary Cooper, John Garfield, John Wayne, William Holden. Only women (and very weak men, or strong men in weak moments) expressed emotions, and when they did it was because they couldn't control them. Controlling your emotions meant not expressing them. So my father didn't use the word *love* a lot. But he knew it mattered, and all our lives we were taught the responsibility of love, what Richard sometimes calls "love's province." Not a feeling, but a way of behaving.

My childhood was full of the usual books of childhood—even now, I can hear my mother's voice saying the words of books I now read my own children. I remember my father's voice, too, although I am not sure they both read to me every night. Stories were important to my family. So were songs, and jokes, and laughter. My father was the best storyteller I've ever seen, and I've seen lots of them. He could be so many different people when he told a story. He'd include every gesture and nuance of a person's character. It didn't matter how many times we'd heard him tell a particular story, we always wanted to hear it again. After a while each story had a name. We would say, "Tell the one about Stabile," or "the one about Shucker," or "the one about Louie Marr and Toley Miller on KP."

When I was six years old we got our first television. It was a box bigger than I was, with a round screen not much larger than my face. We were living in a small three-bedroom house on Kenross Avenue in Silver Spring, Maryland. I remember tall trees and the yard cluttered with leaves. A screen door that shook as though it might come apart when you slammed it. The wind in the fall hissing through the trees, and leaves flying high around the dark eaves of our house.

We were not the first people in our neighborhood to get a television, but still I had never seen one until that day my father brought it home. I think it might have been something he saved a long time to get. He may have been proud of it.

Some of the early television shows became family gatherings. I remember nights when all six of us children sat across the living-room couch, every light out, my father and mother sitting together in a huge chair next to us, popcorn bags rattling, and *The Wizard of Oz* unfolding in front of us like a small, black-and-white dream. (I was a young man before I knew the movie turns to color in Oz. I must have been as shocked as the first movie audience to see the film.) My children can watch that movie anytime they want now, but we couldn't see it any more than once a year. So it was an event and a ritual. It marked the beginning of spring, since that was when the networks saw fit to run it on TV. Sometimes now, when I put my five-year-old son to bed and smell his fragrant washed hair, I remember all of my brothers and sisters, freshly washed and ready for bed, hair wet and combed, teeth brushed, soft and moist white feet lined up on the coffee table, waiting for the first sign of the big tornado that we knew would sweep Dorothy into Oz.

Television was so new back then, people didn't trust it or rely on it as much as they do now. We were never allowed to just occupy ourselves by watching it. In fact my memory of it includes long hours when it was off each day, a blank circle of glass that looked back at me.

We watched "I Love Lucy." My mother reminded us all of Lucy. She looked like her, sang better and more beautifully, and was sometimes just as wildly funny. We never missed "Father Knows Best" or the old "Steve Allen" show. When I was ten years old, my heroes were people who could make my father laugh: Jackie Gleason, Art Carney, Gary Moore, Milton Berle, Jack Benny, Phil Silvers, Martha Raye, Burns and Allen. My father's laugh, even after all these years, still pleases me. I hear it in all laughter, and remember those lazy summer nights, back in the midfifties, lying next to my brother on the floor, watching Bilko outsmart the colonel and feeling really good because my father was laughing.

My mother's singing moved me in the same way. She could have been a nightclub singer. Her voice soothed me. I know she sang to me when I was a baby, and something of that memory haunted me when she'd stand in front of the sink every night and sing a Glenn Miller or Tommy Dorsey song while she rinsed the dishes. All of us children had to help in the kitchen. My father wanted us to "honor" our mother. I thought "honor" was his word.

I think I understand now why "I Remember Mama" was another one of our favorite TV programs. That was about a family of six, struggling week to week, getting along, working at caring for one another in the inevitable confusion and competition of big families. I don't know that we learned anything from watching that show. I doubt it, knowing the quality of TV. Still we developed a sense of our own kinship. Ours was a large family and this show seemed to be about people like us. I don't think it was a situation comedy. It was drama. I remember how safe it made me feel to see a family like that, like ours, offered up to the whole world by TV, facing its troubles and overcoming them. Or, in the better episodes, learning to live with them.

There were eight of us including my parents. Six children always seemed to be the number, although I remember very clearly when my two younger brothers were born. My sister Barbara was the oldest, my parent's first child, born while my father

The Bausch boys at five or six years old; Robert at left

was fighting in Italy. Then came Richard and me, and two years after that my sister Elizabeth. It did not strike me until much later, when I had only two children under five years old clattering around in my peaceful, small house, that my mother managed in a one-room apartment with four of us—Barbara at five, Richard and I running everywhere and getting into everything at three, and my little sister, Betty, one year old, learning to walk in what little space was left.

I don't know if I could identify my earliest memory—or if I'd want to. But there are two images that I have never forgotten which might have happened in the same year, even the same season. One is of me crossing a street I was not allowed to cross so I could play in a tempting forest, and the other is of a little girl, not much older than me, lying under a gray blanket in that street. People standing over her don't seem to move normally.

I don't know if she was killed, but I think she must have been. In my memory, the blanket is draped over her up to her chin. Her hair is brown and her eyes are closed. She lies close to the street, as though she is a part of it.

I was four years old. My twin brother was with me. We watched through a screen from the second floor of a two-room town house my parents rented on Geranium Street in Washington, D.C. An ambulance

came down the street. The image I have of it includes silence—as though it approached out of a spiritual place. It may have been loud with sirens—the old kind that sounded like human wailing—but I don't remember that.

I crossed that street sometime that year. My father told me not to go into the street at all. He was on his way to church, and I was playing with my brother in the front yard. I watched him walk up the sidewalk, wearing a gray fedora, a brown suit. I don't know why my mother was not going with him that day. Perhaps Betty was sick. Or maybe she went when my father came back, because there was no one to stay with us children.

My father had to walk to church because we did not yet own a car. I remember the sound of his shoes crunching the small stones on the sidewalk. As soon as he was out of sight, I walked across the street. Richard said, "You're going to be in trouble."

I don't know how long I stood there on the other side. My memory tricks me and I am handed this image of my father coming back almost instantly. Perhaps I was so excited and amused I forgot the time, but I don't think so. My brother thinks some neighbor named Ruth saw me as she drove to church and that she stopped and told my father and he came back. At any rate, that may have been the first time my father spanked me.

Both of these events come back to me when I try to identify the first things I remember. They don't haunt me, but perhaps something in the danger of crossing that forbidden street and the tragedy of that little girl under the gray blanket colors my vision of things when I am unconscious of my motivations and just writing.

In fact, I rarely write about things that haunt me. If I have guilt over some failure, or terrible fear of losing one of my children, those are things I learn to repress by writing about something else. I purposely think of other trouble and address that. Still, I know we are often moved by things of which we are not even remotely aware. Like most people, I am conscious of almost nothing before the age of three, but the most important influence in my life may have been the reaction of virtually everyone to the fact that I am a twin. From infancy I have been treated as though I were special. People ooh and ahh over twins. Pleased and joyous faces spend a lot of time in front of twins, looking first at one, then the other. In crowds of children, twins are singled out.

I think all those eyes looking with wonder and affection upon me, even during all the days and weeks lost to infant memory, gave me a strong sense of my own value. I am not talking about ego, mind you. I believe I am as flawed as anyone, better than some and no worse than most. I do not think I have any special talent beyond the average salesman's ability to tell a good joke, keep conversation lively, and entertain with a few funny stories. I can draw fairly well, but have no sense of color whatsoever. Words do not come easily to me, but I love them anyway. I think I have a better-than average memory, but I clutter it with things no one cares about.

When I say I developed a strong sense of my own value, I am talking more about confidence, and a willingness to offer what talent I have to the world without fear. It isn't brazenness as much as it is belief. People will pay attention to me because they have always paid attention to me.

When I was fourteen I wrote my first novel. I filled 414 legal-pad pages before I gave up and started to rewrite. I got 60 pages into the rewrite and quit. I was in the eighth grade. By that time we lived in Wheaton, Maryland, and I was attending Belt Junior High School—which, by the way, no longer exists. My English teacher showed no interest in my work, and when I turned it in for a term paper that year—to save myself from certain failure—she gave me a D because it did not have footnotes. I am sure she did not read it. My history teacher—a kind, inspiring man named Mr. Hickman—did read it. He gave me an A and encouraged me to try and publish it. My book was a Civil War story, and this was the beginning of the Civil War centennial.

I have never been as excited about writing, or enjoyed it more, than I did that year. My grades went deeper and deeper into the alphabet, but my parents didn't seem to mind. (My schoolwork never did recover.) The whole family paid attention to what I was doing. I'd come home from school and my mother would clear the dining-room table and I'd sit down and write until dinner. She'd bring me a glass of chocolate milk or ice water and ask me how it was going. I would work nonstop until dinner—usually 5:30 or 6:00. Sometimes I'd work after dinner. My father would come home late and sit down to eat across from me. My sister Barbara was taking typing that year and volunteered to type what I had written. As my handwritten pages piled up, she'd peck on her portable typewriter, trying to catch up to me.

I remember that small house now, the quiet afternoons of work, and I don't see how it was possible. When I was fourteen, all the children had been born. There were six of us. Steve was seven years old. Tim was four. Betty was twelve. Dick was my age, and Barbara was sixteen years old. The house was a small, three-bedroom Cape Cod, with a combination dining area and living room, and a very narrow kitchen. There was no basement. A washing machine was parked by the back door next to the hot-water heater. There was one bathroom. You could not sneeze anywhere in that house without being blessed from some other room. And yet I remember the house pausing for me. Letting me work on my book.

I would occupy all my time in school dreaming of what I would write each day in the silence of those long afternoons. I think I became a writer that year, but I didn't let it stick with me. That summer I got back into baseball and forgot my novel. Perhaps, but for the changes we go through at that time in our lives, I might have finished it and begun another. By the time I was fifteen, the boy who wrote the novel was some other kid way back in junior high. In any case, the experience of high school was so bad I did very well just to keep my interest in reading.

Let me tell you something about public education. As I write this, people are debating whether or not to increase the school year an extra month. Some are advocating going the year round. The objection is, of course, that this will cost lots of money. That would not be my objection. My problem with the idea is that increasing the school year would only provide *more* of a bad thing. Education would not be improved by having more days where teachers are underpaid and classrooms are too full. If anybody really wanted to improve education they'd cut class sizes in half and keep a nine-month school year and watch what happens. Watch how much ground is covered by a teacher working with fifteen students instead of thirty.

School nearly killed my imagination. I had teachers facing too many kids, insisting on the one thing that is counter to both creativity and learning: order. Learning and creativity are chaotic and frustrating and full of passion and wonder. I am not speaking from the position of the writer who naturally tends to simplify things for a balanced rhetorical statement. I have been a teacher since my first year in the air force—more than twenty-five years—and I have observed very carefully how learning takes place. Unless you are teaching math, or some other precise science, not very much learning is achieved by insisting on neatness, correctness, and the proper order of things. I know there are pea-brained people who think learning is lockstepped and orderly—who insist that material should be presented when the teacher is ready to present it, rather than when the student is ready to have it presented—but it just isn't true. I don't know if my writing career might have been rekindled my first year in high school. But I had a teacher who could not possibly respond adequately to thirty compositions from my class, as well as the one hundred and twenty she was bound to collect from her other classes. No human being could respond to each and every one of 150 essays. All she could do was attack its grammar, insist that it be neat, and give it back. Since she could not respond to anything I said, since she could only penalize or reward me according to how correct and neat my work was, and since that seemed to indicate that it didn't matter what I said, but only how I said it, I was convinced very early in my high-school career that I had nothing of any importance to say.

I didn't start writing again until I was in the military.

I spent most of my time in high school playing football and shooting pool, and I still don't know what providence caused me to graduate. I didn't have anything to do with it. I can't remember a single thing I learned in high school. I remember my teachers, who worked very hard I'm sure. I understand what they were up against now. Back then, I thought they were crazy. They didn't seem like people who ever had fun and they always smelled like chalk dust. I called them the "chalk people."

Although I spent no time studying I did read a lot. I loved books about the Civil War. I read them all—Shelby Foote, Bruce Catton, Henry Steele Commager, Virgil Carrington Jones, Douglas Southall Freeman, Burke Davis. My favorite was Freeman. His four-volume biography of Robert E. Lee captured me for a whole year. I loved every page of it. I loved the way those books smelled and felt in my hands, the texture of the pages and the print. I read every footnote, and when I was finished with the whole thing, I read all the source notes in the back of the last volume. I read that book three times before I was in eleventh grade. I also read all of Bruce Catton's books. In fact, I still have books on my shelf that belong to the Wheaton High School library.

Like my father, I didn't read a lot of fiction. I believed reading fiction was a waste of time because you couldn't be learning anything about history or the world from somebody's imagination. I believed this even though I had spent the entire eighth grade writing a novel.

What fiction I did read I enjoyed. I'd think of it as a sort of break from nonfiction. My mother read almost exclusively novels, and a lot of good ones adorned the shelves in our house. I found books by Hemingway, Steinbeck, John O'Hara, and Edwin O'Connor. I read them all, but at the time my favorite was O'Connor. I loved his Frank Skeffington. When I was a senior in high school I read *The Last Hurrah* twice. Then I read O'Connor's other

books at the time: *The Oracle, The Edge of Sadness, I Was Dancing.*

My brother Richard and I used to read late into the night, then drag ourselves to school in the morning. My parents did not want us to stay up so late—my two younger brothers slept in the same room with us, and we were all supposed to be in bed early on school nights—so we'd place a towel at the foot of the door and if my parents walked by they'd only see a dark slot under the door and think the light was out. I don't know if this truly fooled them, but they almost never came to check on us. If they did, we'd hear them coming, snap off the light, and pretend to be asleep. When they opened the door they'd inadvertently push the towel into the corner behind the door, so they never saw it. Once they were gone, we'd put the towel back and turn the light back on.

It occurs to me now that I've talked about them as though it was always both of them who came in to check on us. I remember it was both of them, and now that I am a parent I understand that they weren't checking on us at all. They were just coming in to

"My mother and father, Helen and Robert Bausch," about 1941

Mother with the author's brothers, Richard, Steve, and Tim, 1962

look at us asleep. It is that looking, late at night, while my children sleep in a bed I've provided for them, that I discover my sense of self and fatherhood and balance and even a sort of permanence. At times like that I understand my parents and love them more and wish I had loved them better.

I graduated from Wheaton High School in 1963 (ranked 534th in a class of 536). I had no plans. We moved to Vienna, Virginia, within the month after I graduated. My father had taken a job managing a Ford dealership in Fairfax, and after years of driving to Virginia six days a week, and working until ten every night, we were going to be within three miles of where he worked. Most of my high-school years the only time I saw him was on Saturday nights and Sundays. The whole family was happy about the move, but I didn't want to go to Virginia. All I knew about it was that it was the South. They got out of school for snow more often than we did, which didn't seem logical to me. And one of the counties there, I think it was Staunton, had closed their school system entirely rather than admit black students.

The civil rights movement was well under way by that summer. I remember Martin Luther King's speech in Washington as though it were yesterday. I saw it on television. John F. Kennedy was president and you had this feeling that things were going to

change. It wasn't a bad feeling. Things needed to change. I can remember people using the word "nigger" on radio and television. Fire hoses and dogs and bombs seemed to be the white South's response to integration.

Once I was in Virginia, though, I came to like it. Vienna was a smaller town than Wheaton and our house was a little better, a little more remote. There were trees again—a forest right next to us.

I was eighteen years old, hustling pool for money and not motivated to do much of anything. I didn't want to go to college—that was only more school—and I didn't really need to work. I made sixty to seventy dollars a night shooting pool.

I don't remember much of that first summer in Virginia. But in late fall, just before Thanksgiving, President Kennedy was murdered in Dallas. I remember, as most who lived through it do, exactly what I was doing that day. I was with my mother. Richard had a job at AFL-CIO in Washington, and the other kids were in school. (My sister Barbara was already married.) I was sitting in the living room in front of the picture window reading, and the telephone rang. It was early afternoon. I heard my mother pick up the phone. I didn't hear anything she said. She came calmly into the room and sat down next to me. "Turn the television on, honey," she said. "They've shot the president."

After that it was all sheathed in our black-and-white screen. The lying in state, the funeral, Jack Ruby shooting Lee Harvey Oswald. It seemed as though the whole country had gone mad.

If Kennedy's death was the end of a brief period of idealism and new promise, it also shattered a kind of stillness and lethargy. Everything appeared to speed up and get more complex—as if Kennedy's death set in motion an electronic fantasy. It was as though we were all suddenly swallowed by a television, and the world came at us through a fish-eye lens with loud music and distorted images. It was easy to see the era before Kennedy's death as a kind of happy, simpler time. But it really wasn't. The fuse for Watts and other fires had already been lit. Viet Nam was a serious problem by then.

In any case, Kennedy's death did something to my sense of the future. I made up my mind that I wanted to get into politics and work toward what I believed Kennedy worked for. I remembered the "world of diversity" speech he made at American University and I came to see myself as a convert to the idea. I was eighteen when Kennedy was assassinated, and by the time I was nineteen I had a full-time job. I was enrolled in a correspondence school to study law, and I was making plans to attend Santa

Monica City College in the fall of 1965. I started writing again, but this time it was for the courses in the law. I wrote legal opinions and prepared briefs and legal arguments. These were evaluated and praised very highly by my so-called law professors. (I will not name the school, but I paid $585 for the course and I got the registration form off a matchbook cover. This will give you some idea of the quality of both the school and my naivete.) I completed the course and was awarded an "L.L.B. Degree" in the spring of 1965. I was very proud of myself. I completed a three-year course in only eighteen months. I thought I would be a lawyer without having to go to college. My aunt, who was dating a lawyer at the time, got him to have a talk with me. That conversation convinced me of two things: that I could not be a lawyer, and that I should, as Kennedy always said, cut the cards.

In August of 1965, before I could enroll in college, Richard and I were drafted into the army. My father told us to "stay out of the infantry." He'd been there, and we took his word for it. So we enlisted in the air force on the buddy system.

We were told we would be able to stay together during basic training, but most likely after that we would get orders for different parts of the world. We went through basic training together, then we were sent to Chanute Air Force Base in Rantoul, Illinois. We ended up spending our entire tour of duty at the same place and doing pretty much the same thing— teaching survival techniques and equipment.

In the service I felt cheated. We were being instructed by men who could barely speak the language. Mediocrity seemed forced on all of us. I mean true mediocrity. I am not a person with ultra-high standards, and I rarely think about competence unless I am confronted with true stupidity. I worked for a man who spent every day in an alcoholic stupor, but he always got high ratings because he was near retirement and no one wanted to deprive him of that. His superiors pretended not to notice that he couldn't stand up. The only time he got close to being sober was when he slept a little too long. He never knew what was going on, or even where he was. As far as I know, he did not work a single day in three and a half years. He was the NCO in charge of training.

When air training command announced they were going to inspect the school, we were told to have the students paint it. As long as it was clean, we passed inspection. It didn't matter at all what we were teaching.

Once we had an ice storm. A hard rain, swept by a brutal wind, crossed the pavement, cuffed the small trees, and froze solid. We marched our troops across a flight line where the wind whipped so bad the entire squadron of men seemed to slide back a few inches for each forward step. When we got them to the school, they were all soaking wet and shivering. The heat in the building didn't work. We had nothing to keep warm. Our commander called somebody to tell them of our predicament and ask permission to send the troops back to their warm barracks. A general—I won't name him—ordered the air police to send two blue air force buses to our school to transport the men back to their barracks so they could get warm showers and dry clothing. Then he ordered us to march them back to the school. It was still raining ice, but that didn't matter. The general made his decision and nobody would ask him if it wouldn't make more sense to have the buses wait around and transport them back to the school. His order read that we were to march them back to school and that is what we had to do.

Perhaps now you have some idea why I say the air force felt like enforced mediocrity. Bad orders were given all the time and then we were forced to follow them or face the consequences. Frequently my brother and I faced the consequences.

For some reason I don't remember, early in my term I was told that I had been designated our squadron's volunteer for the base honors team. That too was a consequence, although I can't remember what I did to deserve it. The honors team was really only a funeral squad. We were professional mourners who traveled on blue air force buses to every military funeral within a thousand-mile radius of Chicago. By that time in my air force career, I had begun reading fiction almost exclusively. I read J. D. Salinger, Ken Kesey, Joseph Heller, some more Hemingway, George Garrett, F. Scott Fitzgerald, William Faulkner, James Jones, and Norman Mailer. I also loved the great Russian writers: Chekhov, Dostoevsky, Turgenev, Pasternak, Tolstoy. My brother was so influenced by what he was reading that he had begun to write poetry and songs, but I wasn't doing much writing then. I kept a journal only sporadically. I wrote long letters to my mother.

The funerals began to pile up on me. In the beginning, the honors team was only attending one or two funerals a month, but by 1967, after the Tet offensive, the war sent more and more bodies home and we were going to two and three funerals a week. I've only written one story about that experience, but it is still one of the most disturbing times of my life. The grieving family almost always believed we had come there to honor one of our fallen comrades. If I am haunted by anything from that period it would be all those sorrowful afternoons pretending I was a friend to the man we were burying.

I remember standing outside a church in Chicago. The weather was freezing and the cold air made my eyes water. I felt the tears on my face turning to ice. A man came up to me, steam escaping his mouth in great gasps, and said, "That's my boy in there. That's my boy."

His face was so contorted in sorrow it was difficult to look at him. I must have given the impression that I would talk to him because he kept himself in front of me, waiting. "That's my boy," he said. He took a deep breath that turned into a cry—a lament he was not prepared for. "Oh, my boy." Then he put his hands on my shoulders. I was so embarrassed for him, and sad that I didn't know his son and could not share in his grief.

"Were you with Terry before he—" he sobbed.

"No. I wasn't." That was the first time I had heard the dead boy's name. I knew he was young and he'd not been killed by the war. He'd driven his motorcycle into a bridge abutment.

"Did you know him well?" The man said.

I lied to him. I told him I'd never known a better man than his son. He nodded, wiping away frozen tears.

He thought I was crying. I hated myself for being privy to his most helpless moment, and for pretending I wasn't a stranger who was ordered to be there.

At night the body counts on the news seemed completely unbalanced. When the newsman said, "Only one hundred and ten U.S. troops died yesterday," I felt as though I would have to bury each and every one of them. One hundred and ten funerals whirled in my mind. In places like Dubuque, Iowa, Appleton, Wisconsin, Gary, Indiana, Danville, Illinois, Niles, Michigan, burials were taking place every day. I'd been to every kind of ceremony: Polish, Jewish, Catholic, Russian, Greek Orthodox.

I couldn't stand the trips on the bus. I'd sit in the back and read while the others played pinochle or gin rummy. They joked and laughed until we arrived at the sight. Then they'd get off the bus and behave with proper decorum. I wished I could accept what we had to do with the same blithe attitude, but I couldn't. I suppose most of those men were as bothered about what we were doing as I was, but their diversion was to engage in noise and banter and dirty jokes until the last minute. I did not want to laugh. It seemed disrespectful, and when we got to the funeral, if I had been laughing with the others, I would have felt like even more of a fake.

Military service wasn't all bad. In spite of how much I loathed each day, I met my closest male friend—a thoroughly contrary, droll, and highly trustworthy rogue named Dennis Metter. We have been friends now for over twenty-five years and can still laugh over some of the more bizarre episodes of mediocrity that we witnessed together. We were both on the funeral squad, too, although they knew better than to send us both out to the same funeral. I think that only happened once or twice in the three years we were on the squad together.

When I got out of the service I stayed in Champaign, Illinois. I thought I wanted to continue at the University of Illinois, where I had begun classes during my last two years of service. But I ended up selling new and used cars for Shelby Motors on Neil Street.

I did not think of myself as a writer then. I was marking time, saving money. That's what I told myself. But I had a good job—I only had to be at work one day during the week and all day Saturdays. The other days, I was supposed to be out looking for possible customers. You could do that anywhere: in poolrooms, on the golf course, in bars and restaurants, and even in the library. I spent many days, especially in winter, shooting pool half the day and reading in the library the other half. On the days when I worked—days where the sales floor was mine and anyone who walked into the dealership was a potential sale for me—I got enough leads and sold enough cars to support myself.

"Home on leave," Robert at left, 1967

I liked selling cars. People almost never do that in a bad mood. It's exciting to help somebody pick out a new car and even better to deliver one. Although I still believed I would eventually go back to school, get a real law degree, and then enter politics, my year selling cars was pleasurable enough that I was not in any special hurry. I might have continued in the job, to tell the truth, but sales got worse and worse as Christmas of 1969 approached, so I decided to return home.

My brother went to Boston in the hope of beginning a career in music with the family of his best friend. Dick had begun singing with Dave Marmorstein while we were in the service. They were very good. Dick wrote beautiful and lyrical verse, and Dave set it to music. Dave also created extraordinary harmonies. But while Dick was in Boston that first year, Dave got killed in an automobile accident. Dick came back to Vienna about the same time I did.

We both attended Northern Virginia Community College in Annandale, Virginia. By that time we were both married and beginning to take school seriously. I did not have the same attitude about school by that time. Now I really did want to be educated. I still believed I wanted to be in politics, and my declared major was political science. Later I switched to international relations. Then economics. The whole time I was taking courses in English. I wanted to get credit for much of the reading I was doing, and those were courses I always did pretty well in.

My brother already considered himself a writer by that first year at Northern Virginia. He took creative-writing courses from a writer there named Joe Maiolo, who encouraged and inspired him. I was in an English composition class with an extraordinary woman named Jill Brantley, who told me I should pursue a writing career. I was flattered, but I told her I was going into politics, that my brother was the writer in the family. And, indeed, Richard's reputation, even then, preceded him. People who came in contact with his work liked it enough to talk about it to others.

I didn't see myself as a fiction writer, but I wanted to prove I could do it if I wanted. So I wrote a story called "The Gift." I don't remember much about it now, but I know it was from personal experience, and I wanted Jill Brantley to read it. I had a line in it that went like this: "I tried to open the package without ripping the paper."

When I showed the story to Richard, he pointed to that line and said, "See, that's the fiction writer in you."

"What fiction writer?"

"The one who wrote a novel in the eighth grade."

I laughed then, but now it seems like it was a sort of turning point. I began to examine how I looked at the world. I saw everything in terms of the arch of events—a movement in time toward some palpable denouement. The more I thought about things the more I realized that I viewed my life as a kind of developing story. What happened to me was plot. However adolescent that may sound, it afforded me the luxury of trusting myself to go ahead and begin writing again. It seemed like the sort of development that would best serve the "plot" of my life.

I wrote another story almost immediately. This one was the only truly autobiographical story I've ever written. It was the story I spoke of earlier about my experiences on the military honors team. I called it "Funerals" and in it I told the story of two funerals, one in summer and the other in winter. The summer funeral is for a young man killed in Viet Nam, and the winter one is for an old man, a World War I veteran. In the story, a young man on a military honors team is remembering an earlier winter funeral, waiting for the summer one to begin. The winter funeral was a disaster: ill attended, the honors team ill prepared, nothing went right; the firing squad misunderstood the commands of the new squad leader and some of them fired their guns at the wrong time. The effect of this part of the story is supposed to be hilarious, and I suppose it is. The summer funeral is intended to be tragic. The young man is forced to present the flag to the dead man's widow, who is young and beautiful and whose tears hurt the young man so much all he wants to do is tell her that her husband is not dead. When he presents her the flag and tries to console her with the sound of his voice expressing his nation's cliches about service to country and comrades and loved ones, she throws the flag back at him.

I don't know why I structured the story the way I did. Or why it became about two funerals. I'd been to thousands of them, and these two seemed representative of certain types in my experience. But the story won creative-writing contests at both Northern Virginia Community College and George Mason University, where I later transferred, so I think it may have been what finally convinced me I should write. Ironically, now when I look at that story my principle response is embarrassment. It is so obviously the work of a fledgling writer and there are so many obvious conscious choices in it that I am fairly amazed, even now, that anybody saw anything in it to admire. Still, I consider "Funerals" my first story. It was my first published story, too. I published it in the college

The author (left)—"The day Richard moved to Iowa," 1974

literary magazine at both of the colleges I attended and I still have a copy of the original manuscript.

You might say that since I wrote that story, I have been trying to get back the sense of joy, expectation, and wonder writing gave me when I was fourteen years old and dreaming in all my classrooms about what I would write each afternoon when I got home. Now it is my work and I cannot find anything magical about it. Or romantic. The notion of a muse seems a wry joke on those of us who ought to know better.

While I was in college I worked various odd jobs to keep food on the table. I drove a taxi one year, worked as a waiter for two days, sold appliances in a discount store. I worked in the public library my senior year of college. I was lucky to write one story a year during this time, and I really don't remember any of the pieces I worked on back then. I was not trying to publish, nor did I do much with those stories but enter them in the yearly literary contest in the English department. I had a beautiful daughter, Sara, by the time I got my bachelor's degree at George Mason University. I went right into graduate school

at the same college and majored in the literature of the 1920s and 1930s.

In the fall of that year, 1974, my sister Barbara was killed with her husband in an automobile accident. They were celebrating their twelfth wedding anniversary. They left four children, between the ages of eleven and three years old. If life is divided according to tragic events, 1974 marked the end of that big, charmed family I grew up with. Now the earth was far more threatening, indifferent, dangerous, and merciless. My mother and father took the children in and they became a new family.

My mother never did get over Barbara's death. Our family had been safe from harm, had been so lucky for so long, this was a sort of death for all of us. In some ways I still don't believe it happened, and even now I wish I could talk to Barbara. It thrilled me to make her laugh. Almost everything I wrote was for her approval. I hate it that I never told her how important she was to me. But what still breaks my heart to remember is that after Barbara's death, my sister Betty and I found a collection of manuscripts she had written. In our lives I had been the writer in the family, then Dick was, and then both of us were, and Barbara listened to us, read our stories, praised our work, and she never told us that she was writing; that she was sending her manuscripts out and getting them rejected.

I wish I had asked her, just once, if she ever tried to write anything. She never went to college. I'm sure she was afraid of what we would say about her work. She was the full-time mother of four children when she was killed. I never saw her. She was grown, a housewife, a happy woman. I could talk to her about anything. But I never really saw her. My mother and father raised her children, gave them family legends and traditions and provided all that was humanly possible of love and sane response to needless trage-dy. The children are grown now, and in spite of their broken childhood, I think they are happy.

I tried for years to get Barbara's work published. I still have it somewhere. Maybe someday I'll take it out and try again. It is her voice, sure and honest and full of compassion.

Barbara's courage in sending her work to pub-lishers inspired me to do the same, and from that day I discovered her manuscripts I have been actively trying to publish. The life of a writer is rejection, and I was learning that very quickly.

By degrees I came to realize that I wanted to be a teacher. While I was in graduate school, working toward that end, I thought I was lucky to have completed one story. I got into the habit of compos-ing one or two stories a year, and when I began my teaching career I continued to do that. I believed that was all I was capable of. It took me a long time to write a story because I composed each sentence exactly as I wanted it before I'd go to the next sentence. It could take a month to complete one page. When I finished a story I had to do very little rewriting. Also, I see now, I was not writing the way I did when I was in the eighth grade.

To support my family while I was in graduate school I took a job teaching in a small private high school in Fairfax called Glebe Acres Prep School. The pay was not very good, but the experience was invaluable. Those kids were not allowed into the public schools. Every one of them had been expelled for one reason or another, and since I remembered my own high school experience in public schools, I didn't have any trouble understanding my students. I became a teacher in the year and a half I worked at that school. I came to love most of my students, and maybe some of them will even remember me.

In 1975 I went right from graduate school to my present position at Northern Virginia Community College. It seems a preposterous irony now that I could have hated school so perfectly when I was in high school and yet I have spent all but one of the twenty-seven years since then in a classroom, on one side of the lectern or the other.

I wrote nothing but short stories for the first few years after college. I was teaching five classes at Northern Virginia, and two classes at George Mason University. By that time my second daughter, Julie, had been born and I didn't have a lot of time to write. I was no closer to publication, although I was getting a lot of kind letters from editors at major magazines encouraging me to send them more of my work. I did not think I would ever write a novel.

It seems odd now to remember that former self who looked upon the novel as this opaque and impossible thing. I had written one. The memory did not serve me. It seemed a childhood game, like pretending to be a fireman. I had pretended to be a writer. Now that I knew what that was, there was no way I could actually sit down and devote so much of my life to a sustained effort of several hundred pages. Especially when I had two gorgeous children to play with.

When I was thirty-three, Richard had already started what would become his first novel, *Real Presence*. We talked about how hard it was to break into the market with our short stories. He had gone to the University of Iowa Writers' Workshop while I was in graduate school. While he was there he wrote a collection of short stories for his thesis. Both of us had never truly completed a novel. I came to believe that the only way I could sell my stories was if I published a novel. It didn't seem like publishing one would be very difficult. After all, there are over forty thousand new books published in America every year. All I had to do was write one.

A colleague and friend, Dr. Robert Kilmer, often challenged me to begin a novel. We were both avid organic gardeners, and we both owned small pickup trucks. Frequently we would go together to get a truckload or two of horse manure for our gardens. I figured I needed some impetus and a time limit to complete a novel. One New Year's Day of 1979, Robert and I agreed that if I didn't finish my novel in one year, I would give him one truckload of manure for each day I needed past the deadline to finish it.

I had written a short story called "War Story." It was about this man whose memory of what happened to him in Viet Nam is so terrible it terrorizes him. I sent the story to an editor at *Harper's* who told me I had not "confronted" the conflict in my narrator's life. I decided to make this story the first chapter of my novel—that way I wouldn't have to face the horrible task of writing a first chapter at all. I put a piece of paper into my typewriter and at the top of the page I typed "Michael." In doing so, I both named my character and began chapter two of my novel.

I called the book *Coming Home,* but shortly after I started on it that movie hit the theaters. So I changed the title to *On the Way There.* I worked pretty steadily on it for most of that year. By December, I had ninety pages. I was not happy with what I had, and I had not written a single story that year, so I felt as though my efforts were wasted. But still, I had my deadline. January first was one month away, and I had this novel to finish.

I was done with school by December fifteenth. I was free for the ten days until Christmas and for ten days after that. In a period of fourteen days over that holiday I wrote the last two hundred and forty pages of that novel. I worked from ten or eleven in the morning until five or six in the evening. Each day I did not stop until I had at least twenty pages. If I got twenty pages and it was only four o'clock, I'd keep working another hour and get a few more. I did not take time to think about how things were going as I worked. I still corrected as I went, still revised each sentence until it was the way I wanted, but I would not let myself stop working. I kept at it, even when it seemed as though the English language consisted of only three words and I knew only two of them.

I finished the first draft of the book on December 30, 1979. By that time my brother had already sold his first novel, so I was fairly confident that once I'd rewritten mine, I'd sell it too. It only took me one month to rewrite the book and clean it up. By February of 1980, I was ready to mail it to an agent.

Three different agents saw it. None of them wanted it. I was almost ready to start representing it myself when my brother suggested Nat Sobel Associates, an agency that had tried to recruit him earlier that same year. I sent it to them, and Judith Weber, who loved the book, decided to represent it for me.

Something happened to me while I was writing that first book. For most of that year I kept telling myself that I was writing a NOVEL. I had this huge, generalized vision of the NOVEL hanging over my head governing everything I did. I was unwittingly trying to write all the novels I'd ever read. While I worked I couldn't shake the sense of this fake voice; I felt almost like the eighth-grader who had pretended to be a writer all those years ago, and the memory would paralyze me. I'd let days go by before I'd get the nerve to sit down and try working on it again. Then, over that Christmas holiday when the book

literally erupted, I realized I was not writing a NOVEL. I was writing *this* novel. *My* novel.

I remember the first sentence I wrote after that realization. It was on page 110 of the typed manuscript, and it began the first chapter of part two of the novel. It goes like this:

I have to get rid of the beads of water on the window.

After that, writing that book was like playing in one of those padded, air inflated rooms where you can throw yourself down or up or over in any direction, fall unhurt, and bounce back up. I was free. Free to write that particular book and let it become whatever it would.

I did not sell it right away though. Thirteen different publishers turned it down, and I was pretty discouraged about ever selling it. A year after I'd finished it, St. Martin's Press purchased it for a very modest advance. By the time my novel, which was now called *On the Way Home,* hit the bookstores, Richard's first book had been released and had gotten rave reviews. *Time* magazine compared him to Flannery O'Connor. He had already sold his second novel, *Take Me Back,* to Dial Press.

Still, I was stunned at the attention my first novel got. Although the *New York Times* ignored it, everybody else paid lots of attention to it. A few weeks after the publication date, reviews started coming in the mail every day. Newspapers large and small, obscure and very famous, raved about the book. *Newsweek* called and sent a photographer to my house to take a picture of me. They featured my book in a favorable review the following week.

Through it all I tried to work on my second novel. It was a book I'd started almost immediately after finishing *On the Way Home.* In the year it took to get the first book into print, I'd gotten about seventy pages of manuscript that I was calling *The Lives and Times of Riley Chance.* Again, I started with something I'd already written, a short piece called "Hard Luck Story," about a man who has lived three lives. I don't know where the story came from, except I was bored one Christmas visiting my first wife's family; I'd had a few whiskeys and I decided to sit by myself all day and write. I would not have to face anyone, and I figured I might get something I could use. The story never worked, but I thought it was creative, and I liked the idea of a man living three lives and getting kind of worn down by his third time around. It occurred to me then, as it still does now, that all lives end tragically if you take death as the end of something wonderful and the beginning of nothing. The character in the story says at one point, "having three lives may sound good to you, but remember you also have to have three deaths. Think about that. That's what I do all the time."

That one line led me to *The Lives of Riley Chance*. Composing that book was completely different though because I did not use the story as chapter one and then extend things from an open end. I jumped into the story and pushed out on all sides. It was the frame for the whole novel, so I felt constrained by it, trapped in it. It was the hardest thing I'd ever done up to that time. I worked on it most of the first year after *On the Way Home* was released, but there were several paralyzed months in there. I was sort of swallowed up by my first novel. In spite of its great reviews and a paperback sale to Avon Bard, which kept the book in print right up until 1989, my first novel did not make up its advance, and I never made a royalty payment on it. Somebody at Avon told me it sold thirty-five thousand copies there, but I've never seen a royalty out of them either.

Still, it had gotten so many good reviews. It was very difficult not to expect the same sort of success for my second book. I finished it while I was in the process of divorcing my first wife and marrying Denny Natt, who was and still is the best friend I've ever had. That whole two-year period seems lost to me completely. I truly don't remember writing huge sections of that book or where I composed most of it. I know I worked at a typewriter, that I started another book called *Out of Season* and wrote a hundred pages or so of that before I stalled and came back to *Riley Chance*. But in the spring of 1983 I finished it and sent it to St. Martin's. It was released in 1984, got rave reviews in about twenty or so newspapers including the *New York Times,* and then disappeared.

The Lives of Riley Chance is probably the best book I will ever write. I came to it as myself, with hope and belief. I wrote it without fear. There is not one conscious choice in it. Even now, I can read parts of that book and be surprised that I wrote it. But it got such scant treatment, and sank so fast out of sight, it nearly destroyed my will to write.

I know I was probably spoiled by the reaction to my first book. It was crazy, improbable good fortune to get such wide attention for a first novel, but I convinced myself that my work was worthy of its acclaim. Richard's novel had been reviewed in *Time,* mine in *Newsweek.* We were the fabulous Bausch brothers, embarking on our gorgeous careers.

I came to expect that sort of treatment for anything I wrote. And since *The Lives of Riley Chance*

was the best that I could ever do, I couldn't wait to see the reaction to it. The silence was early and perfect. Nothing after the first month. No reviews in the mail. No phone calls from national magazines. Nothing.

It took me six years to write my next novel, *Almighty Me.* I started work on it in 1985 after a year of writing short stories. I wanted to get away from the novel after *Riley Chance.* I hated the idea of another book. I was still teaching two classes at George Mason University, and five classes at Northern Virginia Community College. I couldn't take the sheer exhaustion anymore. I'd work until two or three in the morning and when I went to bed I'd be trembling so much I couldn't sleep or even get warm. Perhaps it was a function of my age, but I just didn't have the energy for a novel.

In March of 1985, my son David was born. I saw him come into the world and when I held him in my arms for the first time, I remembered and loved all my children. I was fortunate that year to get a letter from a lost child, a young woman born in 1969 who I knew existed but had never met. I will not go into the details except to say that Suzi is my daughter; I always expected she would one day come into my life, but I never dreamed she would be so much like me, or that it would provide me with such joy to know and love her. For the first time in my life, I felt that my own family was complete.

In August 1985, my mother died. None of us were prepared for that. I remember the first time I looked into my father's eyes after I knew my mother was gone, the ache in my heart of seeing in his eyes what had drained out of his life. They had been lovers and friends for fifty years. My father still has the piece of notepaper my mother wrote on when he was a senior in high school getting ready to graduate with honors, and she was in the eleventh grade asking him to remember her.

I couldn't write for a long time after my mother's death. She was an extraordinary woman. When my brother and I were in the service, she wrote a letter to each of us every week. Richard and I would sometimes compare letters trying to see if she ever got lazy and just copied one letter over again. It didn't seem possible that she could write a separate letter each week to her twin boys who were stationed in the same place. Her letters were always different. Always. She'd write the same news, the same queries and discussions of future hopes. But not once, in four years, did she ever copy Richard's letter over to send to me, or vice versa. Not once did she send one letter addressed to both of us. Dick used to look at me and say, "Could you do that?"

My mother and father created our family and it has been terrible watching time defile it, as time always does. My father is still alive and healthy, but he is incomplete without my mother.

I worked sporadically until 1987, when I made a momentous decision concerning my life's work as a teacher. I quit my job at George Mason University, took a leave of absence from Northern Virginia Community College, and began a year teaching creative writing at American University in Washington, D.C.

For the first time in my life I was working for an institution that valued my work. I had the time to write and I was encouraged to do so. The experience at American University gradually brought me back to the idea of a novel.

I got the idea for my next book from one line in *The Lives of Riley Chance*. At one point in the book, Riley says, "What could make heaven so good that you'd forget someone you loved deeply?" I wanted to illustrate that idea. Create it somehow. Even as a child I could never accept the idea that being away from the people I loved would be OK if I was in heaven.

While I was thinking about this idea, I had a conversation about Christ with the poet Gregory Natt, who also happens to be my brother-in-law. We were talking about Christ the man, and I wondered if he didn't take advantage of his godliness just a little bit. It seemed to me that if he was human, and God, he might make some innocent use of his godliness just because of his humanness. Even the best human being would want to avoid, say, tartar on his teeth, gum disease, or a major toothache. It probably got pretty hot in the desert, and even though no one knew about it then, certainly God would know about what was coming a little less than two thousand years hence. Wouldn't Christ have made use of an air conditioner when there was no one around to notice? Just to relieve the discomfort of that awful heat? He was human after all. Therefore, he was not perfect. If he was perfect, he'd be God, but he wouldn't be human. I wondered if he ever trimmed his beard. Every representation we have of him shows him with a perfectly trimmed beard. Who would it harm if he could just wave his hand and have his beard coiffed?

Greg wrote a poem entitled "Christ Trimming His Beard," and I spent the entire year at American University finishing the first draft of a novel I called *Spanking the World*.

I believed I was done with the book, but I wasn't. It was not a very good book and I would have been embarrassed if St. Martin's had published it. My editor advised me to "set it aside." So did my agent. I might have taken their advice—which was good advice—but I'd put almost five years into that book and I couldn't face having to give it up. So I did something I've never done before. I sat down and rewrote the entire book from the first chapter. I spent the summer of 1988 revising and reworking and cutting.

Most of what I cut out of that book was bile. I came to see that I had forgotten my character and lapsed into a bitter attempt to point out all the injustices at the center of things. I had gone after television commercials, politicians, college administrators, salesmen, women, teachers, football players, all celebrities—the list was a long one. Also, my narrator never saw beyond himself. Everything that happened in the book seemed self-absorbed and fake. I wanted to write another Swiftian tale full of irony and wit, and instead I had a narrator so selfish and narrow the irony was completely invisible.

I remember the day I figured out what my story was. I came downstairs and walked into the kitchen, hugged my wife and announced that I had saved the book. I changed the title to *For God's Sake* and sent the book to Tim Seldes at Russell and Volkening, Inc. I had decided that I didn't want to push the book at Judith Weber a second time. I believed in Judith, and loved working with her, but I knew she didn't like the premise of the book and I had not changed that. I felt a change might be best for the book, if maybe not for me.

Sending my book to Tim Seldes was the best thing I ever did. He liked it and said he would be "honored to represent it." Everybody told me I had the best agent in the Milky Way, and at first I thought that was an exaggeration. Tim sent the novel to Janet Silver at Houghton Mifflin in Boston, and after a few conversations between Janet and myself, Houghton Mifflin made an offer.

With the considerable help and influence of Janet Silver, and with her guidance through a lot more editing and revising, the novel became much better than I could have ever made it by myself. It is now called *Almighty Me* and so much has happened to it already I'm afraid to think about my next book. Before *Almighty Me* hit the stands, Hollywood Films, a division of Disney Studios, bought the film rights. It would take me fifteen years in my present position to match the income they offered. Once again I have a book that appears as though it will get a lot of attention. I don't know that I am ready for that, but I am hopeful.

While this third novel has begun to enjoy such tremendous success, Richard recently signed on with Seymour Lawrence and will be with Houghton Miff-

Robert Bausch: "When I could, I used to shoot pool for an hour or so a day, to relax and forget the world; now I only play on my yearly vacations to Canada," 1980

lin now, too. For the first time in our careers we will be with the same publisher and we will both be riding high at the same time.

George Garrett calls Richard and me "the Bausch boys." It's an appellation that stuck and I like it, first because George says it with affection and I value his considerable friendship, and second because it suggests that Richard and I are in this thing together, almost as if we were a team.

Someone once asked me what it was like being a twin. I almost dismissed the question. Twins get used to the foolish line, "Am I seeing double?" And all discussions of being a twin tend to echo that line. But to tell the truth, I wouldn't want to go through life any other way. It's like having yourself and someone else with you at the same time. A person who looks, thinks, acts, and feels like you do, but who is not you. A best friend, a comrade, a competitor, a confidant. We have both pursued the same kind of life, though my writing tends toward the didactic and his is almost

purely art. We joke that together we've produced nine books in the last ten years, but really Richard's work has been the most assured, the most truly beautiful, and almost certainly the most enduring. He probably feels the same way about my work, but I know better.

Still, I can't think of anything I'd rather be than one of the Bausch boys.

BIBLIOGRAPHY

Fiction:

On the Way Home, St. Martin's, 1982.

The Lives of Riley Chance, St. Martin's, 1984.

Almighty Me, Houghton, 1991.

Author of short stories, including "Funerals," "War Story," "Cougar," "The Stag Party," "The White Rooster," and "The Small Good Turn."

Marvin Bell

1937-

Center Moriches—a small, unsophisticated town—lies halfway out on the south shore of Long Island, sixty miles from Manhattan. I was born August 3, 1937, in a hospital in the Bronx, but I was a resident of Center Moriches from the start. My father, mother, older sister, and I first lived for several years on Railroad Avenue on what was considered the "wrong side of the tracks." Center Moriches held about two thousand people. The area was dotted by duck farms, truck farms, and potato fields. There were many roadside fruit and vegetable stands. There were many fishermen. The main thing was water: the Atlantic Ocean, the Great South Bay, Long Island Sound, Shinnecock Canal, inlets and creeks and ponds, coves and spits and sand bars, the docks and dunes, the beach grass, the tides. . . . A thin canal came all the way to Main in the center of town.

My best friend throughout grade school was probably Frankie Holzman, who lived across the street. His father, Frank, Sr., a house painter and the chief of our volunteer fire department, had been a fair first baseman, and he was keen to teach baseball to Frank, Jr., who wasn't all that interested. However, his older sister, Virginia, was, and often they played catch on the lawn in front of their house, with or without Frank, Jr. I'd stand around with my fielder's glove until Frank, Sr., would ask me to play, and then I'd stay as long as he'd let me, sometimes beyond his own children. I was like that: I couldn't get enough play, especially the kind of game in which you couldn't know for sure what would happen next: a ball over your head, a throw in the dirt—a chance for a great play!

What I know of my ancestry dates to the nineteenth century in the Ukraine. My father was the son of Marion Cardon and Mosha Botsian, both of Constantine, Russia. My mother is the daughter of Toba Suvrinsky of Taroscha, Russia, and Reuben Spector of Koshovator, Russia. I have my father's passport. He was a teenager when he immigrated to America, a tough-looking kid with short hair. First (and typically) his father and older brother, Harry, came to America. Once they had a purchase in the New World, the rest of the family followed. They had

Parents, Saul and Belle Bell, 1929

to leave at night, under a wagonload of hay, then ride bareback to Poland. Many other relatives came also, generally settling in New York City or Boston. There was good reason to flee Russia, where both the czar's men and the Bolsheviks liked to kill Jews. My mother's parents had come to America earlier, as young adults. At the time, her father was serving four years in the Russian army. Her mother waited to marry him upon his discharge. But as his four years drew to a close, new fighting broke out, and the army refused to let him go. A generous man from my mother's hometown was financing the move to America, and it was time to go. So my mother's father and his fiancée simply met at the border, from where they escaped to London and then America.

My father did not speak Russian at home, and he rarely told stories of the Old Country. But those few he did, I remembered. I pictured my father slipping through trenches during the day to retrieve the bodies and hiding in the cellar at night while the czar's men and the Bolsheviks had it out. It was a lawless time. My father's family was poor, but his brother-in-law's was wealthy. One day, this man came home to find his family murdered. Afterwards, he took revenge by walking the dangerous streets with his hands in the pockets of a fur coat—a sure sign of money and an invitation to trouble. Told to remove his coat by robbers, he would withdraw two pistols from his pockets and shoot them. It was a chaotic time, too, so that one could always hide in the woods. When the mayor's son bullied my father's sister, my father fought back and had to hide. When one of his brothers went to be examined for induction into the Russian army, and, asked at the end of the line if he had been accepted, lied and said no, the brother hid in the woods until the authorities stopped looking.

My father wanted his son and daughter to be Americans. And that is what I am: an American. I grew up on eastern Long Island, went to school in upstate New York, and later lived in both Syracuse and Rochester, but I no longer feel that I am primarily an East Coaster. I do not feel that I am a dyed-in-the-wool Midwesterner, either, even though I have lived in Chicago and Indianapolis, and have lived and taught in Iowa City since 1965. And I am not a full Northwesterner, though I have been hanging around the Northwest for a number of years and in 1985 purchased a small place in Port Townsend, Washington, where I have lived since, summer and winter, for part of each year. My sense of place comes from many regions of this country. Wherever we have been, I have worked for a living and we have gone exploring. Often we drive long distances: in the past year we have put thirty thousand miles on our car. Each year we drive from Iowa City to the far corner of the Northwest, and later back, sometimes by way of Canada. Often we have reason to follow that with a drive from Iowa City to mid-Vermont and back. And this year we drove from Iowa City to Santa Fe, then to Tennessee and down to New Orleans, and after that to Utah and on up to Port Townsend. Truly, I feel connections to, and differences from, each and every place we have lived, and perhaps because there have been so many, each place is for me inextricably of the whole. I taught a trimester for Goddard College and lived in rural Vermont. I have

lived and taught in Hawaii. I have lived in Santa Cruz, San Francisco, and Santa Fe. Outside the United States, I have lived in parts of Mexico and Spain, briefly visited Cuba, Guatemala, and Nicaragua, and traveled in eastern and western Europe, Morocco, and Australia. I feel that I am an American before I am of any one region—an American poet, with an American childhood, the changing American vision, American successes and failures, troubling American responsibilities. Can one be called a localist but not a regionalist? If so, then that is what I am. Had I traveled more in other countries, I would be pleased to be thought a citizen of the world.

But an autobiography must rest necessarily on one's childhood and early adulthood, for that is the time when emotion and instinct coalesce, and the vision planted then will flower no matter what. And so, in December of 1990, I have returned to eastern Long Island for five weeks to write this report. This morning, walking the roads outside East Hampton near Sammis Beach (called "Sammy's Beach" by some cartographers), I passed a sign for "Hidden Drives." Grasping, some might say, at straws, even as I plucked a stem of beach grass to chew, I sensed a kind of code in that sign. It was signaling me, reminding me that our motives—our drives—remain hidden, as does the great wealth of cause-and-effect by which we arrive at a moment when we look back, autobiographically.

Long Island

The things I did, I did because of trees,
wildflowers and weeds, because of ocean and sand,
because the dunes move about under houses built on
  stilts,
and the wet fish slip between your hands back into
  the sea,
because during the War we heard strafing across the
  Bay
and after the War we found shell casings with our
  feet.
Because old tires ringed the boat docks,
and sandbags hung from the prows of speedboats,
and every road in every country ends at the water,
and because a child thinks each room in his house big,
and if the truth be admitted, his first art galleries
were the wallpaper in his bedroom and the carlights
warming the night air as he lay in bed counting.

The things I did, I counted in wattage and ohms,
in the twelve zones that go from pure black to pure
  white,
in the length of the trumpet and the curves of the
  cornet,
in the cup of the mouthpiece. In the compass and
  protractor,
in the perfect bevelled ruler, in abstract geometry,
and if the truth be known, in the bowing of cattails

he first read his Heraclitus and in the stretching box
    turtle
he found his theory of relativity and the gist of
    knowledge.
He did what he did. The action of his knee in walking
was not different from the over-stretching of an
    ocean wave,
and the proofs of triangles, cones and parallelograms
were neither more nor less than the beauty of a fast
    horse
which runs through the numbers of the stopwatch
    and past the finish.

The things I counted, I counted beyond the finish,
beyond rolling tar roadways that squared the fields,
where I spun on the ice, wavered in fog, sped up or
    idled,
and, like Perry, like Marco Polo, a young man I saw
alone walk unlit paths, encircled by rushes
and angry dogs, to the indentations of his island.
And if the truth be told, he learned of Columbus,
of Einstein, of Michelangelo, on such low roads and
    local waters.
Weakfish hauled weakening from the waters at night,
and the crab rowing into the light, told him in their
    way
that the earth moved around the sun in the same way,
with the branched mud-print of a duck's foot to read,
and life in the upturned bellies of the fishkill in the
    creek.

              (from *New and Selected Poems*)

"My mother, Ruby, and me," about 1940

I can't remember when I started to take walks, to go off alone, talking to myself in my head, and, when I couldn't do that, to say things on paper. Now my father had a small five-and-ten in a small town. After getting his feet on the ground in America, he had left behind the cities where other Jewish escapees from the czar and the Bolsheviks congregated, striking out on his own, setting up shop against local advice in a building where businesses repeatedly had failed. And there he worked hard, happy to "be his own boss," and prospered. By every standard that mattered to him he was a success: he supported his family, the community respected and liked him, and he was free. He had no objection to hard work of his own choosing, and he enjoyed the days, his customers, and his family, no matter what. When I was born, he danced on the counter. He hid from his children the fact that he had heart trouble, and he died of a stroke just after I graduated from college.

But now I was walking out of our house on Union Avenue at all hours, especially at night, heading down to Main Street, away from the stores to the edge of town, then turning toward the Great South Bay on lampless streets, sometimes walking a route several times in succession. There were stops— to see what was in the camera store window, to take books from the small house that several nights a week served as the town library—but mainly I kept walking.

While I walked, ideas went through my head. I couldn't keep from thinking. Every little thing was a small, dry sponge, waiting for some bit of free flowing attention that would swell it to grand proportions. I had a habit of noticing *how* people said things. Nothing about my mind seemed odd or important to me, but it required of me time alone, the walking, and the darkness of night. Years later I would come upon Rilke's concept of an essential solitude, but I already knew that one could be alone in a crowd.

How He Grew Up

He found the corner of town where the last street
bent, and outdoor lights went down a block
or so and no more. In the long list of states
and their products, there was bauxite, rope,
fire engines, shoes, even a prison, but not one
was famous for purposeless streets and late
walks. Often he missed the truth of lists
while gone for a walk, with most lights out
all over town, and no one told him, when he
returned, the ten things it was best to, or
the dozen it was better not to. He knew
the window would be lit most of the night
down at the camera shop, and the gentle

librarian would keep the house of books open
if he stopped by at closing. Up the street he went,
leaving the lamps, each night until he met
the smell of the bay, a fact to be borne home
to sleep, certain of another day. The houses of
friends were dark. He never told, in those days.
Something was missing from the lists of
best and how to and whose town did what.
He figured, when no other was mentioned,
it might be his town at the top of some list:
but it was hard to read things on paper
in the bony moonlight. So he never knew.
People ask him all the time to have been
where what happened happened, that made
the news, but usually the big things happened
while he was out walking: the War, the War, etc.

(from *Iris of Creation*)

At the drugstore, I could buy *Writer's Digest* and *The Writer.* I thought it must be wonderfully free to be a writer. By "writer," I assumed journalist, columnist, or nonfiction free-lancer. I made lists of subjects for articles. The columns of Sydney J. Harris, which sometimes showed a most undaily intellectual bent, appeared in one of our newspapers, and I pictured a life in which one might live anywhere and make a living by mailing back little daily essays.

In fourth grade, when the band instruments had been put on display, I had chosen the trumpet. In a small town with limited ideas of expression, music was to be my first art. Chester Osborne, our public-school bandleader, himself an accomplished trumpet player, was my teacher. He was also a composer, a writer of serious children's books, and an historian. Later, as I approached graduation, he would suggest that I attend music school, or, if I preferred—rarely did anyone from Center Moriches or the nearby towns of Moriches, East Moriches, Brookhaven, Mastic, Mastic Beach, etc., strike out for college—join the Coast Guard band, but I chose not to. Although I didn't know it, he was offering me a chance to find out about the rest of the world. Years afterwards, he would say that, while he had feared at the time that I had thrown away my chances by giving up music, because of my writing things had turned out okay after all.

One day in the middle of an English class, Mr. Berdan, our teacher, suddenly said: "You know that stuff they tell you about these being the best years of your lives? Well, don't you believe it. It gets better and better." I liked him for that remark. I was already developing a sense that the conventional wisdom was often wrong.

I also liked Mr. Berdan for having once changed the requirements of a test in reply to my challenge that the requirements weren't fair. In fact, they were

probably fair enough, but I never forgot the willingness of a teacher to listen, to change and to say, "I think I was wrong, and you are right." As a teacher, I have often said since, "You are right, and I am wrong."

I played in school bands, marching bands, summer bands, fire department bands, orchestras, duos, trios, quartets, quintets, sextets, combos. I often performed solo. In the New York State High School Music Competition, I played Herbert L. Clarke's version of "Carnival of Venice." At graduation, I played Clarke's "Stars in a Velvety Sky," which was used with other Clarke cornet solos in the sound track of *Hester Street*: someone else had noticed the lilting melancholy in that part of each Clarke composition known as the "trio." I played with the Monday Night Band, an adult band which met on Tuesdays in Riverhead. These were good musicians under an admired conductor, Howard Hovey, and, to prove it, at each concert he had the band sight-read one composition. I didn't think about it, but the music was teaching me spontaneity. I was learning about freedom and individuality and beauty, and also the nature of an ensemble—from late nights and jazz. All the while, I kept walking. After I got a used car—it was a '50 Plymouth—I took rides, often ending up at the water just to sit and look out. When a hurricane was reported en route, I would drive through Westhampton Beach to reach Fire Island before the roads could be closed—to see the stormy Atlantic lapping the land.

My sister, Ruby, four years older, was to marry a man from East Moriches whose father was a "ham": an amateur radio operator. One Thanksgiving, Roy Raynor took me upstairs to his "shack," his radio room in the attic. I was transfixed. I sat for hours listening to shortwave stations. Later, I learned International Morse Code, took the appropriate Federal Communications Commission examination on electronics, and received a station license: W2IDK. I built a piezoelectric crystal-controlled oscillator and power supply that put out twenty watts. With it, I talked (in code) to radio operators in California and England, in the Canal Zone and on Saint Pierre and Miquelon Islands. I specialized in handling "traffic" (messages routed by an elaborate circuit of "nets" of operators that meet at designated times and frequencies) and on certain days I served as "net control" for the Swing Shift Net which convened on the airwaves during my school lunch hour. On those days, our homeroom teacher gave me a little leeway as she took attendance and I raced my bicycle up the school driveway. I had a fast and accurate "fist," and, in code, the others could not tell that I was not an adult. I liked that.

Amateur radio operators were odd ducks. I liked that too. I pedaled my bike to nearby towns to meet them. Some took me under their wing. Roy Raynor, W2EBT ("Two Eggs, Bacon and Toast," he called himself, or "Elderly, Bald and Toothless"), was the first. Van Field, W2OQI, lived like a hermit, making radio equipment in a tiny house in the woods. He was a "builder," the kind of amateur radio operator who lives to make equipment from scratch and goes on the air only to test it. I spent many hours at his place, learning, and he helped me to construct my first transmitter. It was necessary then to build one's first transmitter to earn credibility as a "ham." No kits allowed. One chose a schematic, bought the parts on Radio Row in New York City (Canal Street), cut the chassis to accommodate vacuum tube sockets, and went from there.

Another adult friend was Herbert Snell, W2FCH ("Two Females Chasing Herbie"). He gave me rides to and from the amateur radio club and while we traveled he talked. He seemed to me an unconventional mind. All the amateur radio operators of those days seemed to me to have walked away.

Upstairs in their "shacks," whether building, or handling traffic, or trying to work "DX" (distant stations, especially those in other countries), or experimenting with VHF and UHF, or just contacting other hams to chat, they were really escaping to a world in which they could talk to themselves.

I wrote a column about events at the school for the local weekly, and the sports editor let me hang around late at night. While he thrashed his way toward various deadlines, I prepared the baseball and basketball statistics.

There were ball clubs—I played on the soccer and basketball teams at school, and outside of school I played on Police Athletic League basketball and baseball teams. My father bought a small speedboat— an inboard—and sometimes I'd ride my bicycle to the inlet where it was docked and sit in it and daydream. We'd fish together, and for four years he picked me up after school three days a week to drive me to Patchogue, a bigger town than ours, located half an hour west, to study Hebrew and prepare for my bar mitzvah at thirteen. We went to Friday night services, and I attended Sunday school, in Patchogue, with interludes of Friday nights and Sunday school in Riverhead, a town northeast of Center Moriches,

"Mother and Father, with Ruby and me in the middle," about 1948

depending on how my parents felt about the current rabbi. Later, I attended Catholic masses with a Catholic friend, and over the years I have taken part in many different church meetings. Others may at times have identified me as being Jewish, and certainly I was born to it, but I felt eclectic from the start. There were things about every philosophy and, thus, religion, that I liked, beginning with the social utility of churches and the power of belief. I enjoyed arguing intellectually with the rabbi, and I think he enjoyed it also. Later, I heard a speaker at college say that, in Judaism, study was equivalent to prayer, and I thought to myself, "That's the part of me that's Jewish." My Judaism, as I saw it, was realistic, tough but fair, and it had a sense of humor. My father's standard response to criticism of someone else was to say, "Well, he has to make a living too."

"Home on Union Avenue with the addition Mother called a 'sunporch' and Father called his 'office'"

The Israeli Navy

The Israeli Navy,
sailing to the end of the world,
stocked with grain
and books black with God's verse,
turned back,
rather than sail on the Sabbath.
Six days, was the consensus,
was enough for anyone.

So the world, it was concluded,
was three days wide
in each direction,
allowing three days back.
And Saturdays were given over
to keeping close,
while Sundays the Navy,
all decked out in white
and many-colored skull caps,
would sail furiously,
trying to go off the deep end.

Yo-ho-ho, would say the sailors,
for six days.
While on the shore their women moaned.

For years, their boats were slow,
and all show.
And they turned into families
on the only land they knew.

(from *A Probable Volume of Dreams*)

And there were friends. We fished, played ball, rode our bicycles to adventures, and generally enjoyed the safe innocence of that time and place. What did we expect to be? Clerks, store owners, salesmen, mechanics, tradesmen, secretaries, maybe a coach or teacher or nurse. And of course volunteer firemen. Eastern Long Island then, as today, depended on well-trained and well-equipped volunteer fire departments, which competed in special tournaments each summer and formed basketball leagues in the winter. Few of us even considered college. During World War II, I helped watch for enemy airplanes at the official spotter station at the water end of Union Avenue.

Many of the students in our school came by bus, mainly from towns to the west. Few of us stayed in Center Moriches when the school day ended. By high school, there seemed to be even fewer of us from town. Then a friend from Bellport invited me to a band concert at her high school. Bellport was a richer town, west of us and south of the highway, where families lived who had someone working at Brookhaven National Lab, formerly Camp Upton. She knew I was a hotshot cornet player, and she told me that their band had one too and I should listen for the first-chair cornetist. The first chair was good, certainly, but the second chair, who played with an odd embouchure—the mouthpiece off-center, his head thrown back, his eyes looking down his nose—was terrific. His name was Roger Edwards, and we became lifelong friends. Summers, we played in the Bellport, Center Moriches, and Westhampton Beach bands. We formed a trumpet trio with Roland Smith—the "first chair" I had been told to listen for—and with others we formed a "combo" to play in bars. Roger and I sometimes drove to New York City to attend concerts in Central Park by the Edwin Franko Goldman band—James Burke was the trumpet soloist, and I had bought a Bach cornet from Ned Mahoney, Burke's second chair—and then to go to jazz clubs such as Birdland and the Metropole and, also, to the late-night live television of the Steve Allen Show. Roger and I could talk philosophy and laugh at the same time. Later, I learned that Kierkegaard had said that laughter is a kind of prayer. It certainly seemed so.

I came to know others in Bellport, especially Frank DiGangi, another lifetime friend. DiGangi sometimes played drums with us and, although we didn't yet know it, he too was headed circuitously for the world of creative expression. Recently, Frank's wife, Carole Worthington, who grew up in East Hampton when it was potato fields, and not a "second home" in sight, said that Frank, Roger, and I became friends because "there was no one else." An exaggeration, perhaps, but not untrue.

Music Lessons

The best place to hear a cornet played is the local
    gymnasium:
the kind with a basketball court, a stage and a balcony
in which small public schools hold their songfests and
    dances.
The long waxy strips of the wooden floor are very
    like
the golden sounds of the B-flat cornet in bright
    daylight,
and the empty room in which so many bodies have
    passed
accepts and embraces each articulated musical phrase
with that warm sadness known best by the adolescent.

If I had never taken up the cornet, I sometimes think,
beauty would not have taken all my days and filled my
    thoughts.
If I had not had that free hour in the middle of the
    school day,
not selected a mouthpiece with a deep cup for its
    richer tone,
not carried it in my hand to warm it up ahead of time,
if I had never given in to the subtleties of an
    embouchure,
I would not have been blown about by every passing
    song,
each with its calendar and clock, each with its
    beloved.

It takes only a few measures for the dreams to get
    out,
and then you cannot stop them or make them go
    away.
A river of whole tones sweeps from the bell of the
    horn,
containing the sun and moon, the grass and the
    flowers,
all time, and the face of every kindness done to a boy,
and every object of his desire by name, and a single
    smile.
It was my good fortune to be the breath of a magic
    cornet
and my fate to fall asleep to music every night
    thereafter.

(from *New and Selected Poems*)

I applied to Alfred University because two people in town were graduates—a French teacher and a lawyer. I knew nothing about colleges, but my father thought I should go. I went off to Alfred wearing a leather jacket with a switchblade in one pocket. My parents had bought me a briefcase and the Hadassah had given me a suitcase. I assumed that Alfred was close to home—I had never been farther away than Boston and New York City, to visit relatives. Alfred turned out to be four hundred miles from Center Moriches, and I was late to orientation.

Alfred University is located in Alfred, New York, down the road from Alfred Station. Where is it, really? About sixty miles south of Rochester, in the southern tier of western New York. My freshman year it snowed September 14. We called it "Albert" and were amused by the school song, which referred to "Alfred, the Mother of Men."

At my interview for Alfred, which had taken place in a hotel room in New York City, the college representative warned me that in college I would have to choose among activities. I couldn't do it all. But I tried. I asked special permission each semester to take extra courses. I worked for the yearbook and the weekly newspaper, the *Fiat Lux,* and as a senior I edited the paper. I was elected to the student senate. I joined a fraternity, then resigned but stayed a "social" member. I hadn't quite given up cornet, and I took lessons from Dan Clayton, a music teacher who had returned to college to prepare for dentistry. I played with the university concert and marching bands and the town orchestra. On Easter, Dan Clayton and I put on black robes and played Purcell's "Trumpet Voluntary" from the pulpit. (Purcell gets the credit, but he didn't write it: Jeremiah Clarke wrote it.)

At Alfred, men then were required to take two years of Reserve Officers' Training Corps. I went on to advanced ROTC. At the time, it seemed wise—we all expected to be drafted out of college—and the pay for taking the advanced courses came in handy. Moreover, I was a Jew. I remembered Hitler. I had yet to meet a single conscientious objector. In 1957, I went through basic military training at Fort Bragg in North Carolina.

At Alfred, my eyes were opened by another group of "odd ducks." In the State College of Ceramics, located within private Alfred University, the design department had been subverted by artists. I had never known such people, mostly New Yorkers. They had a way of life—their work. It proved impossible to keep the ceramics building locked at night because they would break in to get back to work. During my late-night walks, I included in my route the bottom levels of the long ceramics building where I knew I would find, whatever the hour, printmakers, sculptors, and painters at work. These student artists didn't depend on what others thought. They had a "studio" mentality and so did their teachers—artists together, their lives centered in work and surrounded by good fellowship. To me, it was a revelation, and I watched them. They had talent, they were street smart, and they were actively in touch with their inner selves.

Slowly my eyes opened also to writers and writing—especially journalism. I took one creative-writing course. Dr. Finch required three short stories over the semester. I wrote them late at night in the student union, after it was closed. I knew the student who cleaned up. I'd come in the back door carrying a typewriter, we'd put on the jukebox and cook hamburgers, and then I'd write a story while he cleaned.

My friend and roommate, Lew Carson, wrote the best story of the class. I didn't know what Dr. Finch was getting at when he talked about an image in Lew's story. In it, the main character ended his day at an arcade, shooting a miniature bear behind

"Running in the Honolulu Marathon,"
December 1979

glass—repeatedly hitting the glass eye on the bear's belly with the light ray from his toy rifle, so that the bear groaned, stood up, and reversed its direction over and over. In the window of the machine, the shooter could also see his own face. Later, I understood the image, but not yet.

In *New World Writing*, I found an odd poem. It began with "Fuzz clings to the huddle." And its final line was "We rise and leave with Please." I brought it to Dr. Finch who said he didn't know much about modern poetry and suggested I try Miss Tupper. Miss Tupper didn't know much about modern poetry either, but neither of them disapproved of my interest.

And I *was* interested. We all were. We had the rage to be artists. It was the fifties, a time of many constrictions which then seemed natural but now seem numbing. The part of America that we knew best was becalmed. The Beat Generation was coming and we were its audience-in-waiting.

Roy Glassberg and Mike Moses wrote for the literary magazine. We ran around together and lived in the same rooming house. I knew that my composition teacher had published a novel, though he never mentioned it. One of the students—Charles Froome, one of many military veterans at the school—had published a book of poetry with a "vanity" press, but to me it was a book like any other. I was not part of the literary magazine scene but of the newspaper scene, where I began as a reporter and ended as editor in chief. Along the way, I also began a commotion.

It started with a review—mainly a summary—of a book about sectarian clauses in fraternities and sororities. My article brought a response from the vets on campus, who didn't think that a university should be housing groups that discriminated against minorities. One thing led to another and pretty soon the campus was fiercely divided. By then I was managing editor to Nathan Lyons, a photographer, a vet, and a serious man who talked naturally about both aesthetic and moral activity. I liked reading philosophy more than fiction. One of my heroes was the student who emptied his room, painted it white, and sat for days in a chair in the otherwise vacant room, thinking.

When there was cause, I wrote and mimeographed an "underground" newsletter, which then appeared on the auditorium seats on the Thursdays of college-wide assemblies. At first, few knew that it was I. Later, when people knew, the university tried to seal up the mimeograph machines in town. By then I had succeeded to the editorship and the crusade to get the university to take a position on sectarian clauses—one way or the other—had become even hotter. Newspapers in Buffalo and Rochester sent reporters to Alfred to cover the issue. There were hairy encounters. I wanted the university to make a statement, but I was willing to accept any position they were willing to state, whether or not I liked it. However, I couldn't accept their silence, their refusal even to recognize that discrimination could be an issue. A local minister wrote me an encouraging letter and said that a good editor needs a hide of leather. He told me of a mimeograph machine in the church basement that I could use. But I didn't need it. I had a friend with a key to Hornell High School, where we were producing newsletters in secret in the middle of the night.

Dr. Sibley's ethics class was a favorite. When I asked if I could miss class to attend a talk by Ashley Montagu at the other college in town, the State College of Alfred, he agreed on condition that I report the event to the class. Montagu spoke about "The Natural Superiority of Women," based on chromosomes, and afterwards, in a small informal group, he told an amazing story about two anthropologists from the University of Toronto, Edmund Carpenter and Marshall McLuhan. The story concerned their trip to the Aleutian Islands, and a way of seeing which enabled the Eskimos there to fix car and plane motors without having studied them. He told us how the first issue of *Explorations,* a Joycean magazine edited as a result by Carpenter and McLuhan, came into being.

Dr. Bernstein was a favorite among all the students for his passion. He taught American literature. I took his special graduate course in literary criticism, meeting at night.

Summers, I worked as I always had, in my father's five-and-tens. He had slowly developed a clientele at a second store, in Mastic Beach—a town that filled up between Memorial Day and Labor Day with families from Brooklyn, Queens, and The Bronx. The summer of my junior year, I was scheduled to take army field training at Fort Bragg in North Carolina. The night before I had to go, typically I stayed up late. I had rediscovered an unused, till-then-ignored film-developing kit and now I couldn't put it away without trying it.

Back at Alfred, I began to take photographs, developing and printing in the darkroom of the *Fiat Lux.* I still loved to stay up late. Looking back, I see that there are certain things about me that were true from adolescence on, and have not changed: I like to start work very late at night and then work until dawn, I like a workroom full of tables, and, when I can't sit still, I go for walks. Also, I talk to myself, silently, when alone. Always have. I should probably add to this table of constants the appeal that the arts have had for me, which is to say that I have wanted to try them myself—all of them. But I admit that I could probably be happy in nearly any honest job if my employer would allow me to work late at night in a room full of tables, with walk breaks and some silent extracurricular mental activity along the way.

John Wood was a master teacher among the design students, famous for his great silences and his enormous artistic productivity. He let me take a photography tutorial. First assignment: make a series. I did it—my series involved the horizon, and there were many tricks—and brought it to the design room to show him. It was ROTC day—once a week, we had to wear our uniforms—and I felt conspicuous among those students who were wilder and more artistic than I was. John Wood looked long at my series. He tried switching two prints and then put them back. He tried switching two others and returned them to their places. Then he said, "Good. Make another series." It was a fine tutorial.

As editor of the student weekly, I got caught up willingly in many issues. I believed journalism to be honorable work. So, after graduation, I enrolled in the graduate journalism school at Syracuse University. My old friend Roger was there completing a music degree, and I moved in with him.

Waiting to complete registration, I met another person who would become a lifelong friend, Al Sampson. He and I had considerable experience—Al had graduated college ahead of his class and then served as wire editor for the *Minot Daily News* in North Dakota. We discovered that we both had chosen journalism because of our ideals and because—this was idealistic too, and perhaps naive—we didn't want to ruin literature for ourselves by earnestly studying it for a graduate degree. But Syracuse didn't know what to do with us and made us take beginning copyediting courses and the like, which we soon skipped except for the exams. I liked Professor Root's course in "Social Responsibility and the Press," and I respected Professor Bird's "Research Methods," for which we had to write the equivalent of a term paper each and every week. On class day, Professor Bird would detail the exactitudes of the next assignment while bleary-eyed students straggled in, fell into their seats, and made one final proofreading of the paper due that hour. I enjoyed typesetting with Professor Norton in the Bodoni Labs.

Al and I, and Mary (Mickey) Mammosser—whom I met at an organizational meeting for the campus literary magazine, though neither of us

"Singing with Al Sampson," Port Townsend, about 1986

returned—skipped other classes to read poetry in a restaurant near campus. I think it was called the Italian Villa. We read the Beats—Ginsberg, Corso, Ferlinghetti—and others to one another over afternoon salad and evening pizza. Al soon realized that the journalism courses were taking him nowhere and switched to English, but I decided to finish a semester before skipping out. Next Al realized that he would be better off studying literature at the University of Chicago in his hometown, and he left.

Mickey and I eloped and moved into an apartment on University Avenue. The super was a retired navy boiler man who liked to analyze the serious content of the Steve Allen Show and was "rewriting" the Bible. He had spent a summer reading the *Encyclopaedia Britannica* on a beach. Handing over the monthly rent check to him was always interesting and took time. The dean didn't approve of my having eloped with an undergraduate, and suggested I not return. I intended to leave in any case, and Mickey and I had already moved to Rochester, where we had taken an apartment on Evergreen Street. I inter-

viewed for a job at Eastman Kodak. The interview took place in a small, almost-bare room. It was a small, bare interview. I could feel the weight of the corporation as my interviewer told me about their training programs, the benefits, even the retired employees' sport center.

While in Rochester, Mickey and I began a magazine of literary and visual materials. We called it *statements*, without an initial capital. Nathan Lyons was now working for the Eastman House of Photography and he often employed the word "statement." To me, the word suggested clarity and thought with a philosophical tinge. I felt, even then, that the meaning in words was of more moment than any confusion in the use of words, and that poetry had important content.

Rochester was now a hot spot of creative photography. Minor White, who edited and published *Aperture*, taught at the Rochester Institute of Technology, and Walter Chappell and Nathan Lyons had introduced contemporary work into the Eastman House, while Nathan had thoroughly modernized its house journal, *Image*.

One night Nathan and I went to Minor White's home to attend one of his tutorials. He propped an abstract photograph on a music stand and we "read" it. The remarks had a psycho-spiritual slant, and I only listened. Walter Chappell was experimenting with "thoughtography," a term coined by George De La Warr, who had been working in England, from the premise that the mind gives off a kind of energy that can be recorded—in this case, on film.

Al had been sending us clippings, notes, matchbooks, menus. On them he wrote, "Come to Chicago!" And one night we decided to do it. We loaded the car, put out the garbage, left the rent for the super, and headed off to Chicago. (Within twenty minutes of our arrival at Al's apartment, our car had been burglarized.) There I entered the university and got a job at the law library. We lived in Hyde Park, an area populated by radicals and artists. At first we lived above the Accent furniture store on the corner of Blackstone Avenue and Fifty-third Street. Later, we moved to a third-floor apartment in an old house on the corner of Fifty-second and Kenwood. At work I read law books.

More issues of *statements* appeared. Each issue had its own format—one time we could afford a color cover. I was by now writing poems and still photographing, but I had put aside my cornet and trumpet: I loved music more than I loved the cornet. These were exciting times in Hyde Park: there were continuous political arguments and periodic confrontations. Civil rights were at the forefront. One friend described himself as a "professional radical," and worked for the railroad. Others held office in this or that organization. I joined with them in argument and demonstration, but I held back from anything further. I was still my father's son, and I trusted neither the czar nor the Bolsheviks.

I was still in Chicago in 1959 when my father died suddenly of a stroke. The completeness of it, the finality of it, the look of his corpse, the unsaid, my future never to be known to him—I felt a bottomless emptiness inside, and I still do when I remember his funeral. The town shut down in homage, I said prayers in Hebrew, and then I returned to Chicago.

Ending with a Line from Lear

I will try to remember. It was light.
It was also dark, in the grave. I could feel
how dark it was, how black it would be
without my father. When he was gone.
But he was not gone, not yet. He was only
a corpse, and I could still touch him
that afternoon. Earlier the same afternoon.
This is the one thing that scares me:
losing my father. I don't want him to go.

I am a young man. I will never be older.
I am wearing a tie and a watch. The sky,
gray, hangs over everything. Today
the sky has no curve to it, and no end.
He is deep into his mission. He has business
to attend to. He wears a tie but no watch.
I will skip a lot of what happens next.
Then the moment comes. Everything, everything
has been said, and the wheels start to turn.
They roll, the straps unwind, and the coffin
begins to descend. Into the awful damp.
Into the black center of the earth. I
am being left behind. The center of my body
sinks down into the cold fire of the grave.
But still my feet stand on top of the dirt.
My father's grave. I will never again.
Never. Never. Never. Never. Never.

(from *The Atlantic*)

Mickey had decided I should have a son and bore one in 1960. When, after a year and a half of marriage, we divorced, our son, Nathan, stayed with me. Later, I married my present wife, Dorothy Murphy, who bore our second son, Jason, in 1966. My story since 1960 is forever woven together with the stories of Dorothy, Nathan, and Jason, who have enriched my life enormously by virtue of their great hearts, their uncommon good sense, their goodness, their laughter, and their wondrous minds.

An Elm We Lost

On it we wrote a little essay
about who loved who.
Shade moves in the grass, never still,
and they still do.

(from *Stars Which See, Stars Which Do Not See*)

I took the M.A. slowly, but eventually it was time to complete it. All that remained was the examination, but I would have to be enrolled. I chose a poetry-writing course which met in the evenings at the downtown center of the university. The teacher was the poet John Logan.

Logan was a wonderful teacher for young poets. He read our poems aloud so beautifully that they took on the grace of our intentions despite the awkwardness of our steps. He so seriously discussed the content of our poems—looking at surfaces and underneath—that they took on the substance we had wished for them despite our limited experience.

At the end of the course, Logan invited me to be a member of the Poetry Seminar. It was not an academic course, but an informal group of Chicago poets which met with Logan once a month in the offices of Jordan Miller's newspaper-clipping service. Besides Jordan, at one time or another the group

Dorothy Ann Murphy Bell, 1988

included Dennis Schmitz, Bill Knott, Naomi Lazard, Jim Murphy, Irene Keller, Barbara Harr, Jessie Katchmar, and others. Jessie liked to hold my poems of elastic free verse on their sides and claim that they resembled the skyline of Chicago. She had written a poem about a spider in her bathtub in which she said that the spider was writing on the tub in "spider Gothic."

Paul Carroll was part of the Logan circle. Paul had been the editor of the *Chicago Review* when the administration of the university banned an issue. The banned issue became the first issue of *Big Table*. It was an exciting time for poetry. Villiers, Ltd., printed many of the little magazines in England, and James Boyer May, their representative, edited a magazine called *Trace*, which was full of news of the "littles." Logan began a magazine called *Choice*, to which he had me contribute an article and a photo of the Chicago Water Tower.

It was an exciting time for photography, too. Both Aaron Siskind and Harry Callahan were teaching for the Institute of Design. Many of their students would become well known. I spent lots of time at Rodney Galarneau's small storefront gallery and apartment on the south side near Comiskey Park. Another photographer friend was David Rowinski, who assisted Hugh Edwards, Curator of Photography at the Art Institute.

I had been stalling the army—I would have to go on active duty eventually—and now I wanted to delay it further. I felt I had stumbled on the real thing— poets and poetry—in Logan's seminar, and I wanted more of it right away. Logan told me of something even farther west than Chicago—the Writers' Workshop, it was called, in Iowa City. I decided to apply to Iowa to study for a Ph.D. And I went off to Iowa City to be interviewed by Donald Justice. After awhile, Don, Kim Merker—the printer and founder of the Stone Wall Press—and I went bowling. I must have bowled well because—I was accepted.

Dorothy, Nathan, and I moved to Iowa City at the beginning of 1961 and stayed three years. For most of that time we lived in a tiny house with a big yard on Fifth Avenue in the cheap part of town. Our rent was seventy-five dollars a month. As usual, the front room served as my study, our bedroom, and the living room for company. I taught rhetoric, the course in reading, writing, speaking, and listening required of freshmen. I taught the ordinary course, the advanced course, the remedial course. I turned down a fellowship in the Workshop to teach rhetoric, and I stayed in rhetoric when my peers were thrashing about for "promotions" to literature classes. I early abandoned the Ph.D. program.

Donald Justice and Paul Engle taught the poetry workshop. Justice was a fine teacher, one of uncommon precision, goodwill, and decency. He could describe quality and defend our imperfections at the same time. There were many poets there during those years who would make their mark: Vern Rutsala, Mark Strand, Michael Harper, Lawson Inada, Mary Crow, Charles Wright, Dori Katz, George Keithley, Kenneth Rosen, Van K. Brock, and others. Al Lee was famous among us because he had already published in *Poetry*. Catherine B. Davis had appeared in an influential anthology, *The New Poets of England and America*. William Brady was the best critic among us. Some people seemed to have special standing. But I was busy teaching, writing, and photographing— and soon would be potting—as well as taking classes, and I had a family. In the midst of a swirl of literary fellowship, I still felt that I was following my own road.

The Writers' Workshop had a feeling about it similar to that of the Alfred design department, Logan's seminar, Hyde Park, and the photography department at the Institute of Design. It was a studio program. Writers came because they were writers. People did not come to be made into writers, but to have the luxury of living among other artists as they themselves tested their commitment and their direction. The emphasis was on the writing and the social play that surrounded it. We discussed almost everything about poetry, but there was little talk of magazines or publishers or literary standing. Because Iowa did not then permit the serving of liquor by the drink, and beer was limited to 3.2 percent alcoholic content, the bars closed at 10:00 P.M. weeknights and 11:00 P.M. weekends. Artists and writers crowded together nightly at Kenney's. At closing, there would be a party: if no one had volunteered, the word would simply start from some corner of the room that the party tonight was to be at so-and-so's, and then nothing could prevent it. A few of us also favored Donnelly's, where artists from all over mixed with townspeople. Friday afternoons I joined a group in Donnelly's known as the "seminar"—the name reminded me of Logan's group. I was the group's only poet. We were older students, all apprentices in rhetoric, all given to laughter, philosophizing, and a certain edge of realism.

The fifth and final issue of *statements* appeared from Iowa City, a double number of *statements* and R. R. Cuscaden's magazine from Chicago, *Midwest*. It was a collection of *Iowa Workshop Poets 1963* and contained a single poem by each of twenty-five poets.

On warm weekends the writers played softball. One day while I was fielding ground balls at third base, in between innings, the shortstop—the poet

Keithley—told me of the Bay of Pigs invasion of Cuba then in progress. He knew before the rest of us—he had heard it from a relative by phone—and I was amazed.

John Schulze, a professor of design, started a photography course in the art department. There were many sets of fresh eyes in that group, and we created photographic exercises that were used for years afterwards. I took a film course and, with a partner, made a short movie which began with a highly symbolic egg rocking in a cage and included a woman misapplying her lipstick and Bill Brady in his underwear lifting weights. Years later, I was told that filmmakers from the Polish Academy had come to town and praised it, but I have not seen it since.

Meanwhile, Henry Holmes Smith had decided to organize the creative photographers and called for a meeting at the University of Indiana, where he taught. Paul Engle gave me money from Workshop funds to attend. Dorothy, Nathan, Nathan Lyons, and I shared a storefront apartment in Bloomington. Aaron Siskind came, and Art Sinsabaugh, and Jerry Uelsmann, who was then Smith's student, and Ansel Adams, and many others. We showed our pictures, looked at Maya Deren films projected onto a large wall two at a time, and posed for Sinsabaugh's huge

Son Nathan and Leslie Chapman, 1990

Son Jason and Karen Moeller, 1990

portrait camera, which he had masked to make long horizontal pictures of the Midwest.

I had begun to throw pots. My teacher, Carl Fracassini, was the closest I was to come to a teacher in the spirit of the Zen masters. He could teach without teaching. The pot shop—like the Writers' Workshop, housed in wooden World War II "temporary" barracks—buzzed with activity. The potters made clay in large, plastic garbage cans, and, in other garbage cans, many of them also made beer. An apothecary in town stocked hops.

"Frac," as he was called, also taught a course called "studio," required of beginning art majors and based largely on drawing. I was famous for my inability to write by hand legibly, and I had said that I couldn't draw. Frac insisted he could teach me, and I enrolled in his studio class. By the end of the semester, I better understood drawing, and I had improved, but, no, I couldn't draw. Well, I now know that one can do anything if one keeps at it and does it in whatever way one has to, but I didn't know it then.

One day Frac took me to Vance Bourjaily's farm to shoot clay traps. I could shoot a rifle with some accuracy, but I was missing with the shotgun. Then Frac swung his gun across the sky in demonstration: "Don't aim," he said, "point." Within a few minutes, I was picking off three clay pigeons at a time. That's the kind of teacher Frac was.

The summer that I was throwing only "bottle shapes," Frank DiGangi and his wife, Carole—also an Alfred graduate, a potter and painter—came to visit. School was out, but I had the key to the pot shop. By now, Frank had left engineering—he had arrived at Alfred a year after I did, to attend the ceramics college—and had turned to sculpture. I knew that Alfred required an intense summer potting workshop of its design students. So off we went to throw some pots. And when I looked over at him, this man who was not a potter, I saw someone throwing effortlessly. Clearly, this was the way it was supposed to be. I, on the other hand, struggled to make my pots. Indeed, by throwing only bottle shapes, I was (symbolically?) closing down the opening at the top of each vessel. The next day I broke my bisqued pots and turned in the key, and I have not thrown a pot since. But today, three decades later, Hampton Potters, a pottery on the east end of Long Island operated by Frank DiGangi and Carole Worthington, produces extraordinary ware. The DiGangis estimate that in the past fifteen years they have produced about forty-five thousand pots. They have perfected glazes amazing for their vibrancy of color. And they underprice their pots, in my opinion. They still manifest the studio

mentality I first saw at Alfred and which existed for me later in Chicago and then Iowa City.

*Drawn by Stones, by Earth,
by Things That Have Been in the Fire*

I can tell you about this because I have held in my
   hand
the little potter's sponge called an "elephant ear."
Naturally, it's only a tiny version of an ear,
but it's the thing you want to pick up out of the
   toolbox
when you wander into the deserted ceramics shop
down the street from the cave where the fortune-
   teller works.
Drawn by stones, by earth, by things that have been
   in the fire.

The elephant ear listens to the side of the vase
as it is pulled upwards from a dome of muddy clay.
The ear listens to the outside wall of the pot
and the hand listens to the inside wall of the pot,
and between them a city rises out of dirt and water.
Inside this city live the remains of animals,
animals who prepared for two hundred years to be
   clay.

Rodents make clay, and men wearing spectacles make
   clay,
though the papers they were signing go up in flames
and nothing more is known of these long documents
except by those angels who divine in our ashes.
Kings and queens of the jungle make clay
and royalty and politicians make clay although
their innocence stays with their clothes until
   unravelled.

There is a lost soldier in every ceramic bowl.
The face on the dinner plate breaks when the dish
   does
and lies for centuries unassembled in the soil.
These things that have the right substance to begin
   with,
put into the fire at temperatures that melt glass,
keep their fingerprints forever, it is said,
like inky sponges that walk away in the deep water.

(from *Drawn by Stones, by Earth,
by Things That Have Been in the Fire*)

By the time we left Iowa City, I would have stopped photographing, too. But first I only stopped using film. I took the camera out, set it up on a tripod, adjusted the swings and tilts and bellows and lens, and looked, but I took no pictures. In the darkroom, I used the enlarger to create multiple images by printing through pieces of newspaper: pictures and text. Eventually, I no longer used either the camera or the darkroom. I had abandoned the cornet because for me it was the "wrong" instrument. I had stopped potting because I myself was the wrong instrument. But when I turned from photography, I did it because I felt that I had learned what I could from it. Others might learn more, but I was finished and, if I continued to photograph, could only hope to document what I already knew. I believed that if I ever were to feel the same about writing poetry, I could walk away from it, too.

But then it was time to go on active duty. On New Year's eve of 1964, while the sounds of our friends partying came to us from around the corner, Dorothy and I loaded the largest U-Haul we could rent. At midnight, we dug two bottles of beer from the snow and said a toast. Things were already looking up: just two weeks earlier I had received a transfer from the infantry to the adjutant general's corps.

I reported to Fort Benjamin Harrison, outside Indianapolis. During my training, we lived in a town appropriately called Fortville. I commuted to the post with a sergeant who was about to receive a direct commission to second lieutenant. I had postponed going on active duty so long that I had been promoted to first lieutenant. Our training class had many "noncoms" in it. My commuting partner noted that, as a sergeant, he kept two reminders taped to the rear of his desk nameplate: (1) "Keep the Old Man informed"; and (2) "Don't sweat the small stuff." I felt reassured by his advice. (Later I learned the corollary to #2: "It's *all* small stuff.")

I had been assigned to go next to the Army Information School, then at Fort Slocum on David's Island off Manhattan. But one night, during a class party, a major told me to report to him the next morning and, when I did, he asked me to stay at the Adjutant General School after graduation to become Foreign Military Training Officer. It would be an interesting job—running a liberal arts program for men and women from other countries who had come to take military courses. It would require irregular and sometimes long hours, and the job demanded initiative, so the major was asking me, not ordering me, to take the position. All I knew about my upcoming job at the Information School was that I was to be an assistant to the Director of Instruction.

I said yes. In deciding to favor the job over the location, I made the first of what were to be repeated decisions not to go back east. To my literary friends, it would appear strange to turn down a chance to be near Manhattan, and I wondered if I were making the best decision. Then again, because the major had handpicked me for the job, I had some bargaining power, and I used it to win authority to live off-post. We moved into one side of a duplex on College Street in Indianapolis.

I had a language lab, and authority to take my foreign soldiers on tours of factories, galleries, and museums. For the first half year or so, in addition to being Foreign Military Training Officer, I had other jobs. I was Public Information Officer, Assistant School Secretary, Assistant Security Officer, and I served briefly as Company Commander.

As Foreign Military Training Officer, I set up a weekly series in which foreign soldiers could talk about their countries to the American soldiers. Inevitably, the people from other countries spoke of their countries' art and culture. When it was Major Yoshikatsu Yatsunami's turn, he appeared in a Kabuki costume, and began by leaping from the stage to taunt Colonel Sadove.

In Indianapolis, we met Sue and Terry Friedman. Sue was editor of *Signet,* a little magazine. The Friedmans had adopted children with problems, most recently Jamie, a hemophiliac. As I got to know the Friedmans, I discovered that the Indianapolis Hemophilia Association was so in debt to the local blood banks that they were in danger of being cut off. Yet repeated transfusions were exactly what a hemophiliac needed to prevent the otherwise crippling effects of little falls and such.

The post had its own Red Cross blood drives. But there were always hundreds of "casuals" around who were in between assignments and thus not attached to any local unit. Sergeant Theall was my Information counterpart in the Finance School, also located at Fort Harrison. He and I would line up the casuals and ask for volunteers. On the appointed day, the hospitals in Indianapolis would be ready with extra nurses. Army buses would bring in the donors, Henry's Hamburgers would donate juice and burgers afterwards, and the post photographer would take pictures for the papers. We easily wiped out the debt. And when Sergeant Theall retired, he got the Army Commendation Medal he had always wanted, and deserved.

Dorothy and I made excursions from Indianapolis in three directions: to Ball State in Muncie, to Purdue University in West Lafayette, and, especially, to the University of Indiana in Bloomington. One summer, the School of Letters brought in John Logan, Nathan Scott, and Henry Rago, the editor of *Poetry,* to lecture. I had been coming down to sit in on gatherings of poets—Clayton Eshleman, Mary Ellen Solt, Daphne Marlatt, and others—and we were invited to give a group reading during the week. I was nervous about this because I knew it might mean meeting Rago, who had published me in *Poetry.* It did mean meeting Rago. He was gentle, considerate, and learned, and I trusted him. I came to see how carefully he edited *Poetry,* then a touchstone among poetry magazines. Whether he accepted or rejected one's poems, I discovered, he paid attention and kept track and waited. After I came to know his ways, I made a practice of sending all my poems to him, once a year in a big package. I maintained this practice until his death.

As my time in the army came to a close, I was asked to return to the Writers' Workshop to teach. The news came during the aforementioned session of the Indiana School of Letters, and one night in a restaurant I told Logan, my old teacher. He was delighted, but one of the Bloomington poets who was there was not. I learned from his response that writers who knew nothing about Iowa City or the Workshop nonetheless had many assumptions about it. Over the years, I would encounter this prejudice many times, and it would sometimes affect the reception by others of my poems. As the American poetry scene became more splintered, and the prizes multiplied, I noticed a certain cowardice among my contemporaries. Certain compatriots from my student days, and, later, students from my teaching days, kept their time at the Workshop secret when they broke into print, or they lied about it. I came to see that the success of the Workshop had made it a target. But I also came to see that it was an inevitable part of the literary life to be a target—outside the studio, writers could be envious and paranoid—and, in any case, from experience I already knew the Workshop to be honorable, exciting and worthy.

But now I was being discharged from the army and we were off to Iowa City again, a town I had liked on first setting eyes on it. A letter from Engle helped me to get a three-month "early out" for "seasonal employment." As a member of the National Council on the Arts, Engle had been dining at the White House with President Johnson, Secretary of Defense McNamara, and Attorney General Robert Kennedy, and his letter made note of it. The Vietnam War was heating up faster and faster and there was a rumor that junior officers like myself would soon be frozen for the duration. I was advised to have the documents signed quickly.

I went off to Chicago to obtain one final signature at Fifth Army Headquarters. I stayed with Aaron Siskind, who knew me as a poet and photographer and was amused to see me in the morning in my uniform.

I owed the army two weeks beyond the start of the first semester in Iowa City. We found a house on Iowa Avenue, I greeted my students on the first day of classes, and Dorothy and Nathan stayed while I went back to the post to live in the bachelor officers' quarters for my final two weeks in the army. The day

I was discharged, I drove off the post singing out the car window.

The Vietnam War was growing fast. As Foreign Military Training Officer, my work had involved me with embassies, the State Department, and the Continental Army Command, as well as visiting generals from our country and abroad. Because I often had to get things done quickly, I knew the noncoms—who run things. And so I knew that the military did not want the war. I had been reading dispatches which argued that we didn't belong in Vietnam and couldn't win in any case. Thereafter, I took part in activities protesting the war, but I could not blame just the soldiers. I blamed the government. I blamed all of us.

A Primer about the Flag

Or certain ones. There are Bed & Breakfast flags.
They fly over vacancies, but seldom
above full houses. Shipboard, the bridge can say
an alphabet of flags. There are State flags
and State Fair flags, there are beautiful flags
and enemy flags. Enemy flags are not supposed
to be beautiful, or long-lasting. There are flags
on the moon, flags in cemeteries, costume flags.
There are little flags that come from the barrel
of a gun and say, "Bang." If you want to have
a parade, you usually have to have a flag
for people to line up behind. Few would
line up behind a small tree, for example,
if you carried it at your waist just like a flag
but didn't first tell people what it stood for.

(from *Iris of Creation*)

In Iowa City, I taught with Donald Justice and George Starbuck. Paul Engle was still part of the Workshop but was gradually moving out of it to establish the International Writing Program. There would be many, many colleagues over the years and a stream of talented, interesting, sometimes brilliant students. Donald Justice and I worked together for many years before he left to complete his academic career in his home state at the University of Florida. Robert Dana had restarted the *North American Review,* and for five years (1965–69) I served him as poetry editor. Later, I served as poetry editor for the first two years of the *Iowa Review* (1969–71) under its founding editor, Merle Brown.

Looking back at the years in Iowa City since I returned to teach in the autumn of 1965, I see signals about myself embedded in the decision to return and in decisions since to stay. Iowa City is one of the last of the big-college-small-town towns. I am a small-town person. I like to say hello to people as I walk through town. I like a place where the weather gets "bad" by other people's standards. I like a place where people are less sure of themselves than they are in sophisticated cities. Iowans are truly friendly and believe in schools. Iowa is not at all what some of my friends on the east and west coasts think about it, but I have noticed that people tend to think their own place best and other places inferior. Iowa City is a secret many people know. It's been a good place for us, Iowa City—I'll let it go at that.

Teaching in the Writers' Workshop and elsewhere, reading at venues around the country and sometimes abroad—such activities have put me in the presence of hundreds of known writers. I have seen great modesty and irritating careerism. And I continue to harbor my affection for the studio sense of things—the Alfred design, the Institute of Design model (Moholy Nagy, the Bauhaus), the old Writers' Workshop example. To me, the excitement is all in the writing and in a community of writers.

As a teacher, I have tried to be a student. I take the position of a writer, not an expert. I have tried to remain in certain ways a beginner. My seminars have often included writing assignments, often simply a charge to "be influenced" by a book the members of the class have been reading together. In such cases, I have two rules: (1) No one has to write a "good" poem; and (2) Teacher has to do the assignment too.

In the mid-seventies, the editors of the *American Poetry Review* asked me to contribute a regular column. I called it "Homage to the Runner," by which I meant to signal the long haul and some of the essential solitude from which writing is born. Following my bent, I wrote spontaneously and informally, following my nose while hoping to be useful. Like the teacher who does his own assignments, myself as an example. In other words: no smoke, no mirrors, no lords and ladies. I included poems in the articles. I hoped to demystify what did not need to be mysterious and to protect the unknown. Some of those essays later appeared in a prose book, *Old Snow Just Melting.*

There came a time when I began to run on the roads. I ran marathons and shorter routes and collected drawersful of race shirts. My column title had not meant that. But by the time the editors of the *American Poetry Review* convinced me to write the column again, I had given up running for more walking, and so I was able again to call it "Homage to the Runner."

In 1990, I began again to write these regular essays about the processes of writing and reading. I thought about how things had changed and not changed. I counted up the things I still thought about writing. I looked at the ways in which I had changed, and I wondered how much was due to my writing, and before that to my walks and to my thoughts

alone. I knew that the question was chicken-and-egg and could not be answered. But when I returned recently to Center Moriches High School, to speak about writing, I saw myself and my prospects in the classrooms, and I knew that something had made a difference. And so I tried to recommend, however lightly, my own dumb luck—born of other places and other people.

Down the years of Iowa City as home base, our family has lived elsewhere for short periods. When in 1967 the University of Iowa gave me money just to write over a summer—a bonanza!—we drove to Marfil, a small town in central Mexico up the mountain from Guanajuato, and later to Ajijic. In the seventies I taught a trimester for Goddard College when it was still one of the most radical colleges in the country, and we lived on a road without a name outside Moretown, Vermont. Later on, I worked a semester for the University of Hawaii, following it with half a year in Seattle, where I taught a bit for the University of Washington. We have lived in Spain—in Nerja and Sitges. Work and occasional fellowships have taken us around Australia and Morocco and western Europe. Alone, I have been back to Tangier and Marrakesh, gone to Italy and to Yugoslavia. We have spent sabbaticals in Santa Fe and in California—Santa Cruz and San Francisco. In recent years, Dorothy has often accompanied me on reading circuits and to writers' conferences.

Acceptance Speech

My friends,
I am amazed

to be Professor
in a University

seven times larger
than my home town

and all because
I went away. Meanwhile,

the roots of the ivy
just went on crawling

in the dirt in the dark,
the light that was Brady's

and Gardner's during
our Civil War

became the blaze
in Southeast Asia

and soon everywhere
men lay down

without their women
which is what can happen

when people like me
leave home hoping

to be promoted
and end up promoted

to the rank of Captain
and discharged honorably

just before
whatever new war

we should always have known
was always coming

out of torn pockets and salt
from needles and patches of flowers

out of places for lost birds
night fog and a dying moon

from the work we do yea
(death being

what we don't do).
So to be at work

offending death
which others welcomed

who left home too
and no differently

seems to me half
of a famous story

I have never read
even in school.

(from *Stars Which See, Stars Which Do Not See*)

"With Frank DiGangi, Dorothy, and a friend,"
Long Island, 1984

At the time that the invitation to return to Iowa City arrived, I had my sights set on a job anywhere in the Northwest. I had not seen the Northwest, but it called to me. Twenty years passed. Our second son, Jason, was born in Iowa City in 1966. We moved from the house we had rented on Iowa Avenue into a house of our own on East College Street. Then, in 1985, we purchased a small house in Port Townsend, Washington, at the same time that I was able to stop teaching summer school. Now we live in it between school years. Otherwise, others live there. I call Port Townsend "the Long Island of the Northwest," just as, here on eastern Long Island, I call Long Island "the Port Townsend of the East." Our friends in Port Townsend say about us that we "live in Port Townsend and winter in Iowa."

I come from a long line of people who had to make a living. As for my books: yes, my inner life and some of my outer life are represented or otherwise expressed in them. But my books are the tip of the iceberg: underneath the surface, out of sight, lie hundreds of poems unfinished, poems finished but unpublished or published but uncollected, lectures read to audiences but never printed, notes for essays, pages from journals, unsent letters. . . . *The Escape into You,* a sequence of poems published in 1971, contains but half of the poems I wrote in that mode. The baker's dozen to and about my father—a series

titled "You Would Know," which appears in the collection *Residue of Song*—are only part of a book's worth of such poems. Many poems from earlier books did not make it into the *New and Selected.* And there are poems expressly commissioned to be printed elsewhere: long poems about the photography of Robert Heinecken and the paintings of Georgia O'Keeffe, and a piece for the inauguration of University of Iowa President James O. Freedman in 1982: I titled it "On Second Thought, I Think We Should Keep These Colleges Going." A guitarist, Mark Daterman, and I have made a poetry-and-jazz audio tape together. Frank DiGangi and I will be combining poetry and clay. When in 1990 it came time to publish *Iris of Creation,* I found myself with three books' worth of recent poems. I am one of those who is helpless not to write and helpless not to change.

Yet if all my writing were collected and its content apprehended—of nature, love and politics, the stances, viewpoints and vision, the outer textures, the inner corridors of ideas, the verbal maneuvers (and an alert reader may deduce much)—still much more would remain beneath the surface, out of view. For me—a small-town person trusting dumb luck as much as thought, helplessly receptive to the unconventional and the intimate—writing comes out of a life. In such a rich and difficult world, I feel myself to be of many minds at the same time and to have lived several lives at once. Doesn't everyone?

BIBLIOGRAPHY

Poetry:

Poems for Nathan and Saul (pamphlet), Hillside, 1966.

Things We Dreamt We Died For, Stone Wall, 1966.

Two Poems (pamphlet), Hundred Pound, 1966.

A Probable Volume of Dreams, Atheneum, 1969.

The Escape into You: A Sequence, Atheneum, 1971.

Woo Havoc (pamphlet), Barn Dream, 1971.

Residue of Song, Atheneum, 1974.

Stars Which See, Stars Which Do Not See, Atheneum, 1977.

These Green-Going-to-Yellow, Atheneum, 1981.

(With William Stafford) *Segues: A Correspondence in Poetry*, David Godine, 1983.

Drawn by Stones, by Earth, by Things That Have Been in the Fire, Atheneum, 1984.

New and Selected Poems, Atheneum, 1987.

(With W. Stafford) *Annie-Over*, Honeybrook, 1988.

Iris of Creation, Copper Canyon, 1990.

Nonfiction:

Old Snow Just Melting: Essays and Interviews, University of Michigan Press, 1983.

The A to Z of Poetry, David Godine, 1992.

Contributor:

The Young American Poets (poetry anthology), edited by Paul Carroll, Follett, 1968.

The Contemporary American Poets: American Poetry Since 1940 (poetry anthology), edited by Mark Strand, New American Library, 1969.

The Major Young Poets (poetry anthology), edited by Al Lee, World Publishing, 1971.

Preferences: 51 American Poets Choose Poems from Their Own Work and from the Past, edited by Richard Howard, photographs of the poets by Thomas Victor, Viking, 1974.

The American Poetry Anthology, edited by Daniel Halpern, Avon, 1975.

Heinecken, edited by James Enyeart, Friends of Photography/Light Gallery, 1980.

The Longman Anthology of Contemporary American Poetry, 1950–1980, edited by Stuart Friebert and David Young, Longman, 1983.

The Norton Introduction to Poetry, edited by J. Paul Hunter, 1986, 1989.

The Best American Poetry 1990, edited by Jorie Graham, Scribner's, 1990.

The Vintage Book of Contemporary American Poetry (poetry anthology), edited by J. D. McClatchy, Random House, 1990.

The Bread Loaf Anthology of Contemporary American Poetry, edited by Sydney Lea, Robert Pack and Jay Parini, University Press of New England, 1985, 1991.

Contemporary American Poetry (poetry anthology), edited by A. Poulin, Jr., Houghton Mifflin, 1985, 1991.

Other:

The Self and the Mulberry Tree (sound recording), Watershed Foundation, 1977.

Editor and publisher of *statements*, 1959–64; poetry editor, *North American Review*, 1964–69, and *Iowa Review*, 1969–71. Author of column, "Homage to the Runner," for *American Poetry Review*.

Dennis Brutus

1924-

Dennis Brutus, conducting a poetry reading at Dartmouth College, 1984

Perhaps the most important quality one can have is a sense of oneself as a human being. The value of this is that it gives you confidence in yourself, it gives you the ability to trust others as human beings, and it gives you a sense of being part of an enormous family or community whose wellbeing is your concern: when they suffer, you feel pain. Also, to be human is to be confident of your own creative ability and to believe in the creative potential of others. Perhaps the line which has influenced me longest and most in my own life has been John Donne's: "I am involved in all mankind."

March 29, 1989

This essay ought to have a theme or a focus; but I have been able to find none. Instead I offer some scattered threads which may combine in the mind of the reader to make a pattern. I have sought for one and have come up with several tentative ones, but they seem inconclusive; and so if I offer them here it must be seen as a partial and incomplete statement. I like the fable of the man who woke up one night and found an angel stitching a pattern which he was told was the pattern of his life. When he complained that it made no sense, the angel

53

explained: you are looking at the wrong side. It is possible that patterns only emerge in hindsight.

Born November 28, 1924, in Salisbury, Rhodesia (now known as Harare, Zimbabwe), of South African missionary teacher parents, Margaret Winifred Bloemetjie and Francis Henry Brutus, who returned to South Africa during my infancy, I grew up in the colored-designated township of Port Elizabeth with my older brother, Wilfred, and sisters, Helen and Dolly. "It was a sherded world I entered;/of broken bottles, rusty tins and split roof-tiles:/the littered earth was full of menace/with jagged edges waiting the naked feet:/holes, trenches, ditches were scattered traps/and the broken land in wasteplots our playing field:/this was the world through which I learnt the world/and this the image for my vision of the world" *(Stubborn Hope)*.

I grew up engaged with the quest of social justice for the exploited, which animates my activism in sport, poetry, and academia, and motivates my mission against apartheid, racism, and injustice to help create a world where "pain will be quiet, the prisoned free,/and wisdom sculpt justice from the world's/jagged mass" *(Letters to Martha)*.

Through qualifying for a merit scholarship, I was able to attend Fort Hare University, the only university in South Africa for nonwhites, and earned a Bachelor of Arts degree with majors in English (with distinction) and psychology, together with the College Education Diploma for teacher certification. I served as English master and senior English master at Port Elizabeth's St. Thomas Aquinas High School, my own former Paterson High School, and as English master at Johannesburg's Central High School, which was privately run due to opposition to government policy. I also worked in Port Elizabeth's social welfare department from 1949–1950. In 1950 I married May Jaggers and had eight children over the next eighteen years: Jacinta, Marc, Julian, Antony, Justina, Cornelia, Gregory, and Paula. I was committed to remain constant to my mission against apartheid amidst marriage and growing family: "My continental sense of sorrow drove me to work/and at times I hoped to shape your better world" *(Stubborn Hope)*.

"One of many demos: this one in Chicago," 1983

As a college student on scholarship at Fort Hare University in South Africa, my sport interest brought me into direct contact with black athletes on campus who were among the record-holders for sport ability in the country, but who were barred from becoming Olympic Team contestants because of apartheid sport's all-white competition restrictions. A letter I wrote in defense of two weightlifters whose talents should have qualified them for Olympic competition won me election as secretary for the local weightlifting association.

I carried this spirited campaign against apartheid sport into a larger arena after my graduation. While teaching, I remained active on the question of why black athletes who were scoring the best records in the country were ineligible for the Olympic Team. I pointed out that Fundamental Principle One of the Olympic Charter states that any country that discriminates on the grounds of race, religion, or politics cannot be included in the Olympics. I told the South African Olympic Committee that they might get expelled, and their response was: "Go ahead and try."

That remark was answered, despite its intimidating intent, and SASA (South African Sports Association) was formed in 1958. I became the founding secretary and we launched an international campaign to have South Africa excluded from the Olympic Games if we could not secure membership for all. Correspondence was dispatched to Avery Brundage, president of the International Olympic Committee (governing body of the Olympic Games), and returned unanswered; the excuse being that no correspondence pertaining to the Olympic Games was relevant unless it was from an Olympic organization. Accordingly, in 1963, SASA became SAN-ROC (South African Non-Racial Olympic Committee).

As the campaign started to gain momentum, I was served with further banning orders which made it a crime for me to teach, attend any meeting, belong to any organization, attend a sporting event, or to be with more than two people at any one time. In defiance of these banning restrictions, I was elected to the honorary position of founding president of SAN-ROC, in recognition of my key role in organizing action against apartheid sport. Despite two bannings, I continued organizing strategies in service to the mission for nonracial sport.

In May 1963, I went to the office at the Olympic Association in Johannesburg to raise the question of the exclusion of black athletes. I approached the officials before their meeting began, as my banning order prohibited my attendance or participation at the meeting. As I was talking with the officials, two members of the secret police arrested me.

While on bail pending trial, I fled to Mozambique but was recaptured and returned to South Africa by the Portuguese Secret Police for imprisonment. This created a high-risk situation, as my co-workers and friends were celebrating my escape to carry on the sport struggle outside the country. To make public my return to South Africa, once out of the police car, I sprinted into the 5:00 P.M. rush-hour crowd—away from the two, armed plainclothed secret policemen escorting me to Marshall Square Police Station in Johannesburg—figuring the crowd of people would deter the police from shooting. But when I turned a corner, I ran into one of the secret policemen assigned to guard me and was shot at such close range that the bullet entered my back and exited through my chest—a through-and-through wound. The ambulance that arrived was sent away as it was for whites only, leaving me bleeding on the street, awaiting an ambulance for coloreds. With wounds still unhealed and painful after surgery, I was discharged from Coronation Hospital to the Fort Prison, Johannesburg.

Currently, as president of SAN-ROC and international representative and patron of SACOS (South African Council on Sport) and the South African Boxing Council, I remain active in the campaign for action against apartheid sport, the maintenance of which is necessary through sport boycott until apartheid law's restrictions are withdrawn irreversibly. My efforts are channeled toward the nonracial recognition of all South African athletes, enabling them to take their rightful place in the international sporting arena as equals.

As a consequence of coordinating the campaign to exclude apartheid South Africa from Olympic competition, I was sentenced to eighteen months of political imprisonment on South Africa's notorious Robben Island. There I broke stones with, among others, Nelson Mandela, Walter Sisulu, and Ahmed Kathrada. During this imprisonment, news broke of South Africa's expulsion from the 1964 Olympic Games, evoking a melancholy celebration among the political prisoners, followed by harsh, abusive punishment by prison officials whose anger over this victory was intense. This was followed by house arrest in Port Elizabeth, and exile from South Africa in 1966 on a cancelled exit permit which the government still retains, the status of which is under inquiry due to preliminary negotiations about reform in South Africa.

Upon my arrival in England from South Africa in 1966, I served as director of the World Campaign for the Release of Political Prisoners from 1966–1969, and affected significant improvement in prison conditions through testimony delivered at the Red Cross Investigation of South African prisons. This took place as a result of a letter I wrote to the Red Cross which appeared in the *Times* of London, Tuesday, December 6, 1966:

Sir,

At the time of the Red Cross Inspection by Dr. Georg Hoffman of Robben Island Prison (your report November 28) I was a prisoner on Robben Island.

I have thus some knowledge of the extent to which Dr. Hoffman was misled. I know, for instance, that prisoners who slept on mats alongside the beds in the prison hospital were, for the day of the visit, permitted to spend some hours in the beds. They spent the night, as usual, on the floor.

It has taken two and a half years for this report to be released, and it is probable that if there had not been exposures of prison conditions through the International Defence and Aid Campaign for the release of South African political prisoners, the report might have been kept secret for even longer.

It seems that the report is now being published to rebut the allegations we have made. But the points quoted by *The Times* might easily have the reverse effect:

"At Leeuwkop: Two prisoners out of five . . . complained about occasional beatings;

"At Robben Island Dr. Hoffman picked out seven political prisoners at random. Three complained that they were beaten by warders;

"At Vooruitsig, five of the six prisoners complained about the attitude of the younger warders (beating, smacking, and bad language)."

There is enough material in the report—incomplete as it is—to justify our demand for a U.N. investigation. And it will certainly strengthen the demand of all decent people for the release of those whose crime has been opposition to the vicious regime of apartheid.

The essence of my mission against apartheid can be found in my ten books of poetry. Painfully, through personal experiences etched against her landscape, I have tried to sensitize readers and listeners of my poetry to South Africa's passions of grief and joy, horror and beauty, injustice and innocence as she moves toward liberation, justice, and peace.

Here, thunderheads rear in the night
dominating the awed quiet sky;
on the quiet-breathing plains
fractured metals shriek abandoned wails;
my country, an ignorantly timid bride
winces, tenses for the shattering releasing tide.

(Stubborn Hope)

My first book of poetry, *Sirens, Knuckles, Boots*, was published in 1963 and banned in South Africa upon its release. In an introductory note, the state of deprivation prompting this publication's birth is explained:

Currently working in Johannesburg and studying Law at Witwatersrand University under a scholarship. Banned from all gatherings for five years in October 1961 and also dismissed from a Government High School in Port Elizabeth where I taught English (and some Afrikaans) for the past ten years. Banned this year from teaching in a private school. Banned and gagged by the Minister of Justice, so that no words of mine can be quoted or printed. This is maybe why I have now thought of getting my work published.

Truth defies censorship. "Under green drapes the scars scream/red wounds wail soundlessly;/beg for assuaging, satiation" (*Sirens, Knuckles, Boots*).

My second book of poetry, *Letters to Martha*, consists of poems composed while serving a sentence of political imprisonment on Robben Island. Not allowed to write any publishable material, I transmitted this collection of poems as letters to my sister-in-law, Martha, recounting the prison experience and its echo of South Africa's scarred psyche: "O my people/what have you done/and where shall I find comforting/to smooth awake your mask of fear/restore your face, your faith, feeling, tears" (*Letters to Martha*). As I was discharged from Robben Island, my brother, Wilfred, began serving his prison sentence for similar activities, infuriating the guards who would now have to contend with another tenacious patriot!

After being exiled from South Africa in 1966, my third and fourth books of poetry were published during a visiting professorship: *Poems from Algiers* and *Thoughts Abroad*, which was published under the pseudonym of John Bruin by Troubadour Press, a venture I organized with colleague Ben Lindfors, from the University of Texas, Austin, for circulation of my work in South Africa. *Thoughts Abroad* was sold in bookstores in South Africa until it was discovered that I was Bruin of Troubadour Press, prompting the book's banning. Such a hypocritical process reveals the grotesque nature of censorship laws.

While teaching for approximately one year at Northwestern University, *A Simple Lust: Collected Poems of South African Jail and Exile* was published in 1972; it was unbanned in South Africa in 1990.

Strains and *China Poems* were published in 1975 during my joint appointment as a visiting professor in the English department and African and African American Studies Research Center at the University of Texas, Austin. Also during that year, I launched, with university colleagues Ben Lindfors and Hal Wylie, the African Literature Association, which has since grown to a large, internationally recognized literary organization. *Stubborn Hope* was published in 1978 and unbanned in South Africa in 1990. In 1982, *Salutes and Censures* was published in Nigeria; publication is pending for a U.S. edition. In 1989, during my current professorship and chair of the University of Pittsburgh's Department of Black Community Education Research and Development, poetry chapbook *Airs and Tributes* was published by Whirlwind Press and released in conjunction with my receipt of a deeply appreciated honor: the first Paul Robeson Award for excellence, political conscience, and integrity.

The question has to be asked and answered: How does the exile retain his creativity? In my case and in the case of many others, I would say that it is as a result of maintaining contact with the home country and continuing to make a contribution to the culture and struggle there. It is sometimes asked whether in fact oppression and exile are to be valued because they result in creativity. I would say it is never to be welcomed or desired; those who are creative might be even more creative under more congenial circumstances.

In a country which denies that men and women are human, where the Constitution excludes them as subhumans, the creative act is an act of dissent and defiance: creative ability is a quintessential part of being human: to assert one's Creativity is also to assert one's Humanity. This is a premise on which I have acted all my life and it is the premise I have offered to others as an inspiration (Pittsburgh, March 13, 1989).

Receiving an honorary degree: Doctor of Laws, Northeastern University, Boston, Massachusetts, 1990

I find, on examination, my connection with writing to be a long and continuous one. In my first year at high school, I initiated and edited a school newspaper—something unusual in a school in a deprived ghetto. At college, years later, I was on the editorial board of the revised college journal. When I began teaching, I assumed the duty of editor of the local teacher's journal. Years later, already a banned person, I agreed to edit a journal to keep it alive—its registration was about to lapse. I went on to start a new sport and political journal. Most of these, I should in honesty add, had a very brief life. Years later, when I was released from Robben Island Prison and under house arrest, so that it was impossible for me to hold a job, I wrote essays secretly for the local newspaper. As I was still a banned person, writing for publication was a criminal act. One final note to this particular theme: after I was exiled from South Africa, I published a small collection of poems under a pseudonym and thus was still able to write for people in South Africa although it was illegal for them to read works written under my own name.

The image of Orion, the constellation, recurs in my poetry. One of the poems was written in Nelson on South Island in New Zealand. It is really about Nelson Mandela:

> Here
> on another island
> within sound of the sea
> I watch the moon turn yellow
> or a blurred Orion heel
>
> And remember
> the men on the island
> on strips of matting
> on the cold floor
> between cold walls
> and the long endless night.

(Thoughts Abroad)

Another talks of Orion the Hunter pursuing a vanished or, as I call it, an evanished prey, using a deliberately archaic word. The poem was written, I think, in Dubrovnik, Yugoslavia. It was probably one based in London, working in a London context:

> Orion hunts endlessly
> an evanished prey
>
> but here
> by the still Atlantic
> where Dubrovnik sleeps its medieval dream
> away
> wavelaps throw starglints
> in momentary, fragmentary gleams:

> a near-
> Narcissus
> here
> should he but pause,
> Orion might be less inconsolable;
> Could he but pause.
>
> Orion hunts an evanished prey
> endlessly.

(A Simple Lust)

The most recent poem referring to Orion, a haiku, came to me looking out of my window over the city of Athens in the small hours of the night in September 1988:

> Seeing Orion
> stalk across an Attic sky
> a mosaic fills.

It seems to me that what is happening is that whether I write a poem about Orion in Pittsburgh, or in Dubrovnik, London, or Athens, the strands all pull together, and the focal points are Port Elizabeth and Robben Island. And so, one may knot them all together in something like the poem written as part of *Letters to Martha* about moving one night, after midnight, to try and find the stars, when on Robben Island:

> I remember rising one night
> after midnight
> and moving
> through an impulse of loneliness
> to try and find the stars.
>
> And through the haze
> the battens of fluorescents made
> I saw pinpricks of white
> I thought were stars.
>
> Greatly daring
> I thrust my arm through the bars
> and easing the switch in the corridor
> plunged my cell in darkness
>
> I scampered to the window
> and saw the splashes of light
> where the stars flowered.
>
> But through my delight
> thudded the anxious boots
> and a warning barked
> from the machine-gun post
> on the catwalk.
>
> And it is the brusque inquiry
> and threat
> that I remember of that night
> rather than the stars.

20 December 1965

The theme of stars, and the image of Orion are for me a real element of my thinking. They have always, or for most of the time, been images for me of light, of brightness, of beauty, and of hope. My interest in the stars is more than sentimental. I made a serious effort to identify the constellations and bought books that enabled me to do so. On the other hand, curiosity about the stars and an interest in science led me to the study of astronomy to the point where I knew sufficient astronomy to volunteer to teach a class in the junior high school.

Somewhere I read that what is especially effective about Dante's comedy—so-called "divine comedy"—is the way the portions are unified through the image of the stars, the light that moves the world and all the stars, a unifying image which is found in all three portions of the comedy. I'm not sure that reading that image or reading about that (and I remember reading it years ago in South Africa, at the time I was reading Dorothy Sayers's new translations of portions of Dante) influenced me sufficiently to decide to make the stars a recurring image in my own work. I doubt that. I think this is not consciously chosen. It simply reflects the reality of my personality and state of mind. And on at least one occasion, I've written a poem which asserts the fact that the stars for me are not a poetic ornament, but a kind of constant companion to me. Constant in the sense that they certainly interest me. I respond to them whenever I see them.

Another recurrent thread appearing in my poetry is the theme of religious thought. This seems to be somewhat sporadic in its appearance in my work and to be dependent on particular phases of my life, or arising out of certain circumstances. A poem such as "By the Waters of Babylon" might be a good place to start:

> By the waters of Babylon
>   the brackish wastes of alienness
>   lie like dust on heart and throat,
>   contour and curve of hull and held
>   unspeaking and meaningless
>   as a barbarous foreign tongue
>
> by the waters of Babylon
> we sat down and wept
>   the mind yearns over the low horizon
>   to other familiar friendly haunts
>   not unlike these gracious scenes
>
> when we remembered thee
> O Zion
>   these trees; these hills; this sky, this surf
>   evoke a dearness that lacerates;
>   the heart heels from this wounding loveliness

> how can we sing our songs
> in a strange land?
>   wordlessly
>   one turns from such beauty and such pain:
> weeps
>
> In a strange land
> By the waters of Babylon
> we sat down
> and wept.

(Seven South African Poets)

The poem begins with lines from the Old Testament from the Psalms and then uses these lines, both in the opening and close, to make a statement about exile. The fact that the poem was written in Mali, on the edge of the Sahara Desert or at least was germinating when I was there, and that there were parallels with the Israelites, and the sense of exile, makes it material which I can use to approach obliquely my own sense of exile. Looking back it seems to me to have been a fairly skilled contrivance in trying to make a statement about my own sense of exile when this feeling was still acute. I had at that time probably been out of South Africa less than a year, and at the same time I was back on the continent of Africa, unable to return to my own part of the continent, but nonetheless on the continent. It ends with a simple word, "wept," and then allows the word to resonate in the mind of the reader to make, I hope, a continued statement.

The next poem, sent to Canon L. John Collins, reflects an implied faith and a pun on "canon" and Canon.

> Now that we conquer and dominate time
> hurtling imperious from the sun's laggard slouch
> transcendentally watching the Irish jigsaw
> slip astream dumbly under masking cloud
> green England dissolved in history-grey
> and fanatic old Yeats made mellow by height,
>
> now that all canons of space-time are dumb
> and obey the assertions of resolute will
> and an intricate wisdom is machined to leash
> ten thousand horses in world-girdling flight,
> how shall we question that further power
> waits for a leap across gulfs of storm;
>
> that pain will be quiet, the prisoned free,
> and wisdom sculpt justice from the world's
>   jagged mass.

> 5 August 1966
> En route from London to New York
> El Al Airlines

(Letters to Martha)

Dovetailing with this communal experience of forced submission is the personal voice of "Prayer," which could also take on the persona of a griot's oral history transmission.

Prayer

O let me soar on steadfast wing
that those who know me for a pitiable thing
may see me inerasably clear:

grant that their faith that I might hood
some potent thrust to freedom, humanhood
under drab fluff may still be justified.

Protect me from the slightest deviant swoop
to pretty bush or hedgerow lest I droop
ruffled or trifled, snared or power misspent.

Uphold—frustrate me if need be
so that I mould my energy
for that one swift inenarrable soar

hurling myself swordbeaked to lunge
for lodgement in my life's sun-targe—
a land and people just and free.

3 July 1966

(Letters to Martha)

As a tribute to Mary, Mother of Christ, for the presence of sustenance to endure amidst adversity, I wrote the poem entitled "There are times (1)" I believe while working at Sharp Control while under house arrest in 1966:

There are times
when the pattern of events
in the physical world
falls into such a pleasing design
that I dare be convinced
that they have been arranged
by the tender cajoling hands
of a near-divine maternal graciousness

(Stubborn Hope)

A further thread of this redeeming grace theme is echoed in the poem entitled "Christmas 1965," which is part of the anthology *Seven South African Poets:*

Through the bruises and the spittle
the miasma of invective
and the sealed refractions of our prejudice
painfully man emerges

Straw, shavings, hay
and the mist of the cows' cloudbreath
and through it flickered the lambence
of man's inherent divinity.

Following the thread of this universal statement poem is a personal statement; one, which I note with interest, also centers on and closes with the word "divinity." It appeared in 1989, twenty-four years later, in a poetry chapbook entitled *Airs and Tributes:*

The air
of the universe
enters me:
the great spirit
who encompasses
all existence
enters my being:
where the great spirit
lurks
the divinity within me
aspires to reunion,
to divinity.

Another design of this religious pattern, written postprison and during/after house arrest during 1965–1966, are the following two tributes written to my mother who passed away while I was on Robben Island. I was not allowed to attend her funeral:

Dear wonderful woman

Dear wonderful woman
mother and friend and guide
rest easy now from all the strain
the courageous grasping of our jagged life
or better still—for this I desire
and dare to hope already your reward—
rejoice in bliss to crown your work
that insulates you from our present woe

(Stubborn Hope)

Most gracious exemplar

Most gracious exemplar
weaving your virtues with a modesty
that made them seem unpresent
and waging with a womanly lack of emphasis
tenacious battle with a world
of multiple injustice and evil—
whoever had the blessing of a dearer guide
and yet so little cared—for, little loved?

(Stubborn Hope)

Is my poetry political? Yes. The obligation to influence and change society rests on all of us; so far as we are all part of society and involved in all humanity. I firmly believe that it is not sufficient to describe the world, or even to understand the world; we must seek to transform the world. To depict my landscape in South Africa and not include the political features would simply be dishonest. All my activities: writing, teaching, organizing, creating, are

"At the ruins of a Roman fort, Hadrian's Wall near Newcastle-on-Tyne," 1990

facets of a single personality, are all directed at helping create a better world.

Nicknamed "Professor" during my student days, I suppose, I was earmarked early to teach. As a teacher, I was determined to help and inspire my students to become as well educated as possible to take their place as equals in society, and to impart knowledge with humor, spontaneity, and a relevance to everyday living. Being keenly aware of the inequities between black and white education, I sought to fortify my students with a sense of identity, worth, and accomplishment through education, in defiance of the apartheid government's law requiring nonwhites to be taught that they were inferior and not meant to strive for academic excellence. For defying this prime principle of apartheid, I was banned from teaching.

Even then I continued unofficially until further bannings and restrictions forced shutdowns. I was part of cooperative teams of teachers and parents who created "underground classes" for students in garages and homes to keep the learning process alive. Through a combination of tenacity and sensitivity I

tried to inspire students to interweave life's truths with academic pursuits.

In 1970, while campaign director for the International Defence and Aid Fund for Southern Africa, I received and accepted an invitation to serve as visiting professor in the English department at the University of Denver. This appointment opened the door to university teaching for me in the U.S. up to the present day. From the University of Denver, I became a tenured professor at Northwestern University's English department from 1971–1985 in Evanston. During that period, I also served as visiting professor at Amherst College's English department from 1981–1982 in Amherst; as visiting professor at Dartmouth College's African and African-American Studies department for spring quarter in 1983, in Hanover; and as an adjunct professor with Northeastern University's (Boston) English department in 1984.

From 1985–1986, I served as the Cornell Professor of Swarthmore College's English department in Swarthmore, as well as an adjunct professor for the University of Pittsburgh's Department of Black Community Education Research and Development, where I currently serve as chair and professor of African Literature.

I received Doctor of Humane Letters honorary degrees from Worcester State College and the University of Massachusetts; and an Honorary Doctor of Laws degree from Northeastern University, in 1990.

Granted political asylum in the United States in 1983, after an arduous three-year campaign, I have not traded security for silence. If I had been offered political asylum on condition that I remained silent, I would have rejected it.

During the hours when I was kept in isolation in Robben Island Prison, with no certainty that I would ever be released, and with the strong probability that I would die there, I spent some of my time thinking of places I would like to see if I were ever released from prison and able to travel. There were a number of places, some of them fairly stereotypical. What is curious is how many I have seen since. Reading poetry in St. Paul's Cathedral, London, or the Jerusalem Chamber of Westminster Abbey; walking Hadrian's Wall north of Newcastle, or sailing on Lake Windermere. All these I have done. And St. Peter's, Rome; facing the battlements at Elsinore; passing through the school where Kierkegaard studied; entering the bedroom where Beethoven was born; the Great Wall of China, courtesy of the Chinese Olympic Committee; the West Lake at Hangchow, which Marco Polo called the fairest spot in all the world; the room where Walt Whitman was born; visiting Philadelphia; the Liberty Bell; receiving the Paul Robeson Award. These are things I thought of in prison and wished I might see. The curious thing is that I have done them all. There may be a pattern there.

The following poem was written in prison and is part of the series called *Letters to Martha:*

> Nothing was sadder
> there was no more saddening want
> than the deadly lack
> of music.
>
> Even in the cosy days
> of "awaiting trial" status
> it was the deprivation
> and the need
> that one felt most.
>
> After sentence,
> in the rasping convict days
> it grew to a hunger
> —the bans on singing, whistling
> and unappreciative ears
> made it worse.

> Then those who shared one's loves
> and hungers
> grew more dear on this account—
> Fiks and Jeff and Neville
> and the others
>
> Strains of Eine Kleine Nachtmusik
> the Royal Fireworks,
> the New World,
> the Emperor and Eroica,
> Jesu, joy of man's desiring.
>
> Surreptitious wisps of melody
> down the damp grey concrete corridors
>
> Joy.

This is a poem about music, and starting from a general statement moves to a specific statement about some of the music I missed in prison. I would whistle songs and share my delight in them with others who enjoyed them and were familiar with them as well. And so, one refers to Mozart, to Beethoven, and Bach. The Bach is the little song *Jesu, Joy of Man's Desiring,* and then in closing to suggest the pleasure that music gave to us—notwithstanding our predicament—we were prisoners in the maximum security section of a maximum security prison, each in our single cell. Once we were locked in, unable to communicate with each other, we could be punished by having our food taken away if the wardens caught us yelling at each other from adjoining cells (they would stand hidden in the corridor); we would lose the next three meals, or whatever.

And so, the whole business of talking to each other, of whistling, of singing snatches of melody in a section where this was forbidden, all this generated joy. And so I take the word from the Bach aria, and the word in itself and close with it. *Joy*—and the resonance of the word—is suspended in the air.

A defiance of these prison regulations was a traditional event one day a year: South African Freedom Day, June 26. On this day, all the political prisoners joined in unison to sing Nkosi Sikelela, National Anthem of the people of South Africa. While in prison, I was part of this chorus, and share a reflection of the experience with you in this poem:

> Today in prison
> by tacit agreement
> they will sing just one song:
> Nkosi Sikelela;
> slowly and solemnly
> with suppressed passion
> and pent up feeling:
> the voices strong and steady
> but with tears close and sharp
> behind the eyes
> and the mind ranging

wildly as a strayed bird
seeking some names to settle on
and deeds being done
and those who will do the much
that still needs to be done.

26 June 1967
South African Freedom Day

(A Simple Lust)

I move from that poem to one which seems to me deeply religious, but is not necessarily so perceived by others:

Cold
the clammy cement
sucks our naked feet

a rheumy yellow bulb
lights a damp grey wall

the stubbled grass
wet with three o'clock dew
is black with glittery edges;

we sit on the concrete,
stuff with our fingers
the sugarless pap
into our mouths

then labour erect;

form lines;

steel ourselves into fortitude
or accept an image of ourselves
numb with resigned acceptance;

the grizzled senior warder comments:
"Things like these
I have no time for;

they are worse than rats;

you can only shoot them."

Overhead
the large frosty glitter of the stars
the Southern Cross flowering low;

the chains on our ankles
and wrists
that pair us together
jangle

glitter.

We begin to move
awkwardly.

Colesberg: en route to Robben Island

(Letters to Martha)

This is the poem that describes an incident on the road from Leeuwkop Prison in Pretoria (in the expensive suburb of Bryanston) to Robben Island, four miles from Capetown. And en route, which is

what the poem really is, we stopped at a place called Colesberg that at one time was "distinguished" as being the breeding place for Charles Engelhart's racehorses.

And there, we were taken out of the prison truck in which we were chained together, hands and ankles and barefooted of course in a kind of Bermuda shorts and little vest, after having been stripped and forced to line up naked. At about three in the morning, we were given porridge, which we were required to eat with our fingers since we weren't supplied with spoons, and we sat on the concrete, having travelled about five hundred miles from Pretoria with about another five hundred miles to go. Being in chains at that time of the night, being shuffled between the wardens in the cold and the uncertain, inadequate light, all created a visual picture for me which had somewhere in my mind an equivalent to which I connected it.

And the poem turns again, on the single word at the end. The word is "awkwardly," and I use it in the sense of being clumsy, graceless, without grace, deprived of grace—not only grace which makes one graceful, but grace which puts one in a state of grace.

Dennis Brutus, 1990

And I see the prisoners, including myself, as being without grace, deprived of grace in the sense that Christ was deprived of grace and was desolated at the point when he felt that even his father had deserted and abandoned him and he cried out: Why have you forsaken me? Now that is connected with the poem in a rather oblique way, with the image of the Southern Cross in the sky.

The cross is of course operating in more than one way. It is the familiar constellation in the Southern sky. But it is also the symbol of the cross, of the crucifixion of Christ. And what for me brings it into focus is the sense that the criminals are the innocent persons in this situation. That the real criminals are the guards who are treating the innocent as if they are criminals.

In prison, as Christ was dragged before his persecutors, and accused of crimes, he submitted to the accusations. There is a sense that those who oppose the injustice of the apartheid system are the truly just ones, are the victims.

During all of my teaching appointments, I have been committed to maintain my mission of service for action against apartheid by accepting speaking invitations from churches, community groups, legislative groups, and universities seeking knowledge about South Africa; and by organizing campus and community educational outreach events about South Africa, to prompt calls for divestment, and action against apartheid. I was very deeply touched by the note I received after a presentation about South Africa at the Chicago Theological Seminary. "People found themselves pierced to the heart during the time together with you—which I believe is finally what we all fear, and finally what we all want. Thanks again."

I continue writing, of course, and it continues to be an important if sporadic activity for me.

I strive, through my poetry and activism, to help strengthen the drive to rescue and rebuild a South Africa of freedom, justice, and peace; and to portray the essence of a new South African spirit, one graced by resiliency: "so vibrant and alive/that laughter will come bursting through/as imperious as the sun/and the spirit will survive/resilient as the soil."

Dennis Brutus

BIBLIOGRAPHY

Poetry:

Sirens, Knuckles, Boots (designed and illustrated by Denis Williams; also see below), Mbari Publications (Nigeria), 1963.

Letters to Martha, and Other Poems from a South African Prison (also see below), Heinemann Educational Books, African Writers Series (London), 1968.

Poems from Algiers (also see below), African and Afro-American Research Institute, University of Texas at Austin, 1970.

(Under pseudonym John Bruin) *Thoughts Abroad* (also see below), Troubadour Press, 1970.

A Simple Lust: Collected Poems of South African Jail and Exile (selected poems, including *Sirens, Knuckles, Boots, Letters to Martha, Poems from Algiers,* and *Thoughts Abroad*), Heinemann Educational Books, African Writers Series, 1973, Hill & Wang, 1973.

Strains (also see below), Troubadour Press, 1975.

China Poems (also see below), African and Afro-American Studies and Research Center, University of Texas at Austin, 1975.

Stubborn Hope (new poems and selections from *China Poems* and *Strains*), Three Continents Press, 1978.

Salutes and Censures, Fourth Dimension (Nigeria), 1982, Africa World (New Jersey), forthcoming.

Airs and Tributes (chapbook), Whirlwind Press, 1989.

Still the Sirens (chapbook), Pennywhistle Press, forthcoming.

Contributor; selected works:

Cosmo Pieterse, editor, *Seven South African Poets*, Heinemann Educational Books, 1971.

Frank Mkalawile Chipasula, editor, *When My Brothers Come Home*, Wesleyan University Press, 1985.

David Bunn, and Jane Taylor, editors, *From South Africa: New Writing, Photographs, and Art*, University of Chicago Press, 1988.

Hazel Rochman, editor, *Somehow Tenderness Survives: Stories of Southern Africa*, Harper & Row Junior Books, 1988.

Ann Hope, editor, *Torch in the Night: Worship Resources from South Africa*, Friendship Press, 1988.

Piniel Shava, editor, *A People's Voice: Black South African Writing in the Twentieth Century*, Ohio University Press, 1989.

Catherine Lipkin and Virginia Solotaroff, editors, *Words on the Page: The World in Your Hand*, Books 1–3, Harper & Row, 1989.

Donna Maier, editor, *Treasures of the World*, Scott Foresman, forthcoming.

Algis Budrys

1931-

I was born January 9, 1931, in Königsberg, East Prussia, Germany. My parents were Lithuanian diplomats stationed there, and I am a Lithuanian citizen from birth. In October 1936, my father was transferred to New York City, where he served as consul general of Lithuania until his death in September 1964. I have, then, spent the vast majority of my life in the United States.

I am a speculative-fiction writer. I've done a number of other things professionally, some of them having to do with writing, some of them rather far removed from it. But from the age of eight, I've either been a professional writer of science fiction and fantasy or wanted to be one.

And I consider that this is not merely an attribute I've acquired. I accept no implication that there is some individual in here who is essentially me, and that then in addition he has donned this particular garment. Being a writer of this sort of literature is far more than just my skin.

Now—how does a person get to be this way, and what stance does he maintain in the field of literature generally? In some circles—the number of such circles is open to debate—speculative-fiction writers are considered a breed apart. That much I have always known; my parents were the first to tell me, under the natural assumption they were in primary charge of the twig-bending to be done in my case. They were wrong, but certainly not for want of trying.

Since then, I've had occasion to identify circles to which I am a freak, others in which I'm held in favor, some in which the attitude is wary neutrality, and so forth across the spectrum. Some people who sit behind literary keyboards at least as much as I do, and whose general experience of life closely parallels mine, refuse to believe that I do literature at all. Some other speculative-fiction writers consider that I do the wrong kind of SF. And so on.

I feel I have to deal with this here, because if there's going to be any particular value in this essay, it's in the opportunity to present a picture of what might be called the median-level SF writer. I am not a public celebrity for my work, so simply reciting the facts of my life will not satisfy the reader. I am a very

Algis Budrys, age one-and-a-half, Palanga, Lithuania

good writer of some sort of SF, I'm known for it among my peers, I made myself that way, and I do the needful to maintain that standard, but that's neither here nor there. When lists of the top twenty-five SF writers have been prepared over the years since the middle of the twentieth century, they've run out of room before my byline came up. And that is the value of my being included here.

No great public reputation colors the light cast on me. What validity I have is what my life and work give me. And you can take it that extended observation has convinced me that much of what follows, true in my case, is at least analogously true of almost all of us who at this time are verging on the far edge of middle age and have always been in our *métier* to stay.

I broke in at an unclassifiable time. Between 1926 and 1949, the flag for SF was carried by identifiably wordsmithy people, many of whom wrote or had written for all sorts of pulp-fiction media, and the tone of the penny-a-word free-lance *condottieri* was the tone preferred.

Two newsstand magazines—*Astounding Science Fiction* and *Unknown* (fantasy) magazine—in the late 1930s were in fact showcases for writers who had created something new and different in popular fiction. They rarely sent their work elsewhere, and most had been brought up directly from the ranks of novices by the inventive, vastly seminal, and now-legendary editor John W. Campbell, Jr. But Campbell himself, and many of his writers, rubbed elbows incessantly with people who were wont to call themselves "pulpateers," as distinct from litterateurs. And that rubbed off on all of them, to a greater or lesser extent. If you were a pubescent SF reader at that time, as I was, and particularly if you had every antenna out and quivering for any molecule of information on how real writers walked and talked, it rubbed off to some extent on you.

By 1952, when I sold my first magazine fiction story—to *Astounding*—Campbell's hegemony was broken, the pulps were dead perhaps forever, and I completely failed to grasp either of these vital facts. Another oversight lay in at first failing to grasp the fact that I was not adding myself to Campbell's core group; I was adding myself to an accretion around it . . . and the core itself was riddled with defections. Yet another error was my assumption that no one in his right mind had been thinking Campbell's SF wasn't the very best sort of SF. In all of these things I was wrong. The years had caught up with me while I was still not yet a-wing. But perhaps we'd better backtrack a little.

It was Hitler who started me on the road to being an SF writer. In this, I suppose I am not typical. Watching from my window in Königsberg while he passed in the street below, I saw the good burghers and their spouses lose all control of themselves; some of them ran into the bushes in the park across the street, and some did not quite make it. (Which was a matter of intense interest to me, since I had just recently undergone toilet training myself.) All of them were making this sound, which I ascribe now to an almost endless "Ahh!", and all of them had their right hands stiffly out in front of them. I really had no choice—I decided that I had been born into a world of werewolves.

That being the case, certain things follow. Among them is the fact that no matter how the burgher and his spouse seem pleasant enough when

you are having tea with their daughter, you had better watch out for their expressions when they think you aren't looking. Also among them is the fact that you, too, are a werewolf; people had better watch out for you. So all of life is liable to be a facade . . . friendly, polite, urbane, and about a sixteenth of an inch deep over the ravening beast. Don't tell me it's not true. It is true. The whole point of civilization is to fend off being a beast as best one can, which is not always.

That being the case, all human institutions are more or less transient. They exist only as long as they are convenient; when a different convenience is required, the old one is discarded in a trice and, things being the way they are, the new is declared to have always existed. Very few things actually persist, and none of them are institutions. The things that persist are love, hope, and death. I do not know if we will have death with us permanently; I doubt it. That leaves love and hope. I cannot imagine a human being who is incapable of either. The thing is, with all the love and hope in the world, there is still the werewolf; it is not true that all will be well if we but love one another.

But we were talking about writing.

Writing is one of the great arts, and I am fiercely proud that I do it so well. I do not do it much, mind you—eight or nine novels in almost forty years, and about two hundred shorter works. But it may have something to do with the fact that three of the books are generally considered classics in the field, and the rest aren't bad, all but one. But now I am getting ahead of myself, so let us return to March, 1952, when I sat in my agent's office and learned I had sold my first story, to John W. Campbell, Jr., for *Astounding Science Fiction.*

I had an agent in the first place because of an unlikely combination of circumstances. It *is* true that any agent you can get while an unpublished author is an agent not worth having. But I had Frederik Pohl, who was *the* SF agent of the day, because Jerry Bixby, one-time editor of *Planet Stories,* had said to Fred Pohl, "Why don't you take a look at some of Budrys's stuff; it's not bad." (Jerry, it should be understood, was arranging for me to sell comic-book fillers, so I was not a complete novice. On the other hand, I was undoubtedly the greenest hand around Horace Gold's Friday-night poker table, which was where Jerry said it.)

Fred opined what the hell, I trucked a stack of manuscripts into his office—where I had my first glimpse of Evelyn Harrison's amazing décolletage, Evelyn being his secretary—and in due course, the manuscripts began to sell. Which was a matter of

Age three, Palanga, Lithuania

some amazement to me because, for one thing, the manuscript that John W. Campbell, Jr., bought in its red Frederik Pohl Literary Agency folder was the identical manuscript he had bounced with a printed rejection slip when it came in over the transom three years earlier. But then, three years earlier the market had been tight, and dominated by Campbell; now it was loose, and two other magazines were vying for Campbell's mantle. In fact, my second sale was to *Galaxy Science Fiction,* which was almost brand-new but had some people saying it was already better than *Astounding.* Horace Gold certainly thought so, but then, Horace Gold was its editor.

My third was to *Space Science Fiction,* edited by Lester del Rey, and there were several significant things about that.

For one thing, although the *Astounding* sale was nice, it was with a story that had had plenty of time to get old with me. Then, the *Galaxy* sale, while nice, had been with a story I had written on a bunch of three-by-five cards while taking the Amsterdam Avenue bus from the rough vicinity of Fred's office on Twenty-Third Street to Columbia University, where

I was in the last throes of attempting to please my parents by getting a degree. But the *Space* sale was with a story I really cared about, and considered a serious effort. As a consequence, to this day I often tell people it was my first, and since all three stories came out within a few weeks of each other, what the hell.

But the other thing was that it was sold to Lester del Rey, and Lester and I had had a special relationship for years, though he didn't know me from Adam.

I guess I was about fourteen when I read my first Lester del Rey story, and from then on he was my favorite author. It transpired, years later, that he pointed out this was because he told a weepy, hypersentimental tale most (though not all) of the time. And this is true. And, furthermore, he probably did do it deliberately. But none of that made any difference to the boy who sat on the Vineland High School bus with tears streaming down his face, and to this day I forgive Lester everything.

Also, I had seen Lester del Rey when I was sixteen, and bound for college. In one last fling before departing for Miami—well, Coral Gables; no, farther south than that, as it turned out—I had attended the World Science Fiction Convention in Philadelphia in 1947, and there was Lester del Rey.

Unlike most of the other pros—you must understand that the 1947 Worldcon was not quite as large as Worldcons later became—he was not up on the speaker's platform, which was crowded with John W. Campbell, Jr., George O. Smith, Theodore Sturgeon, and Philip Klass, among others. Unlike the others, Lester was not about to spread sweetness and light. Instead, when he got up from one of the folding chairs in the audience to speak in response to some point, he was acid, sharp-tongued, and—wearing an ice-cream-colored suit—everything the young Algis Budrys wished himself to be. Sell them sweetness and light, but be a waspish son of a bitch in person.

So it made perfect sense to me that when, some years later, I sold him my then-favorite story (it being as close to a Lester del Rey slush-pumper as I could manage), I would bump into him and promptly ask to move in with him. This struck me as perfectly normal. He had things to teach, and God knows I had things to learn.

Now, you must understand something. I had moved out of my parents' home in September, sleeping on the floor of Jerry Bixby's place in Brooklyn, and I now proposed to move in on Lester. To this day, I don't understand, quite, what was in it for Jerry. But to this day, I don't understand at all what was supposed to be in it for Lester, except that he said yes without a moment's hesitation some ten minutes after meeting me for the first time in his life. And in the next nine months, he taught me most of what I know about writing to this day, and editing besides.

We lived a curious life, Lester, and Evvie, and I. In due course, I got jobs—first, as assistant editor at Gnome Press, and later as assistant editor at *Galaxy*—and there were various traumas and triumphs associated with that. But basically the three of us hunkered down as if we were unemployed, living in a cold-water flat on West—far West—Nineteenth Street, with a bunch of cats and very little money. Evvie was the Evelyn Harrison of the décolletage; in due course, she began using the name Evelyn del Rey. She was employed, for a time, and Lester was employed, and even I was employed some of the time, but somehow it was hard to get kerosene for the space heaters, even at fifty cents a gallon.

Nevertheless, in that time I sold quite a few stories, started my first novel, several times wrote two (saleable) stories in one day, and did enough to fulfill many a career, while convinced I wasn't doing nearly enough. And I was right; I wasn't doing nearly enough, at the rates of payment in those days. There was a very steep drop-off once a story bounced out of *Galaxy* or *Astounding,* which, unfortunately, happened now and then. They paid three cents a word on acceptance; *Space* paid three cents a word on publication, and everybody else paid considerably less.

Eventually, I left the del Reys to strike out on my own, with indifferent results; married, in July 1954; moved to Red Bank, Oceanport, and Long Branch, New Jersey; didn't so much as break even until suddenly, in September 1961, everything changed—I got a job. But perhaps we had better go over that ground more slowly.

First of all, you have got to understand that we really were broke. For all that Lester was editor of four magazines, they didn't pay him much. For all that Evvie was employed for a time as Fred Pohl's secretary, that did not last. And for all that I was first at Gnome Press and then at *Galaxy,* the fact is that while I got a tremendous amount of experience, I knew nothing. Soon enough, I knew a little bit, and talked as if I knew a great deal. But that is because I started from scratch. I left *Galaxy* after only three months and did not work another salaried job until September 1961. And all of us—all of us, including Fred Pohl and Horace Gold and just about everybody but John W. Campbell, Jr., and he only relatively speaking—were in exactly the same boat. There was

nothing extraordinary in my being broke—everybody was broke.

At the same time, some of the enduring classics in the field were being written. (Not by me; that came later.) Works like Pohl and Kornbluth's *Gravy Planet,* which became better known as *The Space Merchants,* Ray Bradbury's *Fahrenheit 451,* Alfred Bester's *Demolished Man,* and Arthur C. Clarke's *Against the Fall of Night,* for four. Not a one of them made any significant money until years later. No one in his right mind thought there would ever be any money in science fiction.

Why did we do it? What I have to offer is just a theory; I think we looked at it in two distinct ways. One of them was that of course we had no hope of making money. The other was that SF, done right, was too beautiful not to make money somehow.

I, frankly, was hardly suited for anything else. Among my experiences of this world, already, were innumerable collisions with it, and very little joy. I was handsome, well set up, and far more intelligent than the average bear, and all this meant was trouble. I lacked some essential—in fact, I still lack it—which would let me convert all this into anything much. Except in science fiction. In science fiction, I was a whiz. A little rough around the edges, at first, but I was learning at a truly awesome rate. By late 1954, I was one of the best in the world, although the world did not realize it for the most part.

But that's neither here nor there. What counts is that, for whatever reason, a great many of us were in the same boat. And for some reason, very few of us got out of it. And I don't know how we managed it.

And it was in this condition that I actually sold my first novel, and fell in love.

My agent, Frederik Pohl, quit the agent business very soon after accomplishing the task of selling me to Arnold Hano, the editor of Lion Books. He moved to Red Bank, New Jersey, with Carol, his wife, and one day in 1953, Carol asked me to stay out there a day longer than I had planned. As a matter of fact, it was a Tuesday, a gorgeous fall day, and I saw no particular reason to go back to New York. (I had driven Carol and Mary Kornbluth to the Kornbluths' home in Waverly, New York, on one of those errands that makes no sense in hindsight but seemed perfectly OK at the time. I had gotten back with Carol on Monday.)

Tuesday came and went, and Wednesday came—and Carol persuaded me to stay an extra day—and Thursday, and next thing I knew, it was Friday. At which point Carol asked me to go with her to meet the train from New York, because her old college roommate, Edna, was on it and was coming to stay the weekend.

In fact, Carol spent the better part of the afternoon showing me pictures of *Vogue* models who looked sort of like Edna, and the like, and by the time evening came I hated Edna with the sort of dumb, animal fury that can only grow in the heart of someone who has gradually realized he was being set up.

Well, the train came, and Edna got off it, and she *did* look like a *Vogue* model, and I did hate her, I did. I hated her for several more hours, and then I stopped. We were married about ten months later, and we still are.

I believe the two of us are the only people—including Carol—who gave us a chance of it lasting more than a few months. (Carol was of two minds about the whole thing, it turned out.) But through thick and thin, and for the first seven years it was very thin, she has stuck with me.

My parents came within an eyelash of not coming to the wedding. She was not, after all, Lithuanian. Her relatives were not exactly thrilled either. After all, I hardly held a steady job . . . nor was I Irish.

Algis, age four-and-a-half, Mariampole, Lithuania

But they all wound up coming to the wedding, which was held in Saint Bernard's Roman Catholic church on West Fourteenth Street, and the del Reys were there, and Frank and Polly Freas, and Dave Kyle and the Campbells, and it was all right. It was definitely all right. Without a shadow of a doubt, Edna is the brightest, best single thing that ever happened to me.

We lived, briefly, on the corner of Twenty-Third Street and Eighth Avenue. We might be living there still, I suppose, but Edna came down pregnant.

This strikes me as hilariously funny, now. My cousin, Valyte, had sat me down in the crowded luncheonette on West Fifty-Seventh Street at high noon early in June 1954, and asked me, in her loud, clear, carrying voice: "Do you *have* to marry this girl?" which meant I never felt the same way about Valyte again. On the other hand, we must have been married about five months when Edna did become pregnant, and for quite a while thereafter—about six years—things went downhill in many ways, except that the boys were so lovely.

There were four of them, in the end, although David was born after the worst of the trouble was over, barely.

Jeffrey was the first, and he was born while we were living in Red Bank, New Jersey. Steven was the second, and he was born while we were living in Oceanport. Timothy was the third, and he was born while we were living in Long Branch—specifically, the West End of Long Branch. We never, to my certain knowledge, paid the rent on time, in all that time, and we wouldn't have paid it at all if Edna's relatives hadn't helped us. Nor would we have survived any number of other things.

Meanwhile, my career was flourishing. You see, that was the catch—it kept looking like things were bound to get better anytime, now. They didn't.

My first novel had proved to be a disaster, while we were still living in New York. Through no fault of his own, Walter Fultz, who had succeeded Arnold Hano, had had to cut *False Night* in galleys. He had had to cut it by one-fourth its length, and he had had to cut three other novels over the same weekend. In that way, and only in that way, had he been able to preserve the twenty-five-cent cover prices on the books. But a book that has been cut by one-fourth in galleys shows it, and it was my first novel.

Then, my second novel, *Who?*, was a winner. Written in Red Bank, it was the first of my novels to keep chugging away, going through nearly innumerable editions, and showing no sign of stopping to this day; it has been made into a film (not a good film, but a film), and just when I think it must surely be over at last, somebody else expresses an interest in it. BUT, when I first wrote it and turned it in, Lion Library collapsed entirely before it could be published, and it would be three years before it saw the light of day.

So my third novel, *Man of Earth,* came out before my second novel. And it is a dog. I don't know what possessed me to write it; fortunately, it has shown no sign of reappearing, whatever it was.

In 1958, I wrote *The Falling Torch. Who?* had come out, at last, from Pyramid Books, which had apparently bought Lion's inventory without telling anybody. As it happens, I had just concluded a serial-rights deal with Bob Mills, then editor of *The Magazine of Fantasy & Science Fiction,* which would have brought me $1,500. Unfortunately, when I called Scott Meredith, my then-agent, to give him the good news, he responded with the news that the Pyramid edition was on sale at that very minute, but he would be happy to *lend* me $750.

I could have killed him. Surely he had known, and just as surely he hadn't told me, despite promises to do so. Instead of killing him, I took the $750. And when—for reasons that are still not clear—*Who?* put up an enviable immediate sales record, I signed to do *The Falling Torch* with Pyramid Books, for a snappy $1,500 advance.

The Falling Torch was notable for several things. One, large parts of it also appeared in magazine form, as distinguished from *False Night* and *Who?,* so that I actually made about $2,500 from it on the first go-around. Two, I took so long at the job of actually finishing it that I did not actually finish it; I turned it in with chapter seven missing (being careful to number chapter eight as chapter seven, of course), *and nobody noticed!* Instead, the book went through seven printings and sold over 250,000 copies (I am not making this up). I am not sure whether it is my best-selling book or not. Frankly, I doubt it. But it certainly did very well for a three-legged beast, especially a beast which even Pyramid's own house ads in other SF books of theirs did not include. All they did was change the cover painting with each new printing, and jack up the price a little. And it sold and sold.

Mind you, it took about ten years to sell 250,000 copies. But since I didn't do any more work than had already been done, in the end, so to speak, all was well. And now—just now—I took the time to write the missing chapter, so that it will be out, in late 1990 or early 1991, as *Falling Torch,* and we'll see if it'll sell another 250,000 copies.

But we were talking about a career flourishing, and here I've been presenting evidence for just the opposite. Well, the short answer is that God sees, but waits. The longer one is that I hit a lucky streak just about the time I got married, and began selling magazine pieces like mad, first to John Campbell and then to Bob Mills. (And to half a score of other editors as well, but John, and then Bob, were the principal ones.)

For John, I wrote and wrote, and much of the time he bought what I wrote. There was an understanding between us—including the promise that when he was ready to retire, I would succeed him—that was not as deep, I think, as the understanding between John and the stalwarts of the prewar Golden Age. But it was the best he could do, given the circumstances, which were that for a while I was the only notable new talent that would stay with him. Most of the other bright boys were selling to Horace Gold, while at the same time bitching and moaning about Horace's heavy editorial hand. I couldn't see it. John was paying just as much as Horace, and he didn't edit to speak of.

But he did limit. At first, this didn't bother me because I was inside the limits, which were pretty broad. But around 1957 I got a little restless, which was roughly when Bob Mills came along.

Bob came along in a curious way.

Round about the same time, Damon Knight, James Blish, and Judith Merril invited all the science-fiction writers they could get hold of to visit with them in Milford, Pennsylvania, for no particular purpose, one would think. But an amazing number of us showed up anyway, and it turned out—at this first, ever, purely professional gathering—that we were feeling . . . something. Something that in the end turned out to be a union, or at least a craft guild, but not for some time thereafter; what we felt right away was a sense of solidarity. For no reason in particular, editors and publishers for the first time were courting us, instead of it being the other way around.

Mind you, this was hardly, invariably true. There were plenty of editors and publishers who didn't know about Milford and didn't want to know. But *any* sign that we were not quite the scum of the Earth was welcome, and the fact is that even at the first Milford, there were some editors who let it be known that they were willing to listen to reason. They were even willing to listen to unreason; poor Walter Fultz got lambasted by Cyril Kornbluth for what he had done to my novel, and I raised the hackles of a couple of other people, and God did not strike us dead on the spot.

Sometime around then, Bob Mills made himself felt.

The Magazine of Fantasy & Science Fiction had been around since 1949, the beloved bastard child of

Mick McComas and Anthony Boucher. It was a very strange sort of magazine, with antique rather than slick-finish covers, and a policy against interior illustrations. It was also published by Mercury Press, which had, in its heyday, brought out the *American Mercury,* H. L. Mencken's magazine. At the time of which we speak, its flagship was *Ellery Queen's Mystery Magazine* and a bewildering array of subsidiary crime titles. But by nibbling and cajoling, Anthony Boucher had persuaded the publisher—who either was or would shortly become Joseph Ferman, father to Ed—to try an SF magazine, and this was the result.

F&SF had its ups and downs. But it had more ups than downs, and its overhead was low. By 1956, it was solidly established, and, to the minds of many of us, dull. The fact that it published at least one story an issue that was memorable had nothing to do with the perception. And it is a fact that it paraded an almost endless stream of lady writers before its public—lady writers who were incapable, seemingly, of selling to anyone else.

Well, things had changed. There was now a new editor in the shop, namely Bob Mills, and he had two pieces of news for us, which he gave to anyone at Milford who would hold still. One, *F&SF* had a new companion magazine, *Venture,* which would be interesting and exciting if we chose to make it that way, and, two, he didn't know beans about science fiction, and so would not presume to tell us what to write, provided it was interesting and exciting.

Well, three, actually—*Venture* would only pay two cents a word. But hardly any of us were actually in it for the money.

There began, for me, a period the like of which I have not experienced before or since. It was not that I sold Mills so much, although I sold to *Venture* as much as anybody, I guess, under two or three names besides my own; it was the freedom to write anything I pleased. And the fact that in short order I was his assistant editor. And the fact that he lived in Connecticut, in a house, with a lovely wife and two sweet children, and nobody else I knew did that.

Nobody remembers *Venture* now. But Leigh Brackett wrote for it, and Ted Sturgeon, and Cyril Kornbluth, and Lester del Rey, and a girl named Anne McCaffrey turned up in the slushpile, and it was fine.

Unfortunately, the American News Company was a hollow shell, which fact had escaped the attention of the thousands of magazines that depended on it for distribution, and when it did come to their attention, it was too late. *Sic transit gloria Venture,* and almost as sick was *F&SF,* et cetera. Nor did it help, in any way, that Cyril Kornbluth—who

Age fifteen, Vineland High School, New Jersey

had developed hypertension as a combat machine-gunner during the Battle of the Bulge—shoveled his walk and dropped dead in the train station on his way to take up the first day of his duties as assistant editor on *F&SF.* So died, at thirty-five or so, one of the best of us, and by coincidence, or perhaps not, some of the innocence went away.

But you are still waiting, I presume, for some sort of signal of success. Very simple: Although during this time I made between $1,800 to $4,000 a year, I was steadily gaining in reputation and standing. In 1958, I was considered to be as good as they come—bearing in mind, of course, that one did not speak of the new boys in much the same breath as the cadre that had existed prewar. And bearing in mind that while books were now definitely the wave of the future, there were not so many of them.

In 1957, I had presented myself with a Class A idea, and for three years I tussled with it. I called it "The Death Machine."

"The Death Machine" was an idea so good that it might very well turn out to be the science-fiction novel of the decade (or whatever). And to cap that, I had thought of a new way to tell a story.

A new way to tell a story. Well, we can either have a lecture on writing, which I don't think is the best course to follow, or you can pretty much take my word for it. Essentially, there is a way to tell a story which most writers follow most of the time. And then there is the way I hit upon, and only used this one time, in which the characters act above the usual emotional level, but all act above it at the same degree of exaggeration. The effect is that they appear normal (more or less), but the audience is mysteriously disquieted. Clear? I thought not, but it's the best I can do under the circumstances. At any rate, I set out to write it, in the grip, as they say, of a powerful idea.

Some idea of its power may be gotten from the fact that I did little else for three years. Another idea may be gotten from the fact that at twenty thousand words a year, this translates into roughly two thousand six hundred words a month, which is not quite a living. I don't know why my wife didn't leave me.

You may wonder why I didn't get a job, and write at night. The answer is that it didn't occur to me, or something.

And finally the blessed thing was finished.

The idea had begun with a bunch of people standing around a swimming pool and cutting each other to ribbons, verbally. Actually, I'd had that much of the idea—four pages of manuscript—for some years; I had no idea of what had brought them there, or where they were going afterwards, and it was just one of scores of isolated scenes I've written in my life, most of which come to nothing. Then one day I was talking to J. R. Pierce on the phone, and as I talked, the real idea came to me. Complete, right down to the last line, which was "Oh, no, I won't fall for that—someday I, or someone like me, will hold you in his hand."

Why I was talking to J. R. Pierce is not at issue. The fact that he was director of Bell Labs is, however, because the idea that had come to me had to do with matter transmission—not that J. R. believed for a moment that it was possible, you understand. As for the last line, I had remembered, instantly, a time when I was four years old and, by squeezing my eyes in a particular way, had turned a snowy landscape into a sparkling fairyland—it has to do with moisture in the eye—which, in an instant, became a starry sky as the hero of my idea regarded it, which became, in an instant, either approaching death by strangulation, or tears, or both. And I hung up the phone, and went away for three years.

Well, a couple of interesting things happened to the idea over those three years.

One, the original title absolutely, positively did not fly with Knox Burger, the editor. Certain features of the final draft reflect this; I kept coming up with alternate titles, and two of them resulted in addition to the text. (It did no good; the additions, a New England gravestone motto and a pseudo-Shakespearean portion of a play, survive. But the title was imposed by Knox Burger, it is *Rogue Moon*, and you and I are both stuck with it.)

Two, the book does not end on the original last line. When I finally came to it, I was perfectly willing to stop, but my mind was not. Thus, much to my surprise, the book kept right on going for a while, and much the better for it, I might add.

To be the author of an undoubted classic in the field—which *Rogue Moon* is, no two ways about it—is a curious and perplexing thing. And the feeling does not go away with time, though it mutates.

First, when it is brand-new, there is the irresistible impulse to explain it all, as if, were the book to be cut into enough parts, an infinite number of subsequent books could be produced, just as good. Well, this is a trap, and I fell into it, but fortunately after about the fifth attempt to explain it, I gave up. The book cannot really be explained.

Second, there's the matter of awards. In those days, there was just the Hugo—no Nebulas, no Philip K. Dicks, no half-dozen others—and I coveted one. Suffice it to say I think I was shopped, but the pain of losing went away, since the book has not been out of print in the U.S. for thirty years, and the foreign editions just keep on coming. *Rogue Moon,* horrid title and all, is an undoubted classic in the field, which means it just plain doesn't get old, although its author may be shorter of breath today than he was when he wrote it. More important, the book is bigger than I am; I feel, now, a certain diffidence toward it, and a certain feeling that I am going to be known, if at all, as the author of it. And this is despite the fact that I have continued—at very large intervals, to be sure—to write little and not-so-little gems. In fact, venture to say that if my thirty years since *Rogue Moon* were to be compressed into five, people would marvel at my skill. *Rogue Moon* was an unnoticed watershed in my life; I wrote almost no crap after that; I would not dare.

Well, that is to say I wrote no *SF* crap, but perhaps I am getting a little bit ahead of myself.

In 1961, Harlan Ellison was the editor of Regency Books, which, despite the name, had nothing to do with the Regency period in England. It was a small, softcover-originals house in Evanston, Illinois, bringing out two titles every month, one of which, in due course, was to be *Some Will not Die,* the retitled version of my first novel. In 1961, too, the World Science Fiction Convention was in Seattle, Washington, and I thought, mistakenly, that *Rogue Moon* had a chance to win the Hugo there. I had no money, but I had considerable ambition, and, thanks to a loan from my father-in-law, I set out for Seattle from Long Branch, New Jersey, by Greyhound.

I stopped in Evanston on the way, so that I could collect the money Harlan owed me for *Some Will not Die,* and possibly even persuade him to join me in my trip farther West, he being a nice guy whom I had known for years.

Well, the short version of what followed is that (*a*) I didn't get the Hugo, (*b*) I got Harlan's job in Evanston, and (*c*) Harlan is speaking to me again after some years of speaking about me. I certainly wanted Harlan's job—I wanted any job—but it was not me that caused him to blow up in Evanston and subsequently move to Hollywood, where as we know he sank from sight and was never heard of again.

Getting the Regency job made several permanent changes in my life. For one thing, although my salary at first was slightly less than I made as a free-lance writer, finally, in 1961, it was a good deal steadier. And in short order it was more than I ever made as a free-lance writer.

For another, Edna and the kids moved into the house which has been our home ever since. David, the baby, as a matter of fact, was born two weeks after Edna and Jeffrey, Steve and Tim moved in . . . which does not seem to have bothered either her or him. She was quite a sight, though, getting off the Constellation at O'Hare Field, on January 9, 1962, with three kids in tow, an armful of stuffed animals, and eight-and-a-half months pregnant. Nor did it help that as I drove them from the airport, on a miserably cold day, the heater hose on my father's Oldsmobile broke, directly above my right ankle. I was thirty-one, exactly; not quite half a lifetime ago, but getting close.

We entered upon a long period of gainful employment, punctuated by moments of sheer terror. I worked for Regency eighteen months to the day, then was hired away by Playboy and worked for them eighteen months, to the day. For Playboy, I was one of a succession of editors who tried to run Playboy Press, and the only thing I succeeded in doing, really, was making money, and bringing out Lenny Bruce's autobiography, *How to Talk Dirty and Influence People,* which did not make money . . . or, at least, did not make as much as it could have, by far. In fact, the consistent thing about Playboy Press books in the 1960s was that (*a*) they tended to make money, and

(*b*) they did not make nearly as much as they could have, because Hugh Hefner insisted on going into bookstores, whereas he had a mailing list of four million fanatical loyalists.

At any rate, I tired of this, which is permissible. Besides, my father had died, in September of 1964, and this upset me. After a lifetime of being largely ignored, in recent years I had been able to attract his attention, and I had rather liked it. He was a good guy, our relationship handicapped by the fact that he was in his middle forties, and very busy, when I was born. He continued to be busy until the end, but meanwhile I had learned to break in on him, and the last few years of his life were rather nice for me.

In January 1965, I left Playboy and in fact did not work again until July of 1966. I left Playboy with a considerable golden handshake, for those days; still and all, by the time I went back to work, Edna and I were pretty desperate. I'm not sure, but I believe I sold only a *Saturday Evening Post* story, an *If* story, and a *Playboy* story in the interval, and Edna was not working.

As a practical matter, neither was I. I don't know what the problem was, exactly. Certainly I missed Dad. Certainly I've rarely been a ball of fire when it comes to production anyway. But I think I was trying to die. Instead, for a while I had a space in a downtown Chicago sports-car garage, into which I put a typewriter and a telephone; the theory was I would write novels every day until I tired of it, then go help out in the garage. I still have those novels— that is, I have about two hundred pages of one, and shorter parts of the others—and they were actually great fun to do (they're imitation James Bond), but I gradually spent less and less time on them, and the whole thing died of inertia.

Then I worked on one issue of *Rogue,* a men's magazine published in Evanston, which was the best issue because we all knew it was going to be sold to a Cleveland packager and therefore we could do anything; I got in on it because Frank M. Robinson needed a hand, so many of the employees already having been let go. And for a while Frank Robinson and I had our own publishing company, and we almost made it. But I dropped the ball in the end, I think, though it's difficult to tell, but certainly Frank did all he could to keep it afloat. And then I stayed home and stared at the wall until it came to my attention that we had missed a lot of mortgage payments.

Well, something had to be done. They, as a matter of fact, foreclosed on the mortgage, which is an uncomfortable feeling, inasmuch as you have about three months before you and your family have to move out into the snow. So I got a job in public relations.

Now, what I did was quite simple. I picked up the phone, called the employment agent from whom I had hired proofreaders at Regency, and told him I wanted a job that paid no less than twelve thousand dollars per year and required no brains. Inside of a week, I was suited.

You have to understand I could have done this at any time after January 1965. Why I didn't, to this day, I don't know. (Well, actually, I do; I wanted to make it as a writer, provided I didn't have to do any work.)

At any rate, I went to work for the Theodore R. Sills Corporation, at that time the leading food PR house in the world, and of course the job swiftly progressed from a no-brainer to a fairly complex task, and eighteen months later I quit at fifteen thousand dollars or so and went on to be PR director of an advertising agency shop in Chicago, and then to a job in the PR department of Young & Rubicam, Inc., eventually supervising the International Harvester

Company Truck Division, which was the only department of International Harvester that made money, I believe. I left there in March 1973 to take a job as assistant editorial director and operations manager of the Woodall Publishing Company, arguably the number one publisher to the manufactured-housing consumer, including the consumer of recreational motor vehicles. So in all I spent six and a half years in PR, and I was a hotshot, let me tell you.

I was not, as a matter of fact, anywhere near the hotshot I thought I was. Some reflection in later years has modified my view of the time. But I *was* hot.

In part, it was because in the beginning I didn't give a damn. You wanted a news release about Pickle Week, I was your man; the words flowed—no, they gushed—in a torrent. Thereafter, it was because of Johnny Bohan, my boss at Sills, who to this day is a friend of mine, and my mentor.

John Bohan, who is retired now, was a stroke of God. I have not found another like him, and I know an army of PR men. He put up with my various callow ways in return for my undoubted way with words in a hurry, and in the course of time a

With his mother and father, Regina and Jonas Budrys, and wife, Edna, on his father's twenty-fifth anniversary as Consul General of Lithuania, New York City, 1961

friendship grew that has lasted since 1966. I think if I had to sum it up in a few words, it's that John taught me an immense number of things, and every single one of them was decent.

Not that we didn't have fun, because we had an enormous amount of fun. I will spare you the bulk of it, but the eighteen-foot plastic pickle we gave to the city of Chicago deserves some mention.

The city of Chicago, Richard Daley, Mayor, was inclined to take itself seriously. In pursuit of this, it constantly got itself into peculiar situations, as happened when it contracted for a Picasso statue for Civic Center Plaza.

The Civic Center was new—the rust had not yet fully taken on a homogenous color on its Cor-Ten steel structure, designed to rust to the point where it formed a coating, and then stop—and it faced on a plaza which presented an unbroken granite surface, until someone got the idea of putting a statue on it. And the statue they chose was a Cor-Ten steel structure, of some considerable size, executed from a maquette by Pablo Picasso.

Now, Picasso was an undoubted world-class figure, but there were a couple of things wrong with this, from the public point of view: (1) Picasso was not a realist, and (2) Picasso was not known for his production of statues. But by the time the public even learned that this was contemplated, it was in fact done; the contract was signed, sealed, and delivered, and U.S. Steel was busily welding and carving at its Gary works before the average man in the street had even heard of it.

When he did, he was confronted with newspaper sketches of a steel fabrication that in most of its aspects resembled a dog, or, alternatively, a baboon. Only in a three-quarter rear profile was it revealed as the head and shoulders of a woman, but what woman is not clear, and besides most people look at a statue head-on. Public opinion was approximately evenly divided between the dog theory and the baboon theory, with only a negligible percentage opting for any other choice.

Well, this led to the species of game frequently practiced in Chicago. With a *fait accompli* on its hands, as so often happens, the public pretended it had anything to say in the matter, and for about a week the newspapers were full of controversy and other harmless forms of entertainment, and the occasional sober voice, which was of course not paid the slightest attention. At that point, Bill Moore called me.

William E. Moore had been a Sills PR man many years before, but for many years since he had been executive secretary of Pickle Packers International, 207 members in Seven Free-World Nations (as well as

of the National Kraut Packers, sponsors of the Hero Krautwich). Bill Moore was a rip and genius, soberly plotting some of the most outrageous stunts in the history of public relations, and keeping the public more aware than it knew of the need to purchase pickles (and kraut). What he came up with on this occasion was sheer, simple inspiration: (*a*) the Pickle Fair (a biennial affair at which machinery was displayed to the assembled pickle packers) was occurring in Chicago in a matter of weeks, and (*b*) we would present to the city of Chicago at that time, on its as-yet-bare Civic Center Plaza, an unequivocal statue—the Picklecasso.

I will draw a veil over the actual construction of the statue, which featured a twelve-foot pickle, green, ripe, and juicy, on a stick which in turn led into an ostensibly marble base. In truth, the entire statue, all eighteen feet, weighed at best fifty pounds, and some estimated it as low as thirty-five. It cost us two hundred dollars, and was well worth it.

The actual placement of the statue went off like clockwork. We had of course papered all the newsrooms in town with advance warning; we placed it at high noon, the *Chicago Daily News* followed us from the warehouse where it was kept, constantly updating the story on the front page through several editions, and Burt Thompson and I pulled up in Civic Center Plaza in a rented truck, right on time. Meanwhile, Christine Blackie was in the mayor's office, trying to get someone to accept the deed to the statue; Paul Walker, president of Pickle Packers International, was on hand to be photographed with the statue, various members of Sills were strategically located around the plaza to serve as blockers, John Bohan was standing looking like an ordinary man and part of the crowd, but with, I hoped, bail bonds in every pocket, and I never saw so many people concentrated in one place, including plenty of reporters, photographers, and radio and TV crews.

I flipped open the back of the truck, and pulled the pickle halfway out. At that point, the Civic Center manager screamed at me to get the truck out of there, which was Burt's cue to drive away, the rest of the pickle naturally being unveiled in the process. And naturally with no truck any longer to take it away, I flipped the thing onto its base, sidestepped the open-mouthed building manager, and proceeded to shove it in the direction where the Picasso was to stand.

And stood back. The building manager of course was livid, but the newspaper reporters surrounded him on their own initiative, began firing questions, and began hopping, inconspicuously. The net effect was to move the circle of bodies, with the building manager in its center, out of the way so the photographers could get clear shots of the pickle.

It was the PR stunt without equal in my experience; absolutely perfect. After a while, Burt came back with the truck, we put the pickle on board, and took it out to the Pickle Fair. The pickle was on every TV show and all the print media in town all day, and we were heroes. And from time to time thereafter, the pickle would reappear.

But eventually the pickle was lost. Bill Moore loaned it to a man who wanted to enter it in a canoe race on the Fox River, which ran hard by Bill's door. The man cut a hole in it for a place to sit and paddle; the pickle was hollow, and it maneuvered well, but several miles downstream he was thrown out, and the pickle proceeded unchecked. The Fox connects with the Illinois, which in turn connects with the Mississippi, which connects with the Gulf of Mexico, which connects with the sea. The pickle could be anywhere.

Well, from Sills I went to the Chicago office of Geyer-Oswald Advertising, for which I did PR for a bewildering variety of clients, mostly industrial, and then I spent four years at the Chicago office of Young & Rubicam, Inc., where I wound up as supervisor of the International Truck account. International was the last in a string of nineteenth-century clients, which is not to say it wasn't fun much of the time.

For one thing, it was automotive PR, and there is no finer if you're me. For another, I dealt from strength—International was, and I believe still is, the leading heavy-truck builder in North America—which made a refreshing change.

International, significantly, had at the time a light-truck division, which produced products that ranged from poor to mediocre, (and eventually to awful, about the time I left, and which went belly-up for the light-truck division), mainly because they could not compete realistically, cost-wise, with the car manufacturers. No more than the car manufacturers could compete with them when it came to building the big trucks. But in the dying days of the light-truck division, we actually got some PR going which disguised the noncompetitive nature of most of that portion of the product line, particularly the Scout vehicles and the Travelall 1000.

The 1000-chassis based Travelall (as distinguished from all the other Travelalls) was, actually, a better unit than the Chevrolet Suburban, with which it competed. The Scout vehicle—the Scout 80 and its infinite variations, and then the Scout II—was actually a pretty fair off-road vehicle, competing very well with Jeep, and on the road was more comfortable (in the Scout II), but it was obsolete (including the Scout II, which should have been introduced several years

before it finally made it to market). Anyway, we got a lot of recreational equipment manufacturers to feature Internationals in their catalogs of trailers and pickup inserts, and won what races we entered with the Scouts, and we got some ink on that.

The important thing about all of *this,* as it turned out, was that I got to know the editor of Woodall's, and in 1973 I shifted back from PR to editorial work at Woodall's, pursuing a master plan. I would work at Woodall's long enough to get to know all the other automotive PR men, and then I would quit and go free-lance. I would borrow vehicles from the recreational equipment manufacturers, and the automotive PR men, and I would cruise around the country, with Edna, writing travel articles and vehicle evaluations, and, when the spirit moved me, science fiction. We would meet the kids at major crossroads from time to time, and perhaps we would even have a piece of land—in Wisconsin, say—where we would stop to draw breath in the summertime.

And it would have worked, as far as I can tell. I turned out, for instance, to write a hell of a travel article, and vehicle evaluations were no problem, either. And the science fiction . . . well, modesty forbids. But it all went moot over the winter, when the Arabs embargoed oil. Woodall's *Trailer Travel* lost over 150 pages of advertising literally overnight, and I was out on the street again, as it happens on my forty-third birthday, January 9, 1974.

Technically, I have not worked a day since; my last paycheck came from Woodall's. But I have gotten by.

Several things conjoined to make this possible. Among them, Edna had gone back to work when David, the baby, stopped coming home for lunch, and although at first she only worked part-time, for not too much money, in time this became a very significant income. She is now in her sixteenth year at a medium-sized insurance company, where she is the secretary/staff assistant to the senior vice president in charge of the computer department, among other things, and she makes as much money as I do. And she doesn't have to know anything about insurance *per se,* which strikes me as an advantage.

Then, the kids gradually filtered out of the house, all except for David, who stays because somebody has to do the heavy lifting, and although this did not mean much of a diminution in expenses at first, eventually it began to take effect.

And I hit it lucky.

First, Judy del Rey called me, and asked me if I knew they were making *Who?* into a movie. This news, which did surprise me, was not of immediate significance, because I had sold the film rights years

Algis Budrys as a judge at L. Ron Hubbard's Writers of The Future Contest at the United Nations, New York City, 1988

ago. But it seemed Judy wanted to do the tie-in edition of the book, which had just completed the statutory five years at Lancer Books, so I was able to sell a fresh edition of *Who?* to Ballantine/Del Rey. (The film turned out to be awful, and the U.S. edition by Ballantine contains no mention of it. But the sale was made. And it earned back its advance anyway.)

Then, Ned Chase at Putnam's bought *Michaelmas*, which was a novel I had done the first seven chapters of ten years before—in a period of three days—and let lie fallow ever since, because I couldn't get any interest in it. Ned Chase had the idea he could make me a breakout—that is, he kept the book away from Putnam's SF line, Berkeley, warned the SF editor, David Hartwell, against so much as talking to me, and brought out the book for a dollar less than he would have if Berkeley had published it.

What this strategy was supposed to accomplish, I'm not clear on. The book sold well, but not spectacularly. Ned called me into New York to talk to me about something. I'm not sure what; he spent the entire afternoon talking only about his son, Chevy, who had appeared on the cover of *Time* the day before, and I got back on the plane no wiser than I was. Ned eventually bought another novel from me, but then left the company, and I lost propulsion on the novel and eventually bought the contract back.

But *Michaelmas* sold well enough, between the hardcover and the paperback; a short-story collec-

tion, *Blood & Burning*, sold, and a book of my *Galaxy* reviews of books came out from Southern Illinois University Press. A new book, *Hard Landing* went to Warner's along with reprints of *Who?*, *Rogue Moon*, and *Michaelmas* (although this edition of *Michaelmas* carried on, and in fact exceeded all previous standards, for crucial typos; the book has had only one U.S. edition, the out-of-print Berkeley paperback, that actually represents the book I wrote). *Hard Landing* isn't finished and delivered yet, but it's close. And there was the Donning edition of *Some Will not Die*, which led to the Dell edition of *Some Will not Die*, and the Baen Books *Falling Torch*, which is different (slightly) from all previous editions of *The Falling Torch*, and *Rogue Moon* sold to a television production company, and KMPC paid me to do a script of it, neither of which actually got made, but I got to keep the money. And so forth . . . one way or the other, I've managed to keep my head above water, though I assure you it hasn't been easy, and if Edna were not working it would be grim.

The review book is interesting, because what happened to me is the classic case of the man who thinks he is doing one thing and turns out to be doing another.

Round about 1969 or so, I was approached by Frederik Pohl to do the review column for *Galaxy*, which was one of the magazines he was editing at the time. And though I took him up on it—it was one of my fallow periods, and every nickel counted, for one thing—it was not a smooth relationship. Mind you, as far as I know neither one of us dreamed of terminating it; I certainly didn't. But sometimes I wouldn't review a book at all, and I hardly ever reviewed more than three, and every once in a while I made a mistake of some kind, and in fact I don't know why the readers cared about me. But they did; in fact, I have long since stopped counting how many people claim my column is the first thing they read, and the number of people who claim my column is the only thing they read. I do figure that some of them mean it.

At any rate, Fred long ago stopped editing *Galaxy,* and I stopped reviewing for *Galaxy,* which is just as well considering that *Galaxy* is defunct, but after a short hiatus I switched to *The Magazine of Fantasy & Science Fiction* and have not stopped yet. Similarly, I reviewed SF for the American Library Association and the *Chicago Daily News,* among others, and though Roland Green has held both those jobs for years, now, (switching to the *Chicago Sun-Times* when the *News* went belly-up), I was cajoled into doing a monthly column called *Pop Lit* for the *Sun-Times,* and do it still. It isn't often science fiction, or fantasy—it's best-sellers—but that doesn't seem to hurt my standing any.

The thing is, I do it in my spare time, I do it first draft, and I just toss the columns off. But you'd be surprised how many people think it's the most significant thing I do; you'd be surprised how many people think it's the *only* thing I do, and this bothers me some, though not crucially.

I am, I *am,* one of the best SF writers alive, and if you doubt it don't ask me, ask just about any SF writer. That I don't serve my readers often enough is also true, but when I do serve them, they seem to be satisfied into the dim and distant future; I've never had a book go out of print that I wanted to keep in print.

What have I been doing lately? Well, since 1984 I've been the coordinating judge of L. Ron Hubbard's Writers of the Future Contest. Founded by the man who sold more words than just about anybody, back in the 1930s and 1940s, and sold more SF novels than you can shake a stick at again, toward the very end of his days (he passed on January 24, 1986, which happened to be David's twenty-fourth birthday). The contest represents a philanthropic gesture of some considerable magnitude, and I enjoy being associated with it. The contest depends on the cooperation of a number of very big-name writers, who act as judges. So far, it has brought upwards of one hundred writers

Algis and Edna Budrys, 1990

to the fore, and a gratifying number of them have stayed in the fore. Since 1988 I've also been an advisor to L. Ron Hubbard's Illustrators of the Future Contest, with my old friend Frank Kelly-Freas as coordinating judge. And it's done very well. I edit an annual anthology, *L. Ron Hubbard Presents Writers of the Future,* and so far it's published seven volumes, and done very well. Between times, I go to conventions, teach workshops, and what have you. And I get a certain amount of work done besides, with all kinds of projects.

One of the things I did, with the very first Writers of the Future Workshop, in Taos, New Mexico, was unite Dean Wesley Smith and Kristine Katherine Rusch. It's a long story; it has resulted in Pulphouse, Inc., in Eugene, Oregon, with Dean Smith the publisher and Kris Rusch the editor. Pulphouse has been kind to me, and apparently will continue to be, republishing various bits and pieces, and some original work. Baen Books, as noted, is bringing out *Falling Torch,* the Warner book, *Hard Landing* is well on its way, etc.

Oh, and some time when I was working for Young & Rubicam, Inc., I actually sold another film, and while I no longer have any financial interest in it, and it, too, isn't a very good film, for all that Blythe Danner and Alan Alda were in it, it was based on "The Master of the Hounds," which not only sold to the old *Saturday Evening Post* but won an Edgar Special Award (the polite term for coming in second). Once in a while, somebody reprints "The Master of the Hounds." For that matter, once in a while somebody reprints a lot of my stuff.

I am about sixty as I write these words, but in pretty good shape, barring a fierce tendency to overweight. I think I have some good novels left in me, some good shorter pieces, I work with friends, and I am content. I don't know what else to say for myself.

BIBLIOGRAPHY

Fiction:

False Night, Lion 1953, expanded edition published as *Some Will not Die,* Regency, 1961, revised edition, Donning, 1978.

Man of Earth, Ballantine, 1955.

Who?, Pyramid, 1959.

The Falling Torch, Pyramid, 1959.

Rogue Moon, Gold Medal, 1960.

The Unexpected Dimension (collection), Ballantine, 1960.

Budrys' Inferno (collection), Berkley Publishing, 1963.

The Furious Future, Gollancz, 1964.

The Amsirs and the Iron Thorn, Gold Medal, 1967.

Michaelmas, Berkley Publishing, 1977.

Blood & Burning (collection), Berkley Publishing, 1978.

(Editor) *L. Ron Hubbard Presents Writers of the Future* (series), Bridge Publications, Volumes I, 1985, Volume II, 1986, Volume III, 1987, Volume IV, 1988, Volume V, 1989, Volume VI, 1990, Volume VII, 1991.

Nonfiction:

Non-Literary Influences on Science Fiction, Borgo Press, 1983.

Benchmarks: Galaxy Bookshelf by Algis Budrys (collection of science-fiction book reviews), Southern Illinois University Press, 1985.

Other:

Bicycles . . . How They Work and How to Fix Them, Rand McNally, 1976.

Malay Roy Choudhury

1939-

1

I don't know when I was born. Ma didn't ever go to school and Dad learned his alphabet late.

Eyes closed, holding a tiny steel chisel between forefinger and thumb for cutting my nails, she'd reminisce of a devastating earthquake in Bihar when she lost her pet blackbuck and swan couple. I was born during a lagoon-coloured autumn at Patna in the Prince of Wales Hospital, five or maybe five-and-a-half years after the earthquake that demolished the hutment Dad with five brothers and family lived in. I was called Fauna at home though formally named Malay because the Hindu zodiac indicated *M* on the day of my first rice ritual.

Dad consulted the Hindu almanac, deciding on a holy date at the time of my admission to kindergarten at Saint Joseph's convent, in order to convince the Irish doe-eyed nun of the fact of my birth on October 29, 1939. Ma contested this date till she died of an enlarged heart in 1982, as she thought I was born on a Friday on the eleventh day of the month of *Kartika* with the help of metal forceps nurses used to pull me out of her body, for my legs had come out first.

A devout Brahmin, revelling in his puritanic logic, Dad insisted a Hindu Aryan was born on the date of his sacred thread ceremony and that we were descendents of Bidyadhar Roy, the great zemindar who sold Sutanuti Gobindapur Kolikata villages for a meagre three hundred rupees to the firangi Job Charnok of East India Company, which became the joie de vivre called Calcutta. Dad wished to stay there when young but lived instead 550 kilometers away at Patna, the seat of the Buddhist emperor Asoka during 264–223 B.C.E.

Dad told us about his dad who was a great painter and wanderer, who moved from one maharajah's fort to another maharani's castle with a palette always wet, dragging his caravan of half-a-dozen sons and a daughter from Rangoon to Colombo to Kabul to Cooch-Behar, drawing portraits of Indian kings, nabobs, and their shoals of queens. Granpa was Luxminarayan. His sons Promod, Sushil, Ranjit, Anil,

"My parents, Ranjit and Amita, on their first anniversary of marriage. The year is not known. The photograph was taken by my uncle Anil in Ranjit's own studio in Patna."

Sunil, and Biswanath. His daughter, Kamala. Ranjit is my dad.

The sudden death of the grand old man forced his survivors at Patna, an alien land for them, to eke out collective bread, hawking any damn thing that could be purchased and sold, settling as a last resort on photography, which clicked.

Despite Granpa's adventures, Dad cocooned in an orthodox seed: a vegetarian, devoted to a 333 million pantheon, fasting on the eleventh day of the lunar fortnight, mantras at lunch and dinner, a change of sacred thread once a month, no eating cereals cooked by untouchable castes, a daily mustard-oil bath in cold water.

Granma—Apurbamayee—lived alone at Uttarpara, a suburb twenty kilometers away from Calcutta across the Hooghly River, in an ancestral edifice in ruins habitated by hundreds of wild pigeons and bats, with incorrigible weeds shooting off a miasma of tentacles from the salt-eroded, moss-eaten clay bricks. Here she roamed with a torn napkin around her skinny waist, dried teats dangling on her topless bust. Her companions were single-room tenants using the same toilet and a couple of black cows she milked with her own hands for a living. There were guava and starapple trees, creepers unable to bear gourds—ashgourds, bottlegourds—festooned precariously overhead.

After Granny's death in December 1964, Uttarpara looked deserted except for strange tenants. Seven years later when the roof of a ground-floor room crashed down it became haunted, as Cousin Puti, Uncle Sunil's daughter, unroped the noose of a heifer and hung herself from an exposed wooden beam of the ceiling to be discovered in the night chill by someone who took her to be a flying ghost. Puti

"Grandfather in 1931. The photograph is from his own mobile firm, Studio Bengal, established in 1886 at Calcutta."

was in love with a Marxist revolutionary killed in an encounter.

The brothers had shifted to a double-storied brick house in Bakharganj at Patna after the earthquake, constructed in instalments by Uncle Promod, each brother and his family in a room with a common bath and toilet and water fetched in buckets from a roadside tap. We had a ten-foot-by-ten-foot room facing west on the first floor, a cot beneath which belongings were kept, a packing box used as bookshelf cum table, and a wall-to-wall wire for hanging clothes. Bakharganj was a Hindi-speaking slum area; hoochers and gamblers had their nights, no neighbours' children went to school, women in veils kneaded dungcakes for fuel. Nobody knew of toothbrush paste, we brushed our teeth with fresh coal ash powder using our forefingers.

Uncle Promod's daughters, Sabu and Dhabu, were married before my birth, prompting him to purchase a male infant from a Punjabi prostitute whom he didn't legally adopt and couldn't decide what to do with as the boy grew up to become a ruffian and mugger at fifteen, exhibiting unabashed scorn for everything Bengali to deculturise himself. I was in complete awe of the fearful respect he generated in neighbours. Buro, as he was called, had a country-made revolver spinning on his forefinger. One day he allowed me to shoot at a sitting popinjay—I got my thumb bruised.

I remember Buro brought a whore home with him secretly, double his age, and the thud of the wooden bolt woke up an aunt whose midnight yell pulled out adults and children from their rooms, an event sufficient to provoke Dad and my uncles to dismantle the Bakharganj establishment. In 1953 we shifted out to the locality of Dariapur.

Buro had a sad death. Aunt Nanda, his foster mother, on advice from some sannyasin, devised an enchantment potion made of herbs, fed to him weekly with his food, resulting in slow poisoning. He grew weak and dropped dead. Aunt Nanda wailed uncontrollably over his corpse.

Uncle Promod worked as a preserver of paintings at Patna Museum. I visited it on Saturdays for hours to become a part of ancient and prehistoric mysteries amid granite *apsaras*, Egyptian mummies, fossilised monsters, going back home with him on his bicycle, the only movable asset of the household, cleaned and oiled in turns by the children. I learned cycling on it and in 1956 Dad purchased a bike for me, enabling me to learn by heart the town's alleys and joints.

Uncle Promod loved picnics. On holidays our entire clan of twenty would go out to cook and eat by a slim stream or in a mango orchard or near a wellspring on the outskirts. I carried a book, any book, even a schoolbook, searching for the insect, bird, tree, or grains described therein. Sometimes other Bengali acquaintances were invited to join the picnics, probably as an effort to overcome alienation from mainstream Bengal. One of the ladies would burst out singing, invariably a Hindu religious song, as film songs were taboo and Rabindranath Tagore songs considered un-Hindu.

Since Uncle Promod didn't have a son when he died—in 1966 during an election campaign for an obscure candidate—I performed the rituals by setting fire to the funeral pyre on which lay his cold body embalmed by me with clarified butter. He was a fat man who turned to ashes in two hours in a yelling blaze that licked the horizon on the other side of Ganges River. Satish Ghoshal, our family priest, directed me to collect a few bones from the ashes, which I immersed in the river. This was my first encounter with the beyond, a plight Satish Ghoshal sermoned not to give importance to as it happened when you came to burn or bury the dead!

A couple of years later Aunt Nanda died of burn injuries she received when her cooking stove exploded. But Sabu and Dhabu, scared of my property claims for the last rites performed, sued each other for Uncle Promod's Bakharganj house as well as the assets of their father-in-law, who was the same for both, since they had married two brothers. I used to visit their sylvan house during 1948–50 to play with my nieces Manju, Jaya, and Madhuri in their sprawling garden.

2

As any venture Uncle Sushil embarked upon was a flop, he joined my father at the photography shop on Main Road that shifted later to Dariapur in 1953 when Dad purchased a 1,300-square-foot house. I have recollections of him as a snuff-inhaling afternoon dreamer, customers constantly knocking at his mental absence after his wife died of tuberculosis, leaving behind daughters Dolly and Monu, who flunked school and had to be looked after by Ma. Dolly was packed off in a negotiated marriage I couldn't attend. Monu decided to marry a local non-Brahmin Hindi-speaking boy whom Uncle Sushil didn't approve of, so the responsibility of solemnising the marriage in a Shiva temple befell me. I went attired in a pink dhoti and yellow shawl with collyrium in my eyes and performed priest-directed rituals I was not conversant with. Uncle Sushil died in 1968 of

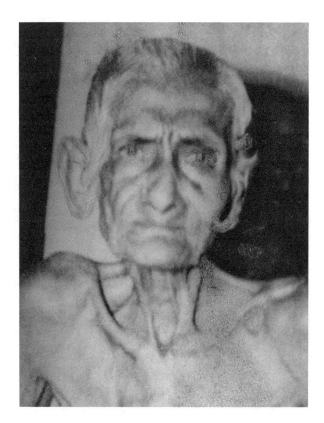

"Grandmother at ninety-eight, a few days before her death. A photograph by my uncle Biswanath."

a hernia he was too shy to get treatment for, on the day of my marriage.

Anil, the brother next to Dad, had a photo studio at Uttarpara at the time of his negotiated marriage with Omiya, a school-educated lady who was already in love with a guy living in the erstwhile French colony of Pondicherry. She continued the relationship despite her marriage, provoking Uncle Anil to abandon his shop and become a recluse. I thought he was nuts when he, along with daughters Shubhra and Rakhi and wife, came down to live with us at Uncle Promod's Bakharganj house in 1947. Aunt Omiya didn't give a damn for Uncle Anil. She took a teacher's job in a grammar school and introduced newspaper reading in the family, creating in us a fascination for her. Among the children she had a strange soft spot for me though I should have drawn her hatred as I resembled Uncle Anil. The daughters were not good at studies; the elder was packed off to boarding school at Mayapur, run by Iskcon, to get rid of her array of boyfriends. She married one, a gambler, then came back divorced, remarried a non-Brahmin, and disappeared. Panicked, Aunt got the second one married to a doctor. Both Aunt and Uncle died of cancer; Omiya had one teat operated upon, Anil's nose had become cauliflower shaped. They stayed on at the Bakharganj house, occupied the room vacated by us in 1953, husband and wife not talking to each other, a menage of dissent with a window opening inside.

Unhappy with his three daughters and three sons, Uncle Sunil, who had a catering job on the Eastern Railway, broke our eating taboo by inducting varieties of forbidden food into the menu for the children, depending on items knocked off from pantry cars. His daughter Puti committed suicide, the eldest son, Khoka, eloped and married the non-Brahmin tutor of his brothers, the second daughter married a boy of the washerman caste, the younger sons flunked school and tried to start a broiler farm in the gloomy rooms of Uttarpara that made the fowls sick and mad. Uncle Sunil died on the day after I met him in February 1989, in unbound glee that he was on the verge of getting out of the mess his incorrect decisions had created.

The youngest of the brothers, Biswanath, who was childless, got himself gifted a small piece of land from Granny that Dad claimed he had purchased for her. Aunt Kuchi used to have religious fits diagnosed by doctors as depression when she was in the Bakharganj establishment. Their prayer for a child at sundry temples spawned in them an insight for having a temple of their own for attracting the gullible, which included my dad also, who thought both his sons had out-Hindued themselves with their way of life and thinking. In 1986 he went to Kotrong to live at Uncle Biswanath's ashram, indicated in brochures printed by Uncle as the place visited by Saint Ramakrishna of Dakshineshwar, though there was a pond forty years earlier at the place marked as the saint's seat in which I had waded in knickers and netted small fish and snails.

Dad's only sister, Kamala, lived in a single-room tenement at Ahiritola in Calcutta, adjacent to the red-light tourist spot Sonagachi. The room had a two-tiered bed for her eight children, seven of whom quit school to be found always on either of the tiers doing nothing by her husband, who would come back from his office every evening high on Goddess Kali brand rice liquor whistling a nineteenth-century tune, alerting neighbours to his drunkenness. It being the only place to stay during a visit to Calcutta, the floor of the room meant for guests was also where we sat and ate steamed rice, pigeon pea pulse, and shrimp fried in mustard oil served on brass plates. The toilet was slippery, without doors, and I used to keep coughing to notify my presence to any intruder. Aunt Kamala

became blind yet continued her cooking routine believing, as she told me, the blindness was for having seen six toes on a woman's feet during a full moon. Her husband was found in a pool of blood on a summer morning in 1967 when he had nightwalked off a terrace during one of his spells; the remains of his body were scraped from the asphalt into a loincloth bundle for the postmortem.

3

Ma was in charge of cooking at Bakharganj, which she did for twenty persons on two coal ovens made of clay placed on the kitchen floor. Through day and night she sat there beside a large wooden box containing spices stored in phials of used medicine and cereals in tin cannisters bought out of a collective fund. She would detect sudden shortages while cooking and haul me up from studies for an immediate purchase in the smallest quantity, which I'd procure in a jiffy to enable her to complete the dish. She loved to apply vermillion on her parted hair twice a day. And her favourite dish was *dhoka*—asafoetida-flavoured cakes of steamed and grinded chick-pea. Unlike Dad she was a nonvegetarian, mainly a fish eater.

Spice pastes were prepared on a stone grinder by our part-time servant Sheonanni, on whose back I climbed while he swayed to and fro pulping turmeric, chilli, ginger, cumin, onion, coriander, garlic, and spearmint for an hour or two in the evening.

Each of my uncles had his own time for lunch and dinner when he ate alone, served by his wife, whereas the children and ladies ate together each on a small piece of mat sitting crosslegged, except for Sundays, which was a meat-eating day, when lunch was late. We ate goat meat or at the most mutton, since chicken, duck, cow, buffalo, rabbit, deer, frog, horse, pig, and turtle meat were prohibited, which later we relished at cheap roadside restaurants when we grew up and accumulated some pocket money. Even some fish like eel and flounder were taboo. Ma never went beyond goat meat though she cooked fowl for us after we shifted to Dariapur.

4

My brother Samir, about five years my elder, was the first individual in our family to complete school and college, as he was sent to our maternal uncle's place in Panihati for studying at Calcutta when Dad decided to keep him culturally uncorrupt. He studied science at City College, joined Satyajit

Ray's drama group, Harbola, and started frequenting joints visited by the reigning Bengali poets of the thirties, about whom he talked to us in bated breath, often brandishing books of verse written in a Bengali diction foreign to our tongue; not even Aunt Omiya used such words while talking to her guests.

Panihati was a boat ride across the river Hoogly, where I was sent during vacation to keep in touch with Bengal as well as to improve my health. The maternal uncles were comparatively richer and educated, had a radio, read the English newspaper the *Statesman,* a status symbol, talked among themselves sometimes in English, and were interested in political developments.

Ma was called Bhulti at Panihati and Amita at Patna. Once while we were crossing the river on the ferry boat, I remember she jumped out into the deep water, presented us with her memory of cross-current swimming, and came out with tiny transparent crablings crawling down her uncoiffured hair. Every time she went to the bank to withdraw her savings, she misspelt Amita in her labouriously practiced signature. Ma was scared of pox inoculation, locking herself up in the lavatory whenever the municipal doctor arrived for the annual prick.

In 1948 I was withdrawn from Saint Joseph's convent and admitted to the Bengali-medium Ram Mohan Roy Seminary, a Brahmo Samaj school, primarily, I learned later, because Dad came to know we were having a prayer class every day at the Gothic cathedral of the convent, meeting with folded hands Jesus Christ in agony in flowing Italian marble surrounded by azure-tipped candle flickers. He didn't have a high opinion about Brahmos though, as the sect had been advocating against idol worshipping. But this might have been the source of my religious pacifism. I don't consider myself an apostate or atheist and may probably define myself as vaguely Hindu without much to do with religious rituals, gods, and goddesses.

Saint Joseph's convent to Ram Mohan Roy Seminary was an unhealing journey of cultural hiatus for me, cause of the schism that still invades my poems; doe-eyed nuns carrying a bleeding Jesus made of soft marble through the bazaars of Patna float in my dreams even at this age.

Ram Mohan Roy Seminary, a three kilometer walk every day, sun or rain, had boys and girls of the same lower middle-class milieu as that of mine to whom I was embarrassed to divulge my fleabag residential area considered infested by criminals, deterring classmates to visit me at home. I was not allowed to mix up with the boys of my locality as Dad thought they were lumpens. I didn't have personal

Malay photographed by Ranjit, Patna, 1941

friends for long and learned to adjust to my loneliness, Samir always at Panihati, Buro away with the ruffians, other cousins very junior to me. Sari-clad girl students were there in my class but the mystery seized me late. I can remember only three girls with effort: Hashi, Juthika, and Bijoya, presumably because of their colourful attire.

Lack of a cricket bat of my own didn't give me much scope to have a place in the school games and I couldn't do well in football either because of a weak physique, so I found my way into the library and reading room, the lady librarian chaperoning my interest to school editions of Homer, Edmund Spenser, Miguel de Cervantes, Shakespeare, Voltaire, and a Sanskrit classics compendium, finding finally in the last year of my school text writings of six persons who changed the condition of my loneliness: George Gordon Byron, William Wordsworth, Samuel Taylor Coleridge, Percy Bysshe Shelley, John Keats, and Alfred, Lord Tennyson. Except for Tagore, the Bengali poets in the text had only moral sermons to deliver whereas Hindi poets talked about the greatness of the creator in a never-changing rhythm.

*"With my first specs in a photograph
by Uncle Biswanath"*

In the final years of school I made friendships with three boys who were themselves unable to make friends, Subarna, Barin, and Tarun. Subarna couldn't afford to have a cricket uniform, white shirt and pants, and was removed from the team. Barin was a myopic. Tarun a short and weak boy who talked little. We sat at the shore of the Ganges River, talked about whatever we knew, pooled resources to see Sunday-morning movies, ate at cheap restaurants, and roamed about from camp to camp during the three-day festival of the goddess Durga. Barin had a good voice, sang Tagore and Atulprasad songs at the riverbank. For three days during the Durgapuja festival, Subarna wore saffron, white, and green shirts stitched out of the silk national flag supplied to his father's office each year by the state government.

Overreading strained my eyesight. I got specs in 1952, the year of my sacred thread ceremony when our family priest gave me a mantra of the goddess Gayatri. My head was shaved and I wore a saffron dhoti. I was required to perform *puja* twice a day, observe celibacy, eat only vegetarian dishes, no cereals, on the eleventh day of the moon, no talking while eating, no eating out, and the sacred thread continuously on my left shoulder. I tried for a couple of weeks, gave up thereafter.

Performancewise I was average at high school, completed in 1954. Then I left home with Tarun, hitchhiking to Calcutta on an illegal truck carrying old and sickly goats for slaughter. As interstate carriage of goats was prohibited by road transport, we feigned ourselves shepherds and herded the goats on the roadside grasslands, heigh-hoing them at the border checkpost into West Bengal where the empty truck was waiting after showing documents at the crossing. We took baths at a village well in a bucketful of cold water. At sundown, stopping at a Punjabi *dhaba,* we ate handmade bread fried in sheep lard, pickled onion, and liquor made of *mahua*—my first taste of an intoxicant. The driver bargained with a suburban whore, went with her into the paddy field under a neap-tide eroded moon while we fought phantoms inside the dim-lit truck.

During 1954–60 we made several such forays in bus, train, steamer, or jeep, visiting Allahabad, Jhansi, Ranchi, Kanpur, a hundred to a thousand kilometers from Patna. Tarun died early of leukemia.

My first two years in college were a real academic disaster. At school I had studied physics, chemistry, biology, mathematics, history, geography, along with Sanskrit, Hindi, Bengali, and English. At college, on Samir's advice, I opted for economics, political science, and mathematics, with Hindi, Bengali, and English; I found interest in none, devoting most of my time at various libraries of the town gobbling up the history of literature of various languages, history of art, philosophy, and the lives of poets; Western and Eastern names started reeling in my brain. For a time I joined the infantry division of the National Cadet Corps and practiced rifle shooting, but I was finding myself unsolvable, rootless, obscure, anonymous. My exam results were weepable.

In 1956 I got admitted in B.A. Honours Economics, regular subjects being English, Bengali, Hindi, and politics. An exclusive room was at my disposal now, a table and chair, a bed, and three *almirahs* on the wall for books on the first floor at the Dariapur house; the complete ground floor was used as a photo studio by Dad; Ma's cooking exercises reduced now to courses for only three persons.

Alone in my room I felt despair for no known reason and attempted in March 1956 to get a few crystals of potassium ferricyanide from the downstairs photo studio used for making sepia prints. The emotion withered on its own. To keep me absorbed Ma purchased a gramophone and some records.

In my B.A. Honours class I met a bespectacled Nepali woman made of snow. Bhuban Mohini Rana was from the royal family and always kept me at a commoner's distance, never allowing me to touch her queenly complexion. The other woman I was in trouble with was Shubhra Ray, of whom I do not prefer to talk.

The years 1957–58 were the period of my introduction to Bengali poetry in a big way. I stumbled upon Bengali poet Madhusudan Dutt, who exemplified moral violence in his epic work *Murder of Meghnad* in such deft rhyming that he proved somewhat curative for me—a stunning perceptual accuracy that instilled purpose. There was something beyond experience in him I became enamoured to. I hero-worshipped him, read the turbulent story of his life, allowed my scanty beard and moustache to grow like his.

5

My memory of India's liberation movement is strewn with opaque scenes of Ma waving a tricolour in a crowd of ladies, horsemen ploughing through a procession, a fat lady donating her bangles to Gandhi under a green canopy, a leader in a marigold garland, and a burned junk of a 1942 van on a road crippled with monsoon weeds. When the British quit in 1947 I was eight years old, a student of Saint Joseph's convent.

Dad had no respect for Gandhi, did not forgive Jawaharlal Nehru, who he insisted was responsible for the partition and eventual plight of the Bengalis. He appreciated Hitler and highly esteemed Subhas Chandra Bose, the nationalist leader. Other uncles also didn't have much political knowledge. A Bengali newspaper I started reading was subscribed to when we went to live in Dariapur.

Prepartition communal riots I do remember: burning hutments, religious howls, shrieks, mutilated bodies seen through a peephole, vultures in the sky, groups being chased, army patrols, caravans proceeding toward nowhere. One day when Aunt Nanda was hospitalised for a tumor operation, Gandhi was murdered. I learned of it in the evening sitting inside mosquito netting and completing classwork, as Uncle Promod told everybody in a hushed voice.

Not until 1957 was I able to get out of the political confusion of our family and allow the formation of my own ideas and views, clashing then with Dad and the other uncles. Samir's progressive and liberal leanings had been worrying them for quite some time.

At the Dariapur residence Uncle Biswanath had presented to me a white puppy with brown patches, which turned out to be a country dog as it grew up. I named him Robert Lingchipula, caricaturing a British name. The dog ate spicy leftovers, became hairless, and died after six years.

Since we had a lot of space at Dariapur, Uncle Promod started an amateur drama group staging nonpolitical works, mainly Hindu mythologies; rehearsals of silky goddesses or woolly monsters barged into my study in gargling voices, characters in beards of jute with wooden swords and tin crowns delivered dialogues in nineteenth-century textbook Bengali occasionally interrupted by a sudden spurt of harmonium followed by a line of a song.

I never heard Dad singing or humming. Ma did a little bit of one line. Uncle Promod, who exuded a sort of holiday gaiety, had a clarinet he took out once in a while but never played a full tune. Aunt Kuchi knew some imitation of *bharat natyam*. That's all. My indulgence in music had to wait. Samir, before he left for studies at Calcutta, sang "Toofan Mail," a Hindi pop song of early movies; that's the name of a fast train of those days.

Whenever Ma and Dad went to Uttarpara, I'd go to the railroad station a few hours in advance, occupy a berth in a compartment attachable to the train, and keep a space for them so that they could join me a few minutes prior to departure. That was the lowest class we travelled in. My first train travelling was inside a compartment full of luggage, no space to drop a pin, myself hoisted throughout the night on a gunnybag from which fresh potatoes peeped out.

6

The result of a B.A. in Honours Economics turned out quite good, making it easier to get admitted for an M.A. in the same subject at Patna University, where in the beginning of 1959 I got a glimpse of Toynbee, Marx, and Spengler. Pages of their books had been removed in several places with the help of a blade in the copies available at the university library. I went to other libraries, took notes, revelling in Spenglerian prophecy taking off from celebrations of decentralisation espoused by Bakunin, Kropotkin, Godwin, and wrote a hundred-page postmodernist treatise, *The Marxist Heritage*. For the moral vacuum laid bare, the printed book gave me shivers. I got all the copies dunked in gasoline and set them on fire, allowing Spengler to haunt me all along.

My journey into realms of poetry had started by literally setting intellectual bridges ablaze. Around the end of 1959 I had been scribbling in my notebook, trying to shape up a few poems.

Samir got a Fisheries Officer's job, posted at Chaibasa, a tiny hilly township of tribals surrounded by green sal, sesame, and teak trees splashed in spring with scarlet splendour of kapok and kino flowers. He was staying in a thatched hut on a hillock touching the moon. Distant cool nights flickered in the villages below amid the sweet aroma of handpounded tribal rice, roasted pig, faint drumbeats, sparkling laughter of Santhal women. During the day, fowls fought each other with knives tied to legs, a tribal gambling sport, and overloaded rickety buses passed by. I visited Chaibasa during vacation, and again after completing my M.A., the results of which were exemplary in view of my preparations. The caste factor didn't allow me to top the batch.

Involved with Bela, one of eight daughters of a local gentleman straight from Emily Brontë fiction, Samir married; I thought it better to keep myself out of the reach of the ladies.

After my disastrous start as an author I indiscriminately stormed through whatever works I could lay my hands on: Rimbaud, Poe, Baudelaire, Apollinaire, Pound, Eliot, Rilke, Mallarmé, Mayakovsky, Lorca. Surrealism thrilled me. I could imagine myself on the streets of Paris, Madrid, or Moscow with a young André Breton or Jean Cocteau. Samir brought for me from Calcutta collections of Jibanananda Das, Bishnu Dey, Buddhadev Bose, Premendra Mitra, Samar Sen, Amiya Chakraborty, Sudhindra Dutta, and little magazines run by mentors of various groups.

From the notebooks I maintained Samir copied a couple of poems and got them printed in *Krillibas* in 1959, for which I feel embarrassed even now as I wanted to do something historical, an entry with a bang, an event to remember in literary history.

My perception of Bengali poetry was that it had a place in the sun, notwithstanding its treatment in Western media as a language of a handful. A Nobel Prize to Tagore was the last glory fifty years back. I wondered about the limitations of Bengali not being talked about in international literature as French, German, Italian, Spanish, Russian, Portuguese were. No doubt the Indian government was spending millions for sponsoring Hindi, which was not my mother tongue; something had to be done in Bengali literature itself, I felt.

I found editors of literary magazines were not conversant with international writing standards, read very little, detested the avant-garde, had contempt for experiments in prose and poetry. Bengali novels thrived on the market of half-literate ladies. Poems were time servers, filling up spaces for which no ads could be procured. Bearded gentries in *kurta* pyjamas stitched of handloom cloth with dirty slingbags passed for poets, even the films invariably depicted them in such fixed attire. The entire corpus after Tagore had been a soft option for the creative writer, articulated in a language not spoken in a common Bengali household. Most of the poets till then were from upper caste, that is, Brahmin or Kayastha from urban areas.

I knew I could do nothing alone. I didn't have money. I didn't have access to reputed periodicals. I didn't have a group. I didn't have a mentor or a sponsor. I didn't know any writers or poets in Calcutta.

I found a queer name in a little magazine in early 1961, Mr. Haradhon Dhara, traced him out in a notorious slum at Howrah near Calcutta, winding my way through a stinky buffaloshit lane onto a hay-roofed mudtiled clayhut with small cane windows nibbled by termites. In the middle of the room lay a high, squeaky antique bed beneath which were stacked magazines gathering dust. Further magazines were sprawled around with no room to move about except for a folding chair offered to me. Debi Roy, which was Dhara's pen name, had worked as an errand boy in a pedestrian restaurant, as a taxi washer, didn't have any knowledge of world literature, had written a few poems rejected by reputed magazines, belonged to a very low caste, and couldn't speak English well. Could be a genuine anchorman, I felt.

We sat together on the clay verandah beside heaps of gourdseeds and pondsnails, I gradually explaining my views of unleashing a literary movement to be called "Hungryalism." I had concentrated on the word *Hungry* from Chaucer's prophetic line "In the sowre Hungry tyme" with a Spenglerian perspective of the assimilation of cultures and ultimate decline thereof in view of the overwhelming infiltration of an alien ethos into Bengali culture. Hungryalism was a postmodern idea, not a philosophy but rather the apotheosis of self-expression, which accepted contradictions as a part of the human condition. Not a theory.

Debi Roy was happy with the coinage from a different perspective, as he thought Hungryalism suited the economic nightmare of a postpartition society suffering from unemployment, shortages of food and clothing, inhuman living conditions of the human individual, hunger of body and soul, mind and being, essence and existence, matter and spirit, known and unknown.

*Bengali poet Debi Roy (back row, center) with his father, mother, wife, brother,
and nephew at his Howrah hutment, 1969*

It was decided to print one-page handouts initially, when and as money permitted, for distribution, bringing gradually within our fold likeminded poets, writers, and artists as a beginning of a multicentered formlessness pervading all diversity where the individual was whole and the whole was individual. We should have sufficient activists to launch a cultural avalanche, we felt.

In April 1961 I got a job in the Reserve Bank of India with a monthly salary of one hundred seventy rupees (ten dollars) which required me to write owners' names on gilt-edged bonds. I wrote a piece on poetry printed on a foolscap paper and arranged for its distribution as the first *Hungryalist* bulletin in November 1961 in the Albert Hall Coffee House on Calcutta's College Street across from Presidency College.

7

The effect of the first bulletin was stunning as it started a swelling of the ranks and provoked editorials and literary headlines in newspapers and periodicals. The *Hungryalist*—later *Hungrealist*—bulletin went from five pages to twenty pages, quarto to scroll size, woodcut-designed cover to offset, black and blue prints to handpaint.

Between 1961 and 1965 about a hundred bulletins were released by participants, of which nine are preserved by Sandip Dutta in the archives of the Little Magazine Library and Research Centre. Poets, authors, and artists who had joined the movement are Subimal Basak, Rabindra Guha, Sankar Sen, Arupratan Basu, Basudeb Dasgupta, Asok Chatterjee, Pradip Choudhuri, Benoy Majumdar, Amit Sen, Amrita Tanay Gupta, Sayad Mustafa Siraj, Bhanu Chatterjee, Utpal Kumar Basu, Tridib Mitra, Phalguni Ray, Satindra Bhowmik, Shambhu Rakshit, Tapan Das, Sandipan Chatterjee, Anil Karanjai, Subhas Ghosh, Karuna Nidhan, Ramananda Chatterjee, Subo Acharja, Saileswar Ghose, Debasis Banerjee, Sukumar Mitra, Mihir Pal, Arani Basu, and Arunesh Ghosh.

I had drafted the manifestoes on poetry, prose, politics, and religion for the Hungryalist movement, reprinted in *Kultchur* 15, edited by Lita Hornick, and *Salted Feathers* 8/9, edited by Dick Bakken and Lee Altman.

Actually I personally didn't know all the Hungryalists as it was Debi Roy and later Subimal Basak who did the organisational work. I knew the authors, however, who came to be known as the major Hungry writers and was in correspondence with them: Debi Roy, Saileswar Ghose, Subimal Basak, Pradip Choudhuri, Subo Acharja, Subhas Ghosh, Tridib Mitra, Phalguni Ray, and Arunesh Ghosh. Later Phalguni died from drugs, Tridib gave up writing, and Subo joined a religious sect. Funny to note, a police informer by the name of Pabitra Ballabh had infiltrated the movement keeping a tab on us; we didn't even notice till he himself spilled the beans.

Till 1963 I visited Calcutta frequently, staying at Uttarpara, Ahiritola, Debi's place, or in Subimal Basak's uncle's goldsmith shop, which did not have a window, ceiling fan, or lavatory, compelling me to go to the nearby Sealdah railroad station, where I used the toilets of arriving long-distance trains. We slept on the cement floor using old magazines wrapped in our shirts for pillows. The shop had a castor-oil lamp that Subimal made use of at night for drafting his novel *Chhatamatha,* written in the dialect of horsecart pullers of Dhaka. Subimal was beaten up in December 1963 at the entrance of the Albert Hall Coffee House by a group of status quoists hostile to our movement.

There were other strange happenings too. A couple of presses refused to print *Hungryalist* bulletins, Pradip Choudhuri was expelled from Visva Bharati University, Santiniketan, for his association with the movement, Subhas Ghose was notified to vacate his apartment, Patiram book stall was threatened by a gang for selling the bulletin. Pressure kept on mounting. Refusal of auditoria led us to recite our poems at street corners, parks, cemeteries to the attention of growing crowds every day. The main theme of hostility to us centered round one single argument that the movement was foreign inspired and against Bengali culture and literary tradition.

In fact all the major Hungryalists were from lower middle-class and came from outside Calcutta. Subimal and I came from Patna, Subo from Bishnupur, Pradip from Agartala, Debi from Howrah, Subhas and Saileswar from Balurghat. Almost all

Novelist Subimal Basak with wife and son on the roof of his brick house in Calcutta, 1980

were first-generation literates. One researcher has argued that the breakdown of the extended family was one of the factors in promoting the Hungryalist movement.

The Indian press harped on the tune that the movement's origin should be traced to the Calcutta visit in the early sixties of Allen Ginsberg, Peter Orlovsky, Gary Snyder, and Joanne Snyder. How far that is correct is a matter of conjecture and serious research. I did meet Allen Ginsberg but not the other people; none of the Hungryalists met any of them.

Ginsberg had been to Samir's place at Chaibasa and stopped over for a few nights at Dariapur on his way to a Buddhist pilgrimage at Rajgir in the summer of 1963. Ginsberg was saintly. Dad took him to be Bishma from the Hindu epic *Mahabharata*. In 1985–86 I translated his *Howl* and *Kaddish* into Bengali. In the sixties I had translated some poems of Lorca, Neruda, and Artaud.

All these three years from 1961 to 1963 I had been working on *Shoytaner Mukh,* a collection of my poems. Samir selected some of them for their ratiocinative abstraction and total effect in terms of sound and sight. Krittibas Publishers agreed to publish them. There were guarded critical reactions to the book at the time. The cover was based on a drawing made available by Margaret Randal, editor of *El Corno Emplumado,* who was in Buenos Aires at that time.

Exploiting Bengali etymology in the costume of a tyrant jester, I wrote a drama—*Illot*—assured of being staged by Nripen Saha of Gandharba. He retained the manuscript for a year then developed cold feet because of its political overtones. I got it published in the first issue of *Zebra* in 1966.

8

Karuna Nidhan and Anil Karanjai, painters, invited me to Banaras where hashish was available in plenty, the visiting hippies having passed on to them marijuana and LSD. Subimal and I took a train to Banaras, stayed there for a few days on top of a garage in smoke and hallucination. All four of us made a trip to Kathmandu where we rented a wooden room with four mattresses made of hay. Basu Sasi of the Royal Nepal Academy took care of our food and drink. I loved *kachila,* made of uncooked buffalo flesh, pickled deer meat, and white rum *ela.* There was unrestricted hashish and opium to float in, cool temples to meditate in, and hilltops to recite poems from. I got rid of the taboos of my milieu but reared instead some lice on my skin and hair.

As my presence became known in the Nepali media, Parijat, Nepal's foremost woman poet of the sixties, sent me a word for poetry, drink, and dinner. She was exquisitely beautiful, reclining on a pillow on a floor mattress, without the black panthers Cleopatra had by her side. Serving super strong homemade liquor in brass saucers, she removed her black woollen robe to show her polio-stricken, cream-coloured legs. I placed my hand on them. She kissed my forehead and informed me she was an admirer of my poems. It was my first literary award.

I attended a few poetry recitations in Kathmandu and met Nepali poets Puskar Lohani, Madan Rengbi, and Padam Sudas. Ramesh Srestha took me to his village, Basantpur, for lunch, flattened green rice soaked in curd, a terrific taste.

Karuna Nidhan and Anil Karanjai talked to the owner of Max Gallery, a black American lady, who arranged for an exhibition of their paintings not for sale. I wrote the brochure. On the concluding day the paintings were placed in one corner and set on fire. Oh, one of the foreign woman spectators cried like a child. Karuna and Anil consoled her. Karuna afterwards became a Maoist, Anil migrated to the United States.

I came back to Patna where Rajkamal, the poet and editor who had introduced Hindi readers to me, was hospitalised. He loved to play chess with me after a pethidine injection. In 1967 he died after a long stint of hospitalisation, monomania, and lack of writing.

9

On September 2, 1964, Sub-Inspector Kalikinkar Das of the Calcutta Police lodged a complaint based on a copy of a *Hungryalist* bulletin—made available to him by Pabitra Ballabh, a poet—claiming that it came within the purview of Sections 120(B) and 292 of the Criminal Code and I should, along with other members of the movement, be prosecuted. Section 120(B) was for conspiracy against society and Section 292 for the sale, hire, distribution, public exhibition, and circulation of obscene writing.

On September 4, 1964, I was arrested by police officers S. M. Barori and Amal Mukherjee, handcuffed with a rope tied to my waist, and paraded on the streets of Patna. A posse of policemen searched the Dariapur house, broke open Ma and Dad's boxes, seized a large number of books, magazines, letters, manuscripts, and a typewriter, which were never to be returned.

I was incarcerated without food and water in a dark cell with crooks and criminals. The corner of the lockup was used as a toilet by inmates, the flow of urine and shit blocked by a tattered rug; rodents moved around in search of food crumbs and bugs crawled the walls. Through the night I stood like a statue of flesh and bone aside the crooks and criminals, who thought I was absurd. The next day I was taken to the local court on foot in handcuffs with a rope around my waist, together with the bunch of criminals, and released on a bail of ten thousand rupees (six hundred dollars) with orders to present myself at Calcutta Court, which I did. At Calcutta I was interrogated by a group of officials and my interview recorded.

The first thing that happened was I was kicked out of the bank job, making money scarce. Worse still, Granny died, so there was no place to stay at Calcutta.

I was not chargesheeted immediately; the police required me to report to them every alternate day. I felt depressed except for some letters of encouragement from Octavio Paz, Allen Ginsberg, Lawrence Ferlinghetti, and others, which were edited and published by Tridib Mitra in 1969. A lawyer, Satyen Banerjee, volunteered to defend me and intervened to stop my visits to police headquarters.

News of my persecution appeared in the November 4, 1964, issue of *Time, City Lights Journal,* and *Evergreen Review.* The *Time* report said the Hungryalist movement was a "growing band of young Bengalis with tigers in their tanks." I appealed to the Indian Committee for Cultural Freedom for help, but they did nothing. Its executive secretary, A. B. Shah, wrote me in January 1965 that he had met the police chief, who informed him that a number of citizens to whom *Hungryalist* writings had been made available wanted action against me. Dipak Majumdar, a poet of the fifties, initiated a signature campaign in my favour, got rebuffed by a senior editor, and gave a hasty retreat. Most of the writers in my group were avoiding me; I was feeling alone, tormented, frustrated, estranged, and abandoned.

I made a trip to Bishnupur, Subo Acharja's place; a devout Hindu by then, he reeled off incomprehensible metaphysics. Went to Mursidabad for a change, discovered a cobra snake atop the mosquito-net roof. I was on the verge of breaking down. Hindi author Sharad Deora wrote *The College Street Messiah,* a novel based on me and our time.

On May 3, 1965, I was chargesheeted under Section 292 of the Criminal Code for my poem *Stark Electric Jesus* in the court of the presidency magistrate, Mr. Amal Mitra. Commissioned by Bonnie

"Karuna Nidhan, Malay Roy Choudhury, and Anil Karanjai on New Road, Kathmandu, 1966. Photograph by Subimal Basak."

Crown of Asia Foundation, this poem was reprinted in *City Lights Journal* no. 3 with an essay on the subject by Professor Howard McCord. It was also published separately in the United States in 1965–66 in three ditto editions by Tribal Press with a verifax cover showing the sorcerer of the Trois Frères. The poem is included in my *Selected Poems,* published by Writers Workshop, Calcutta, in 1989. It is a poem of mourning based on speech rhythms.

The legal battle went on for twenty-to-thirty minutes every week; the prosecution produced witnesses to prove it was my poem, written and circulated by me, seized from my custody, and that it was obscene. Only Pabitra Ballabh testified that it was *vulgar* and that he had seen me distributing it. Defense witnesses were Sunil Gangopadhyay, poet and novelist; Jyotirmoy Dutta, critic and editor; Tarun Sanyal, professor; and Satrajit Dutta, psychiatrist.

Sunil, in cross-examination, told the court that he had read the poem several times and would read it out loud if the court permitted it. *Stark Electric Jesus* was a beautiful poem, he said, the expression of an important poet. Tarun said his students had liked the poem, that it was a piece of creative art. Jyotirmoy testified that it was an experimental poem and not at all immoral and obscene. Satrajit said there was no question of inflaming passion or depraving the mind of a reader.

The judge, Amal Mitra, in his ten-page verdict on December 28, 1965, found me guilty, directed me to pay a fine of 200 rupees (fifteen dollars) or be imprisoned for one month, and gave orders for the destruction of all copies of the issue. It being the maximum penalty, the judge did not permit me to appeal to the High Court. I filed a revision petition at the High Court and started searching for a good criminal lawyer.

Stark Electric Jesus was the first condemned poem in Bengali literature. The judge did not rely on prosecution and defense testimony, but rather drafted his own piece of literary criticism, aware of its going down in our literary history, as evident from this last passage of his verdict:

> By no stretch of imagination can it be called, what has been argued, an artistic piece of erotic realism opening up new dimensions to contemporary Bengali literature or a kind of experimental piece of writing, but it appears to be a report of a repressed or a most perverted mind that is obsessed with sex in all its nakedness and thrives on, or revels in, utter vulgarity and profanity preoccupied with morbid erotism and promiscuity in all its naked ugliness and uncontrolled passion for the opposite sex. It transgresses public decency and morality substantially, rather at public decency and morality by its higher morbid erotic effect unredeemed by anything literary or artistic. It is an affront to current community standards, decency, and morality. The writing viewed separately and as a whole treats sex, that great motivating force in human life, in a manner that surpasses the permissible limits judged from our community standards, and as there is no redeeming social value or gain to society which can be said to preponderate, I must hold that the writing has failed to satisfy the time-honoured test. Therefore it has got to be stamped out.

10

Although *The Searchlight*, a daily newspaper, published a special supplement on the eve of my conviction, with a twenty-thousand-word essay by its editor, Subhas Chandra Sarker, life for me had become miserable all those six months. Living in a dark, damp, dilapidated room at Uttarpara, alone, shrinking, taking a bath once or twice a week in the Hooghly River to get rid of lice, eating at anybody's expense, begging around for money for the court, no editor agreeing to print my poems, in dwindling health, suffering harsh criticisms, and with dementia creeping in, I felt shattered. All these experiences I was putting bit by bit, being a slow writer, in *Jakham*, a long poem alternating sigh and shriek as I abandoned traditional metrics. It was translated by Carl Weissner in 1967, the German translator of William Burroughs, and reprinted by Joan Silva in *Network*, translated into Hindi by Kanchan Kumar.

Jyotirmoy Dutta introduced me to K. S. Roy, a barrister who had practised in London, and said top attorneys required big money. Professor Howard McCord had raised some money from three editions of *Stark Electric Jesus*. Carol Bergé organised a poetry reading at Saint Mark's Church, New York—by Paul Blackburn, Allen Hoffman, Clayton Eshleman, Armand Schwerner, Carol Rubenstein, Gary Youree, Allen Planz, Ted Berrigan, Jerome Rothenberg, Bob Nichols, David Antin, Jackson MacLow—and remitted the collection. Special Indian issues of *Intrepid* by Allen De Loach, *Salted Feathers, Fact, San Francisco Earthquake, Imago, Where, Trace, Work, Iconolatre, Klacto* were printed in the U.S. and the U.K. and the proceeds were sent to me. In Calcutta I got help only from Ashok Mitra and Kamal Kumar Majumdar. I also raised some loans and engaged the attorneys K. S. Roy, Mrigen Sen, Ananga Dhar, and A. K. Basu.

With my conviction most of the Hungryalists started deserting me; it was not possible to hold them together. Debi and Saileshwar, Subo and Ramananda, Subhas and Tridib developed a sort of George Oppen–Louis Zukofsky relationship, making it very difficult to carry on the group with me.

My attorneys were not sure when the case would come up for a hearing, maybe in six months, maybe in ten years. I had drifted around for food and shelter, voyeuring like a fool, depending on remittances from Dad and Samir, straying out to villages, unwanted at the residences of poets and editors, gloomy with plenty of time, when my ill health struck me. Subimal bought me a train ticket for Patna, which I reached in stupor and delirium; Ma weeped at my trauma, and I remained bedridden for a month. Tridib's letters were awaiting my recovery. He had written that Subhas, Saileshwar, Basudeb, Pradip, and Arunesh had launched a new group—keeping Subimal, Debi, and myself out—and that their magazine contained a vituperative attack on us. I felt sad. Phalguni came to

Patna to meet me; I advised him never to come again. The doe-eyed nuns had returned in my dreams carrying Parijat's marble body, the candles were now replaced by castor oil lamps.

My ill health, Ma thought, might be due to drugs and sex, so she informed marriage agents to get me involved. The agents knew of my whereabouts and every now and then presented before me a nervous girl of marriageable age for my consent, I had to quarrel it out with Ma to stop the horrible affair.

Music was there to fall back upon as I came to know Robin Dutta, who drew me first into stories from Palestrina, Monteverdi, Purcell, Handel, Haydn, Berlioz, Franck and then to his discs and cassettes of compositions by Bach, Mozart, Beethoven, Schubert, Chopin, and Brahms, an engaging experience relieving my burden. Dad purchased for me a record player with a sitar recital disc of maestro Ravishankar and *thumri* of Bade Gulam Ali. Ferlinghetti sent me Ginsberg's reading of *Kaddish* and Ezra Pound reading his *Cantos*, which I listened to in the evenings. I had, on doctor's advice, stopped smoking except for a rolled tobacco once in a while.

Subimal's younger brother informed Dad that the hearing at the High Court was fixed for July 26, 1967. I didn't feel like going to Calcutta. The life I had spent there was horrifying; I shuddered at the thought. July 26 came and passed away. Subimal arrived after a week, smiling, with newspaper reports of my exoneration and a certified copy of the verdict of Justice T. P. Mukherji of the High Court castigating lower court judge Amal Mitra for his judicial blunder and the Calcutta police for their harassment.

I felt blank, gave Subimal whatever books, correspondence files he wanted, gave up meeting people, withdrew into my loneliness. My blankness continued. I was unable to write, no images flitted by, lines refused to be composed in my mind. I sat at the table doing nothing, for weeks, for months, nervousness galloped, without a purpose; there was no request from any editor for my poems, no letter from anyone.

11

In the winter of 1968 I was introduced by Sulochna Naidu, a Telugu lady, to her bespectacled friend Shalila Mukherjee, a frail lady of peacock gait, a couple of schoolgirl tresses, deep eyes, and a voice shy enough to make me fumble for words as I controlled myself from placing my head on her lap and weeping. She had lost her mother when a baby; her father had

left her with the maternal grandfather, never to return again.

On my first visit her uncle showed me eight rifles and double-barrel guns, the hides of predators he had hunted, and then whistled for his two pet Pomeranians, Suzie and Caesar. I got the message and obliquely told him to get in touch with Dad or Samir in case he felt uncomfortable about me. He did. Samir was hastily dispatched by Ma to descend to Nagpur, more than a thousand kilometers from Patna, for finalising any nuptial possibility.

I married Shalila on December 4, 1968, reciting full-throated Sanskrit mantras I vaguely understood, prompted by a bearded priest in a saffron robe who had Old Testament-prophet looks, in front of crackling holy fire and smoke, angels, gods, friends, relatives, in a carnival of midnight glory and glamour. The marriage rituals regenerated my lust for life, Wordsworthian fullness, an inspiration to live that was robust. Shalila's cousin married an airport official the same night and the joint marriage created a sort of flutter in the sleepy town.

To avoid the funeral gloom at Patna, where Uncle Sushil had died on the day of my marriage—why such things happen to me I do not know—I made a stopover in Chaibasa at Samir's in-laws' place. I reached Patna to find visitors arriving to celebrate the bridal reception and bereave the dead, provoking Cousin Dolly, Uncle Sushil's daughter, to give me a piece of her mind in chewed verbiage.

I left Patna with Shalila for the tribal jungles of Palamau, four hundred kilometers away by train, in the grip of spring, with a whiff of blooming kino and kapok. We lunched there on coloured rice, barbecued meat, boiled snails, and a dash of liquor made of mahua, rejuvenating my lazy tendencies in pluralist happiness. Pangs of not being able to write were subsiding. Palamau was soothing. The wild elephants, however, didn't give us an audience during the fortnight we stayed.

We made a trip to Shimla by train in February 1969, experiencing the first snowfall I ever saw. Our luggage was placed on the bus top for traversing between Kalka and Shimla and covered with three inches of flakes by the time we stepped down into the knee-deep snow. Then we fetched up a hotel room and finished a full brandy. We didn't have sufficient clothes to go out in the snow, so we remained indoors for the period of our stay.

When we were back in Patna, George Dowden was there, in a saffron dhoti, with the flowing hair of a sannyasin. He was working on Ginsberg's bibliography. Shalila fed him some Indian dishes. I felt a little embarrassed, with nothing to talk about, alienated from what was going on at Calcutta. He excluded me from his India memoirs.

Shalila introduced a Marathi dimension to our Bengali cuisine; we had a dining table now from her Nagpur job savings, curtains on the windows, flower-pots, stainless steel utensils in place of brass, a part-time maid.

Ma was free; she seized the opportunity to revive her interest in Hindu gods and goddesses she had forgotten after coming to Dariapur, sang holy songs in the evenings. Ma and Shalila enjoyed each other's pagan faith, solicited mantras from respective gurus, followed worship rituals. Ma's favourite god was Ganesha, a marble replica originally worshipped by Granny. Ma did abandon her Ganesha later and transferred her interest to stitching a *kantha,* a patchwork bedsheet for my daughter.

Dimple, as we called our daughter, born on September 5, 1969, got her name changed to Anush-ree fourteen years later when a film star named Dimple hit the screen. She introduced me to an infant's universe of wordless communication that I never knew so closely, her vocabulary growing sound by sound, deciphered by Ma and Dad in their new vocation of baby-sitting after Shalila went out to her job as an accounts assistant on a rickshaw. Annoyed with my impatience in teaching Anushree the English alphabet and numbers, she appointed a tutor.

On a day of cloudburst, driblets trickled down from the ceiling and entered the bookshelf, which had been shut for more than a year. I opened it to find corridors of hefty termites revelling through Sade's *Hundred Twenty Days of Sodom* to Genet's *Our Lady of the Flowers.* I felt like weeping; my throat choked, I allowed the white ants to live and spread their colony. Why did I have this acquisitive streak? Since then I have been giving away books and magazines to others after I have read them. Lithe turning of water, Ezra Pound had written.

12

I got a bank officer's job in 1972, conducting credit utilisation studies and impact assessments in deep rural areas I had not been to earlier. I began to understand the life and living of cultivators and artisans. I loved the job. Now I could tell from afar whether a paddy stalk was wheat or barley, pulses of various plants, chillies or *rohu, katla* and *mrigel* fish in pond water; I acquainted myself with the daily life of a farmer's family, the ruthlessness of rural poverty, machinations of caste substratums, village violence, names of birds, herbs, shrubs, and trees I had not

known, men and women ploughing, harvesting, threshing, levelling, jungle-clearing with their own hands. I thought of Whitman, Neruda, Mayakovsky, and the Bengali poets Jibanananda and Sukanta but was unable to write any line myself.

Talking to people was a part of my job—farmers, labourers, social servicemen, government officials, rural headmen, bankers, craftsmen—characters filtering through experience. Hundreds of thousands of kilometers I traversed from village to village—fifteen days a month—on train, steamer, boat, van, bus, horsecart, elephant, camel, bullock cart. Alone on a bed in a hotel or country house, I thought of poetry. I was barren.

Shalila bought me a Lambretta scooter on my birthday in 1973 (we started celebrating it after our marriage; Ma and Dad had not been aware of the custom). We drove into town Sunday evenings entertaining ourselves with Chinese dishes. I had become fond of rum and cola, given up smoking, gathered fat around my waist.

"Shalila in 1968. I took the photograph. In the background are flower plants in wood packing boxes on the roof of the Dariapur house."

Our son, Bappa, was born on February 19, 1975, a caesarian.

Saint Joseph's convent, my first school (where I got Anushree, later Bappa, admitted), had expanded like a deep sea fish out of water: cement crawled to eat up violets, roses, marigolds, dahlias, chrysanthemums; doe-eyed nuns were replaced by serious-looking Keralites; children spilled out like mustard seeds from multistoried blocks onto grassless playgrounds; Saint Joseph's statue was full of crowshit. I visited the other school, Ram Mohan Roy Seminary, in ruins now, physically and ideologically, under a money-making buffoon of a principal, damn it.

The inevitable stroke in the winter of 1975: I pissed blood, my blood pressure shot up beyond limits, infarction of the heart, bedrest for two months, medicines, medicines, oh, pain in my thought process, fear of death, but no poetry came to my mind. Editors and poet friends might have forgotten me.

13

My office, the Agricultural Refinance and Development Corporation, in the summer of 1979 transferred me to Lucknow, city of nabobs during the British raj, which saw to the decimation of the Moslem aristocracy. The town was far better than Patna. I couldn't get a house and stayed for some time with Abdul Karim, a Telugu-speaking Moslem agricultural economist, and afterwards with Prabhakara, an analyst who spoke the Kannada language, who prevented me from lapsing into disorder as I was damn scared of loneliness.

The office gave me a newly constructed bungalow across the Gomti River and adjacent to the Kukrail Crocodile Sanctuary in early 1980 when Shalila and the children joined me. I developed a lawn of Bermuda grass and a rose garden in the front; Shalila took care of a kitchen garden at the rear. I planted guava, jujube plum, banana, papaya, and

"Brother Samir, Kamal Chakraborty, editor of Kourab, *Dr. Uttam Das, Malay, and Bela, Samir's wife, on the eve of Honey's—Samir and Bela's daughter—marriage. They are in ceremonial dress." Calcutta, 1986*

"Shalila and I with Anushree and Bappa in our Lucknow drawing room in 1984. The dog is of papier-mâché and was brought from Madras in 1983. The hanging separators are made of beads from Delhi and mollusc shells from Puri."

horseradish, got the fruits, felt fantastic. On the gate we had multicoloured bougainvillea through the entire year spreading a soft carpet for visitors. I regained my health.

Being the Section in Charge of credit deployment for poverty-alleviation programmes, I found myself in a tension of human misery, unredeemable through post-Keynesian methods. World Bank minions, dizzy with imaginative success, looked like jokers doling out cookies to the dead and dying from their Tutankhamen gold masks, from poems of François Dufrene or Gil Wolman, from paintings by Mondrian or Kandinsky. This entire period from 1979 had been one of regaining helplessness for me. I was a drawing-room intellectual, nuts, retheorising frightening abstractions, suffering from an inexplicable sense of guilt capped with a secret gnawing anxiety of not being able to write, which aggravated my nervous system. I knew that only ten percent of people had the freedom to pursue happiness, the rest were nonpersons, invisible pariahs of our polity. There was nothing I could do, nothing.

Ma and Dad came to Lucknow to spend the winter of 1981 with us, Samir having shifted with his family to Patna. We enjoyed winter, sitting in wicker chairs placed on the lawn, dozing off during sunny, shaded afternoons, disturbed occasionally by a couple of grumbling doves nesting in the bougainvillea. Flocks of low-flying Russian white cranes glided towards Bharatpur Sanctuary a hundred kilometers away, parrots nibbled ripe guava; there were sparrows, swifts, woodpeckers, mynahs, bitterns, thrushes, buntings, cuckoos, falconets, larks, kites, orioles, storks, warblers visiting the garden, and the insects, frogs, butterflies of endless creations, and earthworms and lizards. It was a long way from Bakharganj days.

As the astrologers had predicted Dad would die first, Ma didn't reveal the severe arthritis she was suffering from, detected when her legs swelled, but not before wrong medicines prescribed by a physician led to a massive heart attack, hospitalisation, and death two days after the 1982 Diwali festival of lights. Samir rushed from Patna in response to my telegram, told me and Shalila we had neglected Ma. She was cremated on a funeral pyre the next morning on the banks of the Gomti River, turned into ashes from which I collected a small shining piece of bone and kept it in my purse. I remained in ritual mourning for thirteen days in a single piece of loincloth, barefoot, without shaving or combing my hair, at the end of which I shaved my head, took a bath in the Ganges, and fed Brahmins.

Ma had been in a coma for two days, cut off from us, in her suffering, oxygen pipe in nostrils, eyes closed, soundless. Where was she!

Personal loss is the exact description of the depressive void created by her absence. I brooded in blank anguish and aching insight; no death had absorbed me earlier. A few months later, returning from the office, I found myself weeping one day in the busy market square of Lucknow, overwhelmed by a sudden feeling choking my throat.

I booked train tickets for Dad, Shalila, and the children, journeyed two nights to the temple towns of south India, stayed for a month, and returned confused, mystified, unsettled, words and images in a whirling chaos in me searching for an expansive flow of ideation. I wrote several love poems as they kept on coming, mailed them to Kamal Chakraborty, editor of *Kourab* who had been pestering me for poems during the last couple of years. Floodgates were sprung open.

That spread the word. Poet and researcher Dr. Uttam Das with his wife, Malabika, visited us at Lucknow with the proposal for a book on the Hungryalist movement for which I made available all the material from Patna. His book appeared to stir a hornet's nest again, and I had to give several interviews clarifying my current thoughts on life and poetry, past and present. There was now a generation of poets who were not born or were infants when I was convicted for poetry, and they had their own image of me.

Uttam got the manifestoes and earlier poems collected and published in two volumes in 1985 and 1986, with covers designed by Charu Khan, turning them into avant-garde collectors' items. The manifesto collection was dedicated to Malabika, whose voice resembled Parijat's, and the poetry collection to Bhulti, my mother.

I reciprocated Dr. Das's consideration by a visit to his house and farm at Baruipur near Calcutta, a cool country greened with fruits, foliage, coconuts, and bamboos. Malabika, a teetotaler, cooked steamed prawns for me. I visited Debi Roy and his wife, Mala, and Subimal Basak; they had greyed and become old. Debi, now secretary of the Indian Writers Associa-

tion, had purchased a flat and Subimal had constructed a double-decker house. Debi had become a prolific writer. Subimal had translated the Hindi author Premchand and published an *Anthology of Superstitions.*

On a request from Professor Sibnarayan Ray, a radical humanist thinker, I wrote a story for his periodical recounting the Hungryalist days, leading to an avalanche of special issues of *Godhuli Mone, Swakal, Uttarapath, Jiraffe, Pather Panchali, Goddo Poddo Samvad, Atalantik,* etc., on the movement.

I was now experimenting for a post-Hungryalist, eugenic ethos in my poems, a diction to overcome the musical pattern of Bengali language, a possible perfection in timelessness, closeting myself in the back room when all had gone for work and school.

Prokash Karmaker, painter, who was in France for some years, suggested we bring out a one-page offset magazine with a drawing by him and a poem of mine on the theme of violence. Every month during 1985 and 1986 a sheet was published. These poems were collected, and publisher-poet Mrityunjay Sen of Mahadiganta Publishers brought out my book *Medhar Batanukul Ghungur* during the Calcutta Book Fair of 1987, with a cover designed by Jogen Choudhuri, head of the department of painting and sculpture, Visva Bharati University. The book was a great critical success.

14

Lucknow for me had become a small place now. I moved to Bombay as deputy manager in the National Bank for Agriculture and Rural Development, staying for some time in a house inside a mango orchard in Borivili, shifting later to a Santa Cruz apartment provided by office. I could have gone to Calcutta but didn't, feeling scared of the collectivised response and streamlined thinking of the city and remembering my experience of having lived in squalor, filth, and poverty there despite the fact that my great-great-granpa once owned the city.

Coming to Bombay, I loved it: its fast life, Zoroastrians, Moslems, Goanese, Orthodox Marathis, Iranian restaurants, Gujarati jewellers, the Western cultural inroads, and, above all, the sea. I visited Nissim Ezekiel, the grand old man of Indian poetry in English, Adil Jussawala, and cute Charmayne D'Souza of Bombay's Poetry Circle, dubbed by Professor John O. Perry of Tufts University, Massachusetts, as below international standards.

I have wondered why Indian poetry should be judged by Western native norms. Why can't the

Malay and Shalila in their Santa Cruz apartment in Bombay, 1989. Photograph by Anushree.

editors and critics in the West have a feel of the soil of one's Swahili, Nepali, or Bengali mother! And unless one gains a foothold in the U.S.A. and the U.K., international recognition remains a pipedream.

When Professor P. Lal of the Writers Workshop agreed to bring out my *Selected Poems* in English in 1989, designed by himself with a cotton loom sari cover, I saw the end of the tunnel. The translation is shabby but it certainly opens up the chance to work out my next ventures. Reviews have been wonderful.

Meanwhile, I have kept myself busy drafting my memoirs for Mizanur Rahaman's *Quarterly*—published in Dhaka, Bangladesh—going back in time, hazily remembering people and events, moments of

joy and humiliation, breakdown and despair, challenges of loneliness, and Ma talking of Patna's devastating earthquake in which she lost her blackbuck and swans, five years after which I was born.

March 12, 1990

BIBLIOGRAPHY

Poetry:

Shoytaner Mukh (collected poems), Krittibas Prakashani (Calcutta), 1963.

Amimangshita (long poem), Zebra (Calcutta), 1965.

Jakham (long poem), Zebra, 1966.

Stark Electric Jesus, Tribal Press, 1966.

Kobita Sankalan (collected poems), Mahadiganta (Calcutta), 1987.

Medhar Batanukul Ghungur (collected poems), Mahadiganta, 1987.

Selected Poems, Writers Workshop (Calcutta), 1989.

Hattali (poem), Mahadiganta, 1990.

Nonfiction:

Hungry Andoloner Kavyadarshan (manifesto of Hungryalist movement), Debi Roy (Howrah), 1965.

Letters/Letters, edited by Tridib Mitra, Unmarga (Howrah), 1968.

Chithi Sankalan (letters), edited by Alo Mitra and Tridib Mitra, Unmarga, 1969.

Ishtahar Sankalan (collected manifestoes written during Hungryalist movement), Mahadiganta, 1986.

Plays:

Hibakusha, Pratitwandi, 1966.

Illot, Zebra, 1966.

Napungpung, Unmarga, 1966.

Contributor to periodicals, including *City Lights Journal, El Corno Emplumado, Fact, Imago, Kultchur, Network, Quarterly* (Bangladesh), *Salted Feathers, San Francisco Earthquake, Trace,* and *Where.* Translator of Allen Ginsberg's *Howl* and *Kaddish* into Bengali, 1985. Editor of *Hungryalist* bulletin, 1961–65, and *Zebra,* 1966–67.

Judson Crews

1917-

I

Early Background

My earliest male forebear of record is Jacob Faubion, whose date of birth is unknown, and whose country of origin is not above dispute. The name "Faubion" as such represents a mare's nest in its own right. Whether from illiteracy, perversity, or national chauvinism, it has been bastardized in many tongues. In France, it became variously "La Faubione," though ultimately, simply "Fauve" ("wild beast"). In Germany, it was "Faber" and "Farbin." In Russia, it became chiefly "Faubion-ovitch," though with two or three variations. So it goes, as Kurt Vonnegut would say.

But in Rome, in the time of the caesars, in a senator's chair in the Forum, it is clearly and correctly carved, "Faubion."

I will say for old Jacob, my grandfather five generations removed, unlettered as he was, an honest craftsman, an ironmonger, a man of the lower depths of hell—he did know how to write his own name correctly, though in pre-Revolutionary Virginia, he was contemptuously called "the Dutchman" because he did not speak very good English.

Where did he come from? Is it a self-serving family tradition that he *did* come from Holland, but that he was Norman, not Saxon—that his people were French Huguenots who had been driven out of France in those horrendous times, just as the Moors were driven out of Spain? No one asked me. But only this diaspora could possibly explain the scatteration of these, my people, among so many nations, with so many allied names.

Jacob, in March 1772, in Fauquier County, Virginia, witnessed the Will of one John Rector with his signature. John Rector and Elisabeth Fischbach were the grandparents of Dianah Rector, Jacob's wife (or wife-to-be). "Rector" (sometimes "Richter") is almost certainly German—though family tradition has it that Dianah was an English lady. Her folks were involved in iron-ore mining, smelting, etc., while Jacob was only a lowly blacksmith. Is it very unimaginable that the Faubions and the Rectors intersected

Judson Crews, Pilar, New Mexico, 1982

there in Germantown, Virginia, a few years before the War of Independence?

It seems Jacob and Dianah had ten children, six sons and four daughters, chiefly born in Virginia, but chiefly brought up over the mountains in Tennessee in what later became Cocke County. Of these siblings, I will speak only of the sixth, William Faubion (1783–1839), my grandfather four generations removed.

His courtship was a rare one—it lasted but one evening. It was Indian summer, and the shadows were lengthening, the catbirds still calling. These Vulcans (old Jacob and his apprentice sons) had laid their hammers and tongs aside and banked their coals. A caravan of movers was just coming in on the Warm

101

Springs road, and young William went to investigate. He discovered Rosannah Perthenia Ayers from North Carolina, going west with her family and a whole cavalcade. His mind was riveted by her. Unbeknownst to this young lady, she was to become my grandmother four generations removed.

Old Jacob was no pushover. By law and custom, William had three or four more years of apprenticeship yet to serve. But the old man said, yes, William could use the forge and tools afterhours, moonlighting to earn the keep of this young girl he knew he could win.

Before daylight, with the odor of honeysuckle suffusive, as the train was beginning to form on line, young William went to collect his bride. She consented. The caravan moved out, wending its way into Cherokee country, and Rosannah never saw any of them again.

They bore ten children and it is said it was a happy marriage. Of the ten siblings, Henry Faubion (1815–1892) was the ill-starred one. He was to become my great-grandfather.

Henry (also called "Harry" by relatives) followed in the tradition of his father and grandfather, as blacksmith, wheelwright, and millwright—but later, in Johnson County, Missouri, he was a dirt farmer. He married Eliza Jane Chapman (1824–1863) near Bridgeport, Tennessee, where he was born. She bore him twelve children in all. The last of these twelve was Sabra (1861–1882), my very dearly beloved grandmother who died thirty-five years before I was born. How I have loved her from the learning of the first few facts of her life and character—this only within the past seven years.

W
here, can anyone imagine, did the name "Sabra" come from, in this family of White Anglo-Saxon Protestants—WASPs, if you will? Of course, every literate person knows that "Sabra" means "born in Israel." But wherefrom, there in the wilds of Missouri, even before the War between the States, did this name come, especially in a family which was notorious for recycling given names, male and female, in very short twelve-, fifteen-, eighteen-year generational spans?

Who was this Eliza Jane Chapman (Faubion), who, like so very many frontier women, was already pretty well zapped by age thirty-five from bearing too many children in too short a time? From whence did she get this peculiar name "Sabra" for her twelfth and last child? Sabra was born in a Missouri wildland, only two or three days ride from Indian country. She was born of an almost militantly anti-Jewish and anti-Catholic tradition of more than three hundred

Grandmother Sabra Faubion, Hamilton County, Texas, about 1878

years—so much so that they suffered a diaspora of their own. Would Sabra ever have questioned her mother concerning her name? Did any of Eliza Jane's children ever think to ask her how she hit on the name "Sabra" for this fairy child, this elfin child? There is no record, there is no tradition.

Sabra lost her mother at age two, there on that rambling, disjointed quarter of a section of wilderness in Johnson County, Missouri.

Old Henry (for there was a younger Henry—some prefer to designate them Henry I and Henry II, as if they were of British royal lineage—why not?) remarried soon, with one Elizabeth Ann Ferris (?–1869), who gave him one child who died in infancy, then died herself when her stepchild Sabra was only eight. Henry was already forty-eight when he lost his first wife, and only fifty-three when he lost his second. What a blow this must have been for old Harry.

All the less could this have prepared anyone for Sabra to turn up pregnant at age twelve or thirteen. Barely a generation younger than Hawthorne's Hester Prynne, she epitomized that kind of stalwart woman who would not betray her lover (whether he was indeed lover, seductor, or mere rapist). According to any extant record or oral tradition, Sabra never once during her awful travail revealed who the father of her child may have been.

(Sixty years later, in her early thirties, Anais Nin was pregnant with Henry Miller's child, and he could not stand the thought of it. He wanted an abortion—he would raise the money, *somehow*. Anais would not hear of it. If that were the point, she had the money—or she could get it from her mother, or else from her banker husband, Ian Hugo [Hugh Giyler]—but that was not the point. Instead, she prayed to her unborn child—"Child without a father, I love you, but it is best that you should not be born." He was born dead at seven months or so and tossed over the rail of the houseboat into the Seine—no qualm of conscience for Henry Miller, not that he suffered a qualm of conscience for anything. It was his own ass he suffered for—that only, that always.)

My dear grandmother Sabra revealed no word ever, so her sisters decided upon a putative father—the boy next door. But there were three. The youngest one was too young, and the oldest one was too old, but the middle one was "just right"—so they reasoned. Whether a "Three Bears" syndrome, I would not want to venture. Even so, Sabra would not budge a half inch—and how I reverence her. If I have any guts, and I have not very much, I think I got them from that dear child, frightened as she surely must have been.

Noah was born a perfect male child, but whether in his mother's paternal home or in the home of a married sister is not known.

Old Henry Faubion, that blasted and humiliated old patriarch—was he such a peaceable man that he could not make the move to arrange a shotgun wedding, in accordance with the folkways of that time and place? Or was it the intransigence of that born-in-Israel girl?

At about this time, Sabra's oldest sister, Elizabeth, a widow who had lost one of her two children, moved to Texas with her daughter Eliza Anne, to Savoy, in Fannin County on the Red River, bordering Oklahoma. I would conjecture that Sabra and her infant son Noah (1875–1936) traveled with them.

In 1879, at age sixty-four, twice a widower in less than ten years, Henry pulled stakes of twenty-two years in Johnson County, Missouri, went west into Indian territory, and resumed his trade as a millwright. You think in his trade he didn't know how to handle dynamite? Even so, next thing, blasting a rock emplacement for a grinding mill, he burnt out his eyes with a too-short fuse. Oh, after a few weeks he could tell night from day. He could even tell a horse

from a buffalo, or an outhouse from a barn. In 1881, travelling alone, this blind old man of sixty-seven made his way to Savoy, to the Gorrell place—this was the home of his daughter Ruth Alice and her husband Thompson Vinson Gorrell. It was a safe harbor for many family members for days or weeks or even months in the 1870s and 1880s.

Sabra and Noah were likely there for several weeks, even several months. One thing sure, they were long gone before old blind Henry arrived. Sabra was married in 1879 in Hamilton County, Texas, to one W. L. Dewey, and her name appears not once but twice on the wedding certificate very clearly as Miss Sabra Faubion. Noah was four when his mother married. She bore Dewey two sons and died in 1882 at age twenty-one, when Noah was seven.

According to my sister Ida Marie Buchheit, six years my senior, the 1880 census carries the enumeration of our father as "Noah C. Dewey." All of his adult years my father signed his name as "N. G. Crews," only rarely "Noah G. Crews"—and all of my life I knew the "G" stood for "George." Disingenuously, you would almost have to think, Ida Marie has it figured out in her mind that the "C" in the census report was purposeful and intentional, that it was Sabra's way of documenting the fact that the father of her son was named "Crews." With a creative imagination like this, my sister Ida Marie should have been a theologian. But our nephew, Paul David Call, seems to support her view. And David is the only family member who has done primary research on the Cabble Crews family, which was nearest neighbor to the Henry Faubion acreage in Johnson County, Missouri.

Documentation on the Cabble Crews family is greater than documentation on the Henry Faubion family by a ratio of about five to one. But not yet has any shred of evidence developed to connect that family with Noah C. Dewey of the 1880 census report, the same person who later came to be known as Noah G. Crews. David Call personally interviewed Judge Given Crews III in Pennsylvania some time ago, and Judge denied unequivocally that his great-grandfather Judge Given Crews could have seduced the child Sabra, got her with child, abandoned her—and the matter kept secret from everyone.

After Sabra's death, Dewey was not able to keep his own two sons, much less his stepson. These children were parceled out to three of Sabra's sisters. Noah was taken by his aunt Mary McCormick, who was childless, and who married a second time, to Mitchell N. White in 1890, when Noah was fifteen. I feel the utmost confidence in saying this was the very time that he went back to Savoy, where he had spent several weeks or a few months as an infant. He did not live at the Gorrell place, but in the home of his married cousin Eliza Anne Pate Large (1869–1920), who was only six years older than he.

There are three extant photographs of Noah during his adolescence. The one that I take to be the first is quite faded, but it is of a handsome, intense, full-faced young man I am unable to judge as more than fifteen or sixteen. The distinctively chiseled, unsmiling lips are definitely Noah's, as is the characteristically styled, nicely clipped hair. He is almost sumptuously dressed, with a wing collar, a wide, neatly knotted necktie. The vest is almost elegant, the waistcoat is appropriate, and he is wearing a lapel pin with the initial "N." This is clearly a studio portrait and is mounted on heavy card stock, but there is no logo or date. "Noah G. Crews" appears on the back of the card in a large, easy hand—which could be his, but not necessarily so.

The second print is sepia, smaller, much sharper, but somewhat scratched. This photograph was made by Will S. Thompson in Bonham, Texas, which was the closest large town to Savoy. It was made not more than two or three years later than the first one—but what a change. The face is almost gaunt, and the eyes haunted. The third photograph is a full-length portrait, taken only a year or two later. He looks somehow more mature, adult, but the light is poor and his eyes indistinct. He is well enough dressed, but less formally, though he is wearing a rather flashy necktie, and has a large felt hat in his hand, such as Billy the Kid had worn fifteen years earlier.

Ida Marie and David Call are agreed in reversing the first two photographs, and in dating them later and closer together, in Noah's late teens. This maneuver makes more plausible their contention that Noah travelled to Missouri to find his putative father, Judge Given Crews. Ida Marie believes that he did find him, that Judge confessed and agreed to help Noah financially, but gained his pledge to keep his father's secret, so as not to embarrass his wife and their family. Ida Marie confronted me in a letter, "Where do you think Dad got those clothes? You know he didn't rob a bank." I don't know where he got the clothes. But if he went to Missouri in his late teens, which he may have, it is my guess that what he found out was that Judge Given Crews was *not* his father. What he did find out was something far darker which he would have preferred never to have known, which he never confided to anyone—for the same reason that his mother, Sabra, had never confided it to anyone either.

When Noah returned to Hamilton County, Texas, in the mid-nineties, at almost twenty, he

Father, Noah G. Crews, about 1893

eventually fell in with the Brothers Campbell (Eugene and P. J. [Phillip Judson]). These were to be continuing friendships for the rest of his life. He entered business with them as an itinerant photographer, and it was Eugene who introduced Noah to Tomie Farmer in Mexia, Texas, late in the 1890s. Noah photographed Miss Farmer, her sister Lelia, and her parents, Tony and Ida Maude Farmer.

My mother, Tomie Farmer (1879–1973), had a miscellaneous heritage of vaguely Scotch-Irish people. But in her book it was superior to anything Noah's heritage had to offer. I remember that I asked Mamma early on how it was that all our relatives were *her* relatives—and none of them my father's. She answered easily and quickly: "They just aren't much account." The amazing thing is, at age eight, ten, twelve—even at fifteen or twenty—I just swallowed this bullshit as if it were ambrosia from heaven.

Of course, it must be said that my mother's people were honest and hardworking. Grandpa, Tony Farmer, was a soldier in the Confederate army in the War between the States. He was of age, but he was such a runt that they would not trust him with a musket. He would only trip over it, perchance shoot someone. So they made him a drummer boy. Later, he was a brick and stonemason and a plasterer, and he built half of downtown Mexia in the 1880s and 1890s. At retirement time it was discovered that these buildings, which he thought he owned with his business partner, were, in fact, legally and completely owned by his partner. In the last thirty years of his life, his wife, Ida Maude, supported him by taking in roomers in the big, old family house that had been deserted by all their married daughters. Grandpa scavenged vegetables from garbage bins behind a few friendly grocery stores—just as I have done now for ten years.

(There is a gene that has come up several times in four generations of my mother's people. Ida Maude Vickers Kerley Farmer, my grandmother, had a large birthmark on her medulla oblongata that would flash brightly any time she felt an emotion of *any* kind. My aunt Jenny V. Farmer [Larkin] had it almost in spades. I have it, and often have worn my hair down to my ass to cover it. At Sunport in Albuquerque, a year ago, I saw my nephew Paul David Call for the first time in more than forty years. He is almost blonde and has a crew cut, and the very first thing I noticed was that bright birthmark flashing on the back of his head—whether of embarrassment, or pleasure, or whatever. I mentioned it, and Joann, his wife, answered, "Oh, yes, he has this 'Crews thing.'" Of course, it is not a "Crews thing." It is a Vickers-Kerley thing—which only compounds the difficulty.)

Noah Crews married Tomie Farmer June 19 ("Nigger day" in the South), 1901, in Mexia, Texas, in the home of her parents—a fateful event.

II

Early Memories and Miscellaneous Deductions

My life has been crushed into many varying fragments innumerable times. None very fine or glittering, none sharp-edged or very cutting or piercing—a rather usual sort of lumpish clods or coagulate.

I was born in a tall, red house, on a red-clay hill three miles east of Waco, Texas, in June 1917, a Cancer and a moon child. This old house was a plain landmark for three to five miles west and south—from Lover's Leap, a high chalk bluff in Cameron Park, on the Brazos River north of Waco; from the

third story of the Amicable Life Building (twenty-three stories) on Third and Austin downtown; even from the low delta of the confluence of the Brazos and Tahaukennee, often, in spring, a flooded plain.

Noah put in two dozen small American arborvitae, which we just called "cedar trees," all along our close footage on the Old Springfield road and all around the house. Over the years they grew and grew; eventually they dominated the setting, obscuring the house like some old manse in the Mississippi bayou country. There were also white and purple lilacs, honeysuckle; even roses, early on. Additionally, there were hollyhocks, canna, and flags. In the immediate area there were fruiting pomegranates, and an imaginatively interesting grove of fig trees (the foliage was abrasive and the "milk" could really burn).

In the back field, northwest, there were fruit orchards and several vegetable fields. Between was a small river branch, often flooded in downpours in a day or two, but often diminished to a few muddy crawdad holes much of the year, or a few thin-ice skating places in "hard" winter. The southeast field (fourteen acres) across the road was about two-fifths pasture. We had two or three cows and three or four

Noah G. Crews, about 1898

mules; they could never keep it grazed down. One year (at five, perchance) I inadvertently burned off this silver, sere overabundance. My butt and legs were switched good with a bundle of handy faggots. In spring that pasture was greener and more luxuriant than it had ever been before. But there were still a few charred fence posts.

This was in the moisture-opulent 1920s. How sharply it all changed in the dust-bowl 1930s. Even so, about this time, my father bought an additional seventeen-acre tract—very much against my mother's wishes. After his death in 1936, she often contended that, at times, he would just sit down for a year or two and never put a plow into the ground. He was a depressive, as I have been—but between times, what a creative person. He dug a well, got a big engine, put a good pump on it, and turned several of those acres into a kind of Eden.

He had a greenhouse built for propagating nursery stock. I learned to man it in two summers, as I was finishing high school. I could root about two-thirds of any of the ornamental shrubs that we grew—gardenias, all of the conifers, most of the broadleaf evergreens. I would generally strip naked when I worked—otherwise my clothes would be soaked.

Theodore Roethke's earliest long poem, "The Lost Son," was about life in a greenhouse. His experiences were very different from my own—in this and all things. The greenhouse I worked in was solar, while Roethke's greenhouse was for flowers, and in a cold climate; he always felt the throbbing and clanging in the steam pipes (it was always, somehow, the brooding presence of his father). My poems were never very "sunny," but Roethke's always seemed "brooding" to me.

But I move too quickly. I must go back to age three or four or so . . .

I reached the "age of accountability" early. Or it was thrust upon me. "You know you are lying, *don't you?*" any adult could say, or even neighborhood kids (with my arm twisted and my nose in a cowpie), and I would cry, "Yes, yes." I had no guts.

I was the youngest of seven live births. My two-year older sister, Toolie (Lelia Mae), was my mentor, and she led me by the hand. At three or four (she was five or six) we bathed naked in a No. 3 washtub in the yard, in water she had drawn up out of the well and warmed in the sun. We were oblivious to the road traffic forty yards away. Old Springfield Road had been macadamized and was now Mexia Highway.

My fourteen-year older sister, Ti (Beatrice), was in charge of us, but she was a relaxed late-teenager, already reading "romantic" fiction—*True Story* and

such. She was loved by both her parents and all her siblings. What could be calculated to be more relaxing than that? Soon she married and went away. She was dead at twenty-five after two caesareans.

Lelia Mae went to school at seven—Nalley, a little three-room, eight-grade school on the edge of East Waco. How she changed. Very quickly she was shaping me up to get me ready to go to school. Do this and that. Don't do thus and so. When the bell rings, always get in line quickly. Stand with your feet together, your arms at your side, and your eyes straight ahead. *Never* try to look up little girls' dresses. (She did not in fact say this. She was far too circumspect to even assume this was a problem I had.)

The first rules were easy. The unvoiced but implied rule has always been impossible—even as a septuagenarian.

In school I was never promising. I was well-behaved. But I could not read. I could not add or subtract or multiply. I could only *sit still.* Even in the consolidated school in sixth grade, one well-meaning teacher felt a need to explain me to my classmates: The Lord never intended for Judson Crews to learn anything—but just look at the *sunshine* of his smile. It is true I was always grinning from ear to ear, not only showing two-thirds of all my teeth, but a lot of very ugly upper gumline as well. This was true even in my thirties, until I learned to keep a stiff upper lip and not appear quite so much the jackass that I really was.

Late in sixth grade, at a class picnic in the evening in Cameron Park, I heard a girl behind the bushes screwing with two boys. This was a girl I liked. Her mother had the little store two blocks from the school grounds. Whenever I had the money for a pencil or tablet, I could get permission to go there during the lunch hour. I was thrilled when my friend once asked me if I would like a "kiss," a little paper-wrapped piece of taffy, free on the house. The business in the park troubled me—but I never held it against her. I did subsequently hate the two males very much.

But a year later, in seventh grade, I was the most deeply in love that I had ever been since first and second grade. A simply perfect girl, who obviously liked me also.

At almost this same time, my mother, Tomie, got a "Legal Separation of Bed and Board" from my father, Noah, on essentially a spurious complaint. It was uncontested. (In a Freudian sense, my pre-Oedipal and Oedipal anxieties were so enmeshed, I have not sorted them out in a lifetime.) After my parents' separation (which should have been a private matter, but which was not), Noah lost his place on the school board, where he had served well for several years. I had always been a "private" person—this business compounded it grossly.

It can hardly be contested that psychological factors retarded puberty until my mid-teens. I never had pubic hair until fifteen, and I was sixteen before I ever had a "wet dream." My high-school sweetheart seemed surprisingly faithful to what our feelings had been in seventh and eighth grades, but she did have an "official" other boyfriend the last two years of high school, and I never blamed her. And I loved her still.

At eighteen, I finally began to drive, so I would drive my mother to church. I soon gave in to pressure and joined, and was baptized, a Southern Missionary Baptist. My failure in this undertaking was characteristic of a lifelong career, as you will see.

However much I always wanted to try to look up the dresses of just any girl, I was very idealistic. I would not do this with a girl I "really liked." Even so, when I was baptized—my high-school sweetheart and I were baptized about five minutes apart—it was a different story. She had on an old, faded housedress, without much else under it. She panicked as she was swooshed down backwards in this absurd ritual. She must have sucked in a half-quart of water, though Brother McAuley had his fingers tight-clasped on her nose and his palm tight on her mouth. That dear, good, dedicated young lady came up sputtering, zonked, looking half-drowned. (Did I do much better? Yes and no. I *held* my breath—even though I may have farted.) Even so, no dove descended with a four-leaf clover. The Devil had surely won this first round. Back in the little dressing cubicle, I almost could have clawed the wall down to see her naked, with that soaking rag off, as she was coughing and panting, trying to get the water out of her lungs.

In the next five years, I was to preach three years as a lay minister. There was hardly a month that I was not anguished by some "crisis of faith."

I had barely begun to read by high school. *Treasure Island*, then *White Fang* and *Call of the Wild*. Then *The Good Earth, Main Street*, and *Babbitt*. I picked up early on the *New Yorker*. I copied the sophistication and superficiality of their style, including their covers.

The first "serious" poem I ever wrote was archly sophisticated, very derivative—*and* illiterate:

I've been

Thinking
        about
my elders

Modren
        poetry
is full

Of real toads
        dead
and stenching

Hopping
        with no
strings

Activated
        with in-
trickate

Springs—
        shoot
I'll go for

The globed
        fruit, pal-
itabley mute

Waco, Texas 1935

I was forced to read *Macbeth* and *Hamlet*. Found them the shitz, and still do. Oh, yes, I was reading Agatha Christie, and Faith Baldwin, and Edna Ferber at the same time, and *True Story* and *Argosy* magazines.

However laboriously I read, I read carefully. Soon it was *Esquire*, with John Dos Passos, James T. Farrell, Erskine Caldwell, Ezra Pound, several others. I read Hebrew and Greek scriptures, via the King James version. But slow, laborious reader that I was, I read Spinoza, Schopenhauer, and Nietzsche—at the same time—not to mention Chekhov and Ibsen.

The worst reading disaster I ever stumbled on was Tolstoy—not his fiction, his other stuff. I was already queerly perverted; it perverted me even more. He lay down far harder sex rules than the putative Christ ever had—ultimately to break his own rules.

Going back.

After my sister Beatrice married when I was five, it seemed I was more and more under the spell of my mother, or of her mother, my grandmother Farmer—rare though it was that we ever saw her. My grandmother had seemed peculiarly dominant to me when I was a child; she died in 1931 or 1932. Bad years these seemed to me.

Until my father's death five years later and since their separation, I was far more closely involved with him than I had ever been before. But I was never close to him—too many intervening experiences had essentially estranged us. In fairness, I think he tried to bridge the gap more than I ever did. But there was emotional distance that was never bridged.

After two ineffectual bullets to his chest, and then one to his temple, he died at his mother Sabra's grave in Ireland Cemetery, and was buried there in the fall of 1936.

The same day of my father's death, I masturbated for the first time in conscious memory. This continued, more or less, most of the rest of my life. I felt the deepest sort of chagrin and humiliation—more so since it was kept secret for more than thirty-five years. I prayed, *believing* I would receive divine help, but none was forthcoming. I had already "become a writer," and this too has been more or less continuous to this day. As a compulsion, and a semipublic fact, it has often been more humiliating than the other. Worse, at church, still in my teens, I was pressured into greater and greater commitments—and they became more and more shallow. (I didn't break out of the cloying shackles of this church community until I went into the army in early 1942, at the age of twenty-four.)

In the fall of 1937, I entered Baylor University as a special student, without matriculating—to study theology. But I took courses in sociology and psychology, and soon the Bible was essentially out the window. I was in and out of journalism and won several undergraduate and intramural literary awards. I was neurotic as the devil and grew a beard. I was in love with a perfectly okay girl, if not two or three.

Though a committed conscientious objector, I fled to the army three months after Pearl Harbor—to choose my own branch of service, the noncombatant medics. I adjusted with a will for over a year, but then things began to fall apart. I seduced my understudy in supply; he was rather complacent, but I think it troubled him quite a bit. He soon opted out of supply to become a medical technician at a lower grade.

This was a heavy thing, but there were several other problems—including drug addiction. Ultimately, after two or three episodes in the hospital, they were fed up. At one point, I was evacuated from a desert maneuver area to a rear echelon mobile hospital, where I was treated for psychotic schizophrenia. While at the hospital, I raped a nurse. Due to circumstances, that poor, dear lady never knew who her attacker was and was unable to identify me. I was plagued for two or three days with a compulsion to confess, but I managed to repress it. The episode became a phantasmic nightmare, and, as with "healthy people," I soon suppressed it as just that—a

As a Baylor University graduate, 1941

nightmare. Vague naggings haunted me always, but never was I sure of what actually happened until I wrote of this episode in my Memoir—forty-five years later.

I was mustered out of the army with a Certificate of Disability for Discharge in March of 1944.

I reentered graduate school at Baylor in June, finished my course work, wrote my thesis, and got my M.A. (with honors) at the end of summer. I went to Oregon in the fall and joined the U.S. Postal Service as a delivery person in Portland's Rose City Station. I could not take it for very long. How that wild man Bukowski put up with being a mail-delivery person for thirty years, I don't know.

In January, without a word, I simply absconded and went to Big Sur. I spent most of 1945 there with the "Anderson Creek Gang," variously at Anderson Creek, Slate's Springs (now Esalin), Point of Whales, or Lucia Lodge. The less said of this, the better. Henry Miller *had* invited me, but once I was there, it was his fantasy that his near neighbor Jaime de Angulo, up on Partington Ridge, would run me out of the state of California with a bullwhip. Jaime, as it happened, was a very dear and genteel person, a veritable "Senior de la Coche" of a far earlier order.

Henry summed me up a few years later in *Time* magazine, in a sentence or two, saying I "reminded one, because of his shaggy beard and manner of speech, of a latter-day prophet."

A few weeks after I arrived at Anderson Creek, Wendell B. Anderson joined me from Rose City Station, an offspin from a failed marriage. Out of money, he left for a summer with the U.S. Forest Service in eastern Oregon. Soon I had to join him. But my summer was a short one; with three days' notice I terminated, three days before V-J Day.

I took off for Big Sur again. If it was an Eden perchance, I was too innocent to stand it for long.

Back to my mother's old house outside Waco, Texas. I was back at Baylor for a postgraduate year of art school under the GI Bill. It was one of the worst years of my life. Several things happened; I will detail none of them here. I dropped out in late winter, but I reenrolled for a term so I could attend the Summer Field School of Art, 1947, in Taos, New Mexico.

I had given up writing for art. I left my mother's old house in Waco at twenty-nine, never to return again—except in haunted dreams.

III

Shoestring Publisher

I arrived naked in Taos, New Mexico, in 1947, at close to thirty years of age. Not naked in the literal sense—I had the clothes on my back, plus a change of socks in a battered, discarded suitcase picked up in Big Sur. I had a limping, prewar typewriter and nearly enough cash to get a housekeeping room and a few groceries to last the month. But "naked" in this sense: I had suffered multiple, low-key failures back in Waco, Texas, from as early as I could remember, failures which followed me to the university and the U.S. Army Medical Corps; and, after the army, to Oregon, California, and back to Texas. "Naked" in that I had given up writing after fifteen years of continued effort, after Henry Miller told me my one completed novel was *so bad* he couldn't get through even the first chapter. (I left Taos "naked" twenty years later, in June 1966—at nearly fifty.)

What of Taos itself upon the eve of my arrival? Terms often heard were "the little mud village," "the three cultures," "the artist colony." Or, "the winds of change," "the end of an era." All cliches, all true. In my view, "the artist colony," really, was a fourth

culture. The residents were all "expatriates" in the truest sense. They were never to become a "part." They might marry a local. A daughter might be raped by an Indian or a Mexican. They might live out the remnant of a long, leftover lifetime there. Even so.

As Henry Miller said, "What would anyone want to go to Taos, New Mexico, for—except to see an Indian bite a snake?" Henry, the *oxymoron*.

One thing that surprised me about Taos was the patina of ill-repute that managed still to cling to the image of D. H. Lawrence, two decades after he left. "Lawrence's women," Frieda, Mabel, and Brett, were local darlings—equally. They had all published feverish Lawrentian memoirs. They were old and toothless *friends*—they were above reproach. Yet it was Spud Johnson, of earlier *Laughing Horse* fame, who was the community's literary lion when I arrived.

I left Taos in mid-June 1966. Author Joseph O'Kane Foster penned "A Tribute to Judson Crews" for the *Taos News* the following week (Mildred Tolbert, among others, was to call it "An Obituary"):

> Last Monday morning one of Taos' most important people slipped quietly out of town. . . . Of the writers who have made their home in Taos I consider Crews second only to D. H. Lawrence. . . .

Of course, Joe Foster exaggerated. He *was* writing an eulogy to read above my bier.

The "patina of ill-repute" that clung to Lawrence's Taos image has clung to mine. Of "my women," some have written about me. They are darlings of the community, bless them—they are above reproach.

What further might there be to say? I could say half a million words. In an uncharacteristic rush of modesty, I might hold it to thirty-five hundred—on the subject of *Shoestring Publishing*.

Is it germane that I was found out back in Waco, mid-year in fourth grade, as unable to read twenty two-syllable words in the English language? Further, I could not do arithmetic (not even the multiplication tables, except by rote, beginning, "one times one eekles one"). When I was discovered, you can imagine it was enough to chasten my ebullience for a little while. I was dyslexic—but this learning problem, unrelated to intelligence, wasn't to achieve public attention until forty years later.

In fifth grade, I was transferred to a consolidated school where my father chanced to be sitting on the board of trustees. As such, his voice counted in hiring and firing teachers. Thus, "by the grace of God and

The author, Taos, New Mexico, 1947

two or forty-three! One day she said to me, "What book is that on top of your humongous stack?" "Oh," I said, "that is Neva Whittaker's new collection of poetry. She is a sophomore—but when I spoke to her in the library, she said, 'Kiss my ass—*you* are not a member of Sigma Tau Delta.'"

My friend picked up Whittaker's book, and speaking in a low, hypnotic tone—"What is your life about? What is it you are doing? Who are you? Where is it you want to be going?"—that dear lady interleaved several of the pages with ten- and twenty-dollar bills, and laid it back on my "humongous" pile of books.

She had not mesmerized me. I was totally shocked. It was less than $150, but it was more money than I had seen before, in cash, at any one time in my whole life. Her fingers were firm there for a moment when she returned it. When I retrieved it and fanned the pages, I said, "I can't accept this." She took it from my hand, closed the book, laid it back on the pile again. "You already have," she said quietly.

Her husband came two or three weeks later and took her away, back to the expat community in Mexico City, which she loathed and which she had temporarily flown for a few weeks. This money, little as it might be thought by today's standards, was the beginning of *Motive* magazine, Motive Book Shop, and Motive Press.

M ost notably, *Motive* magazine published several New Apocalypse prewar British poets, J. F. Henry, D. S. Savage, Rayner Heppenstall, etc. It was also one of the first to publish Robert Symmes (later *Duncan*). And, also, one of Norman Macleod's best longer poems. (Norman, a major precursor of my own work.) I carried a very fine short story by John Bovey—of whom I never heard again—and two of the finest poems Alan Swallow ever wrote. I wrote some good reviews of new books by Gertrude Stein, Henry Miller, and others.

When I turned up "naked" in Taos in 1947, this was behind me, including the sinking of all my army savings into several thousand copies of early Motive Press publications that I could not sell—including some Henry Miller. Naked though I was when I arrived in Taos, in the sense that I did not know how to *buy* printing and I did not know how to *sell* the publication once it was produced, I did have the manuscript of Jaime de Angulo's *Indian Tales* in an old leather briefcase and a master copy of Michael Fraenkel's poems, *Death in a Room*. De Angulo was the foremost nonestablishment American Indian anthropologist ever. And it was Henry Miller's appropriation of Fraenkel's "death philosophy" in *The*

the police," so to speak, I graduated from high school (still unable to read except very laboriously, syllable by syllable, and I still could do no arithmetic, though I was pretty good at geometry and loved it—"Euclid alone has looked on beauty bare").

Before I got in through the back door at Baylor University three years after high school (as a special student "to study theology"), I had been publishing *Vers Libre: A Magazine of Free Verse* for a year and a half on a cheap, dumb, rattletrap duplicator. I produced this "free verse" magazine once every two or three months, at a cost of about ten or fifteen dollars an issue. I was working for my father as a bookkeeper, at ten cents an hour.

I made a lot of enemies. This was 1936 and 1937; the very idea of "free verse" was just totally *kaput*. I was already developing a patina of ill-repute. Had I had ten thousand dollars, I could have done little to rehabilitate the term. It was too late. Such special pleading only exposed my ignorance. (Seventy percent of the best poetry to be published during the next forty-five years *was* free verse.)

Two years later at Baylor, I was seen around campus with an "older lady"—twice my age, forty-

Tropic of Cancer that catapulted Miller from a ne'er-do-well, would-be writer in the late 1920s and early 1930s into a major literary figure by the mid-twentieth century.

In Taos, I soon lost the use of a then-borrowed, good, postwar duplicating machine, and I had to give up the thought of publishing *Indian Tales.* I went ahead with the publication of *Death in a Room,* by photo-offset production for about seventy-five dollars for two hundred copies, overall a very attractive job. I never sold more than six or eight copies of it, and I'm not sure what happened to the rest of them. However, this publication supplied the inspiration a few years later for the reprinting of several of Anais Nin's "failed" commercially published novels, in the jumbo volume *Cities of the Interior,* of which Alan Swallow took over distribution, and which may have been the forerunner of the publication of the *Diaries.*

In Taos, in late fall 1949, I became an apprentice printer at $25 a week. (Parenthetically, seven years later, as a journeyman, I was getting $1.25 an hour. And fifteen years later, as a master craftsman, I was getting about $2.50.) The first book (or half a book) which I both printed and published was my own poetry collection *No Is the Night.* Alan Swallow had rejected the manuscript—but he urged me to cut it by half and publish it myself. This I did—and the ensuing ill-repute outlasted the years. I produced the whole damn thing, single-handed—except for manufacturing the paper and the ink. It taxed my new skills to the limit, though for a first effort, it was not half bad.

What then? At one dollar a copy for a thirty-two-page pamphlet, I could not sell it, though New Directions, with its "Poet of the Month" series, was being praised for just such a scheme. I sent out twelve to twenty review copies to editors who had used my work—*Poetry* (Chicago), *New Mexico Quarterly, Voices* (Vinalhaven), several others. None would give me a review. I sent a copy to *El Crepusculo* in Taos. It lay on the desk of Frank Waters, then book-review editor, for three weeks. He never picked it up, though there were no other books there. Finally, Spud Johnson, then editor of *El Crepusculo,* picked it up and gave it a small, front-page news story—in which he gently chided the book-review editor for *not* reviewing it. *This* substantially fixed *my* goose with Frank Waters for all the years to come. This is the way I was; I became a part of the problem of other people's problems. Always.

Of *No Is the Night,* Joe Foster said privately that I was "fighting a battle" that had already been won. He meant self-publishing. Was Joe right? For nine in ten poets across the nation today, it is "self-publish or perish." Of course, for most of these, it is "self-publish AND perish."

I did continue publishing in a variety of formats—books, magazines, pamphlets, often as few as fifty copies, my own work and others. None of these would sell. One extravaganza, in 1951, was a jumbo portfolio called *Taos: A Deluxe Magazine of the Arts,* priced at three dollars a copy, limited to 125 copies. Its publication was made possible only by Marjorie Rogoway going out into the community and selling ads for me at 25 percent commission. It included work by Spud Johnson, Frank Waters, Mabel Dodge Luhan, Dorothy Brett, Becky James, W. S. Hayter, Kenneth Lawrence Beaudoin, Scott Greer, Mason Jordon Mason, Mildred Tolbert, and many others. I do not recall that I sold a single copy of this publication. The last chance copy to turn up that I heard of was bought immediately for fifty dollars.

The beginning of *Suck-Egg Mule: A Recalcitrant Beast* predated *Taos* portfolio. This was a good magazine, though it never succeeded in living up to its name. I managed to print two issues of it at *El Crepusculo* in the first year I worked there, 1950–51. It included mostly good poets—Wendell Anderson, many others. The only thing I distinctly remember was a review I did of a volume of critiques on Ezra Pound and my review of William Carlos Williams's *Autobiography,* which had disappointed me.

After the first two printed issues, *Suck-Egg Mule* converted to a smaller photo-offset format for three or four additional issues over a year or a year and a half. The work was good, mostly unknowns—Joe Wheeler Drennan, San Novit, Hyacinthe Hill, and such. I used a lot of artwork, and I became quite skilled at paste-up.

As I said earlier, *Suck-Egg Mule* never lived up to its name. All the more bizarre that Sidney Alexander, intent on doing an article for the *American Scholar* on the impact of the early anxieties of the "atomic era" on the little mud village of Taos, should hit on *Suck-Egg Mule* for his title. The internal evidence of his article suggests that Frank Waters may have been the only person Alexander talked to: ". . . Waters' outdoorness is genuine, just as he is one of the few genuine Westerners in the Anglo community. . . ."

And then, ". . . The literary exponents of hardiness are also very much in evidence—poets in blue denims who put out 'little' magazines with spit-in-the-cuspidor titles like *Suck-Egg Mule* . . ." For the record, *blue denims were my work clothes for more than twenty years.* For Wendell Anderson they would have been for even longer.

Where was this dude Alexander coming from?

Is it true, as I implied, that the *trouble* with *Suck-Egg Mule* was that it was not living up to its name? Of course, the title was facetious. I never sucked eggs. I mean, not quite—really. I didn't like people who sucked eggs. I don't think Spud Johnson sucked eggs. The community of Taos did suck eggs—particularly the artist community.

A rather special volume, produced in 1955 with Mildred Tolbert and Wendell B. Anderson, was *Patrocinio Barela: Taos Woodcarver.* This volume required an entire year of my life, and every cent that Mildred and myself could put into it, to produce 250 copies, which I priced at the absurd figure of $2.50 a copy. I was concerned with trying to recover the cost of the materials that had gone into the actual production. I feared it would not sell—any more than *Taos* portfolio had. The Harwood Foundation Library in Taos refused to buy a copy. The *New Mexico Quarterly Review* of the University of New Mexico refused to review it. Nonetheless, all copies were gone within the year. Within five years, the occasional copy that turned up sold for $25–$50. What the market value might be today, I have no idea.

Blessedly, this marked the end of my "Mr. Mimeograph" phase—as Stella Masterson had contemptuously called it—and all the third-generation art community had taken up the hew and cry. The mimeograph, generic for the stencil duplicator, was the "mule" of more than twenty-five years of small literary publication—and often it was a "recalcitrant beast." The *Deer and the Dachshund* was mimeographed during its entire two-and-a-half-year life-span, except for a considerable amount of the art-work, which I printed at the *El Crepusculo* shop. *The Anatomy of Proserpine,* a collection of my early Bulltoven poems issued in February 1955, was my last publication before beginning work on the Barela book.

My next major fiasco was *Poetry Taos, Number One* in 1957. It failed so dismally, there was never a number two. No doubt the major feature of this volume was Robert Creeley's classic short story "The Dress." But there were many other fine pieces of work, including a very early reproduction of a painting by Agnes Martin, not to mention William Carlos Williams's fine, brief appreciation of Patracinio Barela and Joe Foster's appreciation of the painter Alfred Rogoway. Also included was the first poem of Max Finstein's ever to be published. I may have done a hundred copies; it may have been two hundred. I was constricted by the cost of materials. All of the work was my contributed labor, occasionally supplemented by Wendell B. Anderson's. Whether

I made more than a cursory attempt to sell this volume is doubtful. All contributors received a copy, as with all of my publications. I gave Bob Creeley ten copies "in payment" for his short story. I gave Rogoway and Barela some copies simply for compassionate reasons. How chagrined I was when I learned Marjory, Rog's wife and manager, excised and saved the Rogoway pages—but put all the rest in the outhouse. She was "ashamed" to have Rog's name associated with two or three nude art reproductions in the publication.

Several of my "lesser" productions were small collections of my own poetry (24 to 48 pages) gathered from recent magazine appearances. These were spiral-bound with board covers. Most were interspersed with photographic reproductions clipped from a variety of sources—predominantly nudes. Fine work by Weston, Brassai, many others. But also some by hacks. A number of reviewers were incensed by this "meretricious" proclivity. It suggested a patina of ill-repute both for the publisher and the poetry. Bob Creeley suggested a truer prospective— "the device," as he characterized it in *Poetry* magazine in 1961, "of occasional photographs, of nudes, of flat building fronts, of many untoward things, let us say, to shock the mind awake with a somewhat wry invitation."

The last magazine I ever published was *The Naked Ear,* the name from a throwaway line by Taos artist Bill Heaton: "The naked ear will hear the sound of the waves we make." It was a "little" magazine indeed, $4\frac{1}{4}$ by $5\frac{1}{2}$ inches, 12 to 24 pages. Only 12 issues ever appeared, yet the contributors list was a long one and included many of the names I have already mentioned, as well as Robert Sward, Charles Bukowski, Diane di Prima, LeRoi Jones, Cerise Farallon, Stuart Perkoff, Alfred Morang, Langston Hughes . . .

In a very generous summation of my thirty years of magazine publishing by Marvin Malone for *Tri-Quarterly,* MM credited *The Naked Ear* with being the very prototype of the *independent,* one-man, shoe-string operation. Whether true or not, I know at least twenty broadly similar publications today. And I consider them, in combination, more important than such corporate enterprises as, for instance, the *Paris Review,* the *American Poetry Review,* and such.

If I should speak to the young, I must point to one thing as central. Paramount, against *all* knowing, the independent publisher must *remain* independent. (Do not misunderstand me. If you can get money, *grab* it—but run like mad.)

I would want the young to be far more concerned than I ever was about distribution. It was only by the benevolence of WCW that *The Naked Ear* turned up on the mailing list of Louis Zukofsky, Ezra Pound, Robert McAlmon, Alfred Kreymborg, and several others. (EP wrote me an acerbic note of ten words—from St. Elizabeth's Hospital—calling me historically doomed. True. In the long haul, we are all *historically* doomed. Political sycophants are always the last to learn.)

Young as Bob Creeley was at the beginning, how very aware he was of *who* the reader ought to be. I mean, *Black Mountain Review* never published more than a few hundred copies, yet half of them fell into the eager hands of very significant readers—not the dusty catch-all bins of a gaggle of *au courant* bigwigs. (How it happened that copies of *BMR* fell into my hands, that is something else.)

Leaving Taos in 1966 was the end of a chapter of my life—or perchance several volumes. It did mark a thirteen-year hiatus as a shoestring publisher. But I did take it up again, with a vengeance you might say, after returning from Africa in 1978. A certain permutation had occurred. Not only had my finances

not improved, they had worsened. Motive Book Shop was ultimately liquidated ten years earlier—after more than twenty-five years with no credits and no debits. It had always been the final resource for publication funding. Now the money was strictly out-of-pocket—a very shallow pocket always.

In five to eight years I have nonetheless issued more than thirty individual booklets. Almost half of them have been my own work. The others represent as broad a range as J. Whitebird, Emily F. Anderson. Others represented once or several times have been Mildred Tolbert, Wendell B. Anderson, Cerise Farallon, Mason Jordan Mason. The basic format of these later publications is 24 pages, but this can extend up to 36 or 48 pages. It is mostly xerox work from clippings and paste-ups on a basic 8½-by-14-inch sheet. Folded once this gives a commodious page for imaginative layout work. Folded twice it is still a pleasing and versatile format. Many individual poems will fit nicely on this 4¼-by-7-inch page, often two to a page. And there is such a variety of "found" artwork that can be used: old photographs, children's drawings, old copperplate etchings, collage, real things—

Judson Crews, Emily F. Anderson, and Wendell B. Anderson, Taos, New Mexico, 1965

even postage stamps, pressed leaves, a wadded bubble-gum wrapper, a flattened segment of beer can, a piece of calico, a discarded condom.

Many of these "books" were produced at a cost considerably less than that of a cheap fifth of scotch. All it takes is a certain disregard for an accumulation of a "patina of ill-repute."

IV

Postscripts

My eighteen years in Taos were not totally involved with shoestring publishing. I married a dear, talented, and charming lady, Mildred Tolbert, a photographer and writer. We went through several pregnancies and two live births (Anna Bush [1948] and Carole Judith [1950]). Our daughters were dear and beautiful always, if sometimes normally difficult.

I was never reconciled to being a job printer in newspaper back shops. Winfield Townley Scott told me in the mid- or late fifties that my career would never change. Bob Creeley implied the same. (He sort of envied me where I was, I think.) But Mae Harover, who had a master's degree in social work, told me I could change it, and so did Joseph Collin Murphey, who had a late Ph.D. from the University of Texas in American studies.

Slowly and bumblingly, I did change it. Arden Tice worked out a job for me at Child Welfare in El Paso, Texas. Several months later, both my wife and I took up courses at University of Texas at El Paso, and it helped us both. I took my first teaching job ever at almost fifty, as instructor of sociology and psychology on the Texas gulf coast, and remained through thick and thin for three years.

Ultimately, though, in Gallup, New Mexico, where I worked as community mental health worker and a lecturer at University of New Mexico Branch College, Mildred could no longer stand it. None of this happened in a vacuum. Off and on I continued to write and publish. Mildred more or less continued with some of her photography, then with medieval English literature at the University of Houston, then with Karl Barth, Martin Buber, etc. Finally we gave up sexually, in spite of my terrible need (or because of it). Three years later, down and out in Gallup, New Mexico, working at minimum wage as a part-time security guard, we ended it—to the relief of both of us, I think. The girls were away at the University of New Mexico and the University of Texas and were pretty much on their own.

In desperation, I wrote Henry Miller. He was now rich and famous. He replied, in substance, Man, you are nowhere. You never were, and never will be. Take it out and burn it.

Did he mean my cock, or my manuscripts? Or did he only mean that big pile of Henry Miller books I had never been able to sell?

I did a little bit of all three.

Only when this final binding-string snapped (he had been a powerful surrogate father for twenty-five years), did I begin to live—in my very modest way. Whether Mildred did or not, I am not quite sure.

I was sort of pushed out of Wharton County Community College, then really pushed out of Gallup Community Mental Health Service. I went on as unit director of intensive care in juvenile corrections at the State School for Girls in Chillicothe, Missouri. I had the confidence of the superintendent, a very bright and energetic lady almost my own age. I did well enough that after seven months they were ready to phase out the intensive care unit. By then I had an appointment in the Oppenheimer School of Social Work in Africa, at the University of Zambia (UNZA) in Lusaka. My daughter Anna Bush went with me.

For four long years in Africa I was continent, though never ceasing to have erotic thoughts of several of my colleagues, and even some of my students. I hated giving up the expatriate life and returning to the U.S. But I had managed to box myself in, with no exit, neither to Guam, New Guinea, Australia, or Namibia in exile.

Six months back in the U.S. I met the *bête noire* of my later years. I will not name her name—under penalty of existing law of libel, slander, and defamation of character.

I was sixty and had never published a book of my poems "not at my own expense" (to use William Carlos Williams's phrase). Larry Goodell, at Duende, and John Brandi, at Tooth of Time, decided to do a "thirty-year retrospective." Then J. Whitebird, at Wings Press in Houston, decided to weigh me in with a volume of recent unpublished poems.

Both volumes were a flop, as was *Clock of Moss,* from State University of Iowa, four years later.

Dare I confess my "influences"? Truly "I am a part of all that I have met"—in literature as in life.

More specifically, junior year in high school, Joe Cox laid the Monroe-Henderson *New Poetry* anthology in my hands. I was enchanted far beyond what I should have been—Sandburg, Masters, Lindsey, a

Mildred Tolbert, about 1946

few others. Amy Lowell and Witter Bynner, surprisingly enough, and also HD (Hilda Doolittle).

I also did dig Wallace Stevens pretty early, and finally Pound (after several years of thralldom with Eliot)—Pound, even with his inane arrogance, and his fascism and anti-Semitism (though this was mostly later in his career). I was never very politically clean—except on sexism; I was always anti-sexist. (As if it mattered.) I was always brutally tarred with several broad brushes no matter what my beliefs were.

Twentieth-century American poetry has been far closer to the needs of my sensibilities than any other—not that I am utterly ignorant of all other. Between high school and university, I studied Greek and Roman mythology for a year, and English versification for a year. I owned the Quiller-Couch *Oxford Book of English Verse* from early on. Two-thirds of about the best in it was by "Anon.", and very much of the rest was very dismal.

Two brief anecdotes about influences:

In the mid-fifties, a fragile young Turk arrived from Black Mountain College, fresh from Olsen, etc.

My Bulltoven poems had just been published in mimeograph as *The Anatomy of Proserpine*. Harvey Harmon picked it up idly, became riveted. His blonde skin pinkened, then reddened. "How could you?" he ultimately burst out in his shallow falsetto voice. "How could you so nakedly appropriate Olsen and Melville?"

In fact, when I wrote the Bulltoven poems five to seven years earlier, I had never read Olsen, nor Melville. The stymied sargasso sea and the raging, mast-wrecking gales both were metaphors for human sexuality. I had even quoted Freud at length in the epigraph, ending, "The *ship* too is a symbol of the female genital."

How blind are those who have been indoctrinated into alternative points of view.

The second case (one of many, at random) is equally ludicrous, though to me more touching.

It has often been my lot to have a twenty- to thirty-year lapse between writing a poem and getting it into print. Time spans are peculiarly collapsible. Many of the young cannot conceive that anything much happened before they were born—Columbus, maybe, George Washington.

One young editor mounted a full head of indignation at a group of poems I sent. "Aren't you ashamed to have so wantonly ripped off this poor young woman who had been hounded to death by a callow and uncaring husband?" he said.

Okay.

Okay, except those particular poems had been written when Sylvia Plath was still a schoolgirl in knickers. Plath's tragedy was a tragedy at many levels—Ted Hughes was a latecomer, but hardly blameless. His guilty conscience shows through doubly in every archival document he has chosen to destroy or suppress.

Where am I now? Do I dare try to define the place? I am back in government-subsidized public housing in Albuquerque. All my neighbors are "ethnics," as they say—Blacks, Chicanos, Asians. I love them all—but how do I cousin up to any of them? I have never told anyone I was an expat in Africa for four years, and I loved everyone—almost fifteen years ago. (My students were all Black Africans, though from five nations, from Nigeria to Tanzania, and including Rhodesia. Several of my colleagues were Asians. Most were Europeans, or Americans, including Black Americans. Styles of discourse, verbal and nonverbal, suffer sea-changes. And I am slow. I didn't have five words of Nienji [the lingua franca of Zambia] after four years. My daughter Anna Bush picked up street Swahili in Mozambique in one weekend, to the amazement of her friends. She is the linguist in the family.)

The big project of my "later years" has been a Memoir. This was something I had *thought* of doing from at least as early as being kicked out of the army at twenty-six. However, it was only in Africa, at age fifty-eight, that I literally took pen in hand and began with a more-or-less chronological narrative of "everything I could remember," *all* from memory—no documents, no research.

At this time I had read nothing meaningful. *The Autobiography of Alice B. Toklas,* Margaret Anderson's *My Thirty Years' War,* John Gould Fletcher's *Life Is My Song*—these were fine in my early twenties; they had no relevance to where I now was. Oh, yes, I had read Miller's "Tropics." But I was already aware that they were useful chiefly *only* in pointing the way not to go. (In fact, Miller changed course considerably, but not sufficiently, in *Rosy Crucifixion*.) I read Benvenuto Cellini's autobiography in Africa, which is eloquent braggadocio—nonetheless a towering human document.

Daughter Carole Crews (left) with friend Kimberly Colegrove, 1965

I finally read Frank Harris's *My Life and Loves*. It is far better than I had ever assumed it was. The man is substantially a fraud, but he had talent and was not altogether without a sense of humor. Additionally, he had a grudge against the vast residue of Victorian hypocrisy—and he was so déclassé by now he could risk some minor assaults upon the barricades. (Dreiser, in America, did it far better—though in "fiction.")

Ultimately, Simone de Beauvoir's *The Prime of Life* fell into my hands. I loved her instantly. Oh, I'd known some of her earlier work and associations. But this was where I lived. (Oh, goddamn, she is a dull writer—or her translator is a dull translator.) She said, "What I write of, I will write of honestly. If I cannot write of it honestly, then I will not write of it at all."

This is my own credo—except it is my commitment to write of *everything* within conscious memory, and to write of it honestly.

Then I read Augustine for the first time—a hundred pages, maybe. I found it the worst quagmire of shit I can imagine the human mind capable of being mired down in.

Through thick and thin for seven years, I hung in with this project. On the island of Malta, in Rome, London, JFK, and O'Hare. In Madrid, in early furious winter—ladies in thigh-high boots and miniskirts, the rest all fur and fluff. In San Juan, Puerto Rico, with three days of torrential rains—the sky *full* of black whales pissing, as Scott Greer would say. At San Juan Ranch near Muleje, in Baja California del Sur. For seven years—one, two, three, five, eight pages a day, maybe ten. For seven years. Even stranded in Taos, when I flipped on ice near Llano Quemado Hot Springs and broke two ribs near my spine and could not shit for two days, I kept writing. My daughter Carole came and fed me Midol for the pain.

Then, in June 1983, at age sixty-seven, I abandoned the domicile of a lady I was involved with, went to public housing in Albuquerque, quit drinking, and quit work on my Memoir. I've taken up the bottle again since, sparingly, but never took up the Memoir again except sporadically, a few times for a few days.

In 1981, after seven years of writing no poetry, and as if to spite the devil, I began to write poems again. Half of the first hundred I did were collected in *The Clock of Moss* for Ahsahta Press in 1983. I have done an additional thousand or more poems in the last seven years—but it seems no additional book publication is in the offing. There have been two or three pamphlets I appreciate very deeply—but this is not the same thing.

For Father's Day in 1984, my daughter Anna Bush sent me a state-of-the-art Pentax from Africa—with automatic mode, which I needed. I wanted to photograph "natural" nudes of all my writer and artist friends—none wanted to. I fell back on self-pictures, mannequins, and three-, five-, eight-minute collages. I had two shows with my friend Diana Huntress—then my camera was stolen, and that was the end of that.

L ast evening, June 29, 1990, a few hours shy of the early-morning daylight hour of my birth, seventy-three years ago, I attended a play at Rodey Theatre on the UNM campus. The play is by Michelle Miller, a very dear friend of more than a decade. The play's title is *The Vintage Erotica Reading Room.* It is about triumphant *losers.* Appropriately enough, my name appears in a line of dialogue near the end of the play—the denouement, as it is said.

Before the play began, as I was urgently rushing out to find the restroom, with the stage darkened but the audience lighted, a dark young man delayed me.

"I met you last evening, at the reading in Old Town. I have just talked with Amiri Baraka—he says you are *still* writing Mason Jordan Mason poems?"

"Am I still *beating* my wife, my ex-wife, I mean?" I expostulated with some steam.

Who is this imposter, *a Miri Baca?*

"Amiri Baraka," he said—LeRoi Jones.

Is this a ghost of forty years ago rising up to haunt me all over again?

But I was pressured to find a convenience, and I never saw this young man again. Though I would have been glad to invite him for a nip or two of cheap brandy after the show.

Mason Jordan Mason has been a kind of recurring nemesis for many years of my adult life. I am sure many would fault me if I evaded speaking of him here. But what is there to say? He was chiefly a phantom, a dervish. He was largely defined by "what others thought"—much of which was adroitly or *unadroitly* manufactured by me "to protect his identity," as I thought. But there is his poetry—however contaminated by my often intrusive editing.

I saw Mason (whom I now prefer to refer to as Thurlow Jackson, though this too was doubtlessly an alias) only about four times, in mid-1946. He was a charmer (though often crass), and I committed myself to work with his poetry. This business quickly soured—even so, I was strangely ensorcelled for several years.

With daughter Anna Bush Crews and grandson Sohrab Bohune Crews-Wilson, 1988

After three or four contacts in Waco, Texas, he "disappeared." He sent me "raw manuscripts" from many blind addresses for another five years. Like a zombie, I was largely under his control. I *worked* with a lot of his things—and many were published.

(In fact, I learned more from these exercises than I had ever known about poetry before. I later used this knowledge in working with material from Patrocinio Barela, Charley John Greaseybear, and the Lusaka Street Tapes. Whether I ever applied much of this knowledge to my own work is highly questionable, though William Carlos Williams was a binnacle, a center, a compass for much of this work—and for my own as well.)

In 1967 in El Paso, I received a telephone call from New York. The caller identified himself as Langston Hughes. He said if I wanted to know who Mason Jordan Mason was, I should go to Africa, and I would surely find out.

The way I am, it was seven years before I got there, to Lusaka in Zambia. In the mid-seventies, this was a cauldron of international intrigue—paramilitary forces of several small Black African nations and would-be nations everywhere. Infighting. Garotting with baling wire. Letter bombs (the editor of *New Poetry Zambia*, in which I was published, was killed by one of these). Car bombings.

My duties at the university (UNZA) were very confining and I hardly had other energies for anything else. Even so, my little Triumph Spitfire was firebombed, or something. And it was quickly known back at UNZA that I was a CIA operative. This was nonsense. But a year later I was forced out of Africa, not wanting to go. Almost a year later my friend Mike Sweeney disappeared, never to be heard of again—dead or alive. He was my build, younger and thinner. He wore a Western shirt of mine, and slender tobacco-colored Levis, and earthshoes, which I loathed.

Might Mason/Jackson be thought an assassin? Who could miss his target this widely? I don't know. In Africa, far stranger things occurred.

In Waco in 1946, Mason zonked me out on drugs—then he and/or a friend sodomized me. They blew town and I never saw him again. I undertook to castrate myself, this was my intent. I only barely one-third succeeded.

I have written in detail much of my memory of summer and fall 1946—perchance the most significant year of my life. This material is "free access" in Yale Archives, and at UNM Special Collections as well. Otherwise, in personal letters or elsewhere, I have never written of it—not even in poems.

What do I know? All I know is that the poetry of Mason, even at its worst, and the person Thurlow Jackson are two apparently distant integers. What I may have done with Mason's poems, or not have done, I am no longer cocksure. It is sure I did a lot. It is sure there was a lot there to work *with*—however hard.

As late as 1975, Joseph Collin Murphey commented that I was holding a certain chagrin against Mason's mid- and late-fifties successes that swamped my own. This was doubtless just. Did I then begin to suppress his work? Of this I am not sure. A third of his work had never been published—some of it his best. His work, at its worst, is compelling.

Personally he was essentially a haunting presence for a very long time. I, at least, was a believer.

BIBLIOGRAPHY

Poetry:

Psalms for a Late Season, Iconograph, 1942.

No Is the Night, privately printed, 1949.

A Poet's Breath, privately printed, 1950.

Come Curse to the Moon, privately printed, 1952.

The Anatomy of Proserpine, privately printed, 1955.

The Wrath Wrenched Splendor of Love, privately printed, 1956.

The Heart in Naked Hunger, Motive Book Shop, 1958.

The Ogres Who Were His Henchman, Hearse, 1958.

To Wed beneath the Sun, privately printed, 1958.

Inwade to Briney Garth, Este Es, 1960.

(Contributor) Fred Baver, compiler, *River*, River Spring, 1960.

The Feel of the Sun and Air upon Her Body, Hearse, 1960.

A Unicorn When Needs Be, Este Es, 1963.

Hermes Past the Hour, Este Es, 1963.

(Contributor) Louis Untermeyer, editor, *An Uninhibited Treasury of Erotic Poetry*, Dial, 1963.

Selected Poems, Renegade, 1964.

You, Mark Antony, Navigator upon the Nile, privately printed, 1964.

Angels Fall, They Are Towers, Este Es, 1965.

(With Wendell B. Anderson; under real name and under pseudonym Cerise Farallon) *Three on a Match*, privately printed, 1966.

The Stones of Konarak, American Poets, 1966.

(Contributor) A. W. Stevens, editor, *Poems Southwest*, Prescott College Press, 1968.

(Contributor) Robert L. Williams, compiler, *Mehy in His Carriage*, Summit, 1968.

(Contributor) Lawrence Ferlinghetti, editor, *City Lights Anthology*, City Lights, 1974.

(Contributor) Paul Foreman and Joanie Whitebird, editors, *Travois: An Anthology of Texas Poetry*, Thorp Springs, 1976.

Nations and Peoples, Cherry Valley, 1976.

Nolo Contendere, edited by J. Whitebird, preface by Robert Creeley, Wings, 1978.

Modern Onions and Sociology, St. Valentine's, 1978.

Roma a Fat At, Instantaneous Centipede, 1979.

Gluons, Q., Namaste, 1979.

(Editor) Charley John Greaseybear, *Songs*, Ahsahta, 1979.

The Noose, a Retrospective: Four Decades, edited by Larry Goodell and John Brandi, Duende, 1980.

If I., Wormwood Review Press, 1981.

The Clock of Moss, edited by Carol Bergé and Dale Boyer, Ahsahta, 1983.

Other:

The Southern Temper, Motive Book Shop, 1946.

(With W. B. Anderson and Mildred Crews) *Patrocinio Barela: Taos Woodcarver,* privately printed, 1955.

Contributor to numerous periodicals, including *Beloit Poetry Journal, Poetry Now, Puerto del Sol, Southwestern American Literature,* and *Wormwood Review.* Editor of several avante-garde magazines in the 1930s, '40s, and '50s, including *Deer and Dachshund, Flying Fish, Motive, Naked Ear, Poetry Taos, Suck-Egg Mule,* and *Vers Libre.*

Louis Dudek

1918-

I was lean and sickly as a child, a tall skinny boy, and a great deal probably follows from this. It made me introverted and hypersensitive from the start, too much concerned with my health— though perhaps with good cause—and too self-conscious for my own good. ("When a hypochondriac is sick," I later wrote, "he is twice as sick.")

"Show me another kid who is any way like you," said one of my cousins to me, sensing my difference from the rest.

"Your family was always superior," said another, many years later. "Always above everybody else."

We were all part of an extended family living in a connected group of houses in east-end Montreal, houses owned by my grandparents and uncles. (My superior family owned nothing, we rented a cold-water flat from Grandma at fifteen dollars a month.) The aunts and uncles very Polish, but mostly Liverpool-born and speaking fluent English from the first generation on. I was second-generation Canadian-born: Montreal, February 6, 1918.

There was Grandma, a large patriarchal mother-figure, and Grandpa, with handle-bar whiskers. A backyard which had a long-stemmed poplar tree going up three stories and then branching out, scattering catkins and caterpillars in spring and summer. There were seven sons and daughters, the uncles and aunts, all but one married and reproducing dozens of grandchildren, who were my sibling cousins. So I lived in a big crowd, though feeling often somewhat isolated and different.

Grandmother said within my hearing, when I was five or six, that I might as well be taken out of school since I would not live long. Adults should be very careful of what they say within the hearing of children: it can be remembered fifty or sixty years later and can still be resented. I have long outlived my grandmother, and I was quite fascinated by her powerful personality, but I never forgot that careless remark.

After all, it flawed my unthinking confidence in life from the very beginning. I was adult from my fifth year, so far as understanding the fact of human mortality is concerned.

Family photo: (from left) Louis, age seven, mother, Stasia Dudek, father, Vincent Dudek, sisters, Irene and Lilian, about 1925

My father was very good to me, though I seemed to see little of him, and yet he too made his slips of speech in my hearing. I was moody and faraway at times, while my two sisters were more alert and lively perhaps. Father would occasionally call me "stupid" when I wasn't quick enough to respond. Some parents do that.

The thought that I was somehow insufficiently quick, both physically and mentally, must have stayed with me, because I have never had much solid confidence in myself. Whatever I have done in later years was partly to prove to my father that I was not altogether a loss, not entirely a disappointment, though my father by then was a long time dead and would not have remembered what that was all about.

(Of course, Father would have been immensely surprised, and shocked, at any time, if he had known that an occasional word dropped, really a reprimand, had sunk so deep. So would Grandmother, who came from a Polish-Lithuanian culture where children frequently died young, and frail ones became predictable white coffins. It was hard common sense to say, "He won't survive." They meant no harm by it at all.)

In my twenties or thirties I invented a "personality test" that depends on childhood memories. Write down the three or four things you vividly remember from your tenth year or earlier (most people will remember no more than that), then interpret these incidents as symbolic memories.

I remember coming home from school in some fear, in my sixth year, having missed a word in an ongoing spelling-bee. (I had lost my first place and dropped somewhere to the bottom of the class.) One of my cousins, or one of my sisters, had run ahead to tell my mother the bad news. I could not face the coming reproaches, and hid under a bed to avoid facing my mother.

This memory indicates a fear of displeasing my mother (who is said to have had a great love for me, in any case, and whom I cannot remember ever punishing me in any way), and also the surprising fact that I stood first in spelling at an early age—but I have no impression of being in any way a superior student, at any time.

Some years later, graduating from Lansdowne School, I missed winning a four-year scholarship to attend high school by a matter of three marks or so. The failure stayed with me throughout my high school and college career, both of which were costly and which we could hardly afford, and it was only much later that it occurred to me, when I sized up the past, that after all I had led the entire school neck and neck with another boy, and came very close to winning! No, actually I had failed.

Another early memory. I cried out loud at closing time on seeing an aeroplane through the school window (they were not common in those days, circa 1925). The teacher kept me in as a punishment, and then I remember walking sadly across the schoolyard, looking up at the sky for the vanished aeroplane.

The symbolism of this memory is a small ecstasy and an irrecoverable loss. It is only in terms of poetry that this event can properly be understood. But it is a central experience.

My mother died, at the mere age of thirty-one, when I was eight years old. My third vivid memory

has to do with the time of her death. I am standing in the corridor of my grandmother's house, before the closed door at the end of it, when an overwhelming realization comes over me that I will never again see my mother. Upon this thought I dissolve in tears. And then, on a sudden I realize, with a kind of thrill, that I am now completely and inescapably free. I block out this thought, but I cannot deny it had passed my mind. In fact I remember it now. To this day I believe I am different from others because of that dearly bought freedom at an early age.

Much later, reading *Sons and Lovers*, I realized how strong my mother's love must have been and how great a hold she had over me. I would have been another Paul Morel. The loss, as well as the sudden liberation, are contained in the symbolic memory. It tells me again and again that I am motherless and free, though I am forever deprived by her death.

In my twenties I looked back over those years and thought I had had the most unhappy childhood imaginable. The loss of my mother was not the only cause. I was always being taken to hospital, or "to see Dr. Ship," to find out whether I was about to die from tuberculosis, whether I would at last undergo that dreaded operation for tonsillitis or for nasal polyps, or some other defect that would either finish me or set me right. At the ripe age of eighteen, when my father managed to get some money together to send me into first-year Arts at McGill, he insisted that I first undergo surgery for adenoids, although by that time I actually had nothing bothering me, and I did have the operation done—like a necessary castration or initiation rite—after which my real life could begin.

After my mother's death, my father brought a maiden sister from Poland to take care of his three children. She was a frail, sensitive, literate person, who told hair-raising stories—some from Pushkin, I later discovered—and could recite many Polish poems from memory that were deeply moving. Her only punishment for me was to make me memorize poems, which was actually a kind of reward I thought, and through her I came to like Slowacki and Mickiewicz, Polish Romantics, before I ever knew Byron, Keats, or Shelley.

In school, in those days (in the late twenties), we sang songs from the English, Scottish, and Irish tradition: "Annie Laurie," "John Peel," "The Minstrel Boy," "Comin' thru the Rye." The words were beautiful and the melodies delightful: a singing teacher visited the schools of the Protestant School Board and intoned the songs in his rich baritone voice, without accompaniment. That's how we learned all the songs of the traditional repertoire, songs of which most students today are utterly ignorant.

I say the Protestant School Board, though I and my two sisters were Roman Catholics. We were actually "illegals" in the Protestant system at that time, just as recently there have been many "illegals" in the English-language school system in Montreal, students whom the law wants to propel into the French school system. Quebec to this day is a narrow and bigoted society which wreaks irreparable psychological damage on little children without being half aware of the harm done. My sisters and I lived in fear and insecurity throughout our childhood, dreading to be "found out" and removed from the school we loved and wanted to be in. We even went to the United Church occasionally and attended Protestant "Sunday School" in order to certify our good standing. But of course we were practicing Catholics in our own community.

In my mind I carry lifetime scars of these early terrors and insecurities. Like Joseph Conrad, I am a lifelong admirer of English civilization, and later, in my poetry, I call England "the best corner of Europe," despite my wasteland vision of modernity. Even in the long poem *Europe*, written in my early thirties, I say that "Courtesy is pleasing . . . And what more pleasant than well-bred English people?" And yet this affection for things English, and for the literature of England, is tempered with a kind of alienation, a feeling that what I most love and admire I really have no proper right to. I am an interloper even where I am most at home.

I should add that, despite my troubles in childhood, I was also something of a pampered darling, as a reputedly ailing orphan, favoured by my aunts occasionally with a slice of rich lemon pie or homemade raisin tarts, and the effect of this preferment has also left its mark. I may take pleasure in "being made much of," even as I suffer from outward signs of neglect.

In the High School of Montreal, for the study of poetry, I had a battered purple-covered book entitled *Poems of the Romantic Revival*. Here I first discovered the great poems of Keats, Byron, Wordsworth, Tennyson, and Browning. Unlike the present time, when students are offered mediocre poems by doubtful poets "whom they can understand," we were given the great poets without any question of watering them down for young minds. Read "The Eve of St. Agnes," we were told, and be ready for the examination. Look up the words. Study the notes.

I also studied Latin and loved it, translating Horace for my beloved teacher and reading her my

translations. (Not Greek, I picked that up later on my own.) But the meaning of great poetry, its timeless beauty, is the same in all ages and in all languages, with the proviso that you have to find your own touchstones, the passages that draw you out, evoke your own nature, and *send you*—"out of this world," as they say 'nowadays. For me it was the ending of Shelley's "To a Skylark," as simple as the Sermon on the Mount, and as pure and perfect as undoctored natural speech can be:

> Better than all measures
> Of delightful sound,
> Better than all treasures
> That in books are found,
> Thy skill to poet were, thou scorner of the ground!
>
> Teach me half the gladness
> That thy brain must know;
> Such harmonious madness
> From my lips would flow,
> The world should listen then, as I am listening now.

To this day, nearly sixty years later, I can remember the exact position on the page—top left side—where these lines occur. They are there for me still, and they have shaped my life and my emotions forever after.

So, too, are the triumphant closing lines of Horace's Fifth Ode in Book Three about the Roman general Regulus, who being defeated and captured by the Carthagenians was returned to Rome on condition that he plead for peace. But he urged war instead, for the future safety of Rome, and then he returned as hostage to the Carthagenians to be tortured to death, knowing what his fate would be. He returned, says Horace, "as unconcernedly / As if they were his clients and he'd settled / Some lengthy lawsuit for them and was going / On to Venafrium's fields / Or to Tarentum, Sparta's colony"—

> *tendens Venafranos in agros*
> *aut Lacedaemonium Tarentum.*

I came to this a little later. In high school we studied the usual Horatian odes: "Integer Vitae," "Exegi Monumentum," "Eheu Fugaces," "O Fons Bandusiae," "Diffugere Nives." (I think those were some of the poems.) Also some Virgil. But speaking of touchstones, let me give you Homer, from the *Odyssey*, Book II, just two lines that for me came to define poetry:

> To them grey-eyed Athene sent a favourable breeze,
> the fresh West Wind, singing over the wine-dark
> sea . . .
>
> *Tóisin d' íkmenon oúron híei glaukópis Athéne*
> *akraé Zéphuron, keládont epì oínopa pónton.*

The first requirement for a student of poetry is to learn the Greek alphabet and to begin decoding phrases like these. *"Glaukópis Athéne"* and *"oínopa pónton"* are standard phrases; but why does the whole thing sound so incredibly beautiful to me?

Not to appear arrogant, I will mention an anecdote. A good deal later, while giving a public lecture in Montreal, I hazarded an off-the-cuff translation of a Latin phrase from Ovid for the benefit of the audience—*si pulvis nullus erit / nullum tamen excute* ("even if there should be not a speck of dust, brush it off," I think that's about the equivalent)— but I mistranslated it somehow, I forget how, and my old Latin teacher, who was in the audience, came up afterward and corrected me, gently, as usual. Well, we never cease to learn from our teachers.

On the subject of *élitism*, since we are touching on it, I say—let's not insult democracy. Democracy was not achieved to make us all mediocre, but to make us free and superior, each in his own way. Élitism is a good thing, and highly democratic, if rightly used, on behalf of the majority.

My father was a hardworking man, at one time a fireman, later driving a truck for a brewery in Montreal, for a time running a hotel and tavern in Hamilton, and in his final years managing a court of roadside cottages in Orilia, Ontario. He was a literate and refined person by nature, but perforce struggling as an immigrant in a new country.

Money pressures at home nearly made me drop out of high school before finishing, but advice from a YMCA counsellor sent me back to school and I completed the course—Grade Thirteen, at that time equivalent to first-year college. I then went to work in a warehouse, on St. Helen Street, in the old part of Montreal, an area of brick, dust, and grime, devoted to tightfisted business operations.

I rubbed shoulders with working people, who were the sort of people I liked best—deliverymen, truckers, salesmen, and typists crowded in busy offices. Some years later I wrote the poem "Old City Sector," whose opening lines well describe my impression of this part of old Montreal:

> This gut-end of a hungry city
> costive with rock and curling ornament,
> once glorious, the pride of bankers,
> reaches each projecting cornice
> over the stomach of empty air, the street
> now deserted.
>
> Here every morning, an old rich idiot
> in a worn, shining suit stumbles,
> ignoring the soft sun, and the imaginary note
> of the chanticleer somewhere singing—

Author, about 1938

> taps his stick on the green-gold morning door,
> then turns the lock with a big key, opens and enters;
> he boards the ugly small safe in the corner
> and on his knees, peels out the dusty dollars—
> the sun on his desk shaking, a pool dripping with
>   mermaids.

My view of work and workingmen is contained in the poem "Building a Skyscraper" written some ten years later, in which I say that someday "They will be celebrated / more than millionaires, since without rich men / nations can run as well, or better, but not without these men." It is not a passing opinion but a permanent belief, of the right order of values. The opening verse of the poem describes men at work:

> By the street's noise muffled, the hammers
> sock silently; a mittened hand
> plucks concrete pieces from the ground,
> throws them with a curse without a sound,
> as automatic these men
> building a skyscraper in the precincts of Wall street
> work without being heard, without headlines, with
>   only
> a truckful of sand making rapids of applause.

At the time, however, work in a warehouse was a dead end, and yet I did not see any hope of ever getting out of it. Then suddenly my father was able to send me to college, I think by persuading his wife, since he had re-married, to help finance my education; and I registered as a sophomore at McGill University.

This was in 1936, three years before World War II, but Hitler was already threatening in Europe and there was civil war in Spain. For me a new life began in the university, a life without parental supervision, a life of freedom and exploration.

I wrote for the campus newspaper, the *McGill Daily*. Saw my editorial articles reprinted in other college papers across Canada. Played chess in the Student Union to my heart's content. Fell in love. Discussed philosophy and social problems with new-found friends, Reg Harris my philosophical cohort, Guy Royer my best friend, a French Canadian from high school, Norman Hillyer a United Church theology student, then a keen socialist who later became a Reverend. (We had great lunches at the Presbyterian College on University Street, bringing our own sandwiches to lunch and sharing tea in common, arguing at the top of our bent.)

My friend Margaret, who thought me "a genius," brought a book of poems by C. Day Lewis to my attention, a book out of the library, but I was slow in picking up the scent. I had been scribbling poems from high-school days. I wrote my first around the age of twelve or thirteen, but these were miserable childish verses. Our parish priest, Father Bernard, encouraged my sister Lilian in poetry, and brought her secondhand books as gifts, *The Complete Poems of Sir Walter Scott*, *The Poems of Thomas Campbell*, *Thomas Moore*, and other nineteenth-century Romantics. I neglected and disparaged these musty tomes.

In the Carnegie Reading Room, subsidized by the Carnegie Foundation, which was a modest room in the Arts building (exactly where the English department offices are now located), I discovered a small anthology of contemporary Italian poetry and in it a poem of about eighty lines, in three sections, which I copied out and soon knew almost by heart. It was by a turn-of-the-century poet named Ceccardo Roccatagliata Ceccardi.

> *Quando ci revedremo*
> *il tempo avrà nevicato*
> *sul nostro capo, o amore . . .*
>
> (When we meet again
> time will have snowed
> upon our heads, my love . . .)

I admired especially the third section, which began—

> *Tu eri piccola e bruna*
> *ricordi? E amavi uno scialle*
> *dai fiocchi lunghi, d'argento*
> *cingere a l'esil corsetto . . .*
>
> (You were small and brown
> Remember? And loved to wear a shawl
> with long tassels of silver
> clinging to your slender bodice . . .)

Ceccardo Ceccardi is missing from most later Italian anthologies. But I carried him around in my head; and some forty years later wrote a poem, "First Love," which echoed his exact phrases:

> You wore a blue coat and white scarf, remember?
> And we walked in the dim night-time, talking.
>
> What does love matter, or all that since has happened?
> What happened is an eternal possession. . . .
>
> (from *Zembla's Rocks*)

A poet may seem to have vanished into oblivion; and yet somewhere, perhaps in a far foreign country, someone may have read his poem, and have lived with it through the years. This is what is called futurity, even if it be in only one reader's memory—immortality, to be reborn in another poet's lines.

Leaving McGill University with a B.A. degree in '39 I had already read Nietzsche, and Ibsen. ("The password is Anarchy" says a poem in the *McGill Daily* in 1951, and I am delighted today, in looking up Ceccardo Ceccardi, that he called himself "an aristocratic anarchist"—though I was neither an anarchist, nor a Marxist, nor even a socialist in any true sense. I argued against the "Reverend" Norman Hillyer, my dear friend, and he called me "a Tolstoyan liberal," whatever that may have meant at the time.) I also carried Walt Whitman into the fields at Charlemagne (some fifteen miles outside of Montreal) and read him aloud to myself, and probably conversed with him in my hallucinations.

At this time (1942) I met with a group of literati and joined in a literary movement of sorts. Canada just then was still doing its spring cleaning of Victorian dust and cobwebs, in the renovation that is called modernism, although our modernism had started a dozen years after the European and American schools of London and Paris, and this was the second wave of "modern poetry in Canada." The Canadian poets A. J. M. Smith, F. R. Scott, A. M. Klein, W. W. E. Ross, Raymond Knister, Dorothy Livesay, and R. G. Everson had started the cleanup in a gentle, quiet way around 1925, writing free verse, appearing in *Poetry* (Chicago) and in other small magazines, writing some vigorous articles, and forecasting the changes to come. Their poetry, however, was less vigorous than their prose. The second wave of poets which I now joined were just beginning, combining their forces with the older boys, to make a more raucous, exciting noise.

The simple idea that modernism was primarily a housecleaning, a sweep-out of sentimental propriety and moral hypocrisy, is now hard to recapture; we have so many complex theories about modernism and postmodernism. But the root problem and the liberation, which the modern revolt brought with it, were then so obvious that the idea could be taken up by flappers and gigolos. "Homme, sois moderne!" was inscribed over a café entrance in Montmartre; and Richard Aldington in his poem "The Eaten Heart" said what everyone in that generation knew:

> We were right, yes, we were right
> To smash the false idealities of the last age,
> The humbug, the soft cruelty, the mawkishness,
> The heavy tyrannical sentimentality,
> The inability to face facts, especially new facts. . . .

In Canada there were already free-verse proponents in 1914. But the main lines of developing modernism can be seen as branchings from the chief modern British and American poets, in a clear order of succession. F. R. Scott and A. J. M. Smith, from 1925 on, are most easily associated with Yeats and Eliot, actually the most traditional and conservative of the moderns. The group with which I became connected, consisting of Irving Layton, John Sutherland (editor of *First Statement* magazine, then of *Northern Review*), Miriam Waddington, Raymond Souster, have a kinship to poets like Whitman, Masters, Sandburg, Kenneth Fearing, or Robinson Jeffers. A much later generation, represented by Ken Norris in the 1980s, shows a passionate devotion, in practice and principle, to William Carlos Williams. (Earlier on, Raymond Souster was also a Williams admirer.) The sequence is fairly simple, with other affinities intervening—to Edith Sitwell in James Reaney; or to Dylan Thomas, in Al Purdy and Alden Nowlan; or to popular ballad and lyric in Leonard Cohen—but it shows a progression, if a bit halting, from tepid modernism to extreme avant-gardism, such as we find in the late poetry of bp Nichol and others, analogous to the experimentalism of Gertrude Stein or André Breton.

For myself, I did not want to take a regressive stance, in which loud vulgarity and forced rhetoric

replace the old sentimentality, although there are poems from the 1940s or early 1950s that might illustrate the road not taken. My particular affinity did not appear until the mid-1940s, and then the magnetic pull was to Ezra Pound, the most complex and difficult of modern poets. What drew me to Pound was his aestheticism and his revolutionary modernism in principle.

There is no creativity possible to man that is not the result of an impress from some preceding work or creation. The infinite potentiality of nature cannot appear in its purity, as something made out of nothing. It can only work upon what is there, since everything in this creation emerges from something that is already there, as a variation or progression in things. An artist, therefore, cannot produce an original work of art in the sense that it resembles nothing known before, that it derives from a different world, from a distant planet, or even from a remote culture which he has not experienced.

My contacts with other poetry, with other literature, with music, with paintings, with powerful ideas, are the only source from which I can develop original poetry, forms of art, or ideas of my own. The vest-pocket copy of *Hamlet* which I carried about everywhere in my college years is one such source; so is the poetry of Whitman, which I recited in my country walks. And there are numerous smaller kinds of "imprinting," from several poets and particular poems—Keats, Wordsworth, Bryant, Spenser, Milton—that have left their mark. Keats's "Grecian Urn," "To a Nightingale," "Splendid Star," and "To Autumn," are such poems. Wordsworth's "Prelude"; William Cullen Bryant's "To a Waterfowl"; Spenser's "Epithalamion"; Milton's "Lycidas" (studied in high school, with "L'Allegro" and "Il Penseroso") are such early poems. Experiences like these evoke from our nature lines of feeling and shaping that we can then make our own: they awaken this or that which is real and specific, from an infinite inconceivable possibility, and what they awaken in us is the only possible branch of progression for the future.

Music had a powerful appeal for me. While still at college I borrowed from the library complete scores of the famous operas and played on the piano the parts which most moved me. The prologue to *I Pagliacci* was one such piece, especially the melody part beginning "Un nido di memorie . . ." (I swooned in ecstasy over such music; come to think of it, my knowledge of Italian, which made me capable of reading Italian poetry, came from these operas.) *Madame Butterfly*, with its wondrous first act, and the great moments in *La Bohème* were made entirely my own, on the piano, in this way. I thought of Puccini's music as "smoke rolling along the ground," with wonderfully imaginative music, and I resented later, and laughed off, Pound's line about "Puccini the all-too-human."

There was Dean Clarke of the Faculty of Music, in those days, conductor of the Montreal Symphony Orchestra, who gave open lectures to interested students in a small, overcrowded room every Friday before the Sunday afternoon symphony concert at Her Majesty's Theatre on Guy Street just above St. Catherine. I could not afford the concerts, but I got a job as unpaid usher and so was able to hear each concert after Dean Clarke's lecture. This was a musical analysis of the themes and development of the main item on the program. I remember especially the lecture on and performance of Brahms's Second Piano Concerto, of which the opening notes still echo in my ears as I pause for a moment in this writing. "Brahms," said Dean Clarke, "was a passionate Romantic at heart, but he held back his emotions— until they broke through in certain passages of his music." There are some things said that one remembers fifty or more years later, whether good or bad, because they are the shaping influences of our lives.

At home we played all kinds of current popular music on the piano, as well as traditional songs. I loved Irving Berlin, and later came to love Cole Porter more than any other current composer. I was a great admirer of Al Jolson. And the singing of Grace Moore, on the screen. A bit later, in my New York years, I discovered the music of Bach, "The Well-tempered Clavier," in the music room at Columbia, where records could be played and music taken out. I played on an upright piano in our rented one-room apartment on 123rd Street, corner of Amsterdam, fingering the music as well as I could, though I'd never had music lessons. Later, I became an enthusiast and collector of the popular songs of the nineties, the songs of Harry Von Tilzer, Paul Dresser, George M. Cohan, and James Thornton. And there was British Music Hall, a great source of social history and fun. And above all, ancient songs from France, beginning with the troubadours, whom I made out on the piano, and going on to the sixteenth and seventeenth centuries, also the melodious songs of French Canada. And finally, English folk songs, in the collections of Ralph Vaughn Williams, songs like "The Banks of Sweet Primroses," "As Sylvie Was Walking," "The Blacksmith," "The Golden Vanity," "The Green Bed," "The Lover's Ghost," "High Germany," and many others. I have, in other words, a strain of the popular and of the traditional life of the people in my poetry, a very powerful strain of

great beauty and universal feeling, but it may be that the people themselves are today cut off from this experience, so that this is not recognized in my poetry.

A visiting lecturer at McGill, many years later, speaking on Theodore Dreiser, remarked about Dreiser's brother Paul, who wrote songs under the name of Paul Dresser, that he was the composer of trivial and unimportant songs at the turn of the century. Sitting in the audience as a faculty member, I could not interrupt the speaker, though I was deeply incensed, for I admired the songs of Paul Dresser with a special kind of joy and nostalgia. Are they collected anywhere? Probably not. And yet, among the stories of Theodore Dreiser, you will find a long short-story—actually a memoir—entitled "My Brother Paul." It gives an excellent account of the music business and of the stirring life of the entertainment world of New York at that time. Paul Dresser's songs were a good part of it, immensely popular, and they are still moving and beautiful, with their gentle and sentimental touch of pathos and melodrama.

At home in our Polish family, or later with my in-laws and relatives after my marriage, there was a custom at Christmastime and on other holidays, when the men and women got a little tipsy, to do some old-fashioned group singing at table. The great songs of the Ukraine, of Lithuania, of Russia, and of Poland would be sounded in chorus, and repeated to one's heart's content, while glasses klinked and drinks were poured out. Some singers of talent, my mother-in-law in particular, sang in harmony with the leading melody, a technique of part-singing which they had learned in the folk villages of Lithuania. This music, too, is part of my inheritance, though there is no way perhaps to recognize its plangent melodies and vigorous rhythms in my poetry. Somewhere it must be there, since nothing is lost that moves us deeply and is part of our continuing memory.

Beauty is international. And the enduring works of art, whether we find them in ancient Egypt, China or Japan, India or Africa, are all recognizable to us because they have a common element, which must be a quality of humanity, called grace or beauty. All these songs of many nations, and the many kinds of music, are part of one essence which is intrinsic to human nature, and which goes by the name of beauty. That is the best word we have for it, though all it means is that we respond deeply with all our being to its surface resonance.

I had shown some poems to Dr. Harold Files, a very fine teacher at McGill, and he had advised me to look up John Sutherland, who was then editing the first numbers of a mimeo magazine, *First Statement.*

At the same time, Irving Layton, whom I knew from his poems in the *McGill Daily* and whom I had met the previous winter, came by chance to know John Sutherland's sister, Betty Sutherland, a young painter who was working briefly as a cashier in the restaurant where he ate his meals. The result was a union of forces in the magazine *First Statement* between a very strong and authoritative critic, John Sutherland, and a very bold and energetic politically-conscious poet— Irving Layton at that time—and a very unassertive lyrical poet, that is to say myself.

I was six years younger than Layton, and in one's early twenties six years counts for a good deal. He was the dominant figure, but I was not inclined to be dominated, so that our conversations for many years took the form of extremely heated arguments. Betty Sutherland, who was a fine realistic painter (her substantial work, alas, is still waiting to be deposited in a permanent collection), used to say: "You two are such different poets, why don't you just let each other be? Why do you have to fight it out over every single point?" (How right she was, yet how impossible to escape this strife of temperament built into our nature.)

The result is that relations between us eventually ceased, in the mid-fifties, which was about a dozen years after we first met. But much water had poured under the bridge (the Jacques Cartier Bridge, where we first parleyed and resolved together to change the shape of Canadian poetry), before that final separation took place.

At the time Layton, Sutherland, and I got together, there were several other young writers working with us: Audrey Aikman, one of the founders of *First Statement*, who soon married John Sutherland (Layton in his turn married Betty Sutherland), Miriam Waddington, who was then wedded to a writer, Patrick Waddington, and Raymond Souster, the poet, living in Toronto, who visited us when he could and with whom we corresponded frequently. Also a number of other interesting young people who have since published poems and books of poetry. We were by then graduated from the university, most of us, or just hanging around its environs like John Sutherland—I was working as a copywriter in Montreal advertising agencies and hating it. So we were able to spend our money and free time debating in local cafés and restaurants and producing magazines and books for the unreading public. Our little magazine, *First Statement,* was in competition—at least we thought so—with a rival mimeo magazine, *Preview,* edited by a brilliant Marxist poet from Oxford, Patrick Anderson, and publishing such senior poets in Canada as F. R. Scott, already a noted jurist-profes-

sor, and A. M. Klein, Montreal's foremost poet in the Jewish community (he was then editor of the *Canadian Jewish Chronicle* as well as a practicing lawyer in the city). Attached to *Preview* were also the poet P. K. Page and the soon-to-be psychiatrist and M.D., Bruce Ruddick, a very forceful writer at the time.

The joint operations of these two magazines, *Preview* and *First Statement,* constitute the second wave of effective modernism in the country, the first being the work of A. J. M. Smith, F. R. Scott, and A. M. Klein in the mid-1920s and after. The first phase is represented by the collection *New Provinces* in 1936, the second by John Sutherland's anthology *Other Canadians* (1947), or more intensively by the three-man book *Cerberus* (1952), by Layton, Souster, and myself.

There is often a short pause between the first phase and the second phase of a significant artistic change, as if "that first fine careless rapture" required the mind or spirit to catch its breath before a second, and stronger, heave could begin. This was true of the modernism of Eliot and Pound, after the *Waste Land,* and it was certainly true of the modern development in Canada. Not only was there a pause after Scott and Smith's first start in the 1920s and early thirties, but there was a pause after the mid-forties which was followed by a new burst of energy after 1951. Collective enthusiasms—that is, creative acts—may come in spurts, for all we know, and this may apply to revolutionary movements as well as literary ones.

During the forties activity I was still in my early twenties, first getting out of college, then working haphazardly in the advertising agencies, scraping a living first as a free-lancer, then as a permanent employee. I married in 1944 and with my wife Stephanie moved to New York, for further study and a taste of bohemian life. My health unfitted me for enlistment in the war, so that I was able to leave Canada and register at Columbia University in New York. Up to that time I had not quite found my direction or voice as a poet, but now things began to take a turn.

I had of course published. Ryerson Press in Toronto had brought out the book *Unit of Five,* in which I was one of the five young poets included. After this, while I was living in New York, the same Canadian firm brought out my first separate book, *East of the City.* However, no book of mine appeared from First Statement Press, where other poets were being published who were my boon companions. I was perhaps already running my own race—a condition which became more marked as time went on.

"Preparing souvlaki on the beach with Stephanie, probably at Cape Cod," about 1945

I eventually entered the Ph.D. course at Columbia and graduated with a doctorate in English and Comparative Literature; but I was ill-prepared for this work, and at the beginning had no such serious intentions. I had no honours training in literature, which would have given me concentrated undergraduate study in the subject. In fact I had wandered all over the lot in the general course at McGill, with courses in political science, psychology, and philosophy, as well as English and French literature, since my notion of education, so far as I had any, was that of self-fulfillment in the broadest sense. I had no practical purposes, beyond poetry and seeing into life as far as possible. Why was I born? In order to know, Socrates had taught me.

As a result, when it came to graduate study for the Ph.D., I had a hard time of it, even though I was an older student than most (almost thirty). I learned by intensive reading what I should have packed away back home in my fresh youth, and this probably showed even later in my orals, where I was still a learner—and mainly a poet, not a concentrated scholar like the rest.

However, I did catch up, to a certain extent. I started at Columbia with courses in article writing, poetry, and even journalism, since I was still an advertising writer and a journalist by trade. But I also took a course in medieval history; and this was so immensely exciting an experience for me that I decided to go solidly into history, and in 1946 I received a master's degree in that field. The subject which I pitched on in history, and which I continued

in the department of English and Comparative Literature, was the history of the profession of letters, a question which interests me to this day and which provides the leading theme for the present autobiographical essay.

Being concerned with poetry, and with the importance of poetry in the past, it has struck me from the beginning of my career that in our time poetry, and in fact any writing with a view to permanence, which is what the arts must have as a first condition of their greater value, does not find a place in the existing culture. While billions of words are being poured out in printed form, in newspapers, magazines, and popular books, little or nothing of this has any lasting value. By definition, then, we are already in, or are entering into, a dark age. Looking over time, periods that have left no permanent record, or little of worth, are negligible; while great civilizations and celebrated moments in history are those which leave durable works of value. I wanted to know the history of this question—the reason why modern culture seems to prefer the journalistic and the ephemeral to the genuine and the durable, in the arts.

Of course, all the arts, in all historical times, are dependent on power and money for their existence. The king or overlord must command architectures and sculptures; the patron must reward the artist; book buyers and readers must provide a livelihood to authors. There is no escape from the real conditions of work and survival, even if your work is some makeshift job like being a librarian or a schoolteacher. But the great periods of art must have a moral quality in the life that supports craftsmen: there must be some integrity in the rulers, or seriousness in their beliefs, that helps to make their works durable; there must be a developed taste and love of art in great patrons; and there must be discrimination and intelligence among readers and buyers of books if there is to be any culture worth the name. (In fact, most people in the present condition of entertainment culture spend their days trying to "fake sincerity" in one way or another, though sincerity is absolutely unfakable by nature—and consumers accept this state of affairs without protest, because they have been made incapable of choice.)

The results of my studies over many years led to the book *Literature and the Press,* based on my doctoral dissertation, and finally published in 1960. I argued that the mechanization of the modern printing press is a much-neglected part of the Industrial Revolution, and that its consequences are seen in the present world of commercial publishing and journalism. That literature has in effect been forced out

At the Acropolis of Athens, 1953

from our society, by the mass production of commercial printed matter and by the stimulation of a taste for such "junk food" as the standard mental fare.

In doing this kind of book, I had little regard for the usual academic requirements that a dissertation be well-focused, on a narrowly defined subject, and that it contribute to so-called scholarly knowledge. I wanted to deal with a huge subject, whose findings were everywhere to be seen, like the ruins of Ozymandias, and whose history embraced everything written and published from classical times to the present. Naturally, I had great difficulty pushing this through, and perhaps I never succeeded in doing it to everyone's satisfaction; but Emery Neff at Columbia was a great supporter, and Lorne Pierce at Ryerson Press was eventually willing to participate in the publication, so the book stands on the shelf as a monument to my passion and fierce devotion to the idea of art.

The most fascinating part of the curriculum at Columbia was a high-powered seminar with Lionel Trilling and Jacques Barzun; but extracurricu-

lar activities were even more engrossing. I met the burgeoning novelist Herbert Gold, as well as the psychologist Zygmunt Piotrowski, as personal friends. With Herb Gold I played some handball in nearby courts and aped the style of James Joyce on the typewriter. But I was a slow poet beside these flashing lights and never made much impression on them.

I wrote to Ezra Pound, who was then incarcerated in an asylum in Washington, D.C., having broadcast to American troops during the war in Italy—all about Usura, the Unwobbling Pivot of Confucius, and the writings of John Adams—so that he was accused of treason, but finally considered *non compos mentis,* unfit for trial. (Oh yes, there was anti-Semitism in these broadcasts, but I didn't find out the extent of that until much later. And yes, he was arguing that America was fighting a futile war. All of which may be very foolish, and mistaken—but is it treason? The case has never been proved.) Pound wrote back, and a kind of correspondence followed which led to my higher education in the reality of modern poetry. (This correspondence, Pound's side of it, was later published in the book *Dk: Some Letters of Ezra Pound.*[1]

Through Pound I came to meet several writers and artists in New York and vicinity (he sent me addresses and telephone numbers which I sometimes followed up—please note that I was up to my ears in graduate work, and from 1947 on I was also teaching English at the City College of New York). I came to know Paul Blackburn the poet, as a friend; and Michael Lekakis the sculptor, whom I valued highly; and Cid Corman, the editor of *Origin,* as well as several other camp followers of Ezra Pound, some not so savory as others. Frankly, I never could understand why I should go chasing after some disciple or other of Ezra's to add a cubit to my stature, so I did not follow up all his recommendations. There was Marianne Moore whom he wanted me to visit with a parcel, but much as I admired MM I used the post instead. And of course William Carlos Williams, whose address I knew offhand—and occasionally exchanged a note with—but I never bothered to visit him. Also E. E. Cummings, whom I did not meet until he came to Montreal for a reading and I introduced him to the audience. I had a distrust of such personal contacts, since the real life is the life of the mind, and there we meet daily with our kind and carry on our conversations.

[1]DC Books, 4238 De Bullion St., Montreal, Canada H2W 2E7.

It was about this time that I translated the famous lines of Catullus *"Vivamus mea Lesbia atque amemus."* Later I checked against the best existing translations in English (there is a collection of them) and concluded with youthful exuberance that mine was in fact the best. Such are the illusions of youth— and yet, who knows, perhaps I was right. In any case, I offer it here as evidence of my progress in New York:

> Let us live, my Lesbia, let us love!
> And all the mutterings of crabbed old men
> weigh as dust, against this one reflection:
> Suns can set, and they can return,
> but we, once our short light has ended,
> one long perpetual night must sleep.

What Pound opened up for me was a great curiosity about contemporary poetry—and its engagement with the cause of civilization. I got out of New York in 1951; my marriage had broken up and went on limping for a while, but eventually it died completely, and I returned to Montreal to teach at McGill University. (I have a son from my first

"Fishing in the Laurentians with primitive equipment," about 1958

marriage, Gregory, who is now a computer scientist in that fine institution.) The return to Montreal began a new productive stage in my career. I was now in my thirty-third year of life and ready to work on poetry and teaching in earnest.

I came to McGill with a mission. It may be that the worst teachers, as well as the best, are teachers with a mission, but I came with the confidence that I had something very important to teach. There were in fact two things. The first was modern poetry and literature, which had evolved fully abroad but which had barely started in Canada with small groups of poets having a limited audience. The message of modernism was to be spread abroad, through students, lectures, and magazines. It was also to be directed at poetry in Canada, at new promising writers; and outlets had to be created for these new voices. Then the second program was the massive movement of European literature and thought since the eighteenth century, with its profound practical implications, which students' minds had still to experience, like buckets of cold water thrown at them from a high lectern.

It was a few years before I was able to teach everything I wanted to teach. But sudden changes in the department made this possible, and as one student (Ruth Wisse, now a prominent teacher herself) said a few years later, "You happen to be teaching all the most interesting courses in the department." I received enthusiastic support from students very often, as many teachers do in their best years, so that it is not entirely vain to record this one remark. Classes grew from twenty or thirty to nearly five hundred in those years before the student revolution, and I was extremely busy trying to keep up with my vast area of teaching.

The subject of my European literature survey was divided into a two-year course (four terms) which many students took in successive years: the period from eighteenth-century rationalism and enlightenment to romanticism and realism; and the period from naturalism to modernism. My six radio lectures, published under the title *The First Person in Literature*, give a fair outline of some of the leading ideas. Also, Emery Neff's *Revolution in European Poetry* provides a good view of the background for the first part; while a recent book like Allan Bloom's *Closing of the American Mind* deals with many of the central books and ideas that formed part of the entire two-year course. In fact, the substance of literature and thought to which American students are now said to be closed was precisely the subject matter which it was my mission at that time to open them.

This huge course—a study, really, of the subversive currents in modern thought—was virtually brought to an end by the student revolution in the early sixties. "What I have been teaching you, and warning you against," I said to my students, "has now arrived, right here in the classroom"—as radical students began to raid the lecture halls and harangue teachers. The course in question was familiarly known as "Journey to the End of the Night," after Céline's novel, which terminated the two-year course—and the night, it seemed, had closed in upon us.

The courses in modern poetry and in Canadian poetry were another thing (there was also one on "The Art of Poetry," a writing course). These were more detailed and analytical, not so far-ranging, although nothing could be more soul-searching and relevant to modern life than the course in poetry from Walt Whitman to Allen Ginsberg. Ezra Pound was of course my personal enthusiasm, for the positive aspects of his aestheticism and his pursuit of enlightenment. One of his early admirations was Voltaire, and he had a wide-ranging interest in rationalism (Confucius) and in the economic roots of civilization. "Consider their sweats, the people's" he quotes in the Cantos, "If you wd / sit calm on throne." I liked this American liberalism in Pound's character, however it may be overlaid with dogmatic irritability.

Beyond the classroom, this activism of my teaching program led to magazine activity and literary publishing of various kinds. With Raymond Souster and Irving Layton we set up Contact Press, derived from Souster's magazine *Contact*, with perhaps a bow to Williams and McAlmon's earlier magazine with the same name. Through this press we published *Cerberus*, our own three-poet book, and after that some thirty of the most promising poets in Canada, a list which came to include most of the established poets in the country: names like Al Purdy, Alden Nowlan, John Newlove, F. R. Scott, Phyllis Webb, Eli Mandel, D. G. Jones, W. W. E. Ross, Gwendolyn MacEwen, R. G. Everson, George Bowering, Milton Acorn, Margaret Atwood, and others. At the university, I started the McGill Poetry Series, which published only ten books, but also launched some prominent names, Leonard Cohen, Daryl Hine, George Ellenbogen, Dave Solway, Pierre Coupey, and Seymour Mayne among the rest, all of whom are still active and writing. And then there was the magazine *CIV/n*, which lasted through seven numbers from 1953 to 1955.

CIV/n was edited by Aileen Collins, with the help of her coeditors Wanda and Stanley Rozynski;

Dudek in his office at McGill, about 1965

but advising these editors, in manuscript-reading sessions, were Layton and myself, and sometimes other people willing to help and assist. There was Layton's wife Betty, soon listed as "Art Director," Jackie Gallagher, an early coeditor, Anna Azzuolo, listed in No. 5 among the editorial staff, and Robert A. Currie, a sharp satirist, active in the later numbers. The title of the magazine came from a letter of Ezra Pound's which I had seen quoted: "CIV/n not a one-man job"—that is, *Civilization*, in order to have it, you must work together and in concert. (This was lightly ridiculed by our old friend Bruce Ruddick from New York: "I hear you have been trying to produce civilization, up there in Canada." But as Marianne Moore wrote in her poem on the same subject, actually entitled "Civilization": "It is not limited to one locality.") There is a reprint of the entire run of the magazine, in the book *CIV/n, A Literary Magazine of the 50's,* edited by Aileen Collins.[2]

After *CIV/n* ceased publication I started the magazine *Delta* in 1957 and continued single-handed until 1966. ("Civilization" had become a one-man job.) Actually, I bought an old Chandler and Price printing press and installed it in my basement in Verdun, Montreal's working-class suburb. The press was not too noisy, I loved the smell of printer's ink, so

[2]Véhicule Press, Montreal, 1983.

that on this press I printed the early numbers of the magazine as well as my own satirical poetry *Laughing Stalks*. Eventually this work became too demanding and I went to a downtown printer for the job, running down at lunchtime from the university to St. Antoine Street or to St. Sacrement in old Montreal (near to Chaucer's "St. Eloi" in that district), to read proofs and grab a quick coffee and sandwich nearby. *Delta* is still a fascinating file of magazines to read through; a reprint of my writings in it was projected by the Paget Press a few years ago, under the title "Louis Dudek: The Delta Years," but somehow the plan never materialized.

For publishing books, I started a small press in 1965, Delta Canada, with my friends Michael Gnarowski and Glen Siebrasse. Gnarowski was one of my earliest students at the university, then a young man from Shanghai, where his father had run a prosperous business. He has remained a close friend all these years, and is now an accomplished scholar and bibliographer at Carleton University, Ottawa, where he is editor of the Carleton Library of university press books. Through Delta Canada we published some thirty-two titles in the years between 1965 and 1971, a list of poets that includes R. G. Everson, F. R. Scott, Eldon Grier, Gerald Robitaille (who brought us in direct touch with Henry Miller), as well as John Robert Colombo, Peter Van Toorn, and the editors Glen Siebrasse and Gnarowski themselves. The press also brought out my *Collected Poetry* in 1971, a book which has remained the principal collection until the publication of *Infinite Worlds*,[3] a generous selection of poetry with a grand introduction by Robin Blaser.

Following Delta Canada, I continued publishing through a small press called DC Books, partly because this name was descended from "Delta Canada" but more so because I had the assistance now of Aileen Collins and the stationery indicated "Dudek / Collins (editors), 5 Ingleside Avenue, Montreal" as an ad-

---

[3]Véhicule Press, Montreal, 1989.

Poets at Dudek's country house in Way's Mills, Quebec, about 1978: (front row) Dudek, Avrum Malus, Aileen Collins, R. G. Everson; (second row) Monique Jones, A. J. M. Smith, D. G. Jones, Marian McCormick; (back row), Daryl Hine, Ralph Gustafson, John Glassco

"Visiting with Michael Gnarowski at Pierrefonds, Quebec, about 1967: (seniors standing) Michael Gnarowski, Dudek, Diana Gnarowski, and poet R. G. Everson; (juniors) Danik, Francesca, and Sybil Gnarowski"

dress. (Aileen Collins and I were married in 1970.) The press published a short list of interesting poets, new and old, in the next few years, among them Henry Beissel, Avi Boxer, and Laurence Hutchman.

I have now given up small-press publishing, having sold DC Books for one dollar (American) to Steve Luxton and his friends, who are still publishing under that name. The method of publication that began with First Statement Press and Contact Press in Montreal has continued and has spread throughout Canada to such vigorous presses as The House of Anansi, Coach House Press (Toronto), Oberon Press, The Golden Dog (Ottawa), Klanak Press, Talonbooks (Vancouver), The Porcupine's Quill (Erin, Ontario), Black Moss (Windsor, Ontario), Quarry Press (Kingston, Ontario), NeWest Press (Edmonton, Alberta), and many others scattered over the country. They are a sociological phenomenon worth some consideration. In my own view, of course, small presses and magazines represent the effort of a literary minority, such as it is, to make a small separate place for itself and to survive in a commercial society.

There is nothing that bothers me more than the rattling off of numbers of copies sold and the huge profits made by popular books. Majority taste is not the only taste. There must be room in any society, as in fact there is, for the more highly demanding preferences of various minorities: it is only by minorities that chamber music, or fine art, or philosophical thought can be encouraged and maintained. And the same can be said, by and large, of poetry. Poetry is not an art that masses of people will turn to easily, unless it's sentimental or sensational in some obvious way, and therefore poetry must be nurtured and supported by the small audience for it which still exists naturally. Eventually, as good poetry ripens, and as its fame spreads through time, it may also reach great audiences. But for the time being we must be content with the readers that exist, and we must provide for them.

It is an awareness of this fact, by the literate few in every country, that has made the small-press movement and the appearance of literary magazines a widespread phenomenon. Public grants and institutional support may have somewhat undermined the integrity of these presses and magazines in recent years, because the motivation for such publications is crucial to their moral and artistic force, but they are still the only hope for a continuing standard of western art—so their reason for being, and their permanence, must be assured.

My own poetry had continued throughout these years, despite the overwhelming amount of work I had taken on, in teaching, student poetry reading, editing, publishing, printing, as well as magazine and newspaper writing. I was writing regularly for the weekend newspapers, vide my collection of newspaper articles *In Defence of Art*, edited by Aileen Collins. I was also guest-lecturing at numerous conferences and universities; and broadcasting frequently over the CBC (the Canadian Broadcasting Corporation, a crown corporation, subsidized and politically free of interference—it actually broadcast and published my heavy lectures *The First Person in Literature*). Other books resulting from this Chautauqua activity are *Selected Essays and Criticism* and the six lectures in *Technology and Culture*.

The notion that a professorial job is an easy one, or is cut off from the real world, is a misconception among people who have never known a busy professor or have never been near a university. There may be some profs having an easy time of it, but in my local experience I have not seen any. Most of them are harried beyond words, trying to keep up with their field of knowledge; and most have social tasks outside their teaching area of work, as well as family and home responsibilities that keep them hopping.

Fortunately, I did not need a vacant mind and perfect leisure in order to write. I wrote when I could and when I had to, which was most of the time, in spare moments between one task and another, during a quiet lunch, or in the evening at home. There is a powerful great self underlying our paltry conscious self, which thinks unceasingly, untiringly, and gives us cataracts and clusters of words from time to time whether we want them or not. We have to edit this stuff, and dispose of most of it as unusable, but it is the source of our best thinking, and our life's plans, and our hope for the future. It is the source from which I have gotten most of my poetry—or rather, all of my poetry, since I have never written a poem consciously from a prepared plan.

There are two stages in the writing of a poem, as I know it: dumping it out, and then working on it. The first stage involves a certain amount of tension and holding one's breath, but one gets over it quickly, whether in a surge or in several short spurts; the second stage demands a good deal of time. My habit

Louis Dudek and Aileen Collins, about 1970

over the years was to write the first draft of a poem and to put it by, then to work on it a few days or a few weeks later. There was not always the free afternoon, or day, to work on a single poem; and in the early days I had often wasted much time laboring over a poem that turned out to be a misguided failure. Leaving a draft to cool for a while saved time, since I would know better after a pause whether the poem was worth laboring on or not.

In this way I perfected the poems that went into my published books, *East of the City, The Transparent Sea, Laughing Stalks, Collected Poetry,* and *Cross-Section: Poems 1940–1980*, and a few other smaller collections. (These do not include the long book-length poems, of which I will give some account.) These books do contain, however, some hefty impressive poems like the poem "On Poetry," or "The Pomegranate," "The Dead," "Meditation over a Wintry City," and "Puerto Rican Side-Street." And there are a good number of published poems scattered in magazines that were never collected in books, since I had the delusion in those years that once a poem was published it was not lost and someone would eventually find it.[4]

The result of this two-stage method of writing, however, was that hundreds of poems in rough manuscript and in sketchy drafts collected in my desk drawers and files, or simply among the papers that crowded my desk. When I retired in 1984 I decided to spend some time cleaning up these unfinished poems, destroying some, putting some aside as unusable, and finishing others, no matter how short, as poems fit for publication. This exhausting work occupied me for several years, but I ended with some five hundred poems that could possibly be considered worth preserving. This is quite a lot, considering that I already had a dozen books in print; and my tentative title for these poems, "Leftovers," was hardly welcome to my publisher, Simon Dardick of Véhicule Press.

Gradually these poems were divided into three books, and eventually condensed further into two. First, Ken Norris, an energetic editor and poet in his own right, assisted Véhicule Press in selecting from the total a manageable book of 141 pages, which was published under the title *Zembla's Rocks.* The remaining poems formed two collections, one of "Satires and Epigrams," and the second of lyrics entitled, with a phrase from Nietzsche, "Small Perfect Things." In the end I tightened up these two sets into one book, and added a section of prose epigrams in the middle, to separate the two sorts of poems. The book has just been published, under the title *Small Perfect Things.* It will be my last book of poetry by all reasonable counts.

My reason for going into some detail about the writing and final gathering of these shorter poems is that it bears on the question of the long poem and the technique, or aesthetic philosophy, that underlies such poems. To begin with, I had no intention of ever writing a long poem. "I wanted to write a poem," as William Carlos Williams once explained. But the poems became a long poem; and why they did so is a key modern instance, in the evolution of poetry.

Of the short poems, many have an imagistic quality, like this very short poem entitled "Metamorphoses":

> Yesterday's snow
> ten white handkerchiefs
> on the grass.

---

[4]A list of such poems can be found in Karol W. J. Wenek's useful bibliography, *Louis Dudek: A Check-List,* Golden Dog, 1975.

> At sunset
> geese will rise
> across the moon;
>
> or whirled out of a locomotive,
> clouds explode
> over tons of iron.

Yet this poem already has a wider implication, as the title suggests. Another brief poem, "Tree in a Street," confronts the urban world with an item from nature:

> Why will not that tree adapt itself to our tempo?
> We have lopped off several branches,
> cut her skin to the white bone,
> run wires through her body and her loins,
> yet she will not change.
> Ignorant of traffic, of dynamos and steel,
> as uncontemporary
> as bloomers and bustles
> she stands there like a green cliché.

And larger social perspectives, even historical concerns for mankind, appear in "The Tolerant Trees":

> Some conspiracy of silence among the trees
> makes the young birds secret,
> or laughing at our infirmities
> in birdlike fashion, they titter in feathers;
> but the uncondescending trees,
> too wise to speak against us, against streamlining,
> against new fashions in uniforms and clothes,
> wear always the same drab leaves,
> preserve a Sachem silence
> toward our puberty rites of golf and war.

This larger load of meaning, coming from various sources, led to my writing a different kind of poem, a poem freighted with sound and a weight of ideas. I offer only the opening stanza from each of two such poems, as examples, the first from "The Pomegranate":

> The jewelled mine of the pomegranate, whose
> hexagons of honey
> The mouth would soon devour but the eyes eat like a
> poem,
> Lay hidden long in its hide, a diamond of dark cells
> Nourished by tiny streams which crystallized into
> gems . . .

And the second from the poem "Puerto Rican Side-Street":

> Morning came at me like a flung snowball,
> the light flaked out of a chalk-blue sky;
> and I was walking down the dilapidated side-street
> like a grasshopper in a field, just born;
> all the rails and pails glistened and deceived me
> with bunches of blue flowers and with silk of
> corn . . .

But I was not satisfied with this development. Actually, "The Pomegranate" took me several months to write, because it is a gradual expansion, verse by verse, of something implicit in the opening idea—a Dantean vision of nature. The second example is overcharged, reality heightened to an extraordinary degree. But in the direction of an earthly vision. The essence of a poem is in the singular insight—the image or song fragment—on which the whole is built. But this brings us to a fundamental question about poetical composition, or any literary composition.

Writing is obviously a mimesis, or imitation, of someone thinking. When we read an essay, we are willing to assume—it is actually our pleasure to assume—that the essay is the thought process of the man writing. He asks a question, pauses, considers various sides of the issue, and perhaps reaches a conclusion. We think this is how he thought the matter through. But actually the essay is a construct; the author designed it carefully to give it that air of naturalness, or reflection—as in Emerson, or Stevenson, or Loren Eiseley—that we take to be his way of thinking.

This is also true of the poem, the novel, the prepared lecture, or even the play. It is a construct that conveys to us an intellectual form, that is, the mode of thought, fictive and conventionalized, of a particular individual. Even a depersonalized, self-annihilating, irrational work must do so. You cannot convey how a tree thinks; you can only convey how you think a tree thinks.

This process of conveying how a man thinks, that is, of communicating from one person to another, has evolved and changed through time. That is why the mode of writing of one period—the poetry of Homer, or the odes of Horace, or the poems of Milton—may at first seem unconvincing. We need to imagine ourselves in their time, to allow the words to seem to be the natural words of a man thinking in that way. (By "man," of course, I mean man or woman, as the English language allows.) Nearer to our own time, Tennyson's or Longfellow's mode is not quite as natural and convincing to us as T. S. Eliot's or William Carlos Williams's. The poet, more obviously than any other artist, conveys to us his own manner of thinking, the very process of his mind. At least, we believe that to be the nature of poetry, and have always taken it to be so.

What actually happens, of course, is that the poet tries to invent modes of communication that sound more authentic, more believable, than the modes of the past, or even the conventions of the very recent past. The success of new poetry—T. S. Eliot's "Prufrock" and "The Waste Land," Allen Ginsberg's "Howl"—depends on their freshness and immediacy of effect, the impression they give that, yes, this poet actually talks straight, he thinks and talks as we actually do think and talk, in the language of today. And the entire history of literature is an attempt to achieve this kind of authenticity, to get nearer and nearer to what we think of as the reality, the actuality of real being.

In contrast to Northrop Frye, therefore, I see the history of literature as a perpetual demolition of the conventions, a dissolution of artificiality, to arrive at the truth of being. The trouble is that all writing is some mode or convention, and there can be no resolution where we would have a one-to-one relation between the literary work and that life which it attempts to represent. In the case of poetry, there can be no poet's voice, no mimesis of a man thinking, that can be the exact equivalent of a human voice, or an exact replica of someone thinking. We can only give an ever more convincing imitation of that kind of thing. And the poem is only art if it is aware of this distinction.

The intensity of my experiences in Europe made for the directness and sweep of the poem *Europe* in 1954. This is a book of about one hundred separate poems, somewhat oratorical and overdidactic in style, but lifted by the rhythms of the sea running through it and the great scope of its subject.

The sea retains such images[5]
             in her ever-unchanging waves;
for all her infinite variety, and the forms,
inexhaustible, of her loves,
she is constant always in beauty,
             which to us need be nothing more
than a harmony with the wave on which we move.
All ugliness is a distortion
of the lovely lines and curves
             which sincerity makes out of hands
                   and bodies moving in air.
Beauty is ordered in nature
             as the wind and sea
shape each other for pleasure; as the just
know, who learn of happiness
             from the report of their own actions.

The autobiography of a poet that matters has to do with the writing of poetry. And this can only be shown by citing actual poems to show the road travelled. Therefore I quote from my poetry in what follows as sparely as possible, but just as much as the story requires.

---

[5]"Such images," i.e. "eidolons of the good," in the preceding poem.

In *Europe*, discursive commentary on history is
consistent with the expository mode:

Time and the wars have destroyed it all, but the
Acropolis
standing there, crumbling with infinite slowness,
in the sunlight,
is all that it ever was, will be, until the last speck
of the last stone is swept away by the gentle wind.
Strange, that a few fragile, chalky, incomplete blocks
of marble,
worn away by time, thievery, and gunpowder,
should be enough, and all that we have come for,
to erect in the mind the buildings
of the Greeks who lived here, and their city . . .

Or, as in "Poem 83," quoted here in its entirety,
explicit ideas are expounded in declarative form:

As for democracy, it is not just the triumph
of superior numbers,
but that everyone, continually,
should think and speak the truth.
What freedom is there in being counted among the
cattle?
The first right I want is to be a man.
It takes a little courage.
The plain truth, I say, not a few comfortable formulas
that conceal your own special lies;
the simple facts everybody knows
are so, as soon as you bring them to the light.
Democracy is this freedom, this light
shining on the human mind,
light
in faces, actions—
as the Greeks once carved it in these stones.

I travelled to Mexico in 1958 in a state of much
dejection. I was now forty years old, my back was
giving me some trouble, I was hit with something
called "urticaria" in Mexico—a red swelling of the
face—and my personal life was a shambles. Enough
to make anyone's poetry fall apart in fragments—and
mine did. Perhaps fortunately.

I could not write any sustained poetry in Mexico.
But I wrote bits and pieces, lines and clusters of lines,
on separate bits of paper, and put them all together
without any order or sequence. When I returned to
Montreal I arranged this fragmented poetry, partly
chronologically (as far as I could remember) and
partly to make a pattern emerge. The result was the
poem *En México*, with its strange, sometimes broken,
associative progression:

They say no more, as language
(art, or faith)
than any other language;
speak as leaves do,

as dogs sniffing,
as the mating glow-worm sending a call.

And may be wrong.
We make advances
toward "humility."

Religion is an open question.

I thought, seeing the layered stones—
how wonderful
the pursuit of knowledge!
When on the lettered rock-face
appeared a skull and bones.

Optimism is foolish. Life can only be
tragic, no matter what its success.

But the universe does not wait
for me to judge it, nor is death itself
a condemnation.

Knowledge is neither necessary nor possible
to justify the turning
of that huge design

that turns in the mind . . .

So strangely, in this time of dejection, I tumbled
on a mode of writing which proved to be a turning
point, a move toward a more authentic form of
inward reflection and of communicating the reflec-
tive state. In a short poem written very soon after, I
began to make this method conscious, a deliberate
aesthetic:

. . . I wrote nothing
I did not first think
complete, as it stands.
Not a poem, but a meditation—
they make themselves, are also natural forms.

This is in a short poem entitled "Lac En Coeur,"
referring to the writing of the larger poem in eleven
sections entitled "At Lac En Coeur" and written in
the Laurentian mountains north of Montreal in the
summer of 1959. ("En Coeur" means literally "in the
heart," suggesting in Quebec a religious association,
which I perhaps echo in the context of the poem.)

Who thinks the living universe?
I think it but in part.
Fragments exist
like those infinitesimal separate stars
I saw, lying on my back on the cushions
last night before the storm:

their union, as powers
but as wheels on the one axle,
and as form—
a drawing by a master hand.

We have united some few pigments
         (all that is in museums)
but the greater part, all life, was there
                    united when we came—
and grows, a copious language of forms.

Who thinks them? . . .
            their being is a thought.

My thought, a part of being—is a tree
of many thoughts, in which a yellow bird sits.

                    *

In the silence, sitting in the silence
I seem to hear the visible language speak
                              a leaf
(a glimpse of paradise perhaps to be)

Here in hell, in purgatorio,
all things suffer this waiting, become
only then whatever they will be:
ecstasies of creation, flowers
            opening ecstatic lucent leaves.

Nothing else matters.
Nothing else speaks.

                    *

So beauty
it says, so quietly in the shadows
that a small bird
            on a red bomb
shrieks a symphonic whistle
just turning its head, without a sound from the
    throat . . .

What followed, in 1961, was the book-length poem *Atlantis*, written in Europe but in no way resembling the work of fifteen years ago. I was now proceeding with a meditative form of poetry, playing over the world of perception and idea—since "pure poetry" is not my vein—and creating a luminous form that corresponds to the mode of thought. *Atlantis* is in many ways an answer to the nihilism of modern literature. What I had been teaching through all those years, of analytic-reductive European thought, had stuck in my craw. I became convinced that there must be another side to the Nothingness (so-called *le Néant*) and the existential absurdism in which modern literature was embroiled; and that this missing element was perhaps the source of the grandeur and the glory of all past literature and art. It could not be wiped out by the skeptical tradition that had taken hold of western man. For the moment, in my long poem, I called this idea "Atlantis."

            Today we passed over Atlantis
                        which is our true home.
            We live in exile
            waiting for that world to come.
            Here nothing is real, only a few
                              actions, or words,
            bits of Atlantis, are real.

            I do not love my fellow men
                        but only citizens of Atlantis,
            or those who have a portion
            of the elements that make it real.

The lines come unpredictably, spontaneously, and rise to a philosophical height at times, only to descend again to the most commonplace actualities:

            These hours are of no interest—
                        I sit and stare.
            Wait for the words to come.

            They appear with new perception, a flash of
                light . . .

                        *

            Marble is the cross-section of a cloud.
            What, then, if the forms we know
                        are sections of a full body
            whose dimensions are timeless
                        and bodiless, like poems,
            whose unseen dimension is mind?

            I want to learn how we can take life seriously,
                without afflatus, without rhetoric;
            to see something like a natural ritual,
                        maybe an epic mode unrevealed,
            in the everyday round of affairs.

            The touch of land, solid under sea-legs,
            touch of the present
                        no matter how sad or poor . . .

The actual world, which is our problem of course (the waste land), yet must be included in the conceptual flow of poetry, is transformed in this meditation:

            In a way, it's one vast slum,
                        the world.
            Or a rich garbage dump
            on which gaudy flowers and delicate pinks
                        sprout, clamber, float—

            a ghostly beauty rising over decay

            on tip-toe stems, hardly touching the earth,
                points of transparent, watery dew.

I try to define the principle of reconception of the hidden reality:

            As pure art, it is Psyche—
                        the ballerina's butterfly body.
            For what is spirit
                        if not the potentiality of things?

And that same hidden unity is then applied to the poem:

Gleditschia   Dietes   Regal Lily

Not that the poem doesn't have a meaning.
            It's what holds the thing together,
an invisible ghost.

Which rises sometimes to an ecstasy, in Kew Gardens,
answering T. S. Eliot (or Céline and Beckett):

Nymphaea and tropical fish

But the rhododendrons were not in flower.
"The rhododendrons were not in flower!"
   "Ah, you must come back another time."

To see the famous roses
   Mme. Butterfly, Sutter's Gold, Masquerade,
   Christopher Stone, Misty Morn

(Was it Mandeville wrote—
   "How Roses First Came Into the World"?)

Primula Japonica . . .

Ah, Waste Land!

From this kind of program there emerges—

Eternal chicken, eternal bread and fruit . . .

The great place of art
      is halfway between this world and some other:
Hals to Hogarth, Giotto to Botticelli—
         including the English pantheon,
         Aristocracy.
But the unknown still remains unknown.

This is our gift, to extricate joy
               from earthly things,
what is distilled of transcendence
               out of the visible.

With Riemann, & Einstein,
with Hoogstraaten's peep-show,
and Vermeer, the fascination of symbolism.

A heap of straw, in which a needle of truth lies
            hidden,
         Turner's "Evening Star"
            over the sea . . .

Turner's evening star is barely visible in the painting, but it is there somewhere. It is the *verbum* of an ultimate reality, as every epiphany of this kind must be. For all things come from that indefinable source:

There, somewhere, at the horizon
               you cannot tell the sea from the sky,
where the white cloud glimmers,

the only reality, in a sea of unreality,

out of that cloud come palaces, and domes,
               and marble capitals,

and carvings of ivory and gold—
                  Atlantis
shines invisible, in that eternal cloud.

These ideas and views may be more common, and more widespread, than I know. Intellectually, I have been isolated in Canada as much as any Robinson Crusoe on his island, with only an occasional poet-companion for a time to talk with, as my Man Friday. I would be extremely happy to know that there were others somewhere of a like mind.

At the end of *Atlantis* there is a passage which promises a continuation:

I said to my friend, "Don't read this,
               it'll make you dizzy."
But she read on, said she couldn't stop.
            "What is it?"
I said: "The vertigo of freedom."

A living thing asks itself
   what milliards of years no plant, bird, or
                        animal . . .
It was never part of their business.

Why stop at all, she said, why not go on?

In nature, beauty is a case of and/or.
There are still the atoms, and the stars
   (and all the crude machines made by man).

"Of course I can't stop," I said.

This led to the final long poem *Continuation*, subtitled (humorously, I think) "An Infinite Poem in Progress," of which two books, *Continuation I* and *Continuation II* have so far been published. There are several pages, and broken lines, of a third book gathering in my desk, but I have no desire to complete this in my lifetime. The poem, in any case, could never be completed; it is a continuation that is imagined as going on without end, like the creation itself.

Continuation I and *II* are simulations of the mind thinking. Of course it is not the actual content of any "stream of consciousness," for that would be chaotic, messy, absurd—no work of art. I accumulate in my notebooks only those lines and passages that come to me unbidden, that drop down from the blue, so to speak, or come up from the word-assembler of the brain. (There is nothing arcane or mystical about this—everyone has words and thoughts that come naturally and unexpectedly—except that I recognize those that have poetical potential, and I screen them for later processing.) I find that the lines accumulated in this way have a peculiar connectedness in their progression, and I shape the whole sequence into a flowing, uninterrupted poem. It *corresponds*, as I see

"With son, Gregory, and Greg's wife, Krys," Way's Mills, Quebec, about 1988

it, to something that is going on in the most erratic and vivacious area of my mind, and it is therefore the stream that is truly poetry, evoked in an unforced and inconspicuous way. I can offer here only a small sample of this poetry, to give the reader some sense of how it looks and sounds, when finished on the page:

> To make the world levitate
>   in a kind of ether,
> to make the real miraculous
>
> The beginning is everywhere
>   The end is everywhere
>
> The child of two, told to 'throw a ball'
>   brings it to your hand
>
> The thought comes to you on the page
>
> One of the mysteries of the creation
>   in which we are embedded
>
> The perpetual coitus interruptus of poetry
>
> Death's jab in the loins:
> "What did you have in mind?" she said
>
> Nothing

> "Human tears are a re-creation of the primordial
>   ocean
>   which bathed the first eyes"
>
> But the heart knows heaven is somewhere
>   far away
>
> The eye "a piece of the brain which has budded"
>
> And what the eye sees the brain records
>
> A blind acceptance of the given
>   flowing happily along . . .

BIBLIOGRAPHY

Poetry:

(With others) *Unit of Five,* edited by Ronald Hambleton, Ryerson, 1944.

East of the City, Ryerson, 1946.

(With Irving Layton and Raymond Souster) *Cerberus,* Contact, 1952.

The Searching Image, Ryerson, 1952.

Twenty-Four Poems, Contact, 1952.

Europe, Contact, 1954, revised edition, The Porcupine's Quill, 1991.

The Transparent Sea, Contact, 1956.

En México, Contact, 1958.

Laughing Stalks, Contact, 1958.

Atlantis, Delta Canada, 1967.

Collected Poetry, Delta Canada, 1971.

Epigrams, DC Books, 1975.

Selected Poems, Golden Dog, 1975.

Cross-Section: Poems 1940–1980, Coach House, 1980.

Poems from Atlantis, Golden Dog, 1980.

Continuation I, Véhicule, 1981.

Zembla's Rocks, Véhicule, 1986.

Infinite Worlds, Véhicule, 1988.

Continuation II, Véhicule, 1990.

Small Perfect Things, DC Books, 1991.

Prose:

Literature and the Press: A History of Printing, Printed Media, and Their Relation to Literature, Ryerson-Contact, 1960.

The First Person in Literature, Canadian Broadcasting Corporation Publications, 1967.

DK: Some Letters of Ezra Pound, DC Books, 1974.

Selected Essays and Criticism, Tecumseh, 1978.

Technology and Culture, Golden Dog, 1979.

Ideas for Poetry, Véhicule, 1983.

In Defence of Art, Quarry, 1988.

Editor:

(With I. Layton) *Canadian Poems 1850–1952*, Contact, 1952.

R. Souster, *Selected Poems*, Contact, 1956.

Montréal, Paris d'Amerique/Paris of America, Editions du Jour, 1961.

Poetry of Our Time: An Introduction to Twentieth Century Poetry, Including Modern Canadian Poetry (anthology), Macmillan, 1965.

(With Michael Gnarowski) *The Making of Modern Poetry in Canada, Essential Articles on Contemporary Canadian Poetry in English*, McGraw-Ryerson, 1967.

All Kinds of Everything: Worlds of Poetry, Clarke Irwin, 1973.

Other:

The Green Beyond (recording), Canadian Broadcasting Corporation, 1973.

"Louis Dudek: Texts and Essays," edited by B. P. Nichol and Frank Davey in *Open Letter*, summer 1981.

Robert Easton

1915-

Prologue

When I received the invitation to do this essay, I was just completing, in collaboration with my wife, a book including many autobiographical pages dealing with my early years. It seemed an artistic and a practical mistake to attempt to repeat myself. So I begin with those pages rather than risk stumbling over a second attempt. I hope you will find I got them right the first time.

Older readers will probably remember hearing the news of the Japanese attack on Pearl Harbor. I hope younger ones will also share the feelings Jane and I had at that moment.

Sunday, December 7, 1941, is peaceful and sunny. We're lunching at the kitchen table in our employee's cottage on a ranch high in California's Coast Range, enjoying a radio broadcast of the New York Philharmonic on our Zenith portable, when the familiar voice of John Daly breaks in. "We interrupt this program to bring you a special news bulletin. The Japanese have attacked Pearl Harbor."

Americans bombed, strafed, wounded, dead—ships blown up, barracks and airfields blasted! We feel as if the floor is being pulled out from under us, leaving us at the edge of an abyss. In our lifetime such horrors happen in other countries, to other peoples: Poles, Danes, Norwegians, Dutch, Belgians, British, French, the Greeks, the Chinese, the Russians. Over our suddenly unappetizing tuna-and-egg salads we stare at each other in stunned silence. Like so many others we'll remember for the rest of our lives exactly where we were, what we were doing, how we felt when we heard the news—and realized we were no longer immune. Bob and millions like him will have to go to war. Jane and millions like her will have to stay home. It seems almost the ultimate disaster, almost like death.

Dazed, strangely mute, we wander through our beloved cottage as if already saying farewell. Piled by the typewriter on the deal table by the fireplace are carbons of stories Bob has sent the *Atlantic Monthly.* Here in the bedroom is the nook by the window where Jane has planned to put the crib when a baby is

*Robert Easton with his grandfather
Warren Olney*

born. We are going to lose this home which has become a cornerstone of the life we are building. We are going to lose each other. What the future holds nobody knows. Our chief consolation is the thought we'll not be alone there, we'll have plenty of company—a whole nation. We sense it, speak of it, rising invisibly around us, feeling the same anger and outrage we do, the same dismay and loss.

Bob: The shadow of war has hung over our marriage of fourteen months. Ours is, we like to joke, the last in this country "arranged" in old-country style. We'd never met but our mothers had a mutual friend who knew us both and put the idea in their heads that we might hit it off. I'd come home to Santa Barbara, that summer of '39, after a disappointing first year at Stanford Law School. I'd concluded that law as generally practiced consisted less in the pursuit of justice than in arguing about other people's property, and at the same time I was breaking up with someone. So the last thing I felt like was "doing something," as Mother kept putting it, "for that nice girl who's over here from Europe and doesn't know a soul."

I spent most of July and August working on a cattle ranch near Santa Maria, writing stories in spare time, and whenever I went home Mother would tactfully suggest: "What about Jane Faust?" Finally to get her off my back I said: "Okay—Ellis and Connie are coming up next weekend. Go ahead and ask Miss Faust if you want!"

So here I am on the station platform feeling a little nervous, looking for a tall blonde girl without any hat—hats were still the fashion—carrying a tennis racket. Doesn't sound too bad. Evidently she's unconventional. Besides she's grown up abroad and I've never met one of those. Sharp at ten-thirty the Daylight Limited comes steaming in from Los Angeles and I see her get off, complete with tennis racket and all-American look, not the least foreign. I notice a shyness but think I see through it to something I may like very much.

Jane: Bob looks handsome in brown tweed jacket and gray flannels—the Ivy League uniform of those days. He doesn't know I've been as reluctant about our meeting as he. When his mother telephoned from Santa Barbara I felt petrified at the idea of a weekend among strangers and glibly pleaded a previous engagement. Afterward Mum scolded: "You've *got* to get over your shyness, get out and *meet* people!" Like most mothers of unmarried twenty-one-year-olds, she was eager to have me meet some young men. We'd just moved from Florence—had been living in Italy for fourteen years—so Daddy could do the Kildare stories for MGM, and I didn't know a soul in southern California my age. But I knew Mum was right. Though I'd been to a girls' school in New York, I felt backward where boys were concerned, embarrassed by my six-foot altitude, afraid I couldn't hold up my end of the line of chit-chat that seemed expected of American girls. Mum's scolding prompted me to phone Mrs. Easton back and say there'd been a change of plans, I could come.

Now my chief sensation is relief that Bob's height is the same as mine. Most of my dates seem to have been around five-five. I'm impressed by the fact he's gone to Harvard and Stanford while I've never been to college, but don't want him to think so and begin

teasing about his driving as he takes us up State Street a little too fast, shifting gears of the Ford V-8 four-door a little too masterfully. He replies as solemnly as if revealing a state secret that the car belongs to his parents—as if that explains everything! Consequently I'm not quite sure how I'm doing but gather he doesn't have much money to spend on cars. The house near the Old Mission is big but not grand. Mrs. E., bursting with energy though over sixty, greets me affectionately. Still it isn't till I've beaten Bob at tennis that I begin to relax.

Bob: On the contrary I let her win a set because she looks glamorous in a short white skirt with those long brown legs. I guess my downfall begins right there. Or perhaps it's afterward on the lawn during our discussion of books and writers. By what seems remarkable coincidence, we've both been reading Chekhov and particularly like his story "The Darling," about someone who needs a special kind of love. I soon realize I've never met a girl I can talk to this enjoyably and find myself confiding my big secret—I want to write and am not going back to law school but to San Francisco and look for a newspaper job. I feel a twinge of regret when Connie and Ellis arrive and interrupt us.

Jane: Before dinner Connie and I change to evening dresses. The men wear black tie and the white tablecloth gleams beneath silver candelabra while we sit in ghastly uncomfortable Chippendale chairs and prepare to eat with sterling knives and forks. Bob's father startles me by saying grace, something I've never experienced. Like Mrs. E. he's short, wiry, a rancher-businessman in his sixties, and also like Bob's mother so full of vitality he seems much younger. Their formal Victorian manners put me off but I see that at heart they're terribly decent and kind, while regarding their only child as a bit unpredictable.

Then we all go downtown to see Herbert Marshall, a popular British actor, on stage in a frothy little comedy called *Ladies and Gentlemen*. It's dreadfully boring. At intermission we troop outside with most of the audience for a breath of fresh air in the portico. Bob and I begin talking again and become separated from the others. When he proposes we step across the street to the El Paseo Bar for a quick drink, it seems only natural. Half an hour flies by before he looks at his watch. Horrified we hurry back, find the curtain up and Marshall on stage, climb into our third-row seats over people's feet to the accompaniment of muttered disapprovals and knowing looks.

Bob: That summer is a turning point for Jane and me as for the rest of the world. A few days later on September 1, Hitler invades Poland. He's been ranting, bullying, breaking treaties, invading the Rhineland, Austria, Czechoslovakia, while England and France back down before him. But we hope it won't lead to war. Of course we want peace. We just think it can be achieved on the cheap, by accommodating a monomaniac. When England and France finally declare war a few days later, that summer of 1939 becomes like the summer of 1914—the summer before World War I—a point from which there will be no return but one to which we and millions of others will long to return—with its unclouded tennis games, its hats, double-breasted suits, unforgettable melodies like "Night and Day" and "Smoke Gets in Your Eyes," movie stars like Fred Astaire and Ginger Rogers, Dietrich, Garbo, Gable, Gary Cooper, its frothy little comedies and grand Broadway musicals, zany crazes like flagpole sitting and dance- and roller-skating marathons, its innocence, and its ignorance of the scope of human evil.

Jane: At first the war seems unreal, it's so far away. It's something you read about in papers, hear about on the radio, see in newsreels at the movies. Nobody calls it World War II. That comes later. It's just "the war," or "the European war" away off "over there." People begin urging us to stay neutral. "It's Europe's quarrel, not ours!" But I feel we might not be able to. I'd been living with a Jewish family in Vienna when the Nazis took over Austria. For weeks there'd been turmoil, pro- and anti-Nazi mobs opposing each other in the streets. Then German bombers flew back and forth overhead. Then from my upstairs window at No. 3 Brahmsplatz I see the goose-stepping invaders march by, hear the welcoming shouts, sense the invisible terror, while Lily Pereira, my landlady, and Iti, her daughter, my age, cower in dread by the radio. When I go out I see "Juden Hier" (Jew Here) scrawled on doors and walls. I feel anger and disgust. I also feel sick at heart for being a member of a humankind that behaves like this. Some of my friends, Jewish and non-Jewish, disappear in the murderous reprisals that follow the *Anschluss*, while others risk their lives to smuggle Jews and other anti-Nazis to the Italian or Swiss borders. With breathless excitement I listen to Franz and Wilfred tell matter-of-factly of these secret errands of mercy and resistance. Their lives are in danger but they continue to do what they feel they must.

Experiencing a Nazi takeover even from the safety of my American citizenship fills me with horror. But afterward like most of the rest of the world I want to get on with my life and hope such evil will never touch me or mine. Now what's happening in Poland makes me think it will.

I liked Bob but we didn't see each other again that summer and in the fall I went to New York to stay with a former schoolmate, Fanny Myers, who lived with her parents in an apartment on Eighty-Sixth Street. Fanny painted her miniatures in the morning while I wrote my stories. Afternoons and evenings we improved our minds, supposedly, by attending lectures on philosophy by Will Durant or visiting art museums whereas actually, like most singles our age, we were on the lookout for husbands. A prosperous young Yale professor asked me home to meet his mother and offered me a job as his secretary. It was either a proposal or a proposition but I declined on grounds of lack of secretarial talent. Meanwhile Fanny and I went to dinner at the apartment of a schoolmate from Spence days, Honoria Murphy. Her parents were wealthy patrons of the arts—Gerald effeminate and artistic, Sara masculine and assertive. They'd owned a villa in the south of France and were becoming celebrated as the Dick Divers of Fitzgerald's novel *Tender Is the Night*. Mum and Pop had known them during our New York days when we'd had an apartment on East End Avenue and Gerald and Pop shared a liking for the poetry of Gerard Manley Hopkins with its unusual rhythms, but Gerald wasn't a published poet like Pop. Now he and Sara were shattered by the recent deaths of two teenage sons and seemed to have little affection left for their remaining daughter.

As my social whirl continues, my bachelor godfather "Dixie" Fish, prototype for Dr. Kildare in the magazine and screen stories Daddy is writing, takes me to Roosevelt Hospital to watch him operate, and dinner and the theater afterward and to rub elbows with celebrities at the Stork Club.

It's all very heady. New York at Christmas time. All the shops aglitter. Everything so glamorous. I fall in love or think I do. Jack is ten years older, lively, witty, a successful stockbroker. We get engaged. Then my girlhood dream of a little red farmhouse on a hilltop—far from the madding crowd with a devoted husband and six children, all of us wearing blue jeans and doing our own work—reasserts itself. Bob too is continually at the back of my mind. We're exchanging copies of our stories. His aren't very good. Neither are mine. But I like his ambition to become a writer and subconsciously perhaps I know I'm going to marry one despite Daddy's admonitions to the contrary. Anyway, when I break off with Jack and head west early in 1940, after that dizzying New

York whirl, something tells me I'll be seeing Bob before long.

Bob: After trying several San Francisco papers I find a job at *Coast Magazine*, headquartered on Bush Street just below Montgomery. *Coast*'s content is largely an imitation of the *New Yorker*'s combined with black-and-white photos like those of the new and highly popular *Life*, and the society gossip of *Town and Country*. It's staffed mainly by ex-Ivy Leaguers, one of whom I'd known on the Harvard *Lampoon*, which is partly how I get my job of associate editor at the glorious salary of fifteen a week. My parents aren't backing my new career so I must watch every penny. I rent a room on the roof of an apartment building at 1228 Washington Street near the top of Nob Hill. It isn't much bigger than a piano box but has a heart-stopping view: the new Bay Bridge, ships coming and going, Pan Am flying boats making their runs across the water, leaving a white wake and taking off for China straight through Golden Gate; and in the middle of it all, Treasure Island, constructed especially for the world's fair then in progress—gleaming out there at night like a veritable jewel.

To get to work I walk down precipitous California Street to our office at 130 Bush, next to the lofty new—all of fourteen stories high—Shell Building, and afterwards ride the crowded cable car back up, clinging among other passengers like bees on a limb, feeling myself part of the picturesque life of a great city. I do most of my serious eating at the Hotel de France in the French district on the north slope of Nob Hill, where a three-course dinner with wine and plenty of bread, common table, costs forty-five cents. In Chinatown, halfway down the east slope, I find equally good bargains; and for social life there are guys and girls I'd known at Stanford plus the *Coast* staff, Innis Bromfield, editor, Christopher Rand our star writer. When we can afford it we go dancing to Jay Whidden's orchestra at the Hotel Mark Hopkins atop Nob Hill, or Ted Fiorito's at the St. Francis down on Union Square. Betty Grable, later a famous pinup girl, got her start as a vocalist with Whidden and used to perform a sensational scarf dance which would hardly raise an eyebrow today.

I'm settling in, getting satisfaction out of seeing my words in print, even if they do no more than advise people what movies to see or where to eat inexpensively, when one of those apparently random events occurs that change our lives. I'm transferred to head *Coast*'s Los Angeles office. There isn't much to head. I'm the only one there besides our advertising manager. But on the frosty morning of February 2,

1940, while walking from my three-dollar-a-week pad in a dilapidated Victorian on the Sixth Street hill, to my office in the Clark Hotel at the heart of downtown, I get a hunch Jane is home from New York and decide to call her. Reaching the lobby I'm amazed to find a letter in my pigeonhole, forwarded from San Francisco, saying she *is* home. It seems an astonishing case of mental telepathy. I go to the pay phone nearby and get her out of bed—it's only 7:45—and agree to come to lunch on Sunday.

Jane: I keep telling myself I don't want to be in love with anybody. I talk it over with Daddy, sitting as usual on the toilet seat while he shaves. We have our best talks then, just as Mum and I do when she's sitting up in bed recovering from one of her migraines. "Do you want another scalp to add to your collection or are you serious about this guy?" Pop demands while scraping his chin. He takes a dim view of my potential suitors. He has something like a cross between Achilles and Homer in mind for me. "Oh, I'm not serious!" I assure him.

Bob: It was a different Los Angeles in those days. No traffic gridlocks. No freeways. No smog. You could see the mountains and you could get almost anywhere in twenty minutes. Now and then a flight of twin-fuselage Lockheed P-38 fighters comes roaring over-head like something out of science fiction, reminders of what's happening overseas. The L.A. aircraft factories are booming with orders from foreign nations and our own military, and Franklin D. Roosevelt, now in his third term, is talking about the U.S. becoming "the arsenal of democracy." But nobody gets very excited. It's not going to touch us, oh, no! It's the period called "the phony war." France and England are playing it safe on the defensive, and Hitler is pretending to do likewise while planning his next blitzkrieg.

Anyway, my pulse rises as I drive out Sunset Boulevard toward the ocean, turn off at Burlingame Avenue in leafy Brentwood and come to a stop in front of a gracious Mediterranean house, half-hidden behind a hedge of Algerian ivy. I've scraped up $120 to buy a secondhand 1936 Dodge coupe, dark green, with spare tire in a well in the righthand fender and a silvery ram rampant as radiator cap. Not quite in keeping with upscale Brentwood, maybe. But my role is that of poor but honest young fellow striving to rise.

Jane looks better than ever. And now we have that shared feeling fate is bringing us together, there's an unspoken understanding between us. Her mother, Dorothy Schillig Faust, is the most exquisitely feminine older woman I've ever met—soft dark eyes, full figure, gently welcoming manner. Her father Frederick Faust comes on like a giant, massively tall, combative jaw, sternly lined face, talking brilliantly in a rich bass voice. I don't know it but under Max Brand and nineteen other pen names he's published over 600 magazine stories, over 130 books, while dozens of movies have been made from his work including *Destry Rides Again* as well as the smash-hit Kildare series; but he prefers to write poetry on classical themes. Twelve-year-old Judy's suspicion of those who come courting her adored sister is formidable. The house speaks to me almost as much as the people in it: it says welcome, it says home—with its book-lined walls and warmly lived-in atmosphere. It's the kind of house I want someday and makes the people who occupy it now seem like relatives.

The author on Cinderella, "a lovely bay with black points," 1941

Jane: We were married in Berkeley in September as bombs rained down on London. France has surrendered. Hitler is preparing to invade England. The first draft law in U.S. peacetime history has just passed Congress. They aren't drafting married men yet but we guess they will soon and want as much time together as possible. The ceremony takes place at 8:00 P.M. in grand old St. Mark's Episcopal Church across Bancroft Way from the University of California. Bob's grandfather was its pastor back in the 1890s and his parents were married there, so a lot of tradition and religion are involved, but most of it goes over my head because we Fausts have no formalized religion and, besides, I prefer living in the present rather than the past.

We've chosen Berkeley because it's near the ranch where Bob got a job after *Coast* folded and because our parents attended college there and numerous friends and relations live nearby. I'm grateful for the way Bob's parents have accepted me as the daughter they never had or, rather, as replacement for one they lost in infancy. By strange coincidence her name too was Jane. It gives me a sometimes eerie, sometimes profoundly moving, sense of carrying on and trying to compensate, even now as I prepare to walk down the aisle. I wear an ivory-satin dress with a train that threatens to trip me and flat slippers to keep me under six two. My only attendant is Judy, still scowling about Bob. My brother John has had to go East to school and can't be best man so Bob's boyhood chum, a Stanford medical student, John Merritt, hefty and even taller than I, holds the ring. He and Bob wear white tie and tails. So does Daddy. As I wait at the back of the church with my right hand on Daddy's arm I see beads of sweat on his forehead that aren't there because it's a warm evening. "You don't have to go through with this!" he mutters grimly. He means it. He likes Bob but is ready to turn and walk out of the church, me on his arm, forever to keep him company. But when I look down the aisle and see Bob I know my future is there—there and in our apartment at Rio Vista, Rio Vista looming like a bit of paradise beyond the reception, the thrown rice, the Just Married sign someone is sure to affix to our old Dodge.

Rio Vista is a tiny town on the Sacramento River just before it empties into San Francisco Bay. Our three furnished rooms occupy a ground-floor corner opposite the grammar school. Down at the end of the street we can see the Sacramento gliding placidly by. The rent is thirty-five a month. I'm so happy I burn the chops for our first dinner. But Bob says it's all right—we're going to live mainly on love anyway.

Bob: In fact I was worried lest Jane might not like Rio Vista or the B. B. Ranch people, having grown up in Europe and knowing nothing of American smalltown or ranch life.

Jane: On the contrary fate was putting me where I'd long wanted to be, among down-to-earth people. They were part of that girlhood dream of a farmhouse on a hill. Ironically the dream first came to me when I was living in a villa in Florence with plenty of servants to look after me, but the servants interested me more than the sophisticated guests who appeared for dinner or to play tennis or swim in our pool. They seemed so much less inhibited, so much more directly connected to life and able to express it without the barriers of manners and education. When not attending Miss Barry's American School, a Florentine institution of long standing, or taking additional lessons prescribed by Daddy as beneficial to body and mind, including fencing and Greek, I spent much time in pantry or kitchen or up in the sewing room on the second floor or out in the garden listening to their talk. Giulia the maid; Elia the butler, her husband, who arranged fresh flowers in the house every day as well as serving meals wearing white gloves; Griselda the second maid; Olimpio the chauffeur, irascible in traffic like most Italians; dear old Berti, age eighty, the head gardener—all seemed inhabitants of another world, one far more interesting than the one I lived in. From servants of neighboring villas they knew what really went on behind all those walls and hedges, and through them I did too. Similarly with the peasants who cultivated the fields adjoining our villa and often sang as they pruned the grapevines or plowed behind white oxen that moved with such dignity under the olive trees and among the grapes. We discussed the crops, the weather, latest births and deaths, and why the oxen wore leather muzzles to prevent their nibbling the vines. "Jane," my mother would reprimand, "you must learn to be more ladylike! The *contadini* and servants are all very well, but you mustn't become too intimate!" Not that Mum and Pop had social pretensions. They just didn't see things my way.

Nor was our villa pretentious. It was a sixteenth-century farmhouse enlarged and remodeled at our own expense. Daddy added three rooms and a tower-study to make it more livable and to accommodate his thousands of books and desire for spaciousness. He wrote every day, poetry in the mornings, prose in the afternoons. We belonged to no clubs, saw few people except those interested in the arts. Arthur and Hortense Acton, our landlord and landlady, who lived in palatial La Pietra across the lane, came for dinners; and Arthur, an Italianized Englishman, painted us all in watercolor, rather badly. Hortense was an American from Chicago. Their oldest son Harold, now Sir Harold thanks to his literary achievements, was away in China but William came to dinner wearing a monocle, which fascinated me. He was to die in the war.

Leonard and Patty Bacon, old friends of Pop's and Mum's from Berkeley days, occupied another of Acton's villas nearby with their three daughters, and John and I and the young Bacons played in the *podere* intervening; and I eavesdropped from the head of the stairs while Pop and Leonard, a Pulitzer poet, discussed writers and poetry late into many nights. And one summer we took a house near the Bacons and Aldous Huxleys on the beach at Forte dei Marmi near Viareggio. Leonard, Pop and Aldous would sit by bonfires on the sand and talk about everything under the sun, and moon, while we children played nearby, sometimes listening, sometimes oblivious as we eyed the distant Carrara Mountains, ghostly white in the moonlight, where Michelangelo got the marble for his statues. Even so I identified less with those talking and writing about life than with the common people who seemed to live it so much more directly and colorfully. Maybe like Tolstoy I saw virtue in peasants because I wasn't one and had a villa to go home to at night. Nevertheless my interest was genuine.

Bob: Again my feelings matched Jane's but with different background. I'd grown up in Santa Maria, a small town north of Santa Barbara, where we kids went barefoot as Tom Sawyer along unpaved streets and alleys, swiped watermelons from neighbors' yards, engaged in bloody fistfights to see who was boss, admired the American Legion when it marched up Broadway in uniform, guns at right shoulder, in the Memorial Day Parade, fresh home from World War I. War was over, war was a thing of the past. The Legionnaires had put it away for good, finished off old Kaiser Bill. The last thing any of us expected was to be involved in a war when we grew up. My mother read aloud to my father and me almost every evening, something out of the *Atlantic* or *World's Work*, plenty of Kipling, Sir Walter Scott, Dickens. On Sundays we attended tiny St. Peter's Episcopal Church which accommodated all of the dozen or fifteen Episcopalians in town. It was so small it had no Sunday school. I didn't care much for church but the words of the Bible and Book of Common Prayer sank in deeply, then or when read aloud by Father at home on Sunday evenings when for some reason we hadn't attended services.

At school I harassed girls much as Tom did Becky, with spitwads of paper propelled by thumb and forefinger, to show mute adoration. My friends included Japanese, Portuguese, Mexican, Italian and Jewish kids. I brought them to our comfortable house at 730 South Broadway and they took me to theirs, more or less comfortable, without altering our basic relationships. There were feelings of prejudice among some of our elders, true, but little of this rubbed off onto us. We regarded ourselves mainly as Santa Marians and dreamed of playing on the high-school football team and becoming millionaires.

Most of us grew up with the work ethic. I earned my first big money, took my first step toward millionaire status, salvaging heads of lettuce and bunches of carrots discarded by local packing sheds and peddling them to housewives for five cents each. Growing older I worked on outlying farms and ranches. What I liked best were vacation trips into the back country with vaqueros of the Sisquoc Ranch, which Father managed, to hunt wild cattle, fish, observe condors and explore Indian caves. Later he and I helped National Audubon Society and Forest Service establish the first refuge for the California condor. The great birds soared into my life and remained there, soaring out from time to time in books and magazine articles. Our backcountry became a spiritual heartland I took with me wherever I went. And about this time, too, I developed a youthful dream remarkably like Jane's—a ranch house on a hilltop shared with a loving wife and numerous progeny. Are there psychic connections? I think so.

Jane: At Rio Vista I spent most of the day with Flora, my neighbor across the hall, wife of an alcoholic oil worker. She taught me how to wash and iron, and when we went to the market explained that string beans were purchased by the pound, not by the bean! Though only my age, Flora had two adorable young children, Billy and Susan, who called me Aunt Jane. Like her I wanted to be a hands-on mother. My parents were so busy when I was young—and Pop so ill with heart trouble and Mum so weak from nervous breakdowns—that they hired a governess for John and me. I loved young children and admired the way Flora managed hers in a realistic manner that didn't spoil them. I'd get everything ready for dinner and wait for Bob to come home. He'd stop in front of the apartment and honk—dirty and smelly from all day at the ranch but looking glamorous in blue jeans and cowboy boots—and I'd run out and we'd drive together to our garage, down by the river, then walk back arm in arm in a blissful moment of reunion, I

carrying his black tin lunch pail. After he bathed and shaved, me sitting on the toilet seat to keep him company and talk, we'd eat. Then I'd read aloud—from *Don Quixote* or *Look Homeward, Angel*—until he fell asleep in his chair, having been up since about 4:30, and then it was bedtime.

Whenever we read the war news in the paper or heard it over our Zenith portable, we realized how fortunate we were, and how bad it was becoming, with England standing alone against what seemed an invincible Germany.

Bob: The B. B. Ranch and Feed Yard where I worked occupied ten thousand acres on the west bank of the Sacramento where it joins the San Joaquin to form the headwaters of San Francisco Bay. The rich delta soil produced tons of hay which was baled and stored in massive stacks as long as city blocks. Twelve thousand cattle were accommodated in pens, separated by alleyways wide enough for feed trucks, in what amounted to a factory in the field, a beef factory. There was a pit the size of a small stadium that contained sugar-beet pulp brought down on barges from a refinery up the Sacramento, and a huge corrugated iron mill that ground up the hay, along with cottonseed cake and molasses and vitamins, into a special formula that was fed the cattle along with the beet pulp.

My job was to ride a dependable sorrel named Barb through the alleyways in company with Dynamite Carter, head cowboy, a colorful character who'd run away from home in Illinois at fourteen on a freight train and knocked around all over the West. Day by day while Dynamite told vivid stories of his experiences, I mounted the bottom rungs of the cattle-business ladder toward, I fondly imagined, an executive position, if the war permitted. I looked forward to a future that might combine writing and ranching. Meanwhile we watched to see the cattle weren't stuck with their heads between fence rails or out of water because of a leaky trough; and when new stock arrived we helped the drivers unload their trucks or the train crew their trains, because the Sacramento Short Line connecting Oakland with Sacramento and the Southern Pacific system ran through the ranch. For reasons best known to those who schedule trucks and trains, these unloadings usually occurred late at night. We got overtime pay at our regular daily rate of thirty cents an hour, and were expected to be at work next morning, seven days a week, no matter how late we'd been up the night before—because cattle must be fed and looked after daily while they gain valuable weight. We shipped the fat ones off to San Francisco and Los

Angeles, steers selling at nine cents a pound, heifers at eight.

Jane: I worry lest Bob's new friends might not accept me. "Just be yourself," he advises as we drive to our first dance along the dirt road that borders Montezuma Slough and thousands of acres of delta marsh beyond it. We pass several deserted farmhouses abandoned when their owners sold out to the B. B. They make me think of solitary gravestones. Finally we come to one that's also been deserted but is lit up for this special evening. It stands in a grove of gloomy cypresses. A dozen or two jalopies of various makes are drawn up around it like the horses and buggies of an earlier era. Though it exudes light and music, this lonely old house which has once been a home seems ghostly and unreal. The wind moans through the cypresses, adding to the eerie atmosphere. Inside I find the most remarkable sight I've ever seen.

Bob's friend Dynamite, small, vibrant, dressed to kill in a purple sateen shirt, red neckerchief and new Levi's, sits on a box in a corner playing a guitar and at the same time a harmonica held to his mouth by a wire frame. With one cowboy-booted foot he's stamping out the rhythm of "Turkey in the Straw." Beside him sits a gaunt mournful-faced man in blue bib overalls sawing a fiddle as if his life depends on it. And shuffling to and fro over the bare-board floor under the pale light of a kerosene lantern that hangs from the ceiling are the dancers—all so gaunt and wild looking. The women wear everyday cotton prints. Later I learn their dresses are often pieced together from patterned bags that contained feed for their chickens. The men wear khaki or denim. These are the Okies, Arkies, Texans driven west by drought, dust storm and hard times—John Steinbeck's people as depicted in his *Grapes of Wrath* published the year before. They move with a strange solemnity as if this is a trance, not a dance. Watchers stand as solemnly around the walls. "They're just warming up," Bob whispers. "Come on!" Soon we're partners in a square dance being called—squealed, actually—by Fritts, the rawboned cattle foreman:

Grab your partner, give her a whirl,
And don't disturb that pretty little curl!
Around and around and around we go,
With a little more swingin' and a do-si-do!

We've never square-danced before but somehow it comes naturally. After half an hour we stop for breath, perspiring and laughing with partners in similar condition, and I feel I'm being accepted. A few minutes later in the kitchen a young woman wearing a formal black afternoon dress and high heels asks politely: "Would you like a little gin, dear?" and pours me half a glassful as a token of sisterhood. The high point for everyone comes toward midnight when delectable "eats"—delicious sandwiches, scrumptious cookies, fabulous cakes, all homemade—are served, and I see Rod Krug, the farm foreman with whom I've recently been dancing, standing in front of me, offering a mug of pitch black coffee, and hear his friendly declaration: "Mrs. Easton, this'll put hair on your chest!" Later Rod gave us an adorable gray female kitten we named Montezuma after the slough we danced beside, that unforgettable night in the ghostly old house.

As I got to know the women of the B. B., helping with their children, accompanying them on shopping trips to Fairfield or Napa where they made pennies count in highly efficient ways, I began to identify with them as with those backstairs or in the fields at Florence. These too were direct, unsophisticated—loving, hating, suffering, enjoying, surviving with courage and cheerfulness. Dynamite's wife, Bernice, for example, lived with their five small children in a house like the one we danced in which the company let them use rent-free. Dynamite made $3.10 a day. With overtime he brought home around a hundred a month. There was nothing left for extras such as doctors and dentists. When the children got sick they simply got well eventually. When Bernice got a toothache she soaked the tooth with whiskey and deferred the inevitable trip to Napa to have it extracted. Dynamite had a roving eye but she put up with it, proud he was the most dynamic male for miles around and sparked the ranch's social life. Sometimes he slapped her, as when she inadvertently let a pregnant sow out of its pen into the hills where it hid its valuable piglets. But she loved her man, her children, life, in a somber gritty way that was enduring as rock. I admired her as I admired Flora and felt my protective cocoon of privilege disappearing as I shared some of their ordeals—and mingled mine with theirs.

Early in November I miscarried. Bob and I had decided against birth control. We wanted children, especially one that might keep me company if he went off to war. It was Flora who explained what might be the matter when I missed my period and then passed a lot of coagulated blood one night in bed. But there were complications and I went to a hospital in Berkeley for treatment. Bob drove down every night to see me. Sometimes when alone I cried for the lost baby we'd wanted so badly. When at last I went home I was weak but our little apartment seemed more precious than ever, our marriage stronger because of shared sorrow, and we decorated our first Christmas tree with joy and hope.

Bob: That winter of '40–'41 was the wettest in California history. Day after day Dynamite and I rode the alleyways in yellow slickers and rain hats. The river rose and broke the levee protecting our lower pens and we had to evacuate cattle to high ground in a hurry. Strange things happened as if triggered by strange weather. Anthrax had been unknown on the delta for so long it had been forgotten. So when a steer dropped as if hit over the head and a trickle of blood ran from its nose, we couldn't imagine what was wrong. Nor could the veterinary. Soon they were dropping like flies. The fact that anthrax could be fatal to humans added suspense when we learned the truth.

Since *Coast* days I'd carried a notebook and jotted down ideas and bits of overheard conversations. Now I began a series of sketches about life on the B. B., getting up an hour earlier to write at our kitchen table. I felt these were better than any writing I'd done because they were more solidly based on actual experience: the ranch life and married life I was living. When Jane's father encouraged me, I decided to make my sketches into stories. Meanwhile world events were catching up with us.

On the scorching hot afternoon of June 22, 1941, while waiting at the railroad station in Lodi for Jane, who'd hurried to Los Angeles after her father suffered a severe heart attack, I saw the headlines announcing Hitler's invasion of Russia. All that spring he'd been extending his conquests—into Yugoslavia, Roumania, Bulgaria, Greece, even the island of Crete from where he might launch an attack on Egypt to support the sensational advance of General Erwin Rommel across North Africa to the Egyptian border. Now it would be global war with a vengeance: Germany, Italy, Japan and their allies against England and the Soviet Union, with China holding out as best she could against the Japanese who've seized most of her territory.

We talk it over as we drive toward Rio Vista, stopping for dinner at Giusti's Italian restaurant on the riverbank where the Lodi road joins the Sacramento levee road. Will Hitler pull it off, or will he

"Jane and the bunkhouse gang at the McCreery Ranch," 1941

151

"Fresh out of OCS with my proud parents, Robert and Ethel Easton," 1942

meet the fate of Napoleon, bogged down in Russia's vast expanse and snowy winter? Over veal parmigiana I remember those fearless young Russians, male and female, I'd seen as a tourist in Moscow in '37 jumping from a hundred-fifty-foot-high parachute tower at the Park of Culture and Rest (now called Gorky Park). They might be hard to beat. I also recall the Germany I'd seen that summer. Aside from the park which was full of gaiety and enjoyment, Moscow seemed like a prison—grim, torpid, oppressed by Stalin's bloody purges then at their height. Once, as we were walking across Red Square, a procession of three black limousines, curtains drawn, shot out of the Kremlin gates and zipped away down a side street like gangster getaway cars—carrying VIPs or dead bodies? We could only guess. Passersby scarcely turned their heads. Probably they were afraid to.

Berlin, by contrast, seemed alight with energy and purpose—of a sinister kind. Swastikas everywhere—on flags, banners, armbands. Uniforms everywhere. Young people marching and singing. And in the dining room of our hotel, middle-aged men in business suits raising right arms in the Nazi salute and muttering "Heil Hitler!" as they entered. Yet on the boat floating down the Rhine, drinking the new September wine with my college mates and me, young non-Nazi Germans—all of us students, all of us full of the optimism of youth—proclaimed that war was absurd and only wine and friendship mattered.

I also remember Italy. There'd been a comic-opera touch, for sure, about black-shirted Fascists marching to music in their shiny brass helmets and

plumes. But Mussolini evidently had strong support and the country was alive with a spirit of militant vigor. In Rome I stood in the crowd at the curb watching the funeral of Marconi, the great Italian inventor of the wireless, and saw a jut-jawed uniformed "Il Duce" pass within a few yards of me as he walked behind the coffin. Mussolini looked tough if pompous. He would later deride our "decadent democracies" as afraid to fight and boast of no breadlines in Italy or Germany, and indeed there were none, the otherwise unemployed being busy on state projects or military service. By contrast France and England seemed listless and defeatist-minded, accepting war as inevitable but unable to muster the energy to do much about it. The "Moose" might be pompous but he was also dangerous.

Just recently during the fall of France, he'd jumped her from behind, while she reeled under Hitler's onslaught, and grabbed a piece of territory along the Riviera; then tried much the same thing in North Africa against the hard-pressed British but got his nose bloodied until Rommel turned things around. And this past spring the gallant little Greek Army had been kicking the dew out of the Italians until, again, the Germans came along. Yet one by one the democracies *had* gone under: Austria, Czechoslovakia, Belgium, Holland, France, Denmark, Norway, leaving England standing alone against Hitler—England and now Russia. Jane and I agreed the U.S. probably couldn't sit on the sidelines much longer.

On the other hand she brought good news. While in Los Angeles she'd met an attractive woman in her early forties, Josephine McCreery, who with her husband, an Englishman, owned a cattle ranch near Hollister, two hours drive south of San Francisco. Selby was a captain in the British army reserve and was being called to duty and Josephine needed congenial company as well as working help on the ranch. So when she wrote inviting us to come take a look we did. The place was perfectly beautiful, golden mountains and a secluded valley three thousand feet high in the Coast Range—Royal Ranch of the Eagles, its original Spanish owners christened it. Josephine's modern one-story H-shaped house, stucco with tile roof, surrounded a bricked patio where honeysuckle and plumbago bloomed. We would have the rustic frame cottage dating back to the mid-1800s. Near it was an almost equally ancient and charming cookhouse where two young Chinese-Americans, Thomas and Roger, presided; and beyond was the bunkhouse, home for three or four bachelors; and then a large barn and adjoining corrals—all set in that high valley dotted with huge oaks, surrounded by peaks of golden grass. It was truly a Shangri-la and we fell in love with it at first sight.

Josephine offered us the magnificent sum of ninety dollars a month cash plus the cottage, our milk and meat free and the possibility of Sundays off now and then. It seemed almost too good to be true. With the war situation what it was, the B. B. job looked increasingly temporary. And at the McCreery we would have improved pay and working conditions and conceivably a home where Jane might stay should I take up soldiering. Furthermore it brought our dream of a hilltop house a step closer.

Jane: We moved in September as Hitler's armored divisions were penetrating deep into Russia and the Japanese were extending their conquests in China and Southeast Asia. There seemed no stopping the Axis Powers, as they called themselves. I rose in the dark each morning at five o'clock when the alarm went off, lit the big black kitchen stove which burned chunks of fragrant oak, and prepared breakfast while Bob went to the barn to water and feed his horses and saddle the one he would use. During the day I worked at my diary or, accompanied by our beloved Montezuma, who like most cats was developing a remarkable personality, I gossiped with Josephine or with the two boys at the cookhouse. Smiling with ancient Chinese wisdom, Thomas and Roger showed me how to soak pink beans overnight in cold water before cooking, then let them simmer until blowing gently on one—held up in a spoon—peeled away its skin and it was properly done.

Little Joe Correia, the choreman, surreptitiously brought me "extra" eggs he'd found in the mangers of the barn where the hens liked to lay, and we kept up this conspiratorial relationship with her approval after I told Josephine all about it. Joe told me about his life. He was especially proud of having worked on a ranch near Carmel for Mrs. Herbert Hoover whom he greatly admired—just as proud as he was of his honorable discharge from World War I. I loved Joe and all the simplicity and good faith he stood for.

Toothpick-thin Weldon Lynch, the foreman, who'd homesteaded on the Mexican border of New Mexico until forced out by drought and bandidos, showed Bob how to handle horses without letting them buck, a departure from Wild West ways; and in the evenings Bob worked on his stories or we read aloud Katherine Mansfield's stories or some of D. H. Lawrence's letters. Lights went out at 9:00 when Josephine turned off the Delco system that generated our electricity. Afterward we could read by kerosene lamp if we wanted but seldom did.

Because the ranch was sometimes isolated for weeks during winter storms, we drove to Hollister, twenty-six miles by lovely if undependable road, and purchased cases of canned food—tomatoes, apricots, peaches, corned beef—and Bob bought two pairs of Levi's for $2.10 each, up from $1.85 because of wartime demand for denim. And thus we began a new life, making friends with our surroundings and its people and feeling accepted as we had at the B. B.—grateful for every day, with the Damocles sword of war hanging over us. Even so, when the sword fell, that peaceful Sunday noontime of December 7, it took us by surprise.

Epilogue

In the foregoing selection from our book, *Love and War: Pearl Harbor through V-J Day*, my wife is no longer covert partner but overt one. She's surfaced at

Jane and Robert Easton with their firstborn, Joan, in Santa Barbara, 1944

last, or we've both surfaced together, after fifty years of surreptitious collaboration during which I've read everything I published aloud to her first, and with typical male chauvinistic shamelessness, used her criticism without publicly acknowledging it, much as I used her emotional and other support. Now the truth is out, now that I've confessed, I feel better. But to resume . . .

Those stories that went off to the *Atlantic* before the bombs fell on Pearl Harbor got published almost by accident. My father-in-law sent them to his agent Carl Brandt in New York where they languished on Carl's desk until one day, when he was away from the office, his right-hand woman, Bernice Baumgarten, wife of the novelist James Gould Cozzens, bundled them up and sent them to the *Atlantic*'s new editor Ted Weeks. Weeks received them enthusiastically and introduced me to his readers as an "Atlantic first," a gimmick he'd invented to hype authors he was "discovering" and publishing for the first time.

Meanwhile I was amalgamating them and others into my first book, a novel, *The Happy Man*, issued by Viking in 1943, my editor there being Pascal Covici, who was also Steinbeck's and had recently published his *Grapes of Wrath*. Covici apparently saw something of Steinbeck in my writing about the California scene. He gave me free rein and published verbatim what I submitted. Covici's encouragement coupled with Frederick Faust's and Bernice Baumgarten's changed my life. *The Happy Man* was generally well received, garnered spacious reviews in *New York Times* and *Herald Tribune* plus a column in the latter by Stephen Vincent Benét, the last words he published, alas, before a fatal heart attack at age forty-five. Benét, a Californian in his youth, generously declared me "an addition to American letters." *The Happy Man* responded by selling a respectable wartime eight thousand copies in hardcover, going through one new edition in quality paperback in later years, and is now poised for a third, I'm happy to say.

Several of its first reviewers noted I was not likely to publish another book for the duration, since I was an officer with a tank destroyer battalion. They were right. Jane went home to live with her parents after Pearl Harbor, and I enlisted in the army as a private, went to OCS and eventually to England and France with the 825th Tank Destroyer Battalion in '44, transferred to the 29th Infantry Division and served the last six months of the war in Germany as a rifle platoon leader. We got close enough to Berlin to see the smoke rising from its ruins. I found that being shot at focuses the mind most remarkably. It also heightens one's appreciation of life, especially of one's wife and children and country. I'm grateful for

The author (standing in background) with members of his platoon, K Company, 116th Infantry, 29th Division, waiting to jump off for the attack on Jülich, Germany, 1945

having survived, and at times feel guilty for doing so while others did not. I'm also grateful that my experience was in a just war, if war ever can be just. My admiration for the American GI, especially the infantry doughfoot-grunt, remains unbounded.

Toward the end of my overseas stay I had the unusual experience of commanding a company that included a platoon of black volunteers, a "fifth platoon" (rifle companies normally consisted of four platoons), whose members had voluntarily exchanged comparatively safe rear-area assignments for combat duty, many of them taking reductions in rank to do so. These black volunteers were widely admired for having performed exceptionally well in combat, and were accepted as friends and equals by their white comrades and vice versa. I found them outstanding in their post-combat conduct as soldiers and individuals, though I was angered and shamed when several told me they weren't planning to go home after the war but to remain in Europe or England where racial prejudice was then negligible. The full story of these volunteers needs to be told. Jane and I tell it briefly in our *Love and War*. I'm glad to say others are doing so more extensively.

Serving with black volunteers reminded me of my maternal grandfather Warren Olney doing likewise nearly a hundred years earlier, also in a war for freedom and justice. Born in a log cabin on the Iowa frontier, he fought in the Civil War on the Northern side as a volunteer private, and later captain of "colored" troops. He too spent four years in the army, most of them with the infantry. Eventually a San Francisco lawyer, he was also a published writer, contributing a variety of articles to the *Overland Monthly*, the West Coast's *Atlantic Monthly*, in the 1880s and '90s. They ranged from California water law to the youth and education of Napoleon Bonaparte. Grandfather bequeathed me his complete set of Sir Walter Scott and his copy of *Man Eaters of Tsavo*, acquired during a visit to Africa, and his love of words and mountains. The Sierra Club was founded in his office. With help from the thousand dollars he left me, I visited London, Paris, Rome, Warsaw, Moscow and Berlin during that summer of 1937, climbed part way up the Matterhorn and looked up toward its craggy white summit as I often looked up to Grandfather.

During and after the war I published stories in *Collier's*, the most prestigious—and remunerative—popular magazine market after the *Saturday Evening Post*. *Collier's* paid us four hundred dollars for our first contribution, twice what the *Atlantic* paid, and eventually as much as a thousand. Multiply by about ten to get today's purchasing power and you see how writers could make a living from magazine work. These were stories with California settings or war stories. I had a war book in mind but time and format didn't jell until much later, nearly half a century.

Meanwhile there was bread to be earned for self and wife and two small daughters. Taking wartime discharge pay and savings nest egg, we set off for the heart of Texas and Lampasas, population five thousand, a charming farm-and-ranch town where Jane and I had lived happily in a hotel room for six weeks in '43 when I was stationed at Camp Hood nearby. Lampasas, deep in the American heartland, far from wartime separations or madding crowds, had become our dream place. We miraculously found a house there when housing was almost nonexistent due to wartime moratoriums on construction, and Jane tended to its operation and continued to realize her ambition of being a hands-on mother and living simply. Our white cottage at the intersection of two unpaved streets, open rangeland adjoining the backyard, had four rooms and a bath, and cost $6,500. Jane made the acquaintance of neighbors and fellow kindergarten mothers, and penetrated the intricacies of local social life, including formal "coffees" in homes at 10 A.M. where you were expected to arrive dressed as for afternoon tea, and evening occasions when women congregated on one side of the room and gossiped while men talked business on the other. Men ruled the roost, often shopping for food and clothing in company with wives and children in order

to supervise the outlay of cash, their cash. Eyebrows were raised when Jane signed her own checks, almost the only woman in town to do so. Notwithstanding differences, people received us with a friendship that remains unforgettable.

I did on-the-job training under the GI Bill of Rights with the editor of a weekly newspaper and eventually became an editor myself, as well as a pretty darn good typesetter, while receiving ninety dollars a month from U.S. taxpayers. I co-founded, co-published and edited the *Lampasas Dispatch*, first as a weekly, later as a semi-weekly. My duties included contemplating, sometimes with dismay, the next-issue deadline; collecting and writing news for it and setting that news in type; soliciting and writing advertising and setting type for and casting the hot-metal cuts (engravings) for that advertising; helping compose and lock up the chases (rectangular metal frames) containing the type and cuts for each page; carrying them from the composing table to the old, black, flatbed roller press; feeding large rectangular sheets of newsprint into the running press that printed what I'd written and composed; feeding the printed sheets into a folding machine and thence into a mailer (stamper); and finally carrying the finished product to the post office. Along with sweeping out our own office and paying bills, it was a wonderfully rich experience that gave me a sense of creating a product from beginning to end such as I've never had before or since.

It also sharpened my writing style and kept me producing readable copy daily in mainstream lan-

"With three incipient baby boomers, Katherine, Ellen, Joan, and our Fiat," Villa Rosina, Italy, 1950

"With Jane Faust Easton and our four girls, Jane, Ellen, Katherine, and Joan," 1972

guage. And it substantiated what I'd long believed: that a man or woman can, perhaps even should, be a citizen first and an artist or something else second. Being editor in a country town where you know and are accountable to your subscribers and advertisers and nearly everyone else on a first-name basis ensures above all that you remain primarily a member of the human race and of your community. The ancient Athenians set us the example, as did the Renaissance Florentines.

Local color abounded in Lampasas as did local issues that were sometimes national and even worldwide in scope. One of our subscribers, Elijah Chambers, a famed rattlesnake killer from far out in the cedar brakes, would periodically walk into our office with eight or ten dead rattlers hanging from his harpoon-like stabber made of flexible copper tubing, before going to the county courthouse in the middle of the nearby square to collect his ten-cent bounty on each kill. And when, with our first issue, we initiated the revolutionary—for Lampasas and many similar communities—practice of *not* putting the word colored in parenthesis (colored) after the name of every

black mentioned in print, nearly all the two dozen or so adult African-Americans in town took advantage of our get-acquainted offer and subscribed to the *Dispatch* for one dollar a year. Real life, real issues, poured in upon us daily and we loved it.

At the same time I was making notes for that war book and for a historical novel about California where my roots ran back to a '49er ancestor who'd found more gold selling vegetables in San Francisco than in prospecting on the American River, and I sold stories to *Collier's* and the big slick new *Holiday*, edited by Ted Patrick, perhaps the first of its kind devoted to leisure and travel as well as quality writing. We loved Texas and the Texans but Texas didn't love us. The allergic asthma which tormented and even killed many in the central part of the state nearly finished off our oldest daughter Joan and our newly born Ellen. When our loyal doctor Rush McMillin made his second successive 4 A.M. house call to give Joan a shot of adrenalin so she could continue to breathe, we began to think of leaving our dream place. Allergies and related asthma were just beginning to be understood in 1949 and no professional allergists existed nearer than San Angelo, 150 miles away. We began looking for a place where we could live cheaply while I wrote full time.

Now with three daughters, we moved to Italy to a small villa on a farm in the Chianti region not far from Florence. It had two stories, eight furnished rooms, and cost thirty dollars a month rent. The *contadini* family who tended its hillside acres of olives, grapes and wheat lived on the floor below us as did their two cows. I continued to write for the magazine market and groped on toward that next novel. Jane gently but firmly criticized everything I wrote and chauffeured the two older children to and from school in Florence in our tiny Fiat stationwagon; while Maria, lovely daughter of the *contadini*, looked after our youngest. We revisited Jane's old home on Fiesole, a headquarters for German SS troops during the war and now a headquarters for the Olivetti typewriter people, and had tea with Arthur Acton in palatial Villa La Pietra across the lane; and later we made the acquaintance, among others, of John Horne Burns whose novel *The Gallery* still ranks high in our list of wartime fiction. Burns also died prematurely, alas. I picked up a few words of Italian as the months went by but never matched Jane's fluency. What we shared equally was a love of the simple wholesome food prepared by our Maria over a wood fire, seasoned with wild herbs from the farm, washed down by Chianti we helped make. I developed an admiration and affection for the Italian people which matched Jane's and has continued to grow.

"In my study with the 1942 Royal Portable at left,"
Santa Barbara, 1990

Children's health problems plus Jane's problematical pregnancy brought us back to Santa Barbara in 1951 and we've been here since. Our red clapboard farmhouse in the hills behind the Old Mission, though built many years before we bought it, uncannily resembles the one we dreamed of when first married—even before we met. We continue to think psychic forces may guide such strange coincidences. Jane's problematical pregnancy proved illusory, resulting in a quite normal fourth daughter, and Jane can now boast of an honorary lifetime membership in our Santa Barbara PTA plus many years' organizational service on behalf of local and regional environments, plus a perceptive memoir in book form of her younger days, *Memories of the '20s and '30s.*

I've helped establish our local environmental defense center and community environmental council, participated in efforts to control offshore oil drilling as well as in city land-use planning and the establishment of backcountry wilderness areas. These activities and others led to receipt of the California Conservation Council's Honor Award, plus a continuing commitment to local and national environmental movements and the effort to preserve the California condor which my father and I helped instigate back in the thirties. I hope to see young birds, successfully raised in captivity, introduced to their natural habitat in our backcountry and a wild flock thus re-created. Meanwhile I've produced numerous magazine stories and a variety of books: biography, history, natural history, environmental history, true adventure, and personal history as well as three more novels. I type everything I publish on my 1942 Royal Portable, sometimes making a pencil draft first, almost always rewriting extensively.

One magazine assignment was supported by a Stern Foundation grant obtained in the summer of '63 to do an article for *Harper's* on the incipient Goldwater-Kennedy confrontation for the 1964 presidency, as previewed in the Rocky Mountain heartland states of Utah, Colorado and Wyoming—where a new and even reactionary conservatism, threatening JFK, seemed on the rise. After two weeks there we found that although the John Birch Society and the Libertarians were factors, mountain conservatism had a predominantly native hue which seemed essentially geographic and nonextremist, more an attitude toward life than a doctrine. Most people we talked to liked Kennedy personally but not the Eastern-liberal-urban establishment he represented for them. I concealed the fact I'd voted for him and that he and his brother Joe had been my collegemates at Harvard. Regardless of politics, what came through overridingly during our interviews was a sense of Western

"Jane and I at three-score-and-ten plus a few"

openness and hospitality. One blue-jeaned rancher, after a relatively brief roadside conversation, asked us home for the night and to help brand calves next day. Our article, titled "Right Turn in the Rockies," scheduled to lead off the February 1964 issue of *Harper's*, was shot down along with Kennedy at Dallas and now rests, perhaps appropriately, at the University of Wyoming at Laramie in the heart of the Rockies.

For several years in the sixties I supplemented our income and experience by teaching English at Santa Barbara City College, first part-time in its adult education division, then as full-time faculty member, acquiring for the latter an M.A. in English at the University of California at Santa Barbara under supervision of Hugh Kenner. I emerged a staunch proponent of the community college system, which provides educational opportunities for almost anyone at low cost, and of Kenner, who excels as scholar-writer-critic-conversationalist. Seldom did I teach a class whose members failed to range in age from eighteen to nearly eighty and include a broad social spectrum: housewives, high-school and other kinds of dropouts, retired people, education-hungry working

people many of them economically or socially disadvantaged and striving to catch up, as well as the normal run of high-school graduates—some university bound, some not. It was a refreshing reminder that public education is at the heart of our democratic system, is democracy in action. As for Kenner, I found him brilliantly familiar with nearly everything in English literature and much outside it. One of his main conversational arguments—with which I disagreed—was that avant-garde contemporary writing could be greatly important, even though comprehensible only to an elite few, much as contemporary astrophysics is comprehensible only to an elite few. I argued that pioneering writing should be comprehensible by a majority of the reading public in order to be greatly important, as most classics were when they first appeared.

Kenner was the first I've known to employ extensively the pile-on-the-floor method of filing books or other material for current or near-current use. There were times when he was barely approachable across a densely stacked office, a condition I often recall when Jane, coming to my open door, advances no farther for fear of stumbling and breaking a leg, while making clear her anxiety in no uncertain terms.

And now in *Love and War: Pearl Harbor through V-J Day*, she and I mingle our letters from homefront and warfront in a kind of dialog interspersed with numerous interpolations and footnotes in our today's voice which, hopefully, help carry the conversation along and clarify it—e.g. What was a ration coupon? What was a buzz bomb? Can love endure? We hope *Love and War* will be a meaningful contribution to wartime literature and to the record of the human experience. What helps make it unique is its woman's view of those stressful and momentous years presented simultaneously with a man's. It will be Jane's second book; my fifteenth as author, co-author or editor.

Along the way I've paid part of my debt to her father in the form of a biography and a forthcoming book of his best poems and have realized that early dream of a California historical novel—not in one volume but in a series which Capra is doing. We call it "The Saga of California." Volumes one and two, *This Promised Land* and *Power and Glory*, have been well received generally and adopted for use in college and university courses; and we are busy with volume three, *Blood and Money*, as we move our characters and their descendants from that moment of first contact between natives and European invaders in 1769 down to present time.

Among friends we made here after returning from Florence were Kenneth and Margaret Millar, both mystery novelists, he writing under the name Ross Macdonald. With Ken and Margaret we drank beer, evenings; took daytime walks along the beach or on Mountain Drive overlooking the city; discussed the human condition and our own. For twenty years Ken and I read and criticized each other's work in manuscript and collaborated in environmental activism. We also participated in the first Santa Barbara writers conferences sponsored by Santa Barbara City College, forerunners of better known ones established later and carried on by Barnaby Conrad and his wife.

Following the disastrous offshore oil spill of 1969, which was to trigger the national environmental movement, Ken urged me to write a nonfiction book about it which I did, titled *Black Tide*. I urged him to write a novel about it which he did, titled *Sleeping Beauty*, perhaps the first environmental novel. Now Ken is gone, but we continue to see Margaret regularly. She was and remains our colleague in various issues.

Not long after we returned from Florence, Aldous Huxley came for dinner and renewed old memories of Italy with Jane, holding us and our daughters spellbound with stories of Frieda and D. H. Lawrence. Though his eyesight was nearly gone, his mind seemed brilliant as ever. What struck us especially was his scientific-philosophical bent. He seemed to have passed beyond literature into what he may have considered more mature interests.

Now as the need for time and privacy seems more pressing, we see fewer people, literary or otherwise. Among them are the prolific mystery writer Dennis Lynds (aka Michael Collins et al.) and his wife Gayle, also a writer; and our longtime friend and publisher Noel Young of Capra Press, one of the country's outstanding small presses and a monument to entrepreneurial courage and skill. Noel has published Henry Miller as well as Kenneth Millar, Ray Bradbury, Edward Abbey, Kay Boyle, Ursula Le-Guin, Gretel Ehrlich and Anaïs Nin among others.

Back in the '50s, Noel was a founding member with me and Ken Millar of the Santa Barbara Writers Luncheon, a fortnightly gathering whose total membership often fitted into one booth at Harry's El Cielito Cafe and watering hole on State Street near the courthouse. The group grew to nearly forty, then split and continued to multiply. Over the years its guests have included such luminaries as William Saroyan, Clifton Fadiman, Jack Schaefer, Alex Haley, and Eudora Welty. Today a small auditorium would be required to accommodate all our local writers, female and male, Sue Grafton being among our latest additions.

During our walks on Mountain Drive, Ken and I used to talk about beautiful, community-conscious, civically and nationally concerned Santa Barbara, nestled there below us by the sea, becoming a center for literature, music and the other arts—the "Athens of the West," as Ken once said. It has moved far in that direction. As one of its few homegrown writers I take special pride in this.

The first part of this essay was excerpted from *Love and War: Pearl Harbor through V-J Day*, by Robert and Jane Easton, published in June 1991 by the University of Oklahoma Press, and used here by permission.

BIBLIOGRAPHY

Fiction:

The Happy Man, Viking, 1943.

The Hearing, McNally & Loftin, 1964.

This Promised Land, Capra, 1982.

Power and Glory, Capra, 1989.

Nonfiction:

(With Mackenzie Brown) *Lord of Beasts* (biography), University of Arizona Press, 1961, Andre Deutsch, 1964.

(With Jay Monaghan and others) *The Book of the American West,* Messner, 1963.

(With Dick Smith) *California Condor: Vanishing American,* McNally & Loftin, 1964.

Max Brand: "The Big Westerner" (biography), University of Oklahoma Press, 1970.

Black Tide: The Santa Barbara Oil Spill and Its Consequences, Delacorte, 1972.

Guns, Gold, and Caravans, Capra, 1978.

China Caravans: An American Adventurer in Old China, Capra, 1982.

Life and Work, University of California, Santa Barbara, Oral History Program and U.C. Regents, 1990.

(With Jane Easton) *Love and War: Pearl Harbor through V-J Day,* University of Oklahoma Press, 1991.

Editor:

Max Brand's Best Stories, Dodd, 1967.

Charles F. Lummis, *Bullying the Moqui,* Prescott College Press, 1968.

(With Jane Easton) *Max Brand's Best Poems: Verses from a Master of Popular Prose,* Fithian Press, forthcoming.

Other:

Contributor to numerous magazines including the *Atlantic, Esquire, Reader's Digest,* and *New York Times Magazine.* Contributor to numerous anthologies including *Continent's End,* edited by Joseph Henry Jackson, McGraw, 1944; *Great Tales of the American West,* edited by Harry E. Maule, Modern Library, 1945; *Out West,* edited by Jack Schaefer, Houghton, 1955; *A Treasury of True,* edited by Charles N. Barnard, Barnes, 1956; *Inward Journey: Ross Macdonald,* edited by Ralph Sipper, Cordelia, 1984; *The New Frontier,* edited by Joe R. Lansdale, Doubleday, 1989; and *Great World War II Stories,* edited by Martin H. Greenberg and Bill Pronzini, New American Library, 1991.

Steve Katz

1935-

Steve Katz—"Boulder in blue shirt," Colorado, 1989

I killed a chicken, a newly hatched chick, that is, two or three days out of its shell. That's my first memory of myself. I grabbed it. It felt downy and pulsed in my hands. I climbed onto a stool in the barnyard, dropped it into a rain barrel, and sprinted away on three-year-old legs. This happened at a place we called the Hardens', where my family would go sometimes in the summer to escape the heat of New York City. The Hardens were a black family that rented rooms and fed a few vacationing New Yorkers on their farm in the Catskills. For my mom I invented a devious story about this little boy who needed to see if a baby chick could swim, my first attempt at fiction, but it was unsuccessful. She had to apologize to the Hardens and pay for the chicken. Although she never hit me I did feel her displeasure, and had to live with

my shame for the rest of that vacation, which seems to go on forever.

The smell of the Hardens' is tucked into my memory, occasionally wafting out on some of my trips into the South, or at some soul-food restaurant, like the old Pink Teacup on Bleecker Street, where I get a whiff of bacon grease and greens, and ham hocks and grits being cooked endlessly on a crusty old stove. My mother was good about my crime, didn't make me suffer much, though I suffered anyway, my first experience of guilt, that involuntary self-indulgence, repugnant, cloying, sweet and unpurgable as a tablespoon of molasses; and it was also thrilling, the first taste of power for a little person, of having made a little death that caused a stir in the commerce of the big people.

161

More credibility should be given to the experiments of three-year-olds. I tried a chicken in a rain barrel and learned it couldn't swim. It died instead, and that gave me my first taste of megalomaniacal ecstasy, which was one of my first reasons for becoming a novelist. Characters are quite like chickens; you can kill them for your sport—fry them if they refuse to come home to roost. They've got minds of their own, but you've got all the weapons. Perhaps that's why early on I submerged my interest in character for other possibilities in storytelling, like the drift of narration, like spontaneity and improvisation, the vulnerability of the narrator, the nature of the page, the look of the book. It's a good thing that there be this profession of novelist, and it is important that it be supported if for no other reason than as a diversion for minor megalomaniacs. Keep them at their desks!

*

I was seven or eight, and she must have been orbiting forty. She was the mother of my sister's friend, Joan. She looked tall to me, and slim, with delicate Semitic features, and a full mouth that she impastoed with red lipstick to play against her blue eyes. A negligee couldn't have been any more provocative to me than the blue-grey uniform of the AWVS (American Women's Voluntary Services) that she wore as she ran that operation from a storefront on Broadway. She introduced me to the war effort. For her I scoured the neighborhood pulling a cardboard box behind me on a rope, knocking on doors to collect scraps of metal foil and worn rubber heels to be recycled into the war effort against the Nazis and Nips. She was the fundament of my patriotism, and I fought my own little war every day through my neighborhood so I could return to her offices to be praised by her for the bits of rubber and metal scraps in my box. Sometimes she'd reward me with comic books—Captain Marvel, Jr., whom I loved for his blue costume, or Archie and his inconsequential romances with Betty and Veronica. (I preferred Veronica for her black hair that made her look more like my muse.) Once she kissed me on the cheek, and I carried that kiss home, my face tilted to the right with the weight of it. "Look at that," said Rita, my sister. "Where did you get that?" She was seven years older than I, and the implications of a kiss were certainly richer for her than for me. I stared at my cheek in the mirror. It was like a brand, a livid tattoo, my badge, my medal. I would never wash it off, and I

didn't, and when I look closely at my face I see it there today.

That was my introduction to what became a long, complicated, and not always happy interaction with the muse. Everything I've done in my life for some cause greater than my limited, tainted self has been for her, to invoke her, to please her, to satisfy her, and I have to admit I haven't got to her yet.

*

Mrs. Makarof was a sexy science teacher at Junior High School 115 in Washington Heights. She often would walk through the classroom asking questions. Her skirt was usually buttoned up the front, but she liked to leave the lower two buttons undone. She enjoyed settling on the desk of one boy or another, usually George Zografi's. He was already shaving and looked almost nineteen. She would plump down on his desk and the fold of her skirt would fall away from her knee as she asked us about the heart of the frog. I sat at the back of the class writing in a composition notebook, a novel about tennis. I had tennis fantasies. My father had once won a city doubles championship, but had gotten sick before he could help me learn the sport. Ray Gangi and I swung at tennis balls on the courts under the George Washington Bridge, fantasizing that in high school we would play on the tennis team while all our New York Bullet buddies were struggling to make the baseball team. We didn't know anyone else who played tennis, had no idea that "rich kids" did it and even took lessons from pros. I never finished that novel, though occasionally in high school I would look at the notebook, astonished at how many words I had put down, and how little I had said. I never made the tennis team either. One day Mrs. Makarof made it to the back of the class and settled onto my desk, right on top of my novel. She asked what I was doing, and when I told her she asked me what that had to do with science. I had no answer. Her lean over me was too intimidating even to be sexy. This muse turned into a writer's block. After that the words wouldn't come for my novel anymore.

*

My father and I listened to the fights. He had a heart condition and at the time this was treated mostly with bed rest. We'd hang out in the evenings in his bed and bet on the fighters. In the Joe Louis–Tami Mauriello fight he let me take Joe Louis, and I won his four bits. I took Jersey Joe Walcott in his first fight against Ezzard Charles, and I lost, but my dad paid me as if I'd won. It was bad training for me as a gambler, but made him feel good. My dad was dead before the third Graziano–Zale fight. I remember bringing scraps of paper to his bed on which I'd written down some little poems. In the tiny apartment we lived in near Jayhood Wright Park in Washington Heights, it felt like a long walk from the bedroom I shared with my sister step by step carrying my poems to his bed. My sister had an anthology of modern poetry, one of the few books in my house, and I was stirred by Walt Whitman and T. S. Eliot and Carl Sandburg and Archibald MacLeish and Dylan Thomas. I thought I would make something with the language that would change the world. My father wasn't much of a reader, but he kept spiral notebooks with messages to himself, and thoughts for his brothers and sisters he didn't dare tell them in person. When I read him my imitation poems I could see his attention wasn't on them, but he told me they were good. After he died I carried his notebooks around with me for years in a sealed box, and when I finally opened them, when I was approaching forty, hoping I'd find in them some answers to the million questions I had about my own life, I found nothing, nothing of interest, no wisdom, but some lists, a banal address to me about being a good kid, which brought a tear, and some grievances against his sisters. I wanted language from my father, but it wasn't there. Whitman was my father in that realm, and William Faulkner, and John Keats, and Dylan Thomas—all of them.

*

The best part of pretending to be a writer at Stuyvesant High School was that if you worked on the literary magazine you didn't have to attend the English classes. Although I wrote a few poems while at the school I put most of my energy into wood shop, working on a table I never finished, or into the jobs I took after school, working as a shipping clerk for Carl Henry Tobaccos, a tiny mail-order company that claimed to sell denicotinized tobacco. Mr. Henry was an old Kentucky gentleman who wore a big white hat, who would occasionally step out of his office, with a fat denicotinized cigar hanging from his mouth, and gaze myopically at the five or six people in his office work force. Once, when the office manager fired me for falling asleep while stuffing flyers into envelopes, he called me into his office and talked disconnectedly about work ethic—"You get paid to do a job, sonny," he said, and then gave me a raise and sent me back to the shipping table. I was fired once as an office boy

"Visionary Boy Scout at eleven years"

for an import-export firm, because, as they said on their pink slip, I had "outlived my usefulness." I was grateful for that, because having outlived my usefulness at fifteen there was nothing left for me but to become a writer, and I think I was a writer from then on, though I didn't yet write much. But as a writer I did enjoy my next job in the city, which was delivering yard goods all over the garment district for two young brothers with a small business on Union Square, wholesaling cloth. They sent me all over Manhattan, either with a cart delivering bolts, or with samples, and it was through that job that I felt my connection to New York grow, as I entered factory buildings through the freight elevators, dealt with receptionists and foremen, ran gauntlets of older workers, fat and boozy and tattooed, and barely avoided disaster in the traffic on Broadway when my cart got stuck in the cobbles.

I spent a lot of time then going to museums, and malingering in front of Rousseau's Sleeping Gypsy, or the Mondrian Broadway Boogie Woogie, or the Picasso Demoiselles D'Avignon at the Modern, or the lucent Vermeers at the Frick, or Hieronymous Bosch

"Visionary college professor at forty-eight years"

mentioned to me that he was going to Cornell to study veterinary medicine. I decided to do the same, because the name of the school rang a clear bell of escape in my mind, and the agriculture school had no tuition, and though I'd hardly ever been near a cow, and never even had a dog, the veterinary profession seemed an honorable one to me, and certainly more attractive than dentistry, which was my mother's ambition for her son. To support my application for advanced freshman English at Cornell, Mr. Astrakhan, the adviser to the Stuyvesant literary magazine, wrote a recommendation that I caught a glimpse of in which he said I wrote poetry of "astounding imagery." I'd never heard the word "imagery" before, or if I had, had never paid attention to it, but now that it was attributed to me, I went back through all my poets—Thomas, Cummings, Whitman, Williams, every poem I'd ever read, and identified the images. They were there. It was something to know. I looked at my own meagre handful of poems to see if I had any, but I couldn't find them. No images. Just thoughts. I felt like a charlatan, and I didn't dare go back to Mr. Astrakhan to ask where he saw the images in my poems, because I wasn't supposed to have seen his recommendation, and I was afraid he would remove "astounding imagery" from the page. I vowed that from then on I would use imagery forever.

*

From my peculiar perspective taking courses in animal husbandry, entomology, and botany at the Cornell College of Agriculture, what went on at the liberal arts campus looked like a joyful pillowfight of the mind. It wasn't long before I ached to be there. I didn't really appreciate until several years after I graduated how rich my two years of education as an "aggy" were. I enjoyed the science courses and was always proud of having learned something about judging cows, sheep, hogs, and horses. When Pat Bell, a young woman from Nevada I met in my freshman year, asked me why I wanted to be a veterinarian, I explained that I was a writer and expected to meet interesting people and have interesting experiences as a vet. After we were married some years later she would frequently bring that up in conversation with other people whenever she wryly explained how peculiar I was.

Since I had no farm experience, the school required that I work on farms in the summer. The first farmer I worked for, Alfred Partridge, who raised Jersey cows on a little over a hundred acres of

at the Met. It was an escape from my neighborhood, which could be full of ignorance and violence, and from my house and my mother, who could ensnare me in meaningless chores. I spent the money I didn't turn into my household usually at Birdland, where once I went five nights in a row, to worship from the peanut gallery at the piano pulpit of Bud Powell. Peewee Marquette, the redoubtable midget doorman and master of ceremonies for that fabled club, exclaimed at the door, "You back again?" and let me in every time, though I was obviously underage. I saw Charlie Parker there, Dizzy Gillespie, Fats Navarro, Lester Young with Billie Holiday, Stan Getz, Slim Gaillard, Miles Davis, Dexter Gordon, Paul Quinichette, Sarah Vaughn, Max Roach, and Clifford Brown, and was so excited and moved by these great artists that I pledged in my heart to make an art with my writing that was as free, and moving, and full in its freedom of formal elegance. I would dedicate books to these men who gave me everything.

It was a last minute decision I made to go to college. I sat next to a kid named Dan Maratos, who steep, rocky Catskill land near Windham, New York, land that has since been turned over to the ski industry, was skeptical about me as soon as he saw my pudgy self let out of the car by the local farm agent. I smelled like the New York City streets. He immediately put a pitchfork in my hand and told me to get up on that wagon and unload that mountain of green hay onto the belt that would carry it into the silo for ensilage. I willingly jumped onto the load with this unfamiliar weapon in my hand, sank it into the grass at my feet, and couldn't move any of it. I grunted and sweated and heaved at it, but the grass wouldn't budge. Occasionally I looked up at Alfred, who was staring at me in bewilderment, and I'm sure trying to figure out how he would endure the summer he had committed to training this urban deficit. Finally he said to me, his voice at that edge where patience borders on exasperation, "You can't pick up the hay that you're standing on, son, try to reach out in front of yourself a little bit. That's why the pitchfork has a long handle." It worked. It was thrilling. I actually unloaded that whole wagon, feeling I had conquered the first elements of farm technology. I followed after him later up his mountain on an exhilarating walk to find and call down his beautiful Jersey cows for the evening chores. I couldn't believe it. The sun was setting, and I was milking cows.

Alfred was a rare person, a new-age farmer way ahead of his time. He had an old Ford tractor he hated to use. Instead he worked a wonderful team of Belgian horses, huge, gentle animals, that I learned to harness and hitch to a wagon, and other implements. I learned prefossil-fuel methods of farming. "A horse gives something back to the land," Alfred said. "A tractor doesn't." This knowledge didn't do very well for me at the Cornell farm practice tests, where they liked their novices to be up to date. Alfred and I got along really well by the end of the summer, and he offered me a small piece of land and a couple of Jersey heifers if I wanted to start "farming it." He saw that his way of life, that he described as independent, self-reliant, and always interesting for its variety, was disappearing quickly. He believed in it and wanted to recruit anyone who was fit to do it. On the few occasions when I went to see Alfred in later years he had refined the stories of my summer with him, and loved to tell them—the one about my standing on the hay I was trying to lift, and one he particularly loved about myself dozing at morning chores and falling into the manure ditch. He liked to explain how I looked, how slowly I fell, like a ballet dancer, and how surprised I was when I woke up in shit. He had refined those stories, given them a fabulous glow in the telling, and a form that finally had little to do with

me, but gave him a good deal of sustenance, and lent shape to his past. I learned from knowing Alfred something of the relationship of the act of shaping experience into story, to the definition and sustenance of the individual human spirit.

*

By my junior year I had transferred to liberal arts, having to work thirty to forty hours a week to pay my back tuition as well as the ongoing costs. Despite that I was happy to be fully flapping my fledgling writer's wings under the grey Ithaca skies. Although knowing the location of organs in a steer cadaver, and the treatment for foot rot and bloat is useful information, it wasn't what I needed to know at the time. More important to me was the kindly and quirky guidance and encouragement of Baxter Hathaway, who managed the modest creative writing program at Cornell. He was a slim, grey man who had been a pole-vaulter in his youth, setting some records for his time back in Michigan. When I knew him he was a championship chain-smoker, and constant coffee drinker, always willing to take a break with one of his writing students, go down to "the Straight," and grind out a conversation in his slow, nasal, Midwestern drawl on whatever interested anyone. There were many excruciatingly long intervals while he sucked on his cigarette and prefaced his thoughts with a dilatory hum and phrases like, "Well, no, if you think about this in another way, Steve, well, on the other hand, I couldn't really say that . . ." He had published one novel and a book of poems, and still wrote poetry, but spent most of his time then writing about transformational syntax and Italian Renaissance literary criticism. He had a great talent for encouraging the young writers around him. He could respect their intentions and leave them alone, and never interfere in their work. I roomed my sophomore year with Peter Dean, who transferred in the next year to Wisconsin and taught himself painting and paints now full time his blazing impasto landscapes and expressionist fantasies. Some good writers were hatching around Cornell at that time. Ron Sukenick, who has become the pope of postmodernism, was two years ahead of me, and Susan Brownmiller was there, and a year behind me, fresh out of the navy, Thomas Pynchon had begun to fashion his juggernaut, chumming with the late Richard Farina. Steve Reich was there, studying Wittgenstein, reading Pound and Williams, and playing drums with the Joe Kurdle quartet. Harold Schimmel, a terrific original poet, whom Nabokov contacted after reading a couple of his pieces in the student literary magazine, was a close friend with whom I later went to live in Italy. He, as much out of his lust for the Mediterranean sun as his Judaism, emigrated to Israel, where he continues to write now in Hebrew. Among the teachers, W. D. Snodgrass impressed me, particularly for a reading he gave from his *Heart's Needle*, when he broke down in tears.

By the end of my senior year I had finished a draft of a novel called *The Steps of the Sun*, a crude, Faulknoid exploration of the Robeson riots in Peekskill, New York. I asked Nabokov to read the novel, and I should have been more flattered than I was that he agreed to do it. The conference over my manuscript took place in his office. He sat me in a dilapidated old velour easy chair, where my butt settled to the floor. Nabokov sat to the right, on a high stool, his long torso leaning over me, so I had no doubt I was in the presence of an eminence. His wife, Vera, leaned against the desk at the other end of the room. In the silence before anyone spoke I realized I was in for more than I had anticipated, and that I was so low in the chair I would have had to hang on to the tail of one of Alfred Partridge's draft horses to get pulled out and escape. Then the torment began. His wife did all the talking, while he leaned over me like the tallest dentist in the world, and occasionally supported her presentation with a word or phrase. I was helpless, miserable. She prefaced her onslaught with the kind phrase—"The talent is there, but . . ."—and all I heard after that was "crude," "comic book prose," "dull repetition," "read Shakespeare, Wordsworth, Keats." In retrospect I think their comments were intended to be kind and helpful, though the physical situation was despotic. All I wanted to hear was praise, all I wanted was for the great Nabokov to ease me onto the first rung of the ladder. I excavated myself clumsily from the chair, and took the manuscript he had scribbled over, and barely holding back the tears that saturated my anger I staggered down the stairs into the life of a nonentity, knowing I would never write again.

That life was short-lived. I sent the manuscript off to Harcourt Brace in competition for a fellowship they gave to first novelists, perversely using Nabokov's name as a reference, without first asking his permission. It made him furious, justifiably so, his wife screaming at me that he was a professional writer, an important writer, and that I couldn't just use his name. "Come on, a name is a name," I shouted back, having recovered my cojones. "They just asked me for the names of people who had read my work, and you were one." It took several years before I could acknowledge that Nabokov was a great

writer, and that this encounter I suffered with him was a terrible privilege. I got a letter back telling me two out of three of the judges favored my manuscript, but they wanted to know more about me, more about my writing ambitions, my philosophy. At the time I was ecstatically in love with Nevada Pat Bell (aka Jingle), and we were fumbling into marriage, and I think a lot of that delirium got into my letter, and I sent it off, forgetting to sign it, and forwarded them my signature on the next day. I didn't get the fellowship, and I don't know if that near miss came because my "philosophy" was goofed up by love, or because, as I suspect, Nabokov's wife wrote to them to withdraw his name as a reference.

My first trip to Nevada to meet Jingle's parents was also my first taste of the West. We drove there in one of the earliest VW bugs, with a tiny rear window, and mechanical turn signals that flipped up at the doorposts like illuminated fingers. The car was unwelcome in the Catskills outside New York, where people remembered it as Hitler's car. To get gas there I had to park around the bend from the filling station and carry a five-gallon can. In the rest of the country it was a great curiosity, one of the first small cars.

My first recognition of the real West came when we stopped in eastern Wyoming for the night, just before crossing the Little Bighorns. We threw our sleeping bags down by a fence near a scraggly town park. I had never smelled air that dry, weedy, and sweet. The snow-capped peaks were hallucinatory, and not to be blinked away. I could see the trace of the narrow road that I was told switch-backed up to the pass. I didn't believe we could make it in this tiny VW. Although Jingle didn't drive, she was a Western girl and had ridden worse vehicles up more treacherous tracks, one-lane dirt, axle-snapping mining roads, where you had to drive in one direction up one leg of the switchback and, with the sheer cliff to your starboard, do the next leg in reverse. I was a faint-hearted city boy, but took some comfort in a sky that showered my face with stars. I wanted to write fiction with this much space in it, with air this refulgent.

Just east of Boise the air was so thick with the scent of sagebrush after a shower I got dizzy. Jingle was looking me over, and I could tell she was uncomfortable about something. I asked her what was wrong, and she wouldn't say. I asked again. "Those pants," she finally said. My comfortable, nerdy driving shorts bothered her. "I can't introduce you to my parents in those pants." She was embarrassed to say that. At the next gas station I changed into jeans and Jingle explained to me how the

Western men wear theirs, as low on their hips as they can without exposing themselves. I was beginning to worry about myself. Was I going to reveal myself as a sissy to this world of Western manhood? Her brother, Woody, later to become a professional rodeo cowboy, worked then as a buckaroo on a ranch near Winnemucca. What would he think of the New Yorker his sister had dragged into the family? A writer? Why?

Jingle's father, Forrest, was frail when I met him, and suffered from silicosis, his lungs full of stone dust, from working with his father and brothers developing the Buckskin gold mine. He talked with some difficulty, always wheezing, struggling for oxygen. I felt privileged to get to know him, one of the last of a generation of independent pioneer men. He was an intelligent, well-educated old sourdough who read a lot, and was informed deeply about the world and whatever interested him technically. For years he had worked alone on his tunnel, eight hundred odd feet in, to try to crosscut the vein of the original Buckskin mine. He said he thought all it would take was another ninety feet before he would hit the high-grade, and to get his wife upset he would threaten to go back into the mine and go that ninety feet. Though he was frail he could still work hard. I remember once trying to dig out the spring that trickled the scarce water used in the cabins we stayed in on his remote Buckskin claims. I worked at it with pick and shovel for about three hours and made little progress. I had never dug in ground that hard, like concrete. When I gave up he quietly went out and finished the job. It embarrassed me to see how much faster than I he could move that earth, letting the pick fall without any wasted motion, the shovel hardly turning in his hands. When some years later I became friendly with some artists—Robert Smithson and Michael Heizer among them—who were called "earth artists" and did various projects requiring excavation in the desert, I often thought of Forrest Bell's thirty-year tunnel stalled ninety feet from an outside chance. Why not call this art!

I fell in love with the sagebrush-covered mountains, the long, pastel vistas, the opposite of Eastern Green, that Jingle often complained leaned on you too heavily. This landscape was aloof and gorgeous. I thought I had married well to be given such a vision as a wedding gift, and was glad to find a job, right there, at these remote claims. I worked for a man named Clark who had begun to develop a small outcropping of cinnabar (mercury ore) at the peak of the mountain. Cinnabar is often associated with gold. He had hauled a trailer to the top and lived there with his Mormon wife and seven kids. He hired me to

help him, and two native Paiutes. Forrest doubted that any of us would ever get paid.

I rode to work every morning on one of the two horses that Wild Bill had left with us to pasture. Wild Bill was an old, one-eyed Basque buckaroo, who looked welded to his horse. As soon as I saw his grizzled old face I wanted to feature him in a novel, which I never did, but Louis L'Amour has probably done plenty. He liked to say, "You can have all those other jobs in the city. I like it out here where it's no further than a hundred feet from the nearest steak." For me those mornings were a peaceful, exotic ritual. I got up before six. Forrest was already up, and had the fire started for breakfast. I climbed the steep pasture and slipped halters on the horses and brought them down, tied them up, fed them a measure of oats, and threw a saddle blanket over the older white one to calm it down so I could ride it to work after breakfast. Forrest loved fixing breakfast, and ballasted me for the workday with eggs and great sourdough waffles or hotcakes. I'd saddle the horse, kiss Jingle, and ride over the mountain to work in the mercury, thinking, "Imagine this life. Who can imagine it for a boy from Washington Heights?"

The work was not so romantic. Mercury is a deadly poison, and exposure to the fumes causes a condition called "salivation." Loss of teeth, hair, memory, and sanity are some of the symptoms. Lewis Carroll's Mad Hatter was mad because of the mercury used in the process of making felt. I can't help but think that any mental lapses I suffer today have origin in my exposure to that mercury. It was, at any rate, more work than I was prepared to enjoy. We worked mostly on outcroppings near the surface, and carried ore out of the mine in buckets, a practice Forrest found funny and suspect. We had a compressor and jackhammers, but no jacklegs for the hammers, so when we drilled a hole into the face we had to brace the hammer against the stone with our chests, and even a short hour of that every day sent me back home vibrating and rattling, hardly able to hold down dinner. It took just a few days of that for me to remember I was a writer. After a couple of weeks I arranged to work half-time, keeping my mornings for my writing. That was when I began to write the stories I later called "Mythologies," that appear in *Creamy and Delicious*. I woke each morning with a mythological name in my mind—Hermes, Apollo, Faust, Wonder Woman, Nancy and Sluggo—and I assigned myself to write a story from beginning to end, with no revisions allowed, each one to be finished in the three hours I had every morning before I had to go to work. It was my homage to automatic writing, and to Greek mythology and to action painting and to pop America, and it was important to my well-being, because it kept me free half a day from having to muscle against that infernal jackhammer.

Clark, it turns out, fulfilled Forrest's suspicions. He was a small-time charlatan who was mining for stock, which means he printed up some fancy stock certificates, took a few high-grade specimens down to Texas or up to Montana, and conned small investors. He also produced a few flasks of quicksilver to show off, cooking the ore in a dangerous, leaky retort that was salivating him faster than it was making him rich. The last time I saw him he had no more teeth, his hair was almost gone, and his wife had taken off with his kids, back to her home in Texas. Forrest died about a year and a half after our first son, Avrum, was born, so he got to be a grandfather for just one summer. After a few years Jingle's mother, Marian, married another miner, Harry Rogan, who went the last ninety feet in Forrest's tunnel, and found nothing, but was convinced that he would hit high-grade if only he could drop a shaft about forty more feet. Silicosis had ruined his lungs too, and Marian would have none of his prospector's ambitions.

I spent another year in Ithaca working as a stock clerk while Jingle finished her degree in sculpture, and I wrote some stories, and I tried to spruce up *The Steps of the Sun,* the novel Nabokov had screened. The following summer we went to work as lookouts, and myself as occasional smokechaser, for the forest service in the Clearwater National Forest, just below the Coeur d'Alene in the panhandle of Idaho. It was a great wilderness job. I don't think they use lookouts like this anymore. We had to pack in eight hours by mule, and the only person we saw for two-and-a-half months was a taciturn mule skinner who brought us our supplies every three weeks. We had a resident black bear who investigated our garbage pit and very politely would close the cover when he left it, and excited the guard-dog instinct in the little black-and-tan dog called Ozark we had adopted on the cross-country drive that took us through Ozark, Missouri. We were adopted by a herd of elk that each morning about 4 A.M. would converse at the base of our tower while they licked up the salt from our cooking water and urine. The only time I ever felt threatened by anything in the wild was by a doe who had twin fawns bedded near the trail I hiked each day, a mile or so down to the spring from where we packed our water. Ozark scared her up once and she got to the trail and identified me as the real enemy and sent me up a tree. As far as I know I'm the only macho writer ever treed by a doe. I had a .22 rifle there and supplemented our diet by occasionally getting a grouse, which was not

difficult. These grouse were called fool-hens because they took cover by freezing in place so you could actually walk up and grab them. I didn't. I shot, aiming for their heads so as not to spoil any meat. I was a lousy shot. The birds would duck and dodge until they got unlucky. The meat was tasty, and except for one porcupine, which we were supposed to kill because they ate tires and small trees; this was the only fresh food we had between mule-train deliveries. That was the only time I ever used a gun. The porcupine, by the way, tasted rather pitchy, and was difficult to skin.

During that summer I read all of *The Remembrance of Things Past,* as well as *Pnin* and *Lolita.* I was so overwhelmed by Proust, I despaired of ever writing again. The little ten-by-ten room of the tower populated itself with the hierarchies of the turn-of-the-century Paris salons. I looked out at the receding profiles of the mountains around the tower and thought how peculiar that there was civilization in the world, and also this. What would the Count and Countess de Guermantes see from this perspective? Lightning storms in the tower were spectacular, especially at night. The tower was grounded so that as much lightning as possible was attracted away from the trees, to be guided down the tower harmlessly into the ground. When we heard a storm coming, Jingle and I had to get out of bed and squeeze together on an insulated stool designed for one while the lightning hit, sending sheets of fire cascading with the water off the railings, off the raised shutters, off the raised hackles of our minds. Nothing like this in Proust's Paris. Nothing like this in Washington Heights.

By the end of the summer we had settled into an affable silence, communicating mostly by gestures. We thought perhaps it would not be necessary ever to use language again. Once we came down from the mountain everyone noted that Jingle had gone away to the tower a slim girl, and came out a pregnant woman. Once out of our silent retreat our talking valves blew, and we aimed streams of logorrhea full force at anyone in our way. We drove out of northern Idaho with our windows open, spraying conversation into the wild. With the help of Baxter Hathaway from Cornell, I had been taken on as a TA in the master's program at the University of Oregon. My other option was to stay with the forest service and work in the elk count. I often trouble myself that at that point in my life I made the wrong choice. I never really liked school, and it seemed to me a danger for a writer to become a teacher. A master's degree in English literature seemed like it would be a stigma. On the other hand, I was soon to be a father and felt the pressure to do something safe and conventional. We drove from sunny Idaho over the Cascades into Eugene, Oregon, slipped under a matting of cloud that covered us until we left three years later, with Avrum and Nikolai in our arms, and Rafael on the way.

*

I went to work there on a long disarray of a novel I called "The Journals of a Summer in Kelly's Thumb," Kelly's Thumb being the name of a Western place, in which I tried to fabulize my Western experiences, particularly Clark, and my mining experience. It rambled for five hundred pages, through several POVs, and I had neither the maturity nor the focus, nor yet an understanding of my own aesthetic priorities, to make that book live. I worked at the same time on some stories I called "From the Childhood of Marcus Morocco" in which I was discovering all the indulgences of the self-referential. These weren't stories I ever wanted to publish, although one of them, the most conventional, appeared in a little magazine, *Epoch*—my first published piece of fiction. I was surprised at how embarrassing it felt to have published something. I realized that an artist has to be satisfied with limited success, to let go of his work at a certain point, because as Paul Valery said, nothing is ever finished, just abandoned. I knew how limited this piece was compared to how I imagined it should be. How presumptuous I was to think I should publish anything. Proust published, James Joyce, Thomas Mann, Virginia Woolf, William Faulkner, Ernest Hemingway. Those guys. Who was I in that company? On the other hand, at the time I thought I was as good as any of them, and they would have to make room. I might not have quite done my best work yet, but I was on my way. My ego was burnished and alight, a useful tool before you've done anything. I didn't mind telling anyone I was the best writer in America. I remember saying it to my sister, to my wife, to my first son after he was born. It was easy to be great as long as I had no work to expose to the world yet. I still get that feeling of embarrassment when a work is published, though it doesn't stop me when I get the opportunity.

In Eugene we supported ourselves at first, almost through the birth of our first boy, on a meager TA's salary, and on a measly income from homemade pumpernickel bread that Jingle baked and I delivered to the homes of some World War II refugees who took it cheap. I did take some good courses at the university, particularly from Arthur Brodeur, who

spent a year of his retirement from Berkeley in Oregon, teaching Anglo-Saxon and *Beowulf.* We also made great hiking trips into the Cascades, one great trip to climb Mount Saint Helens, and frequent runs to the Oregon coast for ocean appreciation and salmon fishing. I waited tables at a steak house called The Branding Iron, which was the only restaurant in Eugene to employ waiters, a place frequented by doctors, dentists, and undertakers. With the slump in the logging industry, they were the only people who could afford the steaks. They tipped well. What started as six months of poverty after our arrival in the rain turned into some prosperity, with always a little loose change rattling in the pocket. It was at this restaurant that I became too well acquainted with Laphroiag, a single malt scotch that consoled me in my moments of self-pity for having married too young and bound myself to family. I learned also there the titillations of philandery, which I pursued too enthusiastically for the health of my marriage. I remember one party where a woman, who had been double-crossed herself in love, and knew of my shenanigans, dumped a full punch bowl over my

"*Lifting Avrum brings flower to mouth,*"
Eugene, Oregon, 1959

head, and Jingle went after her and poured a pitcher of water over hers. I remember my shock at Jingle throwing her own wedding ring into the Willamette River. I remember a confrontation between the other woman and Jingle at another party, when I was backed into introducing them, and I was happy not to be on the receiving end of my wife's stare, which like a disintegrating ray sent this other woman staggering back into the shadows. They were intense, stupid times, made more intense by the close, grey Oregon mists. It was a miracle our marriage lasted. I certainly owed it more to my wife's stubbornness and fortitude than to repentance or self-restraint on my part.

Three years of drizzle and mildew in Eugene, Oregon, turned out to be enough. We had saved some money and returned to Winnemucca for a while to figure out our next move. Jingle was into our third pregnancy, and I needed to do something. I decided that the best thing for us to do was for me to go to Italy to see if we could move there. Italy was on my mind. I had become obsessed with some reproductions of Masaccio frescoes, particularly *The Tribute Money,* that I had in a volume of Renaissance painting.

I thought I needed to go see it. This was 1960. I threw some stuff into a rucksack, and early one morning got on the road that is now Interstate 80, east of Winnemucca, and stuck out my thumb. At noon Jingle came by with some lunch. I remember the look of worry on Avrum's two-year-old face as he stared at me from his car seat. At 5 P.M. she came by again, and I was still there, the exact spot, my thumb a little cramped. She said she was fixing dinner and would come by at seven to get me. I decided that even though I was dedicated to Masaccio, if I wasn't gone by dinner I would cash in my plans and we would all go to Mexico. At six o'clock a man in a Chrysler on his way to Salt Lake stopped to take me with him, starting me on my run to Firenze. In New York I worked at Longchamps, running a little after-hours cafe in the 57th Street store, until I had enough money to book passage on the *Saturnia* to Venice. From there I knew I could hitch to Masaccio, the Carmine, Firenze—wherever.

I enjoyed those few months in New York, getting off work at four in the morning and walking the

With sons Avrum, Rafael, and Nikolai at unfinished cook house, Cape Breton, Nova Scotia, 1972

streets, stopping at some after-hours bars to listen to whatever singer turned up at the piano. On my days off I would go down to the Cedar Tavern, which was on University Place and Eighth Street at the time, because I knew it was where the artists hung out, but I didn't know anybody there, and never got to meet an abstract expressionist. Harold Schimmel, the poet, was my only friend in the city at that time, and he encouraged the Italy trip. He had worked in army intelligence in Verona and was hankering to get back there, where George Schneeman, his roommate in the service, had married and settled, outside of Siena. The only time I was tempted to cash in my ticket, and sign all my traveler's checks away, was a week before departure, when I saw a show of Giorgio Morandi and the gallery director told me I could have a pair of small paintings for approximately all the money I had saved for my trip. They were gorgeous Morandis, quiet, romantic paintings of jars and cups, undulant in their soft grey and pastel elegance. I wouldn't mind owning them now. I had been writing some poems, and I showed this director one I had done for Roy Lichtenstein, which was later published in my first volume of poems, *The Weight of Antony,* a very limited edition. He suggested I show it to Roy, who he said would be pleased, but I was too shy, and leaving anyway in a week. "Ah," said this director. "So you're setting out to have a wonderful life in the arts, of writing and travel in Europe." That made me feel very romantic about myself, Lord Byronish indeed, and at that time my family in Winnemucca seemed very far away. I began to write the first sketches for what was to become my novella, *The Lestriad. Form,* I remember thinking at that time. What was *Form?* Fiction could take the form of a gumball machine, or a pigeon's wing, or a weightlifter's belt. Who was the boss of this? I was! It was important that fiction be like the whole world, no beginning, middle, or end. Before getting on the boat I contacted the Sterling Lord Agency, and they agreed to handle my work. With a sense of mission, and an agent on my cuff, I boarded the *Saturnia* for what turned into three rich Italian years.

*

Without even pausing to look at Venezia, I got on the road in Mestre and caught a ride with a truck driver going all the way to Firenze. The guy wanted badly to talk about the American elections, and kept saying "Kennedy, si. Kennedy, si," hoping I would miraculously sprout some Italian. I took a room in the Pensione Bartolini, where Forster had written and set the first part of *A Room with a View.* My room had a view of a few terra-cotta rooftops. My first few days were spent in the Carmine, looking at Masaccio's *Tribute Money,* and I nearly went blind there because I didn't know that you deposit a fifty-lire coin to turn on the lights. After a couple of days my eyes were badly strained, and I didn't recover till I learned how to say "Vitamin A" in an Italian pharmacy. After a few days it began to sink in, that Firenze was more than just the Masaccio frescoes, that it was a whole civilization, and that I had never seen, felt, smelled civilization before, and I swooned into the Italian experience, with every gesture of a traffic cop, with every stone of Firenze, every hour of the day, every stroll across the Ponte Vecchio, each change of light on San Miniato. At all costs I knew I wanted to stay in Italy. I had to figure out some way to bring my family over.

I visited George and Kati Schneeman at Rencine, a farm on the outskirts of Asciano, near Siena. George was teaching himself how to paint, doing landscapes and portraits, mainly of Kati. They lived the lives of Tuscan peasants, George helping to slaughter the pig, Kati doing the wash in the pond, scrubbing on the rocks, throwing the sheets out on the pond and hauling them back in, and throwing them out again. They had two little kids at the time, and another on the way. I gave George a handful of poems to look at, and a couple of stories. His comments were always sharp and uncompromising. He didn't mind telling you when something stunk. His art, always rooted in daily life, in his marriage and friends, in the stuff he lived with every day, sometimes made me feel I had never grown up to my own work, so tied as it was to a rampaging imagination, so far from life taken a day at a time. As much as I have admired it, and loved him, I have never wanted to make art like his, but have always applied my understanding of what he does to my own sometimes swollen conceptions, like liniment to a sprain. The visit with the Schneemans, and small tour with him of his beloved Tuscan views, made me long even more strongly to expatriate myself in Italy.

I forgot that in my second week at the Pensione Bartolini I had written in application for a job under United States Information Service auspices, teaching English in southern Italy. I had just about despaired of making enough money to support my family in Italy and was getting ready to go home. I had left some laundry that kept getting resoaked in the rain so my departure was delayed a couple of days, just enough for me to get the letter from Bari asking me to come down for an interview. I'd never heard of Bari, but it was a job, I told myself. I wired Jingle, telling her to spend the rest of our savings and buy a ticket and get to Italy. She was almost seven months pregnant, almost past the time they would let her fly alone. It turned out to be a big risk, because I didn't have the job. I was interviewed for it and almost turned back. My pregnant wife and kids were already in the air and the USIS officer told me maybe I wasn't right for the job. I convinced him he had no alternative but to hire me.

The job was in Lecce, a place and situation I wrote about at some length in a later novel called *Wier and Pouce.* Harold Schimmel followed me to Lecce and took a small house in the countryside, and a painter friend of his, Bruce Sharpe, who married a Leccese girl, and later became a dean at Pratt, took a job with me at the institute. George Schneeman and family took a similar job in Taranto, finding a house near a little town called Statte. It was a comfortable coven of expatriates, and a very fertile time for my art. We spent a lot of time together talking vino, talking words, talking pasta, talking landscape. I finished *The Lestriad,* which was composed, I realize, very much like some music I loved, the Goldberg variations, or the late Beethoven quartets, or a jazz number, with the statement of the melody in the opening, a number of solos and excursions in the middle, and the restatement of the theme with a difference at the end. I wanted to explore a form that was resistant to the psychological, a cliche that made much of the literature of the time seem very tedious to me. I wanted the form to be open and free within elegant parameters, and the characters to be figures as if out of allegory, though not allegorical, who moved through emotions and psychologies as if they were territories that each of them could inhabit for a while, but also could vacate. I wanted to deal with the individual more in proportion to the forces that shape him. I don't know if *The Lestriad* did any of this, but I finished it and gave it to George to read, and he said, "Good, now write something else." Schimmel and I found a small press in Lecce and for seventy-five dollars I printed three hundred copies of the novella, and he printed his *First Poems,* his only book in English.

Lecce was a very heady place for me to live, though it wasn't easy for Jingle with the kids. It was an ancient town that seemed permanently cast in its feudalism, its facades a clumsy baroque carved in a soft, golden tufa. I walked around the old streets sometimes drugged with the light and atmosphere, thinking this wasn't real but a movie being shot around me. My Italian friends were mostly gentry who could afford the school, and would take me on excursions, or have fresh ricotta from their farms

With Pat Katz, standing by the tipi at Cape Breton, 1974

delivered to our door. We had trouble, because of Jingle's conviction that the kids should be allowed to run free and get dirty, contrary to the Leccese custom of keeping kids on a tight leash, their clothes spotless. There were very few automobiles, many horse-drawn carriages for taxis. Once we hired one to take us to the ocean, and the contadini working the fields stopped, removed their caps, and bowed to us as if we were some kind of royalty.

After a year in Lecce I got a job teaching extension courses for the University of Maryland at a U.S. military base in Verona. Moving up there was like returning to the twentieth century. Verona is one of the most beautiful small cities in Europe. Its archaeology goes back to the Romans, with an amphitheater second in size only to the Colosseum in Rome, where each summer they have a now re-nowned opera season, but in the early sixties you could wander out on a balmy evening and get a ticket at the door for *Tosca* or *Aida.* My habit on days when I didn't work was to wander downtown and sit at a cafe in Piazza Erbe or Piazza Dante and work on a novel called *Kulik in Puglia,* set in southern Italy. Our time there got less happy when I had to take a job in Germany, and commute for weeks at a time. I enjoyed the freedom and took advantage of it, but for Jingle it was a trial alone with three kids in a foreign country. I stopped in Paris once to visit Baxter Hathaway, who was on sabbatical there, and he asked me if I wanted to go back to Cornell to teach. At the time I thought that with some support I could live in

Italy forever. On the other hand I also thought three years was enough time to be away from my language, and that my kids needed to be educated in the U.S. I didn't like the idea of teaching at a university, but it was an easy way home, and I took it.

We were back in the U.S. in the fall of 1963, and I was teaching at Cornell University. I finished *Kulik in Puglia* and showed it to Malcolm Cowley, who had a visiting appointment there. His reading of it was the best editorial experience I have ever had, like a leisurely stroll through my own neighborhood with an intelligent friend who was alert and interested. He liked the novel, and took it with him to Viking to recommend its publication. They eventually turned it down. I had already begun work on what would turn out to be *The Exagggerations of Peter Prince*, so I lost interest in struggling to publish it. I think sometimes that if *Kulik in Puglia,* which is a straight-forward narrative, a rhapsodic homage to southern Italy, had been published first of my books, I wouldn't ever have had to struggle with the straitjacket of the postmodernist label, which trivializes and falsely stereotypes the individuality of the work of many of my contemporaries.

I got to Cornell in time for the assassination of the first Kennedy and the beginning of political ferment on most college campuses. Doug Dowd was organizing and sending students down to register voters in Fayette County, Alabama. After the Gulf of Tonkin swindle, the Vietnam War protest began to swell and my time on the Cornell campus filled with vigils, teach-ins, protest marches. I did performance-readings voodoo in combat drag, advertised to end the war. It didn't work. The students were educating themselves in the history of Southeast Asia. For one of the few times in my experience, a college campus seemed like an interesting, exciting place to be living one's life, a place where one could further an education in something other than conformity and service to the military industrial complex. It seemed a good place to be writing *The Exagggerations of Peter Prince.*

The rejection of *Kulik in Puglia* encouraged me to explore some more radical inclinations I had in the composing of *Peter Prince.* I was interested in exploring the objectness of the book, its artifacthood. I wanted my book to be telling the story at the same time as it reminded the reader that it was a book, not just a window on an illusionary and imagined space. That was why I tried to make pages and sequences that looked interesting, even intrusive, as they told the story. I tried to float on the text a process of visual signals that worked against the illusionistic narrative

and drew the reader's attention to the surface of the page, so that there were always two things working—the story and the visual presence of the surface. The self-referential aspect of the book had a similar purpose, though it wasn't as interesting to me as the other. This "experiment" seemed to me necessary in response to my modest understanding of new paradigms in the sciences that start from the premise that the nature of the observer, or instruments of observation, influence the results of the observation, that we had to reexamine the idea of the separation between subject and object. I wanted a fiction that operates on the premise that the process be exposed. It seemed necessary if we were ever to reach the candor that Whitman called for.

A lot of good people passed through Cornell while I was there. The poet A. R. Ammons was hired the year after I went to Cornell, and published there his great journal poem, *Tape for the Turn of the Year.* Richard Tum Suden, a painter who was doing strong, witty, beautiful work, and showing it at Tibor De Nagy in New York, taught for a year, as did Charles Ross, a sculptor whose work was eventually to become involved with sky and cosmic phenomena through the use of prisms, lenses, and star charts. Ross is smart, one of the most dynamic and acute intellects of any of my friends. I have learned a lot from the intellectual rigor with which he approaches his art. Tum Suden, with whom I had a deep friendship for many years, after a number of disappointments, dropped out of the art scene, and I have no idea if he is still painting today.

Among the students in architecture and fine arts, some of whom did some writing were Alan Saret, Susan Rothenberg, Donald Evans, Gordon Matta, Joel Perlman, all of whom have since made substantial bodies of work. I did a number of performance pieces in that richly open atmosphere, using costume, slides, adding-machine tape, live voice against taped voice, a film of myself playing handball. I never had the time or opportunity to follow through on those pieces in the bigger world, but I still remember them as part of my work. I remembered one piece that finished with myself buried in adding-machine tape that, without my knowledge or approval, someone set afire.

For one year B. H. Friedman, the novelist and essayist, came to try teaching, as did Jim Dine, the already canonized "pop" artist. B. H. had a dream about the title of *Exagggerations of Peter Prince*, with only one G in the word, and I decided to add his G to my other two, to make Exagggerations, which is often seen as a typo and corrected. It was at a dinner at Jim's house that my "big break" came. Arthur Cohen, who was editor in chief and vice president of

Holt, Rinehart and Winston, was visiting partly to discuss an edition of Apollinaire's *The Poet Assassinated* that Jimmy was illustrating. (One of the illustrations, I'm proud to say, was a snapshot of me, beardless and drunk.) Jimmy had left in his bathroom a copy of the *Chicago Review* containing a piece of *Peter Prince* done in columns, and Arthur Cohen read it there, and emerged refreshed, offering to publish the book if he liked the rest of it. It was 1967. Freedom and experimentation were breaking out everywhere. I sent him an outrageous manuscript, more outrageous than the book that was finally published. He accepted it. I couldn't believe it. These were my most radical ideas. It seemed there was a lesson in that. It was as if the chicken I had killed as a child was going to be published. My elation caused a bad mistake. For one thing I trusted too much the competence of the publishing industry, which at the time planned its projects over six-martini lunches. I didn't realize, or didn't want to realize, that to get what I wanted I would have to be there, holding their hand every step of the way. Instead I went to Turkey and Israel, and sat in Istanbul writing "Three Satisfy-

ing Stories" while the book was being set. When I got back and looked at the design that had been drummed up—I had asked them to follow the manuscript as closely as possible—I was shocked. It was a totally different book. While I was gone a major network had bought Holt, Arthur Cohen had been fired, and my book was turned over to Robert Cornfield, a fine editor, with a lot less clout than Arthur. The book was already in blues, the final stage before printing. I told them I didn't want it to appear in the form they showed me, and Bob Cornfield managed to get production to agree to totally redesign the book. Although it doesn't quite have the energy and edge of the original, and some things were left out, like a thumb movie and maps at the end papers, I know now I was lucky to have been able to realize at all a book so radical in the commercial publishing industry. It would be impossible today; in fact, it became impossible soon after the publication. The book had a lot of prepublicity, was published in September, and got good reviews, but didn't appear in their Christmas catalogs or ads. I don't know what happened, but I always imagine it was a decision

Corn Street porch, Ithaca, New York, 1966 (the photograph used on the jacket of
Creamy and Delicious)

taken somewhere in the antiliterate upper management.

Through Jim Dine I got to meet the photographer Lee Friedlander; his photo of me appears on the book jacket of *Creamy and Delicious*, and I got to write some captions for a section of his photos in *Aperture* magazine. I remember particularly one great afternoon walking up Fifth Avenue with him and watching him wield his Leica. He had the talent of virtual invisibility, could stand practically in someone's face with his camera, without that person even noticing. It was an uncommon thrill to see published some of the photos from that walk.

My history in the commercial publishing world was a series of blunders, and the usual disappointments. The first couple of boxes of *Creamy and Delicious* to come off the Random House presses had Elie Wiesel's *A Beggar in Jerusalem* bound inside the covers of my book. I don't know what reviewers thought when they cracked those covers. The first thousand or so copies of *Saw* that Knopf shipped in its peculiar, half-tacky edition, didn't have enough glue in its "perfect" binding, so the pages fell out as the reviewers read, and of course it caused some witty speculation in the *Times* and elsewhere. I welcomed, therefore, the opportunity to help organize the Fiction Collective, a group of authors who wanted control of their own books, so that when it came time to publish *Moving Parts,* a book that incorporates graphic elements and photographs in an exploration of the interaction of imaginative narrative and documentary, I got to make all the mistakes, and the book looks more or less the way I felt it needed to. By the time I was writing *Moving Parts* I had left Cornell with my family and we'd moved closer to New York City, to Pine Bush, New York, one of those curious redneck cul-de-sacs close to the city, that had an active Klan; in fact, the wife of the local grand Klaven was on the school board, and when that was found scandalous by some, and a new election was called, she was re-elected. I took jobs as an adjunct at various New York city colleges, and went to work with an Off-Broadway director, Leo Garen, on a script for a film of his conception called "Grassland."

Leo was the most obnoxious person I have ever liked, and writing this script was one of the most difficult writing projects I have ever had to do. We labored in tandem over every line and transition. We worked in hotels off Eighth Avenue, in a cabin owned by the producer Max Raab, on Long Beach Island in Jersey, at my house in Pine Bush, in Leo's apartment on Waverly Place. I wish I could say that after all we put into it a great piece of entertainment resulted.

Leo did manage, by convincing them he wouldn't go away until they did it, to get Twentieth Century-Fox to provide a small budget for the film. He cast it well—Keith Carradine, Bobby Walker, Scott Glenn, Gary Busey, all before they'd had any success—and the script was rich enough so it should have been at least some fun, but because of the small budget, and Leo's lack of experience, what resulted was a poorly paced, dimly lit melodrama of motorcycles and half-breeds on the prairie. My poem sequence *Cheyenne River Wild Track* comes out of that experience, particularly from my contact on the set with Henry Crow-Dog, seventy-four years old, a full-blooded Sioux, over six feet tall, classic Native American face, long hair, from the Rosebud reservation, a shaman of the Native American Church, who was hired to be on the set as a "spiritual adviser," and to be seen in a couple of shots. He and I shared a cabin. It was one of those "shocks of recognition" the first time I went to meet him at Crow-Dog's Paradise, where he lived and did sweats and peyote rituals. I walked into his amazing shack by the Little Rosebud River, built of old pieces of corrugated tin, and car parts, and salvaged windows, and refrigerator doors, because he refused to live in the BIA (Bureau of Indian Affairs) prefabs, and a couple of Navajo braves visiting him said "How." That greeting dropped like a stone through my consciousness. It was the first time in my life I was forced to separate these people from the cliche imprinted on me by white American mythology. Living with Henry I realized you didn't need to go to the Himalayas or Sri Lanka to find spiritual teachers. Henry was as exotic and esoteric in his spiritual codes as any yogi, and he was right here in South Dakota. He loved to play the guitar, though he had no conventional training on it. Every night he'd slap and strum and shake the instrument as if it were this ritual implement he had found on the prairie that made some magical sounds. All night he sang his songs for us, and joked with us, while in his own trailer Keith Carradine worked up his song "I'm Easy" that later became a small hit. I remember Gary Busey saying one night, "Thank you, Henry, for helping all of us." "Who says you can help the people?" Henry replied. Knowing Henry taught me that aspect of love, nearly erased from our culture, called veneration.

I wrote a few more scripts, two of which I still like—one about the Haitian revolutionary Toussaint L'Ouverture, the other about Daniel Mendoza, an eighteenth-century British boxer, a Jew, who invented scientific boxing. I doubt they'll ever get made but I enjoyed the research I had to do to write them, taking me to the New York Public Library to plunder images from Gillray etchings and texts about eighteenth-century British life, and to Haiti, where I loved to be, looking for stuff about the great black leader. At the time I was writing as well some of the short pieces later collected in *Stolen Stories*. Many of those pieces focus on the art world, reflecting my circle of friends in New York, including some people who were later to become quite famous, like Richard Serra, Robert Smithson, Philip Glass, JoAnn Akalaitis, Steve Reich, Nancy Graves, Charles Ross, Joan Jonas, Peter Dean, Gordon Matta, Peter Campus, Susan Rothenberg, and others. Some of them have as their setting the camp I had established on Cape Breton Island. When I visited Phil Glass and Rudy Wurlitzer up there one summer, I decided to look for a piece of land by the sea I could afford, and I got lucky. We cut a trail and cleared the place, put up a tipi, and moved a wood cookstove down the beach about twelve miles from Phil's place, sloshing around on a big ocean in his thirteen-foot boat. We built a cook house around the stove out of driftwood, and this little campsite became very comfortable. Every summer for many years we luckily found time to stay in Cape Breton, a place where I did a lot of work, spent time with my kids, talked with other artists, and cleared my mind of noise.

Just after *Peter Prince* came out, I remember sitting one evening in a bar called The St. Adrian Company on Broadway at a table with Richard Serra and his saying to me, "I'm ready to make my move. Next year I'm going to take over the art world." That statement shook me up. I mumbled it to myself all the way back to the little apartment I was keeping then on Morton Street. I had no ambition to "take over" anything. The remarkable thing about Richard was that not only could he say this, but for whatever it was worth (a lot to him, obviously), he did it, and still remains a powerful and controversial force in the art world. I had neither the genius nor the ego. My own lame attempt at wielding some art muscle came as a result of an idea Walter Abish had, to form a group of four writers known for innovative work, with the possibility that we could generate some activity together not possible to initiate individually. We met several times with Clarence Major and Michael Stephens at my apartment then on Crosby Street, and agreed on a name for the group—Projects in Innovative Fiction, or PIIF. We had some stationery printed up, and met once more to divide the stationery, and that was about the extent of our PIIF.

Cape Breton is a great, quiet place to visit with my friends whose careers have taken off in New York, who have little time there to socialize. There were great beach days and stoned dinners at Phil's place

when he was still married to JoAnn Akalaitis, and even now when they come separately. JoAnn at the time worked with Lee Breuer and Mabou Mines, the name of the group taken from a little fishing harbor nearby, where Robert Frank has a house. I always was impressed with what a happy man Phil was. I remember one evening after a long dinner party Jingle and I went out to our car and were overwhelmed by the morass of our own failing marriage, and we sat there for hours weeping into the Northern Lights about how sad it was, and how impossible and painful, and what would happen, and how could we do this to each other, when we really loved each other but still we couldn't go on. We sat there in the warmth and stress of our impasse till dawn, when the door opened and, without seeing us, Phil came out, singing, "Here goaty-goats, here goaty-goats," calling his two goats down to milk, and there was such a contentment in that, that I felt our problems floated away for the moment. Phil is testimony to the truth of the Buddhist axiom that an organized life makes a happy man. He manages to know what he has to do every minute, and usually to keep to his schedule. On a recent trip I went with him to India, to Madras, to the music festival, and following his packed schedule there gave me no time for disorientation. I had to wait till he left, and I was alone in Cochin, to have time for confusion and self-pity—not much of it, but enough to remind me of my own habits.

Moving Parts came out at the time I was leaving New York, for what turned out to be probably a permanent separation from the city that most sweetens my imagination. I had little choice. My adjunct teaching job had been discontinued. New York had become an expensive place to live, and a difficult place to work. Two of my kids had started college—Nikolai already at Chicago, Rafael on his way to Brown—and though they were managing through scholarships and loans to pay their own way, I still had to make up for a little of what they couldn't cover, so I felt it was time to get the money, whatever I could, wherever I could. I took a job at Notre Dame, in South Bend, Indiana. I didn't mind South Bend, ugly as it be. There's something relaxing about living in a place that nobody brags about. I got to spend time there with Jane Jensen, a wonderful woman, native of Mishawaka, and got to witness, at a party given for Tennessee Williams at the Sophomore Literary Festival, a peculiar exchange between the great playwright and William Burroughs, also there for the festival. We were all sitting around a coffee table, and Williams was watching Jim Grauerholz, Burroughs's business manager and amanuensis.

"William Burroughs," he said. "You have a beautiful boyfriend." "He's not my boyfriend," Burroughs said, curtly. Williams slowly lowered his eyes from Grauerholz, smiled a Blanche Dubois smile, sighed softly, and went on. "Life is sad, William Burroughs. Don't you think life is sad?" Burroughs, in his grey suit and black tie, did a quick, mechanical scan in Williams's direction, reversed, and said nothing. "Why, my boyfriend, he's a nice young man, but he just wants to kill himself all the time with those drugs he takes. I think life is so sad, that he should want to kill himself. Why should he want to kill himself, William Burroughs?" Burroughs looked straight ahead, his voice dry as breaking glass. "He doesn't have to take drugs. He can stop if he wants to." Williams paused, sighed again, and looked at his left wrist as if he regretted the wilting there of an imaginary corsage. This was like a confrontation of the parodic queen of Southern decadence with the warrior king of haywire puritanism. "It's so sad," Williams whispered to himself, then to Burroughs. "But he wants to take those drugs. That's what's so sad. I ask him not to, but he insists. He wants to die,

William Burroughs. Nobody can prevent it. That's what's sad. I know it." Burroughs turned to look at Williams this time. "You tell him you don't want him to die. You tell him to stop taking those drugs." "Life is so sad." Williams faded with that last line, and Jim Grauerholz brought over someone else to introduce to Mr. Burroughs.

Notre Dame had a family atmosphere, sometimes a little too cozy; but it was amusing to organize readings for writers like Walter Abish or Jackson Mac Low and have parties for them afterwards at Digger Phelps's house (his wife, Teri, was a graduate student in English), and listen to a conversation in which Jackson talked about chance operations in literary composition, while Digger explained his problems recruiting high-school basketball prospects. Two years in South Bend was plenty. I wrote a few stories there that I included in *Stolen Stories* and began some of the pieces, like "Keeper," that became part of *Wier and Pouce.* Most of my connections and friendships were still in New York City. I was sure I was going to return and resume my life there. I still kept my apartment and spent a good deal of time there. The

"Author as snapshooter—Candy, Phil Glass, Lyn Davis, Rudy Wurlitzer," South India, 1989

problem remained, however, of how to make enough money to afford to help my kids pay their way through school. I knew I could make enough money in Manhattan to support myself and give myself time for my writing habit, but I wasn't sure of being able to afford much else. I was a little weary, too, of the grind of New York life, and didn't realize how much I'd miss it, and that once I pulled out it would be difficult ever to go back. When a job came up at the University of Colorado I felt lucky.

*

Wier and Pouce is my response, in its form, to the sense of discontinuity and acceleration in my life, and the world around me. I feel like I have jumped from one reality to another, to another, with little transition to connect one period to the next. I look back on flashes of disparate contexts and carry pictures from each of these lives as if in a different album in my mind, and to keep connected to the people in any of those different lives takes a lot of effort. This sensation of discontinuity and extreme otherness of the past is exacerbated by the acceleration of change in the environment, in the world. Going back to New York City, if I could afford it now, would be going back to a place that resembles very little what I left not so long ago. I tried a return to Italy, to Lecce, and found even that place that had been so durable, so intractable in its antiquity of monuments and mores, has practically crumbled, all its facades covered to keep them from disintegrating in the car exhaust. The world I lived in there no longer exists. It's now a somewhat unpleasant, small modern city. Because of this sense of disjunctions each section of *Wier and Pouce* was written as if from a separate novel, a different context, each dealing with the same character, offering the general sense that the whole was a bildungsroman dealing with the progress of Dusty Wier. A different formal approach takes on each new stage of Dusty's life.

Most of the book was written in Boulder, Colorado, and Cape Breton, Nova Scotia, with one section done, as is described in the passage itself, while I was living in France, in Montpellier. I met Douglas Messerli at a bookseller's convention in New York, where I was manning a desk for the Fiction Collective. He published a periodical called *Sun and Moon* and intended to expand to publish books. My experience with small presses had been to publish *Moving Parts* with the Fiction Collective, which was a cooperative venture, and with Ithaca House, the small press that published my poem sequence *Cheyenne River Wild*

Track. Douglas publishes books for the right reasons, because he loves them, believes in literature, particularly enjoys "experimental" work, and is himself an innovative poet. I sent him *Wier and Pouce* as soon as it was finished. His decision to publish it came from his belief in the book rather than a calculation of its commercial potential. After some delays it came out, and was reviewed, and sold a few copies, and is still in print, which can't be said for any of the books I published in the power houses. Sun and Moon Press has its problems, the major one being interminable delays before one's book comes out, poor distribution, little advertising; but they do publish books for the sake of literature and the health of the imagination, a refreshing difference in these days of bottom-line arts management.

Boulder, Colorado, is a conservative little college town with a patina of new-age activity and progressive politics. Unlike South Bend, Indiana, it's a place where people congratulate themselves for having chosen to live there. It has some physical beauty, snugged as it is against the foothills of the Rockies. The religion of much of the young, affluent Boulder population seems to be recreation. They are fanatical about what might elsewhere be considered a hobby. The place has great access to skiing, rock climbing, ballooning, hang-gliding, backpacking, cycling, and it's a great place to train for marathons. To be a little overweight and middle-aged is to be conspicuously different in Boulder. Although on the fringes there is a kind of underclass—and you see them, the Hispanics and the Hmong people, doing janitorial work—the feeling of the town is racial homogeneity, and a self-indulgent middle class. Not infrequently racism and anti-Semitism rear up as a bitter aftertaste of the quotidian candy. It's an easy place to live, but not an easy place to feel you are in touch with the problems of mainstream U.S.A. Naropa Institute, the first Buddhist college in the U.S., enriches the climate here somewhat with an interesting flow of visitors, but in order to maintain a sense of the world, and avoid the self-congratulatory torpor this environment encourages, I have to leave as often as I can afford to. Go to New York. Go to China. Go to India. Go to Cape Breton. Go to Detroit. Even going to Denver is a help.

There is a stimulating group of writing colleagues here that makes life more rich, if you don't go too often to the well of their company. Ed Dorn, the poet provocateur; Sidney Goldfarb, a poet turned maniac playwright; Ron Sukenick, who runs his postmodern empire out of his university-sponsored publication center; Robert Steiner, a novelist and theorist; Marilyn Krysl, poet and fictioneer; Linda

Writers Chuck Wachtel, Larry Shainberg, Katz, Jeremy Tarn, Marvin Bell, and Herman Gauggel, "raconteur," in Managua, Nicaragua, 1988

Hogan, poet and novelist; Peter Michelson, poet and essayist; Lorna Dee Cervantes, poet; Reg Saner, poet and nature essayist; and Naropa has in permanent residence Anne Waldman, Anselm Hollo, frequently Allen Ginsberg, Bobbie Louise Hawkins, Jack Collom, and a flow of other interesting writers. I don't miss literary talk here, but I do miss the kind of talk you get on the streets and at the lunch counters of a city like New York. I suppose you don't even get it so much in New York anymore, unless you listen in the black community, the fun of people exercising the language in public, acting it out, giving themselves away. For my connection to the language, Boulder is like life without bread and butter. I wonder, assuming some people will still be interested in my work in fifty years, if they will notice an impoverishment of its language due to this thinner environment.

Perhaps I wrote *Florry of Washington Heights* in order to rejuvenate myself in that street language. It is one of my few conventional narratives, the approach appropriate to the subject matter and the nostalgic tone. What I love about the advent of that book is that it put me back in touch with many of the

kids who grew up with me and were part of the New York Bullets Social and Athletic Club. It was like putting an ad in the personals. People checked in from all over the country, and when a film company bought an option on the novel, I fantasized putting together a reunion of the New York Bullets Social and Athletic Club, but that went the way of many Hollywood dreams.

One pleasant surprise of my writing career was set off by a phone call from a man named Bill Bamberger from Flint, Michigan, who told me he published a few books and wanted to reprint *The Lestriad*. He worked, he said, as a janitor in the public schools, had a doctorate in literature, and was writing a book about the works of Ishmael Reed, Robert Coover, and myself. Here was another who published books because he believed in them. His list is impressive, including Coover, Reed, William Eastlake, Stanley Elkin, Anne Waldman, and myself. He did *The Lestriad* and a book of my poems called *Journalism*. A writer like myself, outside the commercial mainstream, owes a lot to publishers like Bill Bamberger and Douglas Messerli.

Steve Katz "yodelling on the Great Wall of China," 1986

I am working now on *Swanny's Ways,* a sequel to *Florry of Washington Heights.* In my experience it doesn't get any easier to write; if anything, it gets harder. It is more difficult to rewrite something than to get it down in the first place. Getting my new novel right is the most difficult thing I have ever done. I tend to ask more questions of my work, and to want more from it. I suppose there is an advantage in this, that if I ever felt I'd written a perfect work I might stop, and what keeps the writer alive, what keeps the culture alive, is the continual reframing and telling of the stories. Perhaps everything I do as a writer is by way of figuring out in what language to atone for once drowning the Hardens' chicken.

BIBLIOGRAPHY

Fiction:

The Lestriad, limited edition, Edizioni Milella (Italy), 1962, Bamberger, 1987.

The Exagggerations of Peter Prince, Holt, 1968.

Creamy and Delicious: Eat My Words (in Other Words) (stories; illustrated by Richard Tum Suden), Random House, 1970.

(Under pseudonym Stephanie Gatos) *Posh,* Grove, 1971.

Saw, Knopf, 1972.

Moving Parts, Fiction Collective, 1977.

Stolen Stories, Fiction Collective, 1984.

Wier and Pouce, Sun & Moon, 1984.

Florry of Washington Heights, Sun & Moon, 1987.

43 Fictions, Sun & Moon, 1991.

Poetry:

The Weight of Antony, Eibe Press, 1964.

Cheyenne River Wild Track, Ithaca House, 1973.

Journalism, Bamberger, 1989.

Author of screenplays, including *Grassland (Hex),* with Leo Garen, Twentieth Century-Fox, 1972; *Mendoza the Jew; Toussaint;* and *Chicago Needs Show.* Work represented in anthologies, including *Stories from Epoch, Modern Occasions, Experiments in Prose, Innovative Fiction,* and *Statements.* Contributor of stories and poems to periodicals, including *Chicago Review, Paris Review, Northwest Review, Choice, Outsider, Le Nouveau Commerce,* and *In Transit.* Past editor, *Northwest Review* and *Epoch.*

Doris Lessing

1919-

IMPERTINENT DAUGHTERS

I

A photograph of my mother shows her as a large, roundfaced schoolgirl, full of the confidence I have to associate with her being Victorian. Her hair is tied back with a black bow. She is wearing her school uniform, a full white blouse and a long dark skirt. In a photograph taken forty-five years later, she appears as a lean, severe old thing, bravely looking out from a world of disappointment and frustration. She stands by my father, her hand on the back of his chair. He has to sit: as always, he is ill. It is clear that he is only just holding himself together, but he is in a proper suit, certainly because she has told him he must make the effort. She wears a rather smart tailored dress, made up out of a remnant bought in the sales.

The difference between these photographs is what this memoir has to be about. It seems that it has taken me a lifetime to understand my parents, with astonishments all the way. There is a mysterious process, frightening because there is nothing whatsoever you can do about it, that takes you from fierce adolescence—as if parents and you stood at either side of a battlefield, hands full of weapons—to a place where you can stand where they did, in imagination, any time you want.

Only when I sat down to write this did it occur to me that I could write about my father and hardly mention that dread word "class," but with my mother it is a different matter. She never freed her judgements from thoughts of class, but then she did not see why she should. Class was then a straitjacket, an imperative, a crippler. Only that time, that place, could have produced her: London, Britain, the British Empire. But the Empire was in its last days: a thought she would have dismissed as treacherous, wrongheaded, soft.

On a mud wall of the old house on the farm in Africa where I was brought up was a large, ornately framed portrait of my grandfather McVeagh. He is standing beside his second wife. He was fat-faced and overfed, with hair slicked down on either side of a

"My parents, Alfred Cook and Emily Maude (McVeagh) Tayler, on their wedding day,"
December 1918

parting. He wore a tight smug suit, and a golden chain across his chest. I loathed him, this self-righteous prig, with a violence that stopped me from listening to my mother, whose reminiscences seemed only another attempt to bind me to her. Had she, had my father, not escaped from England? Why, then, was she winding me back into that shroud? I closed my ears, and I am sorry now I did. For instance, who was that elegant, fastidious lady he married? She was

Jewish, with a fine curved nose and exquisite hands. Her dress was a miracle of embroidery and little tucks and lace. She came from a different world, by nature if not by class. I think she was a governess. Yet she had chosen to marry him: a thought that didn't enter my head for years, he made two romantic marriages, this philistine bank manager.

Once I had a fit of wanting to know who my forebears were, and before I found what a fussy and tedious business it is and gave it up, I came across birth certificates of McVeaghs from Exeter and Maidstone. They were all called John and Edward and James, and were sergeants in cavalry regiments. In short, my grandfather McVeagh, or his father, had made the jump up into the middle classes, and he was as snobbish as one would expect. Yet his first marriage had been to Emily Flower, the daughter of a contractor for lightering. A marriage for love. There is no picture of Emily Flower. This is because she was such a misfortune. All my childhood I heard of this grandmother thus: "She was very pretty, but all she cared about was dancing and horses." It was said with the little cold sniff that probably derived from the servants who brought the children up after wicked Emily died, which was—my mother's tone said it served her right—in childbirth with her third child. That was in 1888, and she was thirty-two. But how was it that the wife of a suburban bank manager was able to dance all the time and be mad about horses? In Blackheath? Blackheath was where my mother said the tall, grim, cold house was; but on Emily's death certificate it says Canning Town.

My mother, Emily Maude, was the first child. Then came Uncle John. Then Muriel, who disgraced herself and the family by marrying back into the working class. Hardly a surprise, judged my mother, for Muriel was always happiest with the servants. In other words she was not happy in the competitive, striving atmosphere of getting on and doing well.

It was a cold home. Her father, so romantic in love, ruled his children as Victorian papas are reputed to have done, with the rod, and without love. There was no affection from the elegant stepmother, who was dutiful and correct and did not understand children. I never once heard my mother speak of her father with warmth. Respect, yes; prescribed admiration, certainly. Never love. As for her stepmother, she might have been a visitor or a distant relation.

Emily was clever at school, much cleverer than her brother, John, who was destined for the navy, and who found the exams difficult. He had to be coached and pushed and prodded. She loved examinations, came first in class, adored mathematics, and was expected for a time to become a professional pianist.

The children, as was proper in this Forsytian world, were taken to all public occasions of rejoicing or grief; and my mother spoke of Mafeking night, Queen Victoria's funeral, the coronation of Edward VII, exhibitions, the visits of the Kaiser and of foreign heads of government, as if these milestones were the only possible way to mark the passing of a childhood.

If there was little family life, there was an energetic social life full of friends she kept in touch with for years, even from the farm in Africa. She played tennis and lacrosse and hockey and went on bicycle trips. There were musical evenings. They drew portraits of each other and pictures of appropriate landscapes; wrote humorous and sentimental verses to mark anniversaries. They pressed flowers and collected shells, birds' eggs and stones. They visited the theatre with suppers afterwards at the Trocadero. All this went on in London: she was essentially urban, this woman who would find herself on a farm in the veld.

Modern-minded John William McVeagh, proud of his clever daughter, was thinking of university for her, but was confronted with a rebellious girl who said she wanted to be a nurse. He was horrified, utterly overthrown. Middle-class girls did not become nurses, and he didn't want to hear anything about Florence Nightingale. Any skivvy could be a nurse, and if you become one, do not darken my door! Very well, said Emily Maude, and went off to the old Royal Free Hospital to begin her training. It was hard: conditions were bad, the pay was low, but she did well, and when she brilliantly passed her finals, her father was prepared to forgive her. She never forgave him. She had done it all on her own, without him.

Whom, then, did she love, this poor girl brought up without affection? She was fond of her brother, John, but this was a far from simple emotion, and of course he was at boarding school most of the time. Her sister, Muriel, was not her sort. Her many and varied friends? They were good sports, pals. . . . Why did she fight so hard to become a nurse, if not that she needed to care for and to nurture people and to be loved for it? I have only just had this thought: I could have had it before.

Her training completed, she resumed, as far as possible, her social life. She had given up dreams of being a pianist, but continued to play the organ for churches, for instance, in Langham Place. She was part, in a small way, of the musical life of London. "I could have been a real concert pianist," she would say, until the end of her days. "I had my LRAM [Licentiate of the Royal Academy of Music]. The Examiners told me I should go on." I wonder at her energy. Nurses worked harder then than now. Yet there were musical evenings, and concerts, and excursions. Also, holidays—always sea trips, for she loved the sea. She read, too, as did my father. Both knew enough of Wells and Shaw to be affected, and both judged society from a perspective of critical independence. There was a generation of young people, before the First World War, for whom Wells and Shaw played the same tutoring role as Orwell did later.

Then began the War. 1914. She was a sister in the Royal Free Hospital, nursing the wounded soldiers who arrived in trainloads from the trenches. She had an album with verses written by the men she nursed back to life, and she appears as the traditional martinet with a heart of gold.

My father, at that time, was fighting in the trenches. He had two periods there. The first was ended by a timely appendix, otherwise he would have been killed with all his company in the Battle of the Somme. The second, timely again, was when he was wounded—shrapnel in the leg—preventing him from being killed with every other man in the company, at Passchendaele. I do not know exactly how long he was in the trenches, but altogether it was months. He said he was lucky not to have been killed a dozen times over. But the war did him in nevertheless: he lost his leg, and was psychologically damaged. He went into the fighting active and optimistic, and came out with what they then called shell shock. He was in bed for months. My mother nursed him. He was very ill, she said, and what was so worrying was his state of mind. I have a photograph of him in bed in the Royal Free Hospital, a handsome man, but minus a leg and inwardly in torment. Beside him Sister McVeagh sits wearing her full white veil, sewing, her eyes on her handiwork. "Before she was thought of," says the caption, meaning me, their first child. The date is September 1917.

She was thirty-three, a year older than her mother had been when she died giving birth to her third child. Sister McVeagh was facing a hard, a very hard, choice. She had been asked if she would accept the matronship of St. George's Hospital—an honour, at her age. Usually much older women became matrons and ran great hospitals. But she liked nursing: did she want to become an administrator? Besides, matrons were such martinets! She had suffered under these formidable women, did she want to become one? And here was Captain Tayler, of whom she had become very fond, wanting to marry her. There were no men left, they were all killed. Would she be asked again? She had always thought of herself as—had always been told she was—very plain. Did

she want to marry him? Did she want to marry at all, since her real love, the man she ought to have married, was dead?

He had been a young doctor in the hospital with whom, my father confirmed, she had had an understanding. His little picture, torn out of a newspaper that recorded his death by drowning in a ship sunk by the Germans, stood forever on her dressing table. He had a soft, boyish face. The understanding between them, the death, my mother's unhappiness were observed by my father, who always spoke of him with pain. "Your poor mother," he would say, "he was a good chap, that young doctor."

It took her a long time to decide, and she became ill with the strain of it all. As a nurse she should have known what she had to face in a man so damaged. Later she would say, often: "If we knew when we were young what was going to happen to us, then. . . ."

She really had no idea, then or ever, of the mental world my father lived in. I am not only talking of his depression after the war. Quite simply, he had a dimension that she lacked. For a long time I thought it was the awfulness of the war that had given him his sensitiveness to other people, his broadness of outlook. Their experiences, after all, had not been so different. His upbringing had been as bad as hers—savage, I was going to say, and yes, the word can stand: her impatient ruthlessness, I once thought, was the legacy of her childhood. But he had been much beaten at school and at home, over-disciplined, and harshly misunderstood. He, like her, had escaped as soon as he could. Years later I met people who had known him as a young man—and what the war had done was to confirm his essential nature: he had always been contemplative and philosophical. "Your father had his own way of seeing things," cried a former girlfriend, "and I would often rather not have known what he was thinking." And another said, not without ambiguity, that she had never been so well understood. He was kind; he was generous; she had not met anyone like him; but there was something detached in him which was hard to take. And this detachment was a part of his deepest characteristic—an understanding of impermanence, change.

I believe that his nature, so different from hers, was why my mother married him. She knew she had limitations—how could she not, brought up constantly against this magnanimity in everything? "Don't you see, old girl, that's how things *are?*" he would say, amazed at her pettiness, her inability to see: he had been watching Life at it again, working out one of its little games. He was unsurprised, interested: she, always, rebellious.

To put her dilemma squarely: what she respected most in him, what gave her access to a largeness she would never have known without him, was precisely what did both her and him in: these fine ways of thinking, his scope, were always overthrowing her best self, which was a magnificent commonsense. She had married a weak man, then? But his weakness was obviously stronger than her strength, always pulling her further away from what would best suit her. A weak man? Yet he was not weak by nature; it was the war that had distorted him. *Weak!* How else could you describe him? Always refusing to make judgements, take stands; always insisting on what he called the long view—you'd think there was nothing he respected. . . . And yet. Life was not a simple business; she suspected he was nearer to understanding it than she would ever be.

I have an image of them, confronting Life in such different ways. He looks it straight in the face, with a dark, grim, ironical recognition. But she, always being disappointed in ways he could never be, has a defiant, angry little air: she has caught Life out in injustice *again*. "How can you!" she seems to be saying, exasperated, to Life. "It's not right to behave like that!" And she gives a brisk, brave little sniff.

They were married. They did not feel up to a proper wedding. For one thing they were Wells and Shaw people, and white weddings were ridiculous (obviously soon to become obsolete!), and for another, his mother disapproved of Sister McVeagh: she was going to rule him with a rod of iron, said this ruler with the rod. My father was elegant, as always, when he still cared about clothes. My mother wore a dress she clearly had given a lot of thought to: only recently, when I was writing the Jane Somers books, did I realize that my mother (who could, I think, be something like Jane Somers if she lived now) very much enjoyed clothes, even though for most of her life she did not have the money to buy them, or the opportunity to wear them.

It was on the wedding night, they joked, that my mother must have got pregnant, though they were armed with the works of Marie Stopes, and had decided not to have a baby yet, if at all. He was still so low in spirits: he simply did not seem able to pull himself out of his ugly state of mind. And she was ill, she did not know why, but it was probably overwork from the war. And there was all that flu about, so many people dying everywhere: everything was so depressing after the war. It was 1919.

They left for Persia. He had to leave England—he couldn't stand it—so why not Persia? My mother, being a woman of her time, was ready to go off and live in the Middle East, even though she knew nothing about it. A close friend was a missionary in Japan; her brother, John, never at home in the Army—he did not pass the Navy exams—was about to become a rubber planter in Malaya.

Persia was then divided into spheres of influence, mainly French and British. Britain had finance, and my father was going to manage a bank in Kermanshah. Before the war he had been a clerk in a bank, and to have to go back to it was awful for him; but at least he was getting out of England, where he knew he could never live again. Coming back from the trenches he felt as all the soldiers of that war did: betrayed by the politicians who had lied to them and did not keep promises; betrayed by the civilians who talked patriotic nonsense and had no idea of what the trenches were like; betrayed by the jingoistic newspapers; betrayed by the Armistice which would make another war inevitable. It was stupid to treat the Germans like this, one should take the long view. None of the Tommies felt vindictive. Any Tommy could tell the politicians they were being stupid. A funny thing, wasn't it? he would demand all his life (my mother half agreeing with him, feeling that she should, while her nature rebelled): any ordinary person could see it, the politicians couldn't. Why is it that ordinary people have so much more sense than politicians when it is the politicians' job to be sensible?

This was the first time in her life when my mother would need a lot of clothes, and she took trunks full of them. She also took the necessities for a middle-class nursery as prescribed by one Dr. Trudy King and other mentors. The layette for a baby then consisted of dozens of everything. Napkins thick and thin, and napkin liners. Vests long and short, inner and outer. Petticoats of various lengths, of flannel and of lawn, embroidered and tucked and edged with lace. Long and short dresses of pin-tucked and embroidered lawn. Caps. Shawls. Not to mention binders made of thick material which supported the baby's stomach as if it were a wound from which entrails might spill. This layette itself must have been enough to dismay any woman, make her feel helpless, feel at least that an ordeal lay ahead. It all assumed servants of course. Those exquisite dresses alone took hours to iron, not to mention the dressing and undressing of the helpless infant, who was also supposed to be fed every two or three hours day and night, and, if bottle-fed—a recommended practice—the preparations were like those for a surgical operation.

I used to read those lists on the farm in Rhodesia, dazzled by incredulity: I was surrounded by black babies living contented and naked inside a fold of cloth on their mother's backs.

It was "Maude" and "Michael" Tayler who arrived in Persia. My mother had always disliked Emily, I suppose because it was the name of her mother, but she liked Maude, because of Tennyson's Maud. She had been trying to shed Emily for years. She would not have Alfred for my father: a common name. And what did he think about it? I can hear him: "Oh Lord, old thing, who cares? What does it matter? If it makes you happy, then. . . ." He was made Michael because of Peter Pan.

The Westminster Bank allotted Maude and Michael an enormous house made of stone that was carved and fretted, with great arches along the verandahs and arched windows, and surrounded by wonderful gardens. Servants—gardeners, cooks, people who cleaned the house, shopped—did everything. My mother hardly mentioned the servants, except to say that households were regulated by protocol, and that the mistress of the house knew her place and did what she was told. She thought this amusing: not a hint here of what in Africa became a neurotic preoccupation—the shortcomings of the black servants.

For my father Kermanshah was what he had dreamed of: an ancient town on a high empty brown landscape, the high blue sky, the mountains all around with the snow on them. When I went to Granada for the first time I knew it was like Kermanshah: gardens, the sounds of water running everywhere, the smell of the dust. . . . My father was managing the bank; he was not at anybody's beck and call. He rode everywhere, for he would not allow his wooden leg to make him less active. He liked the spacious house and the release, at least to an extent, from English respectability.

My mother was having a difficult pregnancy, morning sickness being only one of the complications. She was expecting a son, Peter John. Why did she not even consider the possibility of a daughter? Her passionate identification with a son was, I think, because of her brother, John, who was not clever, did not care very much what he did, and yet went, was expected to go as if by right, into the Navy. I think she most bitterly envied him, but to feel like this was not being a good sort. She was the one born to be an officer in His Majesty's Navy! She was the clever one, who adored everything about the sea, about ships, was never seasick. She was resourceful and quick-witted. She was decent and good-humoured and able to get on with people. An authoritarian personality, happy in a structured life, she was able to take and to give orders. Of course, the negative aspects of this

particular personality were also hers: the inability to put herself into the shoes of people who were different; a contempt for weakness; a lack of understanding of what she described as "morbid": the ambiguous, the witty, the equivocal—these areas would always be suspect, and she was threatened by them.

I can only guess, hurt for her, at how much she must have felt frustrated as a girl, seeing her slow brother expected to get what ought to have been hers too. And yet she never said anything, except in jolly little jokes, brave jokes. What she felt had to come out indirectly.

The birth was difficult. I was delivered with forceps that left a scarlet birthmark over one side of my face. Above all, I was a girl. When the doctor wanted to know my name, and heard that none had been prepared, he looked down at the cradle and said softly, "Doris?" This scene: the doctor's weariness after the long night, his soft, tactful, but reproachful query, was vividly enacted by my mother, like many other scenes.

Of course I resented it all bitterly, particularly that she did not even see that it was likely to make me angry. How could she stand there, with her customary determined little smile, her brisk social manner, telling me that I was not wanted in the first place; that to have a girl was a disappointment that nearly did her in altogether, after that long labour; that she had no milk for me and I had to be bottle-fed from the start and I was half-starved for the first year and never stopped screaming because she did not realize that cows' milk in Persia was not as rich as real English milk; that I was an impossibly difficult baby, and then a tiresome child, quite unlike my little brother, Harry, who was always so good. And so she let the nurse cope with me, and looked after Harry herself.

Better say, and be done with it: my memories of her are all of antagonism, and fighting, and feeling shut out; of pain because the baby born two-and-a-half years after me was so much loved when I was not. She would recognize none of this, nor accept it. The way she saw it was that her childhood had been cold and loveless, and she would make sure that her children were governed by love. Love was always being invoked; and I became an expert in emotional blackmail by the time I was five. She didn't like me—that was the point. It was not her fault: I cannot think of a person less likely than myself to please her. But it would have been impossible for her to admit it: a mother loves her child, a child its mother. And that's that!

Doris Lessing, about four years old, in Persia

My father hated it when he was transferred to Tehran, to a branch of the bank where he was not manager and had to work under someone else, and where he had to live in a house he thought English and stuffy. But my mother loved it. At last, suitable nurseries, instead of those great stone rooms that curtains and rugs could not soften. I remember the tall, square day-nursery, the heavy red velvet curtains and the lace ones behind them, the brass fender with the tall dangerous fire, the suffocating plenty of things, things, things. And, of course, my brother, the "baby" (he was called Baby until he was seven and fought for self-determination) who was the centre of everything. And the scolding, fussy nurse.

In Tehran my mother also loved the social life, which was like the pleasures of her girlhood over again. About "the Legation set" she would talk wistfully in Africa, while my father, half sighing, regarded her with his familiar expression: incredulity, curiosity, held in check by irony. How could she enjoy those boring jolly evenings with boring jolly people? He loathed musical evenings, with people singing the "Indian Love Lyrics" and "The Road to Mandalay"

to each other, while my mother played. (She played alone, for her own pleasure, music these people found highbrow.) He hated the dinner parties, receptions, garden parties, and picnics; she could not have enough of them. He would tell the story of a certain Englishman in Persia who, urged by his family to let them have a picnic, put his children on donkeys, blindfolded them, and had them led around and around the garden for an hour, when they were unblindfolded and saw the feast prepared for them in a corner of their own garden. Meanwhile he retired to the library. A fellow spirit! My mother only laughed. "Don't you dare try it," she said.

Persia, particularly Tehran, was the best time in my mother's life.

When they had been in Persia for five years, leave was due, after which they intended to come back. He did not much want to: would he really have to work in a bank for the rest of his life? He had had a country childhood, and always wanted to be a farmer.

It was summer, the Red Sea a furnace, and dangerous for children. They decided—which means, my mother decided—to travel back across Russia. Ours was the first family to use that route after the Revolution, through the Caspian to Moscow. 1924, and everything was in chaos. On an oil tanker in the Caspian, my mother sat up all night to keep the lights on us, for there were swarms of lice. A shadow fell on an arm: mine, which became red and swollen with bites. Typhus abounded. The trains were ancient, also lice-ridden, no food on them. On every station were crowds of starved children, orphans; and the peasant women selling a hard-boiled egg or some bread had to defend themselves against these *besprizorniks*, when my mother got off to buy something, anything at all, to eat. She was still on the platform once when our train left without her. I remember the terror of it: she had vanished. It took her a day and a half to catch up. She had to fight her way onto a goods train, had to "tell them what to do—*they* didn't know—I had to make them telegraph our train to wait for me." All in English, of course. At the frontier, informed that we did not have the right visas, she had told the man at Immigration not to be so silly. For years my father collapsed into laughter, remembering the poor ragged half-starved Bolshevik with a rifle "that wouldn't bring down a pigeon," confronted by a British matron. "Oh Lord," wept my father, "I can see it now. Don't be silly, she said, and he was raring to shoot the lot of us." "Did I get us in or did I not?" demanded my mother, not really understanding why he laughed so much, but knowing she was in the right. "Oh, you got us in all right!"

In Moscow, in the hotel, the chambermaids begged to bath and dress us, because they had not seen normal well-fed children. My mother spoke of this with calm, proprietary pride: that the Russians were in this terrible disorganized condition was of course only another proof of the virtues of the British and our Empire.

Six months' leave, in England. My memories of it are many, all of cold, damp, dreariness, ugliness, a series of snapshots illustrating my loathing for the place. My parents took us to visit relations, such as my mother's stepmother, now a distinguished old lady living on a minute pension. They did not enjoy it. My father wanted only to leave England, even more stuffy than he remembered, and my mother yearned to return to Tehran. They visited the 1924 Empire Exhibition at Wembley, and the Southern Rhodesia stand had maize cobs eighteen inches long, and the posters, yards high, claimed that anyone could make his fortune in maize-farming within five years.

My father had about £1,000 capital and a pension because he had lost his leg in the War. This was his chance.

What did they imagine they were going to? Certainly they expected a social life not unlike that in Tehran, for my mother had trunks full of clothes from Harrod's. Also curtains and hangings from Liberty's, and visiting cards. Also a governess, Biddy O'Halloran, aged twenty-one. Perhaps they had heard of the lively goings-on in Nairobi? Not that my mother would have approved of those fast ways. She could not approve of Biddy, who had shingled hair and wore lipstick. These modern girls . . . all her life my mother would use phrases like this, without inverted commas.

It must have been painful, giving up Tehran, to go off to be a farmer's wife in yet another new country. She would not really have minded staying in England—that is to say, London. She was still, every fibre of her, a Londoner. Remembering England, she thought of the streets, buses, trams, theatres, parks, of London. She did not mind the conventional in the way my father did. If he had been prepared to go back into the Westminster Bank somewhere in London, she would have given up the pleasures of Tehran with equanimity. And then she would have lived out her life in conformity with her nature, a useful and energetic middle-class woman in, let's say, Wimbledon.

Instead, she set off for the middle of Africa with her crippled husband, who was steadily getting more prickly and solitary, with practically no money, and her two children, one of whom was born to be a trouble and a sorrow to her. Did she know anything about Africa, or about farming? Not a thing! But it didn't seem to matter.

I think she saw Africa as some little interlude, a station on her way, soon to be passed. Nothing had ever happened to my mother to prepare her for what she would find.

It was a slow German boat. My mother loved the gales that sent the other passengers below, leaving her on the bridge with the captain. This, and the deck games and the fancy-dress parties, made up for her husband, who wanted only to sit and watch the sea, and for her daughter, who was being consistently impertinent, and who cut up her evening dresses with scissors when she was forced to go to bed early so as not to interfere with the evening's good times. The boat loafed around the Cape to Beira, where they caught the train to Salisbury. Outside Salisbury was a place called Lilfordia that boarded settlers while they were buying farms. (Lilfordia was the farm of "Boss" Lilford, later Ian Smith's guide and mentor.) My mother left her children with the governess, and went with her husband by Scotch cart to look at farms. The settlers were being offered land at about twenty pounds an acre (at today's values), the money advanced by the Land Bank. The land had been cleared of the black people who had been living on it: they were despatched to the Reserves, or told to move to land that hadn't yet been allocated to whites. This was "opening up the country for white civilization," a description my mother never could see any reason to criticize.

The farm they bought was in Lomagundi, seventy miles from Salisbury, a modest 1,500 acres, but we were free to run our cattle, and to cut grass and wood on the miles of Government land which remained unallocated all the time we were there. Our farm, then, was at the frontier of "white civilization" with nothing between us and Portuguese East Africa a couple of hundred miles away.

The land was sparsely settled, the farms huge. The nearest farmhouses to ours were three, four, five miles away. It was virgin bush: a few trees had been cut for mine furnaces. Every kind of animal lived there: sable, eland, kudu, bushbuck, duiker, anteaters, wild cats, wild pigs, snakes. There were flocks of guinea fowl, partridges, hawks, eagles, pigeons, doves—birds, birds, birds. Dawns were explosions of song; the nights noisy with owls and nightjars and birds whose names we never knew; all day birds shrilled and cooed and hammered and chattered. But paradise had already been given notice to quit. The leopards and baboons had gone to the hills, the lions

"Our home in Southern Rhodesia, now Zimbabwe"

had wandered off, the elephants had retreated to the Zambesi Valley, the land was emptying.

But it was still a wilderness that my parents were taking on. The farm itself was approached by a disused mine track, a dirt road. The railway was seven miles away. Not one acre had been cleared for planting. The labourers were people who had been savagely defeated in a war thirty-five years before, and who left their villages and came out to work only because they had to pay the Poll Tax imposed on them precisely to make them work.

Having found their farm, my parents came back to collect the children. Their daughter as usual had been very naughty indeed, much worse than ever before: she had lied, stolen, run away, sulked, and screamed. My mother knew it was all the fault of this travelling about: children need an ordered existence. She got us into a covered wagon drawn by twenty or so oxen, while her husband rode alongside it on his horse. The journey took five days. Inside the wagon was everything they possessed.

While the trees were being cleared off the hill where the house was to be built, we lodged at the gold mine just over the ridge.

Settlers always built themselves mud-and-thatch huts, joined by verandahs, which were expected to last only a year or so, to be replaced after the first good season by brick and tin. Our house was a single elongated hut, divided into four rooms. Its walls were

of mud smeared over poles and whitewashed, the roof thatch cut from the grass in the *vleis*, the floor of stamped mud and dung.

All the floors were covered with black linoleum, and furniture was made from petrol and paraffin boxes stained black and curtained with flour sacks that were dyed and embroidered by my mother. In the front room, which had windows all around it, "like the prow of a ship" as my mother insisted, were Persian rugs, Liberty curtains, a piano, and the heavy display silver of the period.

While my mother supervised the gang of black men building the house, my father watched the teams who cleared the bush for planting.

Then there was the business of Biddy O'Halloran, who turned out so badly. She had definitely expected something like Nairobi, and found herself stuck in this lonely and savage place with suitors of the wrong class. Every unattached male for fifty miles came visiting to propose to her, and she did not have as much time for the children as my mother thought was due. There were quarrels, and she departed back home. Then, about a year after the arrival in Africa, my mother became ill and took to her bed and stayed there. It was her heart! It is clear now that she was in an acute anxiety state, was having a breakdown. Neither her doctor in Salisbury, nor she (a nurse) could see it. The worst for her, of course, was the isolation. What my father revelled in—for he had at last found the life that suited him—was destroying her. Having always been surrounded by people, she now had only the blacks, towards whom she had had from the start all the attitudes typical of the settler: they were primitive, dirty, stupid. She was never able to see that there was anything interesting in them. Her neighbours were lower-middle class and working class, mostly Scottish, who had come out before the War and had got rich on maize. She did not want to seem snobbish, but what did she have in common with them? She had no intention of spending her life talking about gardening and recipes and dress patterns. But that was what her life now was, just like theirs.

She got out of bed, complained of a thousand aches and pains, went back again. She complained continually, and it was unlike her, for it simply wasn't done to make a fuss! She lay in a bed specially made by a neighbour who ran a timber mill, with attachments for books and magazines, and summoned her children to her throughout the day, to comfort her. "Poor sick mummy," she insisted, and we responded with fervent but (in my case at least) increasingly resentful embraces.

But this was certainly not all that went on at her bedside. Early childhood is when children learn best, and nothing was going to get in the way of our instruction, according to Montessori. In and out of bed, she read to us, told us stories; she was a marvellous teacher of small children. We were taught geography by means of piles of mud and sand left over from the house building—making continents and countries and mountains that hardened in the sun and that, for oceans and rivers, could be filled with water. She taught us arithmetic with seeds and hens' eggs and baby chicks. She made us understand the solar system through games in which we were planets, the moon, the sun. We were made to notice stars, birds, animals. For a while we were taught by a correspondence course, but its lessons were not nearly as good as hers, and she ordered us books from England, and two periodicals whose impossibly high standards of writing would find no equal today. The *Children's Newspaper* offered news about discoveries, inventions, archaeological finds, beasts and birds, and the *Merry-Go-Round* printed stories and poems by writers like Walter de la Mare and Eleanor Farjeon. It was my mother who introduced me to the world of literature into which I was about to escape from her.

And then my mother got herself out of bed, and went on living. She had been ill for a year. I wonder if she ever understood that her illness had been a way of denying what she knew she had to face. What courage that must have taken! I know it and I admire it, but I can't put myself in her place. It was the farm, the veld, that she hated, that trapped her. She was planning, scheming, dreaming of escaping from it, from the moment she arrived. But the farm, the veld, Africa is to me, quite simply, the luckiest thing that ever happened.

Writing about my mother is difficult. I keep coming up against barriers, and they are not much different now from what they were then. She paralysed me as a child by the anger and pity I felt. Now only pity is left, but it still makes it hard to write about her. What an awful life she had, my poor mother! But it was certainly no worse than my father's, and that is the point: he was equipped by nature for hard times, and she was not. He may have been a damaged, an increasingly sick man; she was strong and full of vitality. But I am not as sorry for him as I am for her. She never understood what was happening to her.

II

In the Twenties, and even more in the Thirties, young middle-class people fled from hard times in Britain where they could not get work, to make a life in the Colonies. Often they had no money, but knew they would be given land and loans. They struggled, and very often failed. If their families at Home sent them their return fares, they went back to what they had left, degrees of genteel poverty, to be rescued, presumably, by World War II. How many of them were there? A great many, I think, for the turnover of white people, certainly in Southern Rhodesia, was always large. There is no way now of finding out about them. What a story! What stories!—and recently I read two of them, for I was sent a couple of manuscripts, memoirs by white women of their lives as white settlers, one in Kenya, one in Southern Rhodesia. These people, without any kind of training, either psychological or practical, found themselves in the bush, usually with not even an acre cleared for planting, in some kind of shack, coping with floods, droughts, fires, wild animals, and black labourers who, having been forced out to work by the Poll Tax, were sullen, angry, inefficient. Not the least of the ironies was that the whites saw themselves as pitifully poor, and the blacks saw them as unreachably rich. Both were right. Now what comes through most strongly in these accounts is that it seems, once these unsatisfactory members of the family had left Britain, it was out of sight, out of mind. The strongest and most frequent note struck is how small sums of money—£50, £25, would often have saved a situation, but money was never forthcoming. That the middle classes tend to be mean to their own is well-known, but never have I seen it so painfully shown as here. Perhaps their families did not have any money to help out with? There was no money to help my parents; all our relatives were just surviving.

These memoirs made me think about the differences between my parents and these settlers who would never have left Home if they could only have found what my father loathed so bitterly and left: a good, safe, respectable job. There were basically two kinds of immigrants: those who could not make it in Britain, and those who could, but who would not conform to British respectability. My father was one of the misfits who provided the landscape of my growing up with colourful characters whose eccentricities, suppressed in Britain, were given plenty of room to expand.

Above all, it was my mother who was defined by these women's reminiscences, all of failure, incapacity, incompetence, muddle. They could not cope with floods and fires and snakes, or having to cook bread in antheaps when the kitchen burned down, or making furniture from paraffin boxes and curtains, and dresses from flour sacks. They could not do more than just suffer what was happening to them, and of course they despised and feared the blacks. With what wails of self-pity and misery did they struggle to impose respectability on the veld, their main drive being to remain what they were—middleclass; their fear being that they could become poor whites, and on the level of the blacks, just as at Home their nightmare was that they might be forced into the working class. As Denys Finch-Hatton said, as he watched the little villas of suburbia marching across the magnificent wildness of the N'gong Hills towards Nairobi, "This continent of Africa has a very fine sense of sarcasm." (*Out of Africa* by Karen Blixen.)

But the fear was real enough. Very often I heard my parents say, in the troubled, grieved voice we use for those whose fate may easily be ours, "So and so's gone bust, he's got a job as storekeeper at the mine, she's going to be a matron—" (or governess or housekeeper) "and God help those kids."

Far from wailing and wincing, my mother enjoyed all the contriving and making do. They complained, "No decent fruit here, no vegetables, our chickens die . . ." Her vegetable garden could have fed a village, and she had fruit trees, chickens, rabbits. She made cheese and the store hut was always full of preserves. She was endlessly adaptable and inventive. She had too much energy, capacity, for her situation. Her fate should have been to run a large organization, a hospital, or even an industry. On the farm she burned herself out.

Five years after we arrived on the farm, this was the situation . . . land had been cleared, and more and different crops were being grown, but we were just as much in debt to the Land Bank. The house, built to last two years, was going to have to stand much longer. Verandahs and additions of all kinds had been made. Her son, aged eight, was still being taught at home; but like all the boys of the district he spent most of his time in the bush. Her daughter, after a couple of bad choices in the way of schools, interminable and unforgettable to the child, but lasting only a few weeks and therefore unimportant to the adult, was in a convent in Salisbury. Convents are more ladylike than other schools. If my mother had known what went on, she would have removed me at once, but there is a convention that children do not tell parents about school. All she knew was that I was very homesick. These days this would be seen as a symptom of something very wrong at home; but in those unsophisticated times she was able to see it as proper and gratifying affection. She did not feel it as shocking, to send a child of seven to boarding school. At that age, children were sent Home from India to board; in England boys were sent at seven to boarding school. And what else could she have done? All the farmers' children went to school in the towns.

Her husband, not her children, was then her main worry. It is hard for the competent—and for those who have all their will behind what they do—to understand those who simply cannot make things work. My father's dreams of getting rich in five years had become a brave family joke. Besides, the Slump had begun. Long past were the days when farmers made sudden fortunes out of maize; still in the future were the fortunes made out of tobacco. Everywhere, farmers were just holding on, nursing their debts to the Government, running up bills at the grocer and the butcher, taking small risks on mixed crops, like sunflower, cotton, peanuts, sun hemp. So in any case things were against my father, but his own nature was worse. He did not really care, and I think she never understood that. War had only intensified what he was, and—from her point of view—that was bad enough. Recently a cousin sent me material about a second cousin of my father, a Victorian who was a melancholy gentleman farmer in Suffolk, writing mellow verses in the Wordsworthian manner about Death, Fate, Life and Nature. A copy is in the British Museum. He and my father even looked alike. So my mother was up against much worse than she had foreseen, though she might have remembered that his father, married to an ambitious, forceful woman, was happy as a bank clerk, spending every free moment playing the organ in the village church. Left to himself, her husband would dream his life away, content, contemplating the African night sky, sunsets, ants at work in a log, veld fires burning their slow way across the mountains in the dry season, the changing colours of the veld and, but a good way behind Nature, the fascinating improbabilities of human behaviour, white and black.

She pushed and she nagged and she made plans. Her aims were simple. Enough money must be made to pay off the debts, and then we must sell the farm and return to England where real life was waiting for her. Talk about what life would be like in England (London, of course) went on all my childhood and was referred to by my brother and myself as "getting-off-the-farm." Not with derision; nor did we ever sit down and analyse the nonsense of it all. It was simply too remote, this talk of good schools and nice houses, of housemaids and buses, theatres and parks.

But my father didn't want to get off the farm. Having reached England, what then? He loathed the Bank, where in any case he might not now get a job. And she could not return easily to nursing, with two children. How would they live? Never mind! All that would sort itself out, once they had got off the farm.

The pressures from my mother to do better caused my father, not to become a successful farmer, but to take a step sideways off this course, into the old dream of finding gold.

It sounds absurd, but it wasn't. The district is called Banket, after a certain type of gold-bearing reef on the Rand, identified by some early prospector. All that country is full of gold-bearing reefs, and outcrops had been prospected everywhere. My brother and I continually came on old trenches dug by some gold-seeker, or rocks where you could see how the prospector had chipped off a sample to pan. There were two gold mines not far from the farm. We could hear the mine-stamps going, day and night, from the mine just over the ridge. Prospectors came through all the time with a gun, a prospecting pan, a hammer, a corner of a sack of maizemeal, and a blanket. They came more often as the Slump deepened and they could not find work. There were many men in those days roaming the bush, self-sufficient and costing nothing, while their wives rode out the bad time as housekeeper somewhere they could have the children in the holidays. Gold was all about us, in the earth, in people's talk, in the history of this area, which was full of old diggings from when the first explorers and missionaries came in. We said they were made by the Arabs. When my father took a hammer with him on his visits around the farm, and brought back samples of rock, then crushed them in the mortar and panned them, he did no more than

most farmers when they came on a likely outcrop or bit of reef. But very soon it became an obsession. Supervising the farm work took second place to gold seeking. He was spending hours of every day stomping over the veld on his wooden leg with the hammer, and the car always came back loaded with rocks. A man was taken off farm work to pound the samples, to dig little trenches after a likely reef, to take a sample into the station to catch a train into Salisbury and the Assay Office. On mail days, when we waited for the results to come back, the tension was painful. Soon it was not trenches, but shafts that were being dug, and not one labourer but two or three were permanently on this work. My mother of course protested that if the same effort were to be put into the farm work, then . . . But nothing like this effort would have been enough to change anything in Slump time. Farmers were going bankrupt, and their land was being bought by more successful farmers, or by combines. This was the beginning of the process that created enormous units of land, hundreds of thousands of acres large, that would shortly be growing not food, but tobacco, making tobacco fortunes, the "tobacco barons."

And then, it was not just prospecting, but divining. My father had discovered he could divine for water. If water, why not gold? If gold, it would not just be a question of finding a gold mine here, on this farm (and that was only a matter of time) but becoming someone to whom the big mining companies from all over the world would come rushing, demanding his services. And then he could train other people to do it, and he could start a school of divining . . .

While all this went on, my mother was trying to maintain what to her was normality. I am sure it had never occurred to her that a lively social life was something one could do without. All her best memories of girlhood, and of her years as a nurse, and then her early marriage in Persia, were of visits and parties and musical evenings and jolly times. Among—this went without saying—*nice people.* The people who farmed around us were not of our class, they had all been working class or lower middle-class people, most of them Scotch. While we visited them, and they us, while she performed all the functions of a neighbor, from exchanges of farm produce to helping during times of crisis, they were not what she had in mind. My brother and I did not understand what she was on about; and our father was not interested enough to enlighten us as to why so much effort had to go into keeping up friendships with people who might be living many miles away, why this was so important to her. What one did was to "spend the day" with whatever family it was, on their farm; or they came to us; but all this was within the limits set by farmwork and the seasons and the school holidays. Some lived beyond one or two rivers which might be impassable when the rains were heavy. We started off early, so as to arrive for morning tea. The men of course talked farming, and the women hungrily talked—and talked—and talked. All the men of the district were guilty when they remembered how their wives starved for the companionship of women. There was lunch. Then tea. All the people in the district kept up the five-meals-a-day pattern of eating, which they had brought from Home. (The Africans called the whites The People Who Never Stop Eating.) In between these meals, we children went climbing *kopjes* or exploring the bush, looking for baboon troops or wild pig. After supper we drove home through the bush where all kinds of animals appeared in the headlights: the different kinds of buck, from little duiker to the big eland and koodoo, wild cats, porcupines, monkeys. My brother and I fought to stay awake.

There was one thing these nice people had in common that I didn't see then. They were survivors of World War I. The men had artificial arms or legs or an eye-patch where an eye had gone. They would discuss the whereabouts of various bits of shrapnel forever travelling about their bodies out of sight, but sometimes appearing from healthy tissue to tinkle into a shaving mug or onto a plate. One woman had had four sons and a husband killed in the Trenches, and was farming with the remaining son. She was dignified, stoical, and the house was full of photographs of dead men in uniform. Another family had two boys whom we played with, but photographs of a third dominated the house and the talk of the parents: he had been drowned in a torpedoed ship. There was a man with a steel plate keeping his brains in, and another who was rumoured to have a steel plate holding in his bowels. They talked about the war, both men and women—the war, the war, the war; and we children escaped into the bush away from it, just as, at home, my brother and I tried to shut our ears against what my father came to call, sarcastically, the Great Unmentionable: "I don't want to bore you with the Great Unmentionable, God forbid that you should waste your time on anything so unimportant." Talk of the war was like this business of *nice people*, with which our mother continually persecuted us. The poor woman was behaving normally for her class and her time, only doing her duty as she saw it by her offspring. There we might be, at the breakfast table, the four of us. My father of course was thousands of miles away, probably in the Trenches, or in some conference of scientists, all of

whom hung on his every syllable. We, the children, sitting on either side of the table, would be regarding her with expressions of embarrassed impatience, while we fidgeted to be off into the bush. "Do listen," she would say, "no, just this once, *listen*. One of these days, when we get off the farm, you'll have to live with nice people, just like everybody else; you won't be racketing around with every kind of person as you do here. Michael—you talk to them! Tell them to listen to me, just this once—*Michael!*"

"What is it?" he would say. "Oh yes, now then you kids, listen to your mother." But he would already be up and reaching for his divining rod, and we went as fast as we could after him, trying not to see the hurt, wistful look on her face.

This business of gold, of divining, meant that the structure of visiting and being visited was always threatened. He would grumble for days at the prospect of having to go off for the day to this or that family: "Oh *Lord*, do I have to? Oh very well, but it'll have to be Sunday, when the boys are off." Or: "Sorry, impossible, we'll be starting the planting, now the rains have begun." But he thought nothing of driving thirty miles on a workday to visit some little mine so as to test out a theory on a reef. It was known exactly how the reef ran underground, where it petered out, what minerals and rock composed it, how much gold it carried. And there my father was, all day in the punishing sun, a shabby but urgent figure walking back and forth over the reef, sometimes for hours, while my mother sat politely talking with a woman she was sure she had nothing in common with, and while we kids hung about the mine which was alien to us, being farming children.

And then we drove back through the starlight, the night air coming in scented from the grasses, but chilled, so that we had to wrap up well after the long hot day. My mother, sitting there in her smart hat, with her gloves and her bag on her lap, would say: "Well, Michael, was it worth it?"

"What, old girl? Yes, I think so."

"We've been there all day," she would persist, in the small unhappy voice she used when she felt that it was her duty to be stubborn, "and there was no one keeping an eye on the farm . . ."

"But it is all information, isn't it? If that reef is going two ounces to the ton, and I was getting that degree of response, then I'll know how to measure what there is when I strike gold at our place, won't I?"

It was not their style to quarrel, shout, raise their voices, accuse or sulk. I cannot remember this ever happening. But I lay awake at night to listen to them arguing. Their voices came easily through the now cracking and loosening mud walls. My mother's voice was patient, persistent—the voice of reason. He stood his ground, but it was a very different one from hers. Her facts and figures were all small sober possibilities with the vagaries of the seasons allowed for. His talk was of great sums of money and gold-bearing reefs like glittering rivers.

In 1935, ten years after my parents arrived in the Colony, this was the situation . . . the house was still upright, a shambling old wreck, its thatch continually being repaired, the mud walls lumpy and patched. In the rainy season the roof leaked, and a bad storm sent water down in a dozen places into pails, buckets, basins. I will remember for ever a certain exquisite hammered copper basin from Persia standing in the middle of the floor on a shabby but glowing Persian rug, like a picture from a fairy tale. Water dropped into it from the thatch, bringing down straws, beetles, and ants that clung to the straws, and laboured their way up them over the edges of the basin, down onto the rug, back across the floor to the walls, and so to the roof.

At the windows the Liberty curtains still hung, pretty but threadbare. In the trunk behind the curtain a dozen evening dresses bought for the fascinating social life my mother had expected to find here lay in their folds of tissue paper with mothballs, when they were not being used for "dressing up." My father's dress clothes lay there too, unregretted. "Good God!" he would say, "just imagine that people are actually prepared to climb into all those stiff collars and suits and go off to spend an evening talking rubbish to strangers they don't care tuppence about. It is hard to believe it all still goes on." The farm was exactly as before, neither successful nor bankrupt. Every year the loan with the Land Bank was re-negotiated. When the money came in at the season's end for the crops, some of the grocer's account was paid off. If the Slump was lifting elsewhere, this did not seem to be happening here, in this district, though a couple of farmers whose fortunes had been solidly based on the maize grown for World War I were doing well. Now, in Zimbabwe, the sons of these farmers are some of the richest in the country.

My father had been talked into doing a couple of seasons of tobacco, and there were two tobacco barns to prove it. To build barns was expensive, but they were standing empty. Getting up at night at all hours to check temperatures, and the steamy air of the curing process (Virginia, not Turkish) had been too much for my father. Now he had sugar diabetes as well. If he had got this disease even a year before he did, he must have died, for insulin had only just been

discovered. He had it very badly. He was supposed to eat only lean meat and lettuce and dry biscuits, for this was the diet in those early days before the doctors learned better. But my mother rebelled and said he would die of starvation before he did of diabetes. She took command and worked out with him how to adjust a variety of foods to the intake of insulin. She was, with every day, more of a nurse again. My father, like many diabetics, had become a hypochondriac. The man who had disdained to make allowances for his wooden leg, climbing trees, riding horses, going down deep mine-shafts in dangerous buckets, now talked of his symptoms with all the intensity he still put into gold and divining. From suffering and resenting the gold-fever, now my mother had become grateful that the passion existed, for it kept my father out every day at his work of divining for gold, and then he wasn't thinking about his rapidly worsening health.

By now he saw the divining as a new science, which he was founding. He used iron rods and steel rods and twigs of various woods from the bush. He "neutralized" the gold in the reefs far under his feet with gold rings held in his hands with the ends of the rods. He tried out silver rings, nuts and bolts from the plough, brass curtain rings, or dipped the rods in water, or in solutions of various chemicals and minerals. He worked at it most of the day, and dreamed of it at night, waking my mother to say, "Listen, old girl, if water neutralises water, and gold, gold, then when the rod pulls down at the end of that trench there, it can't be gold or water, there's something else down there. I wonder what it can be? Chrome? Asbestos? What do you think?" Chrome and asbestos mines were not far off, and lumps of chrome and raw asbestos were part of his equipment. We loved to play with asbestos, alluring stuff, looking like those sweets called satin cushions, or like mermaid's hair, green and glittering.

I wrote about my father, disguised, in a tale called *Eldorado* where the painful passion for gold is described. But by now gold, the lust and the itch for it, had long since become secondary. He was lost in this science of his. He believed he was creating a new method for finding any mineral, gold only one of them. He was alone in the world, so he saw it, with no one sympathetic to talk to, though the children did listen, did try out the rods, and walk with him along the trenches tracking elusive reefs when they were not at school. Only the occasional water diviner who came wandering through the farms, hoping to pick up a five pound note for finding a well, listened to him with understanding—and they started to look polite when he began talking about gold and minerals. He wondered who else, and where, in what continent and country were other people who must be pursuing this line of thought? Perhaps he could advertise in the main newspapers of the world, and make contact with them?

"No, you can *not*," said my mother, "we can't afford it." Why was everyone so small-minded? One day his family would take him seriously: but then prophets are never appreciated by their nearest and dearest.

He sent for books and magazines on metals and mining, ranging from the scientific to the mystical, while my mother protested she needed the money to clothe her children. He regretted he hadn't had the foresight to study metallurgy and chemistry at school: was it too late to study by correspondence course? He brooded about the influence of the moon on metals in the earth, and the influence of metals in the earth on the moon, and on humans and animals.

Whereas once he had refused to have the scotchcart (two barrels on a frame, drawn by two oxen) bring water up the hill to the house more than twice a week, so that baths had to be rationed, now the cart made the journey every day, because so much water was needed for panning the samples. Precious water ran away down the stony hill and made lush plantations of bright green weed among the silvery gold grasses of the dry season. Now, not one or two samples were sent into Salisbury to be assayed, but sometimes dozens. It was all costing a fortune.

But what could my mother do? Her common sense continually outraged, she suffered and rebelled, but mostly in silence, for she, too, was alone, with no one to listen to her. She had all kinds of symptoms herself, particularly bad headaches. She knew that her heart was weak, but no one took this seriously, not even the doctors. She could sleep only when full of sedatives.

And yet . . . gold might be found, even now? Gold *had* been found, not three miles away, and she had gone with her Michael (for she always supported him, no matter how wrong she thought him) to test out a new theory. The miner was a middle-aged Scotchman who had already gone bankrupt several times on farms and on mines, in the way of these days. This was a last gamble, a mere single shaft in the ground, with old and rickety mine machinery. He lived on game shot in the bush, and maize porridge (just like a Kaffir!) and he had the red-eyed sullen look of the compulsive drinker. She knew herself to be lucky, compared with such as he. One day, Michael's ridiculous theories might turn out to have something in them, and then she could get off the farm . . . But what, then, would she do with such a

sick husband? She had accepted that he would never be well, must get worse; and now it was her children who worried her most.

Her son she had got into the only private school in the country that could be compared with real schools in England, a prep school run along English lines. It was expensive, and of course we could not afford it. She had used all her organising abilities to pull strings and get grants. But what would happen to him afterwards? Nothing like an English public school was available, then there would be the question of his career. No money to set him up, no future! She wanted him to go into the Navy, and spend his life with nice people, but when she talked about it, he looked vague and off he went into the bush with his rifle, alone, or with a black boy for company.

Recently my brother came from Africa to visit, and we talked about that childhood of ours, in the old thatched mud house in the bush. A miracle of good luck! We were on land never before farmed, the bush still unspoiled by white and black idiots, surrounded by every kind of wild animal and bird, free to wander as we wanted over thousands of acres, solitude the

Doris at fourteen

most precious of our gifts . . . but our mother lay awake at night, ill with grief because her children were deprived, were not good middle-class children in some suburb in London.

If her son's future was an anxiety, then what could she say about her daughter!

I was always ill at school. Now I know I was ill with homesickness. I did have a couple of real illnesses, malaria and dysentery, but I acquired with my mother's connivance vague ailments that were always taking me into the Convent sickroom with the need to be cossetted. My mother would make her reluctant husband rush her the seventy miles into town—the word "rush" here is relative: in our ancient Overland the trip took hours. There she informed the nuns and the doctor that I must have this or that kind of treatment: *she* knew best, she had been trained at the Royal Free, in London. When I was actually in the classroom, I did well enough, but the pressure of my mother's need that I should be cleverer than anyone else was intense, and I was trying to escape from it. Her schemes for my future had the illusory poisoned glow of the gold mining talk which by then I refused to listen to. The music lessons I took must end on concert platforms, because she could have been a concert pianist. If I hummed a tune, grand opera was waiting for me. Talk of great painters accompanied my attempts at drawing. All this was in English terms. It was inconceivable that I, or any other white child, should learn Shona, or try to understand the lives of Africans. It is impossible to believe now, but a man who travelled around making recordings of African music was considered a Kaffir-lover and a traitor to the whites. A poet who lived in the bush, befriending Africans and liked by them, was hated by the whites, who responded to any mention of him with that loud, uneasy, derisive laughter that means people are feeling threatened. What is the use of exclaiming: "But that's insane!" It was how things were.

I did also write little pieces. But I hid these attempts from her, because I felt that they weren't mine, but hers; for she took possession of them, talking about them to everyone.

When I was fourteen I finally slid out of school on a pretext and stayed on the farm, where I lay on my bed reading, or went about the bush with my rifle. I was supposedly ill with "low fever." Perhaps I did have it. I certainly had a permanent low temperature, lacked energy, and was dosed with quantities of quinine that I am amazed didn't kill me. But there came a rescue. I was sent on a two months' holiday by a charitable organization to another part of the country, right away from home. There I saw certain

things very clearly. One was that there was nothing wrong with me. I knew I had to escape from that house where both parents were ill, obsessed with illness. When I went home I told my mother that I was very well, and said, "It's no good trying to make me ill, ever again." Of course she did not know what I meant, believed that I was, as always, cruel and unfair.

I think now that she was a bit crazy with the menopause. These days she would be given a few pills and remain her normal, humorous, moderate self. She was obsessed. With the deficiencies of her black servants, for one thing. Like nearly all the white housewives then (and now, it goes on still, in South Africa) she spoke to them in a nagging voice full of dislike, much to the distress of my father. "What's the point of making people just out of their villages fuss about teaspoons and cups and saucers that match?" Most of the time she listened, but now she cried: "I suppose you want me to lower my standards!" And she was obsessed with me: my brother was at school and safely out of the way. Everything I was, and did, shocked her. She wanted me to remain a little girl, in a country where girls grew up early. Because she insisted that I wear childish clothes, I earned the money to buy material by shooting guinea fowl and doves for the local butcher and I made my own clothes. They were grown-up clothes and she hated them. I was reading books that I found for myself, no longer the classics and the "good" children's books she ordered for me. I was critical about what I saw around me, the poverty of the blacks, the attitudes of the whites, but in a confused, uninstructed way, and this left me vulnerable to her. But what was really making her ill with frustration was that she needed to project all her energies and talents into her daughter, who would live, for her, the life she had been prevented from living. But the girl had become a sullen, angry wall of rejection, usually silent, and then cracking into rudeness and derision.

"Why do you hate me so much?" she would cry; while I complained to my father, "Why does she hate me? She has always hated me."

Now I understand her state of mind very well. She was afflicted by that common disease of middle life, feeling that everything was slipping through her fingers; she could not grasp hold of or retain anything. Or as if she were juggling far too many balls in the air, and knew that if she dropped one they would all come clattering down.

I put an end to the awfulness of being at home with her by going off to Salisbury and becoming what is now known as an *au pair*. (This used to mean rich families in different countries exchanging daughters

At twenty-six in Salisbury, Southern Rhodesia

III

What I was doing was working all day, dancing or going to the pictures at night, and reading every minute I could. Together with all the other young people of the town (white, of course), I was in a state of accelerating excitement and elation because of the now rapidly approaching war. I see now that we were all rather mad.

When I did go home I found my mother nursing a very sick man. His divining rods hung on the walls, unused. Gold had been found on the farm, but not by him. Nothing very remarkable: a prospector was trying to make pay a reef that ran a few pennyweights to the ton, but it was galling someone else had found it. Galling to my mother. It did not occur to my father to be envious, he was pleased. But he was abstracted and vague and needed more and more to be tactfully brought back from the horrific landscapes of World War I—when he would almost certainly begin talking about the imminent World War II. He and my mother had known it was coming for years. I often wonder what combination of circumstances made them so certain, and on the whole so right, about the politics of Britain. Years before most people, for instance, they knew that Churchill was the only possible saviour for Britain. But while they talked so much sense about home politics, the international scene was a different thing. My father had become a British Israelite. He believed a large number of frightening and contradictory things. Of course my mother did not go along with this talk of Russia and Germany being anti-Christ and destined to ally themselves against Britain, which was scheduled by God to save the world. She did not like Gog and Magog and the Lost Tribe and the seven million dead around Jerusalem. She treated it as a symptom of his illnesses, and put her energies into trying to find ways to save her daughter, a flibbertigibbet who thought of nothing but men, and to get her son into the British Navy.

Very soon, the impossible girl who had said she would not marry for years, talking of a hundred (all unsuitable) careers, came home with a man she said she was going to marry at once. She was nineteen, far too young, he was ten years older than she—and therefore ought to have more sense, said Michael. But this son-in-law—so enquiries elicited—was not too bad, once granted it was possible to marry a Colonial instead of a nice doctor or solicitor in England. It seemed that he had a future in the Civil Service. (In fact he ended up at Master of the High Court, with various other high official posts.) But what was intolerable to my mother was that I never

so that they could learn the language and the customs.) I did this in two different families for eighteen months. It was boring, not too bad; the people were pleasant, everyone got on. But it was a waste of time, and my mother was desperate because her daughter was a nursemaid. This rage and misery of hers reached me wherever I was in very long letters full of improbable threats, such as that I was bound to end up in the brothels of Beira. I had no defence against a mother I could not recognize, except to become cold and indifferent. I went back home to the farm to write a novel. I was the apotheosis of a difficult adolescent. Now I am appalled at how I treated them both—though I could not have done differently. For them it must have been intolerable. For me it was intolerable. I finished and tore up two bad novels and went into Salisbury, and got a job in the Central Telephone Exchange. My mother experienced this as a final defeat: her daughter was a common telephone operator. The life she was leading (not that she told her parents anything, it was necessary to go into Salisbury and make enquiries) was "fast," cheap, and nasty.

mentioned any of the facts in his favour, and seemed to be quite surprised to hear them. As if these things were unimportant, irrelevant!

My mother's sense of occasion was being starved . . . again. How little would have been needed to satisfy it—as I see now. Her nature, her upbringing, demanded properly prepared for and conducted Birthdays, Anniversaries, Weddings, Jubilees. But it was her fate to have a family who temperamentally were indifferent. Her husband did not remember birthdays, and when she did, would give her that long, thoughtful, interested look which meant she was being found petty again. "Birthdays," he could be heard thinking, "Why should anybody care about them? Just another silly convention!" "Oh, our anniversary is it? Oh Lord, I'm sorry, well, if you really think we ought to. . . ." And now her daughter only said, "This is Frank Wisdom, we're getting married next month." It never crossed her mind to get engaged, or to want an engagement ring. Almost at once there was a slapdash and graceless wedding which made my mother miserable.

Then two things happened. Germany invaded Poland, and war was declared; simultaneously the young couple announced that there was going to be a grandchild, but on no account was there to be any fuss about it. There was a war on and, in any case, he was going to be sent up North to fight.

My mother longed to fuss and knit and sew and talk about pregnancies, but when she did, she was merely tolerated. All her natural feelings were being blocked, again. This was not the only way she was being frustrated. A declaration of war is certainly an Occasion, which demands, by convention, certain responses, and she was responding accordingly. All this time on the farm, even when most beset by worry, at her poorest, she had always behaved as upbringing said she should, raising money for good causes, trying to form committees. And now, with the war starting, she rallied her neighbours into various kinds of war work. She was resented for it: Who does she think she is?—was being asked, and by no means for the first time.

But she had succeeded in getting my brother, Harry, into the Navy in England. This had not been easy, and all kinds of strings had had to be pulled: only because it was wartime was it possible at all. Once my brother was actually in Dartmouth he found it hard to keep up: he had not had it in his mind to be in the Navy in the first place, had always wanted to be a farmer. He did not have all the subjects needed for the Navy, and had to study harder than the others.

But he was there. At last something good was happening, something appropriate, linking her with

her upbringing and her old hopes—and for the first time since she had come to this country. Where she still did not feel at home. But she no longer talked of going back Home. In wartime it was not possible: who could say how long the war would last? And her children would be here, for her son said he would come back the minute he could, Africa was where he belonged, and her daughter was married here. Satisfactorily married: even if *how* she did everything was wrong, and calculated only (my mother was convinced) to hurt her, *what* she was doing was no more than the colonial equivalent of what she herself would have liked, and should have done.

For a while it seemed as if this marriage could not really begin until after the war, but then it turned out Frank was not going up North with the others, he was medically unfit. A house was being bought. She was not consulted about the house, though she knew exactly what they needed and should have: plenty of room for children and for entertaining. And they bought such a house. It was in one of the old avenues full of trees, a bungalow in an already outmoded style with rooms spreading about and verandahs and an enclosed back verandah.

The first child was born, and of course the young couple had no idea of how to handle the baby. It was her duty to put things right . . .

My mother did not learn to drive until she left the farm. I found that strange. True that it was rarer then for older women to drive, but plenty did. It was just something she did not, would not, do. As brave as she was I did not believe she was afraid. A woman who thought nothing of holding a revolver straight to a cobra's head to blow it off? It was a mystery . . . but, not knowing how to drive meant that her husband and her children had to drive her about, and it was one way of getting help and support from them: they gave her so little.

The more she brooded about the bad state of affairs in her daughter's house in town, the more often she decided she must go in and take a look. Now that her husband was too ill to drive all that way, she had to find lifts. The day before a trip she spent roasting chickens, making cakes, jam, peanut butter, lemon curd, ginger beer. The neighbour's car would be loaded to the roof with all this stuff. She usually did not ring her daughter before coming, because she was afraid of something new in her: a cool, smiling, impervious politeness. As recently as three years ago the girl had been rude, sullen, tactless—impossible; now she was polite—and impossible. If informed that her mother would be arriving next day, she would certainly be polite, but say she was going to be away or busy or something.

My mother would arrive with food of every kind. She found the larder and refrigerator full. The house was just like every other, at that time. The cookboy was in the kitchen, peeling vegetables. The houseboy, having finished his work by ten in the morning, was probably gossiping with friends at the back in the sanitary lane. The "piccanin" was playing with a toy in the garden or on guard over the pram with the baby in it. And where was her daughter? She might be cooking: she enjoyed that, and husbands came home for lunch. Or she might be visiting with the wives of her husband's colleagues. This seemed to my mother a suitable occupation, proof that I was growing up. At last. Ever since she had been in the Colony she had longed for visits with women—morning tea parties, afternoon tea parties, real companionship with nice women. But her daughter might easily explode with, "If I have to sit through another bloody tea party with bloody gossiping women complaining about their servants, I'll slit my throat." And then seem to remind herself, and pull tight the reins of politeness, putting a smile on her face and offering tea and cake.

My mother would go into the kitchen to check shelves, saucepans, and whether the tea and sugar had been stolen. She spoke sharply to the cook, who went off in a huff. She summoned the houseboy to do a room over again. She complained that it was dangerous to let the "piccanin" touch the baby, because of the germs. She reorganized various bits of furniture to her satisfaction and then, worn out with it all, sat down, lit a cigarette, and waited for a real conversation to begin. But, as she could see, her daughter was being unreasonable again—angry, where she ought to be grateful. Not that she showed she was angry: she sat smiling, smiling if it killed her, and said nothing. Once after a really good going-over of the entire house, she heard her daughter say to the cook: "I am sorry about my mother. She is an old woman. Take no notice." She was furious. In the first place she was *not* old. And she *knew* that the servants took advantage, did as they liked, and the young people had all kinds of silly ideas, paid the lazy black people far too much. She wanted to talk it all over, to have real serious discussions about it all, so that they would listen, and see how wrong they were. She had had experience of servants in England, in Persia, and now here!

She would come rushing into town planning these conversations in her mind: there were a thousand things that needed discussing, quite apart from the upbringing of the baby, and the servants. Every-

thing about that household disturbed her, and it was her daughter's fault: and yet no one could say the girl was lazy. The pantry was full of jams and preserves made by her. There were always guests and a great deal of trouble was taken over food. She made her own clothes (including far too many dance dresses: surely there was no need for them to go out dancing quite so much?)—all her baby's clothes, and her husband's shirts and pyjamas. Why did she not ask her mother to help her? Why did she always say no— politely, of course—to any offers of help? Why did she not understand that her mother's life had always been sacrificed to her and to her brother; a mother's duty is to sacrifice herself to her children . . .

Women of that generation talked easily about sacrificing themselves, to children who were patient, ironical, or rude. A revolution had not taken place: the one that would have informed her that her daughter's terrible homesickness at school was a bad thing; that some of her own symptoms might not have physical causes; that one did not talk about "sacrificing oneself" . . .

But it *was* her duty to sacrifice herself, no matter how much, and how unfairly, she was misunderstood; and she got lifts in from the farm quite often. But it was getting difficult because of petrol rationing. She saw it was time to move into town, particularly as there was going to be another baby, much too soon of course! But what an anticlimax, what a defeat! "Getting off the farm"—that dream full of gold dust and magic—was it really going to become an affair of tamely selling the farm (not too badly, because of the war) and buying a house in town? A house, a mere box of a place, was bought. There wasn't enough money to buy something really nice, once the Land Bank was paid off. And the house was not in the centre, but in a suburb several years off being fashionable. My father was moved in, hating every minute. He did not want to leave the farm, the veld, the space—what he had come to Africa to find. He kept saying there was nothing left for him now, but to die. My mother protested that it was not as bad as that!—but knew it was, very bad. She felt that their lives were ending before they had really begun, for the time on the farm did not really count. She had always been waiting for life to begin when she could move off it.

My brother, Harry, was on the *Repulse* in the Pacific with the *Prince of Wales*, when both ships, supposed to be unsinkable, were sunk in minutes by Japanese bombers. My brother was not drowned, though he nearly was. He was picked up out of the water where he had been floating for some hours, and sent off to Ceylon on recuperative leave. He was soon back in the fighting, in the Mediterranean.

This was very bad for my mother, who blamed herself: why was it she was punished for everything she did? It had seemed such a triumph to get her son into the Navy.

And my father seemed unable to think about anything but the war; sometimes it sounded as if it were he on that ship in the Mediterranean. A good thing he was in town near doctors and hospitals, even though he did hate this house so much. There was nothing wrong with it, my mother bravely insisted, the rooms were quite a decent size, with high ceilings; there were verandahs, there was coolness. But it was no good, he was a bitter, angry, sorrowful, not in years an old man, for he was just into his sixties, but he looked so old, so worn out, and frail. Everything was wrong with him now, and my mother could not leave him for more than half a day.

She knew that this was how it was going to be until he died. Her new life was organised with her usual energy, and courage. Money was short, and soon she was growing vegetables again, and sold them, and had chickens and ducks and sold their eggs. In spite of her husband's illness she was much more cheerful. The long isolation of the farm, which had so starved her gregarious nature, was over. She had friends in Salisbury: she always made friends easily. And there were hundreds of thousands of men in the Air Force camps around Salisbury, and they were homesick and bored. The sons of friends in England soon became visitors, and their friends too. The house was soon full of people and she looked after them, cooked enormous meals and wrote letters to their mothers. She also took on war work.

But her main occupation was, and had to be, her husband, who soon was not getting dressed at all, but lived in his dressing gown, and then took to his bed and did not ever again leave it.

He lay in a room chosen because its windows overlooked what was to him nothing but a painful reminder of what the veld, the bush, ought to be. Town veld, he called it, with far too many people threatening the long grasses, where they made innumerable paths, and the trees, which they were always cutting down. He lay propped up, gaunt and white-faced, and cups of milk slipped through his shaking hands, and if he reached for a pill from among the batteries of bottles on the medicine table near his bed, more likely than not bottles and pills scattered everywhere. He could not be left alone at all, and my mother had to give up war work and visiting, and stay with him.

It had seemed that things could hardly be worse. Then, suddenly, her daughter announced she was going to leave her husband and children. This was of course *not possible*. Such things were not done. But it was happening. She did not get on with Frank, said this terrible, painful, destructive girl—yet she had shown every sign of getting on with him for four years. She could not stand the life, she said; she hated everything about it.

"What does that have to do with it?" demanded the poor woman. "We are not put into this world to please ourselves!"

Not only was the child leaving her husband (but one really ought to stop calling her a child, at twenty-three), she was running around the town with the Communists.

My mother had not known there were any Communists here, in Africa. Unable, as usual, to find out anything from the girl herself, she went visiting all around the town to get information, and found that these Communists were all foreigners, Jews, refugees, and members of the Air Force, a lot of them lower-class people. If they were Rhodesians, they were obviously misfits. Also, there was a certain corporal who had "stolen your daughter away from her husband. A terrible thing, the way all these marriages are breaking up, but what can you expect, with all our own men up North fighting in the desert, and all these Air Force men stationed here?"

Confronted with the corporal, the girl simply laughed and said *of course* she was not leaving her husband for a man, but for the sake of a new society. She then proceeded to deliver what she called "an analysis" of the situation in language that was quite incomprehensible. She had often enough attacked the white way of life angrily, rudely—and of course unfairly. But what she had said had at least been understandable. Now she had acquired a new vocabulary with her new ideas.

What was happening was appalling. The way it was happening was—again—impossible. For again no one was behaving as they should. When she went to her son-in-law to apologise for her daughter's behaviour, she discovered the couple were "seeing each other"—whatever that could mean; and that she was "seeing" her children. My mother understood by this that the marriage might be healed, and behaved accordingly. But when she visited her daughter, she was in a dingy bed-sitting-room, had got a job as a typist, and was earning so little she could not possibly even eat properly on it. She looked ill, and soon she was ill, in bed, reading Communist books and being visited by her new Communist friends who—astonishingly—seemed quite normal people.

The author at thirty

Appealed to for judgement—for satisfactory arrangements of words—my father said irritably that he was not at all surprised. She had been much too young to get married in the first place.

My mother badly needed some kind of ritual throwing-out of the wicked one, condemnation, then contrite tears, then complaints of ill-treatment or of suffering. But nothing like this ever happened, and she could get no sense even out of the mistreated husband.

We talk perennially about the generation gap. But has there ever been a greater gap than between my parents' generation and mine? They believed that the British Empire was the greatest force for good in the world, and that God thought so too. That white people were superior to all nonwhite races, and that British white people were superior to other white people. That the white minority in the Colonies was there with God's approval to civilise and uplift the natives. They believed in Duty. In Patriotism. In doing a job well for the sake of doing it. In staying married. In family life.

What we believed about the British Empire—or any other Empire—and about racism, sexism, in-

equality, and so on, has become the new orthodoxy, and there is no need to outline it. But at that particular time in the war, perhaps because of its awfulness, we believed (our particular kind of young person, and there were—briefly—a lot of us) that very soon, after the war, the whole world would voluntarily choose communism, because of its obvious and evident merits; that war would cease to exist; that the State in every country would "wither away" of its own accord; that (probably within about ten years) there would be a worldwide Golden Age without poverty, injustice, unhappiness of any kind whatsoever.

If my parents had known what was in my head, they would have believed me mad; and I now agree with them. But in addition to the above heady set of Articles of Faith, I personally held some pretty amazing beliefs, generated in me by that long, long nightmare, watching the slow grinding down of my parents. I knew that when I stepped out of the marriage I would be breaking some dark line of Fatality, invisible but invincible, which had forced my father, once healthy, strong, handsome, to become a querulous, war-broken man waiting to die at sixty; had changed my mother from a strong, clever, competent woman into an ailing, neurotic, unhappy one. My leaving the marriage would save my children from following this road, as if I were carrying some kind of gene, not physical, but psychological; or as if I were carrier of an illness that needed decades to reveal itself. These thoughts were shared with no one at all, though I knew when I sat by my father, holding his hand, that he would understand me at once, if I actually put into words what I felt.

Very soon the worst became worse for my mother when the delinquent married again, in the same casual, cheerful way as she did the first time, one of the refugees she was running around with. But he was a German! A German in the middle of a war against Germany! An Enemy Alien. Enquiries elicited that this new son-in-law was "well-connected," even if he was partly Jewish. She could have done worse, if she insisted on marrying a foreigner. When accused of deliberately trying to make them miserable by marrying an enemy, all she said was that since he was a refugee, surely it was obvious he was anti-Hitler? The man himself was dismaying, the epitome of foreignness, even Prussian, being cold, correct, and formal. It was impossible, ever, to know what he was thinking. He was like Conrad Veidt. Why, why, why, this man? You couldn't imagine a greater contrast between the two: this slow, cold, formal man, and a lively quick energetic humorous young woman—so my mother had heard her daughter described, though she had certainly never experienced her like this. This unlikely couple soon announced a new pregnancy, and it was no use asking, "What was the point of leaving Frank and the children if you were going to get pregnant again almost at once?" "You don't understand, Mother!"

No, she did not; and her husband did not. He seemed to see this new awfulness as only another manifestation of the general destructiveness, part of the war, part of what had to be expected in wartime. And no, he would *not* "talk" to the girl; when had that done any good?

The new baby was born, healthy and fine, like the others, and he at once became a favourite of his grandfather, who lay feebly in bed with the child near him, dying interminably, knowing he was, and hating it.

My poor mother yearned for support in that long dying. Her son, perhaps, would give it? He had returned from the war rather deaf from the gunfire in many sea battles. He was slow and smiling and polite and rather absentminded, and he would not talk about the fighting. In fact, he was in a state of shock, as combatants are after a war. He did help her, but not in the way she so badly needed, someone taking responsibility off her, someone understanding what she was going through. He was thinking of getting married, was not much at home.

The new son-in-law Gottfried was always ready to advise about money. He was very good at it: one of the things she had given up trying to understand was how a Communist could be so worldly-wise. But she had no daughter! Of course, this new couple, Gottfried and Doris, would at once come when asked to sit with the dying man, so that she might go off and have a bit of a rest, or go shopping. But there was never any ease in it, never anything she could take for granted . . . she did not know what she would do without them, but it was as if they were kindly neighbours, ready to do a good turn, and this terrible ordeal of a dying man who needed nursing twenty-four hours a day was her problem and not theirs too.

Again, she was up against more than she could imagine.

The group of people I spent my time with shared many assumptions that were never examined, and only some of them were political. What seems remarkable now is how much we did share, coming from so many different countries, different social classes. We all agreed about the family, not yet called "nuclear." To get free of our parents had been our most urgent task, and most of us had been out earning a living very early. It would have been

inconceivable for any of us to live at home with parents. Parents had to be resisted in every way and at all times, not only because they were reactionary (this went without saying) but because they wanted to live our lives for us. The tyrannical father of the last century had been defeated, but had been replaced by the mothers, who were tyrants of the emotions. All the young women I was with had problems with their mothers. We had to fight them: they were leeches who sucked the life out of us. We had all cut free but one, and she was a poor victim, always ill, whose energies were spent not on her husband, but on her formidable mother who never left her alone. But we all knew—by all here I mean our men, as well as the women—what the problem was and how it should be cured. These punishing and pathetic mothers had in their time all been special in some way, had supported the Suffragettes, fought for a career. But had been defeated. Well, it was simple! "Come the Revolution"—(a *mot* which for some reason was being used with increasing irony), there would be proper creches and nurseries and legislation, and this phenomenon of middle-aged women being left high and dry with nothing to do but live through their children would no longer exist.

Meanwhile we—the young women—were frightened. What was to stop us becoming like our mothers? Clearly, strength of will was not enough.

What bothers me now is that my thoughts are not much more evolved than they were then. On the one hand there was this poor woman who—through no fault of her own, and because of one misfortune after another, beginning with the death of her mother when she was three—deserved love, support, cherishing. But on the other hand she had to be fought every minute, otherwise she would have swallowed me up. The thoughts revolve: around and around they go.

But I do see certain ironical aspects I did not then. One is that the Africans on whose behalf we were supposedly fighting would not have understood one word of all this. Old people were respected, and families and clans helped each other; and the idea that an elderly woman with a dying husband could be accused of emotional blackmail because she demanded help would have seemed ridiculous. But that was *then*, before white civilisation had done its work.

The war ended. The men who had gone up North—those who had not been killed—came home. They were in a state of shock. The hundreds of thousands of Air Force men departed to Britain. Southern Rhodesia became itself again, except that many Italian ex-prisoners of war elected to stay. Greeks arrived, escaping from the civil war in Greece.

A great many Afrikaners came in to settle. Was this really still a British Colony? For people like my mother it was, of course; it had to be.

Her son married.

Her husband died. On the Death Certificate it should have said: Of the First World War.

She was a widow. Both children exhorted her to marry again. This was cruel of them and, no, she did not suppose they meant well: they were afraid of her being a burden. How could one marry again when one had been so completely married once? Whether to the man one ought to have married (who of course was the young doctor who drowned in the First World War) or to someone else—it didn't matter: she had been married for thirty or so years to the father of her children. Yes, she did remember how, earlier, on the farm, sitting outside the house of an evening looking at the sunset, or watching the stars (the time and the place for these discussions) she had said, talking of her own stepmother who was living alone in a suburb of London, but wanting (as Maude and Michael knew quite well) to come and live on the farm in Africa, "I am not going to be a burden on my children, I hope I die before then."

But she was in her mid-sixties, strong, full of energy.

Both children urged her to accept the invitations she had to work for organisations such as the Red Cross. Yes, she knew she was good at it, of course she was, but she didn't want to work in some impersonal thing, she wanted to be with her family: it was the duty of women to sacrifice themselves for . . .

But her daughter really did not seem to need her at all. She still spent her time in this group of people, all Communists and Kaffir-lovers, who never seemed to be out of each other's company. Any time of the day or night, anywhere they lived (for Doris and Gottfried always seemed to be moving), their place was full of people—people talking, talking; they never stopped! Gottfried worked a lot. He had two jobs, one in a lawyer's office, and one at the Tobacco Auctions. He was paid badly in both: exploited, it seemed, because he was a German and a refugee: but that was the kind of thing they *would* say. Her daughter worked part-time, and was earning quite well, and the new baby went to a creche and throve on communal living. Offers of help were seldom accepted.

Her son did not seem to need her either: the young wife was as efficient and hardworking as she was herself.

Then, she was told this second marriage was going to end in divorce. Thank God poor Michael was dead and could not have his heart broken over

In London, about 1959

the new tragedy. Which, however, was not being treated as a tragedy. Not only were the divorcing pair the best of friends, but actually went on living in the same house while the divorce went through. And what could one make of a scene where, on a picnic, Frank the first husband, with the two children, and the new stepmother, and the second husband and the new baby and the girl herself all behaved as if nothing much were happening. Nothing was said, nothing explained, no one ever told her anything: or if they did, she couldn't believe her ears.

Her daughter went off to England with the baby, refusing offers of help, either in money (not that there was much) or from relatives there. Gottfried, it seemed, would soon follow,

Very well, she would go to England too. To go Home like this, as an old woman with very little money, and no place or use there, trailing after a daughter who had never been anything else but a source of pain, when for all those years on the farm she had dreamed of how she would go back and take up where she had left . . . well, life was a funny business, as Michael always used to say.

She sold up everything in Salisbury, bought herself a typewriter, and taught herself to type. She would become her daughter's secretary.

There were reasons why she would be pleased to leave. The first novel, *The Grass Is Singing*, had come out. She was embarrassed by it. Of course they would admire that kind of thing in England, but it was wrongheaded and unfair to the whites. People were being tactful, but she could imagine what was being said behind her back. Leaving Southern Rhodesia she would be leaving, too, memories of her Michael's interminable illnesses, the failure of the farm, and the never-ending unpleasantness provided by her daughter. And now there were short stories appearing, every bit as bad as the novel. Never mind, she would live with her daughter, or near her, and sacrifice her life . . .

Two years later she returned to Southern Rhodesia. She had been frozen out. By the climate; for she had forgotten how awful it could be. And by her daughter who just would not accept help, she would not—and yet she needed it, anyone could see that.

She settled near her son. Soon, she died of a heart attack. It was as so often happens when old people die: everyone knows they need not have died at all, if only there had been something real for them to do; if they had felt wanted, needed, by someone.

Parts I and II of this essay are reprinted in entirety from two articles first appearing in *Granta*: "Doris Lessing: Impertinent Daughters," © 1984, 1985, and "Doris Lessing: My Mother's Life (Part Two)," © 1985, 1986, both written by Doris Lessing. Reprinted by permission of Jonathan Clowes Ltd., London, on behalf of Doris Lessing.

BIBLIOGRAPHY

Fiction:

The Grass Is Singing, Crowell, 1950, M. Joseph, 1950.

Retreat to Innocence, M. Joseph, 1956, Prometheus, 1959.

The Golden Notebook, M. Joseph, 1962, Simon & Schuster, 1962, with a new introduction by the author, Bantam, 1973.

Briefing for a Descent into Hell, Cape, 1971, Knopf, 1971.

The Summer before the Dark, Cape, 1973, Knopf, 1973.

The Memoirs of a Survivor, Octagon, 1974, Knopf, 1974.

(Under pseudonym Jane Somers) *The Diary of a Good Neighbour*, M. Joseph, 1983, Knopf, 1983.

The Diaries of Jane Somers, M. Joseph, 1984, Vintage, 1984.

(Under pseudonym Jane Somers) *If the Old Could—*, M. Joseph, 1984, Knopf, 1984.

The Good Terrorist, Cape, 1985, Knopf, 1985.

The Fifth Child, Knopf, 1988.

"Children of Violence" series:

Martha Quest (Part I, also see below), M. Joseph, 1952, with *A Proper Marriage*, Simon & Schuster, 1964.

A Proper Marriage (Part II), M. Joseph, 1954.

A Ripple from the Storm (Part III, also see below), M. Joseph, 1958, with *Landlocked*, Simon & Schuster, 1966.

Landlocked (Part IV), MacGibbon & Kee, 1965.

The Four-Gated City (Part V), MacGibbon & Kee, 1969, Knopf, 1969.

"Canopus in Argos: Archives" series:

Shikasta Re: Colonized Planet 5, Cape, 1979, Knopf, 1979.

The Marriages between Zones Three, Four, and Five, Cape, 1980, Knopf, 1980.

The Sirian Experiments, Cape, 1981, Knopf, 1981.

The Making of the Representative for Planet 8, Cape, 1982, Knopf, 1982.

Documents Relating to the Sentimental Agents in the Volyen Empire, Cape, 1983, Knopf, 1983.

Short stories:

This Was the Old Chief's Country (also see below), M. Joseph, 1951, Crowell, 1952.

Five: Short Novels (also see below), M. Joseph, 1953.

No Witchcraft for Sale: Stories and Short Novels, Foreign Language Publishing (Moscow), 1956.

The Habit of Loving, MacGibbon & Kee, 1957, Crowell, 1957.

A Man and Two Women, MacGibbon & Kee, 1963, Simon & Schuster, 1963.

African Stories (contains *The Black Madonna*, also see below), M. Joseph, 1964, Simon & Schuster, 1965.

Winter in July, Panther, 1966.

Nine African Stories, edited by Michael Marland, Longman, 1968.

The Story of a Non-Marrying Man and Other Stories, Cape, 1972, published in America as *The Temptation of Jack Orkney and Other Stories* (also see below), Knopf, 1972.

Collected African Stories (originally published in *This Was the Old Chief's Country* [and] *Five: Short Novels*, contains *This Was the Old Chief's Country* and *The Sun between Their Feet*), Joseph, 1973, Simon & Schuster, 1981.

The Black Madonna, Panther, 1974.

(Stories), edited by Alan Cattell, Harrap, 1976.

Collected Stories: To Room Nineteen and *The Temptation of Jack Orkney*, Cape, 1978, published in America as *Stories*, Knopf, 1978.

Nonfiction:

Going Home, M. Joseph, 1957, revised edition, Panther, 1968, Ballantine, 1968.

In Pursuit of the English: A Documentary, MacGibbon & Kee, 1960, Simon & Schuster, 1961.

Particularly Cats, M. Joseph, 1967, Simon & Schuster, 1967.

A Small Personal Voice: Essays, Reviews, Interviews, edited by Paul Schlueter, Knopf, 1974.

(With Edgell Rickword and others) *A Garland for Jack Lindsay*, Piccolo, 1980.

Prisons We Choose to Live Inside, Cape, 1987.

The Wind Blows Away Our Words and Other Documents Relating to the Afghan Resistance, Pan, 1987.

Produced plays:

"Before the Deluge," London, England, 1953.

"Mr. Dollinger," Oxford Playhouse, England, 1958.

"The Truth about Billy Newton," Salisbury, England, 1961.

"The Storm" (adaptation of a play by Alexander Ostrovsky), London, 1966.

Published plays:

The Singing Door (for children), in *Second Playbill 2*, edited by Alan Durband, Hutchinson, 1973.

Produced and published plays:

Each His Own Wilderness, Royal Court (London), 1958, published in *New England Dramatists: Three Plays*, edited by E. Martin Browne, Penguin, 1959.

Play with a Tiger, Comedy Theatre (London), 1962, Renata Theatre (New York), 1964, M. Joseph, 1962.

Other:

Fourteen Poems, Scorpion, 1959.

Doris Lessing Reads Her Short Stories (sound recording), J. Norton, 1974.

Also writer of television plays: "The Grass Is Singing" (from her novel), 1962, "Care and Protection," 1966, "Please Do Not Disturb," 1966, "Between Men," 1967, and "Habit of Loving."

David McKain

1937-

WANDERINGS

David McKain with his mother, Ida McKain, at Chautauqua, New York, 1942

I began keeping a journal when I was in first grade. I don't know why I started, but on my fifth birthday my father gave me a bank envelope with a picture of George Washington smiling through an oval window of red berries and holly. The next day, my dollar buttoned safely inside my shirt pocket, I ran downtown to Woolworth's and bought a wooden pen, a bottle of blue-black Parker's ink, and a journal marked "Ledger." The book had a black-and-white marbled cover and swirling purple endpapers. Each page was tinted celery green with a thin red line down the margin and a wide blue line down the center. I didn't know why I bought the ledger,

but keeping a record meant a great deal to me, and I wrote about the experience in *Spellbound: Growing Up in God's Country.*

"Why did you buy a ledger?" my mother asked, perhaps sensing my confusion. "Do you want to become a businessman?" She looked at me and asked me to look at her. I could feel tears in my eyes, but I did not answer. I knew only that I wanted to write down things I had seen during the day so I would always have them, the way I saved oak leaves and horse chestnuts, special stones and rusty railroad spikes. I wanted to keep track of the changes in my life, whatever came into it and whatever went out, but

I did not know that was what I wanted to do. I did not want to show her anything I had drawn or written down, so I hid the ledger in my desk. Keeping a ledger was a little like talking to God. It was secret.

*　　*　　*　　*

My mother's opinion of writers was low. Both my mother and father were ministers. Writers were dangerous. They teased the mind away from our duty of serving the Lord, and however astonishing the revelations of their prose, these discoveries were insignificant compared to the teachings of the Bible. My mother preferred the Apocalypse, that moment of glory when God revealed the mystery of the world and when we all stood singing in a strange luminance that made our mission clear.

The story of everyone who had ever lived or would live was carefully recorded in a book the size of a picnic table—a book sealed with seven seals—so large that it took two angels to turn a single page. God was the Author of all Creation. He wrote down the story of our lives because the treasures of earth would turn to dust and only the Word was to be everlasting. I felt relieved that my story had been written down before I was born, relieved there was no need for me to assume a borrowed role. I had been assigned a role by the Supreme Author. I was free.

God made the Word flesh, and the Word was His seed. Just at the utterance of a single word, the earth brought forth whatever living creature He desired: cattle, fish, and fowl after their kind, or the men and women in Bradford, Pennsylvania, my neighbors. Before the world was created, the word already existed—if not yet spoken or recorded, then alive as seed in the mind of God.

As the world's greatest author, God had several secretaries. He had dictated the Book of Life to John of Patmos the same way that he had dictated the Ten Commandments to Moses on Mount Sinai. Neither fabricated nor imagined, God's stories carried with them the power of the ineffable—the power of life and of death. "And the Lord said, Whoever hath sinned against me, him will I blot out of my Book."

"A man's life of any worth is a continual allegory," Keats wrote in a letter, "and very few eyes can see the mystery of his life . . . a life like the scriptures, figurative." I lived inside a story, watching and listening as the narrative unfolded. The story was a mystery, and I was trying to understand the plot. I paid attention to the smallest detail, to everything around me—searching for clues.

Bradford, Pennsylvania, the town where I grew up, is in northcentral Pennsylvania—a sparsely populated region of the Allegheny Mountains which the promoters, in an effort to lure the flatlanders, call God's Country. "When I recall the past," I wrote in *Spellbound*, "I think about the town of Bradford as much as I think about my parents. The streets were paved with red brick and lined with maple and elm, and I roamed within their protective indifference from one end of town to the other. The demands on my parents' lives to pay the rent gave me freedom. Out of necessity, they turned me over to the streets and hills—the most wonderfully lax set of parents a boy could know." The town was like another person, and each day I went out to meet it, to be in its company. I had become, without realizing it, a chorophiliac—a lover of place.

Place has been the starting point for my poetry and stories ever since I started writing, poems such as "South Mechanic":

> At dawn the snow's mauve light began
> to blue. It blurred above the trees
> and fell so hard I thought of freedom—
> at five thirty, no one owned the street.
>
> I was first on South Mechanic, first
> to smell the snow and taste its iron;
> at Elm I saw Richie Merrie's father
> waiting for a ride to Kendall.
>
> Up close, he smelled like Red Man
> and gun oil, like wool when it's wet;
> he wore a red and black jacket,
> a deer license pinned on back.
>
> I wanted to tell him about a place
> on Quintuple, a flame that burned all night;
> beside it, even winter, grass and flowers
> grew inside a brain of yellow ice.
>
> But he stood there ordered in his space,
> never looking up or down the street;
> he just pulled himself up on the truck
> listening to his hands and feet.
>
> For two years I thought of his hands
> as he shifted the black bucket, wedged it
> between his knees to pay me for a paper
> and then tore off a chew of tobacco.
>
> I wanted to be like him, to drill for oil
> and smell like Red Man—before anyone
> else woke up, to stand out there
> and claim the blue light of the morning snow.

*　　*　　*　　*

I was baptized by my father in the kitchen sink when I was one year old, about the time he lost his church. "Imagine that," my mother said contemptuously. "The kitchen sink! The faucet leaked so bad we couldn't get rid of the silverfish, the cockroaches, and those things with all the legs? Centipedes? And there you were, getting baptized!" My father had worn a green velvet smoking jacket for the occasion and parted his thick black hair down the middle. In a black-and-white snapshot taken on the same day, he was standing under a clothesline in the backyard, his hair slicked flat with Jeris, his face a ghostly white. "Yes, it was green!" my mother said, as though the color had been chosen to deliberately offend her. "A green smoking jacket! A god-awful velvet green smoking jacket!"

That was in Punxsutawney. In Elmo we lived on a narrow county road between Elk City and Fern. The front porch of the house leaned toward the road, a sign of decay my father took advantage of by displaying the parakeets so they could be seen at an angle from the road. The landlords, the MacIntyres, lived next-door. With no electricity, the rent was cheap. In addition to the lovebirds and a few small fish, Dad kept a dog named King, a Chow Chow watchdog chained to the outhouse. We slept on mattresses on the living-room floor because, in the

back of the house, the morning sun would wake us. Dad brought the birds in off the porch at night, and they flicked out seed that ticked onto the linoleum floor—a clock gone haywire.

We were strangers on earth, and our sense of dislocation intensified as we moved farther in time and space from the homeplace that nourished us. Wanderers, we suffered from a topo-psychotic affliction, a condition of the soul known as Placelessness. Today, it's clear, we need doctors capable of understanding the psychological dynamics of a missing landscape or a missing neighborhood, the loss of contour, of familiar weather and climate. We need healers sympathetic to the connection between the self and the spirits of Place. We take the hills and the streets for granted until we are torn from them— dismembered, disjoined, cut up in bits and pieces. The Japanese word *uchi* means "home" and "self," uniting both concepts into a single awareness that reveals the need for the whole.

As a boy I enjoyed stories about adopted children and orphans, about kids raised by foster parents, Indians, and wolves. Like other children, I was

"My father, Charles McKain, in his velvet green smoking jacket, in 1937, the year I was born"

convinced I had been confused with another baby in the hospital, and that my real parents grieved for me in a hollow not far from downtown Amm Street where we lived. By junior high school, I was convinced that my real parents were as rich as we were poor.

By the time I was in first grade, we had lived in five houses in four towns, and I began to take dislocation for granted. Before marrying, my mother had stomped over the hills for the Women's Christian Temperance Union, and my father, born in West Newton, preached in several small churches throughout the two-state Erie Conference. But, they said, it didn't matter where they lived as long as they served the Lord. It didn't matter how confused our history; they wove the fragments of our lives into a narrative whole. Every experience was turned into a story.

There was a war going on when I was growing up, and Displaced Persons migrated to Bradford from Europe in large numbers; my mother called them DPs. Wandering in town became a habit of the place: the practice of berry-pickers, ginseng-diggers, hunters, nut-gatherers, and the dispossessed. In second grade, my teacher, Miss Pike, wrote on the back of my report card, "David wanders about the room and leaves at will."

*   *   *   *

Stories were all we had. We were poor, and words permitted us to live beyond our means. They provided us with both escape and compensation, with familiarity and repetition. We measured our lives not by the seasons or by the clock, but by family tales and the calendar of Christ knocking at a thick door covered with vines: "Ask, and it shall be given you; seek, and ye shall find; knock, and it shall be opened unto you." I marked the year with hymns and carols and verses from the Bible, excited that Caesar Augustus sent out a *decree;* that shepherds, *sore* afraid, were *abiding* in the field; that Herod was *wroth*—inaccessible words that hinted at new beginnings.

"Episodes from my father's life," I wrote in "The Fishbowl," "invented and real, came to me over the years in bits and scraps. He told me he had been a prizefighter, a basketball coach, a race-car driver, and a semiprofessional basketball player on a franchise team for the Boston Celtics. He had taken care of a cow and chickens in Elmo once, too, but he never talked about that. The only sign I ever saw around the house that he had played basketball was a moth-eaten boat-neck in the bottom drawer of his dresser: a bulky grape-colored sweater with a huge

gold *W* in front—a varsity letter from the College of Wooster in Ohio. I found it hard to figure out what had actually happened and what had not. Both my parents had stories which held their lives together and to which they returned for understanding, sad and eloquent tales but stories that made sense nonetheless . . ."

My father signed his name *Reverend* Charles Van Kirk McKain long after he had lost his church. The "Charles" in his name came from the German word for "manly and strong"; "Van Kirk" was Dutch for "son of the church"; and "McKain" identified both of us as direct descendents of the world's first murderer—a man "cursed from the earth . . . a fugitive and a vagabond." And Cain said unto the Lord, "My punishment is greater than I can bear . . ." and my father's punishment—much of it self-inflicted—was greater than he could bear. He called himself "Reverend" to ease the pain. The title redeemed him, renewed him with an air of the holy, clothed him in the sacred, turned his apocryphal collar outward toward the town. "Hi," he greeted strangers cheerfully, shaking hands with a strong grip and looking them in the eye, "I'm Reverend McKain."

I was in first grade when I watched my father sign his name to the note he taped to the door: "At Lunch—Back At 12:45—Rev. Charles V. McKain." I met him at the shop every day for lunch and, before going inside, I caught my breath and stood with my hand extended, ready to open the door at the exact instant he looked up from his crossword puzzles and saw me.

"My father was big," I wrote in *Spellbound,* "half a foot taller than most men, and he weighed nearly two hundred pounds. With his hat on he looked a whole foot taller and marched, he liked to say, as straight and tall as a Prussian soldier. He wore a gold cardigan sweater and a plum-colored tie as rich as any banker's—his socks maroon, his trousers gray, his cloth shoes brown with crepe soles. He looked jaunty among the somber tones of the businessmen and the matching khaki and gray of the men in Dickie's workclothes. But his shirt pocket, the two pockets in his sweater, and the four pockets in his trousers bulged as though he suffered from random growths. His pockets were stuffed with keys, cigarettes, pens, gum, Hershey's Kisses, handkerchiefs, a fat wallet, and two fistfuls of coins he called his silver. There was no cash in the pet shop, not even a cigar box, but he enjoyed it that way, I think. When he had to make change, he smiled and plunged his hand deep into one of his trouser pockets, scooping out a fistful. He spread the pile out across his open hand as though his

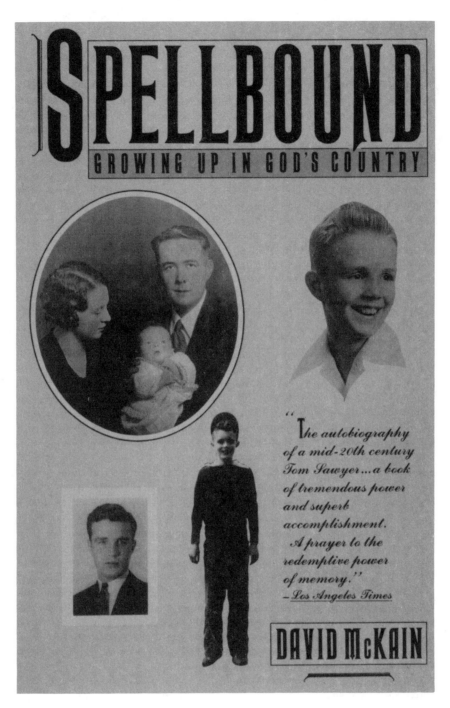

The cover of the 1990 Touchstone edition of Spellbound:
Growing Up in God's Country

palm were a countertop, sliding coins here and there with the tip of his index finger, the nickels, dimes, quarters, and halves all new and shining. He exchanged the old coins at the bank early in the morning each day because, he said, new coins pleased his customers . . ."

Meeting him for lunch was an ordeal. On the way from the pet shop to the drugstore, several children spotted him and ran toward us with their hands out.

"What will it be?" he asked triumphantly, "gum or candy?"

"Smiling, he dug into his sweater pocket and thumbed a stick of Black Jack forward from the pack. I hung back and looked in the window of the Bradford Building Savings and Loan; no one else's father carried gum and candy to give out to children on Main Street. I watched in the reflection of the window as the children laughed.

"My father's smile made me feel uncomfortable. Though endearing, it was bent and slightly hangdog, as though he carried the burden of the world on his broad shoulders. It reminded me of the pained and quizzical expression of Christ on the Sunday school calendar, suffering forth all manner of little children. I did not know what he felt, but I suspect now he reexperienced something of the satisfaction which must have been part of his notion of Christian ministry, of having little and giving much. Whenever I saw him giving away gum and candy, though, I remembered my mother's complaint that he could not even afford to pay the rent without my grandfather's help."

My mother supported us on a take-home pay of twenty-five dollars a week, an income occasionally supplemented by my grandfather. Dressed in a three-piece suit, Grandpa McKain not only paid the rent for the pet shop, but whenever we were strapped, bailed us out—to use my father's idiom. Dad praised his father as "a prince of a man . . . a living saint . . ." and I liked him too. Grandpa sucked a raw egg for breakfast and told stories of climbing up and down redwood trees without using a rope. Every five or six years he and my grandmother drove to Bradford to see us for an afternoon, and at the end of the visit, he would squeeze a ten-dollar bill into my fist as he said goodbye—a gift so extravagant I was convinced he was a millionaire as well as a saint, but I knew enough to give the money to my mother to help with the groceries.

Bradford was an oil town, and during the Second World War, the place was booming. There were two classes of people, rich and poor, and we were of the latter. There are also two kinds of poverty: redeemed and unredeemed. Redeemed poverty opens a world of experience unavoidable in the marketplace, and in all three Bradford rentals, I could sit on the kitchen floor and roll a marble uphill confident it would roll back. I didn't need brothers and sisters—or so I told myself. Stories made life easier, provided memories, prepared me for salvation. I believed in words because I had to, but also because ants and post beetles brought down the pillars of the rich. My own reward would be the Kingdom of Heaven.

When I prayed, I felt as though I was breaking into God's story as the plot unfolded, peeking over His shoulder at the original manuscript as I considered my next move. My mother taught me to kneel each night and tell God what had happened during the day, careful not to ask for favors. God could not be bribed, and even to hint at some special need smacked of ingratitude. The content of my prayers seemed less important than the distance I felt when I said them, and I always wondered if I were getting through. My mother said if I met God halfway, He would talk to me. God, she explained, was always talking, and all I had to do was listen. Although I knew no one had ever seen God, I believed it was possible to hear Him speak, but I didn't allow myself to hope; expectation seemed a denial of faith.

Until I started kindergarten, God was my best friend, and one day when He spoke to me, I wasn't overly surprised. It was an ordinary day, and we were still living in Clarion with my grandmother, and I was on my way home for lunch. The sun was shining, and for some reason I stepped off the sidewalk and stood on the grass. I don't remember the exact tone of His voice, only His words. He said, as I looked up at the sky, "You will live forever. You will never die." Maybe there was no tone, but His words filled me with joy, not just His promise that I would enter the Kingdom of Heaven, but that He had spoken to me.

Dad read me the Bible every day before school, turning the tissue-thin paper as the leather binding crumbled in his lap. His Bible was called *The New Chain-Reference Bible,* and it contained "Thompson's Original and Complete System of Bible Study" with a self-pronouncing text, chain references, pictorial maps, text cyclopedia, a concordance, outlines and charts. "In the beginning was the Word, and the word was with God, and the word was God."

My favorite parable was the Prodigal Son. I loved the story for its improbability as much as for the fear it aroused in me. A boy ran away from home, lived wildly in the city, then came back and was forgiven. "This my son was dead, and is alive again, he was lost, and is found . . ." the father said on the occasion of his son's return. But why did the father kill "the fatted calf" and call for "musick and dancing?" My own father, to use one of his favorite words, would have *throttled* me. Perhaps I enjoyed the story of the Prodigal Son because my own life, by comparison, seemed simple and blessed.

I was a literal-minded child with a wild imagination, and the Bible fascinated me because the world it described didn't wobble. The words held firm on the page, no matter what I had done or what had gone on during the day. Dust gathered in the corners of the house and newborn kittens drowned, but whenever my father opened the Bible, the same black letters were in the same order they had been in the day before. And that was reassuring.

On Sundays I sat on my father's lap as he read me the funnies. He knew I couldn't understand the "Katzenjammer Kids" or "Little Orphan Annie," but he read them anyway, running the tip of his finger from one cloud of words to the next, lifting and lowering his voice to sound happy or sad, young or old, like a man or a woman. The source of my enjoyment was not the story itself but the play of my father's voice, his freedom, for the moment, as though he had escaped the inevitable conclusion of one of his own self-defeating plots.

*   *   *   *

Years go by but the old stories stay with me. Not long ago I had a dream about *Alice in Wonderland*. My mother had read me the illustrated edition when I was too young to read the book myself. I didn't like the illustrations because I made up pictures of my own. "You are just like Humpty Dumpty," my mother said in exasperation. "You just don't listen. Now sit up!" I sat up. She read emphatically.

> "There's glory for you!"
> "I don't know what you mean by 'glory'," Alice said.
> ". . . I meant 'there's a nice knock-down argument for you!'"
> "But 'glory' doesn't mean 'a nice knock-down argument'," Alice objected.
> "When *I* use a word," Humpty Dumpty said, in rather a scornful tone, "it means just what I choose it to mean—neither more nor less."

I hadn't thought about *Alice in Wonderland* until, years later, my daughter reached puberty—and then I had a dream. "Whatever," Megan said flippantly in the dream as the two of us discussed the meaning of the word "glory." Flaunting her contempt, she assumed the person of Humpty Dumpty and scaled a wall, and when I pleaded for her to come down, she fell—yoke, white, and shell in a scramble at the bottom. By the time the King's Horses and Men arrived, it was too late, and they put up a sign in tall black letters: "ADDLED ESSENCE!"

"What?" my wife asked at breakfast when I told her about the dream.

"Addled essence," I said. "Adolescence. There's nothing we can do. When Megan decides to care about language she'll start to care about everything. And not before."

*   *   *   *

One day my father promised he would get well again, and that God would help him find another church. He trained like an athlete hoping to make a comeback, praying day and night. "I could have taught you how to pitch," he said when I was about ten, reminding me that his illness prevented him from pursuing a career in baseball. He rolled up his sleeves and bent at the waist so I could feel the muscle in his arm. "I can still lick anyone in town," he boasted with a twisted smile. "I could walk back into the ring anytime I want."

A prizefighter, he rolled up his shirtsleeves over his elbows, curled his fists, and assumed the boxing stance of John L. Sullivan, an outdated posture I mimicked behind his back. Like an old-fashioned boxer, he slicked down his hair with lard and rose water, parted it down the middle, tweaked an imaginary moustache.

My father's story began when, first born, he was blessed with good looks, an IQ in the 160s, and a father who, he claimed, "was a millionaire many times over." My grandfather, a successful lawyer, quit

McKain and his wife, the poet Margaret Gibson, in Williamsburg, Virginia, 1976

school and began as a logger, then apprenticed with an attorney in Quaker City, Ohio. Those were the days when would-be lawyers "read law," like Nut and Turkey, office boys in Herman Melville's story, "Bartleby the Scrivener." A self-made man, my grandfather believed that if he could succeed starting out as a common laborer, his son, given a pony when he was five, could become anything he chose to be—state representative, governor, senator, even president of the United States.

Becoming president was not out of the question in our family. In Blooming Grove, Ohio, not far from where my father had grown up, Warren G. Harding was raised on a backwater farm. The parallels went beyond their Buckeye past. The Hardings and McKains were staunch Republicans, and through my grandmother's side of the family, the Van Kirks, were related. It didn't matter that Harding was considered one of the worst presidents in the history of the United States, my grandmother was second or third cousin to Warren G. Harding's maternal grandmother, Charity, and, even more than "Reverend," the title "Commander-in-Chief" demanded respect.

"Where's that picture?" my father asked my mother every five or six years.

"What picture?" my mother answered in distraction.

"You know the one. The one where I'm sitting on President Harding's lap eating a drumstick."

The picture was never found, or at least I never saw it, but proof or evidence hardly mattered. My father was convinced he had been chosen for a mission in life, and I believed him because I was his son. But a career in politics was out of the question; my father was too outspoken to win the public's trust. He wrote letters to the *Pittsburgh Press* blaming Roosevelt, "that Jew in the White House," for everything.

A single accident, he said, had ruined his life. "He told me he had flipped his car in a big race in Akron and was lying on his deathbed, his life as good as over. That was when he prayed to God and promised that if God would only spare him he would become a preacher. He would have preached forever, had it not been for the lousy doctors who spliced a major artery with a faulty tube, and so the heart block explained almost everything—why he had become a preacher, his epilepsy, and why he had given up preaching as well."

The lure and power of the church was in the swell of its raucous hymns—joyously stretched and bent notes that straightened me up and out of my pew. The congregation swayed in their seats and

followed the instructions of the founder of Methodism. "Sing lustily and with a good courage," John Wesley wrote in 1761. "Beware of singing as if you were half dead, or half asleep, but lift up your voice with strength." Methodism was a sensual order, a faith manifest in tremulous song. So exciting were the services, my mother and I went to revival meetings in steamy tents pitched in cornfields, hot and steamy as any roadhouse with a rockabilly band in August.

The fervor of the hymns had little to do with doctrine or theology. Their power erupted in long rolling chords, in the play of anguish of the human voice. What did it mean to be lost? The hymns celebrated our confusion: "I Am Weak But Thou Art Strong"; "Gentle Shepherd, come and lead us, / For we need You to help us find our way"; "O for a closer walk with God . . . / A light to shine upon the road"; "I Was Lost in Sin When Jesus Found Me."

Being lost was the first step to redemption, and unless I admitted that I was lost, I could not be found. God could not rescue me unless I cried for help—tied a torn sleeve on a bush, tilted a mirror toward the sun, lit a fire at night. Darkness slid into blindness, and my father trained me for both. In "Seeing in the Dark," I wrote:

> So one day I could see backwards
> better than a fly, my father held
> up one to five fingers behind my back
> while I fixed my eyes dead ahead
> on a tree-spot to count them.
>
> Had there been an ice-cold sea,
> he would have plunged into the water
> on New Year's Day, soft and white,
> the ears of his bathing cap flipped up
> like a pilot's waving from his cockpit.
>
> Living inland, we had to settle
> for whatever truths might be
> wrenched from the mountains, moving
> five times in five years till we found
> a hillhouse with woods behind it.
>
> There, after supper, the two of us
> climbed to the top and watched the town
> flicker below in the darkness, listening
> to leaves and feathers as they settled
> to the ground, adjusting our eyes
>
> so we could practice not knowing where
> we were going. The only light we need,
> he said, is the light that shines inside.
> We don't really need *sight*, he hissed,
> flailing against gnats and cobwebs.
>
> Night after night, we would stumble
> over roots until I learned to feel
> my way with whatever membrane guides us:
> confident in nothing named or spoken,
> believing in the power of darkness.

In "Spinning," an early chapter in *Spellbound*, I wrote about creating my own dislocation. "I stood in the middle of the room with my eyes closed, an arm and finger extended, making myself rigid like a spinning arrow in the center of a gameboard. As the room raced by, I peeked at the dark green shade over the window and at each door: the mudroom door, the pantry door, the kitchen door, the laundry door, the bathroom door, and the Poison Door. Wherever I stopped spinning and pointed, I had to open that door, and I moved like a sleepwalker toward it, feeling my way through the dark."

Controlled confusion filled me with a sense of strength. I was learning to gather uncertainty inside, claim it for my own, give it shape. I could not control the uncertainties of poverty or my father's spells, but by junior high school, I could dance across a railing eighty feet over a ravine by concentrating on the rickety two-by-four beneath my feet.

I was learning. People in Bradford lived at the edge, between extremes. Snow started flying in the Allegheny Mountains in October and covered the hills until May. Winters were long and cold, the ground like iron. People called the winters closed, and sometimes the town shut down overnight. In the spring, when the snow melted, the floods came. Once, on Good Friday, we were rescued by a Civil Defense man in a rowboat, one of a hundred families rescued along Tuna Creek.

The rescue stories sung in hymns at church were part of our everyday lives; in the final stanza of an early poem called "Salvation," I wrote:

Although I don't believe it,
the story's still with me:
that one day I'll hear my name,
there'll be voices and trumpets,
and a hand to take my hand.

In high school I became known as a boy who would do anything, a boy who had nothing to lose. I identified with outsiders, with kids who stayed out all night and got away with it. I wasn't meant to be normal, I decided; I was a McKain, an outcast and a wanderer—a role assigned me by the Supreme Author Himself. My parents did not choose to be different; they were—simply because of their faith. Instruments of the Lord, they had chosen Christ over Caesar. I threw myself headlong from rooftops into snowbanks to prove and test my faith, discovering the thrill of sin.

I was not doing well in school. My teachers gave me *C*s and *D*s, but nothing they could say or do matched the drama of being lost and being saved—of

resurrection and redemption. The stories and hymns made me indifferent to the lesser drama of a well-ordered life. Since God wrote and bound the Book of Life, why, in school, were we wasting our time studying the Wright Brothers and Alexander Graham Bell? Of what significance were the achievements of mankind when one day "the sun shall be darkened, and the moon shall not give her light, And the stars of heaven shall fall . . . and they shall see the Son of man coming in the clouds with great power and glory"?

When my high school history teacher grew angry with me, she warned that if I didn't pay attention to what went on in class, others would go to college and I would find myself "on the outside looking in." But, I knew, I was on the outside already. The lessons of history reinforced the truth told in the hymns we sang so gleefully in church: "knowledge puffeth up . . ." All of us were lost; all of us were on the outside looking in. I did not want to lead the school assembly on Friday pledging allegiance to the flag; I did not want to be president of the Key Club, the Latin Club, or some other club that would help me get into college. I didn't want to go to college. Buoyed up by the luxury of being lost, I didn't care.

"By the time I was in eleventh grade," I wrote in *Spellbound*, "I had been suspended from Spanish class, history class and typing class, and told in each to report to the library. The first two or three times I actually knocked on the library door, but Miss Russo blocked the narrow entrance with her body. She shook her head slowly back and forth, smiling.

"'Never!' she said defiantly. 'Never again, David McKain! Never!' I had been kicked out of the library my sophomore year and I could never go back. Miles Fink, who had been banned from the library as well, nodded from a dark corner of the locker room as he leaned up against the wall, puffing on a weed, a crooked smile on his face. 'S'not bad,' he said speaking in his slow drawl from the hills."

I stopped going to church about the same time I lost my status at school. "In Bradford's terms, at least in the only terms I could see and understand, I was learning to become a man. On some days I skipped school to work, but I was wearing thin from working two jobs and trying to play basketball at the same time . . ."

Bradford was a town of bars and churches. "Men drilled two thousand feet below the ground for oil, and the hills rose up two thousand feet above sea level. They either struck it rich or they lost their savings and their homes. But people had grown accustomed to losing and doing without. During the War there had been no meat, no sugar, no gas, no

David and Margaret, with daughter, Megan, and son, Joshua, 1983

butter, no steel, no money, no rubber, no leather, no
clothes. Instead there had been scarlet fever, diphthe-
ria, polio, meningitis, and the lingering poverty of the
Great Depression. The men in town played it safe,
denying any sign of comfort for themselves for fear it
would be taken as a sign of weakness. In Bradford, a
man showed his toughness not in order to impress
others, but to convince himself he was strong enough
to survive. I admired the slow and sullen men. I
sensed the strength they hid. To me, they were
heroic.''

The men in the ice-cream factory where I
worked bragged about their love lives, pulled up their
T-shirts to show off the scratches on their backs, and
described in detail the wild life of the bars. Working
in construction one summer, I became friends with a
man called Bear.

Drinking Boiler Makers at the Texas Hot

Payday, we'd park our trucks
out back and dive into the river,
washing off the lye and plaster;
we'd air-dry at the bar, our hair
gone limp in ringlets, the sweat
trickling down Bear's bull neck.

Sunburned in ripped T-shirts,
we'd swagger into Greek's
and slap our paychecks down,
stacking the money on the bar:
leaving it there to dance,
sending out word—*we're together*.

For work, we tore the Opera down:
mostly wrecking bar and sledge,
double-strapped two-by-fours,
crowbar, winch, and cat's paw.
In white-face, blinking in the dust,
we bashed the plaster cherubs.

Where once they'd lowered the gods
in paper wings on wires to stage,
I climbed the catwalk on a dare,
only to snap a plank and fall
into the orchestra. Bear carried
me in his arms a mile to the hospital.

After a couple of rounds I'd watch
him squat by the juke box, soulful,
clapping his hands between his knees.
Six-four, two-fifty, he'd wrap his fist
around my arm and whisper, "Bear Cub,"
doing The Walk, touched by *Four Roses*.

The trick was, let him dance;
let him sashay out there alone
on the purple neon floor, biting

his lower lip, singing torch songs.
Soon, I knew, he'd howl off-key
and put his fist through a wall.

*   *   *   *

My bravado was growing thin. I liked Bear, but he frightened me. I never knew when he was going to crush someone, perhaps me. I hung around town for awhile after high school, but I was lucky. I couldn't find a steady job. My mother was delighted. The plot of my life was unfolding the way God had written it. We made a deal. Despite my poor grades and worse attitude, I got to go to college. Entrance requirements were less stringent in the mid-1950s, and I even got a basketball scholarship. I took a special exam to help compensate for my years of drifting, and just like that, I was in.

My father moved to Olean, New York, eighteen miles away. He might as well have moved to Alaska. He didn't drive and I didn't have a car. It is difficult now for me to comprehend, but my father simply drifted off. I hitchhiked over to see him a couple of weekends, but I could only visit an hour or two. He rented a dinky room in a cheap hotel. There was no place for me to stay.

I decided to go to college because the world was falling down all around me. I didn't know what else to do. I was beginning to wonder what would happen to me. I didn't want to end up like Bear, and I was tired of being poor. A friend of mine came back from college wearing a tweed sport jacket, feeling good about himself. That did it. I decided I wanted to wear a three-piece suit, make a fistful of ten-dollar bills, and be a lawyer like my grandfather.

The School of Business Administration at the University of Connecticut required all freshmen to take a course called "Literature and Composition," and we read, among other books, D. H. Lawrence's *Sons and Lovers* and James Joyce's *Portrait of the Artist as a Young Man.* Despite the professor's warning that we would have trouble with Joyce, I read the book as though Stephen Daedalus and I had been best friends. I had seen the girl who stood midstream gazing out to sea. "Her long slender bare legs were delicate as a crane's and pure save where an emerald trail of seaweed had fashioned itself as a sign upon the flesh." Stephen called the vision *claritas.* "You see that it is that thing which it is and no other thing." I was ecstatic. At last the people around me took stories as seriously as I did. I wasn't sure why I identified so strongly with the story of a Catholic boy from Dublin, but in the middle of my freshman year, I became an English major.

For the first time in my life I read books from cover to cover, sometimes two or three times. *My life was a story,* and now I was learning how to take other stories apart and put them back together again. I was learning how to look below the surface to understand how certain words affected tone, how tone influenced voice, and how voice spoke to the heart. Courses in literature legitimized daydream, restored narrative, elevated the significance of story and song.

I lacked the discipline and understanding to become a writer in college, but I tried. I took John Malcolm Brinnin's creative writing class and watched the smoke from his pipe turn blue as it drifted over my head during our weekly conferences. He told me to read William Carlos Williams, and on the sly I read Walt Whitman, Ezra Pound, Chinese poets, and the new voices, Allen Ginsberg, Jack Kerouac. Ready to celebrate life, I hitchhiked to San Francisco after graduation—grew a beard, wore sandals, wrote poems. To earn money I washed dishes, sold books at Brentano's, and wrote reviews for the *San Francisco Examiner,* exchanging review copies for books by Joyce and Faulkner, Lawrence and Pound.

After two years of reading and taking notes, I hitchhiked to New York, borrowed a suit, and found a job as a reader in the trade department at Holt, Rinehart and Winston. Six months later, I became the first editor hired by McGraw-Hill Paperbacks, stayed almost three years, and went back to school to read and study some more. I have been teaching and writing ever since, staying in touch with the story that is my life.

I find that story everywhere, in countries far away. In *Spirit Bodies,* I wrote a poem about traveling through the Soviet Union.

In Soviet Georgia

Heads down, the lambs are staked
inside a triangle of fescue and clover.
The river runs jade-white and cold
in front of the road stop, spruce
and birch rising, leaning
against the sky at the same angle
the dancers lean against the wall.

Four men in small leather caps
sharpen their knives on a whetstone.
The first lamb goes quietly, the thrust
of a single muscle. Two men hold on
as a woman from the bus shudders,
touching her teeth with her handkerchief.
The mountains throw a shadow inside
the thinner shadows of the clouds.
The river air is green and wet.

The last lamb slides its jaw back
and forth chewing on the sweet grass,
the spray of its blood a surprise—
the men jump back as if someone had thrown
a flat rock in the water. They hang
the lambs to drain from a pole—
four curved sprays of wrought iron,
a lamb tree like a plant hanger.

Ready, the musicians finger-roll
their goatskin drums and zithers,
the dancers wigwagging their knives
in semaphore, slashing signals
we don't understand through the air.
Among themselves, the butchers talk,
their backs turned so as not to see us,
to give nothing to the cameras. Up
this high and near the water, ions
charge the air. I would like to stay
and learn the shadows of the mountains,
to fish the cold stream, to take
pride in cutting and carving: one
slit with a blade that hurts no one.

The speaker, identified only as "I," observes the Georgian men slaughter lambs then turn away from a bus load of tourists. The men smoke cigarettes as though they realize their closeness to the land and their work baffles and disturbs us; to rub it in. Although as tourists we arrived as a group, we were brought together by accident. We remain separate from one another. Taken singly—and that is how each of us must view himself and herself—we feel alone. By comparison, the men in small leather caps share a common bond; they form a community unto themselves.

They slaughter the lambs in front of the roadside restaurant because the meat is best when it is fresh, but why do they kill the lambs in public? Because their quick knives set up the dance of the flashing scimitars and swords—because they want to reveal to us our own squeamishness. We have paid them and wish to be entertained; we expect to be dismayed, even shocked. In shocking us, the men help us preserve the myth of our own innocence, reassuring us of how civilized we are, how far we have come.

The men pay us back and pay us off. Confident, they are nearly exultant in their well-being. None of us from the bus has evolved very far from the time when we might have called the peasants "insolent." Without questioning, the woman who puts the handkerchief to her lips might just as well have slapped them or had them punished.

I grew up in a primitive world watched by people who could not, as outsiders, understand. I want to stay in the mountains, raise and slaughter sheep, play the zither and dance, share the integrated life of the men who jump back from the spray of blood because

David McKain, 1990

blood is wet—not because the sight or touch of blood frightens them. The men refuse to play to the crowd, to smile before our cameras, to act the fool or bow. They show no shyness, no vanity, but they are comfortable in the roles assigned them. They have no need to aspire, for posturing, for a borrowed role. I delight in their freedom to insult us. Theirs is the power of those who have been given a story, written off. Theirs is the cold dignity of the artist—of anyone at home in his or her own story.

I have made their lives simpler than they are, and writing this piece, I have made my own life simpler as well—pretending that I followed a short-cut from one place (home) to where I am now. The truth is that I have lived in over fifty different places coast-to-coast, in Mexico and in Greece. The narrative line is actually jagged, elliptical, bent. Someday the line may even circle back to Bradford, Pennsylvania, where it started, like the story of the Prodigal Son. "To know who you are," Carson McCullers wrote, "you have to have someplace to come from." And, as my father's child, as a wanderer and a storyteller, I agree.

BIBLIOGRAPHY

Poetry:

In Touch, Ardis, 1975.

The Common Life, Alice James, 1982.

Spirit Bodies, Ithaca House, 1990.

Other:

(Editor) *Christianity: Some Non-Christian Appraisals*, McGraw-Hill, 1965.

(Editor) *The Whole Earth: Essays in Appreciation, Anger and Hope*, St. Martin's, 1971.

Spellbound: Growing Up in God's Country, University of Georgia Press, 1988, Simon & Schuster/Touchstone Books, 1990.

Contributor to numerous journals, including *Antietam Review, Antioch Review, Colorado Review, Country Journal, Fiddlehead, Greensboro Review, Harvard Magazine, Iowa Review, New Virginia Review, Open Places, Quarterly, Ploughshares, Praxis, Shenandoah, Southwest Review*, and *Unrealist*.

Contributor to anthologies, including *Dear Winter*, edited by Marie Harris, Northwoods Press, 1984; *The Poet Dreaming in the Artist's House*, edited by E. Buchwald and R. Roston, Milkwood Editions, 1984; *Our Roots Grow Deeper Than We Know*, edited by Lee Gutkind, University of Pittsburgh Press, 1985; *Anthology of Magazine Verse and Yearbook of American Poetry*, edited by Alan F. Pater, Monitor, 1986–1988, 1989.

William Meredith
1919-

By Richard Harteis

William Meredith, 1988

EDITOR'S NOTE: In 1983 William Meredith suffered a severe stroke that left him completely paralyzed on the right side. Although his comprehension was not affected, he could not speak, read, or write, and it was only after months of rehabilitation that he regained limited ability in these areas. Meredith himself was thus unable to contribute an autobiographical essay for this series, but his longtime companion and caregiver, Richard Harteis, agreed to write an appro-

priate piece that would, in some measure, capture the essence and spirit of this Pulitzer Prize-winning poet. The following biography was written with Meredith's approval.

The day William Meredith won the 1988 Pulitzer Prize for poetry, we had been travelling to San Francisco for the annual Associated Writing Programs Conference. William was to be honored at the final night's banquet and the trip was a chance to visit some of his family on the West Coast. As we were getting installed in our hotel room, a reporter from the *Washington Post* called asking for an interview. For a moment I thought someone might be playing a bad April Fool's joke. William's friends all felt the honor long overdue, but the reality of it now, at this point in his life, was too wonderful. I gave him a bear hug and cried the good news.

Earlier in the year his new book, *Partial Accounts*, had won the *Los Angeles Times* Book Award and recognition of his work was coming from many different quarters. The attention was having a splendid effect on him. There were parties in his honor and appearances at local bookstores. He had to rise to any number of occasions and the effort was helping to improve his speech. Since William's stroke in 1983, he had struggled with such determination to overcome paralysis and retrieve his speech. Critics were hailing the book as his masterpiece, but I knew what a personal triumph of the spirit it was as well. And now he had won the Pulitzer.

The good news spread quickly among the writers arriving at the conference and added a certain glow to the proceedings. Our suite turned into a nonstop press conference and hospitality center. By the end of the conference, the final banquet became an agape. Extra room was made for all the friends who came to celebrate the extraordinarily humane life and work of William Meredith.

Of the eight speakers on the dais that night, I suppose Maxine Kumin knew William longest— though his old friend William Maxwell had sent a beautiful tribute to be read at the occasion. As Ellen Voigt began to introduce the speakers, Maxine and I calculated that she had first met William at the Bread Loaf Writers Conference in 1963. When it was her turn to speak she pointed out that it was she who had introduced William and me at a party during the conference some years later in 1971.

William and I make a visit to Maxine's farm in New Hampshire each summer to see how the new foals are coming along and catch up on our lives, sitting under the pine trees along the edge of her pond. It's years now since she and Victor moved to those remote hills to escape urban life and raise horses. Summertime is their brief reward for all the hard months tending the farm during the winter. They love having visitors during those golden months, showing off the garden, the new paddock, Victor's latest blue ribbon for trail riding.

Last summer I was bemoaning the biographical article I had agreed to try on William's behalf after

his stroke. How could I discover the details of his early years now that his last relative, his dear sister Kay, had recently died? Given William's limited speech, how could I question him on the intricacies of his relationships with writers like Frost and Jarrell, with whom he exchanged few letters, or even other very close friends like Lowell, Berryman, and Robert Penn Warren, with whom the correspondence is voluminous?

I had shared my life with William for almost twenty years and knew a good deal of his personal history. But how could I muster the objectivity, let alone the particular research skills of the professional biographer? Would I be doing him a service if I were to take an anecdotal approach? The more I reflected on his distinguished career, the richness of his life, the more hopeless the project seemed.

"Why worry about a biography," Maxine said in her wonderfully breezy way. "Just write something you want to write, some part of William's life."

She's often given me good advice and her words seemed to make sense again. How complete can a biography ever be, really, anyway? I'll follow Hemingway's tired injunction to write what I know and look at the two decades since I've met William, delving into the past only where I am pretty sure of my footing. No one is ever totally unbiased when reporting the "facts," I suppose, like the five proverbial blind men each with their individual descriptions of the elephant depending on the part they happen to be holding on to. Recently, I came across some interesting journal entries which might help tell the story, and including some of William's poems will enable him to speak for himself, as it were, in the course of this appreciation.

When I first went to the Bread Loaf Writers Conference in 1971, I had recently returned from two years in the Peace Corps and was anxious to catch up with the revolution that I had missed while I was in Africa. I wore the uniform of my generation: tie-dyed bib overalls, shoulder-length hair, and free-floating skepticism for social institutions and anyone over age thirty. Many of the conferees shared my politics and John Ciardi had all he could do to keep us in line. He was a formidable adversary as the director of the conference, however, a BIG man with a deep voice who radiated authority and had clear ideas of what he expected of people. You couldn't find a more perfect father figure to rebel against.

For Ciardi, Bread Loaf was a school of thought based on firm principles. Presumably, students came there precisely for the sort of approach Bread Loaf represented. If you didn't like the philosophy you could go to Crete or Sparta or Rhodes. But his was the Athens of writers conferences. Writing was a lonely, serious business—some writers were better at it than others—and his workshops were not about to degenerate into mindless praise for mediocrity. My work might be okay, your work might definitely not be okay. Conferees were directed to kindly hang their egos on the door as they came in. He felt no need to incorporate the hippie egalitarian ethic into the rigid structure of the conference. There would be no mixing at the tables assigned to various categories of participants—faculty, scholars, fellows, students, auditors. The bar/lounge in Treman Cottage would remain off limits to everyone but staff members.

Though they remained friends till the end of his life and dealt with each other honorably, William took Ciardi on in the general sessions and became something of the leader for the faculty opposition. William protested once after a particularly brutal bit of public criticism of a student's manuscript in a workshop and made the point that we should try to enlighten a work by our analysis, not merely try to ridicule it. His words were greeted with sympathetic applause as I recall. In a letter to Ciardi in 1970 he defends "the hard line about craft," but he also asks the director to have the staff consider "what it's like to be arrogant and insecure and mildly gifted and destructive and scared and twenty-two before they start projecting their own creative identities as nervously as most of us do."

The student whose work received such harsh criticism later began literally to climb the walls like Spiderman. He buzzed groups of students meeting on the green in the little biplane he had flown from Colorado. Ciardi was not impressed. He'd flown in the war and found the disgruntled student's little "pea shooter" silly. Everybody loved it.

William and Ciardi both seemed larger than life to me. In spite of his populist politics (because of them?), William was a fairly glamourous character. He wasn't my advisor, but one couldn't help following his presence on the campus. He was a snappy dresser, with the patrician good looks of a young George McGovern or Jason Robards. He had arrived in his '62 Mercedes 190 SL with his protégée, a beautiful black writer named Gayl Jones, in the passenger seat. He and Randall Jarrell had each bought a 190 the same year and he kept the car in

Richard Harteis, Maxine Kumin, and William at Maxine's farm in New Hampshire, late 1970s

Robert Frost and William Meredith, Bread Loaf Writers Conference, 1958

mint condition. Not exactly the archetypical social activist.

Still, he had championed civil rights from the beginning and was very proud of the Upward Bound program he had started at Connecticut College, where he had taught since the early fifties. There he introduced his students to black writers and poets as guests in his class. Some time ago I came across the text of a talk he gave at the college chapel and it is a good example of how he was able to speak to the idealism of his students in a literary context. After saying Robert Frost's poem "The Draft Horse," he quoted a Berryman poem to illustrate the "reckless generosity," the response of love he saw in the poet:

"I think what I learned from these two men, that I see witnessed in this exchange of poems, is that there is an appropriate response to anything that befalls us. It is a response that has to do with the love of our fellow man. It is prompted by a personal instinct of love. Its working is mysterious because this instinct is different in each of us. We are constantly being astonished, if we pay attention, at how differently people take their brotherhood. People who

can't take it are non-people: we have cast-out names for them: monsters, zombies, self-lovers. And we can't dogmatize anything very important about love. What's true for me isn't exactly true for you: your instinct has another person for data. It would be dogmatic for me to assert that, at some level, the appropriate response to any crisis is affirmative, though I believe that. It would be dogmatic to assert that the prompting voice is creative, a manifestation of the creative force in the universe, but I believe that. Instinctively, I have come to the role of an affirmative witness."

This kind of talk had us burning in the late sixties. But I suppose it is precisely those instincts he describes that have helped him survive the insult of the stroke and bad health these past years.

William belonged to a number of organizations during that period which tried to bring about change in society and affect the environment, groups such as Amnesty International and an organization which provided financial support for black law students. On occasion he would help pay a needy student's tuition out of his own pocket. He felt a personal responsibility for what American racism had done to blacks in this culture, a need to right the score. His family dates from the country's founding, but I'm not aware of any particular family culpability in this regard.

A great-great-uncle, his namesake, was highly respected as President Taylor's secretary of the treasury just before the Civil War. There's a ten-cent note with his picture on it, looking remarkably similar to William but more serious, with great jowls and muttonchop sideburns. One aspect of his role as consultant in poetry at the Library of Congress was the chance it gave him to perform public service, the way proper, blue-blooded American children are raised to do. At a Thanksgiving dinner, his "imaginary playmate" Hazard (in the sense that Lowell and Berryman chose alter egos to speak for them in their poetry occasionally) said the culture was in later imperial decline and that a lot was expected of him ceremony-wise. He rises to that expectation.

His liberal views were played out within the system, with a sense of history and continuity. Che Guevara he was not. If he had his preference he'd have lived in the eighteenth century, he always said. The restored barn where he lived in Connecticut was filled with antiques and family portraits from the 1800s. The Chippendale china cabinet was filled with amari ware and early Chinese export. The guest book at Riverrun included names such as Robert Frost, Andre Malraux, and Archibald MacLeish, and many of the visitors reflected on the peace and harmony he had created on the gentle acres sloping down to the Thames River. But in spite of the patrician air he projected, his belief in a citizen's responsibility to his tribe synchronized with the values of the young generation at Bread Loaf, and the aspiring writers appreciated his genuine commitment to social change. This commitment didn't necessarily define good poetry for him, however. Poetry was a very large umbrella and covered any number of schools of poetry. In a lecture given at the Library of Congress, he said:

"Poems seem to come into being for various and distinct reasons. These vary from poem to poem and from poet to poet. The reason for a poem is apt to be one of the revelations attendant on its making. 'No surprise in the writer, no surprise in the reader,' Frost said. The reason for a new poem is, in some essential, a new reason. This is why poets, in the large Greek sense of "makers," are crucial to a culture. They respond newly, but in the familiar tribal experience of language, to what new thing befalls the tribe."

Later in the piece he talks of three possible roles for the poet:

"If a poet is committed to an overriding social grievance, as currently some of the best European, Latin American, and United States minority writers are, the poem is best read as a kind of ceremonial rite, with specific purpose. A dissident poem aspires to be an effective ritual for causing change. If a poet feels, on the other hand (to quote an easygoing character in one of my own poems), that the human predicament 'is just a good bind to be in,' the poem should be read as an occasional poem, occasioned by some instance— however flawed or imperfect—of an existing order. An apologist poem aspires to be a celebration. If a poet thinks of himself only as a man or woman speaking to men and women, the poem should be read simply as poem. A solitary's poem is a message written on one person's clean slate to be copied on another person's clean slate as an exercise in person-hood. A solitary poem wants to become a little universe or a charade."

At the end of the Bread Loaf Conference when he roared away in the old Mercedes, I thought that would be the last of the great man I would ever see, but one day a letter came with an invitation to visit in Uncasville. Soon we began to alternate our weekends between Washington and Connecticut, not a very sensible relationship geographically, but the friendship had become more profound. He could be sure of an honest reaction on my part to new poems he sent along. It was a treat to show him off to the English department at my school and eat in restaurants a graduate student could never afford. He helped me keep at the hard work, helped me tone down some of my excesses and be a bit more tolerant. We cooked meals together for his lovely friends, my circle became his in Washington. The friendship was an anchor for me at a difficult time and lent a wonderful glamour to the tedium of student life. On one visit to the farm in the dead of winter, after too much rich food and booze, I got up in the night and managed to scare myself into thinking I saw a ghost coming up from the cellar. William took a candle and performed an impromptu exorcism, explaining to the ghost that I was a friend of the house. And later he gave me a new poem:

The Ghosts of the House

Enabling love, roof of this drafty hutch
of children and friends and pets, and chiefly of the
   dear
one asleep beside me now, the warm body-house

I sack like a Hun nightly in your service,
take care of the haunts who stay with us here.
In a little space for a long while they've walked,
wakeful when we sleep, averting their sad glance
when we're clumsy with one another, they look
at something we can't look at yet, they creak the
  boards
beside the bed we creak, in some hard durance.

And if we're weary at night, what must they be?
Bed them like us at last under your roof.
You who have sternly set all lovers to walk
the hallways of the world-hutch for a lucky while,
speaking good of our short durance here,

wishing our sibling spirits nothing but good,
let them see these chambers once with the daylight
  eyes
you lend to lovers for our mortal time.
Or change some loveless stalker into me
before my bone-house clatters into lime.

The following summer William invited me to visit
him at the Rockefeller Center at Lake Como,
where he was working. Afterwards, we went to
Venice and then on to Kirkestatten to visit Wystan
Auden for a week. Pretty heady stuff for a graduate
student in English literature.

The Villa Serbelloni at that time was run by John
and Charlotte Marshall in the grand manner of a
duke and his duchess entertaining houseguests at a
country estate. John Marshall was a distinguished
gentleman who knew William from the Century Club
in New York. John was a *bon vivant*, author and
exquisite chef, and William loved him like a father.
John's wife was equally cosmopolitan and William
relished the social ambience she created, slightly
formal but appropriate to the varied scholars from
around the world.

At half his age and without any particular reason
to be visiting William, my presence at the villa was
something of an awkwardness—but the Marshalls
made me feel welcome. One political scientist had just
come with his new young wife and we hung out
together like social outlaws. I remember swimming in
the lake with a storm throwing us against the rocks,
but none of us willing to get out the water, lightning
cracking over the lake above, the spirits of Shelley
and Byron egging us on.

The first morning of our visit with Auden, I
seemed to be in trouble for having slept till the

Visiting W. H. Auden (left) in Austria, 1972

ungodly hour of 11:00 A.M. He followed a rigid schedule and my lateness at breakfast kept him from his work, I suppose. In the morning one did one's writing, at lunch one went to the village to collect the mail, and in the afternoon one wrote letters, perhaps had a nap.

In the evening martinis were served—an absolute maximum of two cocktail onions permitted—and then we sat down to one of the frozen gourmet dinners Chester had prepared and stored in the freezer before leaving for Greece. After dinner, William and Auden debated the greater genius of composers, with Auden like a frantic disc jockey, jumping up and down to put on a record to prove his point. Mozart had his charm, but Wagner overshadowed all for his greatness.

William's regard for the master was reverential. He thought Auden bored with life, since there were very few intellects alive who could match or interest him. As a result, Auden held discourse with the brilliant dead in literature. William considered himself a far inferior intelligence and used that to account for the distance he felt with Auden at the end.

After my initial faux pas, I felt very comfortable with Auden. I even had the nerve to read him my poetry, which he politely applauded. At that point in my life I had a hippie's disdain for class distinctions or any structure which placed one person over another even if he *were* the master and I the neophyte. Once William had gone to bed, Auden and I sat up drinking cognac late into the night. He confided that he was breaking doctor's orders, but I think he was glad for someone to break the rules with.

One afternoon the mails brought the galleys for *Epistle to a Godson* and it brightened him enormously. We read through it and he clucked and carried on about the typographical errors that the publisher had made.

A few months after our visit we got word that he had collapsed at the podium in Vienna where he was reading and died. The death was a great sadness for William, but it was not a great surprise.

In 1972 I got a job teaching at a small college in D.C. and had more time and a little money to make my visits to Connecticut more regular. It began to feel like my home too when I made a garden lined with Belgian blocks and helped ball and move trees.

After World War II, William had returned to Princeton for a while but began to look for a place which was a little less intense than Princeton where he could settle more comfortably and do his work. He had rotated through Princeton with other junior faculty like Berryman and was glad for such friendships. But in Connecticut College he could be a slightly larger frog in his own pond. He purchased an 1820s farmhouse and barn situated on thirty acres along the Thames River just seven miles from the college campus. Here he could indulge his love of gardening, and with a friend he planted a private nursery specializing in rare trees and experimented to see what varieties he could raise this far north. Their stock included various sorts of weeping trees (hemlock and beech), dwarf and oriental trees (Japanese maple, Chinese elm), especially grafted trees, such as weeping dogwood and perhaps fifteen types of rhododendron. A number of his poems are set at the Uncasville farm in various seasons of the year:

Winter on the River

dawn

A long orange knife slits the darkness
from ear to ear. Flat sheets of Kansas
have been dropped where the water was.
A blue snake is lying perfectly still,
freezing to avoid detection—no, it is the barge-road.

noon

It's six weeks past the solstice. What
is the sun thinking of? It skulks
above the southern woods at noon.
                                Two ducks descend
on the thin creek that snakes through the plain of ice.
They dream of a great flood coming
to devastate this plastic geography.
We can all remember other things than snow.

dusk

At dusk the east bank glows a colder orange,
giving back heat reluctantly. (The sickle moon
gives it back quickly.) The snake is glacier-green
where an oil-barge has lately churned it.
Tonight unlucky creatures will die, like so many
soldiers or parents, it is nobody's fault.

midnight

The farm dogs bark at a soft crash far up-river:
the ice-breaker is coming down. We go out
in the clear night to see the lights—beacons
on the river, pharos in the sky, and a jewelled
seafarer bringing water to the parched plain.
The hollow roar grows slower than an avalanche.
Her search-light feeling a way from point
of land to point of land, she pulls herself along
by beacon-roots. For a half-mile reach of river
she sights on us, a group of goblins blinking
in front of their white house. Sugary rime
feathers from the bow. An emerald and a garnet
flank the twitching eye.
                                Abruptly she turns,
offering the beam of a ship that has nothing to do
    with us.
A houseful of strangers passes, ship-noise thumping.

Down-river, other dogs take up the work.
They are clearing a path for the barges of cold
and silence which the creatures are expecting.

Many years after William wrote this poem I was reflecting on his aphasia and the irony of those prophetic dogs. I wrote my own poem, a response to William's poem and what his courage was teaching me:

Winter Lesson

There were nights the snow began as powder
dusting the ceramic bulldog on the step
until by morning he wore a white bowler
or was buried altogether. Others,
these gentle fields became moonscape,
a polished crust thick enough to
hold a man without snowshoes. Clear then,
with brittle stars and a freeze so deep
the earth seemed finally irreparable—
you would die if you went too far from home.

Often I lay like a spoiled hibernating bear
after too many nightcaps or excesses
sure the cold would numb me to death, when
the cave grew warmer somehow with dreams of
plump fish hiding in the rainbows of spring streams.

Once I actually woke and stumbled down to
catch you in your father's woolen bathrobe
feeding logs into the wood stove, a dream too.
You could have been counting thousand dollar bills
or preparing the first martini of the day.

Twice a night throughout winter and just before
dawn smashed through the kitchen and required
breakfast, you danced this ritual. Sometimes I came
  down
to smoked ham and eggs over light and remembered
  to
complain how cold I'd been and how your odd
  movements
wakened me in the night. The heat I accepted like
  air.

Now I sit in the same woolen robe
wondering how soon the light will come, and
if these logs will hold till then. You,
can't take the stairs as well anymore. Your
circulation's poor. Sometimes you shake a little
in your sleep. I hold you tighter till it's over
or I stoke the fire. I know the ritual like a
well-trained dancing bear. More than habit though,
sometimes the tenderness I come to as I watch you
curl into the warmth of your sleep feels like perfect
instinct, like slapping the wet air to hook a rainbow.

William began his life as a poet as an undergraduate at Princeton, but it was during World War II that he began to write seriously. In 1944 Archibald MacLeish selected William's first book, *Love Letter from an Impossible Land*, while William was still serving as a second lieutenant in Hawaii. Three short

journal entries from November of that year give an interesting description of his life as a poet/aviator at the time:

"7/11/44—Flew this evening, after what was for here a rainy day; the skirts of rain-squall front lying south of the island. Should like to get into Molokai some time and see where Fr. Damien lived— being put in mind of it by Alexander Wolcott's piece on Ira Dutton, later Brother Joseph, a Vermont man who took over Fr. Damien's work when the latter was dying. Almost every day, of course, I see the island.

"The election returns are incomplete but indicate an easy Roosevelt victory.

"First poem finished in six months to be part of a group called *Ships of the Line* (?), of which only this and 'Transport' are done. This still has filler-words and lines in it: lines 6 and 12 do not satisfy me yet.

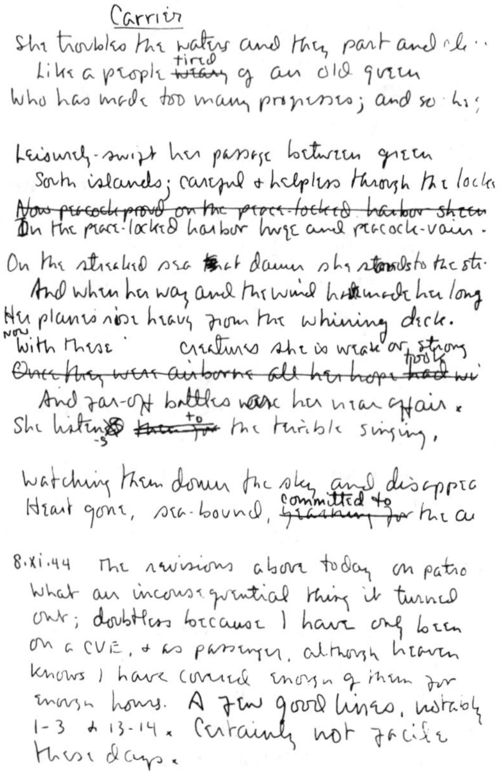

[handwritten manuscript with revisions:]

Carrier

She troubles the waters and they part and cl···
Like a people tired of an old queen
Who has made too many promises; and so his

Leisurely-swept her passage between green
South islands; careful & helpless through the locks
~~Now peacock-proud on the peace-locked harbor sheen~~
On the peace-locked harbor huge and peacock-vain.

On the streaked sea ~~that~~ dawn she ~~stands~~ to the sti·
And when her way and the wind have made her long
Her planes rise heavy from the whirring deck.
With these   ~~now~~ creatures she is weak or strong ~~too~~
~~Once they were airborne all her hope~~
And far-off battles ~~were~~ to her near affair.
She listens ~~for to~~ the terrible singing,

Watching them down the sky and disappear
Heart gone, sea-bound, committed to ~~glancing for~~ the a

8·xi·44 The revisions above today on patio
What an inconsequential thing it turned
out; doubtless because I have only been
on a CVE, & as passenger, although heaven
knows I have covered enough of them for
enough hours. A few good lines, notably
1-3 & 13-14. Certainly not facile
these days.

"8/11/44—The revisions above today on patrol. What an inconsequential thing it turned out; doubtless because I have only been on a CVE, and as passenger, although heaven knows I have covered enough of them for enough hours. A few good lines, notably 1-3 and 13-14. Certainly not facile these days. This evening fighting the rain in S-Plot on duty; by keeping my feet on the legs of the chair I can keep dry. Hope my bed is safely above high water. Wretched job.

"10/11/44—Louis Coxe in from the Marianas yesterday morning, called me just after I got out of S-Plot, and I joined him at the Officer's Club in the Navy Yard. He is thin and pale, with horn-rim glasses and a few wrinkles to contradict his eternal boyishness. We went to the Strovens'—Helen could not contain her pleasure, nor yet Louis his I.W. Harper, and he came back here very tight, nay drunk. Stephen Whiches there.

"Today I joined him late at the Strovens' again, soberer evening. Both sleep at Ford Island tonight. Louis is still marvelously humorous as ever. Signalman on his ship, during a torpedo attack by Jap planes (during which the ship shot down four,) stood on the signal bridge screaming: 'Back the Attack! Buy War Bonds.' ('Buy War Bonds' now used to mean what the hell.) Boatswain who called over the bull horn: 'Now hear this. All those who don't have one, get one; all those who have two, turn one in.' And a ship that signalled during air attack, 'Your line of fire seems to be directed at us; have we done something to offend you?'

"Louis tells of an LCI in their formation going up after a torpedo hit; of the flies, from the great numbers of dead Japs floating off Saipan in the first days; of taking a .45 ashore later so as to escort 6 sailors on a liberty party—a six mile hike on the beach at Saipan, walking the legs off the sailors.

"He thinks his poem 'Dead Marine' very important as do I. He has been through a good deal. Is now skipper, made Lt. this month, was task unit Commander over 9 ships coming back. (His cousin says, he says 'It doesn't care' for it doesn't matter.)

"Talked late about Hopkins, Yeats, a *Blue Jacket's Manual* of his poems and mine, and some commentary. An interesting idea. I think he needs to publish now. I just need to write."

William spent a couple of years at the University of Hawaii after the war, but his poetry took root and flourished in the years after he moved to the farm in Connecticut. Succeeding books dealt with man's relation to nature, human love, and social responsibility. A friend going back to the war years, an artist named Robert Drew, moved to Connecticut, and together they renovated the barn into an exquisite country house. Lowell, Frost, MacLeish, and younger poets Derek Wallcott, Richard Wilbur, and John Hollander, and an endless stream of visitors came to Riverrun and added to the intellectual life of the college. After the death of his parents, William had found a new spiritual home. He worked at the college with the devotion of a medieval monk for his cathedral. For ten years he directed the Upward Bound program to help disadvantaged black students cope with college life. He devised a reading program inviting the great poets of the day to the campus. He could even be seen picking up trash as he crossed the campus as though it were his own private yard. He agreed to take a cut in pay once when the institution was going through hard times. It is hard to imagine such loyalty in a faculty today.

William's devotion and impact as a teacher became legendary, and students began to come from across the country to study with him, as was the case with Michael Collier, a poet who became a close friend and has since helped collect William's works. Connecticut College recently established a Chair in William's name to honor his life as a teacher there. He was a tough grader and would readily admit that he had encountered perhaps only four or five poets with great talent during his career. But he defended the creative-writing courses he taught as a legitimate way of approaching the study of literature, appreciating the beauty and structure of the forms from the inside, as it were. And helping a student organize his life's experience in language was a valuable skill to take away from a liberal-arts education. I don't think William felt strongly enough about the quality of the wistful poem I discovered among his papers to ever publish, but it gives a good idea of how he *liked* teaching, something of a rare quality in English departments today:

His Students

In the warm classroom, they give off heat
It is winter, the lights are on, the pipes knock.
We are studying their youth. I talk.
I don't have a doctorate, but I know
The old way things were done and why.
Formerly I too was young. I sweat.
I've always believed in manners, and to this day
I will defend them. They are a small part of the truth.

I have become fond of this class. Dressed and coiffed
and intellectually equipt like so many Kaspar
   Hausers,
they struggle into the Nürnberg of my Tuesdays,
taxing my powers of invention. Now they are asking
personal questions which do not bear
on youth, which have nothing to do with the subject,
youth. There's an atmosphere of guarded trust
in the room and I don't want to appear pedantic,
but after all, I am the instructor,
they sought me out. Or did I seek them out?
As they ask nosey, characteristic questions
I realize how interested I am in them
as young men and women, in their personal lives.
You can't study youth apart from the world
it has made, personally, out of the damnedest junk.

Nor are they as guileless as they pretend,
all raising their hands at once when I ask
who would like to explain age? Whoever I call on
will say something that sounds like his last respects.

I study them hard, but they will barely consent to leaf
through me, or their stereotype for me.
I wonder if I will ever be read again
after the present generation of teachers retires?
So I read excerpts to them. I read a passage
    about an old war.
It is curiously lacking in violence, (I shy
away from holocaust, just as they are obsessed with it)
but what I read is true and they are impressed.
How much better it sounds when I read it!
Perhaps it isn't really there on the page?
merely a trick of reading, a gift for explanation?

Meantime before the bell I remember to summarize.
(They won't do these things for themselves—
their notebooks are *graffiti,* though I still
ask that they be passed in at intervals.)
I summarize as impartially as I know how,
the essential differences, touched on this hour,
between youth and its opposite, age.

It is becoming clear in the biographies and letters that are appearing these days what an important role William played as a listener and editor during that period for poet friends such as Berryman, Lowell, and Robert Penn Warren. Berryman writes that since Jarrell's death, he can now count on only William for a careful reading of his work. Warren's correspondence is filled with grateful thanks for helping him modify his notion of his work. William's letters were long and quite detailed. The following letter is an example of the sort of nuts-and-bolts discussions they had over many years of hard-nosed friendship and professional honesty:

                              8 November, 1965
                              Ripton, Vermont
Dear Red,

I've been longer about this than surely you or I meant, but mostly because I have been in such admiration of your work as it unfolds. The things I have to say may not be right in particulars, but they arise from a conviction that the best of your poems deserve to be presented to best advantage. This has suggested a good many things, from a quibbling about punctuation on one page to a whole view of the structure of the book. I will save the last suggestion for the end, the one about structure, because I use it partly as a principle to throw you upon your own critical resources.

I think you agreed with me this summer when I said that I felt the most valuable selection of your poems would be the one that made the immediate impact, in effect the shortest compendium of your range and skill. On this basis, (I agree here,

With his sister, Kay, at the family's home in Darien, Connecticut, 1927

I think with your letter, too) the present manuscript is too long. Where I have proposed leaving poems, I've done so on the basis of my own taste which is all I've got but not necessarily yours or right. I'll try to say why, though.

I don't know how you will feel about some of the suggestions I make that seem to impugn the structure of the poems with many parts. If you regard the architecture of those poems as taking precedence over considerations of texture and tone, you will of course not see merit in my suggestion that *parts* be deleted. In *Tale of Time,* I feel that "Something is Going to Happen" is not up to the quality of the rest of "Delight." It seems to me less dense, the way the third section of "Between the Boxcars" is less dense, than the rest of its poem. These are poems I would seriously suggest you reconsider in terms of their total impact:

William's letter goes on for several pages of detailed commentary on twelve poems too long for inclusion here, but ends with more generalized criticism:

The poems at the back of the book should probably be cut back by perhaps as much as 20%, to take an arbitrary figure. I would suggest two grounds to eliminate some of them. There are several that seem to be somebody else's material or written in somebody else's voice. "History" and "Question and Answer" are Audenesque, I feel. "Love's Parable" is what, Ransomeesque? Wilburesque? Not honest Warren, in diction, although honest enough in insight. "Letter to a Friend" is undefinably weak, if only in the company in which it finds itself. The second section of "Mexico" is subject to the criticism of tone I've made about other poems: you are not

Ogden Nash nor was meant to be. "Variation: Ode to Fear" offends me less but offends me. I wish you could hear these two poems as I hear them.

Just two more points. I wish you would try to substitute something for the two lines on the first page of the book where the words fucking and fuck occur. I have no particular quarrel with the word as such but I don't feel the poem digests them and I think it makes a weak introduction to a brilliant poem used sensationally. (In "Dragon-Tree" the tone of "the Belgians sure fucked up" is quite wrong, utterly wrong, to my ear, but that's a mere flaw: in "What Happened" the *image*, the *verbal image*, strikes me as false. You reach for force, you get only violence uncontrolled in those two lines, I feel.) (And the ending of "Shoes in Rain Jungle," while I'm on this point, seems likewise flawed by a wise-cracking tone inadequate to the insight of the poem.)

Final point. If you had time, wanted to take the time, I would suggest that this book might declare itself better—tell you what poems displace others—if you arranged it chronologically except for the new ones. If *Tale of Time: New Poems* were followed by the other books chronologically, the selective process in dealing with *Selected Poems* ('23–'43) might be clearer: what was not yours would show up to you better than it could to me.

William's letter ends with some personal plans for a party to take place as well as the following caveat on Warren's work as a whole:

> I know I need not say deprecatory things about the vast impertinence of these remarks, singly or in battalion. At worst, they can only hint at the seriousness and honor I accord your poetry. Maybe you'd like me to explain or expand some of them, and I can do that, if you like.

Perhaps it isn't fair to look at what are essentially working papers, nor can I say offhand how much of this criticism found its way into Warren's work. But it is an interesting glimpse into the professional relationship between these two poets. Warren's letters to William about his work are equally frank.

Each summer William returned to teach at Bread Loaf, where he built a chalet-style vacation house. But he became more and more attached to his home in Connecticut. James Merrill, a friend going back to their teenage years, lived just across the river (the right side of the tracks, as it were, in Stonington Village), and William often saw other friends in the area, like Mackie Jarrell, Red Warren, Helen and Franklin Reeve, Richard Wilbur, Robert Lowell. He used his stepmother's apartment in New York to

In Hawaii, 1950

maintain his connection with social and cultural life there, particularly his love of the Opera Club. A memoir from that period recently appeared in his selected prose, *Poems Are Hard to Read*:

"In 1958, I invited Auden to a performance of Tchaikovsky's *Eugene Onegin*. I think this was the last time he went to the Metropolitan Opera, and he went reluctantly because of a growing list of grievances against Rudolph Bing, beginning with his production of *The Rake's Progress*. (It would be hard to imagine two men further apart in taste and style. Auden reported with approval the remark of Hofmannsthal's niece about Bing's production of Strauss's *Arabella*, in an English that made Hofmannsthal's elegant Viennese characters sound like the Bunker family, that 'nothing was wrong with it except the style.') (Who was the American industrialist who said, following the successful betrayal of his partners or employees, 'Nothing has been lost save honor'?)

"Anyhow, I wanted Auden to hear *Onegin*. To give Bing his due, it had never been performed at the Met before that 1957–58 season, and I thought it was a fine production. What I had not noticed was that between the many scenes requiring set changes, orchestral interludes had been composed to keep the audience in their seats. In the program it was reported that these had been 'suggested by Mr. Mitropoulos,' but I mistrust that because Dmitri Mitropoulos, who never conducted from a score, who once said that if he didn't know a work well enough to conduct it without a score he didn't know it well enough to have an opinion about it, pored continuously over the score as he conducted these 'musical interludes.' They consisted in rather obvious repetitions of what might be called the hit tunes of the opera, and Tchaikovsky was not a composer to let go of a melody before he'd got his money's worth out of it. The first of these ersatz pieces was loud and vulgar in a fairly ravishing way, and I was sitting there next to Wystan in the gold cave, letting it pour over me like expensive after-shave lotion, unaware of the force of critical rage that was generating beside me. At the noisy end of the piece there was huge applause—nothing that *easy* had happened to this audience in a long time and they were grateful. As the applause faded, a high British voice which I was proud and horrified to realize was my guest's voice—we were in the box of the Metropolitan Opera Club—was heard through the house calling 'Shame! Shame!'

"It did no good to explain afterwards (*Who* is Meredith's guest? echoed in the high-ceilinged club room during the intermission) that he was one of the librettists of *The Rake's Progress*. Mostly we didn't like modern opera. To a man we were too cowardly to call out our disapproval. And which of us would wear sneakers with his dinner-jacket?"

William's recognition in the poetry world grew with each new book, though he worked slowly and claimed to average about two to four poems a year. In 1964 he became a chancellor of the Academy of American Poets and was invited by Marie Bullock to be the sole poet on the board of directors for twenty-five years as well. In 1968 he became a member of the American Academy and Institute of Arts and Letters. He was given the Loines Award, numerous prizes from *Poetry*, and later a senior fellowship from the National Endowment of Arts and Letters.

When William first began to teach at the Bread Loaf Conference he befriended Robert Frost, whose work he greatly admired and whose influence can be seen in William's own work. He accompanied Frost on a cross-country trip to California in the early sixties and stopped off in Tucson to visit William's friends Stewart and Lee Udall. Stewart was about to become the secretary of the interior and asked William if Frost would go for the idea of reading at Kennedy's inauguration. William thought it a great idea and the friendship has deepened over the years.

He accompanied the Udalls on a rafting trip down the Colorado River one summer, which seemed a favorite pastime in the sixties. He dedicated a poem from that trip to the Udalls and later sent out a journal entry as his Christmas greeting:

> *At the Confluence of the Colorado*
> *and the Little Colorado*
> (for Stewart and Lee Udall)
>
> Where the two rivers come together—one cold,
> one desert-warm—the party beached the raft to
>   swim.
> A blue aileron, looking new, lay on the bank
> and Dennis put his shirt and bluejeans in it,
> out of the wind that had blown his hat away.
> Across the canyon, silver in the sun,
> the fuselage glinted. The wreck was ten years old,
> two liners that had come together in broad day,
> dropping their metal feathers,
> and two tribes of travellers who settled then
> where the wind told them to settle.
>
> To that lost Indian tribe, who farmed this dry
>   grandeur once,
> they might have seemed to be surrogates of gods
> (anything but gods, these downcast mortals,
> anything but wrathful, they fell bemused
> at various unfulfillments, at sheer bad luck)
> as they descended, shorn of all human gear
> and taking what they found: the shimmering desert
>   air,
> white water, the hot shale.
>   And the hectoring solitude
> that now made the rafters douse and romp and
>   chatter,
> a solitude that reverts to the subject of death
> whenever the conversation of live things lags.

And in June of 1968 William wrote in his journal:

"The moon came up late, because the sandstone bluff across the river rises perhaps 50 degrees from where I'd set my sleeping-bag. First the cliff behind me took moonlight, then I sat up to watch the canyon wall running NE above us take color. The reds emerged in the light of the full moon, the way I have occasionally seen autumn sumac and maple tell color by moonlight, or I suppose roses must do: I can't recall roses by moonlight though I must have seen them.

"Finally toward the top of the bluff the glow became brighter and at last, only 30 or 40 feet below the top, the moon put out a bright edge, making the dark edge of the bluff dance on the retina. In the course of a minute the full moon showed itself sideways, sharpening the rock profile of a 10- or 20-foot section cleared. How many million times has this night of the planet's tilt occurred before there was a viewer from this crevice in the sand?

"Later I woke and walked across the brilliant sand, past sleepers, to the edge of the bright rapids. Once there was a meteorite in the western notch where the Dipper was going away, lip-first. Then the moon was eaten by the opposite bluff, the one we slept under, having described a low southern arc, like the winter sun's. In the full moon, on my sleeping-bag, I had been able to see to write with this pen a little tetrameter sonnet."

In the Canyon

Under the massive cliffs which the moon,
miser of color, gives color to,
on moon-colored sand at the end of June
hearing the rapids we've hurtled through,
seeing at the base of the talus strand
off the further shore, the whitewater crest
in the frenzy of running water stands,
and Scorpio follows the Dipper west.

As a naval aviator during World War II, 1943

The troubles of cities do not recede
from the mind. Rather, they nag like guilt,
as sometimes when I drink and feed,
in my delicate gluttony I've felt
the spectral hunger of Asia bite
my gut and whet my appetite.

I have had the good fortune to be present for a number of awards that William has received for his work, particularly during his "Bulgarian" phase. When he served at the Library of Congress (1978–80)—now the poet laureateship of the country—William had two main priorities. He attempted to bring more black poets to the reading series, involving the local residents of the nation's capital and reaching out to the black community in the schools. He also was committed to inviting foreign poets from various corners of the world to the Library as well.

A very aggressive cultural attaché had introduced William to the beauty of his country's poetry and in one of the international evenings at the Library, he invited five poets from Bulgaria. The group included the partisan hero who had become the equivalent of vice president, Jeroge Jadgarov. In Bulgaria poetry had attained something of a golden period it seemed, with a wide popular audience and many talented poets writing everything from lyrics to surrealistic epics. The work was somehow apolitical, however, or at least seemed to attack relatively safe targets, such as fascism and the unwieldy bureaucracy. This was in the pre-*glasnost* period, of course, and the ambience was something like living in a novel by Kafka. The relatively noncontroversial nature of the poetry was at odds with the strident prosoviet line touted by its political leaders and revealed a more humane side to this obscure culture.

William came to like these burly poets quite a lot and beauties such as Blaga Dimitrova as well. The Bulgarians were grateful for the opportunity to read at the Library of Congress and the chance to develop an audience in America. William had opened a little window on the West, as it were, and in 1980 they expressed their gratitude by awarding him their highest honor, the International Vaptsarov Prize. Over the years he has traveled to Bulgaria seven or eight times to attend writers meetings and to keep in touch with a few particular friends, such as Kolyo Sevov, Bozhidar Bozhilov, Valentin Kostov, and Lyubomir Levchev, among others. Sometimes friends such as Maxine Kumin were also part of the American delegation. William never shied away from defending our system, but his larger concern has been how we function as members of the human tribe. If poets can't reach out to each other across the walls

*Robert Penn "Red" Warren, Eleanor Clark,
and William, Connecticut, late 1970s*

us transcend our spiritual provincialism and enter into the soul of another people. When William suffered his stroke in 1983 he had finished about twenty translations of Bulgarian poems and had begun to ask poet friends to try their hand as well for a project under the general editorship of John Balaban. There were still too few poems for a book, however, and I wrote to friends like Richard Wilbur, Maxine Kumin, and others for help. To a poet, they dropped what they were doing and helped us meet the deadline for an anthology called *Poets of Bulgaria*, published by Unicorn Press. It's an extraordinary group of translations and a tribute to the friendship of the poets who contributed. We have just received a grant from the Witter Bynner Foundation to publish a follow-up volume with Carnegie-Mellon University Press (working title *Window on the Black Sea*).

One of his own best poems came out of his experiences in Bulgaria and served as an introduction to *Poets of Bulgaria*:

Two Masks Unearthed in Bulgaria
(for Kolyo Sevov)

When God was learning to draw the human face
I think he may have made a few like these
that now look up at us through museum glass
a few miles north of where they slept
for six thousand years, a necropolis near Varna.
With golden staves and ornaments around them
they lay among human bodies but had none.
Gods themselves, or soldiers lost abroad—
we don't know who they are.

The gold buttons which are their curious eyes,
the old clay which is their wrinkled skin,
seem to have been worked by the same free hand
that drew Adam for the Jews about that time.
It is moving, that the eyes are still questioning
and no sadder than they are, time being what it is—
as though they saw nothing tragic in the faces
looking down through glass into theirs.
Only clay and gold, they seem to say,
passing through one condition on its way to the next.

our governments set up, there is little hope that any of us will learn to listen to each other. His journal has an entry dated 25 September 1980 which seems to be the rough draught of the type of official statement conferees were constantly being asked to formulate:

"I believe that the World Parliament of the Peoples for Peace will pass along to the International Conference of Writers at least one continuing challenge: namely, how hard it is to speak exactly, across the barriers of language and culture, of what is in our hearts. Everyone knows that the peace we talk about is more than its basic condition, the absence of war, just as truth is more than its basic condition, the absence of lies. This *something more* is what literature keeps alive in our imagination. Literature reminds us always of that great miracle, our common humanity. It gives us to do the beautiful and difficult work of keeping peace and telling the truth—tasks which only foolish people think will ever become easy."

William believed strongly in the importance of translation to reveal this common humanity, to help

Not everyone has been as generous about William's "Bulgarian Connection," however. One afternoon we were even visited by two beefy FBI agents who were very curious about our visits to the Bulgarian embassy. G-men in my own living room, just like a fifties movie!

I explained the cultural nature of our business and stated the following at the beginning to show just what an all-American boy William Meredith was: Born 1919, New York City. Father a successful stockbroker living in Darien, Connecticut. Mother a southern belle fond of raising cocker spaniels. Both deceased, and his only sibling, sister Kay, as well, an exquisite beauty who had made her life as a writer for the fashion industry in Manhattan.

In 1940 he became the third William Morris Meredith to graduate from Princeton and after a year as a copyboy for the *New York Times*, enlisted in the army. Six months later, he found a physician who overlooked his bad teeth and enlisted him in the navy officer training center in St. Louis to train as a naval aviator. Thirty-two night landings at sea. Later a passionate supporter of Adlai Stevenson and his dream for the United Nations, reenlisted to fight in Korea. Accidentally shot in the back, bullet bounced off the spine and came out the neck. Has written as well about war and death at sea as any writer in American literature. Look at his poem commemorating the loss of our Trident submarine in the sixties, "The Wreck of the Thresher," for example:

Visiting good friend and poet Lyubomir Levchev, Bulgaria, 1984

> *The Wreck of the Thresher*
> (lost at sea, April 10, 1963)
>
> I stand on the ledge where rock runs into the river
> As the night turns brackish with morning, and mourn
>   the drowned.
> Here the sea is diluted with river; I watch it slaver
> Like a dog curing of rabies. Its ravening over,
> Lickspittle ocean nuzzles the dry ground.
> (But the dream that woke me was worse than the sea's
>   grey
> Slip-slap; there are no such sounds by day.)
>
> This crushing of people is something we live with.
> Daily, by unaccountable whim
> Or caught up in some harebrained scheme of death,
> Tangled in cars, dropped from the sky, in flame,
> Men and women break the pledge of breath:
> And now under water, gone all jetsam and small
> In the pressure of oceans collected, a squad of brave
>   men in a hull.
>
> (Why can't our dreams be content with the terrible
>   facts?
> The only animal cursed with responsible sleep,
> We trace disaster always to our own acts.
> I met a monstrous self trapped in the black deep:
> *All these years*, he smiled, *I've drilled at sea*
> *For this crush of water*. Then he saved only me.)
>
> We invest ships with life. Look at a harbor
> At first light: with better grace than men
> In their movements the vessels run to their labors
> Working the fields that the tide has made green
>   again;
> Their beauty is womanly, they are named for ladies
>   and queens,
> Although by a wise superstition these are called
> After fish, the finned boats, silent and submarine.
> The crushing of any ship has always been held
> In dread, like a house burned or a great tree felled.
>
> I think of how sailors laugh, as if cold and wet
> And dark and lost were their private, funny derision
> And I can judge then what dark compression
> Astonishes them now, their sunken faces set
> Unsmiling, where the currents sluice to and fro
> And without humor, somewhere northeast of here
>   and below.
>
> (Sea-brothers, I lower to you the ingenuity of dreams,
> Strange lungs and bells to escape in; let me stay aboard
>   last—
> We amend our dreams in half-sleep. Then it seems
> Easy to talk to the severe dead and explain the past.
> Now they are saying, *Do not be ashamed to stay alive*,
> *You have dreamt nothing that we do not forgive*.
> And gentlier, *Study something deeper than yourselves*,
> *As, how the heart, when it turns diver, delves and saves*.)
>
> Whether we give assent to this or rage
> Is a question of temperament and does not matter.
> Some will has been done past our understanding,
> Past our guilt surely, equal to our fears.
> Dullards, we are set again to the cryptic blank page
> Where the sea schools us with terrible water.
> The noise of a boat breaking up and its men is in our
>   ears.
> The bottom here is too far down for our sounding;
> The ocean was salt before we crawled to tears.

William, Richard, and Mikey sailing the Svetlana *on the Thames River, Connecticut, 1989*

The G-men went on their way and didn't feel the need to bother us anymore.

In his twenty-eight years at Connecticut College, William became a greatly loved fixture in campus life. Year after year students responded to his intelligence, high standards, and empathy. He was very kind without ever slipping into sentimentality or patronizing students. These friendships remain vital to him. Some years ago the college awarded him an honorary doctorate, and one former student, Ellen Bettmann, presented him with a large, gold satin letter *A* on a ribbon, which she placed around his neck. An *A* from Mr. Meredith was one of her highest achievements and now she took the pleasure of returning that mark of confidence.

I've never been an energy snob particularly but when I remember all those years I commuted to Connecticut on weekends the thing I remember most about William was the energy that informed everything he put his hand to. He invariably rose at sunrise—regardless of the number of martinis from the previous night. He seemed as reverential as a high

priest serving Ra as he watched the sun rise, started life up again.

His patience with students seemed limitless, paying such careful attention year after year to their predictable concerns. Teaching sustained him, the way it does with great teachers. I think he'd have taught even if they didn't pay him for his work.

In the early years of our friendship we went to Portugal for the summer, a working holiday, where I was to finish writing a first novel and William wrote most of *Hazard, the Painter.* We each took our corner of the terrace in the morning sun and worked till it was time to go to the beach. It grew a little claustrophobic with only each other for company day after day. On a couple of occasions, because of such cabin fever, and fueled by too much vodka, we'd fight and have to establish the ground rules in the morning again, enabling two strong male egos to coexist. William always appreciates my comments on his work, but I was very goosey about criticism like most young writers. How I wish I'd have accepted his offer to help rewrite that first book before he had his stroke; it might not be collecting dust in a desk drawer now.

In 1989, however, W. W. Norton did publish my account of training for the New York City Marathon, called simply *Marathon* and the story of our life in the past years since William began his own marathon.

In 1982, shortly after a minor operation, he went into cardiac arrest and required an emergency aortic valve replacement and coronary bypass. For a year he did remarkably well, though he pushed himself with the same intensity as usual. In 1983, though, the night before he was to read at a centenary celebration of the Brooklyn Bridge, he sustained a major stroke, leaving him paralyzed on the right side and totally without speech or writing ability. His comprehension was unaffected, however. The irony of his situation was hard for friends to bear, as moving as his extraordinary effort toward recovery, during months of rehabilitation.

The temptation to run on in superlatives over his achievement is great. Friends who have witnessed his courage find it heartbreaking. But his response to life's challenge now is more than luck. I recall lines from *Hazard, the Painter*, which he wrote when he had his health:

Man and artist, he is working on his ways
so that when he becomes set in them
as old people must, for all that their souls
clap hands, for all that their spirits dance,
his ways will have grace, his pictures will have class.

I've known William Meredith long enough to know he is not a saint. There are things in his life he is not proud of, like any man. But I honestly think I've never met a more decent person in my life. I've been very lucky.

In the fall of 1990 we spent a month back at the Villa Serbelloni working on new projects. Upon our return, his new book, *Poems Are Hard to Read*, had just come out with the University of Michigan Press. The Academy of American Poets recently sponsored a tribute for William in New York, where many of his fellow poets read and spoke of his work, his life. The last poem in *Hazard, the Painter* might summarize where William is right now:

Winter: He Shapes Up

Now autumn has finished scolding
with sumac, sun and jays
his heavy-lidded ways,
his drinking and his balding.

Today the first snow fell.
It hung in the hollow air
making space tangible,
showing him how things are.

He watches the yellow larches
guttering on their boles
like half-extinguished torches
as the planet tilts and cools

and the laurel understory
that shields the hill from harm
—the merest rag of glory
will keep ambition warm.

Gnawed by a vision of rightness
that no one else seems to see,
what can a man do
but bear witness?

And what has he got to tell?
Only the shaped things he's seen—
a few things made by men,
a galaxy made well.

Though more of each day is dark,
though he's awkward at the job,
he squeezes paint from a tube.
Hazard is back at work.

BIBLIOGRAPHY

Poetry:

Love Letter from an Impossible Land, Yale University Press, 1944.

Ships and Other Figures, Princeton University Press, 1948.

The Open Sea and Other Poems, Knopf, 1958.

Winter Verse, privately printed, 1964.

The Wreck of the Thresher and Other Poems, Knopf, 1964.

Year End Accounts, privately printed, 1965.

Two Pages from a Colorado River Journal (includes the poem "In the Canyon"), privately printed, 1967.

Earth Walk: New and Selected Poems, Knopf, 1970.

Hazard, the Painter, Knopf, 1975.

Selected Poems, 1977 (audio recording), Watershed, 1977.

The Cheer, Knopf, 1980.

Partial Accounts: New and Selected Poems, Knopf, 1987.

Poems Are Hard to Read, University of Michigan Press, 1991.

Other:

(Librettist) *The Bottle Imp* (opera; music by Peter Whiton), produced in Wilton, Connecticut, 1958.

(Editor) *Shelley: Poems*, Dell, 1962.

(Translator) Guillaume Apollinaire, *Alcools: Poems, 1898–1913*, Doubleday, 1964.

(Editor) *University and College Poetry Prizes, 1960–66,* Academy of American Poets, 1966.

(Editor, with Mackie L. Jarrell) *Eighteenth Century Minor Poets,* Dell, 1968.

Reasons for Poetry & the Reason for Criticism, Library of Congress, 1982.

(Editor) Denise Levertov et al, *Poets of Bulgaria* (translated by John Balaban et al), Unicorn Press, 1985.

Contributor to numerous poetry periodicals. Opera critic for the *Hudson Review,* 1955–56.

Edouard Roditi

1910-

Edouard Roditi in his Paris apartment, 1986

In an interview granted in Toronto in October 1988 to Catherine Bush, Salman Rushdie described himself as a "migrant" rather than an "immigrant" writer because, as he explained, he faced "the problem of not having land to stand on. . . . Writers like Thomas Hardy, William Faulkner, or Eudora Welty, who are very, very rooted in a community and a place, and have that territory which they know is their territory, and simply go on and on mining it and it gives them more and more and more, those are the writers that I really envy."

Of myself, I might well say as much. As I now write these pages, I realize that I'll be eighty years old within a few months, perhaps even dead before the present account of my life gets into print and reaches

any readers. But I become confused when I try to remember what incidents or experiences, in all those kaleidoscopically varied and often busy years, might still deserve being recounted in detail. From what I remember of the past in my dreams, I realize indeed how little of my life that might still be of some historical or more strictly biographical significance has left much of a mark on my psyche. My dreams are composed mainly of distorted memories of past frustrations, and remain peopled above all with the ghosts of those whom I have loved or feared, in fact of men or women who might be of no interest at all to any of my readers. But the many famous writers, artists, or politicians whom I chanced to meet in a long, varied, and busy professional life, whether as a writer or as a conference interpreter, never haunt my dreams. Never do I dream of T. S. Eliot, James Joyce, Salvador Dali, or Marc Chagall, of Gromyko, John Foster Dulles, Konrad Adenauer, General De Gaulle, or Goering, but still fairly frequently of Hetty, who was my English nurse in my early childhood in France, or of some of the French domestic servants who were employed by my parents in our Paris home in my childhood and adolescence, or else of some of those whom I later loved between the age of twenty and the age of seventy. Often, I even awaken in my lonely bed with the vivid illusion that one or another of these loves, several of whom are now long dead, is still lying beside me.

Although I have at various times lived in France, England, Germany, the United States, or Morocco, none of these countries can I now claim, as a writer, as my own special "territory" in the sense that Salman Rushdie intended. In any case, although distorted versions of environments in which I have lived in France or England reappear in my dreams more frequently than any others, I would now experience considerable difficulty in describing any of these settings in truly realistic detail, I mean as Thomas Hardy, William Faulkner, or Eudora Welty describe their own real or fictional "territories." I have become an exile from every environment to which I have at any time been at all emotionally attached. Irremediably uprooted, I can remember each one of these environments only as it reappears, however-much disguised, in my dreams, and if I now chance to return to any of these environments which had once been so very familiar, I feel that I have become a stranger there, in fact that it has ceased to be in any sense my "territory." Only in an increasingly misty or confused past can I claim to have any "territory" of my own.

Night after night, my dreams offer me jumbled or distorted versions of episodes, settings, or persons regurgitated from various periods of my whole re-membered past, but always with some element of their dreamed setting, cast, or plot that I can later recognize as borrowed from my distant childhood or adolescence. From many of these dreams, I thus learn that I lost my own personal paradise at the age of nine, when I was sent away from my family's luxuri-ous Paris home to a boarding school in England. These dreams also reveal to me that more tenderness had been lavished on me throughout my childhood by Hetty, my English nurse, and by some of the French domestic servants employed by my parents, than by either of the latter, both of whom I had even learned to distrust or to fear. I remember my parents now as having nearly always been too busy to pay

much attention to me except, on most occasions, to find fault with my behavior or my appearance or to reprimand me.

Viewed from the lofty peak of my approaching eighties, my whole life reveals itself now in a curiously reversed perspective, like that of a painting by Giorgio de Chirico. Early memories of my most distant past acquire there, as in a psychoanalysis, far more importance than anything that I may have experienced in the last fifty years, busy and eventful as these may all have been in more professional or historical than personal or emotional terms. After reaching the age of thirty, one's emotional life can but rarely be as profoundly affected by new experi-ences as it had already been by the joys and disap-pointments of childhood. Even the bitterest frustra-tions or failures of one's adult love-life or professional career tend only to revive the latent and lasting pain of earlier emotional scars.

Nothing in my immediate family background appeared, throughout my childhood and adolescence, to predestine me to become a poet, least of all, perhaps, an American rather than an English or a French poet. Yet I was an American citizen, although born in Paris, from the moment of my birth, which was duly registered both at the American Consulate and with the French authorities, since both my parents were, at that time, American citizens. Neither of them, however, had ever yet lived in the United States. Born in Constantinople as an Italian citizen, my father came of a Romaniot-Sefardic Jewish family, had been educated in France, and had somehow become, together with his two older broth-ers, Albert and Victor, an American citizen through the naturalization of their father, David Roditi, which occurred about a hundred years ago in Boston while my grandfather's wife and three sons, as far as I can gather, were still living in Paris.

Through her marriage, my mother had also become an American citizen, likewise without having ever set foot on the soil of the United States. Of mixed French-Catholic and German-Jewish extrac-tion, she had become, before her marriage and through the naturalization of her father, a British subject, of which she remained so inordinately proud, although originally born in northern France, that she hastened to become British again in 1937, immediate-ly after my father's death. Of her French mother's family, which came from the region of Roubaix, Calais, and Boulogne in the north of France, I have never known more than a few photographs taken a hundred or more years ago by provincial photogra-phers.

Throughout my childhood and adolescence, my mother never ceased, I remember, to praise everything that was of British origin. Although we lived in France, world-famous for its gourmet foods, she remained one of the best customers of an expensive Paris grocery where she could purchase imported English potted meats rather than fresh French pâté, Stilton and Cheddar rather than French cheeses, and tins of English biscuits or candies rather than those of equally famous French brands. After World War I, my mother and a Baronne Cahen d'Anvers, who was somehow a member of the French Rothschild clan, were both known for a while in Paris society for their insistence on even purchasing their toilet paper in London, from Harrods rather than from any French store.

Soon after his marriage, which occurred in London in June 1907, my father abandoned his very successful career as an engineer on the board of the International Sleeping-Car Company in order to join his father's expanding export firm, D. Roditi and Sons, which had its headquarters in Paris and specialized in supplying American department stores with all their imports of European and Near-Eastern goods. This family firm already had offices, in 1914, in France, England, Switzerland, Belgium, Italy, and the German, Austro-Hungarian, and Ottoman Empires. After World War I, it opened offices also in the Far East, in China and Japan. My father's two older brothers, my uncles Albert and Victor, had already become partners in the firm before my father joined them in it.

Born in Paris on June 6, 1910, I have only a few vague memories of my early childhood, that is to say of the four years that preceded the outbreak of World War I in the summer of 1914. Harold, the eldest of my two younger brothers, was born in March 1913. Although I then ceased to be the only child and, as such, the cynosure of most of the household, I never felt, oddly enough, any sibling jealousy. Instead, it was Harold who, some three years later, began to resent my being older than he. Throughout the sixty years of his none-too-happy life, he tended at all times to treat me as if I were a younger brother who needed his guidance and protection. Perhaps I did. I was indeed a sickly and moody child, prone to frequent and mysterious fainting spells or losses of consciousness which often occurred in moments of stress, but were recognized as a mild form of epilepsy only when I was already fifty years of age. The invention of the electroencephalogram, still unknown in my childhood, had by then made it possible to detect that my left anterior temporal lobe had been slightly wounded, probably by the obstetrician's forceps at the time of my birth.

Of the first nine years of my life, my few memories are mainly of people, as I've already stated, who might be of little interest to readers of these pages, or else of places which I can recall quite vividly in my dreams, but which I might need far too many words to describe here in equally vivid detail. I can remember, however, two incidents which deserve to be related in the present context.

Because my father had originally been a railroad engineer he continued throughout his life to display, as a kind of hobby, a great interest in new types of railroad engines, new models of cars, and new planes. In the summer of 1914, a few weeks before the declaration of World War I, my family was vacationing in Hardelot, a beach resort on the coast of northern France, close to the Belgian frontier. One day, I was on the beach with my father and we were both watching a pilot repeatedly take off, fly a few hundred yards along the beach at low tide, then land again while he tested his plane in these brief flights. After once landing fairly close to us, he removed his goggles to wipe the perspiration off his brow and displayed his face. My father then recognized him as Blériot, the French pioneer aviator who, a couple of years earlier, had been the first to fly across the Channel to England. My father and Blériot then engaged in a friendly conversation about the construction of his plane and its engine. A few minutes later, I found myself strapped into the tiny cockpit next to Blériot as we took off together for a flight of a few hundred yards along the beach. Who else can now, in 1990, boast of having already been air-borne as early as 1914?

But I soon forgot this whole adventure when World War I was declared a few weeks later and the movements of French troops to the threatened Belgian frontier prevented my family's return from Hardelot to our Paris home. We hastily fled, together with a panicky crowd of other French and Belgian refugees, by ship from the port of Boulogne to England. I remember that we then spent some months in a "family hotel" in Hampstead, where I was one day horrified on being served a slice of underdone roast beef and blood-stained boiled potatoes.

Only some fifty years later was I suddenly reminded of my pioneer flight with Blériot when I happened to be visiting, together with one of my young nephews, the Musée des Arts et Métiers in Paris, where all great French inventions are preserved. There, in a former Gothic chapel that has long been abandoned and where pioneer railroad engines and automobiles are now displayed, Blériot's plane, in which he had flown across the Channel to England two years before I accompanied him on a short flight while he was testing a slightly improved model of it, now hangs like a huge dead moth or bat from the Gothic arches of the chapel's roof. Had I really been air-borne, as far back as 1914, in as weirdly primitive and as venerably fragile a vehicle?

Of those nine years that preceded my being sent, in the fall of 1919, into exile in an English boarding school, my only other memory that might still be of some historical significance is that of my brief encounter with, of all people, the great comedian Will Rogers. Soon after the United States had declared war on the German Empire and its allies, Will Rogers, who was then at the very height of his popularity, came to France to entertain the American troops. A friend of the owners of Hollywood's Broadway Department Store, whose Paris purchasing agent was my grandfather's firm, he had been told to contact my father in case of any need. One evening, he thus came as a guest to dine at our home, a huge and very luxurious apartment into which we had but recently moved from the much smaller one where I had been born seven years earlier on the same elegant tree-lined Avenue Henri Martin.

My brother Harold and I had somehow understood that our parents would be entertaining that evening a famous cowboy comedian, and he caught sight of us as we timidly peeped at him through an open doorway when we were both supposed to be already in bed. Very kindly, he gave my mother three tickets for both of us, accompanied by our English governess who by now had replaced my beloved nurse Hetty, to attend his afternoon performance in a Paris theater. Harold and I were both dazzled by his skill with his lasso that whirled around him as he talked, but neither of us understood much of his broadly Western patter.

Until I went to school in England, I had never had occasion to associate much with other children, least of all with boys of my own age and never, as far as I could remember, with any English boys. The circumstances of my peculiar family background—after all, throughout World War I, my mother still had, on her father's side, several close German relatives who were of military age, while my father likewise had relatives serving either in the enemy Turkish or Bulgarian armies—kept us from associating much with French families other than the few that my father had known before his marriage. Of these few families, all the men who were of my father's age were moreover serving in the French armed forces, so that my father's continued status as a civilian could

Portrait of Edouard Roditi, standing, and his two younger brothers, Harold and James, 1921, oil on canvas, by William Ablett

arouse some invidious comment. The two French families with which we nevertheless continued to associate most closely, from 1914 to 1919, had only daughters, no sons. At one point, I was sent, however, to attend day classes in a private French boys' school in our neighborhood, but fear of infection with the deadly "Spanish influenza" which suddenly began to rage in all Paris schools soon put an end to that.

Another circumstance which led to my lack of companions, whether girls or boys, during most of my childhood, was my ability to speak, already at the age of seven, French, English, and Spanish with equal fluency. But I was also of a very withdrawn nature, perhaps because of my epilepsy. Reading and practicing the piano in solitude were my favorite occupations. Never, at the age of nine, as far as I can remember, had I yet engaged in any competitive sport with other boys, nor can I remember ever having yet bounced a ball on my own in solitary play.

A child has little sense of chronology, so that one can later experience as an adult some difficulty in sorting out one's memories of earlier events in their proper historical order. I can thus remember that, at some time in the course of World War I, my mother left our home for a few days on a mysterious errand from which she returned in a particularly uncommunicative mood. Only many years later was the nature of this errand revealed to me, after her death, by a file of old family papers which then came into my hands.

When my mother was still a small child, I then learned, her mother had given birth to a still-born son and promptly interpreted this as a sign that Heaven disapproved of her marriage to a Jew. She soon became a religious maniac and had to be entrusted to the care of nuns in a convent in northern France, where she refused henceforth ever to see her husband or her daughter again. My mother was therefore brought up to believe that her own mother had died.

As the advancing German armies began in World War I to threaten the area of northern France where my maternal grandmother's retreat was located, the nuns to whose care she had been entrusted hurriedly decided to evacuate all their wards, whose surviving relatives were advised to remove them to safer places. As a former German citizen, my maternal grandfather couldn't, however, obtain permission to come from England to France for this purpose, and my mother was suddenly informed that her own mother was still alive. She now had to obtain a special permit, venture into the war zone, and bring the poor woman in these dramatic circumstances to a new retreat near Paris, where my grandmother died only a couple of years later.

Even before this traumatic experience, my mother had been spoiled, headstrong, and subject, whenever at all thwarted, to violent tantrums. Within the next few years, the frequence and violence of these tantrums increased until our whole household, including my father, soon feared to provoke them, and this certainly explains to some extent my father's failure ever to express much opposition to the disastrous decisions which began in 1919 to be taken concerning my education. But were they in the long run so very disastrous? I now realize that they have made me far more neurotic than I need ever have been, and have turned me in many ways into a freak, but perhaps after all into a talented freak.

Be that all as it may, suddenly in the course of the summer of 1919 I was informed that I was destined soon to be sent to a boarding school for boys in England. The prospect of no longer being free to enjoy my solitary reading or piano playing in peace and of finding myself, on the contrary, lost in a crowd of utterly alien English boys truly terrified me. As I have already suggested, I was by nature very withdrawn, in fact inordinately shy or timid, perhaps as a consequence of my epileptic disability.

I can still remember spending a couple of weeks in September with my mother in a luxurious London hotel. Day after day, I was introduced in turn to some of my mother's distant English relatives or girlhood friends, none of whom, however, paid much attention to me, except my maternal grandfather and a French-born Tante Hélène who appeared to disapprove of my being sent to school in England rather than in France. The widow of a German Jew who, like my maternal grandfather, had acquired British nationality, she felt that her two English-born children lacked many of the intellectual advantages that a French schooling would have granted them.

Much of our time was otherwise devoted to the purchase, in department stores of the city's West End, of the clothes and other items required according to a list supplied by the school. In the course of these errands, London's architecture, so much of which is neo-Gothic or otherwise very fanciful and relies to such an extent on brick rather than on stone, already appeared to my eyes, accustomed as these were to the more harmonious architectural sobriety of Paris, disconcertingly alien. Among the many purchases required by the school, two left me particularly perplexed: boxing gloves and football boots for playing soccer. Never had it yet occurred to me that I might someday find myself obliged to engage with other boys in any competitive sport.

I remember also being taken twice on a visit, in a hired chauffeur-driven Daimler, to visit the school before becoming one of its regular inmates. It was situated in Elstree, in a rather picturesque area north of London which was still quite rural, although it has by now become suburban and to a great extent industrialized. The academic year had already begun and the sight and sound of such a boisterous crowd of boys, as I saw them troop noisily into their huge dining-hall, left me quite disconcerted. Even the slangy English that I overheard them speak sounded almost meaningless to me, who had acquired my otherwise very fluent English in Paris from Hetty and my mother, and had but rarely heard English spoken by men or by any boys of my own age.

Throughout the first few weeks of my first term at Elstree School, I was far too intimidated by my environment to make any attempt at communication with other boys or with members of the faculty, or even to respond much to any of their attempts to communicate with me. The noisy promiscuity of the dormitory and of our weekly session in a bathroom fitted with several tubs, the stinking sand-toilets installed in a separate building on the far side of the yard where the boys played rowdily in the brief intermissions between their classes, the unappetizing food offered us in the huge refectory which then echoed with the din of our conversation and the clatter of crockery, all this appalled me. A few weeks later, when the colder and damper weather of an English winter set in, the lack of the kind of central heating to which I had been accustomed at home even during the war years soon led me to develop painful chilblains on my hands and feet. When those on some of my fingers burst so that they had to be bandaged, I was even deprived of the solace of my piano playing as an escape from all this harsh reality in the solitude of the music-room. Instead, I had to rely more and more on my reading and soon found myself able to handle, in addition to English, French, and Spanish, relatively easy classics in either Latin or ancient Greek, especially as, on account of my proficiency in both French and Spanish, I had been excused from all classes in these modern languages and was being offered individual tuition instead, by our Headmaster, in Latin and Greek in his personal and elegantly furnished study.

My losses of consciousness were meanwhile becoming more frequent and already causing the school's physician, a rather bluff country doctor who might have stepped out of a nineteenth-century English novel, some serious concern. He therefore excused me also from participating in any of the school's open-air sports. While all the other boys were now playing soccer on the school's cold and muddy football field to which they had access, on the other side of the former Roman road still known as Watling Street, by means of a subterranean passage which often stank, in particularly rainy weather, like a public lavatory, I was spending more and more time alone in the school library. There I very rapidly read all the available historical novels of Sir Walter Scott and of Harrison Ainsworth as well as some more recent and more blatantly patriotic British fiction by G. F. Henty.

Towards the beginning of December, the signs of my almost total withdrawal from any other activity became so obvious that the progress report on my studies stated at the end of my first term that I "began to hibernate as soon as the colder weather set in." When this weather improved with spring in the course of the following term, I emerged from my hibernation so that this too was noted in the progress report on my studies.

In the course of the intervening Christmas holidays, one of our French servants had caught me at home as I was about to make a childish attempt at suicide by swallowing the contents of a whole tube of aspirin tablets. Far from realizing that my misery in my English boarding school had inspired this act of folly, my mother explained to my father that I was "an impossible child" and that she could under no condition accept the responsibility of keeping me at home. She even suggested that I spend in the future all my holidays away from home, presumably somewhere in England. Fortunately, my father argued that this could be decided later. At the end of this first Christmas holiday, I thus returned sorrowfully to my boarding-school exile in England. Over seventy years later, I continue to be afflicted with an incurable horror of almost everything English except English literature and, perhaps, the best brands of orange marmalade. Both whisky and an English breakfast of eggs and bacon I detest, and many of my nightmares are still haunted by visions of the weirdly ornate Victorian architecture of London's Saint Pancras Station, where we took the special school-train to Elstree at the end of our holidays.

My memories of Elstree School remain nevertheless more pleasant in many respects than those of the years that I spent later, from the age of thirteen to that of sixteen, at Charterhouse, one of England's oldest and most exclusive so-called "public schools." Edward Lancelot Sanderson, the Headmaster of Elstree, was a handsome, mild-tempered, and gentlemanly Greek scholar, a passionate admirer of the novels of Dickens, and a close friend of Joseph Conrad, whom he had known when he was serving in the Royal Navy and who had already dedicated to him one of his most famous novels. Until shortly before his death, Conrad still visited him occasionally on Saturdays, if the weather was fine, and thus chanced to turn up unexpectedly at Elstree one Saturday afternoon when our Headmaster was already busy discussing some problems with the visiting parents of one of the boys. Because Mr. Sanderson knew that Conrad enjoyed speaking French, I was summoned from the music-room to keep the great writer company for a while. For about half an hour we thus walked and chatted together in the Headmaster's private garden, where Conrad tried in vain to remember the French names of some of the flowers of its luxurious herbaceous borders.

I was still too young to have yet read, at the age of eleven, any of Conrad's fiction or even to have heard that he was generally considered one of the greatest prose writers in the English language. As we now chatted pleasantly enough in French, I was completely unaware of how privileged I was to be thus spending a whole half-hour alone in his company. I remember him now as a charmingly amicable but rather sad and elderly gentleman who spoke

French very fluently, though with a slight foreign accent to which I was not yet accustomed, having never associated in Paris with any Poles, Russians, or Romanians. At one point in our conversation, Conrad suggested to me that, with my knowledge of English, French, and Spanish and my obvious facility in learning and handling several languages, I might later become a writer, or at least a translator. He was right.

In my fourth year at Elstree, when I was twelve years old, it was decided that I would have to compete in the annual examinations for an entrance scholarship to one of England's major public schools, since my parents had neglected to put my name on the waiting list for more regular admission to any of them. Although I was by far the school's best scholar in Latin, Greek, and mathematics, I was still known to be so withdrawn and timid that it was feared that I might fail, out of sheer nervousness, in such an entrance scholarship examination, conducted in an alien environment and among unknown boys, for admission to Eton, Harrow, or Winchester, the best and most exclusive of England's public schools. As a mere experiment, I was therefore sent to try my luck first in the entrance scholarship examination to Charterhouse, held in the buildings of the Old Charterhouse, in London's City, although the school itself had been removed in the latter part of the nineteenth century to Godalming, south of London in the county of Surrey.

To everyone's surprise, it was announced a few days later in the *Times* that I had been awarded Charterhouse's First Classical Entrance Scholarship, an honor which it would have been absurd to refuse in the mere hope of later obtaining an entrance scholarship to another school. On the wooden panels which list, on the walls of Elstree School's dining-hall, the names of its graduates who have honored it by gaining such entrance scholarships to other schools, my name can still be seen inscribed in gold letters, a privilege reserved only to those who have won, as I did, a First Entrance Scholarship.

The unhappiness of my first couple of years at Elstree had been somewhat mitigated by the frequent weekend visits of Tante Hélène or of my maternal grandfather, who took it in turn to come from London and treat me to a tasty lunch or tea in the Plough Inn, situated on the main village street of Elstree. There the Victorian furnishings and the hearty food soon began to remind me, when I became better acquainted with the writings of Dickens, of the travels of Mr. Pickwick and of Sam Weller. But both Tante Hélène and my grandfather Felix Waldheim died while I was still at Elstree. I had meanwhile managed, however, to emerge somewhat from the

cocoon of my timidity enough to strike up a few friendships with other boys, each one of whom, I now understand, was in his own way as oddly different from most of the other boys as I. The son of a distinguished and financially successful engineer, Bunny Rodgers was passionately interested in the school's modest theatricals. Later, he became known as one of London's most successful fashion experts when he remained for many years the stylist of Piccadilly's exclusive Fortnum and Mason store. In more intimate circles, he also enjoyed a reputation as, on occasion, a particularly elegant transvestite. My other close friend, Fane Agabeg, was a remarkably handsome, athletic, intelligent, and generous boy of Armenian or Parsee origin from India; after marrying successfully, he was killed during World War II in the Royal Air Force. By going from Elstree to Charterhouse I soon lost all contact with both these friends, each one of whom went from Elstree to another school, while no other boy from Elstree graduated the same year as I to Charterhouse.

Although I had become by now somewhat reconciled with my fate as an exile, during nine months of the year, from my home in France, I proved to be even more appalled by my first year at Charterhouse than I had previously been by my first year in the relatively more friendly and less impersonal environment of Elstree. Situated on a bleak hill and exposed there to the worst vagaries of the climate of southern England, Charterhouse had originally consisted of a small group of rather forbidding neo-Gothic buildings. These included three adjacent residence-halls, a chapel, a library, and a building of classrooms, to most of which one had access, in rainy weather, by means of a sheltered cloister. But the school had considerably expanded in recent decades and, by 1923, consisted of a total of some half-dozen residence-halls as well as of a number of other buildings, while a new and much larger chapel was already under construction. Often, if the weather was stormy, we now became drenched when we were required to wander from one of these newer buildings to the next.

Divided among these various residence-halls where they slept and took their meals, the students at Charterhouse were about ten times as numerous as at Elstree, so that I never managed to know them all at least by sight, as Aristotle recommends for the citizens of his ideal city-state. Because these students had all reached or passed the age of puberty, they tended to be more violent than at Elstree, and many of the older or stronger boys neglected no opportunity of persecuting or even manhandling those who were younger or weaker. Although at the age of thirteen I was still so little interested in sex that I remained unaware of the main physical difference between man and woman, this difference was forced within a few months on my attention by the obsessive interest that other boys displayed in it, and I soon became likewise aware of the practice of masturbation or of homosexuality among many of these. Near the little building where I still went from time to time to practice the works of Clementi on the piano, another small building contained a darkroom reserved for those whose hobby was photography, but it was also used as a conveniently secret haunt by some couples whose hobby appeared to be less innocent, as I discovered one day to my dismay when I was lured there in order to learn, as I was told, how to develop film.

But what shocked me even more at Charterhouse was the brutally feudal institution of "fagging," to which I found myself subjected throughout my first year as a resident of Verites. This was one of the school's oldest halls. Together with a chapel where we attended morning and evening Anglican services every Sunday, these were all built in the same forbidding late nineteenth-century neo-Gothic style and framed three sides of a huge lawn. A statue of Thomas Sutton, a prosperous City merchant and the founder of London's seventeenth-century Old Charterhouse, stood on this lawn, with his back to the school as he faced the bleak landscape ahead of him.

Rigid class distinctions existed traditionally in each house, as in most of England's other so-called "public schools." A privileged elite of boys who had already been admitted, on the basis of their scholastic achievement, to the school's upper classes took their meals in a smaller and slightly more comfortable dining-room where they were served by "fags." These unfortunates were younger boys, still in their first year at Charterhouse, who were also expected at certain hours to wait in the main dining-room until a loud roar, reverberating from the smaller one, announced that the services of a fag were required, to toast bread, shine shoes, or for some other menial task. If this task were not performed promptly or satisfactorily enough, a severe punishment, often a brutal beating, might ensue. Some of the older boys privileged to have recourse to the services of "fags" were still proving, in my time, to be quite sadistic, and there appeared to be no recourse against their whims. They also enjoyed a number of strictly respected vestimentary privileges, so that the whole school aped the character of a rigidly structured class society.

I probably owe the lifelong horror of Fascism that I developed as an adult to my first-year experiences as a "fag" at Charterhouse and to my humiliation when I was later reprimanded, as an upper-class student who could have recourse to the services of "fags," for being too familiar or too humane with them in the eyes of our house's head boy, Jim Vogel. He was a handsome and tyrannical New Zealander who had the physique of a Nazi SS officer and a passion for uniforms and rigorous discipline. Perhaps because of my obviously alien physical appearance, he had instinctively taken an immediate dislike to me.

Much of the time that I spent at Charterhouse I was ill. In the winter months, I continued to "hibernate" as I already had at Elstree, and my grades then justified but rarely my scholarship, but soon improved with the weather so as to satisfy the demands of my teachers, above all in the humanities and mathematics, but certainly not in chemistry. In our chemistry laboratory, I proved to be a veritable dunce, often causing disconcerting explosions over the Bunsen burners.

My tasks of toasting bread as a first-year "fag" over an open coal fire with a toasting-fork had moreover such disastrous effects on my chilblains that I abandoned my piano playing for good during my first winter, above all because my fingers never recovered their lost agility. For a while I then concentrated much of my attention on drawing and painting. In the school's studio, my main rival in displaying some slight creative ambition or original talent was the future cartoonist Osbert Lancaster. As a teenager, he was already an insufferable social snob and had the physical appearance of a character in a Gothic novel of the early nineteenth century. In his published memoirs, he later described me briefly and contemptuously as an "infant Dadaist." Far from yet being in those years at all a Dadaist or a Surrealist, I was still influenced in my own work to a great extent by Leon Bakst and other "World of Art" designers of sets and costumes for the ballets produced by Serge de Diaghilew. But Osbert Lancaster's tastes in art were still too provincial or insular to reach further back in the English past than the designs of Lovat Fraser for a recent London revival of Gay's *Beggar's Opera,* while also displaying an increasingly obsessive nostalgia for England's Regency period.

Repeated bouts of illness in a school which seemed in those years to be ravaged again and again by epidemics of influenza, chicken pox, or mumps that I but rarely managed to escape led my father at last to decide, on the advice of our family physician in Paris, that it was no longer advisable, at the end of my third year at Charterhouse, to send me back there for a fourth year. I had recently managed, in any case, to pass successfully and well ahead of schedule, that summer, my English School Certificate Examination, the equivalent of an American graduation from high school. This entitled me to admission to one of England's universities.

At long last I therefore found myself free to spend a few unbelievably happy months at home in Paris, where my slightly older first cousins Liliane and Georges began to share with me their interests in contemporary French art and literature. Although I repeatedly urged my father now to let me study art, he remained adamant in his refusal to allow me to enter any art school. In a frightening fit of rage, he even began one day to destroy some mildly Cubist watercolors which I had recently produced at home. To the very end of his days, when he died in London almost a pauper as a consequence of his own extravagance and improvidence of the decade of prosperity which immediately followed World War I, my father continued to believe that all artists except a few successful society portrait-painters must inevitably live and die in squalid poverty. It never occurred to him that Picasso, Matisse, or Braque, many of whose works which he despised but could have purchased between 1920 and 1930 for very modest prices, were destined within a few decades to die as multimillionaires.

Meanwhile my family's homes were still becoming increasingly luxurious. In addition to our huge Paris apartment, which was soon destined to be extensively and lavishly renovated, my father had acquired a delightful country residence, a small chateau built, like the one described by Jane Austen in *Northanger Abbey,* next to the picturesque ruins of a Romanesque rather than Gothic priory; also, in Le Touquet, a fashionable beach resort in northern France, a splendid villa where we could spend a month every summer. My father's final extravagance, before being ruined in 1929 by the Wall Street Crash which left him owing such vast sums to his bankers that he was forced to sell everything that he owned in order to repay them, had been the purchase, in Cannes on the French Riviera, of an elaborately ornate garden, with an oval mosaic-lined pool surrounded by a double colonnade of white marble, where he planned to build himself another home for his retirement.

For my further education and my whole future, my parents appeared meanwhile to have not yet formulated any definite plans. For close on a year, I was left to my own initiatives, most of which were innocent enough.

But my mother, it seems, still had other plans both for her own future and my father's as well as for mine. Throughout her life, she continued to be obsessed with the idea, presumably gathered from some nineteenth-century edition of a Karl Baedeker guide-book, that all of southern Europe was infested with fleas, so that she visited Cannes and the French Riviera with my father only briefly and always under protest, loudly proclaiming that she would never resign herself to retiring there in the lavish home which he was destined never to build for himself in Cannes. As for me, she appeared to have not yet abandoned her somewhat misguided ideas of schooling me somehow to become an artificial English gentleman of sorts.

On my return to London from a brief holiday in the New Forest home of a former school friend, I found my mother grimly awaiting me at the Berkeley Hotel with all my clothes and other personal belongings brought from Paris in several suitcases, ready to be shipped with me to Cheltenham, where I was now destined to reside in a small hotel while preparing, under private tuition, for admission by examination to Oxford University's Balliol College. I have never been able to find out how or why my parents first decided to send me to Elstree School rather than to any other English school, or later to Balliol rather than to any other college in Oxford or Cambridge. Their choice, in both cases, appears to have been entirely aleatory, based at best on random information and certainly on no systematic investigation. As for their choice of Mr. Weatherhead, my Cheltenham tutor and a distinguished retired teacher of Latin and Greek, he was recommended to them by the Headmaster of Elstree School, where he had taught for many years before his retirement.

As his only pupil, I enjoyed in Cheltenham the advantages of great personal freedom and, above all, of no longer being exposed to the odious proximity of other boys of my own age, nor being obliged to participate in any of their sports. Not that I was averse in any way to mere physical exercise. On the contrary, I had long enjoyed swimming or horseback riding on my own. But I was at all times too shy or withdrawn to enjoy, as my younger brother Harold did, any sport that was in any way competitive. As I now look back on my English school years, I realize too that, howevermuch I may have been exposed there to the unwelcome homosexual advances of other boys, I was never, it seems, at all sexually attracted to children or adolescents of either sex, so that I remained, at the age of sixteen, oddly innocent and free from sexual desires or preoccupations, in fact still lacking any overt interest in the main physical differences, other than those of mere dress or social status, between the two sexes.

In Cheltenham, I thus spent most of my spare time browsing in the town's second-hand bookstores, reading a great number of books of English poetry and fiction that I gradually acquired there, then already beginning, after some readings of Edith Sitwell, Sacheverell Sitwell, T. S. Eliot, and a few other contemporary English or American poets, to try my hand at writing some very imitative and immature poetry of my own. After first having been frustrated as a musician by no longer being able to play the piano on account of my chilblains, then also as a painter by not being allowed to study art in Paris, I thus fell back on literature as a medium of self-expression that requires a minimum of equipment and space, so that one can even, if necessary, practice the art of writing in secret.

A few months of preparation under the able and friendly tutoring of Professor Weatherhead, who even appeared to be encouraging my nascent literary aspirations, sufficed for him to pronounce me ready to face the test of Balliol College's notoriously formidable entrance examination. By that time, my quite serendipitous readings of Wyndham Lewis's rabid denunciations of James Joyce and Gertrude Stein in an issue of *The Enemy* had aroused my interest in their writings too and led me to acquire a couple of issues of *transition,* the expatriate avant-garde periodical to which they both contributed in Paris. The English essay which I wrote in Oxford as part of my examination for admission to Balliol thus proved to be an enthusiastic defense of the little that I had yet read of the writings of Joyce, Stein, and a few other English or American contributors to *transition.* Moments of almost total recall allowed me even to quote several sentences from the writings of Gertrude Stein and, if I remember right, a whole short lyric by Evan Shipman, one of Ernest Hemingway's expatriate friends whose name appears but rarely in any literary history of that "lost generation."

In spite of some violent attacks of asthma caused by the smog of the Thames Valley, I passed my examinations and was admitted to Balliol College, but then had to spend the next few months at home before I could "go up" to Oxford as a freshman at the beginning of the following academic year. Soon after my return to Paris, I began gradually to realize that I had, at least for the time being, lost all interest in classical Latin and Greek literatures and was becoming more and more passionately interested in contemporary French, English, or American literatures and art.

Within the next few months, I translated from French into English the *Anabase* of Saint-John Perse, without knowing that its translation rights had al-

ready been granted by its author and publisher to T. S. Eliot, who had by now completed the first draft of his translation. Sylvia Beach, to whom I showed my translation, passed it on to Eugene Jolas, the editor of *transition,* who expressed his willingness to publish parts of it, if he could obtain its author's and publisher's permission, which was never granted. To compensate my not being allowed to publish this translation, Sylvia Beach and James Joyce, whom I had met in her Shakespeare and Company bookstore, then suggested very kindly that I try my hand at translating a recent poem by their French friend Léon-Paul Fargue. As soon as I had completed my translation, it was passed on to Jolas, who agreed to publish it, together with one of my own poems, in the next issue of *transition.* Meanwhile Archibald MacLeish, who was spending a year in Paris and later became, in Washington, the official translator of Saint-John Perse when the latter was living there in exile, had sent a copy of my translation of *Anabase* to T. S. Eliot, with whom I thus began to correspond about our different interpretations of some of the poem's more ambiguous passages. Ultimately this correspondence and my various London meetings with Eliot led to his publication of a group of my poems in the *Criterion* in 1934.

Through Pierre Barbe, the fashionable French interior decorator to whom my parents had entrusted the elaborate renovation of our Paris apartment, I met the Egyptian-Jewish French-language writer Carlo Suares, whose apartment Barbe had recently renovated. Suares was then publishing *Cahiers de l'Etoile,* the official monthly publication of the Theosophist French followers of Krishnamurti, who always stayed in the home of Suares whenever he came to Paris. I had meanwhile read some book—was it already one of those of Martin Buber?—on Hassidism. On the occasion of one of Krishnamurti's Paris visits, he was expounding his doctrine to a small group of us whom Suares had invited. I was by far the youngest, but this didn't restrain me from provoking, with the Master, a discussion on the similarities and differences between his own doctrine and some of the doctrines of Hassidism. In a French translation, one of my English poems thus came to be published that year in *Cahiers de L'Etoile.* In the course of those few months spent in Paris, I had also become superficially acquainted with a number of young writers who were members of the dissident French Surrealist group known as *Le Grand Jeu,* among whom René Daumal is now the most widely known to American readers, and likewise acquainted with the older poet Oscar V. de L. Milosz, who was in those years the official diplomatic representative of the Republic of Lithuania in Paris.

By the time I entered Oxford University as an undergraduate in the fall of 1928 at the age of eighteen, I had already published two translations of known French poets and some original poetry of my own in *transition* as well as some original French poems of my own or French translations of my English-language poems in a couple of reputable French literary periodicals. In the eyes of all Oxford, I was a freak. John Betjeman, the future Poet Laureate, was still a student there. In his pictorial biography, published a few years after his death, the Socialist master of Balliol, Alexander Lindsay, is reported apocryphally to have told me that I was "the second Harold Acton and the third Oscar Wilde." In the doldrums of English intellectual and artistic life of the late twenties, any new literary or artistic movement such as Surrealism, which I represented at Oxford in my own naive way, was immediately interpreted as a revival of Oscar Wilde's "New Aestheticism" of some six decades earlier. It was nevertheless in this atmosphere that I wrote "The

Passport photograph, 1929

New Reality" as the first published English-language Surrealist manifesto, which appeared some months later, in June 1929, in the *Oxford Outlook,* when I was no longer a student at Oxford. Sixty years later, a doctoral dissertation on English Surrealism still quotes it and refers to me as its "brilliantly precocious" author.

My memories of my Oxford meetings with John Betjeman remain vague. He was on the editorial staff of the *Cherwell,* the student publication in which the Master of Balliol's above-quoted remark to me was first published. Betjeman may well have been its real author.

Other Oxford poets whom I met during my brief sojourn as a student at Balliol College were Stephen Spender, Louis MacNeice, Clere Parsons, and Bernard Spencer. Only with Clere Parsons and Bernard Spencer did I develop a close association. With Clere, who was two years older than I, this association lasted until his untimely death in 1931.

My studies in the Latin and Greek classics suffered from all my literary activities as well as from the very active social life in which my reputation as a freak or an "aesthete" involved me. My very charming tutor happened to be Roger Mynors, whom I discovered, many years later, to have been one of the oldest and closest friends of Cyril Connolly, who mentions his name often and always affectionately in *Enemies of Promise.* In his very tactful way, Roger Mynors refrained from ever insisting that I become a more disciplined student of the writings of Demosthenes or Theocritus, and attend my lectures on these venerable authors more regularly. He almost certainly felt that, as a nascent Surrealist poet from Paris, I was like a square peg in a round hole in my enforced exile at Oxford and as a student of the Latin and Greek classics.

As the fall weather deteriorated, Oxford's humid Thames Valley climate began to afflict me with increasingly serious spells of asthma, as a result of which I became addicted to drinking more and more frequent and generous doses of sherry as well as to smoking a rather expensive brand of imported cigarettes which, for a reason that was explained to me only many years later in Teheran, somehow made me breathe more easily: in those benighted days, their manufacturer was still allowed to spice them with a very small quantity of hashish, long known to have beneficial effects on certain kinds of asthma, but now officially struck, in our more enlightened age, from the official pharmacopoeia.

By the time I returned home for Christmas, my bad reputation and my unpaid liquor bills had somehow preceded me to Paris, and I was obviously in very bad health too. Our family physician even suspected that I might be afflicted with an incipient case of tuberculosis. I was therefore sent, a few weeks later, to an expensive nursing-home in Switzerland, where the great Austrian poet Rainer Maria Rilke had for a while been a patient a couple of years earlier before dying of tuberculosis. In spite of the reputation which I had so rapidly acquired at Oxford as some kind of new "aesthete" and, as such, presumably as a homosexual too, I spent the next few months in this Swiss clinic as the lover, in quick succession, of a number of attractive older women patients who may well have been succumbing to the well-known aphrodisiac side-effects of tuberculosis rather than to my personal charms. Such was the end of my brief Oxford career and of my ambitions, if any, as a classical scholar.

On my return a few months later to Paris, I found my parents more involved than ever in their postwar frenzy of conspicuous spending, which lasted throughout the summer of 1929 and until that fateful fall's Wall Street Crash. My father's plans for my future seemed, for the time being, to remain very vague, except that they certainly didn't include a literary career, although I was continuing to write both in English and in French and to publish some of my poetry from time to time in avant-garde French or expatriate American periodicals. I was also beginning to associate somewhat timidly with a few writers and artists who lived in older, more romantic, or more reputedly Bohemian Left Bank neighborhoods of Paris than the very elegantly plutocratic Right Bank area where I had been born and where my family still lived. On one such exploratory foray, I chanced to meet, in the Left Bank studio of an American painter, the poet Hart Crane, who was entrusted to my care for the rest of the evening because the painter, his host, had a previous engagement elsewhere. After we had dined together in a modest bistro, the poet, who was already embarrassingly drunk, insisted on dragging me to one of his haunts, which turned out to be a rather rough working-class homosexual bar and dance-hall on the rue de Lappe, near the Bastille. For the first time in my life I saw men dancing together there. At the bar, Hart Crane soon became involved in a none-too-friendly argument with a couple of French sailors and some toughs with whom they were drinking and for whom Crane refused to buy drinks, apparently intent on inviting only the two sailors. The argument threatened to become violent and I was so scared that I ignominiously fled, abandoning one of America's greatest twentieth-century poets to what might well have developed into a fist-fight of the kind

which, as I learned many years later from Crane's published biography, soon led that summer to his arrest, imprisonment, and subsequent expulsion from France as an undesirably troublesome alien.

Was it before or after this encounter with Hart Crane that I likewise met, that same summer, the great Spanish poet Federico García Lorca one evening in the Paris studio of the Spanish painter Gregorio Prieto, on whom I had called quite by chance, after recently meeting him in the art gallery where he was holding a show? Prieto then asked me to stay for dinner so as to meet a poet and painter friend who was in Paris only for a few days on his way from Spain to New York. Over a tasty paella that Prieto had prepared, García Lorca and I exerted immediately on each other an irresistible fascination. Lorca was eleven years older than I, but we looked so much alike that he might well have been my older brother, and our birthdays were but one day apart, so that we had actually been born under more or less the same stars, a fact that appeared to impress Lorca as very significant, especially as we were now meeting under the influence of the same sign of the zodiac, Gemini, early in June. Whereas I now remember my meeting with Hart Crane only as a curious anecdote, the night that I then spent with García Lorca may well have later left a lasting mark on my whole emotional life.

Although already published in a French translation with a small press by my friend Armand Guibert, to whom Lorca later dedicated one of his New York poems, he was still practically unknown as a poet, at the time of our brief meeting, beyond the linguistic frontiers of the Hispanic world. I had not yet read any of his work, but his physical appearance and his whole personality enchanted me. I never had occasion to meet him again, but the news of his murder, when I read it in 1936 in a London newspaper, affected me as if I had lost a close and dear friend.

For my future, my father limited his plans, for the time being, in the early summer of 1929, to having a young French accountant instruct me in our home in the relatively simple principles of commercial accounting, which I learned with ease. Later that summer, I went daily to my father's office, where I worked at first with his accountants, then with other employees in other departments. Whenever he saw me in the offices of D. Roditi and Sons, my first cousin Charles, who was already a junior partner in the firm, made such offensively patronizing remarks that I soon refrained from going to the office on those days when I knew that my father would be staying in our country home in Epernon instead of coming into the city, where I was now living alone, with only one servant, in our huge and deserted apartment.

Toward the end of the summer, some slightly less vague plans for my future began to be expressed by my father. A few weeks later in the fall, I indeed left for America, where I had never yet been, although an American citizen by birth. But I was given no specific travel plans or instructions concerning what I was expected to do or in what cities, nor concerning the planned length of my stay. I had a huge wardrobe trunk, full of the most elegant and expensive clothing for all possible occasions, including both a tuxedo and "tails" for evening wear, a cutaway coat for formal daytime ceremonies, a silk top hat, an opera hat, a grey derby to be worn while riding and a black derby for city-wear, and a veritable wealth of silk ties, a few of which I still own to this day. In addition, I was well supplied with funds, in the form of a letter of credit on an American bank for what was, in those halcyon days, a very considerable sum of money for a young man who had, in any case, so little experience of handling anything but an adolescent's weekly allowance of mere pocket money. Never had I yet had to pay, for instance, for a hotel room, nor had I ever traveled on my own.

Rather than from home in France, my parents sent me off from England, aboard the *Empress of Scotland*, and I landed in Quebec after sighting for the first time a whale in the broad estuary off the coast of Anticosti. My father had instructed me to stay at the Chateau Frontenac Hotel for a few days of sightseeing before proceeding to Montreal. To dine in the restaurant of such a luxury hotel, a man still wore a tuxedo in those days, even if he were alone, as I was on my first night there. While I dined in solitary state, I was greeted by an elegantly dressed woman who was likewise dining alone, at a table near mine. Later, over coffee in the lounge, she came over to greet me by name and admitted that she knew me by sight from Le Touquet, where she had likewise been vacationing, she explained, as the guest of a friend who owned a seaside summer home near my family's. She herself was the recently widowed wife of a young London banker.

Later that evening, I found myself already in bed with her. Two days later, she accompanied me to Montreal and, a month later, from there to Boston too. But our relationship soon began to deteriorate when she ran out of money and insisted on foisting onto me parts of her ample store of jewelry as pledges for all that she was borrowing from me. She was insanely jealous too, accusing me again and again of going to bed with anyone, woman or man, with whom I spent any time, whether socially or on business, on

my own. One morning in Montreal, she even insulted over the phone a friend of my parents in whose home I had dined on the previous evening. Finally, after a series of increasingly violent scenes, I left Boston in a panic for New York one day while she was having her hair fixed. I had paid our hotel bill, but left no forwarding address. I never saw her again, whether in America or later in Europe, and was never repaid all that I had loaned her, although I had scrupulously left her jewelry in the care of one of my father's New York friends, together with her signed receipts for my loans. Before collecting her valuables from this unfortunate man, she unloaded on him, over the phone, such a shower of anti-Semitic abuse that he soon understood with what kind of English "society lady" he was dealing.

After a stay of a few days in New York in the Park Avenue apartment of friends of my parents with whose daughter I had previously had a brief and innocent teenage love affair, I went for a weekend to the Traymore Hotel in Atlantic City. There I chanced to meet, at an auction-house on the boardwalk, an unknown young actress, Silvia Sidney, with whom, chaperoned by her mother, I then dined. The next day I was hastily summoned back to New York in order to return to Paris, where my father, I was informed, was seriously ill.

In exceptionally stormy weather, I traveled first-class aboard an almost deserted SS *Olympic*, taking all my meals in its luxurious a la carte Ritz-Carlton dining-room. I was treated there to almost unlimited servings of caviar that might otherwise go to waste, for lack of other diners. On my arrival in Paris, I then faced at home the first moments of a rude awakening from the Age of Improvidence in which I had been led, throughout my whole childhood and adolescence, to believe firmly that I was destined always to lead the privileged and carefree life of the very wealthy.

Very unwisely, amateurishly, and on an absurdly lavish scale, my father had been speculating "on margin" on Wall Street. With the recent Crash, he had now lost all his holdings in stock, sold overnight by his brokers in order to cover as best they could his indebtedness to them. But he still found himself owing them a very considerable unpaid balance on the original cost of his investments "on margin." In addition, many of his firm's American customers were already experiencing financial difficulties of their own and delaying payments on their imports of the previous summer. For several years, my father had moreover been constantly drawing on his personal account with his firm in order to pay the huge current expenses of his various homes and the extravagant renovation that our Paris apartment was still undergoing. Now the firm's bankers insisted that my father begin to repay what he had thus been drawing on future earnings which could no longer be expected to amount to what they had been in the few years of exceptional prosperity immediately preceding the Crash.

My father was in a panic and had taken to his bed. While administering to his more or less imaginary ills, my mother was already claiming, quite unreasonably, that only my cousin Charles, my father's junior partner in the family firm, was responsible for its present financial problems. He had indeed his share of responsibilities in these, but my mother continued during the next few years to press her absurd claims while also insisting that my father retire from the family firm at any cost. This he finally did after selling all his various assets, his homes, his art collections, and even most of our family silverware, in order to repay his debts to the firm.

Between the beginning of 1930 and the end of 1940, I sometimes found it difficult to make both ends meet, and I often felt profoundly humiliated by the fact that I could no longer associate on equal terms with many of my former friends who appeared to be still enjoying their privileges of before 1929. I've already admitted that I had always, since my childhood, tended to be shy and withdrawn. The humiliations that I now suffered soon began also to affect my emotional life, perhaps as a result of my recent and disastrous relationship in Quebec, Montreal, and Boston, in such a way that I no longer dared approach women as readily as in the past.

It never seems to have occurred to my father that any of his three sons might later benefit from a more formal education which would endow them with any specialized skills. From his own polyglot background as the child of Sefardic Jews from the Ottoman Empire, he displayed a great faith in the mere knowledge of languages, without such a knowledge necessarily implying a knowledge of their history and literature too. At the age of twenty, I was already fluent in both French and English and had a fairly good knowledge of Spanish. In my father's eyes, my knowledge of Latin and of ancient Greek could not possibly be of any practical use. Suddenly, he decided early in 1930 that I should now learn German too. At first, I was sent to work as an unsalaried "volunteer" in a Jewish-owned export firm in Frankfurt-am-Main, where I was expected to learn, in addition to some German, the intricacies of the manufacturing and the wholesale selling of leather goods, costume jewelry, and the kind of gift-shop merchandise known in German as *Galanteriewaren*.

Meanwhile I had already begun to display a surprising fluency in German, due mainly to my own initiative in reading whatever German literature I might already understand. At the same time, I was displaying an ever increasing lack of interest in the business of my employers. My father then decided a few months later to send me to work, likewise as a "volunteer," in a private banking firm in Hamburg. There I met for the first time those few members of my late maternal grandfather's family who were still living in what had been his native city, and I thus began to realize that, although originally baptized as a Roman Catholic in France soon after my birth, and later educated in Anglican schools, I had never been confirmed in either of these Christian Churches. It then occurred to me too that, although I had never had any religious education either as a Jew, I was still a Jew in the eyes of any anti-Semite. Of these, I soon began to sense increasingly the obstreperous presence even in Hamburg, the last of the Weimar Republic's major cities to yield a few years later to the pressures of National-Socialism.

In Hamburg, I continued to learn German with ease and soon became a friend of Herbert List, who had not yet embarked on his career as one of the truly great photographers of his generation. A scion of one of Hamburg's more patrician merchant families, Herbert was still but an amateur photographer. Only as a refugee from Nazi Germany did he become a professional a few years later in Paris, to some extent on my recommendation to a few French or American editors. In Hamburg, I also found myself involved in a love affair with a very enterprising young German woman. The former wife of two bankers and the mistress of a third, whom she visited over weekends from Berlin, she soon persuaded me to visit her likewise from time to time over weekends in Berlin, where she began to introduce me to a number of the German capital's writers and artists. Ultimately, I chanced to introduce her in turn to the young English Socialist journalist and future Member of Parliament Richard Crossman, whom I had known in Oxford and who was visiting me briefly in Hamburg. He later became, much to my surprise, her third husband, in a kind of brief Socialist honeymoon from the banking profession. After World War II, I suddenly met her again as a rather blowsy dirndl-wearing and faded blonde in Worpswede, a famous north-German artists' colony near Bremen. There she had become an artsy-craftsy ceramist and a close friend of the poet Rainer Maria Rilke's daughter.

The more permissive society of Herbert List and most of his friends of Hamburg's avant-garde with which I associated in my hours of freedom from my duties as a "volunteer" in the bank also allowed me to become increasingly aware of the fact that, in spite of my current affair with Erika, I was sexually attracted to men as much as, if not more than, to women. It was thus in Hamburg that I first felt free to have a few homosexual relationships of my own choice rather than by occasionally yielding, often with some embarrassment as at first in the case of Lorca, to the advances of another. Memories of my disastrous Canadian and American experience may moreover have already begun in Hamburg to determine more and more inevitably the real nature of my emotional life, although I still remained until 1934 too scared of its implications to allow myself to become involved in any truly passionate or profound relationship.

It was shortly before my return from Hamburg to Paris late in 1930 that I first heard, if I remember right, from Paul Bowles. In a postcard written to me from New York, he announced his intention of soon coming to Paris, where he hoped to meet me, having already read some of my work in *transition, Tambour,* and one or two other avant-garde periodicals. It now occurs to me that I may well have been the only person in Paris besides Gertrude Stein to whom Paul was thus announcing his forthcoming arrival.

Paul and I first met in Paris soon after my return from Hamburg, and this proved to be the occasion of the birth of our almost legendary friendship which has now lasted more than half a century. My first impressions of Paul were in a way similar to those traditionally attributed to Saint Gregory when, as Pope, he encountered in the slave market of Rome a couple of innocent-looking, handsome, and fair-haired young captives. When he enquired where they came from and was told they were Angles, he is said to have replied: *"Non Angli, sed angeli,"* after which he purchased and liberated these angels before sending to distant England the first mission to convert its inhabitants to Christianity.

Paul was only six months younger than I, but already proved to be in some respects, in spite of his angelic appearance, more mature and independent than I while displaying, in other respects, an almost surprising immaturity or childishness. Concerning his own background, he offered no information. Much of what I now know about it I gathered some four decades later from my reading of his published memoirs. He presented himself to me, in a sense, as a kind of "take it or leave it" proposition, without any explanations except that he planned to study musical

composition in Europe while also occasionally producing near-Surrealist poems, a few of which he actually published, and some equally near-Surrealist line-drawings which, I gather, have remained unknown to this day. From one of the letters that he wrote me while I was away from Paris, I understood that Gertrude Stein was already trying to bully him into writing prose.

I had already met in the homosexual bars of Hamburg a number of unemployed young working-class Germans who admitted their lack of any means of support. Never had I yet encountered, however, any young man of my own avant-garde intellectual environment who freely admitted, as Paul did in Paris, that he was receiving no financial aid from his family and was reduced to living on the kindness of whatever new friends he now made in this alien city. Unable to take Paul into my own family home because of the chaotic conditions in which my parents were struggling to cope with the disastrous consequences of the Wall Street Crash of two years earlier, I hastened to find for Paul another home among my Paris friends. For several months, he was thus able to live peacefully in the apartment of my friend Carlo Suares, the Egyptian-born French-language writer who was already expanding his interest in the Theosophy of Krishnamurti to include some contacts with the French Surrealists and ultimately an interest, a few years later, in the Jewish Cabbalah too. Suares soon reported to me that Paul seemed to enjoy playing with his children at their childish games, and that keeping Paul in their home was almost like having a kitten there. Paul slept on the living-room day-bed, never appeared to need much more than an occasional glass of milk, and somehow managed to scare up elsewhere enough pocket money to cope with whatever needs he might have in the city. Later, I managed to convince two other friends, an American literary agent and an Australian, to assume in turn the responsibility of looking after Paul. One of these he persuaded to take him on a trip to North Africa, where he had already once been, on Gertrude Stein's prompting, in the company of Aaron Copland. But this second trip, I gathered, soon ended with a none-too-friendly parting between Paul and his benefactor.

Was I in love with Paul? I doubt it, although he fascinated me in many ways and my concern over his well-being lasted a good two years, until his return to America. In a way, this kind of obsession with another's well-being still liberated me to great extent from worry over my own problems and future. Only in 1934 did I begin to be fully aware of the disastrous turn of events in my own life. As long as my parents continued somehow to live in one or another of their luxurious homes, I could maintain the illusion of being able to return to the lost paradise of my childhood.

But Paul also happened to be the first young American artist or intellectual of my own age with whom I chanced to become at all intimate. Through him I met Virgil Thomson, the painter Maurice Grosser, the poet Charles Henri Ford, and others who, in one way or another, helped me to emerge from the Slough of Despond where, especially between 1934 and 1937, I might all too easily have been tempted to let myself irretrievably sink.

I was in London in June 1931 when I attained my majority. Suddenly, I then realized why my parents had planned that I should be in London on that occasion rather than at home in Paris or elsewhere. My mother had arranged with an English lawyer that he should apply on my behalf, as soon as I attained my majority, for British nationality rather than French or American citizenship. Having been born in France of an American father and mother who had likewise been born in France, I indeed had the right to choose, on attaining my majority, between French and American citizenship, but no right to British nationality except perhaps on the basis of a residence of several years in England. To my mother and her lawyer, it appears never to have occurred that all my school years in England did not constitute legal residence: as a minor, I remained a legal resident of France, where my parents had continued to reside during all those years. My application for British nationality was therefore rejected. I have never been able to understand how a reputable English lawyer could have accepted to handle such a legally inadmissible application, unless he was either unwilling to argue about it with my mother, whose headstrong character he knew from previous dealings when she had consulted him about contesting some clauses of her late father's will, or else because he was at all times too irresponsibly anxious to collect fees from his clients. Had he been at all conscientious, he should certainly have advised my mother that my application lacked any adequate legal basis.

But I still had an American passport and the right, on now attaining my majority, to opt for French citizenship too. This would have required, however, my serving two years in the French army. My English education unfortunately failed to grant me the privilege of entering an officer's school, like the majority of young Frenchmen of my social background. Much as I had been scared some years earlier at the prospect of entering an English school

Edouard Roditi, 1931, ink on paper, by Yankel Adler. Courtesy of Grunwald Center for the Graphic Arts, University of California, Los Angeles.

and associating there with boys who seemed very alien to me, so was I now discouraged by the idea of soon finding myself associating with young Frenchmen with whom I knew that I would have very little in common. In order to retain my American citizenship, I therefore had to go through the legal procedure of officially repudiating my right to French citizenship, which I did that same year on the occasion of a brief return to Paris.

On my return to Paris, I found myself involved in my poor father's various schemes to solve his financial problems. On my mother's insistence, he had already decided to retire at any cost from his partnership with my cousin Charles in D. Roditi and Sons. With the end of Prohibition approaching in America under Roosevelt's presidency, he now hoped to establish himself as an exporter of European wines and liquors to the United States, but had neglected to investigate under what conditions the sale of wines and liquors had previously been licenced in America and was now likely to be again licenced. Nor had he yet enquired into the cost of warehousing imported wines and liquors as a wholesaler in America. In his plans in this field, he relied exclusively on his past experience as a supplier of the various other imports of department stores. In addition, he now failed to assure himself of the sole representation, for the United States, of any of the better-known French brands of wines or liquors.

Unwilling to quarrel with my father over his way of assuring himself supplies of wines and liquors from French sources, I returned briefly to Germany to assure us of the possible sole American representation of a few well-known brands of German wines, beers, or other liquors. Thanks to my contacts with German private banks, I soon proved to be fairly successful. Early in 1933, my father therefore sent me back to New York, together with a young Frenchman on whose initiatives he relied in another and even more ill-fated business scheme. Within a few days, this other project proved in New York to be totally impracticable, and my French companion returned promptly to Paris, leaving me alone to handle as best I could our projects as exporters of European wines and liquors.

In the course of these few weeks that I now spent in America early in 1934, I had occasion to meet for the first time some of New York's leading writers and artists. At a dinner in the home of an elderly couple who were friends of my parents, I met their niece, Ettie Stettheimer, the sister of the painter Florine and herself a novelist of some distinction under a pseudonym, Henrie Waste. Through the Black poet Countee Cullen, whom I had known through Sylvia Beach when he was in Paris as a Guggenheim Foundation Fellow, I also met most of the writers and artists of the group which is now famous as that of the Harlem Renaissance. The novelist Carl Van Vechten was the link between the Harlem Renaissance and the intellectual society of the three Stettheimer sisters and their very brilliant friends, among whom Max Ewing, an exceptionally gifted and witty young novelist, was a favorite. A veritable dandy of what is now known as the Gin Age, Max had the kind of satirical wit that might have led him to become an American Evelyn Waugh, but he died mysteriously soon after publishing his first novel, *Going Somewhere.*

In Paris I now found myself facing a situation such as I had never yet expected even in my most pessimistic moments. My parents were moving out of their luxurious apartment, unable to afford its rent any longer. My father still failed to realize that the cost of living in Epernon, his country home, and of its maintenance would be so much greater than the rent and maintenance of his Paris apartment that he might

soon find himself obliged to sell it as he did only two years later, hurriedly and at a huge loss.

The fiasco of my application for British nationality meanwhile convinced my father that my two younger brothers should now, over my mother's protests, attend French schools, if only to prepare them to face more readily than I the rigors of French military service should either of them decide, on his majority, to choose French rather than American citizenship. In any case, neither of them had yet visited the United States as I had twice, nor yet developed any American friendships, as I had with young American writers or artists such as Paul Bowles, Charles Henri Ford, Countee Cullen, Virgil Thomson, or Maurice Grosser.

My brother Harold was studying for admission to the French equivalent of the Harvard Business School, and Jimmy, the youngest of my two brothers, was attending a French boarding school in the country in Normandy. For Harold and me, my father rented and furnished a small duplex apartment that we shared, I must admit, with considerable tensions between us. Harold was anything but an intellectual, in fact very *macho* and extrovert, whereas I was becoming more and more withdrawn in my increasing sense of alienation from a social world to which I could no longer afford to belong as well as from the kind of world that I feared that I would henceforth have to face. Events in Nazi Germany and an obscure awareness of a latent threat of Fascism in France were leading me moreover to become painfully aware of all that might soon threaten me as a Jew in the eyes of most anti-Semites.

In London I had already begun as early as 1931 to develop an interest in the writings of Jewish poets, philosophers and mystics of the Middle Ages and the Renaissance. This led to my writing a few poems inspired to some extent by these readings. When I showed a few of these to the editors of the *Spectator* and the *Jewish Review,* they were immediately accepted and published. T. S. Eliot likewise encouraged me to continue writing in this vein and would have accepted one of the sections of my poem entitled *The Complaint of Jehudah Abravanel* had it not already been accepted for publication elsewhere. Few people realize that Eliot's increasingly devout Anglo-Catholicism now precluded his continuing to feel or express the somewhat supercilious anti-Semitism which had cropped up in a few of his earlier writings. After Hitler came to power, Eliot even admitted to me on several occasions the sheer horror that Nazi anti-Semitism inspired in him.

On my return from New York early in 1933, I already found a great number of German refugees in Paris and, among these, several of my Berlin friends, including Lotte Eisner, for whom I soon found a small apartment in the same building as the one that I was sharing with my brother. My Egyptian-Jewish friend Maxime Piha had been in Alexandria the editor of its lavishly published and illustrated *L'Illustration Juive,* to which I began before 1933 to contribute occasionally in French. In Paris, he was now editing *Cahiers Juifs* on a more polemical basis and in a more modest format, and he asked me to assist him in putting together a special issue of protest against Hitler's persecution of the Jews of Germany. My job consisted in finding, among the refugees who were already in Paris, authors capable of writing articles on the Jewish contribution to various fields of German political, economic, scientific, artistic, or literary life. Lotte Eisner, of course, contributed a well-documented article on the Jewish contribution to the German film industry in its heyday, and introduced me to several potential contributors.

But I now needed to earn a living in France and soon understood that this could not be achieved with occasional translations from German into French for *Cahiers Juifs* and other publications and with free-lance journalism in French weeklies to the editors of which my cousin Liliane's second husband, the French writer Paul Brach, was kind enough to recommend me. I needed a steady job, and for this I required, as an alien, a working permit. Unemployment was already beginning in France to threaten the economy, though not yet as seriously as in England, the United States, or Germany, and working permits were no longer as readily obtained as a few years earlier, when France had been glad to import labor. Fortunately, I was able to raise a small sum of money on my share of the capital of my maternal grandfather's estate, of which my mother enjoyed only the income. The French writer Léon Pierre-Quint inveigled me into investing this money in Editions du Sagittaire, the Paris publishing-firm of which he was the majority shareholder. Thanks to this investment, he obtained the necessary permit to employ me in the firm's offices, on a monthly salary which I soon discovered that it couldn't afford to pay me. But with this permit I could work part-time on a reduced salary for Editions du Sagittaire while also working part-time elsewhere. Another French writer friend, Jeanine Delpech, then found me a part-time job as a writer of French subtitles for Metro-Goldwyn-Mayer's American movies in their Paris offices, which were conveniently close to those of Editions du Sagittaire.

As a member of the latter's board, I developed closer ties with the French Surrealist movement, since we were the publishers of André Breton's *Surrealist Manifestos* as well as of most of the novels of René Crevel and two of those of Robert Desnos. When Léon Blum's Popular Front government later came to power in France, we also began to publish a number of books of Leftist political or economic theory and after 1937, when I was already in America at the University of Chicago, a French translation of one of the major works of Leon Trotsky.

Meanwhile my various literary or journalistic activities had somehow brought me to the attention of Alan Byre, the manager of the Paris offices of Metro-Goldwyn-Mayer. My most difficult tasks as a writer of French captions for their films had so far consisted in boiling the text of a French translation of Shakespeare's *Romeo and Juliet* down to the required number of letters for the captions of their version of this masterpiece in which Leslie Howard starred as Romeo, then also in devising sufficiently hilarious captions for *A Night at the Opera,* starring the Marx Brothers. One day, I found myself suddenly summoned to Alan Byre's office, where I was introduced to a dapper Jewish-looking gentleman who might have been in his late thirties and happened to be none other than Harpo Marx. He was visiting Paris for a few days and wished to meet some German refugees, mainly from the Berlin world of theater and movies. Metro-Goldwyn-Mayer would refund me the cost of an informal cocktail party that I might give at such short notice in my home for Harpo Marx to meet a few of my German refugee friends.

With the help of Lotte Eisner and the editorial staff of *Cahiers Juifs,* I managed to round up a good dozen German refugee writers, actors, and movie technicians of some repute, but none whose reputation was at all known to Harpo Marx, since most of the few whose names might have been familiar to him were already in Hollywood or in London. Besides, Harpo Marx could communicate with my guests only in English or else in Yiddish, which he fondly believed to be German. Several of my guests, including Lotte Eisner, were able, however, to communicate with him in English. One of my less fortunate guests in this respect was Zlatan Dudow, a Bulgarian film director who had produced in Berlin, in the last years of the Weimar Republic, a truly remarkable avant-garde movie with Bertolt Brecht. He had recently arrived in Paris with a movie of his own, all of it shot illegally in Nazi Germany and then smuggled out of the country. But Harpo Marx had never heard of Bertolt Brecht and appeared to be unimpressed by the sheer drama of producing a film illegally under a dictatorship and then smuggling it abroad.

One of my French guests was my friend André Ostier, who still owned a Paris bookstore but gradually became after 1945 a famous photographer. With him he brought an Egyptian, Baron Charles de Ménasce, whose cousin, Jean de Ménasce, had already translated and published some of T. S. Eliot's poems in French, and a remarkably handsome Austrian friend of theirs, who invited me to dine with him a few days later. I was far from yet realizing how fateful this invitation was destined to be in my life.

I had for some time been attracted to H., an exceptionally intelligent French heiress who shared many of my interests. I had even considered marrying her. But as the disastrous state of my father's fortunes became increasingly clear and my own future grew more and more problematic, I resigned myself to abandoning all hope of this marriage which, I realized, was less and less likely to meet with the approval of her parents, since my own means of support were still very precarious. Our love thus developed into a very tender friendship which has now lasted some six decades, but I was now left for the time being with a kind of despairing vacuum in my emotional life. Into this vacuum stepped F., the handsome Austrian whom I had just met and who, when we dined together a few days later, very deliberately, expertly, and successfully did his best to seduce me.

I was far from realizing that he was nearly twenty years older than I, already married and the father of a son who was but a year or two younger than I. He was a very successful portrait painter, the heir to an Austrian title and so well connected by birth and through his marriage that most of his models were members of Europe's remaining royal families or of an aristocracy which had not yet lost its hereditary wealth. All this I gradually discovered in the course of the first couple months of our tempestuous relationship which lasted a full two years. To him, in the course of the first year of our relationship, I dedicated those poems which I published privately, under the title *Poems for F.*, in a limited edition in Paris, with Editions du Sagittaire, early in 1934.

M y younger brother Harold's associations and activities had for some time been causing me more and more concern. In his insistence on always proving himself, above all in our father's eyes, more spectacularly virile and energetic than I, he had already, a few summers earlier in Le Touquet, participated rather recklessly in some amateur horse-races in the course of which he suffered a serious fall, though without any permanent injury. Now my

father allowed him in Paris the use of one of his cars, which Harold drove just as recklessly, even becoming involved in a couple of accidents. In the apartment that we shared, he and his shrill girlfriends often kept me awake well beyond midnight, and I was also becoming increasingly suspicious of his activities in the company of some of his rowdier co-students. In January 1934, I became aware of his participating, with some of these French companions, in riots against the French government on the occasion of what became known as the Stavisky Scandal.

In vain I warned my father of the dangers involved in my brother's political activities. He was not yet twenty-one years of age, so that he was technically still an American citizen like his parents. In addition, he was as much of Jewish origin as I, and the French political group, La Solidarite Francaise, in whose ranks he was rioting, was known to be Fascist and at least mildly anti-Semitic. My father paid no attention to my warnings, which he dismissed as absurd, and soon left with my mother, early in February, for London for a few days.

One of my London friends, the writer Derek Patmore, was then visiting Paris on business in which he asked me for some assistance. The great-grandson of the Victorian poet Coventry Patmore, Derek was the son of Bridget Patmore, who had been the companion of Richard Aldington after his divorce from the poet Hilda Doolittle. Derek's mother had thus become for a while a close friend in Paris of Ezra Pound, Ernest Hemingway, and other American expatriates. Although brought up in a strictly literary environment, poor Derek was not a very gifted writer, but earned his living as best he could as a contributor to women's magazines, an author of books on interior decoration, and on occasional windfalls such as the public-relations job which now brought him to Paris.

On the night of February 6, 1934, Derek and I were dining quietly together in a pleasant restaurant on a side street off the Champs Elysées when all Hell appeared to break loose not very far from there. Shots could be heard in the distance, the shrill sounds of police whistles fairly close by, then the stampeding too of apparently panicked crowds fleeing from the Champs Elysées into its side streets. The doors of the restaurant were hastily locked, its lights turned off, and none of us were allowed to leave until the streets might again be safe. When we were at last able to leave an hour later, I accompanied Derek back to his hotel, which happened to be in that neighborhood, but then had to walk all the way back to my apartment, which took me close on an hour. The subway had ceased running several hours ahead of schedule, and there were no cabs in the almost-deserted streets. Later that night, a phone call informed me that Harold was hospitalized with a serious spinal wound suffered in the riots against the government on the Place de la Concorde. I phoned my parents in their London hotel. They returned the next day to Paris. In the course of the next two years, my brother underwent several operations in Paris, then also in Berlin, but remained paraplegic until his death, which occurred four decades later in New York.

Harold's hospitalization had immediate repercussions on my own life, which became within the next few months increasingly chaotic when I had to move out of the small apartment that I had shared with him so that our parents might live there in order to be closer to him. He remained hospitalized in Paris for several months before he could be moved to Epernon, where our parents resided in the country since giving up, a year earlier, their luxurious Paris apartment. For the time being, I moved into a hotel room that I shared for a while with F. in Montparnasse, then into a cheaper hotel near Saint-Germain-des-Prés when F. abandoned me, presumably to return to his wife and children but, I soon discovered, to move later to London, where I found him in 1936 living with another man in Chelsea.

Léon Blum's Popular Front government had come to power in France and was pursuing both at home and in its foreign relations a cautiously anti-Fascist policy. But I was nevertheless becoming increasingly distrustful of Europe's immediate political future. In 1935, I attended in Paris the First International Conference for the Defence of Culture. It was dominated by Communist delegates and fellow travelers. André Malraux was particularly vocal among the latter. Only Robert Musil had the sense and courage to point out in his speech that traditional European culture was as threatened by Communist totalitarianism as by that of the Fascists. A few of his listeners hissed him, while most of the others paid no attention to his warnings.

My activities at Editions du Sagittaire also tended to confuse me intellectually while discouraging me as much as any of Europe's political developments. I had originally joined the firm because of my enthusiasm for Surrealist literature and art, since Editions du Sagittaire were well known as the publishers of André Breton's *Surrealist Manifestos* as well as of the novels of two major French Surrealist writers, Robert Desnos and René Crevel. But Breton's authoritarian and dogmatic leadership of the Surrealist movement was now causing serious political dissensions within it, first

when he insisted that all the Surrealists follow him in joining the French Communist party, then barely a year later when he insisted that those who had followed him by becoming members of the Communist party should now follow him again in his adoption of Trotskyism as opposed to Stalinism. We thus found ourselves still publishing Crevel, who had joined the Communist party and remained faithful to it until he committed suicide, partly as a consequence of his quarrel with Breton, in 1935, and at the same time continuing to publish Breton.

Nothing could be decided in our publications policy without the approval of Léon Pierre-Quint, who was both the firm's majority shareholder and the chairman of its board. But it was becoming increasingly difficult to obtain his approval for the publication of anything of real literary interest. A manuscript by an unknown writer happened one day to be submitted to us and was given first to me to read. I then sent an enthusiastic report of my reading of it to Pierre-Quint, who glanced through it, ridiculed my enthusiasm, and rejected it. The book was Louis-Ferdinand Céline's *Voyage au Bout de la Nuit,* which became a best-seller when another Paris firm, Editions Denoel et Steele, published it a year later. It had previously been rejected by no less than ten French publishers, but it is worth noting that the two readers who had found it worthy of publication, Bernard Steele and myself, both happened to be Americans. In the eyes of most other readers for Paris publishers, it was, I presume, too much unlike anything written by any French writer since Jules Valles or Pierre Darien, two turn-of-the-century anarchists who were in those days forgotten but are now both recognized as classics.

To cover the firm's expenses, we were reduced to a meagre diet of occasional vanity publications of novels or of slim volumes of poems, such as my own English *Poems for F.* and a couple of volumes by Gilbert Mauge, the literary pseudonym of the Duchesse de la Rochefoucauld, a feminist imitator of the poetry of Paul Valéry. With the advent of Léon Blum's Popular Front government, we began also to publish a few books explaining some of its economic programs, mainly in the field of agriculture. All this activity, including reprints of a couple of the firm's earlier successes, barely managed to cover our annual overheads. Not only was I becoming less and less interested, especially after poor Crevel's suicide, in the firm's literary activities, but I was also beginning to realize that it offered me no real future as a publisher. Only some years later in New York did I understand that the firm's decline had been mainly due to Pierre-Quint's drug addiction, which led him to become increasingly withdrawn and incapable of adopting any timely decision in the firm's management.

One of the members of our board was a close friend of André Breton, who was divorced from his first wife and, now married again, was expecting soon to become a father. Whereas his first wife came of a relatively wealthy family, his second wife appeared to have no means of her own, so that Breton was desperate for some immediate financial assistance. At one of our board meetings, it was suggested that we offer him a contract and a sizable advance on a new book. But none of his previous publications with our firm would have justified the kind of advance that he needed. All sorts of suggestions were made by various members of our board and rejected by Breton, or made by him and rejected by our board, until I came up with a proposal that proved to be acceptable both to Breton and to our board. This was for an *Anthologie de l'Humour Noir,* an anthology of macabre humor which it then took Breton close on four years to compile, after which it was ultimately published in

The author, New York City, 1946, "before going as interpreter to War Crimes Trial in Nuremberg"

Marseilles, where Editions du Sagittaire had sought refuge as a Jewish firm in 1940 from German-occupied Paris. Even there, the book was promptly banned as subversive by Marshall Pétain's government, so that Breton soon emigrated in a panic to the United States, while most of the other French Surrealists became courageously active in the French Resistance to the German Occupation Forces and the French Fascists.

My own writing consisted, between 1933 and 1936 when I finally left Paris, at first for London and then in 1937 from there for the University of Chicago, mainly in a great deal of journalism in French for such weekly periodicals as *Marianne, 1934,* Marthe Hanau's notorious *Ecoutez-moi,* and *Voilà,* in addition to the previously mentioned translations from English or German into French and the two previously mentioned books written in French, but both destined to remain unpublished: my novel and *Le Tour de Paris en quatre-vingts jours,* which I wrote in collaboration with Andre Ostier. After writing *Poems for F.* in 1933, the only poetry that I wrote in English until my return to London in 1936 was "Destiny of Israel," originally conceived as the text for an oratorio, the music for which was to be composed by the refugee composer Josef Kosma, who had distinguished himself in Berlin as the author of the music for Bertolt Brecht's only film, *Kuhle Wampe.*

I happened not to be the author, however, of the most sensational article that was published in French under my name. I had known for some years an expatriate American journalist, Sylvia Lion, who wrote features for the *Boulevardier,* a kind of expatriate Paris version of the *New Yorker.* When the *Boulevardier* folded up, poor Sylvia found herself deprived of her only source of income and came to me in desperation for advice. She had written in English a fairly scandalous but mainly true story of the Princes and Princesses Mdivani, all of whom had managed, as penniless Russian exiles whose Georgian titles were even contested, to make very wealthy marriages. I translated it into French and submitted it, under the title *Etalons Or,* which can mean both "Gold Standards" and "Gold Stallions," to a French friend who was editor of *Voilà,* where it immediately went to press erroneously under my name.

All Hell then went loose while two of the most prominent members of the Mdivani family, Barbara Hutton's former husband and the second wife of the Spanish painter José Maria Sert, managed to rouse even the old Catholic poet Paul Claudel, a former French ambassador to Washington, to intervene on their behalf in prosecuting *Voilà* and me. But Sylvia, the real culprit, had meanwhile fled to New York. Without compromising her, I was able to prove, from her manuscript which was not in my own handwriting, that I was only the translator of this article whose real author had been paid by *Voilà* anonymously and in cash.

Who were my closest literary friends in those last years spent in Paris before my deciding to leave Europe for America? Apart from a few French friends such as André Ostier, my cousin Liliane and her husband the writer Paul Brach, Maxime Piha, who edited *Cahiers Juifs* to which I occasionally contributed, the Surrealist poet Georgette Camille, who was destined never to write another poem in all the fifty or more years that she lived after 1940, the film critic Lotte Eisner, and a few other refugee German writers, the young Greek Surrealist Nicolas Calamaris was probably my closest friend. He too was writing a novel in French, but with such atrocious spelling and grammar that I had to correct every page of it, only to learn later in New York that he had never finished or published it. As Nicolas Calas, he then made a fairly successful career in America as an avant-garde art critic. In Paris, I met through him a young Surrealist artist, Brion Gysin, who many years later became in Tangier and Paris a cult figure in the Beat circle of the admirers of William Burroughs. Brion was a man of great charm who wasted most of his real talent, whether as painter or as writer, in endless and often fruitless experiments, each one of which proved in time to be a nine days' wonder, generally as soon forgotten as it had been readily conceived.

My father's obviously declining health already caused me considerable anxiety when I first saw him in his new English home in the course of my brief 1935 visit. A few months later, I therefore sublet my Paris apartment to a friend and moved to London without yet knowing whether I would later travel directly from there to America or return first for a while to Paris.

The few months that I spent in London between the spring of 1936 and the early fall of 1937 were certainly the unhappiest of my whole life. Very soon I became aware of the precariously speculative nature of my father's and my brother Harold's various business ventures. While awaiting the loan which I had requested, I could expect no financial assistance from my family and relied most of the time on the generosity of a few friends who could house me in their home. For several months, I also managed to be employed illegally, without a working permit as an alien, as scriptwriter for British International Films in

the Elstree studios. My task there consisted in attempting to adapt, as an English screenplay, the story of a successful German musical of which they had acquired only the libretto rights, without obtaining rights to the music too. As a circus story, this libretto was so trite that I was well aware of the impossibility of ever turning it into an acceptable English moviescript unless a composer were commissioned to put it to good new music, now that its successful original music had been sold separately to one of the big Hollywood producers. A whole procession of experienced English scriptwriters was later employed at considerable expense in order to salvage, each one in turn, my original translation and adaptation of this dreary libretto before the whole project was finally abandoned.

My father's health was meanwhile deteriorating very rapidly after a brutal extraction of all his teeth, undertaken by an expensive English dentist in whose skills my mother had developed utter confidence, ever since 1919, rather than in those of any of his Paris colleagues. As a result of this surgery, my father developed what appeared to be an irreversible blood-infection which, I now suspect, may well have been a form of leukemia. For several months, he managed to survive only on regular blood transfusions.

Meanwhile other projects for less dreary jobs in the British movie industry never materialized or materialized only later, when I was already in America. The most interesting such project was proposed to me by Gabriel Pascal, a colorful Hungarian-born refugee producer from Berlin who planned to adapt several of Bernard Shaw's more popular plays as movies. He still lacked, however, the necessary financial backing and was meanwhile so destitute that I often had to pay for his marketing and cook meals for him and myself in his office towards the end of my stay in London. But soon after my departure for America, Pascal finally obtained the necessary financing for his production of Shaw's *Pygmalion,* which proved, of course, to be a success. Would I have later made a more profitable career as a screenwriter, had I stayed in London and worked with Pascal on his production of *Pygmalion?* His knowledge of English was still so deficient that he relied to a great extent on me throughout the day as his assistant in almost everything that he undertook, although it sometimes required all my ingenuity to understand his heavily Hungarian-accented German which he often peppered, when we were alone, with abstruse slang, ribald anecdotes, and boastful references to his own virility. He indeed had the physical appearance and manner of a Viennese pimp who might have drifted to the capital of the former Habsburg Empire from one of its more distant Balkan provinces such as the Banat.

In spite of my barely profitable or quite unprofitable occupations in England's chaotic film industry, I was still managing to write a few new poems, most of which were later published as "European Imitations and Inventions" in New York by New Directions in 1949 in my *Poems 1928–1948*. A few of these poems, as well as a number of book reviews, I published meanwhile in London in the *Spectator*, that most venerable weekly which had survived ever since the eighteenth century. If I remember right, I was also occasionally meeting that year in London the poet Dylan Thomas, who had just published his first collection of poems with The Parton Press.

Dylan and I first met quite by chance late one night a couple of years earlier in a crowded Soho cafe where I was seated alone at a table, busily reading a book of poems. A rather sickly young man suddenly asked me whether he might sit at my table and I assented to his request. A few minutes later, he asked me what I was reading, expressed disapproval of my choice of poets, and informed me that he was a poet. I replied that I too was a poet, but had been asked to review this book, which was no choice of my own. When I mentioned my name, he admitted that he had read some of my work in *transition* or elsewhere. I had not yet read any of his, since Dylan had never yet published any poetry in any but local Welsh publications. We agreed to meet a few days later, after which I recommended Dylan for publication in the *Adelphi* to its editor, Sir Richard Rees. The *Adelphi* was thus the first London periodical to accept any of Dylan's poetry, though not the first to publish him, since it was a monthly and Dylan, on the strength of this first acceptance, then submitted a poem to *Time and Tide,* which was a weekly and immediately published it.

Much later, I met Dylan again several times in New York in the company of the poet Oscar Williams and his painter-poet wife Jean Derwood, who painted Dylan's portrait as well as Yvan Goll's and mine in a kind of triptych of poets' portraits. In the fall of 1946, I met Dylan for the last time in London, when we spent an evening together as James Laughlin's guests. Although we were never close friends, Dylan always behaved as if he counted me as one of his very oldest literary friends, which I most probably was.

In addition to my existing psychological and financial problems, two deaths which occurred while I was waiting in London to be able to move to America combined to make me increasingly aware of the fact that the happier world of my childhood and adolescence was now lost beyond recall. A phone-call from Paris suddenly informed me that my cousin Liliane

had committed suicide and, in April 1937, my father died on the eve of his attaining the age of sixty. For me, both these deaths proved to be traumatic experiences. I then realized for the first time that ever since the age of sixteen I had really experienced for Liliane, who had some literary and artistic talent and with whom I had a great deal physically and psychologically in common, an oddly narcissistic love, at all times repressed because she was my first cousin and some eight years older than I. My father's death proved to be a traumatic experience in other respects: after several months of blood transfusions to which he was being subjected every few days, he suffered a hemorrhage of the brain which left him, during the last few days of his life, capable of speaking and understanding only the language of his early childhood, the Judeo-Spanish which he spoke with his mother in his early years in Constantinople or Paris. I was the only member of his environment capable of understanding him or being understood by him, so that I had to remain two whole days and nights by his deathbed, leaving only when, from time to time, he asked for a *mohallebi,* a Turkish rice-pudding which I hastily went to purchase from the nearest Cypriot restaurant.

As best I could, I refrained, during my remaining months in England, from unnecessarily fruitless arguments with my mother and Harold about how best to handle my poor father's few remaining business interests. Early in September, I thus sailed for New York with far too much baggage while still leaving my library, furniture, and art objects in my Paris apartment, for the time being. From New York, I then proceeded a few days later by train to Chicago.

I now realize why I had decided to settle in Chicago, a city where I had never yet been, rather than in Boston or New York. Not only did the University of Chicago offer me the means of obtaining my B.A. more rapidly than any other college or university that I had approached, but above all I felt too profoundly humiliated by the prospect of encountering, in New York or Boston, friends and acquaintances who had known me in my years of apparent prosperity and to whom I would now need to explain my very real poverty.

In Chicago, I indeed had only one friend, as far as I could remember: Edna Horn Mandel, the very charming divorced wife of the son of a couple whom my parents had known as owners of one of the city's better-known department stores. Soon after her divorce, Edna had spent a year in Paris, where she witnessed the rapid decline in my family's fortunes and already proved to be a very understanding and loyal friend. During the next two years in Chicago, she entertained me regularly in her home and introduced me there to a number of her friends, several of whom later proved to be in one way or another of great assistance, above all Lionel Blitzsten, one of America's pioneer psychoanalysts. He helped me indeed to find a suitable analyst when, two years later, I moved to Berkeley and, as a result of anxiety and stress, began to suffer more frequent epileptic seizures than ever before in my whole life.

To the University of Chicago I also owe a great debt of gratitude, not only for the excellent tuition that was dispensed to me there under the presidency of Robert Hutchins, but also for several friendships of many years that I made there as a student. Among these friends, Professor Giuseppe Antonio Borgese later married one of the daughters of Thomas Mann and developed in me, as his assistant in the university's Department of Italian, my lasting interest in Italian literature of the Middle Ages and the Renaissance. Paul Goodman was still but a graduate student there but likewise remained until his death one of my dearest and closest literary friends, and Dean Richard P. McKeon, whose courses in philosophy I had no occasion to follow, later guided me very ably by correspondence in most of my readings in philosophy, so that his influence as an Aristotelian can still be detected in my occasional essays on such philosophers as Spinoza, Lev Shestov, or Martin Buber.

At the end of my first year, I graduated in Romance Languages with honors and a Phi Beta Kappa and decided to continue my studies at the University of Chicago for a second year on scholarships, hoping soon to obtain a Ph.D. without stopping on the way for an M.A. During my first year, I had already found myself less preoccupied by non-literary personal problems and thus began to write short lyrical poems more often, and to publish a few of these, together with occasional book reviews, in *Poetry: A Magazine of Verse.* George Dillon was in those years its very charming and able editor. A minor poet of some distinction, he was unfortunately no modernist and remains perhaps unjustly forgotten. It was also in the course of my first year in Chicago that I contacted James Laughlin in New York and initiated my relationship with New Directions as publishers and my friendship with James, which has now lasted over half a century. The few poems that I wrote in Chicago were later published by New Directions as the first few of the "American Imitations and Inventions" in my *Poems 1928–1948.* To my Chicago discussions with Paul Goodman on the poetics of Plato, Aristotle, and Kant, I owe the distinction

between Imitations and Inventions which characterizes much of my poetry of the past six decades.

With the assistance of George Dillon, Jean Garrigue, Paul Goodman, Stephen Stepanchev, and I founded in 1937 the University of Chicago's Poetry Society. It used to meet one evening a week in the Graduate Lounge, which housed Harriet Monroe's personal library of poetry, inherited by the university. Our activities never met with the approval of Professor Ronald Crane and his cantankerous assistant, the poet Elder Olson, author of *The Cock of Dawn,* a deservedly forgotten volume of pretentious poems. When the university's annual Poetry Prize was due to be awarded towards the end of the 1937 academic year, Professor Crane and his assistant decided that none of the poetry submitted deserved a prize. Four poets who in later years were published with some success—Jean Garrigue, Isaac Rosenfeld, Mat Rosenthal, and Steve Stepanchev—and I, had submitted poems for this prize. My own poem has meanwhile been published and republished three times in volumes of my poetry in the United States as well as in an American anthology of twentieth-century poetry by Jewish authors, and has also been translated and published in French, German, Italian, and Spanish. Poor Elder Olson has never been granted such recognition.

I was making such progress in my studies that I had good reason to hope that I might already pass the preliminary examinations towards a doctorate by the end of my second year at the University of Chicago if I also attended summer school there two years running. But these plans were upset by my mother, first in the course of the summer of 1939.

Soon after my father's death, my mother resumed in London her British nationality, which she had lost by marrying an American. James, my youngest brother, and my sister Ellen were still minors and thereby became British too, though with the option of claiming American citizenship on attaining their majority. In London, my mother meanwhile embarked on a very foolish business project which, if only because of her lack of any business experience, proved disastrous within a few months. In a panic, she suddenly sent my sister to join me in Chicago in the summer of 1938, but with a British passport and no means for her support. Fortunately one of my friends obtained for her, on the basis of her fluent knowledge of French, a scholarship at Rockford College, where I could visit her from Chicago without much trouble or expense, so that I managed to solve this problem for the time being while already applying in Washington at the Department of State for the American citizenship which was ultimately granted to her three years

First Spiritualist Apparition of Madame Verdurin ("*actually, a caricature of Jean Cocteau in drag*"), ink on paper, by Edouard Roditi.

later, when she reached the age of twenty-one. This premature application made on her behalf allowed her meanwhile to stay in the United States on an indefinitely prolonged visitor's visa.

But my mother then turned up in New York and a couple of weeks later in Chicago too in the summer of 1939, with such a medley of inane business projects and financial problems in which she involved me by cashing bad checks in London through my account with a local bank that I very soon found myself unable to face the additional strain of final preparation for my proposed preliminary examinations towards a doctorate in Romance languages and literatures. Fortunately, I had in any case applied for a teaching assistantship for the following year at the University of California in Berkeley, just in case anything might delay my graduate studies, which were perhaps over-ambitious. My being granted this providential teaching assistantship at Berkeley allowed me to escape

from my mother, while leaving her and my sister to fend for themselves in New York, where my mother soon returned after withdrawing my unfortunate sister from Rockford. My sister had made friends there and would certainly have been happier as a sophomore at Rockford than in New York in the increasingly hectic immediate environment of my mother.

The stress that I was feeling as a result of the constant demands made on me by my mother led me, in my last few weeks in Chicago, to experience more frequent losses of consciousness or seizures than ever in the past. One of these occurred in the home of my friend Edna Horn Mandel, when my mother suddenly interrupted an otherwise pleasant farewell party in my honor by phoning to make further hysterical demands on me. Edna immediately informed our friend Lionel Blitzsten of the circumstances which appeared to have caused my loss of consciousness, and Lionel insisted that I consult one of his psychoanalyst colleagues in San Francisco as soon as possible.

While undergoing what turned out to be a fairly successful analysis, although interrupted several times and conducted later by other analysts in New York and in Paris, I still suffered several more such seizures in the first few months of my studies at Berkeley. These were nevertheless proving to be as fruitful as my studies at the University of Chicago. Two of my new professors were particularly encouraging: Haakon Chevalier, a specialist in contemporary French literature, and Ernst Kantorowicz, a truly remarkable medieval historian who, before emigrating from Nazi Germany, had been a close associate of the great German poet Stefan George.

Although I never shared Haakon's incurable and in many ways almost adolescent faith in Communism, a number of circumstances led us to remain friends until his death, which occurred in Paris nearly fifty years later. I was a frequent guest at Berkeley in his home, where I met Oppenheimer on several occasions and, from their conversation and that of a number of their closer friends, soon became fully aware of their common involvement in Communist or fellow-traveler activities. Haakon even tried to involve me in some of these, but this led to our first ideological disagreement at the time of Soviet Russia's invasion of Finland. Haakon and his friends then asked me to join them in some pro-Soviet and anti-Finnish protest, which I refused to do. After that, I very soon dropped out of a Californian organization of Leftist writers which Haakon had recently persuaded me to join. In Los Angeles, this organization was running a periodical in which I published a pro-Loyalist poem inspired by an incident reported from the Spanish Civil War. Many years later, my very innocent association with Haakon and my publication of this poem were among the causes that led to my troubles as a victim for a long while of the FBI's fumbling investigations.

I was meanwhile becoming increasingly distrustful both of my mother's apparently irresponsible activities in New York and of my brother Harold's feverish speculations, of which occasional reports were reaching me by mail from England. On the one hand, I determined to assume the responsibility of supporting my young sister, if necessary, as soon as I might afford it; on the other hand, I did my best to discourage Harold from becoming involved in further ventures, and even sought legal advice about measures which I might take in order to protect him, as a paraplegic, from the consequences of his less felicitous initiatives. But it appeared that I could dispose of no legal means, as his older brother, to protect him. Less than three years later, he was imprisoned for his debts and bankruptcy in wartime England as an undesirable alien who could no longer be deported to German-occupied France, of which he was still a citizen.

The German invasion of Poland in 1939 and the declaration of what later became World War II made me even more despondent. I then began writing my longest poem, "Cassandra's Dream," which some readers still consider my best in spite of its many hidden references to my readings, some of which, I must admit, were truly obscure. Its title is thus borrowed from the *Alexandra* of Lycophron, perhaps the most difficult and cryptic of all the poets of ancient Greece. In Lycophron's *Alexandra,* a messenger repeats to King Priam the ravings of Cassandra who, in a trance, has predicted the whole future Trojan War. Some passages in my poem also refer, among other sources, to my readings of Homer, of the medieval French *Roman de Troie,* of Dante, of Shakespeare's *King Lear,* and of the philosophy of John Scotus Eriugena, who proposed that God can be defined only by negation, that is to say by listing all that is known that God is not. Like God, the future, I suggest in my poem, can be defined only be negation, since it can never be exactly like anything that we have already experienced in the past or the present. Unlike Eliot or Pound, however, I refrained in "Cassandra's Dream" from quoting any of these sources directly, but always assimilated them, as Milton and others had always done before me, into my own poetic idiom, whatever this idiom may well be worth.

Nobody would now believe that I was able to live in Berkeley on a teaching assistantship which paid me

only fifty-five dollars a month. I can no longer remember how I came, in the course of that year, to correspond with Clarence Decker, the very young, enterprising, and ambitious President of the University of Kansas City, now the Kansas City campus of the University of Missouri. Suddenly he offered me a job to teach French and Spanish there for a salary of nine hundred dollars per year. I accepted it immediately as this would allow me to support my sister in Kansas City instead of leaving her in my mother's care in New York. I was so poor that I could only pay for the shipment of my belongings from Berkeley to Kansas City while I managed to hitchhike there as best I could. In Cheyenne, I somehow attracted the attention of three cowboys in a bar where I had stopped for a cool drink. One of them suddenly asked me where I came from. When I said that my original home had been Paris, they were so impressed that they took care of me over that whole weekend.

In Kansas City I managed to rent a one-room furnished studio apartment where my sister joined me a few days later from New York. For that whole academic year, we lived together in one room. I slept in the "Murphy" bed, which was raised by day to disappear in a closet, while she slept on the couch. After a while, she managed to earn small sums of money on her own as a tennis coach in a girls' school or by tutoring a few students in French conversation. I soon managed also to obtain a slight raise in my salary by agreeing to teach a first-year night-class in Portuguese, mainly to employees of local businesses which were dealing with Brazilian firms.

My memories of Kansas City remain, on the whole, very pleasant in spite of the many problems which I still had to face there, especially after the German occupation of Paris in 1940. I then found myself overwhelmed with requests from former Paris friends for assistance in obtaining visas to emigrate as refugees to the United States. On one occasion, I was able to return for a few days to Chicago to visit old friends. On a brief visit to Washington University in Saint Louis too, I first became acquainted with the poets Clark Mills and William Jay Smith, with whom I had been corresponding, mainly about a project for a book of translations of selected works of the French poet Yvan Goll, whom I had known in Paris and who was already a refugee in New York. My friendship with William Jay Smith has now lasted half a century. Still practically unknown in America, the great Hungarian composer Béla Bartók gave a concert one evening at the University of Kansas City. At a reception in his honor in the home of Clarence Decker and his wife, Bartók later sat at the piano and very modestly enchanted us all with an enthusiastic performance of selected works of Mozart rather than any works of his own.

The painter Thomas Hart Benton dominated the artistic life of Kansas City and was proving in those years to be a most generous sponsor of all refugee European artists or intellectuals who happened to drift to that whole area of Middle America. Often I now regret that we somehow failed, perhaps because I was still too shy and withdrawn, to remain as close friends as we might have become. Although already recognized as a master of American Regionalist art, Benton remained devoted to the work of those Cubist masters whose works had inspired him to develop in Paris his own very personal sense of sculptural volume in everything that he depicted, and he very gladly discussed with me, on several occasions, his memories of the time he had spent as an art student in the French capital.

I spent the beginning of the summer vacation in New York in the home of Edna Horn Mandel's brother, the poet Edward Horn, whose booklet of *Poems for Small Apartments* I had persuaded the press of the ill-fated James A. Decker, who later died under such mysterious circumstances, to publish in Prairie City, Illinois. At a party in Edward Horn's apartment, I first met the poet Oscar Williams and his wife: they were enticing every one of the other guests in turn into another room to panhandle us all by explaining that they were both starving poets. At the same party, I also met someone who knew Colonel William Donovan, who was then organizing for President Roosevelt what later became the Office of War Information and also the Office of Strategic Services. Impressed by my knowledge of European languages, he recommended me there to Edd Johnson, a former United Press journalist, for a job. I was promptly asked to work as a multilingual shortwave radio-program monitor in a listening post where one summarized and recorded the programs of European stations. The salary offered me was more than double what I was being paid by the University of Kansas City, so I resigned from there and decided at once to accept this offer and move to New York.

There I would at least be able to resume my psychoanalysis, which I had interrupted by moving from San Francisco back to the Middle West. Little did I realize that, by becoming a civil servant of the federal government, I was signing a Faustian pact whereby I sold my soul to the Devil and would henceforth, for the duration of my employment by the government and for several years after that too, find myself constantly the object of the often weirdly misguided attentions of the Federal Bureau of Investigation.

Some thirty years later, I finally obtained from the Department of Justice several pages of Xeroxes of my FBI file. Over half of their contents had been blacked out as still "secret," while much of the rest was purely malicious nonsense, even confusing me sometimes with other members of my family and attributing to me, for instance, some of the French Fascist associations of my brother Harold or my Parisian cousin Georges and some of the less reputable business activities of my cousin Charles. Nowhere in all these pages did I find a single reference to any of my own activities as a writer, publisher, or editor. Everything there appeared indeed to have been compiled by busy illiterates.

When I first became a member, in the early fall of 1941, of the skeleton staff of Colonel Donovan's New York office on Madison Avenue and East Forty-first Street, he was President Roosevelt's newly appointed Coordinator of Information, whose future responsibilities and activities were still very vague. Soon after the Japanese attack on Pearl Harbor forced us a few months later to become belligerents, Colonel Donovan's office was divided into two separate units: the Office of War Information, where I continued to be employed in New York under Elmer Davies, and the Office of Strategic Services, which remained headed by Colonel Donovan mainly in Washington and which some years later spawned the CIA. During the four years of my employment in the offices of the Coordinator of Information and then the Office of War Information, I never set eyes, as far as I was aware, either on Colonel Donovan or on Elmer Davies. My immediate supervisors were, in turn, Edd Johnson, a tough, mildly alcoholic, very authoritarian, and overtly Leftist former news reporter with United Press, then Leonard Carlton, a former local New York radio commentator and the son of the once mildly notorious leader of one of New York's many turn-of-the-century Lower East Side Socialist splinter groups, and ultimately, last but not least, Pierre Lazareff, former editor of the most widely read daily newspaper in prewar Paris and a refugee in New York since the German occupation of the French capital.

As early as the summer of 1941, it was clear that the United States, even if it might still avoid becoming overtly a belligerent, could not remain strictly neutral in its political sympathies and would inevitably find itself committed sooner or later to some kind of wartime activity in favor of Great Britain rather than of Nazi Germany and its allies. Part of even such a relatively peaceful activity would consist, of course, in official propaganda intended to explain and justify it. But the United States still had no experience at all in this field. News of American activities, whether official or unofficial, was traditionally reported or explained to the rest of the world by privately owned and commercial agencies and publications or shortwave radio stations. One of the primary duties of the newly established Office of the Coordinator of Information therefore consisted in studying the official propaganda devices of the belligerent nations and, to some extent too, of those few neutral powers, such as Franco's Spain, which likewise had recourse to such propaganda activities. On the basis of this preliminary study, the United States planned to undertake, if and when necessary, its own official propaganda activities.

Because of my fluency in a number of foreign languages, I was at first employed as a monitor in the CBS listening post on Madison Avenue, since the United States government still operated no such posts of its own. My duties there consisted in listening to foreign shortwave news broadcasts while at the same time recording them and also summarizing them in English on a typewriter. Any news item in my summary that was considered important was then translated word for word from my recording and transmitted both to the CBS news desk for possible use in domestic programs and to our own offices in New York and Washington. To the truly acrobatic skills that I thus acquired as a monitor translating foreign-language shortwave broadcasts on the spur of the moment I owe the ability as a multilingual conference interpreter which allowed me later to earn most of the time, from 1945 until 1985, an easier living than many other American poets of my generation.

After a while and as a consequence of a tiff which occurred between me and Edd Johnson in one of his more drunken, authoritarian, or overtly Leftist moods, my responsibilities were shifted to likewise monitoring any existing American shortwave broadcasts of news or commentary. These were still being handled exclusively on a public-relations or non-profit basis by a few private enterprises. Among these, Station WRUL operated from Boston and was by far the most politically mature and efficient, especially in its shortwave German-language programs, broadcast by Hans Jacob. He had been French-language interpreter for the Weimar Republic's Ministry of Foreign Affairs in Berlin until Hitler came to power, then employed as a refugee by the French government to handle its German-language broadcasts until the German occupation of Paris sent him again into exile, this time in the United States. After 1945, Hans Jacob settled in Paris and remained until his retirement

chief interpreter for UNESCO, where I often had occasion to work for him.

From New York, NBC and CBS were broadcasting fairly efficient shortwave news programs. Those broadcast in German by NBC, I soon discovered, were written and spoken by the young German novelist Ernst Erich Noth, who had been one of my close friends in Paris between 1934 and 1936. From Schenectady, General Electric was likewise broadcasting news programs over its exceptionally powerful station, but the quality of these programs, especially those beamed in Spanish to Latin America, remained so unbelievably amateurish that many of their listeners must have wondered whether the United States was at all aware of the fact that a major war was already being waged in Europe.

Immediately after the Japanese attack on Pearl Harbor, announced over my radio while I was taking a leisurely Sunday morning bath in my New York apartment, the Office of War Information went into action, assuming control of all existing shortwave broadcasting stations in the United States and producing its own official programs, those of the Voice of America, in English and a limited number of foreign languages, from offices in New York and, on the West Coast, in San Francisco. Because our New York office was not yet staffed to handle foreign-language broadcasts and could not employ overnight as civil servants without the necessary previous "clearance" all the linguists needed for its first foreign-language broadcasts, I had the honor of acting as announcer for the Voice of America's first experimental news programs recorded in French, German, and Italian. Whether these were actually broadcast I was never informed. In any case, who would have heard them, unprecedented as they were, except perhaps a few radio hams? A few months later, I became an editor, under Pierre Lazareff, an intensely cheerful, over-active, and friendly midget, for the French-language shortwave radio programs of the Voice of America.

Because these were beamed to so many different areas in Europe, Africa, the Near East, the Indian Ocean, the Far East and New Caledonia, and French Polynesia in the vast Pacific Ocean, as well as to the French territories in the Caribbean, in Guyana, and off the coast of Canada, our French radio programs had to be broadcast on a daily twenty-four-hour basis. A skeleton staff even remained on duty at night so that these programs would always include the very latest news from the various war fronts as soon as it reached our office. Pierre Lazareff managed our activities regularly all day, often including Sundays too, sometimes for a good twelve hours at a stretch.

Towards the end of the afternoon, he expected me to phone him in order to find out when he wanted me to come and receive his instructions before relieving him overnight. In periods of stress, Pierre and I worked seven days a week, each of us in turn. From 1942 until 1945, no candidate proved capable or willing to replace either of us on the basis of three eight-hour shifts per day instead of our exhausting schedule of two daily shifts.

The staff of the French radio department consisted to some extent of celebrities of literature or of the arts. André Breton, the founder of Surrealism, was one of our announcers. Throughout the years of his employment by the Voice of America, he insisted steadfastly that he was not engaging thereby in a political activity. He was only "leasing" his voice as an instrument for reciting before the microphone news items that were fed to him without his ever having to select or draft them, so that he remained, in his own eyes, free of any intellectual or moral responsibility for them. The absurdity of this argument never occurred to him, not even when, in the course of a conversation that I held with him one day in our office, he accused in the most violent terms the Surrealist French poet Robert Desnos of being a despicable Collaborationist because he was accepting payment in German-occupied Paris, like Breton in his exile in New York, as an announcer for entertainment programs broadcast by a Paris radio station controlled by the Germans.

One of Breton's announcer colleagues in the French programs of the Voice of America was the distinguished Purist painter Amédée Ozenfant; another was the art historian Georges Duthuit, the son-in-law of the Fauvist master Henri Matisse. Other announcers included the future film-star Yul Brynner and the young actor Sasha Pitoïef, scion of a veritable dynasty of Russian and French actors. The writers of our French radio programs included René Etiemble and Denis de Rousemont, both already well known in France as avant-garde authors, and the art critic Patrick Waldberg, who distinguished himself in Paris mainly after 1945. The multilingual poet Yvan Goll and the Greek poet and art-critic Nico Calas were also employed in the French radio department as its archivists. André Breton always studiously ignored Goll's presence although their paths crossed several times a day in the limited space of our offices, much as they had both ignored each other's existence for many years in the much vaster area of Paris. From time to time, the famous American-born French novelist Julien Green also made a brief and discreet appearance in order to broadcast a special commentary addressed to his many readers in occupied France. Other French celebrities made occasional appearances in our office: among others, the Arctic explorer Paul Victor, who amused us by producing a collection of photographs of his Eskimo friends and explaining that one of them, who looked like any other Eskimo and distinguished himself in his physical appearance and dress from no other male Eskimo, was, believe it or not, a homosexual.

Between the fall of 1941 and the spring of 1945, my heavy work schedule in the offices of the Voice of America left me little leisure for social or literary activity. In my free time, I was also continuing to undergo in New York the psychoanalytical treatment which I had begun in 1939 in San Francisco and interrupted a few months later when I moved from there to Kansas City. This treatment, occasioned mainly by my frequent and otherwise unexplainable losses of consciousness, led in New York to my rejection by my draft board, before which I came up in 1942 with a letter from my analyst stating that I had been undergoing treatment under him and a San Francisco colleague ever since 1939. The New York draft-board physicians were unimpressed by this statement and put me through a rigorous series of physical and psychological tests which caused such a serious condition of stress that I lost consciousness there and then, after which I was hastily dressed and driven in an ambulance to the office of my somewhat surprised analyst. This proved to be the abrupt end of what might perhaps have been a brilliant military career.

During these busy years in New York, I nevertheless managed to write a few new lyrics, mainly on themes suggested to me by my fears concerning the fate of relatives or friends who remained in Nazi-occupied Europe. These lyrics were all ultimately published by New Directions in 1949 in my *Poems 1928–1948*. I also contributed during the war years a few new prose poems, translations of texts by French avant-garde writers, and critical essays of my own to *View*, which was edited in New York by my friends Charles Henri Ford and Parker Tyler and of which I was also a contributing editor, as well as to *VVV*, a more orthodox Surrealist publication edited by André Breton, Yvan Goll's bilingual *Hémisphères*, to *Poetry: A Magazine of Verse* in Chicago, to Cyril Connolly's *Horizon* in London, and to the *Journal of Aesthetics* and a few other more learned than strictly literary publications.

Because I was generally kept at work nearly all night, I slept most of the day and thus had little opportunity to join in the social activities of most of my New York friends, such as Charles Henri Ford, the painter Pavel Tchelitchev, Paul Bowles and his wife Jane, John Latouche, Virgil Thomson, the three Stettheimer sisters, the poet Oscar Williams, and the painter Kurt Seligmann. My closest friend remained, in those years, Paul Goodman, whom I had first met in 1937 in Chicago. Through my sister, who shared an apartment with me on the corner of Madison Avenue and East Sixty-seventh Street and was ultimately likewise employed in the offices of the Voice of America, I occasionally associated with a couple of younger poets, Howard Nemerov and John Pauker, whom she numbered among her own friends. For Charles Henri Ford's View Editions, I translated a selection of the poems of André Breton, which Ford published in an edition illustrated by Arshile Gorki and with a jacket designed by Marcel Duchamp. Undertaken in our rare moments of respite during office hours, this job of translation was no easy task. Breton knew practically no English, tended to distrust me as his translator, and constantly submitted my translations, for their approval, to French friends whose knowledge of English he appeared to trust more than mine. Over four decades later, I now feel sorely tempted to revise these translations and publish them, if possible, in a version which would no longer be subjected to this interference, in fact without the alien "improvements" on which Breton and his French friends insisted.

One of my colleagues of the French news desk of the Voice of America was Louis Kouindjy. Before the war, he had been an interpreter for the International Labour Office of the League of Nations in Geneva. A skeleton staff of this organization now remained practically dormant in its exile in Montreal since the beginning of the war. Early in 1944, the prospect of an Allied victory and of peace roused it from its slumber, and it then invited all its Allied or neutral member states to send delegates to a Conference on Postwar Labor problems, to be held on the campus of Temple University in Philadelphia.

Kouindjy obtained the agreement of the Office of War Information to loan me as an interpreter to this conference, which proved to be my first experience of both consecutive and simultaneous interpreting, with English, French, and Spanish as the official languages of its deliberations. On the very eve of the Conference, Kouindjy asked me whether I knew in New York any other linguist who might prove to be both available and competent as an interpreter. Haakon Chevalier, one of my former professors of French literature at the University of California in Berkeley, happened to be on a sabbatical in New York, so that I recommended him for this task. The ILO's Philadelphia Conference thus proved to be the

Edouard Roditi, 1959, oil on board, by Josef Herman, of the Royal Academy, London

start of the career as a conference interpreter on which Haakon too embarked a few years later, when he moved to Paris and took out French citizenship after his mysterious involvement as an alleged Soviet agent in the atomic energy scandal arising from his earlier association, together with his friend Robert Oppenheimer, in their somewhat immature and amateurish Leftist activities in Berkeley before 1940. Nor did it ever occur to me, in Philadelphia in 1944, that I too was destined to earn my livelihood as a conference interpreter during most of the time in the next four decades.

My own life in New York was meanwhile becoming increasingly difficult. Although I had managed to obtain official recognition of my sister's American citizenship and no longer needed to support her since 1942, I still had to offer my mother occasional financial assistance and had become involved in a very complex action on behalf of my paraplegic brother Harold. In wartime England, where he still claimed French citizenship, he had somehow managed, as a result of his business dealings with some very dubious English associates, to be declared a bankrupt and was even imprisoned as an undesirable alien who could no longer be deported to German-occupied France. I then undertook in Washington the necessary steps to prove that he had never resigned his claim to American citizenship by filiation. In the State Department's Passport Division, the notoriously awesome Mrs. Shipley, with whom I had already had dealings on behalf of my sister, now proved truly sympathetic. Because wartime censorship could not allow the publication of sailing dates of any transatlantic passenger steamers, I was suddenly informed late in 1944 that my brother and his German-born wife had already landed on Ellis Island and, within a few hours, would be brought to my New York apartment unless I made arrangements for them to be housed elsewhere.

After a few days, I moved out of my apartment to stay with a friend, but still had to support in my apartment my brother and his wife in full or in part for close on two more years, in fact as long as they proved unable to earn enough on their own. Such financial responsibilities as well as other personal problems discouraged me to a great extent from undertaking, between 1940 and 1960, any major literary project other than my critical study of the writings of Oscar Wilde, published by New Directions in 1947 in its Makers of Modern Literature series, my 1949 *Poems 1928–1948,* likewise published by New Directions, and a number of translations from French, German, Dutch, or Turkish.

The propaganda activities of the French desk of the Voice of America had reached their peak on my birthday, June 6, 1944, the day of the Allied landings in Normandy. For a full twenty-four hours, I was kept at work in the office, supervising our broadcasts or replacing our exhausted speakers, with only brief pauses for my meals. Many of my colleagues had already been transferred to London or to North Africa, to prepare from there, with more readily audible broadcasts, our landings in Sicily, on the Italian mainland, in Normandy, and in southern France. These broadcasts often included hour-by-hour instructions to the civilian population or the Resistance in the areas of our landings.

After the liberation of Paris, the volume of our activities began rapidly to decline. Many of my French colleagues who were still in New York began to prepare their return from wartime exile to their more normal life in France. In spite of a lot of foolish shilly-shallying, both Churchill and the American High Command and government had meanwhile forgotten their flirtations with General Giraud, who never enjoyed much support from the French Resistance. However unwillingly, they all came to terms with General De Gaulle. Towards the end of 1944, I began to entertain some misgivings concerning my own future in the peaceful activities, if any, of an ever more sparsely staffed Voice of America. My financial responsibilities, after the arrival of my brother and his wife, considerably increased these misgivings.

Early in 1945, I was led to believe that the problem of my professional future was solved. The Department of State suddenly remembered that I was one of the very few Americans with any previous experience of conference interpreting and requested my transfer from the Office of War Information to its own staff for a conference to be held within a few weeks in San Francisco, but without specifying that my employment would be only temporary. This conference turned out to be the one in the course of which the Charter of the United Nations was debated, drafted, and finally approved.

Throughout the Conference, I was repeatedly shocked by the incompetence of most members of the Secretariat supplied from Washington by the Department of State and by the ineptitude and vanity of all but one of the official American delegates. In moments of boredom, Senator Vandenburg filled whole pages of paper with doodles of an unconsciously obscene nature. These I patriotically hastened to gather and burn in ashtrays as potentially "restricted" documents at the end of each meeting, lest they fall into none-too-friendly hands. Senator Connally proved to be veritable innocent in the complex and delicate field of international politics and diplomacy. He always spoke in a hortatory tone, as if he were addressing an audience of ranchers in his native Texas. John Foster Dulles raved in most of his speeches like a trial lawyer trying to convince a jury of nincompoops. Only Harold Stassen displayed at all times a rare mixture of statesmanship, common sense, and courtesy. I have often wondered, ever since 1945, what contemporary history and the destiny of the United States might have been had Stassen been later elected to the presidency rather than such unworthy heirs to the tradition of our earliest presidents or of Abraham Lincoln as Nixon or Reagan.

The Department of State's choice of its Spanish interpreters likewise proved to be infelicitous. Most of them were young Puerto Rican or Filipino playboys who may well have been perfectly bilingual in terms of Café Society chitchat, but who had absolutely no experience of the terminology of international politics or diplomacy. Highly recommended to the Department of State by senators or other bigwigs who were acquainted with their families, these young exquisites failed miserably on the job or fled in a panic within the first few days of the Conference.

The opening speech of the first meeting of what later became the Trusteeship Council of United Nations was given by its Chairman, the Chief of the Australian Delegation, who spoke uninterruptedly for no less than one hour and fifteen minutes, while I feverishly took notes of what he said as best as I could. I then summarized his speech in French in slightly less than half an hour, and was followed by my Russian colleague, who was a bit more brief. This Russian summary was followed by an embarrassing silence while he and I scanned the horizon in search of our Spanish colleague, who appeared to have fled. A Latin-American delegate then demanded a Spanish interpretation. On the spur of the moment, I rose undaunted to my feet and very briefly summarized the Chairman's whole speech in what I fondly believed to be fairly idiomatic Spanish. Later, one of the Latin-American delegates kindly complimented me on my excellent accent, but asked where I had learned my rather oddly idiomatic Spanish. Only then did I realize that I had expressed myself in my late grandmother's Judeo-Spanish, full of archaisms and of words borrowed from Catalan, Portuguese, Italian, French, Modern Greek, or Turkish!

The chief of the Conference's Secretariat was the ill-starred Alger Hiss, whose wartime ideals of lasting friendship and peaceful cooperation with Soviet Russia were not yet disturbed by premonitions of the impending Cold War. In one of the subcommittees where I happened to be interpreting, the Soviet Delegate, Comrade Manuilsky, always expressed himself in very correct French, so that my job consisted in both interpreting him into English and some other delegates into French. At one point, a bitter discussion arose between the American and the Soviet delegates, and I interpreted it almost word for word. Later that day, Hiss summoned me to his office and reprimanded me for "deliberately embittering" their exchange of remarks. I replied that my job consisted in interpreting as best I could what had actually been said, without ever presuming to edit or soft-soap it.

As the Conference progressed, I was becoming increasingly aware of some of the absurdities of the United Nations Charter that we were so busily drafting. Why, for instance was Soviet Russia being granted three memberships and three votes, one for the Soviet Union as a whole, then one for the Ukraine and one also for Byelorussia, as if these two were fully independent and sovereign nations? Why wasn't the United States likewise claiming sovereignty and full membership and vote, say, for Texas and California or for Hawaii and Puerto Rico too? The veto powers granted to the Security Council's permanent members assumed, I also felt, too readily that these would agree on most problems of real urgency. Within a very few years, the United States actually ceased to agree with the Soviet Union, then with Communist China too, on almost every major issue that came up before the Security Council, which thus found itself powerless for close on four decades. I was also disturbed by the disproportion between the population of member states and their representation and power in the General Assembly, where many a nation with less than five million inhabitants is empowered to a full vote while far more populous cities, such as New York City, Mexico City, Calcutta, Shanghai, London, Sao Paulo, Lagos, or Hongkong, are granted no such powers. The insistence of the American delegation on the inclusion, here and there in the English text of the Charter, of some purely rhetorical and untranslatable catchwords tended moreover to render such passages very ambiguous, if not quite meaningless, in terms of international law since the French, Spanish, Russian, and Chinese versions of the Charter were reputedly as valid as this original American text. No longer officially a civil servant, I felt ultimately free to express some of these reservations in an article which I published, soon after the conclusion of the Conference, in New York in *Tricolor,* André Labarthe's English-language Gaullist periodical.

Towards the end of the Conference I was asked by its Secretariat to fill an application form for a job on the staff of United Nations. Nothing ever came of this application. When I enquired over a year later what had become of it, I was informed that no trace of it or of any other such application filled with the Department of State's San Francisco Secretariat could be found in the new Lake Success headquarters of United Nations. I had in any case been meanwhile surprised to discover, at the end of the San Francisco Conference, that my transfer from the Office of War Information to the Department of State had been permanent in the eyes of the former, but only temporary in the eyes of the latter. The Voice of America no longer needed my services in the reduced peacetime activities of its New York office, while the Department of State dismissed me overnight, offering me only my travel expenses back to the East Coast and vacation pay corresponding to the brief period of my employment.

For the time being, I chose to remain in California, at first for a few weeks visiting old friends in the Bay Area, above all Kenneth Rexroth in San Francisco and Ernst Kantorowicz in Berkeley. Later, I moved down to Los Angeles, where I soon found myself working, mainly in the University of California's William Andrews Clarke Memorial Library's unique collection of Oscar Wilde memorabilia, on the critical study of his writings which James Laughlin had suggested that I undertake for publication in the Makers of Modern Literature series of New Directions.

I have often been asked why I chose to write this book on Wilde, as a "Maker of Modern Literature." I had originally proposed to Laughlin, when he first approached me for a book of this nature, a very different study, on Luigi Pirandello as both dramatist and fiction writer. Laughlin agreed that Pirandello was truly one of the makers of modern literature, but he objected that too few American readers were yet aware of his importance, so that New Directions would not be able to sell enough copies of such a book to cover its production costs. To this I replied that the general public, alas, was familiar only with the names of such writers as Shakespeare, Byron, Browning, Wilde, and George Bernard Shaw. "Yes," Laughlin concluded, "but Shakespeare, Byron, and Browning can scarcely be called Makers of Modern Literature, and I already have someone writing a book on Shaw for my series, so why don't you write one on Wilde?"

As a result of what had been a mere quip, I thus found myself, in a way, wedded for life to Oscar Wilde, since my critical study of his writings remains the only one of the whole Makers of Modern Literature series to have now been reprinted, though in an expanded version, four full decades after its original publication. It proved also to be one of the very few such books to have deserved, when first published, the main full-page review in the *New Yorker,* though it has also earned me some less advantageous publicity. After I had panned Edward Dahlberg's *Flea of Sodom* in a review that pointed out its bad spelling and faulty proof-reading, he accused me in print of being a homosexual on the mere evidence of my having written a book on Wilde. I replied that Bernard Shaw was no female saint, in spite of his having written a play on the theme of Joan of Arc.

While writing my book on Wilde, I stayed in Los Angeles in a house on Benton Way. It was what a few years later became known as a commune, run by the Indianapolis poet Charles Aufderheide, whom I had first known at the University of Chicago as a close friend of the gifted poet Jean Garrigue. Whenever we could afford it, we gave poetry readings or musical evenings there, and some of these were attended by the great German poet Bertolt Brecht, who was still living in exile in southern California and whose son Stefan I first met there as a teenager. Brecht then suggested that I undertake translations of some of his poems. Early in 1946, I had just about finished work on my book on Wilde and was ready to begin translating Brecht from German into English when the Department of the Army, in a long-distance call from Washington, offered me what appeared to be a more lucrative job as an interpreter for the War Crimes Trial of the International Military Tribunal in Nuremberg. There I would be replacing Haakon Chevalier, already weary of his task and anxious to return to his family and his teaching in Berkeley. Some years later, I learned that Brecht, when he decided to return to Europe from his exile in California, stored much of his library, until he found a new permanent home in East Berlin, in the basement of our Los Angeles "commune," a compromising fact that was duly recorded in my FBI file as well as in the files of all the commune's other occupants.

Although unemployed since the end of the San Francisco Conference, I was still, on my savings and my cumulative pay for unused annual leave or sick leave from the Office of War Information, helping to support my brother and his wife in my New York apartment. Without further ado, I therefore accepted, at least for the time being, the new civil-service job offered me. After first being administered by mistake, in an Army Infirmary in Los Angeles, the required inoculation shots for service in the Far East and then, after my papers had been counterchecked, those too for Europe, I developed for a couple of days a high fever, from which I soon recovered enough to be sent by air to my port of embarkation, which happened to be New York, where I was to await further travel orders.

These were preceded by a plethora of instructions concerning required inoculations, which had already been administered all too generously in Los Angeles, or else listing the items of military uniform which I had to acquire and the baggage which I was allowed to take. When I had satisfied all these requirements and my travel orders finally arrived, I learned that I was destined to travel to Le Havre aboard SS *Argentina,* the hold of which proved to have been temporarily equipped as a troopship while all the cabins on the decks above were reserved for private passengers. As we boarded the ship, I recognized among these passengers a few friends or acquaintances, including Nina Ricci, one of the most charming stars of Parisian "haute couture," and an American family of distinguished prewar expatriates who were returning to the splendid home which they had been forced to abandon in German-occupied Paris.

I was thus privileged to take at least one meal a day as a guest in the first-class restaurant instead of already subsisting exclusively on GI cuisine. When we landed in Le Havre, I discovered that I was the only passenger with travel orders to proceed from there to Nuremberg. The officer who should have instructed me concerning my further transportation happened to be away on temporary leave and I was vaguely instructed to proceed to Paris and find out there how best I should solve my problem. My American friends were meanwhile experiencing some problems with the French customs officials on account of the vast quantities of their baggage, which included even gardening tools and floor polish to replace all that had been used or looted in their home by its wartime German occupants. My American uniform and fluent French worked wonders on their behalf on the customs officials, but my own foot-locker was nowhere to be found, officially having already been forwarded, I was told, with other US Army shipments, to the American Zone of Occupation in Germany. Actually, it had never even been shipped across the Atlantic, but was ultimately found, close on a year later, in Kansas City, of all places, in an American army depot for lost property.

A privately rented truck awaited my friends to transport their baggage to Paris, while their own prewar Rolls Royce, abandoned in their garage by the hastily retreating Germans billeted in their home, stood ready to drive them to Paris, though with a new chauffeur. My friends insisted that I accompany them, so that I spent the next three nights in the guest-room of their suite at the Ritz Hotel, which already had central heating while their own home still lacked fuel.

It took me some time to locate in Paris the responsible officer for my further travel to Nuremberg, and some time for him in turn to figure out how best to send me on my way there. When he asked me where I could meanwhile be reached, I gave him my room number at the Ritz, and he was duly impressed. While I awaited his instructions, I was busy visiting old Parisian friends and seeking a few of my relatives who had remained in occupied France. I was horrified to discover that one of my father's first cousins had been arrested by the Gestapo, together with her husband and their two sons, and all deported to Auschwitz, from where they never returned. Several more distant relatives as well as a number of friends, including the Surrealist poet Robert Desnos had likewise been either victims of the Holocaust or had died in German concentration-camps as political prisoners, or else had died fighting in the Resistance. I thus began to wonder how, within the next few days, I would begin to react as an interpreter for the trial of the major Nazi war criminals in the very city

whose German population was long reputed to have been vociferously anti-Semitic readers of the rabble-rousing rag, *Der Stuermer,* which Jules Streicher so successfully published there.

My few days of respite in Paris meanwhile made me feel that "Cassandra's Dream" and several of my other wartime poems written in America were shockingly prophetic. My trip from Paris to Nuremberg then proved to be, in a way, a kind of absurd parody of an eastbound trainload of doomed Jews deported from France to Auschwitz. Although not in an overcrowded and sealed cattle-car, I was transported aboard a troop-train in what had once been a first-class compartment, but without any light overnight and with no heating or glass left in its windows, so that the wind blew the snow, sleet, or rain onto me. Again and again, the train stopped, often for a long while in dark and apparently deserted railway stations. For hours on end, nowhere could I detect in any of these a place where I might procure any food or drink. At first I had the impression of perhaps being the only passenger on this weird troop-train, until a burly American soldier suddenly entered my compartment, surprised to discover there a fellow passenger in the dark. He was an enlisted man, I soon gathered, and somewhat bibulous, but had exhausted his own store of liquor and was now in search of further supplies. I had none that I could share with him, but he had a blanket and suggested that we wrap ourselves in it and lie side by side on the floor to keep warm. In the dark, he became aware of the fact that I wore an officer's uniform, after which he began to address me as "Sir," although I soon felt that he was surreptitiously seeking to have sex with me.

Fortunately, his fumbling attempts were interrupted when our train stopped in what appeared to have once been a major station. From the platform, a sergeant informed us that we should all disembark for breakfast. A bedraggled small group of uniformed men then gathered from the train's many carriages. We were greeted in the grey dawn by an even more bedraggled crowd of displaced Volksdeutsche women and children. Emerging from cattle-cars sidetracked there, they sought to engage us in barter deals. From what I gathered, they had been deported from some rural area Croatia.

I was the only passenger wearing an officer's uniform, which surprised the mess sergeant responsible for our breakfast. He asked me how I happened to be on this troop-train. I showed him my travel orders. Some asshole, he concluded, had snafoo'd: I should have been shipped from Paris to Nuremberg by air. Be that all as it may, it took me a full twenty-four hours to reach my final destination from Paris. Such was my first experience of the American army's efficiency in everything but the use of weapons.

Too much has already been written and published about the International Military Tribunal's trial of the major Nazi war criminals for my own memories of its procedures to be still of much significance. Only a few personal observations or experiences may still prove to be of some interest. Several of my interpreter colleagues subsequently made brilliant careers. Among my Soviet colleagues, Trojanovsky, who spoke perfect American English, later rose to the rank of Ambassador and was permanent Soviet delegate to United Nations in New York, while Mamedov, a dark and handsome young man of apparently Islamic origin from the Caucasus or central Asia, spoke fluent French and, I'm told, subsequently made a brilliant career in Moscow in the planning and administration of Soviet radio programs to Western Europe.

Among my colleagues employed by the American, British, or French elements, George Wassilchikof, a polyglot Russian prince who could speak fluent English, French, German, and Russian, as well as some Lithuanian, was afflicted with a disastrous stammer whenever engaged in a private conversation and obliged to express his own views, though he could overcome this disability as soon as he interpreted another speaker's statements or opinions. Later, George Wassilchikof made a successful career in United Nations in various semi-diplomatic posts or missions and also wrote and published a number of historical works.

My own duties consisted in interpreting from French into English in the Tribunal's open sessions in the courtroom, and from English into French in the closed sessions when the eight judges met, sometimes with the chief prosecutors too, in order to discuss whatever legal or other problems arose in the course of the trial. As Haakon Chevalier had now left for California a few days after my arrival, I was the only interpreter who had any previous experience of simultaneous interpreting with its still relatively rudimentary IBM equipment. A few of my colleagues, however, above all those from Soviet Russia or those recruited from Geneva, appeared to have some experience of this equipment or of similar equipment from their training in the few schools that already offered courses in interpreting. But only Haakon and I, of all the interpreters employed in the International Military Tribunal's Nuremberg Trial, had actually used this equipment professionally, at the International Labour Office's Philadelphia Conference in 1944, and no other interpreter who had previously

used it in the ILO's meetings in Philadelphia, Geneva, or elsewhere was now employed in Nuremberg.

My personal impressions or experiences of the Trial are as varied as they are limited. I was impressed by the dignity of Goering, who clearly displayed contempt for those among his co-defendants who, like Kaltenbronner among others, repeatedly disclaimed responsibility for incriminating documents which appeared to bear their signature. Although responsible, as former chief of Hitler's Security Agency, of perhaps more crimes against humanity than any of the other defendants, Kaltenbronner even argued, in the case of some such documents, that he had never seen or signed them and that, in fact, they had been signed with a routine rubber stamp imitating his signature. Goering, on the contrary, admitted responsibility for all such documents which appeared to bear his signature. For those among his co-defendants, such as Schacht and Papen, who assumed throughout the Trial that they should never have been accused of any crime against humanity or war crime, he likewise displayed great con-

Portrait of Roditi, 1980, mixed media on paper, by Yüksel Arslan

tempt. Both Papen and Schacht ultimately managed to be acquitted.

One of my colleagues who interpreted German into English happened to be ill when Robert Jackson, the Chief American Prosecutor, accused Goering of having ordered the Berlin police, after the looting of the city's leading Jewish-owned jewelry store in the course of the historical *Kristallnacht,* to recuperate as many of the stolen diamonds as possible because, as Jackson rather foolishly claimed, Goering desired them for his own famous collection of precious gems. Goering's defense lawyer then pointed out in German that the looted diamonds were nearly all mounted on relatively modest engagement rings, in fact stones that were mostly of half a carat or one carat. Goering had been asked to issue this order to the police by the insurance companies representing manufacturers who traditionally delivered such rings on consignment to this jeweler and who were not all likewise Jews. While I was interpreting this lawyers long and detailed argument from German into English, I could see that Goering was listening to it with one ear and, through an earphone, with the other ear to an interpretation, whether English, French, or Russian, of his lawyer's speech. Later his lawyer came up to me in one of the court-house passages and complimented me, on Goering's behalf, on my exceptionally accurate interpretation of this whole argument. When I thanked him in German, Goering's lawyer added: "Well, your German reveals that you must originally have been a Berlin Jew, so that you of course knew this jewelry-store and understood my whole argument." Actually, I could well remember the store from my Berlin holidays of some fifteen years earlier.

Robert Jackson's *chutzpah* throughout the trial was sometimes quite ludicrous. From one of his close associates, I heard that he fully expected his assignment as United States Prosecutor in the Nuremberg War Crimes Trial to lead him soon to the White House. An ungrateful nation later neglected to appreciate his achievements and voted instead for Eisenhower. Never, in the course of the many months that he saw me almost daily in the court-house or elsewhere in Nuremberg, did he have the courtesy to respond to my greetings or those of any of my interpreter colleagues. With Francis Biddle, the Senior American Judge, my quarrel was of a different nature: although he always greeted me politely by name, it never appeared to occur to him that I was, as his interpreter in the closed sessions of the eight judges, the same Edouard Roditi as the young American poet whom his wife had befriended and entertained in their Washington home as one of the patro-

nesses of *Poetry: A Magazine of Verse,* to which I had by 1946 been contributing for well over ten years.

As I now look back on the Trial with almost half a century's hindsight, I realize how much it was inspired by merely journalistic notions of public relations or of political expediency and, as far as the American prosecution was concerned, by a very national misunderstanding of the nature of international law. Founded to a great extent on Roman law, international law requires that a defendant be accused, tried, and condemned for actions that were illegal or criminal at the time or in the place where they were committed: *nulla poena sine crimine* means that no condemnation can be valid without a previous formulation of the crime. The leaders of National-Socialist Germany who were on trial in Nuremberg could therefore not be validly accused of conspiracy as conceived under American law, since no such crime exists under German law nor indeed under French or Soviet law. Nor could they be validly accused of genocide, since the whole concept of genocide as a crime against humanity was first formulated only after they had committed it on the Jews and the Gypsies of the Third Reich and of German-occupied Europe. In the course of the closed sessions which I interpreted, the French judges went to great length to convince their colleagues that parts of the American prosecution's initial argument had to be dropped because founded on such misconceptions of international law.

Robert Jackson, as American Prosecutor, had moreover prepared and formulated his case on the basis of a very hasty and superficial study of captured enemy archives. Again and again, while the Trial was progressing, more compromising documents than those previously quoted were turning up. Nor is this true only of the Trial itself. Only in 1990 was it finally proven and universally admitted that the Soviet rather than the German authorities had been responsible for the massacre of the unfortunate Polish prisoners of war in Katyn. True, this had been, in the course of the Trial, a very controversial point, hotly contested by the German defense until the American, British, and French judges rather ignominiously yielded to the pressure of Soviet rhetoric and, we now know, fallacious evidence. The whole Trial might indeed have been more brief and conclusive had it been more carefully initiated, perhaps with a delay of only three more months of preparation. In any case, we now begin to realize that, according to the ancient Latin principle of *vae victis,* only a vanquished nation will ever be accused and convicted of war crimes or of such crimes against humanity as the American bombing of Hiroshima.

If only for a few days at a time, the Trial was attended in turn by a veritable procession of senators, congressmen, star reporters, and other celebrities of one kind or another. Among these, the Russian-born and French-language novelist Elsa Triolet turned up to report on the Trial for the French Communist press when Hoess, the former Kommandant of Auschwitz, was scheduled to appear in Nuremberg as a witness, but not as a defendant.

The wife of the novelist and poet Louis Aragon, who had abandoned Surrealism a good ten years earlier in order to play an active part in the French Communist party, Elsa Triolet was already suspected of being a secret KGB agent and of exerting some mysterious influence on her husband. Only after her death did it gradually become known that Aragon had long been a guilt-ridden homosexual and that their widely publicized love was politically rather than emotionally inspired.

Be that all as it may, my immediate superior, an American naval officer, delegated me to make it quite clear in French to Elsa Triolet, who had previously protested in the French Communist press that Hoess should, in her opinion, now be one of the defendants in Nuremberg, that he had been tried and condemned to death in Poland, the scene of his crimes, and was in Nuremberg only in order to testify briefly on his mere implementation of policies formulated at a higher level by some of the defendants, after which he would return to Poland to be executed.

I explained all this very clearly to Elsa Triolet, even quoting to her the text of the four-power Allied agreement according to which the defendants now before the International Military Tribunal in Nuremberg were those Nazi political or military leaders who were accused of having formulated criminal policies, whereas those who, like Hoess, had only implemented them locally were to be tried and condemned where such crimes had been committed. Again and again, she interrupted my argument, refusing to listen to me. On her return to Paris, she published in the French Communist press a violently anti-American article, still protesting indignantly that Hoess had appeared in Nuremberg as a free witness in the stand instead of being a defendant as one of the major war criminals.

Our performance in Nuremberg proved to be a trial run for the system of simultaneous interpreting. In the few years that followed, this system, originally used experimentally under the old League of Nations only by its International Labour Office, was soon adopted by United Nations in its temporary home in Lake Success and by all its specialized agencies except the International Court of Justice in The Hague, as well as by an ever greater number of other international organizations of one kind or another. Immediately after the conclusion of the International Military Tribunal's Nuremberg proceedings and Goering's sensationally mysterious suicide on the very eve of his proposed execution, I was sent on temporary leave to London to interpret a United Nations Conference on International Trade and Tariffs. On the basis of our team's success in demonstrating here the advantages of simultaneous interpreting, United Nations soon decided to adopt this system in its new Lake Success headquarters rather than the older, more spectacularly eloquent but much less rapid system of consecutive interpreting which I had practiced at its original San Francisco Conference in 1945.

Our whole team then moved from London to New York, to be employed by United Nations at Lake Success. Only I remained in Europe, content with my American civil-service status and having previously agreed, on a brief visit to Berlin while still employed in Nuremberg, to return from London to Germany to work as interpreter for the American Element of the Allied Control Council in Berlin.

On my brief preliminary Berlin visit from Nuremberg, I had met Alexander Koval, a young German writer of some ambition and talent, who was destined to play in the next ten years an important part in my life. On my return from London with my mother, I found Alexander in fairly desperate straights and immediately assumed the responsibility of solving some of his problems as best I could.

One of my interpreter colleagues in the American Element of the Allied Control Council was the French-language poet Alain Bosquet, whom I had previously met briefly in New York as a co-contributor to Yvan Goll's bilingual *Hémisphères*. Alain's creative genius and literary ambitions couldn't allow him to remain content with the limited intellectual scope of our work, which consisted to a great extent in endless quibbles over interpretation of the original Allied Potsdam Agreement of 1945 or over details concerning the administration of the four Allied Zones of Occupation of Germany. While I was already employing Koval to revise and then proofread the German translation of my book on Wilde which Herbert Kluger Verlag was about to publish in Munich, Alain approached me to undertake with him the task of editing *Accord*, a little magazine where he planned to publish contributions by writers who happened to be employed in Berlin by the four Allied occupying powers. For its first issue, we obtained, as Americans, fairly adequate cooperation only from a few of our British or French colleagues, but none yet from any Russians. It included Alain's translation of the first section of my poem entitled "Cassandra's Dream." For the second issue, we already began to encounter financial and other difficulties. Finally, we managed to publish it only as a supplement to the Berlin edition of the US Army's daily *Stars and Stripes*, most of whose readers displayed little interest in our venture.

We soon became aware of the very limited extent of *Accord's* real audience. I then suggested to Alain that, with Alexander Koval's assistance as our German-language co-editor, we should publish in German a truly avant-garde periodical which would set out to reveal, without any concessions or compromises, to interested German readers the kind of German or foreign literature that had generally been forbidden throughout the twelve years of Nazi dictatorship. No German editor or publisher had yet managed to establish, with foreign writers, editors, and publishers, the kind of contacts that Alain and I already enjoyed or could readily establish with the help of Karlheinz Henssel as our Berlin publisher, *Das Lot* was thus founded as a series of irregularly published volumes, if only because technical or financial problems of one kind or another still discouraged us from publishing it as a regular periodical. The first of *Das Lot*'s six issues was published in West Berlin in the fall of 1947 and soon sold out, so that it had to be reprinted two years later.

Our six issues of *Das Lot* are now generally recognized as one of the most significant contributions to the revival of purely literary activity in western Germany in those few immediate postwar years. Interviewed many years later as their publisher by a journalist for the popular Hamburg weekly *Die Zeit*, Henssel nevertheless objected, with oddly unconscious irony, that our selection of foreign authors had generally been untimely for the immediate postwar, by including too many Surrealists and not enough Existentialists. He had forgotten that he pusillanimously refused to publish one of Sartre's stories from *Le Mur* or Sartre's existentialist text on Genêt, which I had submitted to him for translation and publication with Sartre's consent, that he then failed to obtain in time the translation rights of a text by Albert Camus which we had likewise proposed to translate and publish, that we convinced him only with great difficulty to publish a selection of the writings of Cioran, and that we still planned to publish Beckett in a forthcoming issue when Henssel suddenly decided to suspend further publication of *Das Lot* under our joint editorship.

Without much success and without Koval's, Bosquet's, or my editorial assistance, Henssel later undertook the publication of a new and rather undistinguished series entitled *Das Neue Lot*, in which one of his favorite foreign authors proved to be the rather namby-pamby South African author Lawrence Vanderpost, and his most daringly avant-garde experimental writer the French prose poet Francis Ponge, a somewhat compulsive author of painfully detailed descriptions of such still-life objects as pebbles or a glass of water.

With the currency reform in Germany's three Western Zones of Occupation, the Allied control council ceased to hold regular meetings with the Soviet Element in Berlin. I soon found myself declared "surplus" as an interpreter and sent to Bremerhaven for shipment back to civilian life and unemployment in the United States. A few days before my embarkment, I was summoned back, however, to Berlin because of my knowledge of German, which appeared to have become known to my superiors as a result of my entirely unofficial activities as one of the editors of *Das Lot*. But my duties were no longer those of an interpreter.

Offers of new jobs as a conference interpreter soon began to abound and I moved back to Paris, where I lived between jobs for several months in various modest hotels.

In 1954, I at last found a suitable apartment on the narrow but historic rue Grégoire de Tours in the Saint-Germain-des-Prés neighborhood, in the same block as the building where the poet Théodore de Banville had once rented for Rimbaud, when the latter first came penniless to Paris, the cheap room in which the future author of *The Season in Hell* allowed himself to be seduced by the poet Paul Verlaine, a considerably older married man.

The rue Grégoire de Tours appears indeed to have always attracted poets. Gérard de Nerval is known to have haunted one of its taverns in the few weeks of tragic insanity that preceded his suicide. In my own twenty-five years of tenancy on that street of only two short blocks, I was host to Alexander Koval and Paul Goodman as house-guests on several occasions, once too to Harold Norse, and also entertained Kateb Yacine and Paul Celan to lunch or dinner. In a hotel on the other side of the street and in the same block, the poets James Broughton, Robert Duncan, Jean Garrigue, and Stanley Kunitz stayed at one time or another, while the French poet Guillevic lived for many years in an apartment on the other block, across the Boulevard Saint Germain, of the rue Grégoire de Tours. Of the many prose writers whom I entertained to lunch or dinner in my home, Eugène Ionesco, Arthur Adamov, Alfred Chester, and Yashar Kemal

Charles Henri Ford and Edouard Roditi, Paris, 1983

are perhaps the most famous. The rue Grégoire de Tours may well be able to claim by now to have housed or entertained within its two modest blocks more poets or prose writers of various languages or nationalities than any other street in the world. It was even in my apartment on this street that Paul Celan and I collaborated on our translation of a selection of poems by Fernando Pessoa from Portuguese into German. These translations are now regularly reprinted, under our joint names, in all posthumous editions of Celan's complete works.

As I was preparing, early in 1954, to move into my new Paris home, I was suddenly appointed chief of a team of interpreters engaged to handle English, French, Italian, and Spanish for a conference of growers of citrus fruits which was about to convene in Algiers. The colleague originally scheduled to be its chief interpreter had meanwhile accepted a more lucrative job in Venice, leaving me to fill at the very last moment a few vacancies in the team. For lack of a better candidate, I hurriedly appointed Haakon Chevalier to fill one of these vacancies. I knew that he was equally fluent in French and English and he assured me that he could also interpret from Spanish, but that he knew no Italian. His interpreting from Spanish proved nevertheless to be far from satisfactory, so that I often had to relieve him by working in turn in one booth as interpreter into English and in another booth as interpreter into French. While the Confer-

ence was still being conducted in Algiers, poor Haakon was suddenly reported extensively in the French press to have been a Soviet atomic spy when his friend Oppenheimer became headline news in what has meanwhile been proven to have been one of the most hysterical American episodes of the Cold War.

Before leaving Paris for Algiers, I had requested a telephone for the apartment into which I was not yet ready to move as it still needed to be entirely renovated. I was then informed that I might have to wait a good two years before obtaining a phone line, unless I could bring proof from an employer that I needed a phone for professional reasons. My old friend Hans Jacob, still Chief Interpreter at UNESCO, then promised to supply such a statement on my return from Algiers. But I was then surprised to find that a phone had meanwhile been almost miraculously installed in my unfurnished but already renovated apartment while I was away in North Africa.

In the course of the next couple of years I had occasion little by little to realize how ingenuous I had been, as an American poet, an admirer of Philip Freneau, Melville, Thoreau, Whitman, Henry James, and Veblen, and a friend of, among others, Paul Goodman and Kenneth Rexroth, in having originally accepted, in 1941, to be employed in New York by the federal government and thereby exposing myself, even when no longer one of its employees, to the constant investigations of as ineptly unimaginative and fundamentally malevolent an organization as the Federal Bureau of Investigation. Within the next few years, I was indeed destined to become a victim of persecutions of which the real nature and full extent were revealed in the daily press of Western Europe, above all in Italy, France, Belgium, and Spain, only as late as the last couple of months of 1990.

Again and again, between 1954 and 1958, I complained that there appeared to be unexplainable disturbances on my telephone line, producing odd sounds which were also heard by persons who were conversing with me. Then my Translators' Union asked me one day whether I would be free to translate into French in its Paris office a recording of a conversation in Portuguese. To my great surprise, this turned out to be a barely audible recording of a long-distance phone conversation held a few weeks earlier by myself with Lisbon's Ministry of Public Health, which was enquiring whether I would be free to interpret in the Portuguese capital an international conference on tropical diseases. When I now presented my signed bill for this little job and had to be paid by the interested French intelligence agency, the shit hit the fan. I was summoned to the offices of the "Direction de la Sûreté du Territoire" on the rue des Saussaies, which had been occupied from 1940 until 1945 by the Gestapo, and questioned for almost a whole day on all my activities past or present. I was asked, among other things, whether I was a Jew, as if this still happened to be at all pertinent now that the Gestapo no longer occupied these sinister premises. From a number of other questions, I gathered that my phone had long been zealously tapped. Was I a Communist, since the writer Antonina Valentin had phoned me several times for information on Picasso, a notorious Communist, whose biography she now planned to write? No, I wasn't a Communist, only an art critic and historian who could advise Antonina Valentin on bibliographical source material concerning Picasso's early relationships with the collector Alphonse Kann, the dealer Daniel-Henri Kahnweiler, and Gertrude Stein. Oh, but all these names sound Jewish. Does this mean that Picasso too is a Jew, like so many other Communists?

However nonsensical much of this long interrogatory proved to be, I emerged from it thoroughly shaken and, from many of the questions raised, well aware that my stay in Algiers together with Haakon Chevalier had inspired this whole investigation, although some questions already suggested to me that this French intelligence agency might well be acting on behalf of the Federal Bureau of Investigation. I

was asked, for instance, whether I considered myself a political refugee in France, why I hadn't returned since 1950 to live in the United States, and why, in America I had signed an affidavit of moral sponsorship on behalf of the French-language writer Vladimir Pozner, who was then seeking refuge as a Jew in the United States from German-occupied France, where he was well known as an authority on Russian literature and as a novelist of some talent. With the Paris firm for which I worked from 1933 to 1936, Pozner had published a very competent history of twentieth-century Russian literature and I therefore limited the affidavit of moral responsibility which I signed on his behalf to a brief statement about the nature of my professional relationship with him as one of the more distinguished French writers whose work I had assisted in publishing in Paris.

Only an American intelligence agency might now, in 1954, have still known that I had signed this affidavit for Pozner so many years earlier in Kansas City, and could still be at all interested in enquiring further into the nature of my relationship with Pozner. All this, of course, as well as my occasional associations, at first in 1954 in Algeria and then in the ensuing years in Paris too, with a few French-language writers of Algerian origin, such as the novelists Mouloud Mammeri, Mouloud Feraoun, Mohammed Dib, and Kateb Yacine, or the French poet Jean Sénac, born in Algeria of a family of settlers of European origin, now aroused the suspicions of the French secret police too, although I was able to explain, on the occasion of either my first interrogation in 1954 or of the second one four years later, that I had originally been recommended to most of these Algerian writers, at the time of my trip to Algiers, by Albert Camus, himself Algerian-born, like Sénac, of a family of European settlers. Why had I later allowed Sénac to stay for several weeks as a house-guest in my Paris apartment? Again, because Camus had asked me to put Sénac up in my spare room until he would obtain a sufficient advance from his Paris publisher. Why had I invited Yacine to dine in my home? Because Sénac had suggested that I invite him . . .

All this smacked indeed of "disloyalty" in the eyes of the interested American authorities in those dark days of ideological witch-hunts, and of "subversive activity" in the eyes of the French government. The latter was already unofficially involved, at the time of my infelicitous conference in Algiers and subsequent brief holiday in the spring of 1954 as a tourist in the picturesque countryside of Kabylia and then in Oran and Tlemcen too, in what later became known as the Algerian War of Liberation, which was indeed raging sporadically here and there in the mountains of Kabylia, where I spent a week as an innocent and unsuspecting tourist, actually on the advice of the official French Tourist Agency in Algiers. In my ignorance of any existing political tensions in Algeria, I even believed that the few armed natives whom I then happened to meet while hiking from Fort National, where I had dined with the writer Mouloud Feraoun, and the town of Azazga, where I found a bus to drive me to Bougie on the Mediterranean coast, were either poachers hunting partridges or hares, or rural policemen.

Within the next few years, I became increasingly aware of the fateful nature of these few weeks spent in Algeria, not only in my own life but also in the life of some of my interpreter colleagues at the citrus-growers conference and of some writers with whom I associated in my spare time in Algiers or later as a tourist elsewhere in Algeria. Fedor Ganz, one of my interpreter colleagues in Algiers, was expelled a few months later as an undesirable alien from the Swiss canton of Geneva after being subjected there to a mysterious interrogatory about the nature of his relations with me. Another colleague, a German who resided in Bonn, was likewise questioned at length about the choice of the hotel where she had stayed in Algiers. Although the writer Mouloud Feraoun had remained, throughout the Algerian War of Liberation, overtly opposed to all violence and an ardent advocate of a peaceful settlement, he was brutally murdered by French Rightist thugs shortly before the end of the conflict, while the poet Jean Sénac, who had always expressed his sympathy for the Algerian Liberation Front and even opted, after its victory, for dual Algerian and French citizenship, was likewise murdered in his home in Algiers as the capital of an independent Algeria, although in such mysterious circumstances that nobody knows whether he was the victim of a political act of vengeance or of a sex crime.

The interest displayed in me by the French secret police lasted, as far as I have been able to ascertain, from 1954 until 1960. Its real nature was revealed to me, however, only some thirty years later, in November and December 1990, while I was holidaying in Morocco. A series of scandalous official admissions reported in the Belgian, French, Italian, and Spanish press, above all in *Le Soir, Le Monde, La Stampa,* and *El Pais,* as well as in radio and TV programs of these nations then led all of Western Europe to realize how much the CIA, in its anti-Communist frenzy of the years of the Cold War, had violated civil liberties in its investigations, under some secret terms of the Atlantic Pact, of any person

suspected of being within the frontiers of America's NATO allies, at all politically dissident or unreliable.

These official admissions and the ensuing controversies that they inspired within the next few weeks in 1990 in Belgium, France, Italy, and Spain all concerned the operations of a top-secret network of agents named *Gladio* in the Italian press and *Glaive* in the Belgian and French press, which reported extensively that such agents had continued for several years to be trained in a special camp situated in the Canary Islands, where it was placed at the CIA's disposal by the Spanish government under Generalissimo Franco. Their training consisted mainly in acquiring techniques of resistance and sabotage to be used in case of a Communist take-over in their native land. Only the imminence of the Gulf War put a stop, early in 1991, to the controversies that arose as a result of these revelations.

Between 1954 and 1958, I was also beginning to write more and more frequently for French-language publications, above all for *Preuves,* an overtly anti-Communist literary monthly which later proved to have always been to some extent financially sponsored, like all the other publications of the Congress for Cultural Freedom, by foundations acting on behalf of the CIA. While the latter's right hand thus continued to pursue its investigations of my life and professional activities, its left hand was still publishing my writings fairly regularly as those of an intellectual who appeared to be politically quite harmless.

In addition, I was often appearing in those years in a weekly French radio program entitled "Etranger, mon ami" together with such well-known writers as André Maurois, Albert Camus, and Eugène Ionesco, among many others. Organized by the distinguished literary critic Dominique Arban, this program was devoted mainly to discussions of recently published French translations of works by eminent foreign writers. Because of my familiarity with English, American, German, Italian, Spanish, and Latin-American literatures, Dominique Arban had come to rely on me more and more frequently as one of the participants in her program.

Whenever I was in Paris between frequent trips abroad as a conference interpreter, I was thus a rather busy man whose many and varied social and professional occupations and associations were scarcely of a nature which might appear at all suspect in the eyes of the French secret police, if at all adequately investigated. Only one aspect of my life as an alien resident of Paris might still appear at all questionable: I seemed to have studiously avoided ever registering officially as a resident alien and to be thereby evading French taxation on whatever income I might be drawing from French or foreign sources. But further investigation would soon have revealed that here too I had acted in good faith and indeed attempted, though in vain, to register as a resident alien and thereby obtain the required "carte d'identité" soon after finally acquiring the lease on a permanent home in Paris.

But the responsible official at the Préfecture of the Paris police had explained to me that I could apply for registration and obtain a "carte d'identité" as a resident alien only after staying without interruption within the frontiers of France for three whole months, and my work as a conference interpreter, mainly elsewhere in Europe, Africa, or Asia, still prevented me from ever staying three months in France without thereby suffering a loss in my earnings by refusing employment abroad.

In spite of unpleasant memories of my first encounter with the French security police in its sinister headquarters on the rue des Saussaies, my conscience remained fully at rest from the end of 1954 to the end of 1957, when I decided to return on holiday to the United States after an absence of seven years. Some doubts had recently been raised by the American Consulate in Paris about my right to renew my American passport, which was about to expire. Under the recently enacted McCarran Act, a naturalized American citizen who had been living seven consecutive years in his country of birth without meanwhile returning to the United States could be deprived of his American citizenship. But I had never been, as I pointed out, a naturalized citizen. Born in Paris of an American father and registered soon after my birth at the American Consulate as a citizen by filiation, I was not subject, as such, to the provisions of the McCarran Act.

While the validity of my citizenship was being verified in Washington, I took the precaution of also enquiring what steps I might take, in case of need, in order to acquire another citizenship. I thus discovered that I needed only to establish residence in Italy in order to file a claim for Italian citizenship, my paternal grandfather having been a citizen of the Grand Duchy of Tuscany and then of the reunited Kingdom of Italy before emigrating to the United States and becoming an American citizen in Boston in 1887. Under Italian law, one can indeed lay claim to Italian citizenship by filiation, in fact by *ius sanguinis* (by blood), as well as by *ius terrae* (birth on Italian soil). Far from being exposed to the risks of statelessness, I could even produce some vague claims to Spanish and Greek citizenship too. Both in Madrid and in Athens, influential friends assured me of their

support in obtaining my citizenship after first establishing residence there.

More readily and rapidly than I feared, the Department of State recognized, however, my claim to full citizenship by filiation, and I was promptly issued a new passport while I was still in New York. But I now preferred to return in the future more regularly on holidays to the United States, if only to consolidate, come what may in an increasingly unpredictable age, my claims to the citizenship of the only nation of which I feel that I remain a somewhat marginal or dissident writer.

While I was visiting my family in New York and Washington and renewing contact with old friends, I decided to ship to my Paris apartment much of what remained of my library in my mother's apartment as well as a few pictures. The French Consulate advised me, since I was born in France and now had a home in Paris, to file an application for a visa as an immigrant in order to qualify for the advantages of a duty-free removal of household goods, and I was assured that I would be granted such a visa within a few weeks.

But the weeks went by without any reply to my application from Paris. If only on account of a couple of contracts for work as an interpreter in Europe in the immediate future, I finally packed my books in some twenty grocery cartons and my few pictures in a suitcase and returned to France by ship, since I now had too much baggage to travel conveniently by air. With the French customs in Paris, I encountered no difficulties: most of the books contained in the cartons opened for inspection happened to have been published in France.

The real trouble arose suddenly a few weeks later, when I was awakened early one weekday morning in my Paris apartment by plain-clothes French policemen summoning me to dress hastily and follow them, as it later turned out, to the same sinister headquarters on the rue des Saussaies as on a previous occasion. There I was again questioned for several hours in an increasingly hostile manner and finally handed, at an hour when all good Frenchmen interrupt their day's work for a copious lunch, a paper ordering me, as an alien whose activities threatened dangerously the nation's security, to leave France by midnight of the same day.

A pusillanimous official at the American Consulate refused an hour later to undertake any official enquiry or other action on my behalf. In the course of that afternoon, I reported to François Bondy, the Swiss editor of *Preuves*, the French-language monthly of the Congress for Cultural Freedom to which I had for the past few years been a fairly regular contributor, that I had been questioned at great length in the rue des Saussaies about his activities, opinions, and presumably Jewish origin. He then recommended me to a French lawyer who received me immediately in his office and demanded that I pay him there and then a fee in advance, which I did; after which he advised me to leave France immediately, as stipulated in my expulsion order, while trusting him to act on my behalf with the French authorities in my absence. For two whole years, he then failed to answer any of my letters addressed to him from abroad and always remained extremely evasive if I phoned him long-distance from England, Belgium, West Germany, or Switzerland.

Following his advice, I left Paris that same day, by the last night-flight to London, after informing my brother by phone of the probable hour of my arrival. In Paris, I abandoned a fully furnished apartment, a large personal library that included a number of valuable first editions, and a small art collection of some value too. For the time being, I settled in the London home of my brother James while Harold, my other brother, undertook in New York a vast action on my behalf, collecting written testimonials and protests from some fifty reputable American writers, editors, and scholars who knew me personally or were acquainted with my work. Wystan Auden was one of the very few who failed to respond to my brother's request for a testimonial, although Auden had known me since 1930 and should have remembered that I had been the very first to translate any of his poetry into a foreign language when I published some of his work in French in the Belgian *Journal des Poètes.*

Copies of all these testimonials and protests were submitted in Washington to the Department of State, which replied politely that it couldn't interfere in what appeared to be purely domestic French affairs, a point of view which, if at all valid, would likewise have prevented it from intervening far more actively at all times in our age in the domestic affairs of equally sovereign states such as Vietnam, Cambodia, Chile, Nicaragua, Granada, or Panama.

While I was in London, my professional reputation as an interpreter continued to serve me in good stead. I soon found myself employed almost as frequently in England or on the Continent, with the exception of France, as previously there or elsewhere from my Paris home. An English friend soon brought my predicament to the attention of the editor of the *New Statesman and Nation,* which devoted a brief but indignant note to the arbitrary manner in which I had been expelled from France without further explanation. This proved to be the only mention of my case to appear in the press anywhere in the world, but

The author, 1985, ink on paper,
by Judith Clancy Johns

even this brief paragraph had repercussions which were mysteriously revealed to me from Vienna, of all places, some thirty years later.

Meanwhile an American lawyer consulted in New York by my brother Harold pointed out an odd anomaly in the text of the order expelling me from France: it had been drafted, signed, and dated while I was still in the United States, but served on me by the French security police only some weeks later after my return from New York to Paris. If the French authorities, this lawyer argued, had nothing better to do than to expel from their territory aliens who happened not to be in France, they could be kept busy for a long while expelling some 500 million Chinese citizens who had never yet set dainty foot on French soil, and most of whom were never likely to be tempted to come and view the Eiffel Tower. I was therefore advised to return to France and risk arrest there: in the ensuing legal proceedings, I should point out, by producing my American passport which clearly bore the stamped date of my return from the United States to France, that my expulsion order lacked validity because signed and dated at a time when I was not in France.

I managed to return twice to Paris before being finally arrested in 1960, on the occasion of my third re-entry into France, in the French frontier town of Annemasse, across the border from Geneva, where I was working for a few days for the International Labour Organization. The French police then drove me as a prisoner from Annemasse to the nearest administrative center, where a surprised Public Prosecutor happened to know me by name as a French writer, listened sympathetically to my story and refrained, for the time being, from detaining me in the local jail while awaiting trial. Instead, he sent me back to Geneva, promised to phone Paris for more ample instructions concerning the whole matter, and assured me that he would inform me in Geneva within a few days whether I would still need to return for an appearance in court.

The French Fourth Republic's last tottering government, which had expelled me from France in the course of one of its crises arising from the Algerian War of Liberation, was by now a thing of the past, already replaced by General De Gaulle's Fifth Republic. When I appeared a few days later in court in France, I was briefly but officially informed that I was free to return in peace to my Paris home, in fact armed with a new official statement proving that my former expulsion order was no longer valid.

As I learned many years later, General De Gaulle, soon after his accession to power, had denounced the involvement of France, as a sovereign nation, in the subservience of other European members of the Atlantic Pact to America's Cold War activities as implied in the CIA's secret *Glaive* or *Gladio* policies. Overnight I therefore ceased in France to be the object of constant investigations as an alien considered suspect in the eyes of the CIA and therefore, by delegation, in those too of the French Security Police. For a while I continued nevertheless, in the course of my travels, to be the attention of the security police of a few other member nations of the NATO pact. While undergoing treatment for a dermatological ailment in a London hospital, I was visited in my sickroom by an agent who claimed to have been sent by the Home Office in order to find out whether I had entered England in order to benefit as a tourist from its program of nationalized medicine. Without actually questioning me, he could easily have found out that I was being treated for an allergic reaction to something that I had apparently eaten and was paying for my treatment out of my own resources. But he also insisted on asking me questions which clearly revealed the nature of his other inter-

ests in my life. In Brussels too, some months after my return to live in France, I was suddenly summoned by the Belgian Security Police in order to be questioned at length on the reasons for my expulsion from France and how and why I had obtained the annulment of my expulsion order. Both Great Britain and Belgium, as I later learned in 1990 from the Belgian, French, Italian, and Spanish daily press, had continued to cooperate in the CIA's secret *Gladio* or *Glaive* activities long after General De Gaulle had officially banned them from France.

When I was free to return to Paris from my temporary exile, much of all this was discreetly hinted to me by one of my childhood friends, who was then a Minister in General De Gaulle's cabinet. Intrigued by the weird nature of my whole involvement with the French Security Police, he had requested the temporary loan of my file from the interested ministry and was so astounded by the vast amount of documentation accumulated in the course of several years of investigations that he asked a member of his staff to summarize it for him. My security police files, he discovered, consisted mainly of vicious gossip and of details concerning my private life and professional activities which, on the whole, could not be interpreted as having any possible political significance. All this, he admitted to me, had been diligently gathered by the French Security Police in response to repeated requests for information about me emanating originally from an American intelligence agency.

My two-year exile from my Paris home proved, however, to have exerted in the long run a positive influence on my life as a writer. While living in exile in London, I began, between interpreting assignments in England or abroad, to interview in English, French, German, or Italian a number of contemporary painters and sculptors with the intention of adding these to an earlier interview of Marc Chagall in a volume which was ultimately published in London as *Dialogues on Art* by Secker and Warburg and then reprinted in New York by Horizon Press, again in Santa Barbara by Ross Erikson Publishers, and, ultimately, in a somewhat revised edition almost thirty years later in San Francisco by Bedford Arts. At a considerably later date, I interviewed the painters Victor Brauner and Max Ernst as well as a number of other painters for later editions of my *Dialogues on Art* or for its ill-starred sequel, *More Dialogues on Art*, published in Santa Barbara by Ross Erikson shortly before that firm's financial collapse.

These interviews led me, beginning in 1958, to become ever more active as art critic, art historian, and lecturer on art. As an art historian, I can now pride myself on having discovered and identified a few old-master drawings which I subsequently sold through dealers to reputable museums; also on having discovered and identified, in an obscure London auction, an unknown small painting, *The Destruction of the Golden Calf,* by the great English Romantic visionary artist John Martin.

With my return to my Paris home, my literary activities began to increase concurrently with my regular work as a free-lance conference interpreter. In addition to regular contributions as its art critic to *L'Arche,* the illustrated monthly of the Federation of the Jewish Communities of France, and frequent contributions to *Arts Magazine,* edited in New York by Hilton Kramer, as well as to a few other American or English art journals and literary periodicals, I was suddenly commissioned by a Paris publisher, Editions SEDIMO, to write *De l'Homosexualité* in French.

Although now outdated in the light of a great deal of research undertaken in this field in the past twenty-five or thirty years, *De l'Homosexualité* remains, I'm told, a pioneer study because of its strictly biological and sociopsychological or even mildly behavioristic approach. A survey of all species in which homosexual behavior had previously been observed led me to conclude that, with very few exceptions among arthropods in the insect world such as dragonflies and bedbugs, homosexuality appears to be practiced, under a variety of sociopsychological circumstances, almost exclusively by vertebrates. Overcrowding, shortages of food, or constant exposure to such nuisances as noise can bring about phenomena of collective anxiety which, in various species of vertebrates such as sticklebacks or some rodents, in particular, soon lead to readily observable disturbances in the hormonal secretions of the secondary sexual attributes of males or females and ultimately to a more frequent incidence of homosexuality, of cannibalism, or of both.

Ethnological and other cultural factors exert, however, an important influence on the incidence of cannibalism or homosexuality in human societies, although the homosexuality of "deviant" members of a society which condemns or represses it tends to be determined by more specifically individual factors of a physical or psychological nature. Among the Amlash tribesmen of New Guinea, both male homosexuality and cannibalism are traditionally not only tolerated but actually encouraged in certain specific contexts which would require too many details to be satisfactorily defined here.

A few winter months spent in Istanbul while translating Yashar Kemal's novel into English also inspired in me a kind of love affair with Islamic history civilization in general. Within the next few years, this increasingly passionate interest began gradually to extend beyond Turkish history, literature, and art in order to include also, to some extent, those of the Arab world, of Iran, and, on the occasion of a couple of UNESCO missions further East, of India, Pakistan, and Afghanistan. In addition to editing a special Turkish issue of the luxuriously illustrated Swiss-German periodical *DU,* I thus wrote little by little those twenty short stories which were later collected in a volume as *The Delights of Turkey* by New Directions.

My own love affair with Islam soon led me to become, for a number of years, an addict of Tangier. I hadn't been back there since 1929, when I spent a couple of days there in the company of my parents. Back there in 1962 for a few weeks as a guest of the Dutch painter Guy Harlof, I revived my friendship with Paul and Jane Bowles, who had established their home there some years earlier. Returning now to Tangier two or three years running, I soon became rather unwisely involved in purchasing a house and garden in a predominantly middle-class neighborhood. Its traditionally Spanish or Moroccan-Jewish residents were moving out of it and emigrating, since Tangier was no longer the capital of the so-called International Zone and had become integrated into the Kingdom of Morocco, now fully independent and no longer divided into a Spanish and a French Protectorate and a small International Zone. Real estate had thus become temptingly cheap not only in this neighborhood into which middle-class Arab families were moving, but everywhere else in Tangier.

I became inveigled into this purchase by a local Moroccan-Jewish lawyer, Carlos de Nesry, who had some pretensions as a French-language writer and author of a couple of published books on Tangier. When I purchased the house, I agreed to allow its former owner and his family to continue occupying the apartment on the upper floor, where they lived, until the end of the school year, while I transformed an occupied shop on the ground floor into a small independent apartment for my own use and, perhaps later, for the use of tenants or guests.

But the former owner and his family continued to occupy the upstairs apartment for three or four more years, in fact until he died. In addition, I discovered that Nesry had meanwhile failed to have the deeds for my purchase of the property duly registered in my name and simply pocketed the money entrusted to him for the payment of the necessary fees. After the former owner's death, I finally had to undertake a lengthy lawsuit in order to evict the widow and her children. Out of sheer spite, they smashed all the windowpanes, as well as the bathtub, washbasin, toilet bowl, and kitchen sink when the police came to evict them by force, after which I had to renovate the whole apartment at considerable expense for my own future holiday use.

In spite of these worries, I then managed to spend a number of pleasant summer vacations in Tangier, though I soon began to weary of the constant increase in the expense of maintaining such a home away from home. In my absence, the house was being robbed nearly every winter of all its house linen and cutlery and the roof began again and again to leak during the rainy season. Meanwhile, many of the European or American residents of Tangier with whom I associated either died or moved away. The last years of illness and the death of Jane Bowles, then the return too of Peter Spencer-Churchill to England, where he soon died, all tended to reduce my social life to the point where I began to regret having purchased the house and thereby committed myself to returning every year to Tangier and depriving myself of holidaying anywhere else.

Some fifteen years after purchasing this home away from home in Tangier, I was glad to be rid of it at a loss and in otherwise somewhat disturbing circumstances. A young Moroccan, whom I had frequently befriended during his years as a student in a French university and with whose family in Tangier I had long been acquainted, availed himself of my hospitalization in Tangier for phlebitis to make me sign, while I was in a state of reduced mental alertness from the effects of analgesics, a financial agreement whereby he acquired the house on terms which later proved to be illegal so that I had no recourse against him when he failed to respect his financial obligations. Although I resented at the time having thus been fooled, I soon began to be greatly relieved by no longer having to pay for the maintenance of this house or feeling obliged to return as often to Tangier. On my few brief returns in the past ten years, I have found Morocco in general, and Tangier in particular, ever less attractive, with the possible exception of Marrakech. In any case, I had meanwhile acquired another "home away from home," in Dieppe, on the coast of Normandy and within much closer reach from Paris, although I'm now beginning to regret this purchase too.

In the course of the first decade after my return to live in peace in Paris, I gradually undertook the task, between frequent trips abroad on interpreting assignments, of collecting and editing all my poems for publication in three projected volumes which would include many new poems written since the publication of my *Poems 1928–1948* by New Directions in 1949 as well as some older poems which had never yet been published or had been published only in periodicals. Black Sparrow Press has now published only the first two of these three projected volumes. *Emperor of Midnight* contained most of my earlier more-or-less Surrealist writings and is now out of print. *Thrice Chosen,* published a few years later, included all my poems on Jewish themes except those that I've written in recent years. *A Private Life,* the third of these three proposed volumes, remains for the time being unpublished. In addition, Asylum Arts will be publishing in California in 1992 a volume of my prose poems or fables, *Choose Your Own World,* that illustrate what I'm tempted to call my Surrealist Poetics of the Absurd, while CLOUDFORMS, a small press in England, will likewise be publishing in 1992 *The Journal of an Apprentice Cabbalist,* one of my old Surrealist texts of 1931 which had long been lost but suddenly surfaced again a couple of years ago.

In addition to thus becoming increasingly active as a writer, I began around 1968 to interpret less frequently or preferably on short-term assignments in Paris for UNESCO or in Brussels for the European Common Market, while also returning more regularly to the United States. After a first full-year assignment to conduct courses in both English and French literatures at San Francisco State University, I was invited within the next two decades likewise to teach at Brown University, Oberlin College, the University of California at Santa Cruz, the graduate school of Columbia University, the University of California at Los Angeles, and twice at Bard College.

After teaching at San Francisco State University and then interpreting a conference in Mexico City and another in Seattle, I was engaged from California to interpret two more in Australia and returned from there to Paris via New Guinea, the Philippines, Hongkong, Japan, Taiwan, Cambodia, Sri Lanka, India, Pakistan, Afghanistan, Iran, Lebanon, Syria, and Turkey.

I had previously visited several areas of India as well as parts of Nepal some years earlier, while vacationing for a few weeks after interpreting a conference for UNESCO in New Delhi. Unlike Allen Ginsberg and a number of other American intellectuals of the last few decades, I was appalled rather than at all attracted by Hinduism. Only with some of the Sikhs, Mohammedans, or Parsees of India have I ever felt any sympathy. My reaction to Hinduism remains, in this respect, similar to that of a Mohammedan philosopher whose name escapes me and who, soon after the first Mohammedan invasion of northern India, attempted in vain to come to some intellectual understanding with Hindu thinkers and concluded: "How can one argue with people who not only ignore the rules of logic, but have never even felt the need of them?"

Following my teaching job at San Francisco State University and my interpreting jobs in Mexico City, Seattle, and Sidney, my round-the-world trip had lasted, all in all, close on two years by the time I finally returned to Paris, where my home had meanwhile been occupied much of the time by the painter and writer Mary Guggenheim and her two daughters. While in San Francisco, I had lived in Kenneth Rexroth's apartment on Scott Street throughout the whole of his own round-the-world trip, accompanied by his two daughters and the poet Carol Tinker, whom he later married.

Soon after my return to Paris, I undertook, under a grant from Lisbon's Calouste Gulbenkian Foundation, the necessary research, in the excellent library of Lisbon's Sociedade de Geografia, in the Portuguese National Archives of Torre do Tombo, and in Seville's Archives of the Indies, for a biography of the great sixteenth-century navigator Magel-

Edouard Roditi, New York City, 1987

lan. Much of the first draft of this book was written in the course of a winter in my Tangier home, if only in order to be closer to Seville or Lisbon in case of need of further research. The final draft of this biography was then delayed for a year as a result of my mother's illness and death in London, where she had returned some months earlier after living most of the time since 1938 in the United States.

My *Magellan of the Pacific* was ultimately published in London by Faber and Faber in an edition that soon sold out after being favorably reviewed in the *Economist* and elsewhere. It was never reprinted, however, in England because Faber and Faber were discouraged by the lack of success of most of the similar biographies of great travelers which they had published in the same series. In New York, an American edition of my *Magellan of the Pacific* was later published somewhat unwillingly by McGraw-Hill, which found itself committed to this task after buying up Herder and Herder, which had originally contracted to publish the American edition of my book. Mursia later published in Milan an Italian translation, which was enthusiastically reviewed at great length in the *Osservatore Romano*, the Vatican's official daily newspaper. The illness and death of the Portuguese publisher who had originally undertaken to publish it in translation in Lisbon then delayed for several years its final publication there by Assirio e Alvim.

I should perhaps pride myself on having been Magellan's only biographer to have scrupulously refrained from any speculations, such as those hazarded some years earlier by Stefan Zweig, concerning the great navigator's psychological motivations, which have been attested by none of his contemporaries. On the contrary, I limited myself, throughout my account of Magellan's life, exclusively to the few facts available in the historical sources, such as Antonio Pigafetta's Italian diary of the whole expedition, which I was able to consult. In addition to studying all the maps which might have been known to Magellan, and finally identifying the only one which probably misled him into believing that the estuary of the Plata River, now separating the Argentine Republic from Uruguay, might be a straits leading from the Atlantic to the Pacific, I also undertook extensive research into the knowledge of the stars of the Southern Hemisphere that might already have been known to him as guides for navigation as well as into the whole field of the navigational instruments available to him in the first quarter of the sixteenth century.

In addition, I proved to be Magellan's only biographer to have so far been able or willing to consult Turkish naval historians and Istanbul's Naval

Museum in Besiktas in order to obtain more detailed information concerning the naval battle of Diu, in which Magellan is reported to have participated off the Indian coast of Gujarat against a Turkish fleet while he was still serving in Portuguese India. This Turkish fleet, I thus discovered, had been handicapped in its movements by the size and weight of its cumbersome new bronze cannon, which a Venetian engineer had but recently taught the Turks to produce in the newly established foundry of the Ottoman naval base in Besiktas.

While progressing in my research in such technical details concerning Magellan's life, I became increasingly aware of how much I still owed in my approach to historiography to the teachings and the example of Ernst Kantorowicz, the great medievalist whose seminars I had attended as far back as 1939 in Berkeley. Ever since the publication of my *Magellan of the Pacific,* I have again and again been tempted to undertake some similar task of historical research, but my later choices in this whole field appear to have so far met with little encouragement from the various foundations and publishers to whom I applied for financial assistance.

My fields as a guest lecturer or teacher in American universities and colleges varied considerably. In addition to being invited to conduct creative-writing seminars, in the efficacy of which, I must admit, I have never had much faith, I also taught courses in English or French literature or else in art history. The most popular of these courses have proven through the years to be those on Marcel Proust, on the Gothic novel, on Surrealist literature and art or on Symbolist literature and art. In my seminar on Symbolist literature and art conducted at Oberlin College, my best student proved to be Larry Kanter, now Curator of the Lehman Collection in New York City's Metropolitan Museum of Art. Other former students of mine have made careers which, without being quite as spectacularly successful as Larry's, yet owe much of their success, in their own expressed opinion, to my teaching and the guidance which I later continued to grant them.

While still interpreting and occasionally teaching between 1970 and 1980, I developed an increasingly regular activity as a writer, whether in English or in French. This activity included a great deal of criticism of literature or of art, above all of the work of contemporary Jewish painters or sculptors in my monthly contribution in French to *L'Arche,* but also more and more editing, for final publication, of much of my writing that had long remained fragmentary or otherwise unfinished in my archives.

Between 1970 and 1980, I thus managed to collect, for publication by Black Sparrow Press, my two previously mentioned volumes of poems, *Emperor of Midnight* and *Thrice Chosen,* as well as most of the third book, *A Private Life,* which remains unpublished, and also a collection of a few of my very early poems, *In a Lost World,* which Black Sparrow Press published as one of its *Sparrow* pamphlets. For publication by New Directions I then managed likewise to revise and collect the twenty stories of *The Delights of Turkey.* In the ensuing decade, between 1980 and 1990, I likewise collected and edited for final publication the prose and verse contained in *The Journal of an Apprentice Cabbalist,* originally written in 1931, which Cloud Editions is now publishing in England, as well as the texts contained in *Choose Your Own World,* which Asylum Arts will be publishing in California, while also beginning to work on the memoirs which all my friends have long been urging me to write.

Still following the advice given me some four decades earlier by T. S. Eliot, I continued during all these years to be active as a translator of poetry, whether into English or into French, and of prose too, from so many different languages that I should modestly blush, were I called upon to list in greater detail the full range of these "five-finger exercises." Among the more important such tasks, I should mention again my two small volumes of translations of poetry from Turkish, the one, *The Wandering Fool,* into English, and the other, selected poems by Sultan Suleiman the Magnificent into French. The more important such tasks included, in addition to a great number of translations of poems from various languages for publication in periodicals or anthologies, a French translation of Horace Walpole's *Hieroglyphic Tales,* which Jose Corti did me the honor of publishing in Paris with my long critical introduction in his almost inaccessibly exclusive publishing house, and now a more important volume of translations into English, still unpublished, of selected verse and prose by James Joyce's close French friend Léon-Paul Fargue. This last volume includes a long introduction containing my personal memories of meetings and conversations with both Joyce and Fargue in the "expatriate" Paris world of *transition* and of Sylvia Beach's now historic bookstore.

Long before 1980, friends were already urging me to undertake the task of writing my memoirs. I thus began to write and publish here and there, in American or European periodicals, accounts of individual episodes of my past life, above all of my meetings with T. S. Eliot and my subsequent association with him, or else of my meetings with George

Orwell as a still very needy journalist named Eric Blair. Soon after attaining the age of seventy, I also began to feel increasingly the physical and nervous strain of long sessions of simultaneous interpreting, and I was more and more often bored by the sheer repetitiousness of the deliberations of most of the European Common Market's meetings in Brussels. With the expansion of the European Community to include new member states, the number of its official languages was increasing and I now found myself more and more often expected to interpret into French not only English, German, or Italian speakers, but also Portuguese or Spanish speakers with whose native language I had lost, for lack of practice, much of my former proficiency as an interpreter.

A few of the less serious physical handicaps with which one tends to become afflicted with age were also incapacitating me from time to time in my work. At the age of seventy-four, I suddenly realized that I was by far the oldest free-lance interpreter still employed occasionally by the European Common Market, which retires all its own regular full-time interpreters, together with other permanent employees, as soon as they reach the age of sixty-five. I could also claim quite justifiably some kind of seniority in my profession as an interpreter for international meetings. No colleague who was still employed permanently or on a free-lance basis could, as far as I knew, claim to have worked on and off in our profession, as I had indeed by now, ever since the spring of 1944, when I first worked as an interpreter in Philadelphia for the International Labour Office.

I therefore decided in 1984 that it was high time that I retire from this exhausting and intellectually less and less stimulating profession, which never exerted on me the kind of fascination which I had for many years observed that it appeared to exert on so many of my more ambitious or vain colleagues. In the course of the next six years and until I reached in June 1990 the age of eighty, I still remained active, however, as a teacher, in the graduate school of Columbia University, at Bard College, or at the University of California at Los Angeles, as well as an increasingly productive writer, both in English and in French.

In recent years, in addition to still writing some poetry and, whether in English or in French, a great deal of critical prose as well as, from time to time, a few short stories, I have been increasingly concerned with the writing of my memoirs. As I now look back on eight decades of an exceptionally busy and varied life, I begin also to realize how much its evolution has been determined by unpredictable

chances or else by often all-too-hasty choices, many of which may well have proven in the long run unwise.

Throughout my childhood and adolescence, my upbringing and education might have prepared me for the life of a gentleman of leisure or a successful career as a scholar, a creative writer, or an artist, perhaps even a scientist, but certainly not for the kind of future as a businessman which appears to have been the only ambition entertained for me by my parents. Nor did my schooling, in a privileged and sheltered upper-class English environment, prepare me to face with ease and equanimity the economic and political upheavals so soon to disrupt the family background which I had learned to take for granted. As I now look back on the various problems that I repeatedly found myself facing and having to solve between 1930 and 1960, I often wonder how I managed almost miraculously to cope, most of the time in an entirely unfamiliar environment, with some of the heavy responsibilities that I assumed, towards my teenage sister, my two younger brothers, and my mother, in the years that followed my father's death and my realization that nothing was left of what once appeared to be my family's great wealth.

In spite of many handicaps, discouragements, or unwise choices which I might still regret, I have by now been able to write and publish, whether in English, French, or German, some thirty volumes of my own writings or of translations of works by other writers, as well as perhaps as many as two thousand critical essays, book reviews, and articles of one kind or another. These remain scattered in a great variety of European or American periodicals, some of them only in translation in Judeo-Spanish, Portuguese, Italian, or Turkish. Most of these publications in periodicals are now preserved, should posterity ever be interested in them, in the Special Collections Division of the Research Library of the University of California at Los Angeles.

In the few more years that I may yet be privileged to live, I suspect that I'm unlikely to complete the task of writing final drafts of the ten or more books of which the preliminary drafts await further development in the extensive literary archives still preserved in my Paris apartment. Nor am I ever likely to select, revise, and finally edit for publication some four or five more volumes of interviews of artists or essays of one kind or another which I might wish to select from the mass of critical writings, whether in the field of literature, of art, or of philosophy, which remain dormant in my archives at UCLA.

My most urgent problem as a writer remains that of somehow licking into shape the final version of my

With Susan Sontag, New York City, 1988

memoirs. These, I now fear, may well fill as many as three or more volumes. What can I claim that the ultimate meaning of my whole life may have been? Of the turmoil of events in which I've often found myself involved and that I've somehow managed to survive, what remains of real significance in my own eyes or in those of my potential readers?

As a Jew, I'm endowed with a memory and a sense of history that should embrace, according to the traditional doctrine of *Zakhor,* much more of the past than my own puny lifespan. But I've lived in an age so obsessed with its own importance and its daily news that it tends to reduce us all to a kind of behavioristically induced collective amnesia. Often, I now feel that, if I had been privileged to live, for instance, in the Italian Renaissance, perhaps in Florence at the court of Lorenzo the Magnificent, I might perhaps have achieved, as a humanist thinker, scholar, or creative writer, a kind of immortality that appears to be denied in my age to American writers of real substance. All too readily and busily, we acclaim many nine days' wonders whom we just as readily and quite properly forget. Where indeed are most of our best-sellers of yesteryear?

My friend Kenneth Rexroth once remarked that poor Paul Goodman, had he lived in Paris and written in French rather than lived in New York and written in English, would probably have become world-famous in his lifetime and as widely read and respected in translation in America as Jean-Paul Sartre or Albert Camus. Himself one of the greatest American poets of his generation, Rexroth has never enjoyed the same acclaim as Allen Ginsberg, Gregory Corso, or Lawrence Ferlinghetti, who certainly make fewer intellectual or real emotional demands on their far more numerous readers. Paul Bowles now owes much of his celebrity as a major American fiction writer to his successes in England or in French, German, Italian, Portuguese, or Spanish translations, or else to the international success of a film version, directed by an Italian, of his first novel, which remained for several decades ignored or out of print in his native America.

Was I originally destined to be Christian or Jew, heterosexual or homosexual, French, English, or American? And what have I finally become? As an American poet, I'm consistently neglected by nearly all American anthologists, who appear to believe erroneously that I'm either English or French. French and Italian anthologists, on the other hand, sometimes include me in their anthologies of contemporary American poetry. Only the FBI and its sinister offspring, the CIA, and the latter's *Glaive-Gladio* changeling, have at all times considered me American enough to deserve the dubious privilege of their attentions.

BIBLIOGRAPHY

Poetry:

Poems for F., Editions du Sagittaire, 1935.

Prison Within Prison: Three Elegies on Hebrew Themes, James A. Decker, 1941.

(With Paul Goodman and Meyer Liben) *Pieces of Three*, 5 x 8 Press, 1942.

Poems 1928–1948, New Directions, 1949.

New Hieroglyphic Tales: Prose Poems, Kayak, 1968.

Emperor of Midnight, Black Sparrow Press, 1974.

In a Lost World, Black Sparrow Press, 1978.

The Temptations of a Saint (prose poem), Ettan Press, 1980.

Thrice Chosen, Black Sparrow Press, 1981.

New Old and New Testaments (prose poems), Red Ozier Press, 1983.

Etre un Autre, privately printed, 1983.

The Journal of an Apprentice Cabbalist, CLOUD, 1991.

Other:

Oscar Wilde, New Directions, 1947, revised edition, 1987.

Dialogues on Art, Secker and Warburg, 1960, Horizon Press, 1961.

Joachim Karsch, Gebrüder Mann (Berlin), 1960.

Selbstanalyse eines Sammlers, Galerie der Spiegel (Cologne), 1960.

De l'Homosexualité, Editions Sedimo (Paris), 1962.

(Editor) Ambrose Bierce, *Mein Lieblingsmord*, Insel (Frankfurt), 1963.

Magellan of the Pacific, Faber, 1972, McGraw Hill, 1973.

The Disorderly Poet and Other Essays, Capra Press, 1975.

(Editor) Hamri, *Tales of Joujouka*, Capra Press, 1975.

The Delights of Turkey: Twenty Tales, New Directions, 1977.

Meetings with Conrad, Press of the Pegacycle Lady (Los Angeles), 1977.

More Dialogues on Art, Ross Erikson, 1983.

Propos sur l'Art, José Corti (Paris), 1987.

Dialogues (contains revised selections from *Dialogues on Art* and *More Dialogues on Art*), Bedford Arts (San Francisco), 1990

Dialoge über Kunst, Suhrkamp (Frankfurt), 1991.

Translated (from English, French, German, Portuguese, Spanish, or Turkish, into English, French, or German):

André Breton, *Young Cherry Trees Secured Against Hares*, View Editions, 1946.

Albert Memmi, *The Pillar of Salt*, Elek, 1956.

Ernest Namenyi, *The Essence of Jewish Art*, Yoseloff, 1960.

Yashar Kemal, *Memed, My Hawk*, Harvill Press, 1961, Pantheon, 1961.

Pablo Picasso, *Toros y Toreros*, Thames and Hudson, 1964.

Robert Schmutzler, *Art Nouveau*, Thames and Hudson, 1964.

Carlo Suares, *Genesis Rejuvenated*, Menard Press, 1973.

Yunus Emre, *The Wandering Fool*, (selected poems of a medieval Turkish Sufi mystic), Cadmus Editions (Tiburon), 1984.

(With Paul Celan) Fernando Pessoa, *Selected Poems*, Suhrkamp, 1983.

Horace Walpole, *Contes Hiéroglyphiques*, José Corti, 1985.

Suleiman the Magnificent, *Soliman le Magnifique, Poète* (selected poems), Dost Yayinlari (Istanbul), 1989.

Contributing editor of several periodicals, including *Antaeus, Arts in Society, European Judaism,* and *View.* Cofounder and co-editor of literary journal *Das Lot,* 1947–52. Art critic for *L'Arche, Arts,* and *Pictures on Exhibit.* Contributor to periodicals, including *Asylum, Caliban, Encounter, Europe, Exquisite Corpse, Midstream, New Directions Annual,* and *Pardes.*

Eve Shelnutt

1941-

Sisters Cynthia, Eve, and Anne Waldrop, 1949

It was the season when odors rose like invisible flame against the landscape of suffocating heat. Beneath the burnt grass and withered kudzu, rodents, skunks, knots of insects were dying, for we saw daily buzzards circling the folds of the hills. The hills lay belly-up and reddish against the skyline, the kudzu, with nothing to hold it, having slipped like a robe downward. As if to anchor these dead or sleeping Buddhas, an occasional tree rose from their navels. Without the trees, they might have rolled down into the valley, leaving the horizon deserted and more still.

I began one short story this way. While writing, in this instance the story "Voice," I know where I am—memory released, for without fiction and poetry, its power both to save and to transform, my past would be closed to me. Before I wrote, I believe that I lived with little separation between the past and the present, and, without perspective, the past is a second skin. With writing came a sloughing off. I have saved the skins, toughened, stretched.

The place of "Voice" is my grandfather's farm outside Landrum, South Carolina, but not *the* farm where I had followed him as he plowed by mule; not the rock house he had built where we visited and later lived during occasional summers after he had died and my grandmother Waldrop had moved over the hills to Greer.

That land retains for me my memories of him, all benign, for my grandfather Waldrop was the kindest of men, taken up not as his wife was by the noisier forms of the Baptist religion, but by his mind. He was a reader, my father says, and it was he who wrote me letters when we had a fixed address; I who took dictation from my grandmother at the table by the stream when she "wrote" to her children scattered as distantly as California.

I saw my grandfather at work or pausing for water at the spring. He had lost a business during the Depression; the farm was what he bought with the last of his hard currency, or perhaps it was borrowed; my father never said. While he cleared the land for crops and built the stone house, he and his family lived in a clay-floor, one-room clapboard house across the primary dirt road, high on a hill, on land too steep for mules. It was that miniature house that became the avenue to the story.

I have no knowledge of how many children my grandparents had then; indeed, no knowledge of how many children he and my grandmother had altogether—how many had survived. Seven, eight?

Father, James Marion Waldrop, 1961

The question is telling: I could ask one of my parents, but when I was a child, questions were discouraged by the emotions they set off. It was better to ask nothing. Observe, and wait.

I was born into my parents' restlessness, bred of my father's need and ambition and of my mother's grudging allegiance, if not to motion, then to him, or maybe to her idea of Family that resolved into a configuration hard to bear for its difference from her aristocratic background.

We came to live for a summer in the one-room house on the hill, and yet I have no idea when or why. Presumably my grandparents still occupied the rock house below. Since my grandfather died when I was eleven or so, I would have been young.

For many years I had retained in memory a picture of how the house sat on the hill, and—invented?—an image of my older sister and mother standing outside the house looking down to the road below. It was that image I wanted to pursue. I suspect now that the image issued from my imagination; nevertheless, it had taken on a life similar to that of a memory. At the least, I had made a picture in my mind from an ambience, an emotion, a yearning that the image of my sister and mother on the hillside defined.

In the story, a man similar to my father is away on a trip; his wife and children sleep on pallets on the cool, clay floor. Then strangers move into the farmhouse across the narrow dirt road, bringing their differences as people that will unsettle the mother and children. At stake is the middle child's definition of sexuality.

Now, when I visit my father, my husband and I wind up the recently paved road, past brush that obscures the rock house crumbling into bottom land, and we arrive on the site of The Little House. Just as I had remembered, a white farmhouse sits under oaks across the narrow road. Waldrop Road, it is called on a green-and-white marker, for my father holds the deed to the land, knows his congressman and how government works, and has cared enough that his father's name identify the road.

Did I write the story "Voice" before or after my father had built his house where The Little House once stood? I can't remember; when I first saw my father's house, built upon his retirement, I was startled. I have driven by other sites of my childhood and been disturbed when the image that had seeded a story displayed its life, ungentled by memory and clearly purposeful, apart from my use of it in fiction. A disjunction occurs, a severing, and, always, I promise myself, I won't seek such a wrenching again. My memory, it seems, is to serve my fiction and poetry, not the social self that would like coherence, sequence, "history."

We have family photographs; they overflow from boxes and fill a wall of my mother's house in South Carolina. But my father's image is missing from the photographs on the wall and, I believe, from the boxes, for she has in recent years sent to my father the photographs no longer relevant to her life now.

Yet pictures of several houses remain, especially of the good house, the "real" home of my parents' first years of marriage, the Dutch-colonial house in Douglaston, on Long Island Sound. My grandfather Waldrop visited us there, as did my grandfather Brock, each pictured holding the hands of the, then, two grandchildren. It was a grand house, of antiques and polished wood floors. The children appear pampered, untroubled, beloved.

My father worked at NBC then, when radios were companionable, when reporting the news was a sacred trust. Television was a mere advancing idea, and to display talent of more than voice required the long trek to Hollywood. My father served in radio his apprenticeship to all his travels. My older sister, Cynthia, and I are photographed in bunny suits on either side of a microphone, with the initials "NBC" prominent. In our hands are baskets filled with candy eggs. We look entirely confident.

But World War II came nightly over the radio waves; my father, who had suffered polio as a child, broadcast at night for Voice of America, after his long days at NBC. When the bomb was dropped over Nagasaki, my mother was in the hospital having my younger sister, Anne, and the horror entered her as if it were my sister's twin. "You have no *idea* what the world was like before," she often said to us as we grew. Although it was years before the facts behind her words wounded us, tone can convey the weight of knowledge that is coming; my mother had been stricken by a force being born. Her last child was its anodyne.

And, over the years, like a balancing agent, the house in Douglaston took up a life inside my mother too. During the writing of a story, I remembered the dining room as she had described it, with its broad table onto whose wood light streamed from large windows. A plate of fudge sits on the table; Father will be arriving on his bicycle from the train station; my mother is in high heels, lamps are lit above the two easy chairs slipcovered in blue linen. Outside, Cynthia, the eldest daughter, is ice-skating on the small pond beneath the trees. . . . *Home at last*, my mother may have thought, for that house alone had the solidity of her parents' home.

Mother, Evelyn Brock Waldrop, 1980

My mother's mother, Grandmother Brock (I don't know her first name), was killed by an automobile as she walked hand-in-hand with my mother along a road in Spartanburg, South Carolina. The car dragged her along as my mother, age ten or eleven, watched. Almost immediately my mother was sent alone to a boarding school, her much-older sisters having already married and moved away.

The death was, I think, the single transforming event of my mother's life; it shadowed her as a young woman, as a bride, and, later, as a woman raising her children alone. We heard little, initially, of Grandmother Brock and, later, when the wound was partially healed, scarcely more. She was tall, elegant, classically beautiful; photographs testify to this, as does the beauty of her three girls, Romona, Pauline, and my mother, Evelyn. She ran for her husband an ordered establishment, a large house common to the South when various relatives might be in residence for months or years.

She was, apparently, beloved by all, not for the patina of goodness an early death uses as cover, but for all that she was and gave to others—a woman of great refinement, educated in mind and spirit and manners, and generous with similar visions of the lives of her girls, all of whom would be, appropriately, musicians. Her family, the Kuykendalls, came from Holland; she possessed a great Dutch strength of body and bequeathed the same to her daughters, all of whom are still living, all vivacious, the eldest in her late eighties.

Grandfather Brock owned a transport firm and, during the Depression, kept all of his men employed. He too was fine in appearance, tall, strong, and gentle looking. In our photographs taken outside the house in Douglaston, he must stoop a long way to grasp our hands. By then his full hair was white. When he was overseeing the removal of a bank safe, it fell, crushing him. Not many years had gone by since his wife's death, too few certainly for devastation not to seem doubled for my mother.

One of his properties in Spartanburg, the place of my birth, became our family's then, and we moved into it. I have no knowledge of why my parents had lived previously in Spartanburg, or where. The house we moved into was large, set back from the sidewalk, with a sun porch on one side. At age four I roller-skated outside with vestiges of whooping cough, scaring my little friends. In that house during nap time, I opened a heating grate in the floor and fell through to the living room below, barely missing the peaked mantle clock that accompanied us through all of our travels and still sits in my mother's house.

I watched my mother faint on the long walk to our door late one night when I had been lost, then found popping corn across the street in the lighted kitchen of a neighbor's otherwise dark house. As my mother later explained, a "Negro" ball game was being played that night; the fact increased her fear. And yet it was unusual information for my mother to impart; she had been raised by various Negro household help, had loved in particular a cook whose physical strength and verbal skills were the source of endless stories. As we girls grew up, my mother employed various black women to iron, and men to do yard work. When we rebelled, citing progressive politics and our own capabilities, she said, "Someone must employ them."

Yes, we did receive a "Southern" education regardless of how much both parents did to ameliorate it. By practice, great force of will, and the demands of the job market, my father had trained himself from the telling speech patterns and intonations of the South; my mother's years of singing had given her, too, a diction almost unidentifiable. As children, we were trained to enunciate clearly, and it set us apart. We were not to stoop so low as to

denigrate Negroes regardless that our schoolmates did. We were to learn music and proper posture, and if we were taken on various Sundays to homes where Negroes in uniform served us from the left on huge white platters—well, who knew? It might be training we would need one day. It was better, our mother said, than the Southern custom of women without servants standing while guests ate, at the ready themselves with second helpings of chicken and ham and mashed potatoes. We tried to believe her, but the "White" sign still hung over the water fountains at Woolworth's.

My father was filled with prejudice, the sort that spans the globe. Even now at Christmas we search for sweaters made not in Japan or China but in Scotland or England, or stamped "Made in USA." Yet he had and has impeccable manners that allow no rudeness to anyone. Indeed, he is interested in any individual; it is group mores that sometimes anger him. Yet he recognizes that the world has changed. He said in the midseventies of Washington, D.C., where the women handling the documents he wanted were black, "I thought to myself, 'This is Martin Luther King's dream come true.'"

In the ninth grade, I argued with him; somehow, as the middle child, stubborn by nature, I was the one always asking him to pause in his knowledge and arrogance. We were in Orlando, Florida; I was in a civics course. After our long and fruitless debate, my mother took me aside to tell me that he was wrong, but unchangeable. Often, in our cars, she merely shook her head covertly in our direction to say, *Pay no attention.*

But there was no way to disregard either parent. Much of the time we traveled so extensively across America that our home seemed to be our two cars and their trailers of open metal slats where our belongings were. Indeed, they *were* our home, since we had emptied the rented house and were on our way to another not yet found. These trips often lasted for months; sometimes we would live temporarily with relatives, divided among their houses—once in a house built and abandoned by a relative—then move on. We often entered school in midautumn, and usually in a different state than we had lived in the previous school year; always in a different town.

Sometimes my father moved with us; often my mother moved us alone to the town where she would teach that academic year. Or my father would accompany us, stay a day, a week, several months, then be off again while my mother honored her contract with whatever public school would keep us in food and clothing. Once we moved into an apartment only to move from it the same day, going on to a different state because my father had gone to the television station where he was to be employed and found irregularities in the terms of employment. Probably it had to do with a weather program; he never liked doing the weather. Or maybe it was a dispute about a "talent fee," for as children we were familiar with the term.

My mother never liked public-school teaching; her upbringing had prepared her to be, as my older sister has said of us all, "a drawing-room woman" who plays a little violin, speaks a little French, and presides graciously over the long dining-room table for family and guests.

And yet she had, during those years, a prodigious strength of character that made it always possible for her to find a job, feed and clothe us when my father's jobs came to an end. Besides the public-school teaching, she gave private voice and violin lessons and conducted the choirs in many towns' Baptist churches. She sewed our clothes, baked our bread, canned our food; and despaired of our father. Ours was not the life she had planned for herself or her children.

Still, vestiges from the house on Long Island remained. In our trailers, and used weekly for Sunday dinners when we came to a halt, was the antique Wedgewood china, sterling-silver cutlery, crystal glassware; around us the antique clock, the Chinese vase, the harp, violin, the sheet music, the hardbound books, our good clothes. Clothes were important, my father's particularly elegant since he was the one before the camera. But my mother's, too, were fine, a suit being worth having a snagged spot rewoven by a tailor.

Above all, we had books, and it was typical that eventually—having married one another twice and twice divorced, their three children solemnly in attendance—it was the *Webster's* unabridged dictionary that was the one contested possession of my parents. The argument concerning the dictionary dates my proclivity to consider fairness in a dispute over a possession less a factor than who wants the object more. It was my father who should have had the dictionary, for he used it with great delight and frequency.

He had quit high school in the tenth grade and, although he had planned to, he never went to college, since my mother became pregnant early in their marriage. My mother, as all of the women in her family, had received a college education. It was a difference between them that we children knew existed; sometimes, hearing my father on the radio, my mother would catch a mispronunciation and correct him. His pride was such that he was bothered

greatly; a most-familiar line from my childhood was his order to us about a word: "Look it up." The *Webster's* was our most-used book. It was very early in my childhood that my father ceased needing to have his use of language corrected, he who has treated education as a lifelong, natural pursuit certainly not confined to schools or universities.

We children were told almost nothing about the reasons for our travels, as, indeed, we were told little of my father's career. Along with the *New Yorker* and *Saturday Review*, copies of *Variety* were stacked on tables. We had seen publicity photographs of our father in which, invariably, he was pictured with a Camel cigarette, the brand he has smoked all of his life, unfiltered then and now. Early we were conscious of his admiration for Edward R. Murrow. We knew that he loved the theater and saw plays in New York. We had lived in Oxnard and Venice, California, for reasons of his career. Or did we know that then? I'm not sure.

We crossed America numerous times, from New York or the South to California, and I do know that my father, for some period of time, sought to become a film actor, and may have been in several films. I went to kindergarten in California; later there in the second grade, having lived in the South in between. But I doubt, now, that I had any knowledge of why we were in California. Our trips West had been leisurely, for we spent time in state forests, magnificent in the era before such camping out was commonplace.

My father loved America's natural beauty and shared his wonder at it with such enthusiasm that I assumed we were simply traveling in order to see our country. We slept sometimes in our cars, for the Nash Ambassador had a fold-down bed in the back and the Packard seemed equally large. Often in national parks when the weather was good we slept on the double mattresses that were positioned on top of our crates of belongings. And we slept in motels after my father had investigated the quality of the beds and the establishment's cleanliness. In the era of independent motels, it was not easy to find a proper set of rooms or decent meals. My father always took it upon himself to speak to the managers or the cooks if they had represented themselves by something unworthy. He did it kindly, as an obligation: a lapse might well be understandable if one were ill or had unusual problems, but honorable service was surely the aim.

On one stay in California, my mother taught in a public school whose student body was primarily poor Mexican children; she was horrified that, due to their hunger, the children devoured the white paste stored in a huge jar on a closet shelf. In the market nearby, I saw Chinese women with two-inch-long fingernails, and had no idea what to make of it. With Mexican children, I went trick-or-treating, running wildly with cayenne pepper-dipped toothpicks stuck in my mouth. We lived in a row house; my mother despised it. I was five during one California foray; seven during another. Of my two sisters during our times in California, I have no memory at all.

In the first grade, as I remember now, I went to school in Columbus, South Carolina, not far from where my father had rented a gentleman's farm between Tryon, North Carolina, and this tiny South Carolina town. The stone house was huge and elegant, surrounded by trees and with a stream running in front of the house at the bottom of the sloping lawn. Down the road were the tenant farmers who worked the farm, although my mother kept several cows for milk, grew turnip greens to sell in Tryon and from which to brew the pot liquor we loved.

I think that she was not teaching that year; that my father returned occasionally, for I remember his deep-red hunting boots and our Irish setter at point. Were we short on money that year? Why, otherwise, would my mother raise and sell turnip greens? Yet, even if we had been, she did not neglect to make candied orange-peel confection for our teachers, beautifully enclosed in glass, paper doilies, and ribbon. When mine broke, Cynthia waited for me as I ran home crying to have it fixed; I remember Cynthia well that day. We had missed the school bus by the time I returned. Cynthia led me over a small mountain, a "shortcut," she said, to school. We arrived hours late, our legs scratched, our feet cold. And yet I was confident we would arrive; Cynthia kept saying so; very early, she possessed a great authority.

We must have begun our travels from the house in Long Island, then to South Carolina and on to California with money from the sale of the several houses and a portion of my mother's inheritance. Then it dwindled and finally ran out, for our rented houses and apartments were suddenly less grand. Our belongings gave off a telling history: we were not really meant to be *here*.

Always we were permitted to buy books. Socially, we were not like the children we lived among. What to make of "who" we were, when even our formal education in school was not of prime importance? "They can read, can't they?" my father would ask my mother when she wondered when and where her children would next be in school. Going from state to state, we studied history out of sequence,

geography from our cars in tandem over America's roads.

If the relatives from my mother's family, whom she took us to see when we found ourselves back in the South, found our situation as children odd, they were circumspect enough not to tell us. We did well in school; in fact, in each school we entered, no matter how late in the school year, the principal wanted us to skip several grades after reading our test scores. Indeed, Cynthia went to college at age fifteen and graduated at age nineteen, which soon my parents came to consider a bad idea, and so I was permitted to miss only the twelfth grade. School hardly mattered at all, for the lessons came too easily and, clearly, could not help us understand our lives.

We were in a way classless, and yet my mother insisted on our aristocracy in the manner in which she dressed us; in what she refused to let us do, such as go to a fair or become a cheerleader for a junior high school football team; in the manners she suffused us with; in the assumption of good school grades; in our violin, voice, piano lessons; in our church attendance when a church was nearby.

I became convinced at some time in my youth that we knew little of what our father did professionally because being a radio broadcaster and appearing on television was newfangled as an American profession and transgressed on my mother's image of what proper men did. I was twenty-two before I saw a film clip of my father at work. The result has been my astonishment as an adult that personalities in the media become heroes to some.

Yet surely it was the qualities my father was offering without a formal education—his wonderful voice and extraordinary handsomeness—that had attracted my mother. Somehow, we learned very early not to inquire, and this too was in keeping with our mother's sense of her social standing: well-bred people were private.

When we found ourselves in a new school, I learned to give a short version of where we had previously been to school; not only because the forms were inadequate for such travels, but I felt very strongly that it was no one's business where we had been, who we were, what we were like. Ours was a family in which what was most important happened in gesture, in inflection; in sudden moves without explanation; in horrifying arguments between our parents; in their making up in order to enjoy the immense attraction for one another they had; in my sister Cynthia's sullenness about our living arrangements that contained a greater force of memory than mine of the "better days"; in my younger sister Anne's sunny nature. Above all, our family was not to be inquired into: we five had great pride and dignity. It was what I felt without question.

When my mother collaborated with Carl Sandburg on arranging some of his children's songs for the Autoharp, we went casually with her to look at the goats while they worked, from our house nearby in Mountain Home to his outside of Hendersonville. It was not unusual to us that our mother somehow would know him.

We had lived in Orlando, Florida, during my fifteenth year, my tenth grade of school, during which my mother had taken herself back to college for a master's degree in education, I believe, at Rollins College in Winter Park. Or perhaps she simply needed additional courses in order to qualify for a Florida teaching certificate, for she was teaching that year in a public school. My father came and went, doing what, I had no idea. Then, abruptly, it was all over. My mother decided to leave him a second time.

What I did not fully understand, for it had happened so gradually, was that her immersion in music was almost over. We had sat through so many concerts, choir rehearsals, recitals, music lessons, that music seemed irrevocably a part of my mother.

We sold our belongings; I remember in particular the round oak table my mother had refinished, like so many others similarly sold before a journey. We put the china, books, musical instruments, and our trunks of clothes into a small trailer and set off for the "real" South, to Greenville, South Carolina, the major city near our relatives on my mother's side. We lived for a time in several apartments; my father came, went. And then my mother bought a small house on the good side of town, a house far too small for five people, even for the three who were now the family. And we were told that the marriage, again, was over. This time it was true.

I was probably the only one who found the new living arrangements far worse, a diminishment of who we were, for I had appreciated my father's élan, his sense of expansiveness that allowed him to enjoy small wonders in the midst of indirection. Our lives seemed to narrow when he was no longer permitted inside the house; meeting him at Howard Johnson's for ice cream seemed pitiful. My mother worked for a time at a radio station, moderator of an interview program, and then at an advertising agency. She directed a Baptist church choir. Yet everything had changed. I began to skip school now and then, hanging about with a distant cousin, a boy younger than myself but more worldly, I thought. On days when the city park was too cold, we sat in the Christian Science reading room or in the Catholic church balcony.

The author's first husband, James William Shelnutt, 1961

I had been told in a thousand ways that of course I would go to college; my older sister had graduated the year we moved to Greenville. But no one mentioned where the money was to come from. And then, one day, I realized it wasn't to come from anywhere, not then. Because I had enough credits to graduate after the eleventh grade, I signed up for a typing course and began working at several stores downtown, imagining that I could save enough for college. Finally, in January, my mother permitted me to choose either Furman University in Greenville or Carson-Newman College in Jefferson City, Tennessee, and so my college years began. Or so I thought.

We *were* Baptists; Carson-Newman was a Baptist college. And yet I was wholly unprepared for its strictures, both in terms of its rules and in what was taught in courses: the Bible, in the course The Bible as Literature, was to be interpreted literally, which put a crimp on interpretation. It was at Carson-Newman that I fully understood how truly secular our upbringing had been, how relatively cosmopolitan in comparison with the lives of students I met at Carson-Newman.

I began to understand that our travels, our voracious reading, our ruthless condemnation of all that was not in good taste or high in quality had affected me. We knew, for instance, only classical music and hymns and art songs for the voice competitions we entered. We knew no slang; we owned no baubles; we had had no telephone; the one television had long since been discarded in a move. I had gone to church because my mother had worked in churches and because it was a place to make friends of whom my mother would approve.

I lasted at Carson-Newman College one semester. Back home, I worked and took classes at Furman University, and then, in 1961, married a boy whose family lived in Greenville. When I met him, he was home for a holiday from Flint, Michigan, where he was an engineering graduate student at the General Motors Institute. I hardly knew him when we married. What mattered was that he lived in the North and that his family was a decent, upstanding family, although of the working class. My first husband was, and is, a fine person, who had no idea himself what

*With her son, Gregory William Shelnutt,
in Greensboro, 1973*

the background of his wife would come to imply in terms of his vision of a family.

The families blessed us, my father arrived from somewhere to give me away, and we moved to Flint. At last, I imagined, I was free of the house in Greenville, the site of my greatest distress. My younger sister, Anne, was entering high school; I hardly gave her a thought. My older sister was living in Atlanta and working as a secretary after majoring in music at college.

In Flint I took classes at Flint Community Junior College and at the Flint extension of the University of Michigan, receiving a junior college degree, which meant nothing to me at all since I had no idea what I wanted to study and treated my classes as casually as I had all of my previous education. The classes were easy; not to be taken seriously, surely. And yet I wanted an education, if I could discover what the word meant. To me, nothing I had experienced in school related to that word in my mind.

What education meant to me, I believe, was whatever was in the minds of the writers whose books I loved, the Russians, particularly, and Conrad, and several poets. Walking two miles a day, six days a week to Furman University, I had carried a little book of poems, choosing one each day to memorize as I walked. I later began to memorize, too, sections of plays whose language I particularly liked. I believe, too, that the writers in *Saturday Review* influenced my conception of education, for I understood them only partially.

But before I began to answer what discrepancy lay between the education I had gotten and my idea of education, my husband was drafted; he chose to join the air force. Suddenly I was pregnant and back in my mother's house while he went to officers' training school. Then we were stationed in Fort Walton Beach, Florida, where, unknown to me, he tested, I now believe, Agent Orange. My son, Gregory, was born; we were transferred to Wright Patterson Air Force Base in Dayton, Ohio, where the Sac bombers rattled the windows.

A cousin I had come to know over a period of years when my mother took us back to see relatives in the South had been in the Korean Conflict. He had been the lone survivor from his platoon. He returned quiet, immeasurably changed in ways almost imperceptible and therefore alarming to a girl accustomed to watching others for the least sign of change. He had somehow taught me the horrors of war through nuance of gesture, through all that he would not say.

The dentist who lived next-door volunteered to go to Viet Nam; during the day I listened to his wife wailing and, outside, in the glorious sunshine, tried to

Son, Gregory, at thirteen

distract her four-year-old daughter while my son learned to walk.

I tried dutifully to play bridge with the officers' wives, but they talked about the pilots they knew who had been killed in Viet Nam. I wore the long, beautiful dresses appropriate to the officers' dinners, but I was stiff when shaking the generals' hands at the reception line. A resentment was building, and I lived fearful that my husband would volunteer for service in Viet Nam. I chose, then, not to have a second child, and I signed up for a course at Wright State University.

Because of my husband's idea of what proper wives did with their days, I was permitted to take a university course in the evening, after I had put our son to bed, and it would be best, he suggested, if I returned home by eight. As I looked at the offerings, it was obvious that the only course possible in the time allotted to me was one in creative writing. It was taught by the poet Dick Allen, now at the University of Bridgeport in Connecticut, and it met one evening a week. Our first assignment was to write a short story by the following week.

Of course my husband, an engineer, could have had no idea what changed in his wife that week. Suddenly, as I struggled with my story, I knew what I wanted to do with my life; I had no doubt. I had been trained in the violin by my mother and had given it up, having asked myself one day if I would ever play as well as Jascha Heifetz, her standard of excellence. Nothing I had encountered in school had been as difficult as the violin until I tried to write the assigned story. Here I was on familiar ground.

I wrote with my son beside me at the typewriter or when he took his naps. Dick Allen invited the poets John Woods and Conrad Hilberry to our class to read their poetry; I met for the first time, as an adult, writers who had published books. As children we had, through my mother's encouragement, written letters to the authors of the children's books we read, receiving answers that we prized. Then, later, I had been disappointed to understand that the writers whose books I read were dead, for, after childhood, we read the classics. I memorized John Woods's and Con Hilberry's books. The class became more important to me than anything except my child and, indeed, one afternoon while writing I forgot to pick him up at nursery school. I became the editor of the Wright State literary journal, *Nexus*, and took my son with me to help peddle issues. I became a reader for another journal issuing from Wright State, the *Mad River Review*.

When Dick Allen required the women in his class to submit to the *Mademoiselle* Fiction Award, then open only to women, I sent in my one story, which won the award. It was a most unsophisticated story. When it appeared and an agent wrote to ask if I wanted her to represent me, I had written all of three stories. No, I had nothing to represent.

My husband was disturbed by this turn my life was taking; surely it was a hobby I would tire of. On the basis of the single publication, I began teaching in the afternoons at a federally funded arts program, the Living Arts Center—my first job. I took my son along; the visual artist Bing Davis let him finger-paint in the art room while I taught three afternoons a week the junior high and high school students who came to the school. I began to review books from time to time for the *Dayton Daily News* and wrote an article for the Sunday supplement on area libraries.

My husband talked about volunteering for service in Viet Nam; I answered that, if he did, I would leave him. We joined a Unitarian Fellowship and tried to keep the marriage whole. But something had broken irrevocably; I had become filled with long, pent-up greed for my own education and development. I had no patience.

It was my mother's fierce standards for musicians that permeated me. When I read what I wrote, it was obvious that had it been a musical score rendered by a second-rate conductor, singer, violinist, pianist, she would have said, characteristically, "Sheesh!" But how did one become better as a writer? I was voracious, suddenly, for an education, whatever that meant.

In 1968, eight years after our marriage, my husband, William Shelnutt, and I divorced. I took day classes at Wright State and worked as copy editor at *Dayton, USA*. I had never written a check, paid a bill, driven on a four-lane road. Over and over, I dropped out of my classes. I began writing nonfiction for several Dayton papers; I became for a short time the editor of the alumni newspaper at Antioch College; I went to the Bread Loaf Writers Conference on a scholarship. I hated everything that I wrote, and I wrote day and night.

At the Living Arts Center, I had met a journalist who had studied in the Masters of Fine Arts program at the University of North Carolina at Greensboro,

Eve Shelnutt, 1976

with Fred Chappell. I read Chappell's novels and eventually wrote to him asking what was required to study writing at Greensboro. I moved with my son to Cincinnati to complete my B.A. degree, taking classes while my son was in school, with money I had saved from the Antioch College editor's job. Upon graduation in 1972, my son and I moved to Greensboro, where, under the auspices of the Randall Jarrell Fellowship, I studied for a year, receiving an M.F.A. degree in 1973.

But these facts hardly convey the psychological underpinnings of a circumstance. At Greensboro, Chappell imparted some kind of permission for me to break out of the tedium of the prose I had been writing so that I could begin to suffuse it with the music that had been the constant attendant to my reading as a child. I was able to begin writing stories that captured my experience in the world, and, for the first time, my enormous greed to learn found an answer. It is impossible to convey such a situation, coming as it does in the mind and feelings as they coalesce with literary form.

The forms of the short story and poetry, for I studied poetry with Robert Wallace in Cincinnati and

Louise Glück in Greensboro, released my past for me, not so much as material for writing but as that which could be contemplated. I stepped back from myself; for the first time I had the means.

In the Greensboro program, students without master's degrees were not permitted to teach; to have time to write with little distraction was a great gift, for while my son was in school I had only to attend a few classes and produce writing. For the first two months, I had nothing at all to write, and I was nearly speechless. It seemed that I had given up language altogether. I rode my bicycle and thought, wholly disinterested in the fact that, having written stories before, I knew that I could get something down on paper.

In Greensboro, because of Fred Chappell's presence as a person and the shocking affirmation of my hopes for myself that studying with him represented to me, I refused to write the kind of stories I had written before. I wrote nothing until, ever so mildly, Mr. Chappell suggested that those of us who had not turned in a story might consider doing so before Thanksgiving.

I remember well my rage: how could he possibly make such a request? I was attuned to some other logic. But it was my fury that prompted me, as if a lifelong fury at language culminated in a release. Mine had been a most verbal family; we children used language ruthlessly for comment on everything that passed before us. With no linear history given to us by our parents; no vision of the future or ways to judge the past; no ways to place ourselves socially, we used words for judgment on all that we saw, thereby trying out criteria by which people such as we might be could make an evaluation. It was self-definition by verbal trial and error, for my older sister would tell us quickly how stupid we were, when we were stupid. She told us nothing in detail but, rather, presented herself as one who knew what a proper life was supposed to be. Her disgust at our father was supreme, if not wholly convincing; and, but for his ideas, we would be in Douglaston, Long Island, in better surroundings. Our mother wouldn't cry or be snagged again by his wiles. Or, at least, the Douglaston house would have protected her.

Language had been used by me to ferry between my love for both of my parents and this sister's superior knowledge, bred of memories I had no access to. She was also the gifted musician, a fact not to be discounted. Her fury had a purity to it that never failed to impress me, no matter it rendered what she saw different from what I saw. Because of her temperament, her life among us five was difficult, and yet how could one discount a fury so pure as to

have a certain beauty about it? When she played Beethoven on the piano, the fury was there and was a part of what made her playing so compelling. We could hear that; it was at times heartbreaking, at others disturbing.

We all had talked and talked; it had gotten none of us anywhere. And that language was useless to me as a writer, even the kind of details the eye took up ravenously for dissection. I needed to look inward; I had no recent practice. Then my fury released me into a different kind of language, a different arrangement of materials for a story. It seemed, suddenly, as if a childhood spent reading and listening to music had a rationale, even my training in harsh judgments, for I practiced it on what I wrote. In my avarice for writing of my own that I could bear, I took on some of my older sister's attributes, used for a different purpose.

It was an odd sort of student-teacher exchange that I had with Mr. Chappell, for, taken as I was by my own process of liberation, I had little interest in what he had to say about an individual story. And yet every

Husband Mark Logan Shelton

299

Eve Shelnutt, 1988

word he said mattered to me immensely, simply not about *that* story, or *that* one. So the months passed. I made no real friends in the program among the other students; they were barely present to me, for I felt both frightened and in a terrible rush to learn as habit through writing what this new relationship to language felt like. I spent the time stamping its sensations on myself and, for the first time, the act of writing began to feel like a wholly physical enterprise, so melded was my brain to a story's emotion and its form, which had its own demands. And I loved the dictates of form; I loved the slight wedges of freedom I could wrest from it. That freedom must have represented for me whatever freedom I had taken in my family for the forming of my own personality in the face of so few outward inquiries about how I was developing.

After Greensboro, my son and I moved back to Cincinnati for a year while I worked again at nonfiction writing for a living and fiction and poetry in the evenings. My son had discovered sculpture as a passion and was enrolled in the Mount Adams School for the Performing and Creative Arts. His father, having resigned from the air force, was studying for a Ph.D. in psychology at the University of Cincinnati; we mourned together the loss of our marriage and celebrated our friendship.

In 1974 I was invited through the recommendation of John Woods to teach at Western Michigan University in Kalamazoo, where I completed my first story collection, *The Love Child*, and slowly worked on poetry. John and I talked little about writing, but he read my stories, his very presence in the department important to me. Shirley Scott, teaching literature in the department, also read my stories as I wrote them, and later wrote several essays on my story collections that seem to me unusually perceptive. Her husband, the poet Herb Scott, introduced me to contemporary art and helped me learn how to encourage my son's interests.

I continued to send my stories to Fred Chappell to read, which he did out of the uncommon generosity that so many writers have received from him.

Just after receiving tenure at Western Michigan University, my son entered college, and I moved, in 1980, to the University of Pittsburgh in order to support his education better. There I published my second and third story collections and published my first poetry collection with Carnegie Mellon Press, Gerald Costanzo, the publisher, having received it from my agent before my move to Pittsburgh. My fiction I published with Black Sparrow Press, because, although having sought no other publishers, I felt that John Martin knew what my fiction was about. I have never met him and yet he has generated immense loyalty in me not only for his to my work, but for the admirable work, particularly that of Paul Bowles, that he so carefully publishes.

With me in Pittsburgh was the writer Mark Logan Shelton, whom I met in Kalamazoo. He became my second husband; we have been married for ten years: one of my fortunes.

My son teaches sculpture at the University of Mississippi in Oxford; his own sculpture evidences his love of literature and history as well as the depth of character that enabled him so cheerfully to accompany me as I went to school and filled our houses with the sound of typing. My father, in the house that he built on my grandfather's property, is writing a four-volume study of the Waldrop family, having retired from, toward the end of his professional life, a job as a speech writer in Washington. His understanding of how government works is evident in the letters that he writes to Washington officials in protest over various political decisions.

My mother, in Greenville, South Carolina, owns her own advertising firm, and if I lament her having put music away, it is my lament; she is obviously happy. My younger sister, Anne, is married to a physician and lives in Atlanta with their two children. My older sister, having married a photographer from whom she is divorced, works for a government agency and plays the organ for several churches in Virginia, not far from her two children.

My husband and I live in a house filled with my son's art, in Athens, Ohio, where I joined the faculty of Ohio University in 1988. The town is as bucolic as Pittsburgh was bustling. We travel widely as we both give readings of our work; our literary friends are scattered throughout the country and so we practice the old-fashioned art of letter writing.

Having inhabited several towns for a long period, I often sense that, despite the order I maintain in daily life, my true place is on the road, if this time it could be with my husband, so long as we could stop now and then to receive letters—from my son, my father, and Fred Chappell, whose amusing notes let me know that the writer most crucial to me is still there.

Otherwise, place for me is language and form, and a true education is always just out of sight, over the next rise. In writing, how to capture what cannot be said in any language sounds elusively in the ear, an echo like music from an imagined source of wholeness that by its persistence as desire earns respect and endless labor.

BIBLIOGRAPHY

Fiction and Poetry:

Sparrow 62, Two Stories, Black Sparrow, 1977.

The Love Child (stories), Black Sparrow, 1979.

Descant (chapbook), Palaemon Press, 1982.

The Formal Voice (stories), Black Sparrow, 1982.

Air and Salt (poetry), Carnegie-Mellon University Press, 1983.

The Musician (stories), Black Sparrow, 1987.

Recital in a Private Home (poetry), Carnegie-Mellon University Press, 1988.

First a Long Hesitation (poetry), Carnegie-Mellon University Press, 1991.

Nonfiction:

The Magic Pencil: Teaching Children Creative Writing, Peachtree Publishers, 1988.

The Writing Room: Keys to the Craft of Fiction and Poetry, Longstreet Press, 1989.

(Editor) *Writing, The Translation of Memory*, Macmillan, 1990.

(Editor) *The Confidence Woman: 26 Women Writers at Work*, Longstreet Press, 1991.

Raymond Souster

1921-

GETTING ON WITH IT

First Appearance

From what I've been told our family physician, elderly Dr. Hunt, was all set to retire for the night when his telephone rang. After taking the message, he no doubt grumbled to himself as he dressed again. Then, picking up his hat and black bag, he left his warm house for the bitter winter winds of Toronto blowing outside. A College street-car took him to Rusholme Road, where in one of the rooms of the very cramped Women's College Hospital his patient, Mrs. Norma Souster, was experiencing heavy labour pains. In spite of this, Dr. Hunt still had time to doze off several times in a chair, for it wasn't until almost eight o'clock that chilly January morning in 1921 that he was called upon to bring me onto the scene. No doubt I made my arrival known to everyone within earshot—these were the lungs that would one day bellow across the diamond at my baseball opponents . . .

Shaking The Family Tree

Before going any further, it might be a good idea to give a few branches of my family tree a quick shake or two. But I should point out that my name is Anglo-Saxon rather than French in origin, my father's nickname as a young man being "Souse," a good old English term if ever there was one.

My maternal great-grandfather, James Elder, Sr., was born in 1839 in Ballymena, Northern Ireland. It must have been a very sobering experience for this father of nine to set sail for the New World in 1875 with his wife Elizabeth. The former gentleman farmer, now willing to work at any job available, first landed in Boston. He found, however, no work there in a city teeming with Irish immigrants. The decision was then made to try Toronto, Upper Canada, where it was rumoured jobs were to be had.

Toronto was then a bustling city of fifty-one thousand. He quickly found work as a yard hand for the newly formed Canadian Pacific Railway. The

Raymond Souster reading at Swansea Public Library, 1985

family had now grown to ten: five boys and five girls. He and his wife found themselves more than busy making a comfortable home while stretching out one meagre salary.

I was never able to meet either great-grandparent, both dying some years before my birth. Of their children—my great-aunts and uncles—four would touch my life considerably in later years.

On my father's side of the tree the first name that crops up is that of my great-grandfather, John Souster, Sr. What we know about him is very sketchy; even his birth and death dates aren't known. His

"My paternal grandfather, John Souster, Sr., with his wife, Mary Holmes McGhie, and three of their four children," 1903

family, apparently, immigrated from Fenny Stratford, England. As a young man he fought for "King and Country" in the Canadian militia during the Lower Canada Rebellion of 1837 (part of Canada's comic-opera civil war). After this he returned to the small town of Mount Forest in Upper Canada (Ontario), having somehow qualified during the intervening years as a high-school mathematics teacher. He married, raised a family, and wrote hymns of a deeply religious nature, one of which has luckily been preserved.

A son, John (destined to be my grandfather), was born in 1870. At age eighteen he moved to Toronto. Here he found work at first in a variety of manual jobs, ending up for the rest of his life working at Massey-Harris, the large farm-implement manufacturers. He married Mary Holmes McGhie, and in a few years had a family of four, Aunt Gertrude, Uncle Cecil, my father, Austin Holmes Souster, and Uncle Iner.

The earliest photograph of my father shows a pleasant looking young man with an abundance of black curly hair, taken at the age of twenty-one or

twenty-two. Raised at the family home on Fennings Street, he attended Givens Public School, excelling more at the pole vault than his lessons. At the age of seven he sold one-cent newspapers for spending money; at twelve he began full-time work as a delivery boy for a downtown corset factory.

Then at the age of fifteen, just out of knee pants for the first time, he was accepted by a local bank as a teller-ledgerkeeper. Mastering this quite demanding job fairly easily, he considered it an easy way to make a cool three-hundred-dollar-a-year salary. He was to remain at that main branch of the bank for fifty years until his retirement at sixty-five.

Now one last shift to the other side of the family. Our focus is on Jane, the youngest girl of the ten Elder children, or as I was to know her, Grandmother. Born in 1870, she'd met at the age of twenty-two a young, handsome piano-repairer, Alfred Maximillian Baker. Born in Toronto as the son of a market-gardener, he had a natural green thumb, and in his spare time was an amateur actor and violinist. He was immediately attracted to grandmother from their first introduction, marrying "his Jenny" shortly afterward. Their first child, Norma Rhodesia, was born in 1896, and four years later a son, Sydney Raymond.

Norma was a bright, attractive child who took special pride in her penmanship, winning the competition in her class at the Canadian National Exhibition. After adding to her public school education with six months at a business college, she became at age fifteen a stenographer and bookkeeper at five dollars per week.

Then shortly after the outbreak of the First World War she met my father at an evening arranged by Iola Elder, her cousin and best girlfriend. Dad had been coaxed by his chum Ken Stark, then dating Iola, to go along; he liked the girl he saw and their courting began from that night. This clean-cut young man, my mother discovered, was a bank teller downtown, who by a fortunate chance lived only a block away.

For the next two years the couple spent much of their spare time together. Canoe rides on the Humber or Rouge rivers, movies two or three times a week at a local motion-picture theatre, church every Sunday night, where he listened to her singing in the choir. All this time a fierce war was raging overseas. Recruiting sergeants were stopping men in the street not in uniform. Late in 1916 he and Ken Stark enlisted in the 70th Battery, Royal Canadian Field Artillery. Now almost every evening he'd appear at my mother's house with spurs clicking, swagger stick swinging, but needing a good soft pillow under his sore buttocks before he could sit down on Mother's sofa.

The spring of 1917 his unit was shipped overseas to Whitley Camp, Aldershot, England, where he and Ken were switched to infantry training. The one standout event in all that endless marching in the mud was the visit of a lone German fighter that swooped down out of nowhere one breakfast time, creating a great loss of dignity among the scattering tent-dwellers dodging machine-gun bullets.

Finally, in the puzzling way that armies operate, my father and his chum were separated, being shipped out to different artillery units at the front. So it was with the 43d Battery, RCFA, that my father served out the rest of the war on the battlefields of France and Belgium, returning with that outfit to Canada in the spring of 1919. Arriving in Toronto on April 7, he was discharged from the army on the very same day. We can only imagine what a heartfelt reunion took place that evening between the young couple.

Within a week my father had reported back to the Standard Bank to find his old job waiting for him. He was dead broke, needing money badly to get

"My maternal grandmother, Jane Elder, with my grandfather, Alfred Maximillian Baker," 1919

married. It wasn't until April 7, 1920, one year to the day after his return, that the couple were married in a very modest ceremony in the bride's home. There was so little money to spend that no wedding pictures were taken. So I've had to imagine just how lovely my mother looked that day in her bridal gown.

A Young Boy's World

Almost the first memory I have of childhood is of the great, endless rooms of our Indian Grove house. Or so they seemed to a child first crawling, then slipping, then struggling to his feet only to crash down with a thud a few steps later. Another impression that's remained is being wheeled in a stroller by my mother to nearby High Park, where apparently I was fascinated by ducks on the pond, monkeys in the zoo, birds, flowers, and green grass. Another equally fascinating trip was to shop in The Junction, a section of Dundas Street between Keele and High Park Avenue. Here I marvelled at streetcars, automobiles, and the long, colourful aisles of Loblaw's Groceteria.

At age three I made friends with the boy next door. His name was Joe Spring, and he was every bit as curious and over-energetic as I was. One day we fought; he swung his toy shovel in a rage and came close to slicing into my left eye. I still have the scar to prove it. Another day we wandered off "to see the trains" at West Toronto Station, where police and distraught parents found us hours later.

All this happened sometime after the birth of my brother, Kenneth John, December 30, 1922. I remember looking down at him in his crib and thinking what deep blue eyes he had.

At age four my mother took me along with my brother on an ambitious midweek outing. This was a forty-mile train trip to a friend's farm near Waterdown. My mother carried Ken; I was half-dragged along by the hand. We both had our first train ride, which was my most thrilling experience to date; I never quite got over the wonder of steam trains after that. Halfway through the afternoon at the farm I wandered away into the nearby barnyard, where I was eventually found in a pigpen with two puzzled porkers. Unfortunately no picture exists of me sitting

"My father, Austin Holmes Souster, at twenty-four, in the uniform of the Royal Canadian Field Artillery"

there, hands, feet, and clothing plastered with mud. Years later my wife would recall a similar experience of her own involving chickens rather than pigs that happened almost in the same year on a faraway Alberta farm.

But by far the clearest memory of those infant years is me setting out on my tricycle two or three times a week beginning that same summer to visit my mother's two dearest lady cousins, whom I called simply "Aunt Theresa and Augusta." Aunt Theresa, a retired china-shop owner, and her niece, Augusta Hewitt, who worked nearby as a private stenographer, lived together a block and a half away on Indian Road Crescent. They had a beautiful garden full of vegetables and flowers, a big three-storey house with an unusual chestlike music box that played three tunes, one after another. It was Aunt Theresa who introduced me to her favourite game of dominoes, which we played on the large, smooth kitchen table. No matter how badly I was beaten at the game there was always the consolation of a delicious dish of homemade ice cream after I'd visited the "boneyard" for the last time that day.

When I was four-and-a-half I started kindergarten, my mother walking me over to the nearest school every afternoon. I was just beginning to remember the names of some of the boys and girls when my grandmother, who'd lived with us as long as I could remember, bought the Colbeck Street place, situated a mile or so to the west in the Runnymede area. It was a brand new, semidetached, solid brick house I learned much later. It was to be my home for the next fifteen years.

I finished the rest of my kindergarten year at Runnymede Public School, seven long blocks from our house. It was to be a walk I would get to know so very well. The new school was a huge place, with three floors and endless rooms. That fall I started in the Junior First Grade. The boys and girls had separate playgrounds, and in class we sat on opposite sides of the room. The first game I learned used hardened horse chestnuts on a string; throughout the winter I froze my fingers perfecting the fine points of marble shooting. School was a whole new world to me.

The following spring and summer my brother and I began playing in the whole block of uncleared land we called "The Field" right behind our house. Or we'd check out the sandpiles at "The Dump," a covered-over landfill site further down Jane Street. And we began our first timid explorations of the Humber Valley and its river, not more than a ten-minute walk away.

I was given a baseball glove for my seventh birthday, a pair of hockey skates for my eighth, not the usual order for a Canadian boy. My father was a big baseball fan and had me trying to catch a small rubber ball at six. It certainly rubbed off, for I played some form of baseball until age forty-three. Indeed, the greatest thrill of my public-school days was in making an impossible over-the-shoulder catch as a twelve-year-old right fielder on the Runnymede senior softball team. What made it remarkable perhaps was the fact that all the other players were fifteen or sixteen years old.

The one other major event in my young life was my grandmother's decision to give me the small library of books my uncle Syd had read as a boy. The volumes I would treasure most were a dozen or so by G. A. Henty, an English writer of boys' stories popular at the turn of the century. Mixing fact and fiction, these historical adventure novels covered a wide range, with such titles as *The Cat of Babustus, With Lee in Virginia, With Wolfe in Canada,* and *With Clive in India.* Along with baseball, reading now became my most cherished hobby.

New Horizons

At age twelve I became a member of Runnymede United Church, and almost sixty years later still have my membership there. As well, at my parents' insistence, I wrote competitive exams to enter the Lower Fourth Form at University of Toronto Schools. My great-uncle Jim offered to pay my tuition fees there if I was admitted. I managed to pass and became for the next five years a student at a boys' day school of five hundred students administered by the city's largest university.

What I remember today of UTS is a strange mix indeed . . . The large, buttered bathbuns covered with vanilla icing which sold for eight cents in our school cafeteria; winning my first payment as a writer for the best review of the school Shakespeare play, a ten-dollar cheque; coming suddenly upon Archibald Lampman's unsurpassed Canadian poem "Heat" in our literature text *Shorter Poems,* and deciding I wanted to write poems like that. Equally vivid memories began a year later with me leaving a notebook of my first poetic efforts in my history teacher's office, then getting it back a few days later with the terse comment: "You do have the poet's eye—now you need to find out about rhythm and rhyme," good advice I did my best to follow; the way our cadet corps used to stop all eastbound traffic on Bloor Street as we paraded to Varsity Stadium; finally, the

"My mother, Norma Rhodesia Baker, at eighteen"

library that "Bunny" Baird had assembled on the second floor of the building, where I read *The Sun Also Rises, The Great Gatsby, Of Human Bondage,* and poets like John Masefield, W. W. Gibson, Archibald MacLeish, William Butler Yeats, and Edwin Arlington Robinson—not bad for a high-school library . . .

All through these years of my early teens I'd been honing my skills as a baseball player. When it came to pitching I didn't have nearly enough beef on me to be able to deliver a real fast ball. Instead I relied primarily on a big-breaking curve, "roundhouse hook" in baseball slang. As I had almost perfect control with my specialty, I began to get a lot of strikeouts. In 1936, at age fifteen, I signed up with the West Toronto Nationals, a bantam (under sixteen) team playing in the Toronto Baseball League. By a great coincidence our home field was on a vacant lot across from the Canadian National Railways roundhouse on St. Clair Avenue West; I had a joke about throwing third strikes when a pall of black smoke would suddenly blow across the diamond.

After winning twelve games in a row, which took us to the city finals, we were badly beaten in two straight games by Columbus Boys' Club. It was a sobering experience for me having my fancy curve-ball hit all over the lot. I'd learned the hard way what every pitcher finds out sooner or later—you need at least three different, well-mixed pitches to hope to survive for long on the mound.

That happened to be one year before my father copied out in his neat handwriting what I considered my best poem to date, then sent it in to the "Little of Everything" column of the *Toronto Star*. To everyone's great surprise the short poem, titled "In Winter," appeared the following week. I would go on to publish another thirty-six poems in three Toronto papers over the next three years.

Then, in 1937, after finishing third form at UTS with a mediocre set of final-term marks, my parents decided that I'd do just as well at public high school. So that fall I enrolled at Humberside Collegiate Institute, entering the world of coeducation. It took a bit of getting used to, having girls in the classroom. But I was now at an age to welcome such a distraction.

Basketball had become my winter game since the age of thirteen, when I found out I couldn't stand the pain of being on skates for any length of time. It was then I learned that I had fallen arches, which explained why I didn't have that quickness on my feet to become a runner. This was a considerable handicap at basketball, but I compensated for it by perfecting my shooting and learning to get rid of the ball fast in passing situations. I made the junior team at Christmas, playing centre most of the time. This last was no easy assignment for a player only five feet, ten inches tall.

The summer of 1938 I managed to squeeze through with a pass on my junior matriculation exams. My old Latin teacher, Miss Nora Belcher, gave me what she thought was good, honest advice when she told me, "Souster, don't press your luck by coming back for anymore Latin next year," but then as always I was never one to distinguish wise counsel when given to me.

Instead, I dug my heels in and swore I'd show the old so-and-so. I took Latin along with French, German, English, and modern history for my last high-school year. Slowly I began to realize that getting a high-school diploma would be a very necessary document to have in the years ahead. Then my failure to make the senior basketball team not too long after meant I had one less distraction interfering with my studying. I hit the books that winter and spring like I hadn't for years. When my final results

came in the mail in late July, I was too nervous to open the envelope from the Department of Education. Instead my mother read out the nine marks one by one. My lowest was a 58 in Latin grammar. I think I went half-crazy with joy for the next few minutes. I was through with school at last . . .

Getting Down To Business

Tomorrow," my father announced at the supper table one night in the first days of that August, "Ray and I are going to start looking for his job. We have three interviews to do by the end of the week."

With much trepidation I visited those offices with my father in the days that followed. With the continuing depression jobs were even harder to find, he told me. It turned out he had an "in" at each place, having worked years ago with the men who saw us now. In effect he was coming to them with cap in hand, begging for a job for his son. Along with the interview I filled out an application, taking pains to make my writing as legible as possible, for in those days penmanship was highly regarded in business.

Two weeks later a call came to me at home. I was to report to the Imperial Bank of Canada on September 1. I'd be on three months probation at a salary of five hundred dollars a year. Little did I know at the time that I would retire from the same bank forty-five years later.

I began work at 8.00 a.m., Friday, September 1, 1939. I found myself assigned to the mail desk, joining two other busy clerks. The main job was getting the incoming correspondence around to the proper recipients. Besides that there were a dozen other tasks to keep us busy.

I've mentioned that particular date of September 1 with good reason. When I stepped out later into the lunchtime crowd along King at Bay the headlines on the newspapers the newsboys held out to us read: "NAZIS INVADE POLAND." Of course I had to buy a paper even though I couldn't really afford one. It would come in handy later that night. At five o'clock the whole staff was told to stay. The whole office by this time was in worse confusion than ever. Apparently all currency trading had been suspended.

All evening we three mail clerks sat around doing nothing. I had time now to remember Mrs. Rochat's German classes at Humberside Collegiate. There we had listened intently several times a week to her compact shortwave radio broadcasting Hitler's tirades against everyone but himself. "His accent is poor," our teacher said, "he's very hard to understand." The rest of us caught only the odd word here and there. This Hitler was an unpredictable madman, a bully whose power-hungry threats had gained him country after country. But would he fight? We rather doubted it. Now I could see how wrong we students had been.

Two months later I was transferred upstairs to the clearing department, where I was to spend almost two years. The new job meant a lot of night work; overtime pay was then unknown. Surprisingly I soon began to settle into this new routine, finding it fairly agreeable. At least when I finished the day's work the rest of the time was mine to do what I liked. That winter I found myself writing dozens of poems in a new vein prompted by observing eye-opening, challenging life in the downtown streets during my lunch breaks. I discovered a great new American poet, Kenneth Fearing, rediscovered an old favourite, Stephen Spender. I made two new friends at the bank, Don Thornton and Charlie Barker, and through Charlie a third, Gord Galloway. Don was then living with his numerous brothers and sisters in a big old house on High Park Avenue; we shared a common love of books and sports. Charlie had become the owner of a Model T Ford, and along with Gord, the three of us "curb-cruised" at Sunnyside Beach and anywhere else where girls were in evidence. We drank a few beers, made fumbling, innocent passes at girls who unanimously refused to take us seriously. We talked very knowingly about how long the war would last and, even more to the point, how long we'd be able to keep out of it.

The summer of 1939 I'd pitched juvenile baseball for Keele playground at Perth Square, my second and last year. Now a year later I managed to land a pitching job with my old arch rival of bantam days, Columbus Boys' Club. Our coach was a swarthy Italian-Canadian in his early thirties, a former semipro pitcher. I was to learn more about pitching from Carmen Bush in my first year with him than I'd picked up all along the way. It was also a real thrill for me to be playing at Willowdale Park, or "Christie Pits" as it was more usually called, the same park where sandlot heroes Jake Moon and Frank Cater had performed. Columbus Boys' supplied real uniforms (which had to be handed back after each game for use by other teams), and real baseball stockings with most of the feet cut out. But gloves, spikes, and caps we still had to provide ourselves. Those were still depression days.

Then in August, at the end of a disappointing sandlot season, my first "serious" poem, "Nocturnal," was published in the *Canadian Forum*, then the leading literary monthly. It was only years later I learned it was poet Earle Birney who was behind the

acceptance. And, to give the magazine its full due, they ran a short story of mine, "It Can Happen Here," in the November issue, one of two of my early prose efforts to see the light of day. These appearances had an enormous effect in reinforcing my self-confidence. Remember that at that time I was working entirely alone, knowing no other poets or writers of any kind.

It was, however, in 1941 that my greatest encouragement came, this time from the United States. I read somewhere that the *Providence Sunday Journal* was interested in publishing poetry and (almost unbelievable) offered payment for same. My first poem accepted, "Twentieth Century," appeared in August, which followed my critical assessment "Report from Canadian Literary Front Line" published in June. These were the first two in a number of contributions published through the kindness of the late Winfield Townley Scott. Some of them would even appear after I was in uniform.

In Air Force Blue

Nineteen forty-one was also the year I had to choose to remain a civilian or take the big jump into military life. By then enlistments in the Canadian army had fallen off, and everyone sensed that conscription was inevitable before too long. My chum, Charlie Barker, a year older than myself, decided in October that he didn't want to wait any longer to join up. No bloody army for him when he could volunteer for either the navy or air force. Gord Galloway and myself, nineteen and twenty respectively, didn't feel the same pressure. But we had by then become like the Three Musketeers, and it didn't feel right to stay out when Charlie was going. The upshot was that we three were sworn in as recruits in the Royal Canadian Air Force on November 11, 1941.

After languishing around Manning Depot in Toronto for the next month, we were selected as standard tradesmen, Charlie as an armourer, Gord as a security guard, and myself as an equipment assistant or storekeeper. We went our separate ways for training, never to see each other again for several years.

After completing a twelve-week crash course in six weeks, I was shipped off one thousand miles to the east. One cold February morning I stepped off the train at Sydney, Cape Breton, Nova Scotia. Here at RCAF Station, Sydney, a home-war air base located eight miles from town in a reconverted swamp, I would spend the next two years. I was one month past my twenty-first birthday.

"Three airmen of the Royal Canadian Air Force: Bud Devins, 'Scotty,' and myself,"
Sydney, Nova Scotia, 1942

After spending the rest of the long winter in a barrack block always smelling of coal-gas fumes, I received an unexpected, very welcome break. The station was about to expand to triple its size, and offered us the chance to live out at the air force's expense. I jumped at the chance, quickly teaming up with a fellow bunkmate from Toronto to look for a room in Sydney. Bud Devins, an ambulance/crash-tender driver, agreed that the big, front attic room we looked at on Prince Street was all we needed, besides fitting our budget. Bud mostly worked the night shift, while I had nights only once every two weeks. That meant there was plenty of time for me to work at and read poetry in quiet surroundings, impossible in the barracks. Down at the main stores building I had the use of a typewriter at all times, so I found I was sending out more manuscripts than ever, many to little magazines in the U.S.A.

And while there was no baseball at Sydney, I eagerly took up softball that first summer with much of my old enthusiasm. I easily made the station team, playing either first or third base.

Most of the year the brass really had the wind up. It was feared that being so close to the Atlantic our air base might be raided by German submarine personnel. Nazi U-boats were being sighted everywhere in the Gulf of St. Lawrence, so every airman was ordered to carry a rifle with him wherever he went on the station. But our rifles were useless, as no one trusted us with ammunition.

It must have been early June when Bill Goldberg was posted to Sydney. He came into our stores building one day to introduce himself. A radar operator, he was the poet Irving Layton's nephew. When I told him I was going on annual leave in two weeks he gave me Irving's address. Stay over a day and get to know him, he suggested.

I slept over my one night in Montreal at Irving's flat on University Street. He proved very easy to talk to. I chatted as well with another Montreal poet, Louis Dudek, up from New York and his graduate studies at Columbia. I also met John Sutherland, editor of a new little mag, *First Statement.* As a result I went on to Toronto feeling I wasn't the only poetry nut in eastern Canada.

Spring 1943 I had my first poem appear in John's magazine. It was "The Hunter," still one of my most widely anthologized poems. That summer four or five Sydney airmen suddenly decided to publish a literary magazine entirely on their own. With myself and Bill Goldberg as chief instigators we eventually produced one hundred copies of a mimeographed little mag which we called *Direction*. It appeared in November 1943, and would be the only issue to appear at Sydney. Shortly after, my fellow poets of the radar unit would be posted out, their radar operation at the base being closed down. Bill Goldberg ended up at Port Aux Basques, Newfoundland (then a British Crown Colony), where he somehow managed to get eight more issues out at considerable effort and expense. *Direction* managed to publish Irving Layton, Pat and Miriam Waddington, while issue number 4 was an entire Henry Miller production. We utilized portions of his *Tropic of Cancer*, perhaps its first North American appearance. And I mustn't forget Kenneth Patchen. In answer to my request he sent two short poems from California for our first issue. Patchen had become my god of the American poetry world. I'd read his magnificent *First Will and Testament* among the books I'd begun to order from the Gotham Book Mart in New York City. The two Kenneths, Fearing and Patchen, both so completely different poets, would continue to be my twin poetry idols until the sixties.

With the war going better for us by the end of 1943, I was even more satisfied with life at Sydney. Although my living-out allowance had been cancelled by then, I found I could still manage to live out as I'd advanced to the rank of leading aircraftsman with Class A trades pay. I even had a room to myself at the house on Prince Street. But on December 1 disaster struck. I was posted to No. 4 Repair Depot, Scoudouc, New Brunswick, a good 250 miles away in the middle of nowhere.

I arrived there after a huge snowstorm; it was a desolate place twenty miles from Moncton, the nearest city. I was to spend almost a year in this prisonlike setting, living in barracks again with my precious privacy gone. I became an aircraft checker, working mostly out on the breezy runways at all hours. My one bright spot in the next year would be my surprise appearance in a small, clothbound volume issued by Ryerson Press of Toronto. Titled *Unit of Five*, it had poems by five poets, three of whom, Louis Dudek, P. K. Page, and myself, are still publishing regularly. My first appearance in book form, it was a much better launching than anyone could have expected at the time.

By November 1944 I was beginning to wonder how much longer I could stick it out at Scoudouc. Now I knew why my fellow airmen claimed its English translation was "Place of Mud." The powers-that-be came to my rescue with a patriotic call for volunteers to switch over to the Canadian army, then desperately short of infantry reinforcements. I was fed up enough to accept this appeal. Along with twenty other airmen I was sent to the nearest army reception centre at Fredericton. After a week of leisurely tests I was told I was unfit for the infantry but okay for the army service corps. No thanks, I said, and ended up back at Scoudouc. But coming back in the railway station at Moncton I happened to meet an old friend now stationed at Eastern Air Command, Halifax. I explained how I was climbing the walls at the repair depot. "I'll do what I can, but I can't promise anything," he said, and he was as good as his word. On January 4, 1945, my posting overseas came through.

After thirty days' embarkation leave in Toronto, I reported back to the Y Depot, Moncton, New Brunswick. For once the air force moved swiftly. Within a week I was on a troopship with ten thousand Canadian army troops. Seven days of zig-zagging on the Atlantic aboard the *Aquatania*, the last of the four-funnelers, brought us to Greenock, Scotland. From there a frantic twenty-four-hour train ride using secondary rail lines brought us to Bournemouth, on the southeast coast of England. Here I'd spend the next ten weeks living in two different commandeered hotels, not doing much that resembled work. But Bournemouth had its beautiful seafront, the Pavilion, fabulous meals, free tickets to dances, chocolate rations, private film showings. I could have stayed there forever.

But as the expression goes, the fickle finger of fate was to strike again. One day before V-E Day, May 8, I was posted to RCAF Station, Topcliffe, Yorkshire, a Canadian training unit attached to 7 Group, RAF.

Here I played third base for the station's softball team, and signed up for every request for specialized help to serve in a civilian role in Germany. But my longtime wish to see Europe continued to be denied. In frustration I was one of the first in our unit to volunteer for Eagle Force, being formed to take part in the final campaign against Japan. Near the end of June several hundred of us were loaded onto trucks, and in one six-hour drive sped north to good old Greenock, Scotland, where we were the last of thousands of bodies crammed on the S.S. *Île de France*. I'd been exactly ninety-three days in England, three more than I needed to receive the Maple Leaf clasp to my Canadian Volunteer Service Medal.

I had thirty days' disembarkation leave in Toronto before reporting back to RCAF Station, Dartmouth, Nova Scotia, where my section of Eagle Force was forming up. Little did I know then that history would unfold one of its most momentous events in modern times, the atomic bombing of Hiroshima and Nagasaki in late August. Suddenly I, along with the rest of Eagle Force on the base, was discharged from the service almost overnight. Our country no longer needed us, almost giving the impression it wanted to forget all about us as soon as possible. We understood that, because we felt exactly the same way about the military. Besides, we had a lot of wasted years to catch up on.

Back Home Again

It was wonderful being home again for good in Toronto. I felt I wouldn't mind if I never left it again in my life. When you were away from home it was the little things you'd taken for granted that you'd missed the most. My own room, my own bed again.

I'd come out of the air force with a small nest egg of Victory Bonds in the bank, but with little cash in my pocket. After a couple of weeks of complete leisure I knew I had to get back to work. My bank job was waiting for me, according to law, but I was hoping for a change at this point in my life.

During the next month I was interviewed for a number of job offerings. At McClelland and Stewart, the publishers, which had not advertised for employees, I even offered to work for nothing on a trial basis. No one expressed the slightest interest in acquiring my services. Very reluctantly, as the bank was now pressing me for a decision, I returned to work there in November.

I'd hardly worked a week at the bank when I got a very welcome letter from John Sutherland in Montreal. He wanted to publish a small poetry manuscript I'd sent him from Scoudouc through his newly established First Statement Press. This meant that my first verse collection would be published the following March. It was the encouragement I needed coming at the right time. No setback in my writing would bother me after that.

The bank sent me right back to the same department I'd left almost four years before. When the former male staff had left to join the armed forces, "temporary" female employees had been hired to fill the gap. Now I found my old clearing

department was almost entirely staffed by young women, all of them in their early twenties. I was very much in favour of this, especially when I noticed a particularly attractive girl with long, lustrous black hair. I found out she was twenty-one, had moved East from Alberta hardly a year before, which explained her very friendly manner.

Having spent most of my teen years in a boys' school, then working in an all-male environment at the bank, I was extremely timid about approaching her. And no doubt the fear of rejection also had something to do with it.

So, believe it or not, it wasn't until May 1946 that I made a serious move. The clearing staff were in the habit of getting together two or three times a year for corn roasts, sleigh rides, and Christmas parties. This particular occasion was a birthday party for two of the girls, one of them being the girl I had my eye on. Learning that she lived only a few blocks away from the hall we were having the party in, I offered to walk her home. After that night it became an established ritual to be with her every evening. We would be married a little over a year later.

In August 1946, I had a reunion with my good friend Bill Goldberg. I took the train to Montreal and stayed at his home for a couple of days. I saw Louis Dudek, up as usual from New York for the summer. When he heard Bill and me talking of going there for a look around, he offered us his apartment at Amsterdam and 125th Street. The two of us left a day later, taking the slow train through Vermont and western New York. New York City was in the grip of an intense heat wave, and we seemed to spend most of our waking hours dodging from one bar to another drinking ice-cold beer. The second night we ended up in a big, noisy place on 125th Street. It wasn't until we'd been sitting at the bar for over an hour that we realized we were the only whites in the place. It didn't seem to bother the other patrons, as no one gave us a second look. Although big city boys, we both gasped at the endless rows of tall skyscrapers in Manhattan, took every excuse to use the subway, marvelled at the number of speakers seriously addressing the crowd at Columbus Circle. Tired and dead-broke we returned to Montreal. That trip with Bill would whet my appetite for further visits.

Bill had by this time run off the tenth and last issue of *Direction*, our air force little mag. He'd done most of the work and deserved full credit for it.

That fall I submitted a poetry manuscript to Ryerson Press, and got a friendly letter back from famous editor Lorne Pierce, stating they would like to publish *Go to Sleep, World* in the spring of 1947. Heavily influenced by Kenneth Patchen, as Kenneth

"Wedding day: the Geralde and Souster families, with Lia's maid of honour, Pat Brock," 1947

Fearing had been my obvious influence in *Unit of Five*, it showed a young poet still groping for his own voice.

Also appearing that spring was John Sutherland's First Statement Press anthology *Other Canadians*, featuring the best of what he considered the "new" poetry. I was very generously represented in this book, whose introduction perhaps raised more critical eyebrows than the poems themselves.

In the meantime I'd become engaged to Rosalia Geralde, and we decided to marry June 24. Lia was then living in rooms with her mother. The momentous decision was made to buy a house; the two of us immediately began reading the real-estate ads. After a weary round of house-hunting we made a lucky find. We bought a semidetached six-room house in the village of Swansea, located directly south of my old Runnymede district. Here we would live for the next seventeen years.

Lia and her mother moved into the new house on June 1; I visited them after supper every night, cleaning and polishing floors, stripping off old wallpaper. Then on the twenty-fourth, with my brother as best man and Lia's father a surprise visitor from the West, we were married by the family minister. By now we had used up all of our cash. With no reservations at Niagara Falls available, we made do with an overnight jaunt to Hamilton as our honeymoon.

Two days later, in an unexpected move, Lia's mother decided to return to the West with her husband. My poor wife suddenly was left in charge of running a house, something she was entirely unpre-

pared for. But she was able to rise to the challenge immediately, surprising me and even herself by taking charge of our little household.

Nineteen forty-eight would be the year I founded Enterprise Agency. I was looking around for some way to make extra money on the side. I answered an ad from some small British publisher looking for a Canadian sales representative. To my great surprise I found myself receiving a large shipment of books by mail from the Falcon Press and the Grey Walls Press of London. Before I gave up this time-consuming, close-to-unprofitable venture two years later, I was representing no less than eight English publishers. But there was very little Canadian interest in quality books, many slanted toward an English audience, and I was more than happy to turn the whole thing over to the British Book Service, then forming in Canada (they would give it up as well, but years later). I wrote the whole thing off to experience, vowing never to hawk books again to booksellers. Like most of my promises, to myself or others, I ended up breaking that one as well.

In the fall of that year I submitted a novel about an air force veteran titled *The Winter of Time* to a new Canadian paperback company, Export Publishing Enterprises Limited, whose first books had appeared on Toronto newsstands. Ryerson Press and Macmillan of Canada had already rejected it. Imagine my surprise to get a letter of acceptance a month later. A payment of two hundred dollars would be made on publication, a lot of money in those days. The book appeared the following January, but the story of how I finally collected my payment is too long, too incredible to record here.

One other pleasant experience of that year was a meeting a few months earlier on a torrid summer day with the two editors of *Here and Now*, a new literary quarterly being published in Toronto. It was in a damp basement room somewhere near St. Mary's Street that Catherine Harmon and Paul Duval told me of their ambitious plans for their magazine. Surely the most handsomely produced magazine to ever appear in Canada, it printed my poem "To the Crows outside My Window" in its second of four issues.

It was now the turn of my friend Louis Dudek, still in New York City, to brighten up the literary scene with his poetry mailbag circuit. The concept was simplicity itself: you received a bulky envelope of manuscripts, read the poems, made any comments you cared to, enclosed four or five of your own poems and mailed it off as quickly as possible to the next poet on the list. The one I received contained work by Louis, William Carlos Williams, and Samuel French Morse, among others. Who the Canadians were beside myself and Louis I can't remember, but surely Irving Layton was included.

The hope was that the mailbag would go around the circuit in a couple of months, so it could be dispatched again from scratch. This hope was dashed, however, when I forwarded the mailbag to Paul Blackburn in New York City. The story goes that he went to work one morning leaving the various manuscripts spread over his bed and elsewhere. When he returned that night he found that his seven cats had shown their displeasure with the poems littered around the room by leaving their own unmistakable rejection notices. Most of the manuscripts were too badly soiled to save. Paul was forced to type most of them over—at least that was his excuse when Louis finally got him to pass them along almost six months later. A second mailbag tried a year later only confirmed the fact that many poets from necessity are too self-centred to be of much use in cooperative enterprises. And perhaps what we need today are a few more sensitive cat packs free to exercise their literary judgements as Paul Blackburn's were!

Contact Days

In August 1951, my wife and I travelled to Montreal on holiday. There we accepted an invitation from Louis Dudek, now in Montreal for good, to drive out to his grandmother's farm at Charlemagne on the banks of the Little Jesus river. John Sutherland also came along, but Irving Layton declined for some reason. And it was at the outdoor picnic table that Louis threw down issues Number 1 and Number 2 of Cid Corman's *Origin,* saying, "This is typical of what the nuts in New York are doing these days." I flipped through them casually, then handed them back; I was in no mood for things literary that day. But near the end of the year I saw the magazine mentioned favourably, and for some reason sent to Boston to order them. A month later I'd begun a correspondence with Cid that would reshape my whole poetic life.

Little magazines were definitely on my mind when I wrote Louis Dudek in October to tell him I would launch the first issue of a mimeographed poetry journal, *Contact,* in the following January. And appear it did, all ten 9-by-14-inch sheets neatly stapled together, folded in half, then stapled once again at the top, addressed on the blank side of the back page, and dropped in the mail with a three-cent stamp attached. Two hundred copies were run off, in which the opening editorial by Louis began: "Poetry

in Canada needs a new start," and ended with, "Why are the young poets at a loss for words?"

That issue featured four poems by Irving Layton, "Three Little Poems" by Kenneth Patchen, five by Louis himself, and a fine poem by Alfred G. Bailey—none of the poets appearing "young" except at heart. But it was my hope that the young ones would soon follow.

By the third issue Charles Olson, Paul Blackburn, and William Bronk had appeared, while Robert Creeley would be published later, all thanks to Cid Corman's unselfish interest. And of course Cid's numerous translations which graced all succeeding issues were an education in European poetry in themselves.

Meanwhile, in Montreal Louis Dudek and Irving Layton had put their heads together and decided it was now high time to launch Contact Press as a natural offshoot of *Contact* magazine. So in February 1952, I was invited to submit seventy-five poems toward a book the three of us would appear in together. The title *Cerberus* finally surfaced, and soon it was ready for the press, with Betty Layton's linocut featured on the cover. My address at the time, 28 Mayfield Avenue, Toronto, was used on the title page because my Montreal comrades feared trouble from the straight-laced, repressive administration of Premier Maurice Duplessis, then ruling the Province of

"Afternoon at Charlemagne, Quebec: Lia, myself (in front), John Sutherland, Stefi and Louis Dudek," 1951

Quebec like a veritable dictator. As it turned out it would remain the permanent address until 1958.

Contact Press went on over the next fifteen years to publish forty-seven titles, all poetry but one. Seven would appear under my name (five of them mimeographed booklets), while three others would be edited by me. As I was a silent third party in the Montreal operation, with no funds to contribute and living in Toronto as well, the real responsibility for the press fell on Louis Dudek and Irving Layton. After the first few years Irving would gradually withdraw from the business end of it, although he did continue to publish frequently. Louis was therefore left to shoulder the burden physically and financially, which he tackled with his usual energy and commitment. It wasn't until 1958 that he handed over management of the press to Peter Miller, a promising poet and fellow worker with me at the Imperial Bank. Thus Contact Press became a Toronto operation, with Peter assuming the financial and actual publishing end of it, while I tried to help as best I could, mainly with coediting. To sum up: the two guiding forces behind Contact Press were Louis Dudek and Peter Miller, and this is the way it should read in the record. I've always winced ever since when someone erroneously refers to it as "Souster's Contact Press."

And right here I want to acknowledge the fine letter received in June 1952 from William Carlos Williams. He complimented me on two or three poems from my section of *Cerberus* and ended his letter: "Have confidence in yourself. You've got it." Those seven words from a poet who was even then a modern American master were to sustain me through good times and bad in the years ahead.

I went on to publish *Contact* magazine until March 1954, when I decided it had finally fulfilled its mission. The tenth and last issue was one of our fattest and strongest, proving we were a going concern right to the last.

Nineteen fifty-six is the year I'll always remember for my few visits to see John Sutherland at the Toronto General Hospital. John had moved to Toronto two years before to begin religious studies at St. Michael's College. But now his short life was coming to an end. He'd written a study of Canadian poet E. J. Pratt for Ryerson Press, and every effort was made to put a printed copy of the book into his hands before his death; they didn't make it by much. He edited a last issue of *Northern Review* from his Stryker frame; I sat beside his bed sipping the ice-cold beer a nurse magically produced from a small refrigerator John's father had had installed in the room, along with an air conditioner and a tiny TV set John could watch even while lying on his back. After three trips to the hospital I couldn't bear to see him anymore; when he died I couldn't bring myself to go to the funeral.

In the following year I found I hadn't kicked the little magazine-editing habit yet—with Cid Corman providing the title *Combustion*, I began another mimeographed little magazine. In its fourteen issues, the last of which appeared in 1960, it featured poets like Margaret Avison, Gregory Corso, Robert Duncan, Theodore Enslin, Lawrence Ferlinghetti, Allen Ginsberg, and LeRoi Jones, among others.

Then by April of 1957 we were ready to hold our first Greenwich Gallery poetry reading. Av Isaacs, the generous owner of this avant-garde gallery on Bay Street above Gerrard in downtown Toronto, offered us its free use one Saturday night a month. We paid for the rental of the folding chairs along with cleaning and polishing the Gallery floors after use. We began with Doug Jones, whose Contact Press book *Frost on the Sun* had just appeared. Poets weren't paid, but we managed a little expense money for those travelling from out of town. Other poets in that first series were James Reaney, Irving Layton, and Louis Dudek, with Jay Macpherson, Peter Miller, and Kenneth McRobbie following in the spring. A second series began in November 1958 with F. R. Scott, then myself, and concluded with an evening of contemporary Hungarian translations.

For our third series, now called the Contact Reading Series, the newly formed Canada Council awarded us $845 of $1,312 requested. Which meant we could now pay the poets a reasonable fee, even bring in some poets from the U.S.A. Ralph Gustafson gave his first reading to open the series on October 3; Denise Levertov became the first American poet to read on November 28, while Charles Olson closed out the series on April 30, 1960. One highlight of this series had been two French-Canadian poets reading in their own language in March.

For the fourth series the venue changed to the YM-YWHA (Young Men's and Young Women's Hebrew Association) at Spadina and Bloor, where Nathan Marcus was the director. Among the fine poets reading that winter were Louis Zukofsky, George Johnston, Cid Corman, and Theodore Enslin. The following year a fifth and final series saw us return to the Isaacs Gallery, Av Isaac's new and spacious location on Yonge Street above Bloor. Two of the readings merit special attention here. The first, Robert Creeley's understated and haunting lyric statements, as he took to the platform in place of Allen Ginsberg. The second, Charles Olson's unforgettable wave-crashing renderings from his *Maximus Poems*. This performance even overshadowed a virtuoso rendition by Marshall MacLuhan of Gyula Illyes's

"Of Tyranny In One Breath" in an outstanding translation by Margaret Avison, delivered during the Hungarian poets' evening of April 1959. And it was fitting that the last Contact reading, held in April 1962, should be by James Reaney, second reader in our original series.

Nineteen sixty-two was also the year Lia and myself took the long, two-day train journey to Fredericton, New Brunswick. We shared a roomette on a train that seemed to go around one sharp curve after another; as a result we didn't get a wink of sleep all night. Dr. Desmond Pacey had invited me to read at the university's commencement day in mid-May. After Des and his wife had plied me with homemade dandelion wine, I read to a large audience, feeling quite relaxed. We left two mornings later, my wife and I enduring a very bumpy bus ride to St. John, where we lunched with Kay Smith, a fine poet from the First Statement Press days. Late that same afternoon we took the *Ocean Limited* for Montreal. It was only at the last minute that we discovered that our sleeping berths were not available. That meant we

were forced to sit up all night. That gruelling trip was to cure us of train travel forever.

Early the following year I took a gamble and submitted a poetry manuscript to my old publisher, Ryerson Press. To my great surprise the new editor and old friend of mine, John Robert Colombo, wrote me favourably. He even suggested that I include all previously printed poems in a volume which could be loosely called "collected." So it was that in March 1964 *The Colour of the Times,* my most popular and widely circulated verse collection, was published.

A nice surprise for both my wife and myself that May was an invitation for me to read at Western Reserve University in Cleveland. Gwendolyn MacEwen replaced Margaret Avison (if my memory serves me correctly) as a second poet; the three of us flew down and back together. Gwen was fascinated by being close enough to Hart Crane's birthplace of Garrettsville, Ohio, to visit it during our Cleveland stay. It was my first and, as it would turn out, only poetry reading in the United States.

Another short journey for Lia and myself which gave us some very agonizing moments was our flight to Ottawa, the nation's capital, in May 1965. The occasion was the presentation to me of the Governor General's Award for Poetry in English for 1964. Fog held up our 1.00 p.m. departure from Toronto for an hour, but this didn't worry us, as we weren't expected at Rideau Hall, the Governor General's residence, until 4.00 p.m. for the presentation. But imagine our dismay on arriving at Ottawa airport to find someone else had taken our one large suitcase from the baggage carousel, leaving us a similar though smaller one in its place. The Air Canada officials got busy at once but couldn't manage to locate our bag-switcher. It was 3.30 p.m. when I phoned Rideau Hall and explained our plight to an aide-de-camp. He was very reassuring. Tell your wife to come exactly as she is, he said. The Vaniers will put you completely at ease. But get in a taxi right away and hurry.

We made Rideau Hall at exactly four o'clock. When we entered the big reception hall it looked as though they were waiting for us to arrive to begin the ceremony.

My wife felt very self-conscious wearing a very plain jumper in a roomful of people appropriately dressed for the occasion. But after, at the reception, the Governor General and his wife were so charming that we found ourselves laughing at our little mishap. Then, following the reception when we returned to our hotel room, we found Air Canada had returned our suitcase to us. My wife, therefore, was able to wear the dress she had brought for the occasion at the banquet at the Chateau Laurier that evening. We had

"Lia and myself beside the Humber River," Étienne Brûlé Park, Toronto, 1965

a fabulous dinner, and I was handed a thousand-dollar cheque which no one had told me I would receive. Next day we drove back to Toronto with my publisher. At least we'd ended the journey with the same luggage!

Nineteen sixty-five also marked my close involvement with *New Wave Canada,* an anthology of the new Canadian poets of the sixties. Edited and produced by myself, I benefited from much sage advice from Victor Coleman, then editing a little magazine, *Island,* as well as Island Press. By riding herd on a procrastinating local printer I had the 167 pages ready to collate by April 30 of the following year, which quite by chance was two days after Lia and I had moved into our new Baby Point Road home. A dozen or more volunteers arrived early that Saturday morning. I had spent the previous evening removing all six inside doors of our bungalow, then making crude tables of them in the basement with whatever came to hand. These were then piled high with the pages of *New Wave Canada* in exact order. We were printing 900 copies, 160 clothbound, the balance in paper. All day long the group toiled faithfully at their collating task in that cool basement. My wife served up a supper of steaming pasta, with a couple of cases of beer standing by. The following day only four of us toiled at the piles beginning to shrink significantly; the third and last day I worked alone, finishing the now-hateful job early in the afternoon, then collapsing into bed with a bad head cold. I would never again get physically involved with any more of the books I produced—I would let the machines and the proper professionals handle them.

Nineteen sixty-six still had one more memorable twist to it. During a summer holiday trip to Montreal, Lia and I joined a small group of fellow poets on August 20 at Ralph Gustafson's lovely home in North Hatley, Quebec. Here in one short session we put together the ground rules for an organization of Canadian poets which was shortly to be christened rather logically the League of Canadian Poets. I went on to serve as first elected chairman of the league for the first four years of its youthful struggle for survival, with strong assists by Doug Lochhead, John Robert Colombo, and many others. This year of 1991, it will celebrate its twenty-fifth Silver Anniversary.

Then what was perhaps the watershed year of my poetry career came in 1969 when Oberon Press of Ottawa published my collection *So Far So Good.* Today I can only re-echo that title, as Michael Macklem at Oberon Press has been my publisher ever since, with twenty-one poetry titles (all but one in both cloth and paper) issued to date. My latest,

Founding meeting of the League of Canadian Poets: Lorna and Ron Everson, Ralph Gustafson, Lia and Raymond Souster, and Louis Dudek, North Hatley, Quebec, 1966

Running Out the Clock, is due this spring of 1991. Who knows how much more hot lead from his faithful printing press Michael may still use to fashion more pages of mine?

A Final Note

The reader may have noticed that I've said nothing about the decades of the seventies and eighties. That's not to slight them or take anything away from those years in any way. It's only that for the most part I still feel too close to that period to be sure what events deserve a place in this narrative.

If, however, I had to choose one personal literary highlight of those times, it would have to be the decision of Oberon Press to publish my collected poems. Michael Macklem and I first discussed it in correspondence in 1978–79: the first installment appeared in 1980 as the *Collected Poems of Raymond Souster,* Volume 1, 1940–1955. Volume 6, 1984–1986, appeared in 1988. Originally a four-part set, the *Collected Poems* is now an open-ended concept, limited only by my ability to write meaningful new poems and by the desire of readers to keep buying my books. In 1984, to complete the package, Oberon commissioned Montreal poet and critic Bruce Whiteman to compile an exhaustive 240-page bibliography.

Finally, from time to time I hear some poets complain about "the poems drying up." Surely it is rather the poets themselves who are going through this process. For as long as man is still capable of emotion, be it love or hate or fear or great joy or sorrow, poems will cry out to be written, and somewhere and somehow poets will spring up to write them down.

BIBLIOGRAPHY

Poetry:

When We Are Young, First Statement Press, 1946.

Go to Sleep, World, Ryerson, 1947.

New Poems, Enterprise Agency, 1948.

City Hall Street, Ryerson, 1951.

Shake Hands with the Hangman: Poems 1940–1952, Contact Press, 1953.

A Dream That Is Dying, Contact Press, 1954.

Walking Death, Contact Press, 1954.

For What Time Slays, Contact Press, 1955.

Selected Poems, edited by Louis Dudek, Contact Press, 1956.

Crêpe-Hanger's Carnival: Selected Poems, 1955–58, Contact Press, 1958.

A Local Pride, Contact Press, 1962.

Place of Meeting: Poems, 1958–60, Gallery Editions, 1962.

At Split Rock Falls, American Letters Press, 1963.

The Colour of the Times: The Collected Poems of Raymond Souster (also see below), Ryerson, 1964.

12 New Poems, Goosetree Press, 1964.

Ten Elephants on Yonge Street (also see below), Ryerson, 1965.

As Is, Oxford University Press, 1967.

Lost and Found: Uncollected Poems 1945–1965, Clarke, Irwin, 1968.

The Mirror and Late Arrival, Unicorn Press, 1969.

So Far So Good: Poems 1938–1968, Oberon, 1969.

The Years, Oberon, 1971.

Selected Poems of Raymond Souster, edited by Michael Macklem, Oberon, 1972.

The Colour of the Times [and] *Ten Elephants on Yonge Street*, McGraw-Hill Ryerson Limited (Toronto), 1973.

Change-Up: New Poems, Oberon, 1974.

Double-Header, Oberon, 1975.

Rain-Check, Oberon, 1975.

Extra Innings: New Poems, Oberon, 1977.

Hanging In: New Poems, Oberon, 1979.

Collected Poems of Raymond Souster, Oberon, Volume 1, 1940–1955, 1980, Volume 2, *1955–1962*, 1981, Volume 3, *1962–1974*, 1982, Volume 4, *1974–1977*, 1983, Volume 5, *1977–1983*, 1984, Volume 6, *1984–1986*, 1988.

Going the Distance: New Poems 1979–1982, Oberon, 1983.

Jubilee of Death: The Raid on Dieppe, Oberon, 1984.

Queen City (with photographs by Bill Brooks), Oberon, 1984.

It Takes All Kinds: New Poems, Oberon, 1986.

The Eyes of Love, Oberon, 1987.

Asking for More, Oberon, 1988.

Running Out the Clock, Oberon, 1991.

Editor:

Experiment 1923–29: Poems by W. W. E. Ross, Contact Press, 1956.

Poets '56: Ten Younger English-Canadians, Contact Press, 1956.

New Wave Canada: The New Explosion in Canadian Poetry, Contact Press, 1966.

(With John Robert Colombo) *Shapes and Sounds: The Poems of W. W. E. Ross*, Longmans, Green, 1968.

(With Richard Woollatt) *Generation Now* (poetry anthology), Longmans Canada Limited, 1970.

(With Douglas Lochhead) *Made in Canada: New Poems of the Seventies*, Oberon, 1970.

(With Woollatt) *Sights and Sounds* (poetry anthology), Macmillan (Toronto), 1973.

(With Woollatt) *These Loved, These Hated Lands* (poetry anthology), Doubleday (Toronto), 1975.

Vapour and Blue: Souster Selects Campbell (selected poetry of William Wilfred Campbell), Paget Press, 1978.

Comfort of the Fields: Archibald Lampman (selected poetry of Archibald Lampman), Paget Press, 1979.

(With Woollatt) *Poems of a Snow-Eyed Country*, Academic Press of Canada, 1980.

(With Lochhead) *Windflower: Poems of Bliss Carman*, Tecumseh Press, 1985.

(With Lochhead) *Powassan's Drum: Selected Poems of Duncan Campbell Scott*, Tecumseh Press, 1986.

Other:

(Collaborator with Dudek, P. K. Page, and James Wreford) *Unit of Five*, edited by Ronald Hambleton, Ryerson, 1944.

(Under pseudonym Raymond Holmes) *The Winter of Time* (novel), Export Publishing, 1950.

(Collaborator with Dudek and Irving Layton) *Cerberus,* Contact Press, 1952.

(Under pseudonym John Holmes) *On Target* (novel), Village Book Store Press, 1973, New American Library, 1982.

(Collaborator with Lochhead) *100 Poems of Nineteenth Century Canada* (poetry anthology), Macmillan (Toronto), 1974.

(With Douglas Alcorn) *From Hell to Breakfast* (war memoirs), Intruder Press, 1980.

Flight of the Roller Coaster: Poems for Children, edited by Woollatt, Oberon, 1985.

Souster's papers, which include manuscripts and correspondence, are held at Lakehead University Library, Thunder Bay; the Rare Book Room at the University of Toronto Library; and the McGill University Library, Montreal.

Gael Turnbull

1928-

Gael Turnbull, 1985

1

I am a white Caucasian male, born mid-morning, 7 April 1928. Height: 5 feet, 10½ inches (180 centimeters). Weight: 10½ stone (147 pounds or 67 kilograms), rarely varies whatever calorie intake, but has been as low as 9 stone when ill or not eating for other reasons. Hair: once brown, now almost entirely white and absent over the vertex. Clean-shaven, but beard formerly with a reddish tint. Eyes: greenish brown. Moderate astigmatism. Need glasses for any close work or ordinary reading. Teeth: slightly stained and irregular, almost intact. Hearing: not what it was, but usually adequate. Pigmentation: light with moderate freckles. No gross distinguishing marks.

Habits: generally a good sleeper and crave a lot, feeling best with at least nine hours in twenty-four. Poor waker, usually with resentment at being summoned back from oblivion, except after a daytime nap. Dreams not often recalled, rarely fearful or of apparent significance. Take less and less alcohol, but enjoy glass of wine with a meal, occasional whisky, beer. Was social, even moderate smoker, years ago, mostly tobacco, rarely cannabis.

Enjoy physical activity and need it. Swim, walk a lot, cycle, but none of it competitive, with myself or others. A Morris dancer for many years. Heterosexual.

Good sense of rhythm, but almost tone deaf. Have serious difficulty remembering tunes and cannot reproduce them at all, though able to enjoy

321

"With Mother," Aberdeen, 1928

several days. Can distinctly recall supposing in brief intervals of consciousness that I was about to die, then the moment when I realised that I was going to live after all. At the time, it seemed only a matter of passing curiosity, either way. Luckily, it has left me with only mild wasting of both thigh muscles and lower trunk muscles, and few limitations as to what I can do. (2) Internal haemorrhage in 1981, fortunately not so massive that I could not get to neighbours for help. Required several units of blood, but I escaped laparotomy. Cause officially unknown, but I suspect side effect from an analgesic I had taken. No problems since.

2

We are all many selves and lead many lives. The difficulty is in where to start, what to exclude. There is also the observation, "Biography is inevitably inaccurate and autobiography is . . . unbecoming as well."[1] Yet the attempt, if not "accurate," can be revealing, intentionally or not, even for the writer. Or is it to be considered as any writing, that is, fiction, a manipulation of experience, at whatever remove, expressed in words?

To begin with the surname: Turnbull and its resonance, which has always been strong for me, from my earliest memories. Reference books about the origins of names tend to be sceptical, but traditions have their own power. Boece (1527) mentions the story, that a man called William de Rule saved Robert Bruce shortly after his coronation in 1306 from a wounded bull, near Callander, northwest of Stirling, on the edge of The Highlands. This same man is also described, perhaps more convincingly, as having been killed just before the battle of Hallidon Hill, outside Berwick, in 1333. He is said to have swaggered out and rashly challenged an English knight to single combat. I have always taken this as a caution against over-presumption, as a warning to "stop while you are ahead." He was certainly called "Turn-ye-bull" and there is other evidence that a man called William de Rule held land in the valley of Rule Water, what is now Bedrule, just southwest of Jedburgh.

In 1451, Glasgow University was founded by a Bishop Turnbull who came from Bedrule, and the motto on his coat of arms (three bulls' heads) was "I saved the king." I like to think that as a family crest, the verb, being in the past tense, implies no current or future obligation. Even today there is an unusually high concentration of the name in the area and south across the border into Northumberland.

music, the simpler the better. Short-term memory loss about average for age, but have always had problems remembering personal names. Only art form which I have serious difficulty enjoying is ballet, traditional or contemporary.

Hate feeling dependent on a car. Never learned to fly. Love sailing, though it frightens me. Owned a dinghy once. Still have daydreams of owning a small seagoing or coastal boat, preferably a Drascombe.

Accent: this used to fret me more than it does now, especially since being told that I have a "disturbed accent," which is at least a useful label. Medications: none. Dependencies: sleep (see above) and morning tea, several mugs, milk, no sugar. Food: enjoy it and do some cooking and always have. Only aversion is to oranges as a fruit (juice or flavouring, no problem).

Injuries: only minor, more by luck than judgement, except for slight concussion in 1957. Nearest escapes from disaster (1) when climbing on Pavey Ark in Cumbria as a student in 1946 and (2) when nearly shipwrecked on Ithaca in 1986.

Two life-threatening events: (1) poliomyelitis in summer of 1957, when I was semiconscious for

Though not so famous as other Border families, such as the Armstrongs, the Eliotts, the Kerrs, we are mentioned in one of the ballads, which records how Sir Andrew of Bedrule turned up in good time for the "raid" of Redeswire, near Carter Bar, in 1575, "With all his Trumbills at his back." At least it was only ten miles for them to come, on that occasion.

David Lindsay mentions them in his "Ane Satyre of the Thrie Estatis" (1552) among other Border families who were well known for their freedom with others' property, and there is a contemporary account of James IV rounding up all the Turnbulls in 1510 for justice at Jedburgh. I was always told that he hanged every tenth man as a token of impartiality.

Through my father's immediate family, I am a hereditary Freeman of Berwick-upon-Tweed, technically in Northumberland since 1482, but the natural county town for Berwickshire or Merse, as it used to be called. The earliest name in our line of which there is record in the Freeman's Book at Berwick is a John Turnbull, "admitted 27 April 1798." He is listed as being an "apprentice cooper," thus still young, and cannot have been "given" his Freedom at such an age, so must have claimed it as a right through his father, but there are no earlier records available.

Originally, Freemen in effect governed the Royal Borough and had all sorts of rights and privileges. There is still a Freeman's Guild and minor privileges if you live in the town and even a fund to help with the education of Freemen's children. As I have no son, nor has my brother, we cannot pass it on, but there are many distant cousins and even one second cousin of about my age, of the same name, though he still spells it "Gale."

All this is not totally irrelevant to my sense of myself, as a Borderer, though perhaps of borders beyond those of Scotland; and the ambiguity of Berwick, north of the Tweed yet annexed to Northumberland, has something congenial in its situation.

3

My father's parents were both born in Berwick, Thomas Turnbull in 1867 and Phyllis Ewart in 1866. They were married in 1888 and had three sons and a daughter. My father never knew why, but they moved to Edinburgh, where my grandfather had his own butcher's shop for many years on Leith Walk on the northeastern edge of the New Town. However, when my father, the third child, was due to be born, my grandmother went down to Berwick for the

birth. There may have been family reasons why it was more convenient.

My father was born on 3 March 1901 and named Ralph Gale Turnbull, after his mother's mother, whose maiden name was Eliza Ralph Gale, and who is said to have been at least partly Welsh. Thus, when I was born I was given my father's middle name, and it had that spelling on my birth certificate. I am not sure at what age the spelling was changed, probably when I was twelve or thirteen, perhaps when we moved to Canada, and I suddenly became aware that it was more commonly regarded as a girl's name.

I can remember episodes of being teased about this by other boys of my age. This was particularly so when I was for brief periods at a boys' boarding school and the inevitable letter would turn up labelled with the wrong gender. What strikes me now as strange is that I cannot ever recall being in the least humiliated or ashamed, rather the reverse. I took any confusion as merely showing the ignorance of the rest of the world.

According to my mother, my grandfather Thomas Turnbull, although he worked long hours in his butcher's shop, was not a good business man and was noted more for spending time reading books than "keeping his books." My father remarked, half joking, that there was "some astringency, economically." Though originally Church of Scotland (Presbyterian), by some time after settling in Edinburgh they were attending a nearby Scottish Episcopal Church, Saint Paul's on York Place, where Thomas Turnbull, who had a fine bass voice, sang in the choir, and my father eventually with him, in the boys' choir.

Two events then occurred, both with consequences for my as-yet-unimagined life. When my father was about thirteen or fourteen, having done well at school and won some prizes, he was put in to take the exam to go on to one of the secondary "colleges" and was offered a place. It was a moment in his life which he never forgot. There was some sort of family conference and the expenses for books, uniforms, and other incidentals were considered. Reluctantly, it was decided that it was not possible, or perhaps his parents thought that the alternatives offered a better future.

He was sent instead as an apprentice, on a seven-year scheme, to learn the farm feed and fertiliser business with a firm in Leith. Although this loss of educational "advantage" left him with an obsessive commitment that no child of his should ever be deprived in that way, he always spoke highly of his years in business. He had ability, worked hard, received rapid promotion, and was given considerable responsibility at an early age.

The other critical event was in 1914, when he was thirteen years old. There was a revival "crusade," with one of the two evangelists being an American, Wilbur Chapman; and my father had a profound "conversion experience." With his parents, he began to attend Charlotte Chapel (Baptist) on Rose Street and came under the influence of a well-known preacher and writer, Dr. Scroggie, who loaned him books of all sorts and encouraged his education, both religious and secular. By the time he was sixteen, the sense of a "calling" towards some sort of ministerial work began to develop strongly, and before he had finished at Leith he was used to taking part in and even helping to lead meetings and services of various kinds.

At some time during this period about the end of the First World War, his own father gave up his shop and took a salaried position with Thomas Liptons on Princes Street. This may have eased the financial pressures. Certainly towards the end of my father's working days in Leith, he was able to save a useful amount and about then the family moved to a flat on

*"My grandparents Turnbull," Edinburgh,
about 1925*

the other side of the city, which they eventually owned.

Scroggie had spent time in America, and at the Moody Bible Institute, and highly recommended it; and the American evangelist, Chapman, had made an enormous impression on my father. In 1923 he set off for Chicago. The ship took six days, the train from New York another two. Thus he arrived at last in the "New World."

4

My middle name, Lundin, comes from my mother. It is pronounced: Lun-deen. Her parents came from Sweden. Her grandfather was born and grew up on what might be called a croft or smallholding in a village called Åsen, in Älvdalen (a river valley) in Dalarna.

When he was born in 1862, in that area, as in so much of Sweden, there were no surnames. His father's name was Lars, son of Lars, of Grav, or more formally Grav Lars Larson, though usually just Lars Larson. Thus my grandfather's name was Olaf Larson, and his sister's, Anna Larsdotter.

The village is on what is known as the "copper-mine" road, running north and slightly west towards the border and the copper-mining area in the north of Norway. It is virtually the last area where some farming is still done before the northern forest closes in completely. The ground is poor, rocky, and rarely flat. They kept some cows, pigs, and chickens, grew oats and hay, but mostly survived by working *i skogen*, in the forest in the logging industry, through the long winter months. I shall always remember him, as an old man, remarking on the contrast with the rolling, fertile fields of Minnesota.

In 1880, when he was eighteen, his father and mother, with his sister and others from the area, set off for America to join friends and relatives already there, settling a few miles south of a small town to the west of Minneapolis called Dassel, which at that time was as far as the railway extended west. Their first winter was spent in a "dugout" shelter on the side of a hill and they began the long process of clearing and ploughing.

It was not long after the Sioux "uprising," and my grandfather's sister married a man, Ben Brown, who could remember as a boy how near he came to being killed. It was impossible for any of them to conceive that the Indians had any "right" to the land, even less any "use" for it. It had appeared to be unoccupied. For my grandfather, it was quite simple and a great wonder. In his words: "This has been a very good land to many poor people" and he, like so many others, worked very hard to make it so.

He married, in June 1885, a girl of perhaps a more genteel background, two years his senior (though he never liked to admit it), also a recent immigrant, who came from a town in a more southern area of Sweden, Torsby in Värmland. Her name had been Kirsten Neilsdotter, but she signed her marriage certificate as Christin Nelson, the surname she had taken. My great-grandfather and his family also had to choose a surname and my mother did not know why they chose Lundin, but "the Lundins" they became.

There were seven children, of whom only one, the youngest, died young, aged four, of a cancer of the eye. My mother, Anne, or Annie, born 4 February 1901, was the youngest surviving.

Thus she grew up on the farm, speaking Swedish at home, and even when she was at high school in Dassel, she and her friends of her own age spoke Swedish among themselves as much as English. She could remember as a young girl walking the miles into town, sometimes through woodland paths, helping to carry butter and other produce for sale, even for barter. Though no longer a "pioneer" area in any strict sense, there were those who told stories of the "early days," and some who could claim to have been the very first settlers, even before the railway.

The Swedish Covenant Church was a very central part of their life and my mother remembered the controversy when some English was first introduced into a service.

She then trained as a teacher and came back to teach at the local country "redbrick school," only a couple of miles from the farm, where she had been a pupil herself when young. In the autumn of 1922, she left home again and started a two-year course at the Moody Bible Institute in Chicago.

5

When my father arrived in Chicago in 1923, my mother had already completed her first year. They were both outstanding students, and when my mother graduated in 1924, she was "valedictorian" for her year, as my father was for his in 1925.

By 1926, my father had completed a year of studies at McCormick Presbyterian Theological Seminary in Chicago, supporting himself by a variety of jobs, including a period as a student pastor, and was firmly committed to becoming a fully trained and ordained minister.

He was also engaged to my mother. He had visited her family and the farm at Dassel, the start of what was to become a steadily increasing attachment to the place in future years. There must have been much discussion, and much prayer, about their future life together.

My father returned to Scotland ahead of her, to his parents' in the ground floor, or "garden flat," at 1 Valleyfield Street in the Tollcross area by the Meadows, and it was here my mother eventually came, and where they were married on 7 December 1926.

Two aspects of their life at that time become more and more present to me. The first, what a shock and adjustment it must have been for my mother, not only the vastly different life in another country far from her own kin, but also the experiences of marriage, pregnancy, childbirth, and motherhood. The second, how they survived financially. Even they marvelled, in later years, looking back. Quite simply, nothing went to waste, every penny was accounted for.

When I was born in a nearby nursing home in 1928, they were living with friends in a first-floor flat at 16 Comley Bank, having their own bedroom but sharing otherwise.

By then my father was a student at New College, the divinity school associated with Edinburgh University, finishing studies he had already begun in America. During 1928–29, he was at Aberdeen University, because they were able to live in a house there for a year, helping to look after some children whose parents were abroad. From 1929 to 1931, they were back in Edinburgh, where he was completing the requirements for his M.A.

During all of this time, he worked as a "supply preacher" at weekends and in the holidays. He had amusing stories to tell of some of his experiences visiting remote parishes in many parts of Scotland. Occasionally he had the satisfaction of finding that they wanted him to come back, or even to consider a "call," but he was determined to complete his degree.

My mother always spoke of those times with particular warmth, especially of the holidays we spent at Kelso, on the Borders near Jedburgh, with a family, the Gleeds, at Union Street. Evidence of strains and problems came later. Perhaps it was simply the resilience of youth, the sense of adventure and new beginnings. They were living as much for the future as for the present.

She did make one visit back to America to see her family, when I must have been two or three. I retained one or two dim memories of the farm. It was during this trip that I achieved my first *bon mot*. On the train someone asked me where my father was.

Remembering the photograph that my mother carried, I replied, "In my mother's handbag."

Although the details of all these early years were not explicit for me until much later, the atmosphere was very real and strongly conditioned my life as I grew up.

6

My father finally began his formal ministry at the Baptist Chapel in Jarrow-on-Tyne. It was 1931 and they arrived just as the worst of the Depression made itself felt, and Jarrow was one of the places most severely affected in the entire country. The famous "Jarrow March" began there for that reason, when unemployed men walked in demonstration south to present a petition to Parliament.

The church was active in relief efforts, with soup kitchens and the distribution of used clothing. During this period my parents acquired a reinforcement of their existing antipathy to "drink," which they saw as a frequent factor in making the plight of the unemployed even worse than it already was. Though never obsessively "teetotal," it was many years before they could be relaxed about even occasional social drinking.

But there was much laughter too in Jarrow and, from almost the first day, a deep bond of friendship with a local dentist and his family who lived only a few doors away on Bede Burn Road which lasted for the rest of their lives.

The first of my two sisters was born there, on 24 February 1932, and I can remember first attending school: the expanse of playground, the thronging feet and bodies of the other children. I was teased initially about my Edinburgh accent, but by the time we left, it had transmuted into almost "Geordie," that is, a Tyneside and Durham accent, the first of many such adaptations.

There is a notebook, probably my first, which has survived, most of the pages blank or scribbled on by my sister. There are typical boys' drawings of aeroplanes and red Indians. On the front page I had carefully written my full name and address and, underneath, the words "I love my baby sister Esther Jen."

However, as a child, this was transmuted to "Tesser," and she is now known and signs herself as Tess.

The links with Jarrow and the Tyneside were to continue. Twenty or so years later, staying with those same friends of my parents, I would call nearby on Basil Bunting.[2]

"With my grandparents Lundin,"
Minnesota, 1931

7

In 1934, when I was six, we moved to Blackpool, a very popular seaside resort in Lancashire, on the Irish Sea. My father became minister there to a larger, and it seems in my memory, more well-to-do church, the Baptist Tabernacle. Like the chapel at Jarrow, it is now disused and boarded up.

After a time at a school in the north part of town, I attended, as a "day boy," Arnold Preparatory School, for three years, followed by a year in the main school. This was what used to be called a Public School, now an Independent, and by continual economy, and my father doing other occasional preaching during the week elsewhere, my parents managed to pay the fees and keep me in uniforms.

At first we lived on the north side of the town, and I had a long journey on the trams, changing by the North Pier. This could be exciting in winter, with high winds off the Irish Sea, waves and spray over the Promenade, once so violent that I had to get the help of a passer-by just to cross the open space from one tram to the other. Later we lived on Coniston Road, in an area known as the South Shore, rather more upper-middle-class as I recall, within easy walking distance of the school.

We had no car and my father made his pastoral visits, even to the church, by tram or bus or on foot. A well-to-do neighbour, prominent in the church, often gave us a lift in his car on Sundays.

But we did have a maid. Her name was Madge and she had in effect "joined the family" when we were in Jarrow, after my sister was born. She lived in, with her own room. It seems unimaginable now but was not remarkable then. All my early memories include her though there were aspects of her situation which sometimes troubled me even at that age.

I became aware that she had an "afternoon off" once a week and found it impossible to suppose what

"With Father," Berwick-upon-Tweed, 1939

she did with herself. Vaguely I knew that there were such things as going to the pictures, but it seemed more like a banishment. Then by the time I was nine or ten, I knew in theory that "maids" usually had "young men," but I could perceive no sign of one for her.

The sands at Blackpool are vast and the tide, when it comes in, is rapid. Madge had taken my sister and me down there one afternoon, perhaps for a picnic. It was not far to walk. All of us must have been enjoying ourselves, and without Madge realising, the tide had come in behind us, into a long, narrow depression in the sand. By the time we had gathered our things and started back, she had to carry my sister and I had to wade through; it seemed almost up to my waist. I remember how I clutched her hand and how frightened we were, and even yet I wonder how near I came to drowning. Perhaps it was only up to my knees, but I can remember the fear, perhaps hers more than mine, and how cold and powerful and dark the water was.

I was quick at school and seemed to learn without effort and even won a prize one year, 1938, which I still have: a beautiful edition of Kipling's *Puck of Pook's Hill*, which I never tired of reading. I was fairly good, but not competitive, at games. Most improbably, I remember excelling at boxing.

I was generally eager to please and enthusiastic in the Cubs (Cub Scouts), where I became a "sixer" and industriously collected more badges than anyone else, so that my "six" won the trophy in the last year, much to my surprise.

There was also a model theatre which I devised, of my own "invention," such as that was, and I can still feel the glow of praise from comments of the school staff.

I read a great deal from an early age and had a very active fantasy life, perhaps no more than most children. Yet I was gregarious also, busy devising and taking part in games with other children on the street. There was even conscious playacting and I remember something about Joan of Arc and, another time, some sort of "murder mystery."

I had great fondness for making plasticine models, sometimes with my sister, and I devised a whole "world" of imaginary creatures—with kings and heroes, adventures and dynasties, but also humbler details of villages, houses, carpets, furniture. There were books too in that "world" and I began to compile and write a history for it, in minute script, on pages hardly bigger than a large postage stamp. But like most of what I did, the book was not carried through to completion and I can still see how eagerly

Gael (center) with sisters, Tess and Karin, and brother, Stuart, Winnipeg, 1943

I began the first sheets, then the blank pages later, never filled.

My father's study was the downstairs front room of our classic late twenties or early thirties "semi." Home always included an awareness of his books and his typewriter, though he had as yet written and published nothing. (His first book, a collection of sermons, did not appear until 1943, but he published many after that, almost every year; one in particular, *A Minister's Obstacles,* was frequently reprinted.)

I had little sense of what he actually "did" except officiate and preach twice on Sundays, plus prayer meetings and other events in the evenings during the week. I do not remember that he was ever remote nor did it seem in the least strange that the person who officiated in a public pulpit was the same as the one I knew at home who would sometimes joke with me or help with my homework. He also played cricket with the church team. Once he came home after a Saturday match with an injured hand, which had been struck by the ball while he was batting. In my memory, I was told he had a broken bone and I looked with awe at the swelling and the bruising, which I can still see vividly in my mind.

One particular detail of my mother persists, of a different sort. There was always a prayer at bedtime, and from a very early age my mother must have been in the custom of repeating a children's verse in Swedish as she tucked me in. That sequence of sounds, in a muffled form, is a permanent part of my mind, even to this day, though I know no Swedish beyond a few words. Eventually she stopped doing it, perhaps by the time I was speaking fluently in English, and she never made any persistent effort to teach me further. Thus it is like some enigmatic writing, in unreadable yet fantastic script, stamped into the basic level of my consciousness.

After her death, my sister Tess came on a diary that my mother had kept for a time, starting in September 1934. On the flyleaf she had written: "In the hope that the contents of this little book might be of interest to Gale and Tesser in later years." Entries continued, with some breaks, until June 1936.

I had always been aware of how inadequate she sometimes felt in coping with those "duties" so often expected of a minster's wife. Not that there is any suggestion that there was any pressure from my father, rather, from her own wish to be "of use."

There were also the problems of being an American in 1930s England. I may imagine it, but I don't think she felt quite the same in Scotland. To some extent this was compounded by an awareness of her Minnesota farming background, of which she could be both proud and yet defensive. All this comes out, often obliquely, in many of the entries, and though often poignant, was not too surprising. What did surprise me is the intensity of her feeling about, not Sweden, where she had never been (though she finally went in the summer of 1936), but her lack of contact with others who spoke and understood what was, after all, the language of her growing up.

But there is much happiness in the diary too, even fun, and glimpses of that six-year-old boy who eventually became the person who writes this now, as in the first entry:

Sept 1, Sat., Took children with me shopping; it is difficult carrying on a philosophical conversation with Gale on the streets of noisy crowded Blackpool guiding a pram etc. Today the subject has been "traffic officers" which closed "Why don't they make cars that couldn't go faster, then there would be no need for speed officers. What's the use of making cars and having men to keep them going slowly?"

My childhood was happy. I was not conscious of the significance of this until many years later. Whether it is always such a good preparation for life, I sometimes wonder, since the world in which we must actually live is often far from happy, in fact does not function on such terms at all.

8

The date 3 September 1939 has a significance for me beyond what can be read in the history books. That "the war" was coming had been obvious even to a boy of ten, towards the end of 1938. I can still remember the smell of the rubber of the gas masks, it must have been in the spring of 1939, with which we were all fitted at school, and the little flapping valve on the canister and my scepticism that it would work. But it was exciting too, the sort of drama, even heroism, that happened in books, which might at last become real.

Our well-to-do neighbours, who had a car, actually built, of red bricks, an air-raid shelter. There was some mockery along the street that this was ostentation, even an invitation for bombs to come.

Seeing it, I was disconcerted by the design, thinking that if a bomb should land on top, it was manifestly not strong enough.

My younger sister, Karin Anne, was born in January 1938 after an earlier pregnancy when my mother lost twins. She was pregnant again in 1939. I don't know how long my parents had been considering leaving England, nor all the reasons, but there are some factors of which I do know.

First, they were apprehensive about the coming war. Then there was my mother's family, from whom she had been separated for so long and from whom the war might cut her off completely.

There were also dissatisfactions on my father's part with what he saw as limitations to his ministry in an English or Scottish context. His time at Moody and McCormick had impressed him with a more enterprising and imaginative approach to evangelism. He had never been entirely happy with the Baptists and some of his closest friends were in other denominations. There may have been specific problems in the church at Blackpool of which I am not aware.

Suddenly I was told that we were "going to America," specifically, to my grandparents' farm in Minnesota and I was delighted at the prospect. It was an "adventure" as exciting as in any book. My image of what it would be like was more conditioned by the stories of R. M. Ballantyne, and my mother's tales of her life as a girl, than any reality. In my imagination, there would surely be Indians in the woods, somewhere, in spite of what my rational mind tried to tell me.

I have no memory of any pang, for my own sake, in regard to what I might be leaving. Anyway, I was not "leaving home," it was merely home that was moving. Painful uncertainties as to what was "home" would only come much later.

My mother with my two sisters went on ahead in the late spring and my brother, James Stuart, was born in Minnesota in June 1939. I finished my year at school and my father, significantly, knowing that it might be his last chance, finally made the time and arrangements to go to Berwick to "claim" and be given his Freedom.

Our maid, Madge, who had lived with us for five or six years, wept when my mother and sisters left. My parents had invited her to accompany us, offered to pay her passage, with I do not know what other commitments, but she had refused, probably wisely. I had pangs because of Madge. This was not for my sake, as I had surprisingly little or no personal attachment, but for hers. What would become of her? In fact, with the coming of the war, she went into the

Auxiliary Territorial Service, and began another life altogether.

My father and I were due to sail early in September, I think on the *Mauritania.* Then all sailings were cancelled. On that Sunday, the third of September, we were staying with old friends in Bournemouth and had been to church. As we came back to the house in their car, it must have been 12.30 or so, their maid met us at the door, tears streaming down her face. "War has been declared!"

It was a particularly fine and sunny early autumn day, not a cloud in the sky, as I remember, and this gave the moment a peculiar intensity. At one o'clock, we all sat listening to the news and rebroadcast of Chamberlain's speech: "We are now at war with Germany."

I was old enough to appreciate some of my father's anxiety, with all sailings cancelled and my mother with my two sisters and the newborn son he had never seen in America. Almost at once came the news of the sinking of the unarmed passenger ship *Athenia.*

My father took the train up to London. By literally walking ahead of the queues, intruding himself into some office, insisting that he speak to some official, explaining his situation, for all I know no worse than many, he was able to get us a place on one of the few passenger ships still sailing, the *Aquitania.*

As we went aboard, workmen were busy bolting two guns onto the deck at the stern, the last nuts tightened only a few hours before we sailed on the tenth of September. I remember thinking that they looked absurdly small and exposed and ineffective, with no one standing by ready to use them. The irregular zigzag of our wake probably expressed a more realistic precaution.

Six days or so later we disembarked into the bustle and peacetime world of New York, and almost another life altogether.

9

In what follows, I am aware that this account of that "other life" since September 1939 may perhaps appear cursory, but there are limitations of space and attention. There are also many areas, important enough to me and which I would not wish to deny, about which it would be difficult to write, sometimes because painful, sometimes simply because obscure even to myself. And my "beginnings," rightly or wrongly, appear more significant than much of what

has happened since. Not all silence is cowardice; not all candour helpful.

For the last three months of 1939, I was a pupil at Dassel High School in Minnesota. In January 1940, we all moved north to Winnipeg, in Manitoba, Canada, where my father became pastor of Elim Chapel on Portage Avenue. I was at one of the city schools, Laura Secord, until the summer of 1940 and then started at Saint John's College, modelled on an English boys' "public school." I was a boarder there for the first few terms, I don't know why.

Though physically small for my age and assigned to play sports with boys two years younger, I was academically very successful without any conscious effort. This made me intellectually lazy later on. When taking the Manitoba end-of-high-school exams, I won the Provincial Governor General's Medal, in the summer of 1943.

Partway through the next school year, my parents arranged for me to return to England to attend the Perse School in Cambridge. (For the reasons for this and associated consequences, see part 10.) I arrived there, after crossing the Atlantic on a light cruiser with a group of returning "evacuees," in April 1944. I was supposed to live at the nearby Saint Paul's Vicarage, but this arrangement fell through, so I became a boarder at the School House for the following year, took my Higher School Certificate in

"My former wife Jonnie," Montreal, 1953

June 1945, and entered Christ's College, Cambridge, in early October, as a Natural Science student.

In the winter of 1946–47 I made a bizarre visit to Philadelphia. My parents had moved there in 1944, where my father was pastor of Bethlehem Presbyterian Church, scarcely six months after my arrival at the Perse School. This was over an extended Christmas holiday, two weeks of which were spent in travelling by Cunard and train. I had, I realise now in retrospect, become quite depressed, but managed to finish the rest of the year and gain a 2/2 (lower second class) degree in the summer of 1947.

If I had stayed on in England, I would have begun my clinical work at a London hospital. Instead, I rejoined my parents in Philadelphia, and my two sisters and American-born brother. By then eight years old, he was virtually a total stranger and would remain so until we finally "met" when he was twenty-three, and we became good friends.

In the autumn of 1947, I began at the medical school of the University of Pennsylvania, where I finally graduated with an American M.D. in 1951. During the first two years I lived at home with my parents. In 1949, my father became professor of Homiletics (preaching) at the Western Presbyterian Theological Seminary in Pittsburgh, so I was in lodgings for the last two years, not far from the university. I partly supported myself in that period by working at various medically related jobs in term time, and elsewhere in the holidays.

From 1951 to 1952, I was doing an internship in Pittsburgh, and in June 1952, married a girl from California, Jonnie May Draper (born 9 October 1927), who was doing a playwriting course at the Carnegie Institute of Technology. Due to sudden and unexpected harassment[3] by the Pittsburgh Draft Board (the Korean War was still on), we "fled" to Montreal, where I took the Canada Council Exams in September 1952, and I accepted a job with a practice in a small town in northern Ontario, Iroquois Falls.[4] Our eldest daughter, Christine Anne, was born there in April 1953.

When I was able to save some money, we left in the autumn of 1955 for London, where I set about finding work, first at the Manor House Hospital and then for nine months at the West Middlesex, where our second daughter, Julie Alice, was born in July 1956. For practical reasons, that year in London was mostly a disaster and it was with great relief that I accepted a job as Senior House Officer in anaesthetics at Ronkswood Hospital in Worcester, where a flat went with the job. I took my Diploma in Anaesthetics while there, and except for the "polio" (see part 1), those were a happy two years with friends nearby.

"At Ronkswood Hospital," Worcester, 1957

But there were no long-term prospects for work and most of my contemporaries seemed to be emigrating. As Jonnie had hardly seen her family except for brief visits, and as I had the necessary qualifications to practice there, we went out to California in the autumn of 1958, driving across the continent from New York. We were able to use her parents' as a base and once again I set about finding work. This turned up at the county hospital in Ventura, on the coast just south of Santa Barbara.

The actual place and much of the work was pleasant, if demanding. Our youngest daughter, Shari Ione, was born there in September 1961. Though happy in many ways, I could not settle and I made a visit to Scotland and England in the summer of 1963, which confirmed my decision to return to Britain.

It was hard on my wife, and had unsettling consequences for the children, but at least by returning to the Worcester/Malvern area there were friends and familiar associations. I had managed to save some money again and there was capital out of the house we had sold in Ventura, which went towards a house in the country just outside Malvern. I had a year or two working part-time or intermittently.

Through those years, first in Ventura and then near and in Malvern, the children were growing up and much of our lives centred on them. In particular, there were many holidays together, while in America along the West Coast and into Arizona and New Mexico, then later around England, Scotland, and nearby Wales. Once for three weeks, we went to Sweden, to visit Älvdalen and Torsby, as well as friends in Västerås and Stockholm.

These were usually touring and camping holidays, in an ageing VW "mini-bus," for which I may have had more enthusiasm than my family, but for which I hope they retain at least some cheerful memories.

Eventually I joined a practice in Worcester as a "half-partner," and did some regular sessions of anaesthetics at Kidderminster as well. In 1974, we moved into a house actually in Malvern. By 1981, our eldest daughter had left home and was married and living in California, with our first grandchild born there; our middle daughter was married, and the youngest was working as a secretary with the BBC in London.

At the end of July 1981, I separated from my wife, fortunately on friendly terms, which have continued. Toward the end of that year I met Pamela Jill Iles (born 8 May 1936), formerly Norman, herself also separated, and we were married in December 1983. She has two sons and a daughter, of similar ages to my children.

We lived in Stratford-upon-Avon for a while, where Jill had a house. I had resigned from the practice in Worcester at the end of September 1982. In September 1983, we both found work in Barrow-in-Furness, Cumbria, living in nearby Ulverston.

My father died suddenly and peacefully in December 1985 and then my mother less easily in August 1986. They are both buried only a couple of miles from the farm where she was born in Minnesota.

Jonnie, my former wife, having come to love the area, still lives in Malvern. My youngest daughter, Shari, is now settled in New York and my eldest daughter, Christine, with my granddaughter Jonna-Rose Annas Turnbull (born October 1980), is still in Los Angeles. Julie lives with her husband, Simon Bundred, in Nottingham with their two children, Samantha Eileen (born October 1984) and David Peter (born April 1986).

I was finally able to give up the doctoring at the end of June 1989 and Jill and I moved to Edinburgh on the fifth of July.

10

If there is very little about poetry in all this, that is because a bibliography probably says all that needs to be said, and more concisely. In the end, poems must speak for themselves, shift for themselves,

survive or shrivel away quite separate from the living person who made them. Yet since it is because of certain poems which I have written that I now write this, some account of how the writing came about is indicated, closely linked to my experiences when I went to the Perse School and to Cambridge, and thus probably to that decision of my parents in 1944.

To send their son, barely sixteen, all those miles away, in wartime and for an indefinitely long time, was a decision about which they must have thought and prayed for a long time. The consequences of that decision were profound and disturbing, in many ways for them as much as for me.

How the possibility came up, I cannot remember, but undoubtedly it had much to do with a friend of my parents, then in Canada, who was returning to his home in Cambridge and could provide me with care. They could not have guessed how this would break down, or all the circumstances. I was eager to go and they were eager to do "the best" for me. I was academically forward (if emotionally and physically rather the reverse) and Cambridge appeared to be that "best."

If I had not gone, and had finished my year at Saint John's College, I might have continued as a boarder, or followed my parents to Philadelphia when my father moved to a church there at the end of 1944. The course of my life would have been radically different and it is most unlikely that I would be writing this memoir.

For my part, intensely unhappy as part of the experience was, I feel an immense gratitude to my parents, and respect for their courage (others might say rashness) in sending me; the full consequences in some respects were very far from what they had hoped. I grew away from them in certain ways, and at crucial years of my life, though I did my best to cover up, even persuade myself otherwise. This separation was most critically felt in areas of religious belief and expression, and I know that there were ways and times, particularly for my mother, when they thought it had been a disastrous mistake, even as they were pleased for all that I had got out of it and proud of my Cambridge degree.

I don't think that, growing up, I wrote much more than many others of my age, or took that much greater interest in poems. What I do remember clearly is a particular moment, perhaps significant more in being remembered than because it would have seemed so remarkable at the time.

It must have been in the summer term of 1945 while I was a boarder at the Perse School House. I was reading a late nineteenth-century volume of *Selected Poems* by Robert Browning, which I had bought at a stall in the market in the centre of Cambridge. There are even associations with a particular poem, but that may be an accretion from later reading. I was sitting on the grass by the farther side of the tennis courts at the back of the School House. How far all this may be true, as historical detail, I have no way of knowing; but it has another sort of "truth." From that moment, or some such moments which my memory has attached to that particular one, something began which has continued.

That "something," one might call it a "calling," was undoubtedly fitful at first but certainly connected with the experience of reading poems in a new way that related to my own writing of them. I have textual evidence, from a year later, of a notebook used in this way, and very consciously so.

One other book deserves mention, a little *Selected Poems* of Ezra Pound, which I bought some time during my two years at Christ's, possibly in 1946, and which I still have. This made an enormous impact, but one difficult for me to analyse, even now.

My first three published poems were in a student literary magazine at the University of Pennsylvania, in 1951. One of these had been written at Cambridge, thus before 1947. It has a simple lyrical quality which, though immature, I can still admire and even envy.

Before that, I had submitted poems to both the *New Statesman* and *Partisan Review*. I think I was more surprised than discouraged when they were rejected. My conviction of whatever it was, perhaps not so much "ability" as something nearer to "destiny," was beyond such trivia.

Then, I had a group accepted by Peter Russell, from London, in March 1952, for his magazine *Nine*, with a generous letter. I was an unknown name and writing from far-off Pittsburgh, and I shall always be grateful. The poems, in fact, were never printed, a not-uncommon happening, for whatever reason.

Later in that year, by then in Canada, I submitted some poems to *Northern Review* and John Sutherland printed a generous group in 1953, and again in a subsequent issue.

The consequences of this first real publication were considerable.[5] I was confirmed in my mistaken impression that one only had to publish poems for them to be read and remarked upon. Only later did I learn how rare this is. By the time I left Canada for London in 1955, I was in contact with a circle of largely American and Canadian poets, but also with some in England and Scotland. My ideas about the construction of poems, of the priorities and values involved, had been greatly affected, for better or for worse, by writers who were "contemporaries" in a

way that had not been true previous to those years in Canada.

Though I thought of myself as British, even Scottish (I had been in correspondence with and had written a poem for MacDiarmid), even occasionally perhaps English, my work was often perceived as Canadian or American. I had had poems in early issues of *Origin* and in *Black Mountain Review*. Some years later I would remark to a friend, somewhat bitterly perhaps, that I thought my destiny was to be the poet laureate of Rockall.

Surprisingly to me now, a few poems from those years seem to have survived, to the extent of occasional editors finding them of sufficient interest to reprint.

11

It is necessary to backtrack again in order to understand how I came to qualify and work as a doctor. This was largely, I think, through reading the book *The Microbe Hunters*, by Paul de Kruif, when I was thirteen or fourteen. This told of the pioneers of microscopy and bacteriology, in a rather romantic and dramatic way. I got a toy microscope for Christmas and even read massive biographies of Louis Pasteur and Claude Bernard.

Eventually my parents bought me a real and expensive microscope. I spent many happy hours peering down it, mostly in a sort of fantasy, learning and accomplishing very little. By 1943 or 1944, my idea that I would become a doctor was linked with the idea that I would do medical research, perhaps bacteriology.

Even then, however, I was very interested in the arts, drawing and painting and writing, mostly stories. I am sure that my parents never put any pressure on me but encouraged what interests I had. There were chemistry and mineralogy sets, as well as the trains and aeroplanes natural to a boy.

At the Perse School and then at the university, I did Natural Science, even though I knew that I would write poems. I had one very good friend, also doing Natural Science, who was equally interested in literature and poetry. I cannot speak for him, but I think that I even had some scorn for those on the "art side" at school, as opposed to us on the "science side," and felt that the discipline which I was in was superior, or had advantages, even in regard to reading and writing poems. This may seem preposterous now, part of the arrogance of youth, even as it has its filament of truth.

"My daughters, Chris, Julie, and Shari," California, 1990

There was also the motto of William Morris, whose writings and life and personality and ideas, each in turn, I came to admire: *Al Ich Kann*. He did it all, or almost, so why not I? Thus, as part of the turmoil of those two years and "long vac" term at Cambridge, I spent much time in the university library reading other things when I should have been in the anatomy lab, or dreaming in my "digs" over poems when I should have been finishing a physiology essay.

By luck, bluff, and short-term memory, I got through the final exams. This did not help to curb an intellectual arrogance which had crept up on me, or teach me to concentrate my energies, rather the reverse; and the effects have marked me for the rest of my life. *Al Ich Kann* contains the implicit questions: In how many directions? and, How well can you?

Later, after three years at the University of Pennsylvania, and a more rigorous discipline of teaching, I went through a crisis, not easy to discern now. It may not have been so much a conflict between medical studies and trying to write poems so much as a nausea with education itself. However, I was

increasingly aware of a gulf between my interests and attitudes and those of nearly all the doctors with whom I found myself forced to associate.

After a summer job was finished, in 1950, I hitchhiked through part of Canada, and spent a few days with a friend who was working for the summer in the gold mine at Snow Lake, in northern Manitoba. I was overwhelmed to encounter someone of my own age who was actually living in the real world, able to earn money, doing the things he wanted to do, being just who he was. I was entranced by Snow Lake and the almost "frontier" life.

The thought of another year of medical school, then internship, seemed intolerable. Suddenly I did not want to become a doctor. I just wanted to live and write poems. How serious this was, I have no way of estimating now, but I remember the pain of it clearly enough. Out of courage or cowardice, wisely or unwisely, and probably largely through inertia, it was easier to continue than to stop. Somehow I finished my degree.

In the last year, I became involved with research projects in the pharmacology department, though the focus was primarily physiology. I suddenly enjoyed my role in the department, learned much respect for the particular doctor for whom I worked, even won a prize with two other students for a project and got my name on a couple of papers in the *American Journal of Physiology*.

In a sense, this was a return to an earlier course and during my year at Pittsburgh, doing my internship, it was arranged that I should start, early in 1953, at the Babraham Institute of Animal Physiology outside Cambridge, in England again.

For gratuitous reasons beyond my control, this plan had to be abandoned, and in October 1952, just married, I found myself working as a general practitioner in northern Ontario.

Thus, general practice, and later anaesthetics, became the means by which I earned what is called "my living." I found it initially full of interest and challenge and learned to take some pride in trying to do "a good job." For some years, while in California, I even taught anaesthetics, but by 1965 or 1966 I had come to terms with the fact that in my heart, I had no ambitions in that direction and had not for many years. Some false expectation had driven me on, and possibly the idea that it might enable me to earn the money I needed more easily.

Full-time general practice was beyond my ability to survive, that is, it left no time or energy for my own life. Thus I contrived in the end, with the generosity of a practice in Worcester, a role where I could go in to work in the morning, work hard at a 35- to 40-hour week, but have my evenings and weekends to myself.

For a while it worked, and at times I even enjoyed the double life. Unrealistically I would daydream that in some way there would be an escape, that the poems would miraculously achieve some public happening, that I would be offered I scarcely knew what.

In the mid 1970s I suddenly found myself unable to go on. The practice generously gave me some leave of absence and I took my annual leave as a unit, and I paid out of savings for a "locum" to cover my duties.

I had twelve weeks when I did not think of the doctoring once. I remember finishing work on a Saturday at 1.00 p.m. as usual, and driving back to Malvern. It was as if a switch was turned off. What I wrote mostly turned out to be nothing: a full-length play, other things; only a few fragments survive.

Suddenly, one Sunday evening, I realised that I had to go back into work on Monday morning. It seemed unimaginable. Then, as the first patient came through the door, there was that "click" and the familiar words began to come out of my mouth. It

was a bit like a long-running play in which I could take some satisfaction, even amusement, at playing a successful part. And as a way of earning a living, one could do much worse.

But that "break," and a few others, kept me going. I am grateful enough, even though I went through many years of resenting what seemed a bondage from which I could not break free, despising myself that I diffused what time and energy I had, or finding myself consumed by foolish and dreadful jealousies of those of my contemporaries who seemed to have "succeeded" with Arts Council grants or as writers-in-residence.

As for those working in teaching, I could envy them their long holidays but not the circumstances of teaching, especially "literature," especially "poetry." On that count, I would rather be doctoring. How could I teach it? There were difficulties enough trying to write it.

12

Of the many lives we all live, or at least that I do, and the many "selves," there is that role in which I only exist in relationship to those others whom I consider as "friends." Not to mention them might seem to deny their importance, even their existence, but it is impossible to include all and perhaps invidious to select.

Yet there are some of particular importance in regard to the writing of poems. Most of these are still alive and thus part of a continuing process. Of these, to be inconsistent, three stand out as particular comrades over more years than I care to number: Roy Fisher, Matthew Mead, and, most unwearied of correspondents, El Cid (Cid Corman).

Of others, it is to the dead I would make salutations, and in the order of their going.

John Sutherland: always independent of opinion and against all fashion, who so generously published my first poems, and occasioned so much else.

Louis Zukofsky: again, ever generous with comment and in friendship, and patient with my inability to grasp what so many of his own poems were trying to do.

Robert Garioch: *makar* above others, and man, always generous reader, and ever providing good company on occasional visits to Edinburgh.

Hugh Creighton Hill: poet, almost entirely neglected and forgotten, whose commitment nevertheless continued, his words fewer, always sharper, as the years went on, and whose example sustained me through many lean times.

"With my wife Jill," Cumbria, 1986

Basil Bunting: for twenty-seven years, ever patient with my vanities and digressions, whose hand on my shoulder at our last meeting I would wish to return, as one might salute an old shipmate at the end of a long voyage.

Robert Duncan: whose own poems are mostly so alien and yet who was so generous to me, as exemplar and reminder of the importance of all that, by natural inclination, I might unjustly neglect.

Norman Nicholson: some of whose early poems appear in notebooks of mine from 1948 and 1949, and who became a "neighbour" across the Duddon estuary for the last years of his life.

Two others also remain firmly in my mind. That they were friends seems a presumption, and yet their friendship to me, as to so many others, was real, as was and still is their example and influence as poets: William Carlos Williams, whom I only met the once, but vividly enough[6] and Hugh MacDiarmid, whom I met on a number of occasions. His repeated invitations to visit Brownsbank I never took up, perhaps out of diffidence, perhaps in not unreasonable apprehension of what might have been at least a memorable occasion.

One final salutation: when I saw the announcement of the publication of the Lorimer New Testament (into Scots) in 1985, I had it on my mind to order a copy. Then a letter came from my father, almost at the same time, enquiring about it, so I ordered two copies and sent one on to him.

Sadly, it arrived a few days after his death. Yet the evening on which he died, I had been reading my copy and thinking of him; and particularly, in my mind, sharing Lorimer's jest in an appendix, where he has an alternative translation of the Temptation in the Wilderness, all in Scots with only the Devil speaking in "standard" English.

How my father would have laughed, and in a sense, I shall always share that jest with him, in spite of whatever separation "death" may claim to make.

"Man shall not live by bread alone."

NOTES

1. Ian Hamilton Finlay in *The Best of Scottish Poetry* (Edinburgh, 1989).

2. "Resonances and Speculations," *Kulchur* 7, (Autumn 1962), pp. 23–6.

3. "Charlotte Chapel, the Pittsburgh Draft Board and *Some Americans*," *PN Review* 28 (1982), pp. 9–11.

4. "Memories of Northern Ontario," *Northward Journal* 50–51 (1989), pp. 73–81.

5. See notes 3 and 4 above.

6. "A Visit to WCW: September 1958," *Mica* 3 (1962) and *Interviews with William Carlos Williams*, New Directions, 1976, pp. 91–96.

BIBLIOGRAPHY

Poetry, except where noted:

(With Eli Mandel and Phyllis Webb) *Trio*, Contact Press (Toronto), 1954.

The Knot in the Wood and Fifteen Other Poems, Revision Press (London), 1955.

Bjarni Spike-Helgi's Son and Other Poems, Origin Press (Ashland, Massachusetts), 1956.

A Libation, The Poet (Glasgow), 1957.

With Hey, Ho . . . , Migrant Press (Birmingham, England), 1961.

To You, I Write, Migrant Press, 1963.

A Very Particular Hill, Wild Hawthorn Press (Edinburgh), 1963.

Twenty Words, Twenty Days: A Sketchbook and a Morula, Migrant Press, 1966.

Briefly, Tarasque Press (Nottingham, England), 1967.

Walls, privately printed, 1967.

Seven from Stifford's, privately printed, 1968.

A Trampoline: Poems 1952–1964, Cape Goliard Press (London), 1968.

I, Maksoud, University of Exeter, 1969.

Scantlings: Poems 1964–1969, Cape Goliard Press, 1970.

Finger Cymbals, Satis (Edinburgh), 1972.

A Sea Story, Byways (Saffron Walden, England), 1973.

A Random Sapling, Pig Press (Newcastle-upon-Tyne), 1974.

Witley Court Revisited, Migrant Press, 1975.

Wulstan, Blue Tunnel (Bradford, England), 1975.

Residues: Down the Sluice of Time, Grosseteste (Pensnett, England), 1976.

Thronging the Heart, Aggie Weston (Belper, England), 1976.

If a Glance Could Be Enough, Satis, 1978.

What Makes the Weeds Grow Tall, Five Seasons Press (Hereford, England), 1978.

Some Resonances and Speculations, Migrant Press, 1979.

The Small Change, Migrant Press, 1980.

Rain in Wales, Satis, 1981.

Nine Intersections, Circle Press (Twickenham, England), 1982.

From the Language of the Heart, Mariscat Press (Glasgow), 1983; Gnomon (Frankfort, Kentucky), 1985.

A Gathering of Poems 1950–1980, Anvil Press Poetry (London), 1983.

Traces, Circle Press, 1983.

Circus, Peacock Press (Malvern, England), 1984.

A Year and a Day (journal), Mariscat Press, 1985.

Spaces, Satis, 1986.

A Winter Journey, Pig Press, 1987.

As from a Fleece, Circle Press, 1990.

While Breath Persist: New and Selected Poems, Porcupine's Quill (Erin, Canada), 1991.

Works translated:

(With Jean Beaupré) Paul-Marie Lapointe et al, *Poems*, privately printed, 1955.

(With J. Beaupré and Jill Iles) Jean Follain, *Twelve Poems*, Moschatel Press (Nailsworth, England), 1983.

Cumulative Index

CUMULATIVE INDEX

The names of essayists who appear in the series are in boldface type. Subject references are followed by volume and page number(s). When a subject reference appears in more than one essay, names of the essayists are also provided.

INDEX

INDEX

INDEX